Stalingrad

Stalingrad

City on Fire

Alexey V. Isaev

Edited and Translated by Richard W. Harrison

Pen & Sword
MILITARY

First published in Great Britain in 2019 by
Pen & Sword Military
An imprint of
Pen & Sword Books Ltd
Yorkshire – Philadelphia

ISBN 978 1 52674 265 0

A CIP catalogue record for this book is
available from the British Library.

Printed and bound in the UK by TJ International Ltd,
Padstow, Cornwall.

Pen & Sword Books Limited incorporates the imprints of Atlas,
Archaeology, Aviation, Discovery, Family History, Fiction, History,
Maritime, Military, Military Classics, Politics, Select, Transport,
True Crime, Air World, Frontline Publishing, Leo Cooper, Remember
When, Seaforth Publishing, The Praetorian Press, Wharncliffe
Local History, Wharncliffe Transport, Wharncliffe True Crime
and White Owl.

For a complete list of Pen & Sword titles please contact

PEN & SWORD BOOKS LIMITED
47 Church Street, Barnsley, South Yorkshire, S70 2AS, England
E-mail: enquiries@pen-and-sword.co.uk
Website: www.pen-and-sword.co.uk

Or

PEN AND SWORD BOOKS
1950 Lawrence Rd, Havertown, PA 19083, USA
E-mail: Uspen-and-sword@casematepublishers.com
Website: www.penandswordbooks.com

Contents

List of Maps

List of Illustrations

Acknowledgements

The author wishes to thank A. Yeliseenko, D. Golubev, N. Vlasov, P. Kozlov, O. Kuznetsov, I. Ostrovskii, A. Tomzov and D. Shein for their invaluable help in working on this book.

Translator's Introduction

This study contains a number of terms that may not be readily understandable to the casual reader in military history. Therefore, I have adopted a number of conventions designed to ease this task. For example, major Soviet field formations (i.e., Western Front) are spelled out in full, as are similar German formations (i.e., Army Group South). Soviet armies are designated using the shortened form (i.e., 62nd Army). German armies, on the other hand, are spelled out in full (i.e., Sixth Army). In the same vein, Soviet corps are designated by Arabic numerals (3rd Guards Cavalry Corps), while the same German units are denoted by Roman numerals (e.g., VIII Corps). Smaller units (divisions, brigades, etc.) on both sides are denoted by Arabic numerals only (147th Rifle Division, 75th Infantry Division, etc.).

Given the large number of units involved in the operation, I have adopted certain other conventions in order to better distinguish them. For example, Soviet armoured units are called tank corps, brigades, etc., while the corresponding German units are denoted by the popular term 'panzer'. Likewise, Soviet infantry units are designated by the term 'rifle', while the corresponding German units are simply referred to as infantry.

Elsewhere, a *front* is a Soviet wartime military organization roughly corresponding to an American army group. Throughout the narrative the reader will encounter such names as the Western Front and South-western Fronts, etc. To avoid confusion with the more commonly understood meaning of the term front (i.e., the front line), italics will be used to denote an unnamed *front*.

Many of the place names in this study are hyphenated, such as Verkhne-Kurmoyarskaya. In these cases, the names are separated by a single hyphen, which is to distinguish them from the recitation of a particular line of individual locales, often countered in such works, such as Yevseev – Maiorovskii – Plesistovskii. In the latter case, the individual villages and towns are separated by en-dashes.

The work subscribes to no particular transliteration scheme, because no entirely satisfactory one exists. I have adopted a mixed system that uses the Latin letters 'ya' and 'yu' to denote their Cyrillic counterparts, as opposed to the 'ia' and 'iu' employed by the Library of Congress, which tends to distort proper pronunciation. Conversely, I have retained the Library of Congress's 'ii' ending (i.e., Rokossovskii), as opposed to the commonly-used 'y' ending. I have also retained the apostrophe to denote the Cyrillic soft sign.

The work contains endnotes by the author. They have been supplemented by a number of appropriately-identified editor's notes, which have been inserted as an explanatory guide for a number of terms that might not be readily understandable to the foreign reader.

Preface

In studying the battle of Stalingrad, I could not shake the thought of how it resembled the well-known film *The Terminator*. Paulus's army, like a robot made for killing, methodically destroyed everything in its path. It attacked with panzer corps and hundreds of tanks, while more and more fresh and full-blooded rifle divisions were put up against it. But the tank attacks did not produce any visible effect, while the divisions fell back, bleeding. The Terminator stubbornly moved forward in search of Sarah Connor, while the Sixth Army just as purposefully moved toward the Volga River and Stalingrad. When the tanker exploded (the encirclement ring closed), the grating noise that chilled the soul sounded once again and the isolated army restored the front line. The burnt machine, which had been turned into a metal skeleton, nevertheless continued to move. The Sixth Army influenced the operational situation. Even after the failure of Manstein's operation to relieve the 'cauldron', and deprived of any hope of rescue, the army retained its combat capability. In the same way the robot, torn in two, continued to stubbornly crawl toward its target. Only after the hydraulic press of Operation Ring did the sinister red fire in the 'eyes' of one of the most powerful German armies go out.

Despite the fact that the battle around Stalingrad is primarily associated with street fighting, tank units and armoured formations played an enormous role in it. The open terrain favoured the employment of tanks and they were actively used in all phases of the battle. For example, on 1 September 1942 the Stalingrad and South-eastern Fronts contained eight tank corps. There was one tank corps in the Bryansk Front on the same date, while the Voronezh Front had four and the *fronts* in the Caucasus had one. Only the Western Front along the most important Moscow direction had this number of tank corps (eight). In all, there were twenty-one tank corps in the entire active army at that moment. This means that Stalingrad and the Moscow direction attracted 80 per cent of the Red Army's independent tank formations. On 1 December 1942, at the height of the conduct of Operations Uranus and Mars there were three mechanized and four tank corps within the Kalinin and Western fronts on the approaches to Moscow. The South-western, Don and Stalingrad Fronts contained, correspondingly, four mechanized and five tank corps. At the same time, as opposed to the positional fighting around Rzhev, the corps were employed around Stalingrad for manoeuvre actions in the depth of the enemy's defence. The battle of Stalingrad actually became the first truly successful employment of Soviet mechanized formations in combat.

It would seem that absolutely everything should be known about the battle that took place three-quarters of a century ago. However, the history of the war is being written anew, often from zero. As early as 1967, A.M. Vasilevskii complained in a conversation with K. Simonov:

> It's amazing how little we take advantage of documents. Twenty years have passed since the end of the war and people remember and argue, but they often argue

without the aid of documents, without the kind of checking that one could easily do. Quite recently, while looking for some papers, I came across an enormous amount of documents in one of the General Staff's sections. Reports and conversations about the most important operations of the war testify with absolute accuracy as to how things actually happened. But these documents lie where they were from the end of the war to this day. No one looks at them.

Unfortunately, forty years later, Vasilevskii's words remain relevant. If in 1967 there were still some barriers to acquainting oneself with the basic combat documents, then today there are practically none. But for many operations of the Great Patriotic War, they continue to pull in different directions. In the 1990s German documents became accessible for Russian historians, while 21st-century telecommunications have made access to them even simpler.

It is namely documents that allow us to reconstruct the picture of events, placing the accents on objective data about the situation. Memoirist and politically-engaged researchers have been able to 'shine a light on' or 'put in the shade' this or that episode. Besides, by no means did all participants in these events leave memoirs. Thus the centre of events in the memory of descendants could shift to that area where the man who left such absorbing memoirs was active. Quite the opposite, a person who was located in the centre of the hurricane of events might not have left memoirs or simply remained silent about this important page in his biography. Such a seemingly insignificant event might substantially alter our impression of the battle. Authors of reports and operational summaries and accounts, without realizing it themselves, were writing letters to the future, to their descendants – you and me.

From the operational point of view, the battle of Stalingrad may be conventionally divided into three major periods. The first is the manoeuvre battle on the distant approaches to the city. It covers the time from approximately the middle of July to the end of August 1942. The second period is the fighting for the city and the Stalingrad Front's counterblows against the Sixth Army's flank. This period is the longest and runs from the end of August to 19 November 1942. However, it should be noted that the intensity of combat activities during this period gradually eased. Finally, the third period covers the encirclement of Paulus's army, the repulse of Manstein's attempt to relieve the encircled troops and their destruction during the course of Operation Ring. This lasts from 19 November 1942 to 2 February 1943. The book is correspondingly divided into three parts, in each of which the narrative is divided according to axes of advance and in chronological order. I devoted the greatest attention in my work to the fighting for the city and along the close approaches to Stalingrad as the culmination of the sides' armed struggle and the turning point of the Second World War.

Part I

The Art of Sowing the Whirlwind

Chapter 1

Thermite Rain

(Maps 1–3)

As opposed to many other epic land battles, the battle of Stalingrad began with the absence of a fixed front line, where the opponents' main forces did not even see each other. In the endless steppe of southern Russia a small forward detachment from the 147th Rifle Division collided with the Germans advancing eastwards. The detachment's core was a company of T-34 medium tanks and a company of T-60 light tanks from the 645th Tank Battalion. Two platoons of automatic riflemen, four platoons of riflemen, six anti-tank rifles and three anti-tank guns and their crews also made up the detachment. Two hours after the unloading of the tanks from trains, on 15 July 1942 the detachment headed in the direction of the Morozov farm and Morozovskaya station. The hilly terrain enabled the enemies to close on each other unnoticed. At 13.00 the detachment arrived at the Golden farm, which was 8km south-east of Morozovskaya station. At 17.40 on 16 July three T-34s and two T-60s were fired upon by enemy anti-tank guns while reconnoitring the Morozov farm and destroyed them with return fire. The tanks returned following the reconnaissance, towing one T-34. This was not yet a combat loss – the tank's gearbox had simply broken down.

A more serious collision took place a few hours later. At 20.00 four German tanks stealthily approached Golden farm and opened fire on the detachment. The first fight of the battle of Stalingrad lasted 20–30 minutes. The tank crews of the 645th Tank Battalion reported destroying two German tanks and their crews, while knocking out another and destroying one anti-tank gun. The Germans evidently did not count on immediately running into two companies of tanks and had sent only four vehicles forward. The detachment's losses were one T-34 burned and two T-34s knocked out. The first fight of the bloody, months-long battle was not marked by anyone's death – the two tank companies' casualties were eleven wounded. The tank detachment returned, towing the two knocked-out tanks. The first shots of the great battle had sounded.

On that same day, when the forward detachments collided with the enemy, the commander of the Stalingrad Front (renamed from the South-western Front), S.K. Timoshenko,[1] signed Operational Directive No. 0023/op, in which he defined the tasks of the *front's* troops. The German command's goals along the Stalingrad direction were defined in the directive as follows: 'It is most likely that the enemy will shortly, following the arrival of his operational reserves, set himself the objective of capturing the Stalingrad area and reaching the middle Volga.' Accordingly, the *front's* task was to 'retain the Stalingrad area at all costs and to prepare forces for a counterblow to the west and south-west'.

In accordance with Timoshenko's directive, the 63rd and 38th Armies were to occupy the line of the Don River. The 21st Army had been pulled into the reserve and was to reform the remnants of its formations into four rifle divisions. The 62nd and 64th Armies were to cover Stalingrad from the west.

The 62nd Army, which consisted of the 33rd Guards, 192nd, 181st, 147th, 196th and 184th Rifle Divisions, the 644th, 645th, 648th, 649th, 650th and 651st Independent

Tank Battalions, the 1185th, 1186th, 1183rd, 508th, 652nd, 614th, 555th and 881st Light Artillery Regiments from the High Command Reserve, four armoured train battalions (eight trains), and four regiments from cadet schools, occupied a defensive position along the line Malokletskii – Yevstratovskii – Kalmykov – Slepikhin – Surovikino.

The 64th Army, which consisted of the 214th, 29th, 229th and 112th Rifle Divisions, the 66th and 154th Naval Rifle Brigades, the 40th and 137th Tank Brigades, four artillery regiments, two anti-tank artillery regiments from the High Command Reserve, two armoured train battalions and four regiments of cadets, was to occupy and defend the line Verkhne-Osinovskii – Sysoikin – Pristenovskii and then along the eastern bank of the Don River as far as Verkhne-Kurmoyarskaya, with its left flank joining the North Caucasian Front.

The 18th Rifle Division, along with the 133rd Tank Brigade (four companies of KV heavy tanks), and the 131st Rifle Division, with the 158th Tank Brigade (four companies of KVs) were allotted to the *front* reserve. The 3rd Guards Cavalry Corps, which was located in the area of Kalach, was also part of the *front* reserve.

Timoshenko's directive as yet only outlined the contours of the defence being constructed along the far approaches to Stalingrad. At the moment the directive appeared the 64th Army was still in the process of concentrating. By 20 July only the 154th Naval Brigade and the 29th Rifle Division had reached their designated defensive areas.

However, Timoshenko was not to lead the defence of Stalingrad. On 23 July 1942 he was recalled and placed at the disposal of the *Stavka*,[2] and his place was taken by V.N. Gordov.[3] The reasons for his fall are obvious: the South-western Front's failure at Khar'kov in May 1942, the subsequent retreat and, finally, the encirclement around Millerovo. The true scope of the latter catastrophe had become evident by 20–22 July and the reaction of the supreme commander-in-chief[4] to Timoshenko's blunder was predictable. The decision to remove Timoshenko from his position was perhaps hurried and premature. Gordov lacked sufficient experience to command a *front* under difficult conditions. Moreover, he failed to cope with this task and A.I. Yeremenko[5] later commanded two *fronts* (Stalingrad and South-eastern). Marshal Timoshenko appears as a more suitable candidate for commanding the Stalingrad Front, at least during the defensive phase of the battle.

On the same day that Timoshenko was removed from command of the Stalingrad Front, there appeared Directive No. 45 from the supreme commander-in-chief of the German armed forces on continuing Operation Braunschweig (the name of Operation Blau from 30 June). As regards the plan for activities along the Stalingrad direction, it stated the following:

> 4. As ordered earlier, Army Group B will have the task, besides outfitting defensive positions along the Don River, of launching an attack on Stalingrad and defeating the enemy group of forces concentrating there, seizing the city and also cutting the isthmus between the Don and Volga and disrupting communications along the river.
>
> Following this, panzer and motorized troops are to launch an attack along the Volga with the objective of reaching Astrakhan' and there to also paralyze movement along the Volga's main channel.
>
> These operations by Army Group B have the code name 'Fischreiher' [grey heron. Author], and the degree of secrecy is 'top secret – only for the command'.[6]

The task of attacking in the direction of Stalingrad for the purpose of seizing it is usually tied to this very directive. However, as regards Stalingrad itself, it only affirms decisions adopted earlier at the army group level. For example, as early as 20 July 1942 Army Group B's operational section (Ia) sent outgoing Document No. 2122/42 to the Sixth Army command, which was signed by Weichs[7] and which contained the following in black and white:

> In a telephone telegram from Army Group B to the Sixth Army's corps, the task has been assigned of taking advantage of the enemy's current weakness for a non-stop pursuit and to defend the front on the Don with minimal forces. At the same time, particular attention is devoted to anti-tank defence along the most threatened crossings.
>
> Following the **seizure of Stalingrad**, the Sixth Army's task will be the holding of permanent positions between the Volga and the Don, which will allow us the unlimited use of the Morozovskaya – Stalingrad rail line, as well as the defence of the line of the Don from the area north-west of Stalingrad as far as the army's left boundary.
>
> The defence of the southern front south of Stalingrad should be organized approximately along the line of the Kotel'nikovo – Stalingrad rail line.[8]

The phrase 'following the seizure of Stalingrad' (*Nach Erreichen von Stalingrad* in the original) does not allow for any other interpretation. The decision precisely to seize, and not to neutralize, Stalingrad was taken by the German command at least three days before Directive No. 45. Moreover, as we can see from the cited text, the Sixth Army's defensive lines in the Stalingrad area had already been approximately defined in Army Group B headquarters. However, Document No. 2122/42 was printed in only two copies (Directive No. 45 in six copies) and remained in the shadows, which afterwards allowed people to speculate in an unrestrained fashion on the theme of the 'raging Führer's' unforgiveable mistakes.

Such figures of speech as 'the enemy's weakness' and 'non-stop pursuit' are also worthy of attention. The Army Group B command obviously underestimated the Soviet forces along the Stalingrad direction at this moment.

The operational plan with which the Sixth Army entered the fighting in the great bend of the Don had been outlined in an order signed by Paulus[9] on 20 July 1942. If the order of 19 August 1942 for the final lunge at Stalingrad is quite often cited in the literature, then the order by which the Sixth Army began its march toward the city on the Volga is much less well known. However, it is precisely this order that determined that the famous battle began. The description of the opposing Soviet forces in the 20 July order was, let us say, far removed from reality: 'Only a weak enemy with tanks is facing the army's eastern front.'[10] Based on prisoner testimony, the presence of fresh forces was assumed only along the bridgehead in the Kalach area. It's clear that these conclusions were based on the results of the fighting with forward detachments. Despite the traditionally critical evaluations of the actions of the Stalingrad Front's forward detachments, they played a definite role in wrapping in the 'fog of war' the actual disposition of the Soviet forces in the great bend of the Don.

The Sixth Army's task was formulated in accordance with the evaluation of the enemy in Paulus's order: 'to occupy Stalingrad as quickly as possible and to also firmly hold the Morozovskaya – Stalingrad railway. The army's main forces are to immediately attack toward the Don and beyond it and along both sides of Kalach. A part of the forces will cover the northern flank along the Don.'[11] Here, once again, it is impossible not to draw attention to the formula 'to occupy Stalingrad', which was employed prior to the appearance of Directive No. 45.

According to the plan, the main attack was to be launched by the XIV Panzer Corps, which had been ordered 'to cross over the Don along both sides of Kalach and to seize Stalingrad'. Great significance was attached to the seizure of intact bridges over the Don, particularly the railway bridge east of Rychev[12] and the paved bridge near Kalach. The VIII and LI Corps were to cover the shock group of forces from the north and south, respectively. They were also to force the Don. In light of the prospect of forcing the Don, the XIV and LI Corps had been significantly reinforced with engineer equipment as early as the beginning of the battle: the first received ten and one-half pontoon-bridge columns and the second nine pontoon-bridge columns, while seven of these were subordinated to the corps on 23 July.

On 22 July the 24th Panzer Division from the Second Panzer Army's XXIV Panzer Corps was transferred to Paulus.[13] It was precisely this that may be called an actual consequence of Directive No. 45. The change in the composition of forces brought about a certain correction in the plans, but on the whole the operational idea remained as before – 'An offensive over the Don and the main attack on either side of Kalach'. As before, the XIV Panzer Corps was oriented toward forcing the Don in the Kalach area. The mobile formation newly transferred to Paulus was given a task in accordance with the overall concept: 'The XXIV Panzer Corps' 24th Panzer Division is to first reach the area west of Nizhne-Chirskaya, in order to then, upon being reinforced with one or two infantry divisions, attack toward Stalingrad together with the XIV Panzer Corps.'[14] Nizhne-Chirskaya is located far to the south of Kalach and such a choice for the direction of an attack can in no way be called a desire to encircle anyone.

Thus the opinion, quite widespread in the literature, that Paulus planned from the very beginning an encirclement battle in the great bend of the Don, with the closing of the 'pincers' in the Kalach area, seems insufficiently grounded and at odds with the Sixth Army's documents. Even the distribution of reinforcement equipment (pontoon-bridge columns in such numbers are not needed for an encirclement battle) contradicts this. The Sixth Army's plan for the beginning of the battle of Stalingrad may be characterized as a 'cavalry swoop' – a rapid breakthrough to the city on the Volga over the Don. This can be explained by the fact that from the point of view of the Sixth Army's headquarters, the army was located along the outer encirclement front around Millerovo and serious resistance from behind by the South-western Front's armies was not expected.

The optimistic estimation of the enemy held until the last moment. Even in the note in the OKW[15] war diary of 23 July, Soviet forces in the great bend of the Don were evaluated in the following way: 'According to intelligence data and aerial observation, the enemy has unloaded in the area of the inhabited locale of Kalach (75km west of Stalingrad) a division with up to 200 tanks. This division has orders to delay the German forces' offensive from the west along the line of the Liska River, in order to win time for creating a defensive line between the Don and Volga rivers.' That is, instead of the 62nd Army's six divisions, the presence of only a single large division was assumed along the approaches to Kalach.

By 23 July the Stalingrad Front's armies occupied the following positions.

- Lieutenant General V.I. Kuznetsov's[16] 63rd Army was along the left bank of the Don along the sector Babka – the mouth of the Medveditsa River, with an overall frontage of about 300km;
- Lieutenant General V.N. Gordov's 21st Army was east of the 63rd Army, along a front of over 60km as far as Kletskaya;

- Major General V.Ya. Kolpakchi's[17] 62nd Army was deployed along a 100km sector of front from Kletskaya to Surovikino;
- Lieutenant General V.I. Chuikov's[18] 64th Army was deployed south of the 62nd Army and was defending an 80km sector from Surovikino to Verkhne-Kurmoyarskaya, with its left flank on the eastern bank of the Don River.

The strength of the former reserve armies was at a high level. For example, in the 62nd Army the strength of the formations' rank and file varied from 11,428 men (196th Rifle Division) to 12,903 (184th Rifle Division), with an authorized strength of 12,807 men. Correspondingly, in the 64th Army the strength of a division varied from 10,795 men (131st Rifle Division) to 12,768 men (112th Rifle Division). For the sake of comparison, the 300th Rifle Division numbered 844 men and the 304th Rifle Division 1,100 men. The situation with weapons was satisfactory. The number of rifles and sub-machine guns was close to authorized strength. More exactly, they were a little short of rifles, while actually having a surplus of sub-machine guns. The days when the 1941 Red Army relied on the semi-automatic Tokarev[19] rifle were far in the past. As of 18.00 on 1 August 1942 there was not a single Tokarev semi-automatic rifle, not a single sniper's rifle, nor a single carbine, but only 60,629 ordinary rifles.[20] There were 3,853 Nagant revolvers, and not a single Tokarev pistol. The situation with machine guns was even worse: heavy machine guns were at three-quarters of authorized strength, and light machine guns at two-thirds. On the other hand, the number of mortars in all divisions in the two former reserve armies actually exceeded the authorized strength for this type of weapon.

The reserve armies' formations were formed according to the new strength table No. 04/200 of 18 March 1942. In comparison to the previous one, No. 04/750 of December 1941, the authorized strength of a division increased, as well as the number of field guns, machine guns and anti-tank rifles.

At the same time, one has to say that a miracle had not taken place and that the substitution of the forces encircled around Millerovo with the reserve armies was not equivalent. The matter is not even in the units' combat experience: the South-western Front had primarily lost reinforcement artillery. The arriving armies disposed of only the divisions' authorized artillery and were reinforced only with anti-tank and anti-aircraft regiments. If in March 1942, before the Khar'kov disaster, the South-western Front disposed of 117 152mm gun-howitzers and 40 model 1909/1940 152mm howitzers and 25 model 1938 152mm howitzers,[21] then as of 20 July the Stalingrad Front's forces had only 21 152mm guns of all types.[22] Moreover, this artillery was concentrated in the 28th and 38th Armies, which were being pulled back for reinforcement. By way of comparison, in the Sixth Army's infantry divisions alone there were 144 150mm field howitzers. There was no heavy artillery (these were usually 203mm howitzers in the Red Army) at all in the Stalingrad Front.

Each of the reserve armies' rifle divisions had an authorized artillery strength of forty-four field guns: twelve 76mm regimental guns, twenty 76.2mm divisional guns, and twelve 122mm howitzers. In the majority of cases, the numbers on hand corresponded to the authorized number. However, at the same time Soviet divisions did not dispose of 150–152mm howitzers, which were in every German division. As regards equipment, one should note that the ZIS-3 divisional guns, which became one of the Red Army's symbols, were not yet widespread. There was not a single ZIS-3 in the 62nd and 64th Armies, and all divisional guns were 1939 model 76mm guns. The *front's* forces had only 56 ZIS-3 guns and the majority of guns (913 pieces) consisted of 1939 model 76mm guns, while there were even a few old models – 41 1902/1930 model and one 1900 model.[23]

If one looks at a map and correlates the defensive front with the forces available, then the Stalingrad Front had almost no chance of withstanding a powerful enemy attack. The reserve armies covered a major breach in the Soviet forces' front, but they were unable to do so in sufficient density. The Southern Front, which had earlier occupied a front along approximately the same latitude as Stalingrad, was now deployed with its front facing north and was falling back to the Caucasus Mountains. It was as if a door had opened up before the German forces attacking east.

The formation of a new front was not a simple task. Even with the movement of all the divisions into a single echelon, the density of the defence was approximately 17km per division. In actuality, a defence requires the echeloning and the detachment of forces into a reserve for parrying crises. In the 62nd Army the 33rd Guards Rifle Division and the 192nd, 181st, 147th and 196th Rifle Divisions occupied a defence along their designated front of 100km, with the 184th Rifle Division in the second echelon. In each first-line rifle division two regiments were in the first echelon, with one in the second.

One could have increased the firmness of the defence by guessing the axis of the attack and thickening the troops along it. Kolpakchi, the commander of the 62nd Army, concentrated the efforts of his defence along the army's left flank, blocking the axis along which Stalingrad could be reached by the shortest route. Accordingly, the thickening of the left flank was achieved at the expense of lengthening the 192nd Rifle Division's front along the 62nd Army's right flank. The 184th Rifle Division, which had been pulled back to the second echelon, was also located behind the 62nd Army's left flank, astride the railway. It only remained to hope that that it would be this axis that would be chosen by the enemy.

One must say that the Soviet supreme command soberly evaluated the prospects of holding a broad front with the reserve armies. The *Stavka* removed divisions from the Far East even before the formation of the Stalingrad Front. On 8 July 1942, *Stavka* Directive No. 9944101 ordered the commander of the Far Eastern Front:

1. To dispatch from the Far Eastern Front the following rifle formations to the supreme High Command Reserve:
   the 205th Rifle Division from Khabarovsk; the 96th Rifle Division from Kuibyshevka and Zavitoi; the 204th Rifle Division from Cheremkhovo (Blagoveshchenskii District); the 422nd Rifle Division from Rozengartovka; the 87th Rifle Division from Spassk; the 208th Rifle Division from Slavyanka; the 126th Rifle Division from Razdol'noe and Putsilovka; the 98th Rifle Division from Khorol'; the 250th Rifle Brigade from Birobidzhan; the 248th Rifle Brigade from Zakandvorovka, Far Eastern Province, and; the 253rd Rifle Brigade from Shkotovo.
2. Begin sending the formations on 10.07.1942 and finish it on 19.07.1942.[24]

The soldiers and officers of the Far Eastern Front, who before this could only greedily listen to Sovinformburo[25] reports, were now fated to get into the thick of things. We shall have the opportunity before long of meeting the majority of the enumerated formations. They arrived at the height of the battle and were employed along various axes.

By the start of the offensive on Stalingrad the German Sixth Army was the most powerful on the Eastern Front, with a strength of about 320,000 men. Only the Eighteenth

Army around Leningrad could boast of a comparable strength – 306,000 men, while the remaining armies were nowhere near 300,000 men. This came about as the result of the gradual reinforcement of the troops subordinated to Paulus: at first the VIII and LI Corps from the Fourth Panzer Army, and the XIV Panzer Corps, with two divisions, from the First Panzer Army, were transferred to it, and then the Fourth Panzer Army's XXIV Panzer Corps (24th Panzer Division).

However, it is expedient to employ these figures in comparison to other German armies. If one sets oneself the task of comparing it to Soviet forces, then it's necessary to use other figures closer to the methodology of counting in the Red Army. In this case, the most informative way is the so-called 'ration strength', by subtracting the number of prisoners of war on the army's rolls. According to a report by the Sixth Army's chief quartermaster of 20 July 1942, its strength according to the number of rations was 443,140 men. This number was broken down into the following categories.[26]

	Men	*Horses*
Army	358,350	100,050
Luftwaffe	40,000	–
Foreign formations (Croats, Slovaks, Hungarians)	6,600	800
German civilian employees	16,750	–
Foreign civilian employees	8,350	–
Prisoners of war	12,910	–
Total	443,140	100,850

This data show that the strength figure of the Sixth Army of 270,000,[27] which is sometimes encountered in Russian literature, does not fully reflect the condition of Paulus's army before the start of the battle to the fullest degree. In reality, this figure is closer to 400,000 men, even without counting the XIV and XXIV Panzer Corps.

By comparison, as of 20 July 1942 the Stalingrad Front numbered 386,365 men, including rear units and establishments and the 29,947 men in the 8th Air Army.[28] The *front's* combat troops numbered 298,895 men and 45,577 horses.[29] In comparing these figures one may arrive with confidence at the conclusion that one should not speak about any kind of numerical superiority of the Soviet forces over the enemy, at least at the beginning of the battle.

An important event for the Sixth Army on the threshold of the battle of Stalingrad was the delivery of two types of 75mm anti-tank guns: the 75mm PAK-40 and the 75mm PAK-97/38 (before this, infantry divisions did not have 75mm anti-tank guns). The guns arrived in several shipments during the period from 23 May through 24 June 1942, and in all a total of 111 PAK-40s and 63 PAK-97/38s were received.[30]

Before long the new guns were tested in battle. The Sixth Army's 75th Infantry Division reported destroying fifty-nine Soviet tanks (four KVs, four light tanks and fifty-one T-34s) in fighting on 13–19 July 1942, of which thirty vehicles were destroyed by the forces of an anti-tank battalion armed with 75mm guns,[31] and another eight vehicles by the 177th Assault Gun Battalion.[32] The testimonials about the new guns, according to the results of this fighting, were, if not rapturous, then on the whole positive, despite the inevitable 'teething troubles':

The effectiveness of the 7.5cm PAK-40 is amazing; however, in many cases problems arose with loading and other unreliable aspects of the guns, about which it will be further reported.

The effectiveness of the PAK-97/38 with a hollow-charge shell was also good, not counting the case of eight hits on a KV-1, not one of which penetrated the armour, as well as hits on the same tank from assault guns with the same munitions.[33]

The outfitting of all of the infantry divisions in Paulus's army with the 75mm PAK-40 and the PAK-97/38 signified a qualitative leap in its anti-tank capabilities. Now the troops were no longer dependent on the presence of 88mm anti-aircraft guns and the soldiers' training. The fight against Soviet tanks was becoming more of a trade than an art. Soviet tank attacks without the suppression of the anti-tank defence's artillery were virtually doomed to failure.

However, at first ammunition was a serious problem for the new German anti-tank weapons. A directive had already been distributed to the troops, in which it stated: 'It is permitted to fire munitions only against the heaviestw tanks, insofar as their delivery in the course of the next few months will be carried out only in minimal amounts.'[34]

The Sixth Army had also been liberally supplied with heavy artillery immediately before the offensive on Stalingrad. On 24 July there were five battalions of 210mm howitzers (about forty barrels), three battalions of 105mm guns, and four battalions of 150mm FH18 howitzers as reinforcement equipment.

The state of the Sixth Army's tank park is shown in the table.

Table 1: The Strength of the Sixth Army's Tank Park as of 21 July, 1942[35]

	Panzer II	*Panzer III (short)*	*Panzer III (long)*
16th Panzer Division	–	17	70
60th Motorized Division	16	–	34
3rd Motorized Division	10	–	28

	Panzer IV (short)	*Panzer IV (long)*	*7.62cm Sfl1*	*Total*
16th Panzer Division	7	15	–	109
60th Motorized Division	–	4	8	62
3rd Motorized Division	–	4	4	46

The twelve self-propelled tank destroyers (7.62cm Sfl1), which formed part of the XIV Panzer Corps, were captured 76.2mm Soviet weapons, modernized and mounted on a Panzer 38(t) chassis and then on the chassis of the obsolete Panzer II.

After the battle had already begun, the 24th Panzer Division was transferred to the Sixth Army. According to a report of 26 July, it numbered six Panzer IIs, five short-barrel Panzer IIIs, seventy-two long-barrel Panzer IIIs, six short-barrel Panzer IVs, and three long-barrel Panzer IVs.[36]

Aside from the tanks, a battalion of assault guns was also part of the Sixth Army. According to a report of 24 July, the 244th Battalion of *Sturmgeschützen*, which was subordinated to the 24th Panzer Division, numbered seventeen StuG IIIs, and in the 177th Battalion, which was subordinated to the VIII Army Corps, there were eleven long-barrel and five short-barrel StuG IIIs.[37]

In Search of a Creative Decision

Realizing the difficulties with the construction of a firm defence in place of the collapsed front, the Soviet command reinforced Kolpakchi's army with tanks and anti-tank weapons. Powerful independent tank battalions, which included forty-two tanks (twenty-one medium and twenty-one light) each, lent a distinctive coloration to the 62nd Army's makeup. One each was attached to each of the 62nd Army's formations, with the exception of the 196th Rifle Division. Not one other army had independent tank battalions in such a proportion as one per division. Each of the 62nd Army's rifle divisions was also reinforced with an anti-tank regiment (twenty guns each).

Essentially, even the forward detachments that had been moved up were an attempt by the Soviet command to find some kind of solution for the problem of predicting the enemy's actions. A creative decision, or a 'masterpiece' was necessary, and these were the forward detachments. They were theoretically capable first of all, of delaying the enemy, forcing him to move in combat and pre-combat formation, and not in march columns. Secondly, they were able to feel out the enemy's really powerful group of forces and determine the axis of its movement. One cannot describe this idea as a successful one. The depth of the forward detachments' (PO) mission was 88km from the forward edge of the defence line along the 192nd Rifle Division's sector, 66km along the 33rd Guards Rifle Division's sector, and 82km along the 147th Rifle Division's sector. This was a very great distance for rifle formations. As a result of the shortage of motor vehicles, the detachments' mobility was low. At the same time, up to 25 per cent of the divisions' strength, with reinforcement equipment, was allotted to the forward detachments. Upon coming into contact with the detachments, the Germans tied them down from the front with small forces and outflanked them. As a result, the forward detachments were defeated in detail by the Germans moving to the east. Their remnants fell back chaotically in small groups to the forward edge of the defence. For example, the 33rd Guards Rifle Division's forward detachment fell back to the 192nd Rifle Division's sector.

Major Kordovskii, a General Staff officer with the 62nd Army, wrote the following about the activities of the forward detachments in his report to A.M. Vasilevskii:[38] 'As a result of sending the forward detachments to a great distance, the army has lost a large number of personnel and equipment, before the beginning of the fighting along the forward edge. The forward detachments carried out their task very poorly.'[39] The normal alternative to the forward detachments was effective aerial reconnaissance. However, it appears that the Red Army's supreme command did not particularly trust 'Stalin's falcons', which were quite often mistaken in their identification of ground targets. To feel out the enemy by moving up small subunits seemed a more reliable means of determining his group of forces and plans.

One must say that the story of the 62nd Army's forward detachments was a stone thrown into the garden of the advocates of the strategy of the 'deep preliminary defence' as a means of the effective defence of the border in 1941. The attempt to hold the Germans' advance by small detachments in the space between the old and new borders would have led to exactly the same result as the activities of the forward detachments around Stalingrad. The small detachments were unable to hold the enemy for the time necessary for deploying the main forces. The units that made them up would be destroyed and thus taken from the ranks of the active army. Infantry detachments possessed very limited mobility and the motorized ones were an unproductive expenditure of forces. The idea of a preliminary defence to a depth of 100–300km in front of the main defensive zone should be consigned to the realm of fantasy.

'In the capacity of a powerful reserve ...'

The loss of the forward detachments was not the Stalingrad Front's biggest problem. It was deprived of the opportunity of operating actively, that is, to attack. This freed the enemy to launch attacks along the Soviet forces' defensive line in the Don bend. The commander of the Sixth Army, General Paulus, was able to pick any point along the 62nd or 64th Armies' front and strike it, while leaving only a thin screen along the remainder of his front. The German Sixth Army was able to extend itself, without risk, into a screen, while concentrating a fist in conditions of the Soviet troops' enforced passivity. Given the even density of its formation, the 62nd Army was simply unable to put together either an attack fist or a stable defensive front with its forces. The defenders' only hope was to create large, mobile reserves, which they could manoeuvre along the front and launch counterblows against the enemy who had broken through.

Formally, there existed a manoeuvre formation in the 62nd Army for parrying crises that arose. In its Order No. 0095/op of 23 July, the Stalingrad Front command transferred the 13th Tank Corps to the commander of the 62nd Army, 'in the capacity of a powerful reserve against the enemy's tanks that are breaking through'. At that moment the 13th Tank Corps included the 163rd, 166th and 169th Tank Brigades, and the 20th Motorized Rifle Brigade (consisting of one company). Since 17 July the corps had been commanded by Colonel T.I. Tanaschishin, who before this had commanded only a brigade. He replaced the previous commander, Major General P.Ye. Shurov, who had perished in the beginning of July. If one judges only by the number of tanks, then the 13th Tank Corps was a serious argument against the enemy's breakthroughs. By the beginning of the fighting its three brigades numbered ninety-four T-34s, sixty-three T-70 light tanks and ten armoured cars.[40] The tanks were distributed equally by brigade, with thirty-two T-34s and twenty-one T-70s. Only the 166th Tank Brigade was short two T-34s, which had been left behind in the assembly point due to technical problems.

However, as an integrated formation, the 13th Tank Corps did not deserve the rating of 'excellent'. In reading the corps' documents, one gets a firm feeling of *déjà vu* regarding the mechanized corps of 1941. In a written report on the matter of outfitting the 13th Tank Corps, its commander described the tank troops' training as follows: 'The outfitting is satisfactory, but the drivers have only 3–5 hours' experience in driving. It's extremely necessary that the corps should have at least 30 drivers with 30–50 hours' experience.'[41] Mention of these few hours of driving experience in the new tanks is often present in descriptions of the actions of Soviet mechanized units in June 1941. For example, D.I. Ryabishev, the commander of the 8th Mechanized Corps, wrote in his summary report on the corps' combat activities around Dubno: 'The majority of the drivers of KVs and T-34s have from 3 to 5 hours of practical driving experience.'[42]

The description of the state of the 20th Motorized Rifle Brigade leaves the same feeling of *déjà vu*. Tanaschishin wrote of it as follows: 'The brigade has only 27.2 per cent of its rank and file ... The brigade is not combat-capable without the full complement of the rank and file, particularly in the motorized rifle battalions. The shortage of equipment makes it impossible to bring the brigade up to strength, even if I hurry.'[43] The corps commander was by no means lying. As of 22 July 1942 the 20th Motorized Rifle Brigade numbered 857 men, as opposed to an authorized strength of 3,258, while its motor transport consisted of only 70 trucks.[44] Thus the corps' motorized infantry was weak, which could not but tell upon the effectiveness of its activities. There was also no rocket artillery in the corps, while the artillery park numbered only sixteen 76mm guns and four 45mm guns. Compared to an average German panzer division, with 105mm and 150mm howitzers in an artillery regiment and a powerful motorized infantry contingent, the Soviet tank corps appeared quite weak. Thus the 62nd Army entered the fighting, having as a mobile reserve a formation quite weak in infantry and artillery.

From Tank Corps to Tank Army

In any event, a single tank corps was not the most reliable means of holding a sufficiently broad front. Aside from its limited (compared to analogous German formations) combat capabilities, there were quite evident limitations from the point of view of its employment. It was cruel to dump the task of controlling several corps on the army commanders. They could not always cope with a single mobile formation. A major defensive battle required the commitment of two to three tank corps in one area against the German breakthrough. Accordingly, it was necessary to control them at the *front* level with an intermediate army command (the necessity of supporting the corps' rear echelons, communications, etc.). Thus within the depths of the Soviet military machine a more promising decision was taking shape – the formation of tank armies.

It is not yet clear who was the author of the idea of creating tank armies on the Stalingrad Front. The earliest document found by this author, in which this idea is sounded out is a 1 July 1942 coded message by Y.N. Fedorenko[45] to Stalin. He wrote: 'It is necessary to create a tank army [in] the Stalingrad area, consisting of: three tank corps, one independent tank brigade, two rifle divisions, two anti-tank regiments, and two anti-aircraft regiments.'[46] Fedorenko suggested a proposed date of 1 August for putting the tank army in readiness. Such a deadline was relatively realistic, particularly when taking into account the fact that it was proposed to deploy the tank army's headquarters on the bases of the headquarters of one of the former South-western Front's combined-arms armies. Fedorenko's proposal was quite rational. The three-corps tank army, with an independent tank brigade, became the Red Army's actual standard during the concluding period of the war in 1945. In 1944–5 they abandoned the inclusion of the three rifle divisions in the tank armies and a substitute was found in the form of the mechanized corps, with a powerful complement of motorized infantry. Fedorenko also from the very beginning included in the tank army an independent tank brigade for resolving local missions without involving the tank corps. The independent tank brigade, directly subordinated to the army commander, would become a component part of the tank armies during 1944–5.

The question of whether there were to be or not to be tank armies under the Stalingrad Front was decided a few days later. During the course of wire discussions between Stalin and the *front* command on the evening of 23 July, the supreme commander-in-chief confirmed the proposed plan for forming and concentrating the 1st and 4th Tank Armies. They were to be formed according to Operational Directive No. 0096/op, issued at 00.23 on 24 July by the headquarters of the Stalingrad Front. Each of these armies was to consist of two tank corps, three rifle divisions, two anti-tank artillery regiments with 76mm guns, two anti-aircraft regiments and one Guards mortar regiment.[47] The 1st Tank Army was to be formed by 26 July, and the 4th Tank Army by 1 August. The armies' headquarters were to be created from the headquarters of the 38th and 28th Armies. Accordingly, the tank armies inherited the commanders from the combined-arms armies. Major General K.S. Moskalenko[48] became the commander of the 1st Tank Army, and his deputy was

Major General of Tank Troops Ye.G. Pushkin. V.D. Kryuchyonkin[49] became commander of the 4th Tank Army, and his deputy Major General of Tank Troops N.A. Novikov. The remnants of the two armies, which had broken out of encirclement in the Millerovo area, were to be transferred to the 21st Army.

The 13th and 28th Tank Corps were to be subordinated to the 1st Tank Army, and the 22nd and 23rd Tank Corps to the 4th Tank Army. Of the six rifle divisions which it was planned to include within the new armies, only the 131st Rifle Division from the *front* reserve was being transferred to the 1st Tank Army as early as 20.00 on 24 July. The remaining five divisions were supposed to arrive from the *Stavka* reserve. The 126th, 204th, 205th, 321st and 422nd Rifle Divisions were supposed to arrive in the Stalingrad area from the Far East on 26–27 July. It was namely these divisions that it was planned to employ for the new formations. The 1st Tank Army was to concentrate in the area of the crossings over the Don at Kalach, while the 4th Tank Army was to concentrate along the near approaches to Stalingrad, near Voronovo. Thus the Soviet command was creating reserves with which they could launch attacks from the depth, or at worst, to cover the most vital points against immediate seizure by the enemy who had broken through.

The early Soviet tank armies compared poorly with the German panzer corps and were distinguished by a smaller amount of artillery and their lesser power. Also, the Red Army lacked a class of formation similar to the German motorized division. A German panzer corps usually included three mechanized formations, two panzer divisions and one motorized division or two motorized and one panzer divisions.

However, the Stalingrad Front command no longer had any time to build the tank armies or to bring the 13th Tank Corps even close to authorized strength. As opposed to the Kursk salient in 1943, where the Central and Voronezh fronts had a tank army apiece as a support for the defence, the Stalingrad Front began combat operations with only a packet of brigades, united under the control of the 13th Tank Corps, and with several tank battalions, which were scattered among the rifle divisions. Within eleven days of the formation of the new *front*, the first blows of the German troops advancing on Stalingrad fell on the 62nd Army.

The Steamroller

If we are to be honest, the mobile formations of the German XIV Panzer Corps attacked as though there was no kind of defensive line covering the great bend of the Don along their path at all. In the Sixth Army's war diary, the first collision with the 62nd Army's defensive line was described as follows: 'The XIV Panzer Corps began its attack at 02.30 [23 July]. The 16th Panzer Division in the XIV Panzer Corps' zone was fighting at 06.00 with enemy rearguards north-west of Kisilyov.'[50] That is, the enemy's fresh forces at first took them for the retreating units' rearguards. Only later did they take 33rd Guards Rifle Division, which had been under attack, for a 'reinforcing' enemy. It is also necessary to note that the positions of the 62nd Army's formations were not attacked at the same time: the 3rd and 60th Motorized Divisions were still located to the south of Serafimovich early on the morning of 23 July. These two formations attacked and broke through the 62nd Army's defence only at about midday.

The fact that along the 62nd Army's left flank the 192nd Rifle Division was occupying a very broad 42km front and, to its left, the 33rd Rifle Division was defending a front of 18km, played into the Germans' hands. Moreover, both of these divisions had been weakened by approximately a third by the dispatch of the forward detachments. As a result, the 'unfavourable, flat, tank-accessible, and open' defensive line along the 62nd Army's right flank was broken through at several points and three German mobile formations arrived in its rear areas.

However, this breakthrough did not resemble the breakthroughs of the Soviet front so typical of 1941–2. First of all, the infantry divisions, which widened and held the base of the breakthrough, were absent. Behind the XIV Panzer Corps' back were the 113th and 100th Infantry Divisions, which were attacking along a broad front. As a result, the breaches made in the Soviet defence were closed off, at least partially. As noted in the Stalingrad Front's morning operational report of 24 July: 'Despite the breakthrough by individual enemy groups of tanks, the front occupied by our infantry is holding along the former line.'[51] The results were not long in manifesting themselves. As was noted in the Sixth Army's war diary for 24 July, the 113th Infantry Division, which was attacking on the heels of the tanks, collided with 'major enemy forces, which are putting up stubborn resistance along positions covered by minefields, and with the support of numerous tanks'.[52] At 18.00 on 24 July this note appeared in the Sixth Army's war diary: 'The XIV Panzer Corps is reporting by radio: the offensive by mobile divisions has halted due to a shortage of fuel.'[53] The 16th Panzer Division also radioed that 'a fuel convoy has been destroyed by the enemy'. This division was in the worst situation, while the 3rd and 60th Motorized Divisions had broken through a less dense front.

As so often happens in defensive operations, the uncertainty as to the enemy's plans sowed some disorder and vacillation. On 22 July, Hoth's[54] Fourth Panzer Army, which was attacking south, forced the Don near Tsimlyanskaya. This event immediately fixed the attention of *Stavka* and the two adjacent *fronts*. The headquarters of the Stalingrad Front, in its Combat Order No. 009/op of 07.25 on 23 July, which was addressed to the 8th Air Army command, directed the aviation to launch strikes against the crossings: 'To shift from the morning of 23.7 the main efforts of all of combat aviation's forces to the destruction, both night and day, of the enemy's crossings over the Don along the Filippovskaya – Romanovskaya sector, and preventing at all costs the crossing of his artillery to the southern bank of the Don River.' Moreover, Gordov was ordered to take immediate steps to rebase part of the Stalingrad Front's air force to the North Caucasus Front's territory 'in order to reduce the flight radius and to increase the number of air attacks against the enemy'. These actions materially weakened the *front's* aviation along the attack axis of the German Sixth Army's XIV Motorized Corps.

In an evening conversation by wire on 23 July with the Stalingrad Front command, the supreme commander-in-chief spoke of the developing situation as follows: 'The enemy has diverted our attention to the south by throwing his units to the Tsimla area, while at the same time he was quietly bringing up his main forces to the *front's* right flank. The enemy's military stratagem succeeded because of our lack of reliable intelligence.'

This reproach as to the absence of 'reliable intelligence' may just as easily be addressed to Paulus's headquarters and that of Army Group B as a whole. However, the battle was just beginning. Having reported the situation to Stalin, Gordov reported on the measures being taken by the front:

> The 62nd Army is carrying out the following measures in this situation: it is concentrating the tanks, rocket artillery and anti-tank weapons at its disposal along the front of the 33rd [Guards Rifle Division] for preventing enemy tank attacks;

it is moving the 184th Rifle Division to the right flank to thicken the 192nd Rifle Division's combat formation along the Yevstratovskaya – Kalmykov sector; it is moving the 196th Rifle Division, which has been relieved by units of the 64th Army, into the reserve behind the army's centre. From the morning of 24 [July] 50 per cent of the *front's* aviation is being dispatched to the 62nd Army's front for opposing and eliminating the enemy's attacks.[55]

Thus it was planned to reorganize the army's formations in order to parry an attack along its weak right flank. Gordov planned to employ the remaining 50 per cent of the *front's* air force against the crossings at Tsimlyanskaya and Nikolaevskaya, that is, a certain inertia in planning remained. Stalin did not support this decision, pointing to the *front's* right flank as the most important axis, requiring the concentration of all forces. The supreme commander-in-chief concluded his conversation with the Stalingrad Front command with a warning regarding the new commander: 'Tell Gordov the following: keep in mind that Kolpakchi is a very nervous and impressionable person, so it would be good to dispatch to Kolpakchi someone a little stronger to keep his spirits up, and it would be even better if Gordov himself would go and see him.' In short, the *front* command received, one should openly say, from higher up an unflattering description of two army commanders along the Stalingrad direction. One should mention that the *Stavka* did not limit itself to the naturalist's observations. After this, when it became clear that the enemy was developing the offensive along the Stalingrad direction, Generals A.I. Lopatin[56] and M.S. Shumilov[57] were dispatched to the front.

Both sides were in a very strange situation. Both the XIV Panzer Corps in the depth of the Soviet defence, and the 62nd Army's right-flank formations had ended up with partially blocked supply routes in the absence of a continuous front. The Germans' situation was somewhat allayed through supply by air (a request for air supply had been sent to Army Group following the receipt of the above-mentioned radiogram from the 16th Panzer Division). At the same time, both the Soviet forces in the Don bend and the forward formations of Paulus's army were being gradually reinforced by bringing up fresh forces from the rear. The question was who could more rapidly achieve a decisive result and more quickly commit the arriving formations into the fighting.

'A powerful means for counterblows'

As a result of the enemy's breakthrough along the 62nd Army's right flank, the 13th Tank Corps entered the fighting even before completing the formation of the tank armies and was transferred to the 62nd Army on the evening of 23 July. At first, the corps was to concentrate along the expected axis of the enemy's main attack, approximately along the axis of the 62nd Army's railway leading to Stalingrad. Thus on 23 July it avoided colliding with the German mechanized formations breaking through to Kalach. However, as early as 24 July the 13th Tank Corps took part in 'sealing off' the front following the breakthrough by the German 16th Panzer Division. The corps launched a counterblow with the forces of the 166th and 169th Tank Brigades in the Pervomaiskoe area, halting the advance of the 113th Infantry Division and announcing the destruction of other 'motor vehicles with fuel and ammunition' – the very same destroyed convoy.

The 163rd Tank Brigade had been withdrawn into the reserve of the 62nd Army's commander and very quickly was employed according to its calling. The 16th Panzer

Division's combat group had spread deeply into the 62nd Army's rear, having reached Kachalinskaya and created a threat to the army's headquarters and the communications of not only the 33rd Guards Rifle Division, but even the 181st Rifle Division, which as yet had not been attacked from the front. Before long two of the 13th Tank Corps' motor vehicles had become victims of German elements in Kachalinskaya.

The threat to the rear communications had to be eliminated. Correspondingly, the 163rd Tank Brigade was moved up for a counterblow against the enemy that had broken through. The first pressure against Kachalinskaya was unsuccessful and the brigade's losses for 24 July were ten T-34s and six T-70s.[58] The success of the German forward detachment can be explained to a great degree by the effective support from the air, as is shown by an entry in the Sixth Army's war diary for 25 July: 'The enemy repeatedly attacked the combat group in the Kachalinskaya area from the north-east, supported by tanks, which we were able to repel with the aid of "Stukas".'[59] Whatever the case, the 13th Tank Corps entered the fighting in a unique situation, when its various brigades were operating in opposite directions: two with their fronts facing to the west and one with its front facing east.

However, the problems in the Kachalinskaya area and in the rear of the formations in the centre of the 62nd Army's combat formation paled in comparison with what was happening along its right flank. The breakthrough to the area to the north-west of Kalach by the XIV Panzer Corps' mobile formations led to a situation in which the 184th and 192nd Rifle Divisions, a regiment from the 33rd Guards Rifle Division and the 40th Tank Brigade ended up being deeply outflanked on both sides. Besides this, as a result of the Germans' breakthrough toward Verkhne-Buzinovka, the headquarters of the 192nd Rifle Division was routed and the division commander, Colonel A.S. Zakharchenko, was killed in the fighting. In order to coordinate the actions of the encircled formations, the chief of the 62nd Army's operational section, Colonel K.A. Zhuravlyov, was dispatched to the 'cauldron' by aircraft. Upon arriving at his destination, he established communications with the army's headquarters through the 40th Tank Brigade's radio set and as early as 25 July had taken the control of the encircled forces upon himself. Thus was formed the so-called Colonel Zhuravlyov's group. It consisted of the 676th, 662nd, 427th, 753rd, 294th and 297th Rifle Regiments, the 88th and 84th Guards Rifle Regiments, the 616th Artillery Regiment, the 1177th and 1188th Anti-Tank Artillery Regiments, the 40th Tank Brigade and the 644th Independent Tank Battalion.

If the encirclement of the Soviet divisions had been part of the Sixth Army's offensive plan, then the 'cauldron' that formed probably did not cause any problems. However, in reality the 'cauldron' arose spontaneously and was creating problems for the XIV Panzer Corps' communications. Besides this, the route, along which the 16th Panzer Division broke through into the depth on 23 July, remained blocked. The Soviet 13th Tank Corps was interfering with the restoration of supply lines along this axis. The chief axis for Tanaschishin's corps during 25–26 July remained the Pervomaiskoe area, where his west-facing front opposed units of the 113th Infantry Division. It was an irony of fate that it was precisely along this axis that the Sixth Army had the German army's most powerful self-propelled anti-tank guns on the Eastern Front. There were two 128mm self-propelled guns – 12.8cm K.40 (Panzer Sfl.) – in the 521st Anti-Tank Battalion and one 105mm gun. They were capable of destroying any Allied tank at a range of greater than 2,000m. The self-propelled guns were first developed for dealing with the armoured parts of the Maginot Line's[60] structures, but they arrived too late for the campaign in France. As of 24 July 1942 the 521st Anti-Tank Battalion was subordinated to the XIV Panzer Corps,[61] and on the 26th it was subordinated to the 113th Infantry Division and had one 128mm self-propelled gun and one 105mm gun listed as combat-ready.[62] At the same time, the 113th Infantry Division had been rearmed with the latest 75mm PAK-40 gun. It was difficult to achieve success in attack against an enemy with these kinds of anti-tank weapons. Nevertheless, the tank attacks by Tanaschisin's corps interfered with the 11th Infantry Division's advance and its linkup with the XIV Panzer Corps' mobile formations.

The Threat along the Left Flank Grows

The non-simultaneous and staged arrival of the Sixth Army's formations in the defensive zone of the Soviet reserve armies became a characteristic feature of the fighting in the great bend of the Don. The entry into the fighting of the XXIV Panzer Corps (24th Panzer Division) in the offensive sector of the Sixth Army's LI Corps on 25 July did not yield a decisive result. The XXIV Panzer Corps command radioed the Sixth Army's headquarters in the evening: 'The enemy is defending in deeply echeloned positions west of Solyonaya. As of 16.30 there is a sensation of increasing resistance.'[63] The 62nd Army's 229th and 214th Rifle Divisions, which had not been weakened by the dispatch of forward detachments, were defending along this axis and they confidently held off the first thrust by the German infantry and tanks. However, this could not continue indefinitely and as early as 26 July the LI Corps' 297th Infantry Division, having broken through the Soviet forces' defence in the Sulatskoe area, reached the Chir River along both sides of Blizhne-Mel'nichnii and formed a bridgehead there along the eastern bank of the river.

In any event, by 25 July it was already evident that the planned 'cavalry lunge' on Stalingrad, with the forcing of the Don, was not coming together. It was absolutely necessary to change the formation's objectives. The necessity of overturning the initial plan and drawing up a new plan 'on the fly' always causes dissatisfaction at headquarters. Paulus's headquarters was no exception in this regard. General Wietersheim became the initiator of a change in plans 'from below'. The discussion of this question on 25 July was preserved in supplements to the Sixth Army's war diary: 'The commander of the XIV Panzer Corps considers the situation of the new divisions, which are engaged in heavy fighting with Russian tanks along a front to the south-west of Kalach, to be serious. He requests that we dispatch the 24th Panzer Division to the north-east, west of the Don, in order to ease our division's situation.'[64] However, at this stage Paulus and his chief of staff remained deaf to these quite sensible demands from below. Their arguments sounded thusly: 'To give up the seizure of the bridges south of Kalach by the forces of the 24th Panzer Division would mean missing our chance. The attempt to resolve both tasks – the seizure of bridgeheads and an attack to the north to aid the XIV Panzer Corps, would mean a dispersion of force and a lack of success along both axes.'[65] The decision was put off until the next day, 26 July.

Moving forward, we should say that on 26 July Paulus's headquarters decided nevertheless not to give up on their previous plan. In a note in the Sixth Army's war diary, it is noted: 'The impression is forming that the Russians, as has so often been the case, are attempting to cover the withdrawal of their infantry and other units with tank attacks. The 24th Panzer Division's task of attacking over the Don south of Kalach toward Stalingrad remains.'[66] Such an evaluation of the situation may be described as an attempt to substitute the desired result for the actual situation and the Sixth Army command's desire to follow its original plan with all its heart, despite the obvious lack of correspondence of the present situation with its evaluation in the order of 20 July. The inevitable correction to the plans was only put off and prolonged. One more day was required for this.

The adoption of emergency measures was required for parrying this enemy attack. Chuikov, who at this time was serving as deputy commander of the 64th Army, recalled:

> I immediately made the decision to eliminate the enemy's breakthrough and particular for securing the boundary of the 64th and 62nd Armies: to quickly move the 112th Rifle Division, which was resting in the area of the Logovskii farm, with ten KV tanks from the 137th Tank Brigade, following a night march, along the railway bridge over the Don. They were given the task of occupying a defensive line from Staromaksimovskii along the Chir River to its mouth and to consolidate along favourable positions. It was necessary to immediately and reliably secure the boundary between the 62nd and 64th Armies and to prevent an enemy attack against the 62nd Army's flank and rear. This manoeuvre was successful. By the evening of 26 July we had managed to cross over the 112th Rifle Division and bring it up to the line of the Rychkovskii – Staromaksimovskii rail bed, where communications were established with the 229th Rifle Division.[67]

Chuikov is speeding up events somewhat. The 137th Tank Brigade was removed by him while on the march, but somewhat later. At first the brigade's mission was to move to Tsimlyanskaya for launching a counterblow, but part of its forces (a battalion of KVs, minus a company of light tanks) was committed on the right bank of the Don only on the evening of 27 July. It's unclear who made this decision but it's possible that this was M.S. Shumilov. By the morning of 28 July the T-34s, which had been returned from Tsimlyanskaya, joined the ten KVs. The attacked developed according to the usual scenario: the infantry did not follow the tanks and the latter could not consolidate the success on their own. Losses, by the way, were moderate – two KVs and one T-34 burnt, and one KV and one T-34 knocked out.

By moving up the 112th Rifle Division and the 137th Tank Brigade, the 64th Army command managed to prevent an immediate breakthrough by the Germans into the depth of the Soviet forces' defence in the great bend of the Don. However, the attack by the Sixth Army's southern group was nevertheless very powerful and led to grievous consequences for the Soviet side. The plan of the attacking Germans was quite simple: to drive the Soviet forces to the bank of the Don and destroy them. The very necessity of making it to the crossing before they were cut off had a demoralizing effect on the troops. Chuikov describes what took place as follows: 'It seemed that we would nevertheless manage to halt the enemy, preventing him from reach the Don and Chir rivers, and to close the breach that had opened. But someone reported to the medical battalions, artillery parks and the units' transport, which were located on the right bank of the Don and Chir rivers, that German tanks were two or three kilometres away. Many rushed to the crossing.'[68] The command had on hand only a company of T-60s and a motorized rifle battalion taken from the 137th Tank Brigade, which had been removed from the march and dispatched to occupy defensive positions near Nizhne-Chirskaya. They were unable to offer serious resistance and the Germans managed to break through to the crossing. This was a rehearsal for the tragedy which happened before long with the 112th Rifle Division. The company from the 137th Tank Brigade was almost completely destroyed: three T-60s sank when the crossing was blown up, two T-60s were knocked out by artillery fire, and one T-60 failed to cross and went missing in action.

By the evening of 26 July the crossing over the Don near Nizhne-Chirskaya had been destroyed by German aviation. The 214th Rifle Division and two of the 64th Army's naval rifle brigades remained on the western bank of the Don without a place to cross. They organized a defence along the right bank of the Don and under the cover of this defence the crossing of units and the occupation of positions along the river bank took place. But the withdrawal behind the Don nevertheless did not occur without serious losses. On 25 July the 214th Rifle Division numbered 12,267 men and on 30 July 7,762 men. For the Germans, the squeezing back of the Soviet units beyond the Don along this axis meant securing the safety of their right flank while attacking the 62nd Army's rear. Now the Soviet command simply lacked a bridgehead along the right bank of the river from which it could launch an attack against the enemy's flank with Tank Corps.

The Tank Army Enters the Fighting

The first and natural reaction by the Soviet command to the enemy's tank lunge was to cover the crossing near Kalach at the expense of its reserves. According to Order No. 00101/op of 24 July by the *front's* headquarters, a regiment from the 131st Rifle Division (the division's overall strength was 11,041 men as of 25 July) and ten tanks from A.V. Yegorov's 158th Tank Brigade (forty KVs) was to move to the approaches to the crossing. The division's and the brigade's main forces were to remain along the eastern bank of the Don. Crossing the Don became a problem: the existing bridge and steam ferry were not able to handle heavy KVs. It was necessary to build a special steam ferry. By 12.00 on 25 July they had managed to get only three KV tanks to the right bank of the Don River. By 05.00 on the 26th one tank company of nine KVs had crossed.

However, after the first careful step, more decisive actions followed. First of all, V.N. Gordov's staff decided to commit the 1st Tank Army into the fighting prematurely, before the completion of its formation schedule. By Order No. 00190/op from the headquarters of the Stalingrad Front, it was sent into the fighting as early as 25 July: 'The 1st Tank Army, consisting of the 28th and 13th Tank Corps, the 131st Rifle Division, two anti-tank artillery regiments, two anti-aircraft artillery regiments, and a guards mortar regiment is to destroy the enemy that has broken through by a decisive attack in the direction of Verkhne-Buzinovka – Kletskaya and to restore the situation along the line Kletskaya – Yevstratovskii – Kalmykov. The beginning of the offensive by the 28th and 13th Tank Corps is 14.00 on 25.7.' Secondly, it was decided to commit into the fighting the 21st Army, which had absorbed the remnants of the 28th and 38th Armies' forces. In Combat Order No. 0015/op at 19.00 on 25 July, it was ordered that: 'The 21st Army, along with reinforcements, is to launch an offensive on the morning of 26.7.42 over the Don along the Serafimovich – Raspopinskaya sector to the south in the direction of Verkhne-Cherenskii.'[69] In this way it was planned to close the breakthrough along the 62nd Army's right flank with attacks along converging axes. The 1st Tank Army's was assigned a task to a great depth, but in a larger sense Gordov did not have much of a choice – an empty space was simply yawning in the Sirotinskaya and Trekhostrovskaya area along the flank of the enemy shock group of forces.

The good condition of G.S. Rodin's 28th Tank Corps offered grounds for hope. Its strength level in all aspects was far better than Tanaschishin's corps and was almost better than all of the corps taking part in the opening phase of the battle of Stalingrad. Its 39th, 55th and 56th Tank Brigades numbered on 25 July 68, 71 and 69 tanks respectively, while the corps contained a total of 208 combat vehicles.[70] The 32nd Motorized Rifle Division, which was part of the corps, numbered 3,147 men and 133 motor vehicles. Such strength for a motorized rifle brigade was a rarity among the tank corps which took part in the counterblows in July and August 1942 around Stalingrad.

The most serious shortcoming among the forces being gathered for the troops' counterblow (which distinguished them from the Germans' XIV Panzer Corps) was their weakness in artillery. On 25 July K.S. Moskalenko's army contained the 233rd, 1251st and 1262nd Anti-Aircraft Regiments and the 1254th Anti-Tank Regiment. The army contained neither howitzer nor gun artillery regiments. As of 25 July the 1st Tank Army lacked guns heavier than 76mm, even according to the authorized strength of those units and formations that had been subordinated to it. On the whole, the instruments for suppressing the enemy's anti-tank defence and defensive system in a tank army of July 1942 were extremely weak. The situation for including rifle divisions in the army was getting a little better, but they predominantly added 76mm guns and only a dozen 122mm howitzers each.

As regards infantry, the German 16th Panzer and 3rd and 60th Motorized Divisions numbered fifteen motorized infantry battalions. The Soviet 28th Tank Corps and 131st Rifle Division could theoretically put forward 12 battalions (3+9), and by counting the tank brigades' motorized rifle battalions – 15 battalions (6+9). At the same time, one should take into account the fact that a Soviet rifle division's full-strength battalion numbered 700 men, while a German motorized infantry battalion numbered 900–1,000 men. The tank brigades' motorized rifle battalions were even weaker, so it would be more correct to say that the equivalent of 13.5–15 battalions was being allotted for the counterblow. Thus, even when taking into account the losses suffered earlier by the Germans, one cannot see a significant numerical superiority here. Zhuravlyov's group had been to a significant degree neutralized by the cutting of its communications and pressure from the front by the Germans' infantry units. Thus one may state that the Soviet 1st Tank Army did not possess a decisive superiority in forces over the enemy and was even inferior to him in artillery. There was no reason to expect a major success from it.

The *front* counterblow began on the morning of 26 July, precisely according to the 'Prokhorovka' variation.[71] One company of KVs from the 158th Tank Brigade, a company from the 131st Rifle Division and the 28th Tank Corps attacked the forward units of the German 3rd and 60th Motorized Divisions and forced them to fall back. A radiogram from the 3rd Motorized Division sounded almost panicky: 'A powerful attack along the entire front, especially on the 60th Motorized Division's right flank. There is no ammunition for the tanks.' At the same time, one should not exaggerate the Germans' ammunition problems: the XIV Panzer Corps expended 50 tons of ammunition on 26 July.[72]

As a result of the counterblow, Soviet units liberated the settlements of '10 Years Since October' and Lozhki. Of the 158th Tank Brigade's nine KVs that attacked, six were lost, including three burned up. The 13th Tank Corps' 163rd Tank Brigade, which took part in the counterblow, won back Kachalinskaya, which had been unsuccessfully attacked earlier, and according to Soviet data five serviceable German tanks were captured. The 163rd Tank Brigade's losses over two days of fighting were twenty-one vehicles, including ten tanks lost due to air attacks.[73] On this day air support showed its limitations. In the Sixth Army's war diary the situation at that moment was described in the following manner: 'Mobile formations north-west of Kalach are engaged in uninterrupted heavy fighting with major enemy infantry and tank units that are constantly being reinforced from the south and south-east. Significant losses in personnel and the insufficient supply of fuel and ammunition are preventing us from continuing the offensive to the south and south-east and on 26.7 the vanguards have to be temporarily pulled back.'[74] At that moment Paulus's original plan for seizing the crossings at Kalach had essentially collapsed. But this was only the first round of the battle.

At the same time, the Stalingrad Front command made the decision to throw both tank armies into the fighting before the completion of their formation. In Operational Directive No. 00121/op from the *front* headquarters at 20.30 on 26 July, it was ordered:

The commander of the 1st Tank Army is to launch a decisive offensive with the forces of the 13th and 28th Tank Corps, the 196th and 131st Rifle Divisions and the 158th Tank Brigade in the general direction of Verkhne-Buzinovka, with the mission of destroying the enemy and arriving with its main forces in the Verkhne-Buzinovka area by the close of 27.7

The commander of the 21st Army is to begin an offensive with the forces of three rifle divisions from the Serafimovich area to the south and south-east in the direction of Karaichev.

The commander of the 4th Tank Army is to cross the 22nd Tank Corps, together with the attached 133rd Tank Brigade, over to the western bank of the Don River on the night of 27.7 and attack with the mission of destroying the enemy's forward units and reaching the Golubaya River with its main forces by the close of 27.7. Its subsequent task is to attack toward Verkhne-Buzinovka from the east, in conjunction with units of the 1st Tank Army, and to destroy the enemy's main group of forces and to restore the situation along the 62nd Army's right flank.[75]

If one compares this text with the preceding directive (see above), then the reduction of the depth of the armies' task is obvious. Now, instead of a powerful attack on Kletskaya, an attack to a lesser depth, on Verkhne-Buzinovka from the north-east and south-east, is planned. They managed to include the 196th Rifle Division in the shock group of forces by freeing it up with the 64th Army's units that occupied its positions. Thus the Stalingrad Front command was seeking to defeat the enemy by attacks along different axes before he could be reinforced.

Organic shortcomings only exacerbated the situation with the delay in concentrating forces. The counterblow of 27 July, which was conceived as a crushing offensive from several directions, became essentially a continuation of the attack near Kalach with the forces of the 1st Tank Army, and even these were limited.

The strongest participant, in the sense of armoured equipment, in the 27 July counterblow was the 158th Tank Brigade, which was equipped with heavy KV tanks and which had been crossed over to the western bank of the Don in full strength and supported by units of the 131st Rifle Division. The main mass of the latter's infantry was gradually being brought up as the battle was already going on, while the division's artillery had only partially occupied firing positions and the vast majority of it was still on the march and on the crossings. The 158th Tank Brigade's KVs attacked without having a sufficient amount of infantry and lacking artillery support, as well as the absence of air support. Before long the weak infantry was cut off from the tanks by machine gun and artillery fire and the KVs moved on further alone. In June–July 1941 almost thirty KVs would have been a serious force. However, on 27 July 1942 the units of the 3rd and 60th Motorized Divisions, which were defending along the axis of the 158th Tank Brigade's offensive, disposed of more than enough anti-tank weapons: 76.2mm anti-tank guns and their own tanks, including ones armed with long-barrel 75mm guns.[76] As a result, the KV attack was halted along the line of Height 169.8 – Height 174.9 to the north of '10 Years Since October' and the 158th Tank Brigade lost that day twenty KVs burned-out and five knocked out, that is, almost all of its available tanks.

Yet another powerful participant in the counterblow of 27 July was the 196th Rifle Division, which together with the 649th Tank Battalion (forty-two tanks) attacked from the '10 Years Since October' State Farm to the north. The full-strength division with tanks managed to force the Germans to fall back. In the history of the 16th Panzer Division, this fighting is described in the following manner: 'The division was torn into three parts, each of which was drawn into heavy fighting and cut off from supply. This was a time of true testing! Latmann's and Wietzleben's combat group was supplied by air by He 111 aircraft. Surrounded by forty-five tanks, Wietzleben's combat group was forced to fall back from Ostrov to Gureev and finally to Yeruslanovskii.'[77] Despite the dramatic description of the supply situation, the artillery remained the strong element in German mobile formations – the XIV Panzer Corps expended 70 tons of ammunition in a day.[78] As was noted in the Sixth Army's war diary: 'Bitter fighting erupted north-west of Kalach, during the course of which all of the enemy's attacks were beaten back, partly by counterblows, while 39 enemy tanks were destroyed, including 28 heavy ones.'[79]

On 27 July Tanaschishin's corps ended up being completely excluded from the shock group of forces. The subordination of the 13th Tank Corps to the 1st Tank Army and the receipt of a new mission required its withdrawal from the fighting with its front facing west. However, it was decided 'to destroy the opposing enemy with a decisive attack in order to begin the fulfilment of a new task'.[80] The attack was set for 03.30 on 27 July. This time was held to, with the exception of the 163rd Tank Brigade, which was 40 minutes late. The commander of the above-named 521st Anti-Tank Battalion described the morning attack thusly: 'Our eyes try to pierce the morning mist. At a distance of 1,500 meters the silhouettes of the Russian tanks can be made out: first one, then the second, and the third … The steel giants attacked from out of the mist, firing from all guns.' The battalion's 128mm and 105mm self-propelled guns let the Soviet tanks pass through and occupied positions along their flank, opening fire against their sides. All three of the 13th Tank Corps' brigades attacked the enemy, but they were unsuccessful. The corps' losses for the day were nineteen T-34s and ten T-70s.[81] According to the report by the commander of the 521st Battalion, cited by the historian T. Jentz, in repelling the Soviet attack, fourteen Soviet tanks were knocked out by two of his heavy self-propelled guns and anti-tank guns in a short time, while two tanks that had broken into the depth were knocked out by anti-aircraft guns. The following was noted in the Sixth Army's war diary: 'There was heavy fighting opposite the 113th Infantry Division and the 16th Panzer Division's western group, and 46 medium and heavy tanks thus far have been destroyed, according to available data, while our losses are significant.'[82] However, the 13th Tank Corps' potential was already practically spent – on the evening of 27 July only twenty-seven T-34s and thirteen T-70s remained in service.[83]

The 21st Army took part in the counterblow of 27 July with the forces of the 300th, 124th and 278th Rifle Divisions, which numbered as of 27 July 878, 7,625 and 1,080 men respectively. It was difficult to achieve success with such worn-out divisions, and there was no miracle – the Germans evaluated the attacks near Serafimovich as 'a reconnaissance in force' and they were beaten back by the forces of the 305th Infantry Division, which had arrived from the west.

The Soviet attacks on 27 July finally convinced the Sixth Army command of the necessity of altering its plans. At midday the following order was dispatched by telephone telegram:

> The LI Corps must immediately, while advancing through the heights north-east of Rychov, establish contact with the XIV Panzer Corps west of Kalach. We must clear the terrain south of the Chir of the enemy. As before, it is important to seize undamaged the bridges in Rychov and to the south-west. The corps must prepare for crossing over the Don on both sides of the mouth of the Chir. The 44th Infantry Division remains subordinated to the LI Corps, aside from which the 24th Panzer Division is temporarily subordinated tactically to the corps.[84]

One sees a certain half-heartedness in the order – as before, missions are laid down for forcing the Don. However, for the first time we see the mission of attacking to link up with the XIV Panzer Corps near Kalach.

Finally, on 28 July the 13th Tank Corps was finally deployed along the flank and rear of the Germans' XIV Panzer Corps: it received an order to attack toward Maiorovskii and Verkhnyaya Buzinovka and was ready to carry it out. To be sure, by this time there were only forty tanks in service in the corps. On the morning of 28 July the brigades of Tanaschishin's corps were breaking through to the Maiorovskii area and establishing communications with Zhuravlyov's group. The group managed to deliver twenty-one vehicles with fuel and ammunition. The 13th Tank Corps' combat vehicles were essentially carrying out the role of protecting supply convoys.

The ease of the breakthrough by Tanaschishin's tanks to Maiorovskii forces us to consider whether it would not have been more expedient to employ the 13th Tank Corps for attacking the enemy's flank earlier. However, one should admit that holding the 113th Infantry Division's offensive was also an important task. To turn one's back against it and counter-attack in the direction of Verkhnyaya Buzinovka would have been, at the very least, reckless. Following the withdrawal of the tanks from its front, the 113th Infantry Division moved forward and during the second half of the day occupied Yevseev, essentially cutting off the 13th Tank Corps' path of withdrawal. It's most likely that the tank armies were committed into the fighting late.

Following the link-up with Zhuravlyov's group, the 13th Tank Corps continued to attack in the direction of Verkhnyaya Buzinovka. From 14.00 to 18.00 it advanced as far as Verkhnyaya Buzinovka, crushing everything along its path. According to the report by the corps commander, during the course of this attack thirty-one guns, including nine heavy, were destroyed, as well as 'many motor vehicles and transport'. Heavy guns are not a needle in a haystack. If we consult the enemy's documents it becomes clear that on the day the Sixth Army really did lose three FH18s, one 1eFH18 and three anti-tank guns.[85]

However, further advance was checked: subsequent attacks by the 13th Tank Corps' tanks from 18.00 on 28 July through 22.00 on 29 July on Verkhnyaya Buzinovka were without result. The attack by thirty-five tanks from the 40th Tank Brigade, along with infantry from Zhuravlyov's group, brought success. Late in the evening of 29 July they managed to win back Verkhnyaya Buzinovka, capturing thirteen guns and 'cars and transport vehicles'. Among the 100th Light Infantry Division's lost weaponry were eight light field howitzers, which were included among the Sixth Army's losses for 29 July, as well as about thirty motor vehicles.[86]

According to the Sixth Army's war diary, the breakthrough to Verkhnyaya Buzinovka cut XIV Panzer Corps' lines of communication and units of the 376th and 305th Infantry and 100th Light Infantry Divisions were dispatched to restore them, as well as units of the 113th Infantry Division and a tank company from the 16th Panzer Division from Yevseev. Not long before midnight on 29 July, Tanaschishin received an order to break through to Osinovskii to link up with the 1st Tank Army's units.

Relief of the 13th Tank Corps by the 23rd Tank Corps.

The forced employment of the 13th Tank Corps as a means of holding the enemy facing the west forced the Soviets to re-examine the initial composition of the 1st Tank Army. Despite the fact that according to the command's plans the 13th Tank Corps was supposed to have been part of the *front's* second tank army (4th Tank Army), the situation forced it to move it up to Kalach and to subordinate it to K.S. Moskalenko's headquarters. On 27 July the corps included the 99th Tank Brigade (seventeen T-34s and sixteen T-70s), the 189th Tank Brigade (twenty-six T-34s and sixteen T-70s) and the 9th Motorized Rifle Brigade.[87] As in many other tank formations in the Stalingrad Front, the corps suffered from a shortage of motorized infantry. According to a report on the state of the 9th Motorized Rifle Brigade's combat and numerical strength on 26 July, there were 1,190 men, as opposed to an authorized strength of 3,258. A large part of the shortage was felt in the enlisted ranks, and in the corps' report the capabilities of the motorized rifle brigade were listed as only 254 'bayonets'.[88] Due to the low level of manning, the motorized rifle brigade was left on the left bank of the Don. Major General Abram Matveevich Khasin, a sufficiently experienced tank commander, headed the 23rd Tank Corps. As early as the beginning of the 1930s, Khasin completed the Military Academy of Motorization and Mechanization, commanded various tank units, began the war in the Baltic States, and presided over the awarding of a guards designation of his 1st Tank Brigade in September 1941.

By 04.00 on 29 July the 99th and 189th Tank Brigades crossed over the Don and arrived at their jumping-off positions for a counterblow. The corps was given the following mission: to attack in the general direction of Osinovskii to link up with the 4th Tank Army's units. In this manner it was planned to encircle the enemy's mobile formations that had broken through to the approaches to Kalach. However, at the last moment an order arrived cancelling the offensive and rerouting the 23rd Tank Corps to the Surovikino area, that is, in the direction of the attack by the Sixth Army's LI Corps. To judge by this, at that moment Operational Directive No. 00129/op of 02.00 on 28 July from the *front* headquarters reached the headquarters of the 1st Tank Army. It stated: 'The 23rd Tank Corps and the 204th and 321st Rifle Divisions are to destroy with a vigorous attack the enemy who has crossed to the left bank of the Chir River and by the close of 28.7 reach the Chir River along the Bol'shaya Osinovka – Nizhne-Chirskaya sector.'[89]

The shift in the direction of an attack was a reasonably common practice. However, this was not accomplished without the kind of disorderly movements characteristic of defensive battles. At 10.00 on 29 July, when the corps' units were already on the march to their new concentration area, there followed an order from Moskalenko for the 189th Tank Brigade to turn back. On a map affixed to the corps commander's report, there was written 'returned by Khrushchev's order'.[90] The corps was actually to be divided in two: one part was to operate against the Sixth Army's northern shock group, and the other against the southern one. In order to do this, they had to make a 150–300km march, during the course of which up to 30 per cent of their equipment was put out of action and they remained another 3–5 days undergoing repairs. These losses were linked, in particular, to the drivers' lack of experience, many of whom had only four hours of practical training. A no less vexing loss was that of time. The 189th Tank Brigade returned to its jumping-off positions only by 16.00 on 29 July and the attack was rescheduled for 04.00 on 30 July, that is, it was shifted an entire day from the initial plan for the counterblow. At 16.00 on 29 July the movement to Surovikino was finally cancelled. As opposed to what is maintained in some memoirs and even historical studies, the 23rd Tank Corps did not take part in the repulse of the enemy's southern shock group. This is what Moskalenko wrote: 'The 23rd Tank Corps and 204th Rifle Division soon arrived and were also dispatched to the designated area and committed into the fighting along the boundary between the 62nd and 64th Armies. They played a decisive role in repelling the enemy's attack from the south-west. The enemy divisions suffered heavy losses and were thrown back from the Novomaksimovskii area and beyond the Chir River.'[91]

It's unclear what kind of decisive role he's speaking of here, when the 99th Tank Brigade was returned that same day to its former area for counter-attacks against the Sixth Army's northern shock group. As a result of the change in plans for employing the 23rd Tank Corps, on 29 July a pause actually ensued in launching attacks against the enemy's mobile formations along the approaches to Kalach. The 158th Tank Brigade, with four KVs, together with units of the 131st Rifle Division, went over to a general offensive. Upon reaching Heights 174.9 and 168.9 the tanks were met with heavy anti-tank fire and, lacking support from the infantry and artillery, fell back to their jumping-off position. The 196th Rifle Division attacked, but was halted by fire from 'buried tanks'. These two lunges were more like pinpricks than counterblows. This was all the more vexing in light of the fact that on 29 July the XIV Panzer Corps' rear services had been disorganized by the actions of Tanaschishin's corps and Zhuravlyov's group and its defensive capabilities had been reduced.

Tank Army II

The date for completing the formation of the 4th Tank Army had initially been set at a later time (1 August) than for the 1st Tank Army. The army was also being formed along the near approaches to Stalingrad. Thus V.D. Kryuchyonkin's army entered the fighting later than did K.S. Moskalenko's army. The later date for forming the army led to a situation in which they managed to take from the 4th Tank Army the 23rd Tank Corps, which had been designated for inclusion within it. It was reassigned to the Kalach area in Moskalenko's army, while Kryuchyonkin's tank army got only Major General of Tank Troops A.A. Shamshin's 22nd Tank Corps. At this time Shamshin was only 34 years old, although he had been associated with the tank troops since the beginning of the 1930s.

The Soviet command once again employed the method of subordinating freshly-formed brigades to the headquarters of a mechanized formation with combat experience. The corps, made up of the 13th, 36th and 133rd Tank Brigades, had taken part in the battle around Khar'kov. Now the 173rd, 176th and 182nd Tank Brigades were subordinated to Shamshin. The latter two brigades had been formed in the spring of 1942 in Gor'kii and were transferred to the Stalingrad area by rail. By the close of 26 July the 182nd Tank Brigade had concentrated in the Ilovlinskaya area and the 173rd Tank Brigade was located in the place where it was being formed – the Kachalinskaya area. The 176th Tank Brigade was late and arrived in the area of combat activities on 27 July, and not fully formed – the 2nd Tank Battalion and the motorized rifle battalion caught up with the brigade only on the third day of fighting. That is, the brigade found itself without even minimal infantry support. The 22nd Tank Corps' motorized rifle brigade, which had been caught halfway through it formation, was able to send 200 active bayonets and one (!) 76mm gun to the area of combat activities. At first there were simply no rifle units in the area of the 22nd Tank Corps' area of operations. Essentially, the situation in the northern part of the great bend of the Don, around Sirotinskaya, was typical of this small battle – at first there was no continuous front at all.

For the newcomers, there were shortcomings in being subordinated to an experienced headquarters. The brigade's final composition became known only on the evening of 26 July, and at the time the combat order to launch a counterblow was received the commanders of the corps and the brigade commanders did not yet know each other by sight. Having begun the crossing over the Don on ferries at 11.00 on 27 July, the 22nd Tank Corps' units completed it only by the close of 28 July.

After the crossing over the Don there followed the march to the designated concentration area for the counterblow. Some of the tanks fell out during the march due to breakdowns,

Table 2: The 22nd Tank Corps' Strength and Losses, 27 July–2 August 1942.[92]

Brigade	Tank Model	Present at Start of Fighting	Combat Losses by Days							Total Losses
			27.7	28.7	29.7	30.7	31.7	1.8	2.8	
173rd Tank Brigade	T-34	32/23*	–	–	10	4	–	1	3	18
	T-70	21/19	–	1	2	1	–	1	6	11
	T-60	13/13	–	–	–	3	4	–	3	10
Total for 173rd Tank Brigade		66/55	–	1	12	8	4	2	12	39
176th Tank Brigade	T-34	32/19	–	–	16	–	–	3	–	19
	T-70	16/10	–	–	8	–	–	–	–	8
Total for 176th Tank Brigade		48/29	–	–	24	–	–	3	–	27
182nd Tank Brigade	T-34	32/21	4	2	15	8	–	1	1	31
	T-70	21/8	–	1	6	4	4	–	3	18
	T-60	13/12	–	–	–	4	–	–	2	6
Total for 182nd Tank Brigade		66/41	4	3	21	16	4	1	6	55
Total for 22nd Tank Corps		180/125	4	4	57	24	8	6	18	111

* The figure in the numerator is for 27 July, while the figure in the denominator is following the march, at the time of meeting the enemy.

both due to the fault of the producing factory and to the drivers. The state of the 22nd Tank Corps' tank part can be seen from the table opposite.

One can easily see that as a result of the tanks falling out of line on the march the corps' offensive capabilities by the time it came into contact with the enemy had materially fallen. For example, of the 180 tanks available, 125, or 69.4 per cent of initial strength, were on hand ready to enter the fighting, while the share of T-34s was even a bit lower at 65.6 per cent – sixty-three vehicles out of ninety-six listed.

The 22nd Tank Corps' mission was to launch a counterblow from the north against the enemy's group of forces which had driven a wedge between the 21st and 62nd Armies, with 'the main attack along the axis Os'kinskii – Verkhne-Buzinovka'.[93] One cannot say that the delay in beginning the counterblow immediately led to a radical change in the situation. The Sixth Army's infantry formations were still on the march to the great bend of the Don and the Soviet tank troops' main enemy remained the units of the XIV Panzer Corps.

During the first encounter the 22nd Tank Corps' brigades attacked 'in the best traditions' of 1941, that is, tanks without infantry. The few motorized battalions of the brigades of Shamshin's corps were pulled apart for covering the left flank along the Don River. They formed a sort of screen between the tanks' shock fist and the bank of the Don. At the same time, it is hard to reproach Shamshin for employing his motorized infantry in such a fashion, since the enemy's breakthrough to the crossings over the Don along the army's left flank could have resulted in a real disaster.

In the 4th Tank Army's first fight on 29 July all three of its brigades advanced along a broad front, actually having no contact with each other. The 173rd and 182nd Tank Brigades advanced a few kilometres, while occupying Os'kinskii and losing thirty-three tanks (see the data on the losses of the 22nd Tank Corps above). The events of 29 July developed most dramatically in the 176th Tank Brigade's attack zone. The brigade's first echelon, headed by the commander and consisting of fourteen T-34s and eight T-70s, was advancing in the direction of Sukhanovskii and ran into the Germans' anti-tank defence in the Osinovskii area. One of the 16th Panzer Division's combat groups had a strongpoint in Osinovskii with an all-round defence (the so-called 'hedgehog'). Eight T-34s and seven T-70s were immediately lost. The brigade commander was killed. The operational group of the brigade's headquarters was advancing behind the first echelon under the cover of four T-34s and two T-70s. It was fired upon from the flank and all the tanks and wheeled vehicles were destroyed.[94] This was an obvious case of ignoring intelligence on the enemy. Also, a large part of the command and rank and file was in combat for the first time had no experience and training and manoeuvred poorly on the battlefield. The absence of radio tanks led to a loss of control at the start of the attack. The result was the massacre of the 176th Tank Brigade as early as the first fight.

Nevertheless, the tank attacks made a definite impression on the Germans and in the Sixth Army's war diary it states that 'the 16th Panzer Division, while covering Liska, is fighting in Verkhne-Buzinovka and near Os'kinskii against superior enemy tank forces'. One cannot say that the tank attack without infantry was completely without result. The 173rd Tank Brigade reported destroying twelve anti-tank guns and two tanks and capturing twenty-five motor vehicles, nine radio sets, fuel tankers and a mortar battery. If a full-blooded mechanized formation, with powerful motorized infantry and artillery, had been in the place of the 22nd Tank Corps, then its attack could have been nearly fatal for the XIV Panzer Corps. However, the attacks by tanks alone only pushed back the German units, because the tanks were unable to occupy and hold terrain by themselves.

Judgment Day

July 30th 1942 became the climax of the *front's* counterblow, when the Stalingrad Front managed to mobilize significant forces for attacks on the enemy's breakthrough.

For ten hours from the early morning of 30 July the 13th Tank Corps and Zhuravlyov's group were fighting for Osinovskii – that same inhabited locale near which on the previous day the first echelon of the 22nd Tank Corps' 176th Tank Brigade had been destroyed. At that moment the fighting was going on literally within a few kilometres from the 1st Tank Army's units attacking from the south. It was admitted in the history of the 16th Panzer Division that 'never had the division's situation been so critical'. According to the Sixth Army's war diary, the attacks on Osinovskii on the morning of 30 July had been repulsed and eleven Soviet tanks were reported destroyed. The failure to break through and link up with the 1st Tank Army forced Yefim Pushkin to redirect the 13th Tank Corps to the north in order to link up with the 4th Tank Army. This order was carried out and at 21.00 on 30 July the remnants of Zhuravlyov's group and those of the 13th Tank Corps reached Os'kinskii. The most combat-capable elements of Zhuravlyov's group broke out of the encirclement. However, the less combat-capable elements, probably the rear services, for the most part remained behind. As was noted in the Sixth Army's war diary, '[The VIII Army Corps], in conjunction with units of the XIV Panzer Corps, captured more than 2,000 prisoners in the fighting for Verkhnyaya Buzinovka and destroyed 38 tanks and captured or destroyed 25 guns and much other equipment'.[95] On the whole, the situation had changed in the Germans' favour: the 100th Light Infantry and 113th Infantry Divisions had established secure contact with the mobile formations of Wietersheim's corps that had broken through to the Kalach area.

At the moment the 4th Tank Army was ready to launch an offensive again on 30 July, the defence of the opposing German forces had been significantly strengthened. First of all, yet another of the VIII Army Corps' divisions – the 305th Infantry (with two regiments) had reached the Don bend. Secondly, the 13th Tank Corps' breakthrough to Zhuravlyov's group had freed up the 113th Infantry Division and it had moved up to occupy defensive positions with its front facing east.

A result of the shifts in the enemy's camp was that on 30 July Shamshin's tank corps attacked with all three brigades but collided immediately with the defence of three German divisions. The 182nd Tank Brigade attacked the right flank of the 305th Infantry Division unsuccessfully on the offensive's right wing, and according to German data of the thirty attacking tanks twelve were destroyed, while the remaining eighteen 'were scattered by the fire of assault guns and a strafing attack by Ju 87s'. In the centre the 173rd Tank Brigade unsuccessfully attacked units of the 113th Infantry Division. On the 4th Tank Army's left wing, the 176th Tank Brigade attacked units of the 16th Panzer Division. According to the results of the day, the 4th Tank Army was only partly reinforced by the worn-out 184th and 192nd Rifle Divisions from Zhuravlyov's group and the remnants of the 13th Tank Corps – twenty-two tanks. On the following day, 31 July, the reinforced German group of forces not only defended, but also began an offensive.

On 30 July the 23rd Tank Corps, which was the last of the tank armies' mobile formations committed into the fighting, also took part in the *front* counterblow. At first, only the 189th Tank Brigade took part in the offensive, as the 99th Tank Brigade was covering the flank of Khasin's corps by facing west. The brigade's losses for the day were eleven T-34s and twelve T-70s, that is, more than half of its initial strength. The situation remained unchanged along the old axis. Having received a reinforcement company of nine KVs, on 31 July the 158th Tank Brigade attacked in the previous direction and the tanks broke into the depth of the enemy's defence without infantry. Ten KVs were burned by 'thermite' (most likely hollow-charge) shells.

On 31 July the 23rd Tank Corps once again attacked, this time with the 99th and 189th Tank Brigades. The attacking tanks were met with anti-tank defensive fire and fire from tanks dug into the ground. A tank battalion from the 99th Tank Brigade broke into the depth of the enemy's defence to Sukhanovskii, but communications with it were lost and its fate remained unknown. In the Wehrmacht[96] high command's war diary these events were described thusly: 'In the area north of Kalach our attacking forces are repelling attacks by the enemy's tank groups, partially by those shifted from other sectors and partially by those trying to break out of encirclement.' In a diary entry for 31 July, Halder[97] wrote: 'The Sixth Army's situation has improved. The enemy is once again attacking, bringing up fresh forces, but all his attacks are being beaten back. The situation with ammunition and fuel is normalizing.' The attacks against the XIV Panzer Corps' main forces were a difficult and exhausting affair, and the hopes for success illusory.

At the end of July the commanders of the reserve armies, who were considered insufficiently prepared for waging battle in a difficult situation along the most important direction, were relieved. Lieutenant General A.I. Lopatin (who earlier commanded the North Caucasus Front's 9th Army) replaced V.Ya. Kolpakchi as commander of the 62nd Army, and M.S. Shumilov replaced Chuikov as commander of the 64th Army. On 5 August the task of controlling the Stalingrad Front's forces was simplified: according to *Stavka* Directive No. 170554 the South-eastern Front was created, which included the 64th, 57th and 51st Armies.

Infantry instead of Tanks

At the beginning of August the Soviet forces along the right bank of the Don were still attempting to seize the initiative and defeat the enemy's tank group of forces that had broken through all the way to Kalach. The 1st and 4th Tank Armies continued to attack the enemy who had penetrated all the way to the Don. With the creation of the South-eastern Front, units of the 1st Tank Army were to be transferred to the 62nd Army.

If during the course of the 22nd Tank Corps' first counterblows there had been practically no infantry in the 4th Tank Army, then in the beginning of August the situation had improved considerably, mostly by the transfer to the army of the 'Far Eastern'[98] divisions that had arrived at the front. As of 1 August Kryuchyonkin's army included the 18th Rifle Division (the *front* reserve, numbering 12,024 men), the 205th Rifle Division (11,826 men) and Zhuravlyov's group (the worn-out 184th and 192nd Rifle Divisions), which had emerged from the encirclement. The 4th Army was also to have transferred to it the 321st and 422nd 'Far Eastern' rifle divisions. However, here events along the *front's* southern flank intervene, and the 422nd Rifle Division had to be crossed back over the Don and thrown in the Abganerovo area (see later).

As of 1 August 1942 the tank park of Kryuchyonkin's army was by no means in a brilliant condition (see table).

Table 3: The Availability of Tanks in the 4th Tank Army's Units on 1 August 1942.[99]

Unit and Tank Type	Muster Strength	In Service	Left on Battlefield	Irreplaceable Losses	Undergoing Repair
173rd Tank Bde					
T-34	32	9	7	2	9
T-70	21	12	2	1	4
T-60	13	9	–	–	2
Total	66	30	9	3	15
176th Tank Bde					
T-34	32	3	–	–	–
T-70	16	2	–	–	–
Total	48	5	–	–	–
182nd Tank Bde					
T-34	32	7	–	9	–
T-70	16	7	–	5	–
T-60	13	7	–	6	–
Total	61	21	–	20	20
Total in 22nd Tank Corps	175	56	–	–	–
133th Tank Bde					
KV	40	40	–	–	–

It's apparent that a large portion of the 22nd Tank Corps' tank park now consisted of light and small tanks. The 176th Tank Brigade, which was facing the 16th Panzer Division, had suffered the most in the fighting. The remnants of the 13th Tank Corps, which had broken through to the 4th Tank Army's lines, had been reformed into a single 169th Tank Brigade, which was subordinated to the 22nd Tank Corps. The 133rd Tank Brigade, which is shown in the table, was formally subordinated to the 4th Tank Army but was soon removed from Kryuchyonkin's command and dispatched to the area of the '74 kilometre' railway siding to the south-east of Stalingrad due to the breakthrough by the German Fourth Panzer Army. Nevertheless, quite a large number of tanks undergoing repair still remained in the 22nd Tank Corps.

On 2 August the 22nd Tank Corps attacked together with the infantry from Zhuravlyov's group that had broken out of the encirclement. For the first time since the commitment of the corps into the fighting its actions were supported by infantry and artillery (up to sixteen 76mm guns). On this day all four tank brigades subordinated to the corps took part in the fighting, but only managed to advance 2–3km.

The report by the commander of the 22nd Tank Corps stated: 'The rifle units, which were operating in conjunction with the corps, were poorly organized and did not demonstrate tenacity in the attack. Upon the first fire encounter with the enemy's fire resistance, they halted their attack and part of them fell back into the *balki*,[100] and part of them entrenched along the line they had reached.'[101]

Taking into account what we now know of the VIII Army Corps' artillery capabilities, the 'first fire encounter' was terrible. During the next few days, up to 3 August, the 4th

Tank Army continued its attacks, but they were already doomed to failure, as the Sixth Army's VIII Corps had established a solid defence from the Kletskaya area to the Don. Moreover, the corps' formations had been materially reinforced. For example, the 113th Infantry Division, which was located along the axis of the 4th Tank Army's main attack, disposed of, as reinforcements, the 521st Anti-Tank Battalion, the 177th and 244th Assault Gun Battalions (both of the ones in the corps!), the 733rd Battalion with 210mm howitzers and the 631 Battalion with 105mm guns.[102] As of 30 July the two battalions of assault guns included five short-barrel and eleven long-barrel StuG IIIs.[103] Besides this, the corps' reports spoke of six 88mm anti-aircraft guns used as anti-tank weapons. Thus, both the anti-tank and artillery capabilities of the German formations opposite Kryuchyonkin's army enabled them to hold the front with confidence and to repel attacks.

On 3 August there were only forty-three tanks in line in the 22nd Tank Corps: fifteen T-34s, ten T-70s and eighteen T-60s.[104] One should stress that the main losses were suffered from the enemy's artillery fire, while losses from air attack were seven vehicles. At the same time, it can't be said that the game was completely one-sided. As of 2 August thirteen short-barrel and five long-barrel StuG IIIs were considered ready for combat.[105] That is, the Soviet tank troops managed to somewhat thin out the park of the long-barrelled *Sturmgeschützen*, while at the same time vehicles, which had been knocked out earlier, had been repaired and put back into the line with long-barrel guns.

Unfortunately, the significant reinforcement of the 4th Tank Army's infantry component by means of the 'Far Easterners' was very late. First of all, in light of the loss of the greater part of its tanks, one could only conditionally call it a tank army. Second, Kryuchyonkin's army now faced three of the VIII Army Corps' infantry divisions, the 305th, 113th and 384th, which had recently been committed into the Don bend.

Basically, at that moment the time had already arrived for declaring the game over: the German group of forces had been reinforced, tanks had been lost and the chances for a decisive result had been reduced to zero. What motives was the Soviet command guided by? During discussions between the *front* headquarters and the Red Army General Staff on 2 August, Gordov formulated the reasons for continuing the offensive in a quite straightforward manner: '… we are getting an influx of reinforcements simultaneously with the enemy. I can't sit and wait until forces are concentrated, because the enemy may become stronger and roll up the 62nd Army's right flank. This is why active operations are not ceasing here, although I know that this is resulting in mutual pulverizing.'[106] Further on Gordov expressed the hope that with the arrival of reserves the balance of forces would swing in the direction of the Red Army, which would enable him to take the offensive in his hands. It is also necessary to stress that during these discussions A.M. Vasilevskii openly demanded 'broad and active operations' from the Stalingrad Front's headquarters.

The next series of attacks followed on 5–8 August. This time the fresh 'Far Eastern' divisions took part in the offensive. However, at this moment the 22nd Tank Corps tank park presented quite a pitiful sight. On 5 August the 182nd Tank Brigade attacked with a strength of two T-34s, two T-70s and five T-60s, while the 173rd Tank Brigade numbered just eleven tanks. Given such weak tank support, one could not count on crushing the enemy's defence. Just as weak was the artillery support (compared to the VIII Corps' artillery). August 6th and 7th were spent in regrouping and on the 8th a new offensive began, with a slight change in the axis of the main attack. But it also suffered a reverse. Following this, the 4th Tank Army went over to the defensive.

The 1st Tank Army had entered the August fighting with a significantly reduced number of tanks. The condition of its units at that moment was only a little better than that of its sister, which was operating at this time to the north (see table).

Table 4: The Availability of Tanks in the 1st Tank Army's Units at 21.00 on 1 August 1942.[107]

Availability of Tanks by Model				
	T-34	*T-70*	*T-60*	*BT*
28th Tank Corps				
55th Tank Brigade	13	1	–	16
39th Tank Brigade	4	1	10	–
Total in 28th Tank Corps	17	2	10	16
23rd Tank Corps				
56th Tank Brigade	24	24	–	–
99th Tank Brigade	5	6	–	–
189th Tank Brigade	9	–	3	–
20th Motorized Rifle Brigade	7	–	–	–
Total in 23rd Tank Corps	45	30	3	–
Total in 1st Tank Army	62	32	13	16

In contrast, the Sixth Army's XIV Panzer Corps' armoured equipment park remained powerful (see table):

Table 5: The Strength of the XIV Panzer Corps' Tank Park on 1 August 1942.[108]

	Panzer II	*Panzer III (short)*	*Panzer III (long)*
16th Panzer Division	6	19	75
60th Motorized Division	12	–	31
3rd Motorized Division	9	–	25

	Panzer IV (short)	*Panzer IV (long)*	*7.62cm Sfl*	*Total*
16th Panzer Division	6	12	2	118
60th Motorized Division	–	3	3	49
3rd Motorized Division	–	5	7	46

The stability of the strength of the tank formations in Wietersheim's corps may be explained both by the timely recovery of knocked-out vehicles on territory controlled by German forces and by the correct employment of tanks while being supported by motorized infantry and artillery.

Despite the change in the situation, the Soviet command still hoped to turn the course of the battle in its favour. On 2 August the 23rd Tank Corps once again attacked according to the 'Prokhorovka' model, that is, practically in the face of the enemy's shock group. The losses on this day were twenty T-34s knocked out and seven burned, six T-70s knocked out and one burned, and fourteen T-60s knocked out and three burned. One of the 56th

Tank Brigade's tank battalions, consisting of six T-34s and four T-60s, penetrated into the enemy position and simply disappeared. However, one cannot fail to note that according to the results of the 2 August fighting, the number of combat-ready tanks in the XIV Panzer Corps changed somewhat (see table).

Table 6: The Strength of the XIV Panzer Corps' Tank Park on 3 August 1942.[109]

	Panzer II	*Panzer III (short)*	*Panzer III (long)*
16th Panzer Division	–	19	65
60th Motorized Division	12	–	21
3rd Motorized Division	8	–	25

	Panzer IV (short)	*Panzer IV (long)*	*7.62cm Sfl1*	*Total*
16th Panzer Division	5	16	–	105
60th Motorized Division	–	2	3	38
3rd Motorized Division	–	5	6	44

In the first days of August Moskalenko's tank army also received a fresh rifle division – the 399th. This was yet another fresh division that was committed into the fighting and which numbered on 5 August 1942 12,322 men and outfitted almost entirely at authorized strength. It was committed immediately into the fighting on 5 August and suffered heavy casualties, which, according to the Red Army General Staff's officer with the 62nd Army, amounted to 'more than 3,000 killed', although he was most likely speaking of both killed and wounded.

At the same time, one must not think that all of these counterblows by the 1st and 4th Tank Armies resembled tossing fine tableware against a concrete wall. Dërr evaluated the situation as follows: 'The enemy's fresh forces attacked along the army's northern flank from the Don bend in the Kremenskaya area and began to threaten from the rear our divisions north-west of Kamenskii. Units of the VIII Army Corps were forced to begin a withdrawal under enemy pressure, insofar as a security line along the Don did not yet exist.'[110] On 5 August Halder wrote in his diary: 'Paulus is reporting serious enemy counterblows against the XIV Panzer Corps from the south. The enemy is waging even more serious attacks against the northern sector of the XIV Panzer and VIII Army corps.'

Table 7: The Expenditure of Ammunition by the VIII Army Corps.[111]

Weapons	5–15.08.1942		18.07–04.08.1942
	Rounds	per cent of Combat Load	Rounds
Infantry Weapons	472,600	18 per cent	933,507
Anti-Tank Guns	952	17 per cent	2,931
Heavy Infantry Weapons	9,337	37 per cent	9,032
Light Field Artillery	12,487	260 per cent	10,172
Heavy Field Artillery	4,305	102 per cent	2,320
Rocket Artillery	1,918	53 per cent	–
Tank Guns[112]	8,247	157 per cent	3,780

The entry of 6 August is shot through with alarm: 'Paulus is involved in heavy defensive fighting along the northern sector.'

One can trace through these data the high percentage of ammunition expended by the field artillery and assault guns. Soviet tanks were beaten off by a hurricane of field artillery fire. It's hardly surprising that the words 'The enemy is putting up heavy fire resistance' sounded as a refrain in the General Staff's reports dealing with the 4th Tank Army's August offensives.

On the whole, the events in the bend of the Don developed much in the manner of the counterblows of 1941. Soviet tank formations launched a flurry of attacks on the enemy, but did not achieve decisive results. Following the exhaustion of the mechanized units' forces, the enemy had the opportunity of realizing his plans. Thus, for example, during the course of the battle around Uman' at the end of July 1941, the 2nd Mechanized Corps was able to delay for a period of time the offensive by Kleist's[113] tank group into the rear of the Soviet 6th and 12th Armies. After the corps lost its tanks the Uman' 'cauldron' followed.

Order No. 227

On 28 July 1942, at the height of the fighting in the great bend of the Don, there appeared the infamous Order No. 227 by the people's commissar of defence 'On Measures to Strengthen Discipline and Order in the Red Army and to Prevent the Voluntary Withdrawal from Combat Positions', which is also known as 'Not a step backwards'. It became sadly famous in light of the strong link between it and the introduction into the Red Army of the very harsh practice of employing punishment units and machine-gun detachments. Signed by Stalin, the order was brought to the attention of literally every soldier and commander. The battle of Stalingrad took place under the impression of this order and to fail to mention it in our narrative would be a major mistake.

For the first time, perhaps, Stalin addressed the entire army with such a harsh evaluation of the situation at the front. Now it's quite difficult to imagine with just what amazement they listened to Order No. 227 along the stable sectors of the front and in units that were preparing for an offensive along the north-western and western strategic directions. In its capacity as a measure for stabilizing the situation and preventing a withdrawal, it was planned to introduce punishment companies and battalions, as well as to organize blocking machine-gun detachments with orders to fire on retreating troops.

A positive evaluation of Order No. 227 predominates in Soviet and Russian historical literature. In this regard, historical studies have something in common with the troops' operational documents at the end of 1942, in which it was common to rate highly the results of carrying out this order. However, such an almost exalted appraisal of Order No. 227 seems poorly founded. Fighting withdrawals continued, and from 28 July through November 1942 Soviet forces fell back to the Volga, having lost a large part of Stalingrad. In the Caucasus, the withdrawal was halted around Vladikavkaz (Ordzhonikidze) and along the Terek River. In a word, there was no immediate effect.

To justify the appearance of Order No. 227 by the necessity of adopting harsh measures and machine-gun battalions does not correspond to the realities of war as they had come to pass by 28 July 1942. Blocking detachments had appeared in the Red Army as an initiative from below as early as the first weeks of the war. These groups had existed long before Order No. 227 and instructions from Moscow. Of course, their activity was not strictly ordered, but they existed. One can see no extraordinary necessity to solidify this practice by publicly making it known to the entire rank and file. Moreover, there was already the *Stavka* of the Supreme High Command's Order No. 270, of 16 August 1941, which was also signed by Stalin and the members of the State Defence Committee.[114] Order No. 270 was directed at the struggle against abandoning positions, voluntary surrender and desertion. It proved to be quite sufficient in the 1941–2 winter campaign.

The reference to the enemy's experience in the formation of punishment battalions seems just as controversial. It sounded, at the very least, strange and had quite an ambiguous effect on the morale of military personnel. There was no urgent need for a declaration on the formation of punishment units in such a form in connection with a description of the difficult situation at the front. Punishment sub-units could have been introduced through individual orders without such widespread publicity and ambiguous motivation.

On the whole, one must admit that Order No. 227 showed to a great degree the critical situation along the fronts that had arisen in July 1942 and the recognition of the critical situation by the country's leadership. This was first of all by Stalin himself, who had experienced at that moment a certain loss of spirit and disappointment in intelligent commanders, and it was not for nothing that the order began with the loss of Rostov, abandoned by the forces of R.Ya. Malinovskii's[115] Southern Front. However, in the final analysis it was not Order No. 227 that halted the German offensive to the Volga and the Caucasus. It was halted by quite traditional means, including measures adopted before July 1942. This was the formation of reserve armies, the solution of the problem of the quality of tank production, the improvement in the work of military industry, and evacuation as a whole.

Chapter 2

Heat. 'The Cauldron'

The turn by the German Fourth Panzer Army toward Stalingrad (see below) was exerting an increasingly greater influence on the Stalingrad Front. By 6 August 1942 the Soviet command required an army headquarters and the choice fell on K.S. Moskalenko's staff. Before long it had become the staff of the 1st Guards Army. Correspondingly, by Front Directive No. 00209/op at 00.15 on 5 August, the forces of the 1st Tank Army, the 131st and 299th Rifle Divisions, the 23rd and 28th Tank Corps and the 158th Tank Brigade were to be transferred to the 62nd Army.

The removal of the tank army's headquarters and the plans to employ it by no means meant an abandonment of offensive plans. On one hand, the 62nd Army's tank park was a pitiful sight. On 6 August 1942 the 23rd Tank Corps contained one T-34 and ninety motorized riflemen in the 189th Tank Brigade, two T-34s, two T-70s and sixty bayonets in the 99th Tank Brigade, six T-34s and two T-70s (five tanks in working order and four not) and twenty-five automatic riflemen in the 56th Tank Brigade, and ninety-two bayonets in the 9th Motorized Rifle Brigade.[1] There remained in the 28th Tank Corps' 39th and 55th Tank Brigades one and two tanks, respectively, while the 32nd Motorized Rifle Brigade numbered 1,730 men.[2] Perhaps the most powerful at that moment was the 158th Tank Brigade, which, thanks to tenacious work by the repair crews, by 7 August had twelve KV tanks in line.[3] On 5 August there remained 4,772 and 6,279 men in the 196th and 131st Rifle Divisions respectively. Of their former power, nearly 100 per cent strength, there remained only memories.

Nevertheless, the 62nd Army was assigned the task of 'attacking on Sukhanovskii and Nizhne-Buzinovka'. At first glance, this might seem to be madness, but in fact it was part of a plan and the 21st Army was to become a new and powerful player in the fighting in the great bend. The 96th, 98th and 87th Rifle Divisions from the 'Far Eastern' forces, which were being unloaded along the Filonovo – Archeda sector and which were to move to the army's defensive front by 4–5 August 1942, were to be transferred to the army. Correspondingly, it was planned that 'a small fist from three fresh and well-trained rifle divisions and two new tank brigades is to be created along the 21st Army's sector'.[4] The 96th, 98th and 87th Rifle Divisions numbered on 5 August 11,796, 11,878 and 11,753 men respectively.[5] It's unclear what brigades they were speaking about, but they transferred three independent tank battalions (eighty-six tanks) to the 21st Army. It was planned to cross the three divisions over the Don and to employ them in a new offensive with decisive aims against the flank and rear of the German forces in the great bend of the Don. The 21st Army's overall strength increased to approximately 85,000 men. By way of comparison, on 20 July the army had numbered only 29,000 men.

In evaluating the situation then from the point of view of what we now know, we can state that the 21st Army's offensive had a fair chance of success: the XVII Army Corps' 376th Infantry Division was defending around Kletskaya. This corps disposed of neither heavy artillery nor *Sturmgeschützen* as support weapons. The start of the offensive was set for the morning of 6 August, but on this day the fresh divisions were still in the process of concentrating and it had to be postponed.

However, on the other side of the front offensive plans were also being hatched. Dërr writes: 'Finally, on 7 August the remaining combat units arrived. The army's supply was secured to such a degree that we could begin an offensive against the enemy's positions west of the Don.'[6] Of course, the accumulation of ammunition and fuel was an important matter. Just as important was the bringing up of the Sixth Army's infantry into the bend of the Don. This enabled the Germans to remove the 16th Panzer Division from the front line and to prepare it for the offensive. In all, five infantry, one light infantry, two panzer and two motorized divisions were to be brought in for the offensive.

On the morning of 7 August the German Sixth Army's northern and southern shock groups went over to the offensive along converging axes. The northern group of forces broke through the defence of the 62nd Army's 196th Rifle Division, and the southern the 112th Rifle Division (8,107 men as of 5 August) of the same army. The main attack was launched by the XIV Panzer Corps' 16th Panzer Division, attacking from the Maiorovskii area. Its combat groups 'rolled through' the 100th Light Infantry Division's positions. In essence, the Germans managed to launch an attack against the weakest place – the 196th Rifle Division had been greatly reduced in the previous fighting. Having broken through its defences, as early as about midday on 7 August the German tanks reached the Ostrov area, forced the Liska River and streamed toward the approaches to the crossing over the Don at Berezovskii (near the crossing in the Kalach area). In this way the 62nd Army's shock group had its flank deeply turned and a threat appeared to the crossings over the Don. At first the army put up tenacious resistance and in the Sixth Army's war diary it is noted that: 'During the latter half of the day the 3rd Motorized Division joined in the offensive by the 60th Motorized Division, which is moving to the south-east following the seizure of Skvorin. The division is heavily engaged with the entrenched enemy disposing of tanks. Numerous minefields are hindering its offensive.'[7] However, as early as midday on 7 August the turning of the flank led to the upsetting and gradual collapse of the defence. The 23rd Tank Corps' 99th Tank Brigade was encircled and German tanks reached the corps' headquarters.

The 297th, 76th and 71st Infantry Divisions and the XIV Panzer Corps' 24th Panzer Division spread out like a fan from the breach made in the 112th Rifle Division's defence at Chir station. The 112th Rifle Corps was thrown back to the east and forced back against the Don. As early as 10.00 on 8 August the division began to cross over the Don along the railway bridge. The bridge was set afire by a hail of shells and the crossing of the troops proceeded over the burning bridge. But this was only the beginning of the disaster. The German tanks broke through to the bridge behind the retreating tanks of the 121st and 137th Brigades. Three KVs, four T-34s and four T-60s remained in the 137th Tank Brigade at that moment. The bridge was blown up between 14.00 and 14.30 on 8 August 1942 in order to keep it from falling into enemy hands. A mass of the 112th Rifle Division's men and equipment remained along the right bank of the Don in front of the blown-up bridge.

During the night of 7/8 August the XIV and XXIV Panzer Corps' 'pincers' linked up (according to an entry in the Sixth Army's war diary, a radio telegram from the 16th Panzer Division, which reported on the closing of the 'cauldron,' arrived at 05.45 Berlin time on 8 August) and the 62nd Army's units and formations defending along the western bank of the Don were surrounded.

The formations that remained outside the 'cauldron' fell back over the Don in a greater or lesser degree of order. The remnants of the 23rd Tank Corps covered the crossings and twenty-one tanks, 70 per cent of which were immobile, were moved up to the defence. In the morning report to the Red Army General Staff on 8 August, it was noted that 'the 399th and 196th Rifle Divisions crossed over the Don River in small groups'. During the day on 8 August the crossings came under artillery fire from the German 16th Panzer Division. It's not difficult to imagine what kind of hell broke out along the crossings over the Don at Kalach at that moment. To the north, near Rubezhnoe, KV tanks from the 158th Tank Brigade were facing west and defending the crossings for the withdrawal of the 131st Rifle Division. At that moment the XIV Panzer Corps' main forces were deployed facing east.

Thanks to the tanks, the complete destruction of the retreating units was averted. By the evening of 8 August a large part of the 158th Tank Brigade's KVs had been burned by 'thermite' shells, and the last three vehicles were destroyed by their crews on 9 August. However, the tank troops were able to save a number of lives. On 10 August the 131st Rifle Division retained 2,933 men in line, approximately half of its strength on 5 August. The fighting along the approaches to the crossings at Kalach was just as stubborn. In the fighting on 9 August the 23rd Tank Corps' remaining tanks were practically all burned or knocked out, but 150 carts and motor vehicles managed to get across before the morning of 10 August. Nevertheless, the 62nd Army's formations that had fallen back to the eastern bank of the Don were in a pitiful state. According to reports on 10 August, the 196th and 399th Rifle Divisions numbered 1,190 and 2,114 men respectively.[8] This meant, essentially, that both divisions had been routed. The rout of the 62nd Army forced the Stalingrad Front command to give up any plans to employ the 'Far Eastern' divisions in the 21st Army's offensive (which by this time was losing its meaning with the loss of the positions in the bend of the Don). They were to be pulled out for occupying defensive positions along the eastern bank of the Don in the 62nd Army's sector.

Attempts to Break Out

As a result of the completed encirclement manoeuvre, the German forces reached the line of the Don to the north and south of the railway leading to Stalingrad. A bridgehead from Kletskaya to Peskovatka, occupied by the 4th Tank Army, remained along the right bank of the Don. Further on, the external encirclement front, which was occupied by the Germans' 3rd Motorized, 24th Panzer and 71st Infantry Divisions, ran from Peskovatka to the south toward Nizhne-Chirskaya. As early as 9 August the 'cauldron' was hemmed in by infantry formations and the encircled forces had almost no chance to break out of it.

Significant forces from the 62nd Army ended up in the 'cauldron': a regiment from the 33rd Guards Rifle Division, the 181st, 147th and 229th Rifle Divisions, the Krasnodar military school, five anti-tank and three tank regiments. The strength of the encircled forces (minus the 33rd Guards Rifle Division's regiments and the Krasnodar military school) was estimated by the Stalingrad Front's headquarters at 28,000 men. This figure included:

The 147th Rifle Division (9,575 men as of 5 August);
The 181st Rifle Division (11,142 men as of 5 August);
The 229th Rifle Division (5,419 men as of 5 August);
The 555th, 508th, 881st, 1185th, and 1252nd anti-tank regiments:
The 645th, 650th and 651st tank battalions.[9]

The encircled troops disposed of 157 field guns and 67 anti-tank guns, 17 T-34 tanks, 39 T-60s, 354 motor vehicles, and 4,562 horses.[10] The 33rd Guards Rifle Division's 88th and 84th Guards Rifle Regiments avoided encirclement. They fell back together with Zhuravlyov's group and were fighting as part of the 4th Tank Army.

The encircled formations broke up into several groups, which sought to break out in different directions. Two-way communications with the army and *front* headquarters was absent. In a report by the Red Army General Staff's officer on the 62nd Army's activities, it was noted: 'The front landed scouts with radio sets from aircraft for communications with the divisions, but there is no information from the latter.'[11] According to a report by A.I. Utvenko, commander of the 33rd Guards Rifle Division, at 19.00 on 8 August a radio telegram was received over the formation's radio ordering him to attempt to break out to the north together with the 181st Rifle Division. Major General T.Ya. Novikov, the commander of the 181st Rifle Division, was appointed to head the group. The 147th and 229th Rifle Divisions formed yet another group. A.A. Vol'khin, the commander of the 147th Rifle Division, had no communications with the command and received the breakout order from the commander of the 229th Rifle Division, Colonel F.F. Sazhin. These two divisions were to break through to the east and south-east by the railway bridge over the Don.

The first step was an overall withdrawal. The 33rd Guards Rifle Division left its old positions and began to fall back, breaking contact with the enemy. It was already impossible to reach the designated area. Division commander A.I. Utvenko described ongoing events in a letter to K. Simonov:[12] 'At the moment we received the order to break through to the east I had up to 3,000 men, 17 guns and 13 light tanks. We set out in two columns straight ahead through the *balki*. We were towing out guns by hand. We broke through along a narrow front, losing about 300 men. During the night and morning the Germans threw in an infantry regiment further east and once again closed the ring.'

There was no supply by air to the encircled forces and ammunition was running out, while the artillery had been completely destroyed. The 33rd Guards Rifle Division's last fight was from 05.00 to 11.00 on 10 August. Utvenko wrote Simonov: 'We resisted to the end. I reloaded my Mauser five times. They slashed away with automatic rifles. Several commanders shot themselves. Up to 1,000 men were killed, but they sold their lives dearly.' The remnants of the division scattered among the *balki* and creeks and tried to break out of the encirclement in small groups. The Sixth Army's war diary noted: 'By the evening of 10.8 the Russians had been crowded into a space approximately six kilometres in diameter. He is putting up very tenacious resistance, particularly north of Savinskii and he has to be destroyed in his positions.'[13]

One should note that the memories that the Germans retained of this fighting were by no means rosy ones. In September 1942, while planning a new operation, the Sixth Army command stressed: 'Battles for the encirclement of the enemy run into the local terrain, which is teeming with *balki* and great difficulties. This does not mean the formation of the cauldron, but clearing it out, a process which takes up a lot of time and will be linked to significant losses. At the same time, we will only be able to employ tanks in a limited fashion, in the best case. The infantry will have to carry the main burden of the fighting.'[14]

The 147th and 229th Rifle Divisions began withdrawing at 21.00 on 9 August. However, The Germans had already erected a screen facing west across the path of Vol'khin's and Sazhin's retreating divisions. The rear units of the 229th Rifle Division were moving in panic toward the retreating columns. They were attempting to find a way to the north in order to save themselves. The 147th Rifle Division's main forces were soon isolated in Gracheva *Balka*. There were no woods, which had become a refuge for those encircled in Belorussia, near Vyaz'ma and Uman', in the bend of the Don. Only the deep *balki* offered some protection.

The decisive fight took place on the night of 9/10 August. Units of the 147th and 229th Rifle Divisions moved to break through the 76th Infantry Division's screen near the Liska River, putting the headquarters of the German 230th Infantry Regiment, which lay along their path, on the brink of destruction. But this tactical success could no longer change the overall situation. More and more wounded filled up the *balki*. Thirst tormented everyone. It was decided to undertake yet another attempt to break out of the encirclement as a single detachment. Vol'khin, in his report on the fighting in encirclement, wrote: 'The soldiers and commanders welcomed this decision and declared "It's better to die in the field than in this trap".' They rolled out some guns to open positions, But there was already no chance of breaking through the dense screen of German infantry. The two divisions' units were scattered and small groups were able to break through to link up with the 62nd Army's main forces. Colonel F.F. Sazhin, the commander of the 229th Rifle Division, perished on 10 August near Pyatiizbyanskii farm.

The 112th Rifle Division, which had been pushed back against the Don near the blown-up bridge, was routed simultaneously with the destruction of the encircled formations. In the combat report by the division's headquarters at 20.00 on 11 August, it was stated:

> As of 11.8.1942 the following are in the three rifle regiments: 152 senior and junior officers, 154 NCOs, while there are 504 enlisted ranks in the line sub-units and 180 rear-area personnel.
>
> One 45mm gun and 87 rank and file remain in the 156th Anti-Tank Battalion.
>
> The 436th Artillery Regiment has ten 122mm howitzers, four 1939 76mm guns, and 12 anti-tank rifles. There are 692 rifles, 847 rank and file and 469 horses.[15]

The situation was somewhat better with the division's auxiliary elements, which lost up to 25 per cent of their strength. It would not be excessive to remind the reader that as of 5 August the division numbered 8,107 men. The commander of the 112th Rifle Division, Colonel Ivan Petrovich Sologub, who had headed the formation since the beginning of its formation in the Siberian Military District in December 1941, perished in the fighting near the crossing on 10 August.

But there was no immediate checking of the soundness of the hastily re-established defence. The Germans did not hurry to force the Don. Following the encirclement of part of the 62nd Army along the right bank of the Don, quiet once again descended in the attack zone of Paulus's army. The Germans were methodically grinding down the encircled troops. By 23.00 on 13 August only 160 men from a signals battalion of the 229th Rifle Division and 27 men from the 147th Rifle Division, headed by the commander, Major General Vol'khin, had got out of the encirclement. In Operational Report No. 90 by the headquarters of the 62nd Army at 18.00 on 14 August, it states: 'No new information has been received about the situation of the 33rd Guards, 181st, 147th, and 229th Rifle Divisions. Individual small groups have been crossing to the eastern bank of the Don River in the 131st and 112th Rifle Divisions' zone.' General T.Ya. Novikov, the commander of the 181st Rifle Division, was taken prisoner on 15 August. He perished in captivity in December 1944.

The supreme high command manifested an interest in the fate of the encircled forces on 15 August 1942. In *Stavka* of the VGK Directive No. 170569, Stalin stated: 'According to reports from the headquarters of the Stalingrad Front, the 62nd Army's 181st, 147th and 229th Rifle Divisions continue to fight in encirclement in the Yevseev – Maiorovskii – Plesistovskii area. Despite this and the *Stavka*'s repeated instructions, the Stalingrad Front has still not rendered them any assistance. The Germans never abandon their units encircled by Soviet forces and try at all costs with all possible forces and equipment to break through and save them.'[16]

Unfortunately, this *Stavka* directive was far too late. By 15 August the group of forces encircled along the western bank of the Don had already ceased to exist. Densely pressed from all sides, the divisions were destroyed. Whatever Stalin said, the Stalingrad Front had no forces with which to relieve the 'cauldron'. The 4th Tank Army was able to put forward only two rifle divisions. Reserves, in the form of the 1st Guards Army's divisions, arrived too late in order to somehow influence the fate of the 62nd Army's encircled units.

This was not a matter of any kind of special feelings of comradeship, but rather in the Germans' powerful technical equipment. The Germans could supply any of their surrounded groups of forces with the aid of a large transport aviation park. And the quantity and quality (the weight of the payload) of the German transport aircraft materially exceeded analogous indices for the Soviet U-2s, which were usually brought in for supply operations.

Nevertheless, one had to react somehow to the supreme commander-in-chief's instructions. At 06.00 on 16 August it was reported from the 62nd Army's headquarters: 'We have not been able to establish communications with the 33rd Guards, 181st, 147th and 229th Rifle Divisions. They do not reply to radio messages and do not broadcast.'[17] By 18.00 on 17 August it was noted in operational report No. 96 by the 62nd Army's headquarters: 'It has been established from interrogations of the commanders of the 33rd Guards and 147th Rifle Divisions that under enemy pressure the divisions have been split up into small groups, which are moving toward the eastern bank of the Don River.'

In a report by the Sixth Army's headquarters to the headquarters of Army Group B, the results of the battle were described in the following manner:

> The battle in the cauldron along the Don west of Kalach is over. The Reds' 62nd Army and major parts of the 1st Tank Army have been destroyed. Seven rifle divisions, seven tank brigades and two motorized rifle brigades have been routed, while another two rifle divisions suffered heavy losses. The enemy lost in the fighting from 7–11.8, according to available data, 30,000 prisoners, 270 tanks and 560 guns, including anti-tank and anti-aircraft. The enemy's losses in killed are high and the amount of prisoners and booty continues to grow.[18]

The battle in fact did continue. On 11 August the Sixth Army's war diary noted: 'The clearing out of individual *balki* in this area and also along the western bank of the Don south-east and east of Chir station continues.'[19] By 20 August 418 men had gotten out from the 33rd Guards Rifle Division, 171 men from the 147th Rifle Division, 28 men from the 181st Rifle Division, and 278 men from the 229th Rifle Division.[20]

In conclusion, I should like to comment on a phrase from Dёrr's book on the Stalingrad campaign. In summing up the results of the battle, he writes that 'On 10 August the Sixth Army won a complete victory, the last one in a battle in open terrain. The author has not managed to determine for what reason it was not employed for the immediate forcing of the Don.'[21] A study of the Sixth Army's operational documents, which may not have been available to Dërr at the time he wrote his book, enables us to easily answer his question. By the beginning of August the initial plan for forcing the Don to the north and south of Kalach had already been abandoned. In informing the command as to its subsequent plans, Paulus's headquarters noted: 'We must strive to seize bridgeheads west of Kachalinskaya, if possible, on the heels of the retreating enemy.'[22] The plan for subsequent actions was also corrected in comparison with the order of 20 July. Now the following was planned: 'Following the seizure of bridgeheads south-west of Kachalinskaya, the XIV and XXIV Army Corps[23] are to attack along the string of heights stretching to Stalingrad to the north and south of Stalingrad, in order to establish contact with the Fourth Panzer Army in the area of Voroponovo station.'[24] An entire series of factors evidently became the reason for the change in plans: acquaintance with the terrain, the entrance of Hoth's Fourth Panzer Army into the battle, and others. The result was that it was planned to force the Don following the elimination of the Soviet bridgehead in the Sirotinskaya area, about which further on.

The 1st Guards Army Enters the Fighting

The crisis that arose following the rout of the 62nd Army along the right bank of the Don forced the Soviet command to forego its initial plan to commit its arriving reserves to the fighting. The 1st Guards Army, which was destined for the South-eastern Front, was now to join the fighting along the right bank of the Don. Major General K.S. Moskalenko, who had been appointed commander of the 1st Guards Army and who had arrived at the headquarters of the South-eastern Front to get acquainted with the situation, returned to take over the army's forces in their new concentration area. In his memoirs, Moskalenko wrote:

> It was already night when I parted from A.I. Yeremenko and F.I. Golikov,[25] and at dawn the car was hurrying me to the area of Frolovo station. Somewhere out there was the headquarters of the 1st Guards Army. Not far from this station, as well as Ilovlya, as I understood it, the army's forces arriving by rail were unloading. I could not help but think: once again I'll be taking command and leading an army which is only just forming. This premonition was more than justified.[26]

However, it should be stressed that the 1st Guards Army stood out among the other reserve armies. The army's former chief of staff later wrote:

> In the next few days, as comrade Stalin promised, the 1st Guards Army, consisting of first-class divisions, will be thrown in here.
>
> Yeremenko sorted through a pile of papers on his table, pulled out one of them, ran over it quickly with his eyes and, not without pride said:
>
>> 'Six rifle divisions are part of the 1st Guards Army. All of them are guards divisions, with five of them formed from airborne corps. The strength of each division is 8,000 men. Communists make up half of the rank and file, while the remainder, with rare exception, are Komsomol[27] members. This is a magnificent field force, the first guards army formed in our armed forces ...'[28]

Here S.P. Ivanov (or A.I. Yeremenko, in his account) is somewhat mistaken. The average strength of the 1st Guards Army's divisions at the time of their arrival around Stalingrad was around 10,000 men, according to reports. In the new army's Guards divisions the number of sub-machine guns was above authorized strength, although they were short of light and heavy machine guns. The formation's strength may be, on the average, rated as high.

The disaster that befell the 62nd Army also forced the Soviet supreme command to reconsider its opinion of V.N. Gordov's capabilities for leading a *front* along a strategically-important direction. According to *Stavka* Directive No. 170562 at 23.00 on 9 August, at 0.600 on 10 August the Stalingrad Front was to be subordinated to Yeremenko. At the same time, Yeremenko was to remain the commander of the South-eastern Front. The South-eastern Front's success in holding the enemy's breakthrough around Abganerovo evidently played a role in this appointment.

Initially, the plan for employing the 1st Guards Army was only slightly corrected. Instead of preparing positions behind the South-eastern Front's 64th Army, which had been attacked by Hoth, the army was to be turned with its front facing west. In this way, Moskalenko's army was to become the *front's* insurance policy along the near approaches to Stalingrad. This variant did not suit the *Stavka* and they pulled the army back to the right flank of the Soviet forces along the Stalingrad direction. The concentration of the divisions of Moskalenko's army in the Ilovlya area would enable them to employ the 1st Guards Army along either the eastern or the western bank of the Don, depending upon the situation. However, the temptation to launch a counterblow against the Sixth Army's flank was too great.

Chapter 3

The Results of the Tank Battle in the Great Bend of the Don

At first glance, it would seem that the battle in the great bend of the Don had been an unqualified success for the Wehrmacht. On 11 August 1942 Paulus reported to the headquarters of Army Group B that: 'The defence and offensive west of Kalach since 23.7 has yielded 57,000 prisoners, with more than 1,000 tanks destroyed and 750 guns of all kinds captured.' The first question that arises in studying the fighting along the Stalingrad front at the end of July and beginning of August 1942 is 'Where did the tanks go?'

Much has been said earlier about the character of the tanks' actions in this battle, when they were forced to attack without sufficient artillery and infantry support. This, of course, had a bearing on the losses. However, also of interest is the question of what were the Soviet tanks getting hit by during this period; so we turn to the data of the Sixth Army's chief quartermaster regarding the expenditure of ammunition during the period from 20 July through 10 August 1942. The absolute leader, strangely enough, are the hollow-charge 75mm Gr.Patr.38 rounds for the 24-calibre guns of the Panzer IVs and *Sturmgeschützen*, of which 7,062 were expended. The summer of 1942 became for the Germans a period of the massive employment of hollow-charge ammunition. The production of ordinary calibre armour-piercing 75mm shells for long-barrelled tank and anti-tank guns was developing slowly. As a result, hollow-charge shells, on the whole, comprised 67.6 per cent of the ammunition production designated for fighting armoured targets for self-propelled *Sturmgeschützen* in 1942.[1]

The next most common rounds expended by the Sixth Army from 20 July through 10 August 1942 were the 50mm armour-piercing shells for long-barrelled tank guns and PAK-38 anti-tank guns, or 5,488 and 5,609 rounds respectively. A total of 967 and 1,354 sub-calibre rounds for these two types of guns were expended respectively. Yet another leader (particularly in taking into account the numbers in this artillery system) were captured 76.2mm guns: 1,135 same-calibre and 130 sub-calibre rounds were fired by them. As opposed to these, the firing of 3,594 calibre and 1,194 sub-calibre rounds from the 37mm PAK-35/35 guns was quite low. The new means of fighting were to a certain extent outsiders: the Sixth Army fired off 1,649 75mm rounds from long-barrelled tank guns and 608 rounds from 75mm PAK-40 guns. To judge from this, they sought to fire on tanks recognized as KVs from the PAK-40, as instructions recommended. In comparison with these figures, a large number – 766 – of hollow-charge rounds for the 105mm howitzers were fired.

It is clear from the data cited that the Sixth Army had more than sufficient means for hitting the numerous Soviet tanks of various types, from KVs to T-60s and BTs, which were committed into the fighting by the Stalingrad Front command. Without the suppression of the anti-tank defensive system by artillery, tank attacks inevitably led to heavy losses in armoured equipment.

One of the problems of the summer and autumn of 1942 was the loss by the Soviet tanks of that relative 'invulnerability' they possessed in 1941. Our tank troops sometimes called the new types of shells 'thermite rounds'. Now the German artillery knocked out even heavy KVs with confidence. In a report by the commander of the 158th Tank Brigade, it was stated: 'The enemy has a new anti-tank gun similar to our 57mm, which easily penetrates the armour of a KV from a great distance (1,200m) and its round ignites the vehicle.'[2] He is most likely speaking here of hollow-charge shells for the 75mm tank and anti-tank guns, which were mentioned above. The 57mm figure was arrived at by measuring the diameter of the shell hole from the hollow-charge round.

It would also seem that secondary elements in the tanks' construction, such as observation equipment and mistakes by the artillery spotters, worked against the Soviet tank troops. In a report, written about the results of the fighting around Stalingrad in July–September 1942, by Tanaschishin, the commander of the 13th Tank Corps, the following shortcomings of the T-34s were pointed out:

5. During the fighting it was clearly established that the observation equipment of the T-34 tank does not allow for sufficient observation in conditions of broken terrain.

6. The T-34 tank's gun penetrates the armour of all German tanks at a distance of 1,200 meters and less. The German self-propelled gun penetrates the armour of the T-34 tank at a distance of two kilometres. In order to enjoy equal firepower, it is necessary to mount on part (one-tenth) of the tanks an 85mm anti-tank gun, which is equal to the German self-propelled gun. Moreover, it is necessary to shield the vehicle's front and turret, bring the sum total of armour to 250–300 millimetres and securing the top of the turret and the body with 100 millimetres of armour.[3]

Overall, the matter was not to be found in general principles of employing the tank troops, but in their correct tactical employment. The rapid transfer (often under their own power) and commitment into the fighting from the march was a mechanized corps' typical mission. Soviet and German tank divisions or corps almost always entered the fighting in detail, as they arrived in the area where a defensive operation was being conducted. Moreover, this applies not only to failed but also to quite successful defensive operations. For example, the SS *Totenkopf* Division was committed to the fighting in detail during Manstein's brilliant counterblow around Khar'kov in February-March 1943.[4] The problem of securing the effectiveness of a mobile formation's employment for a counterblow lay in its organizational structure and tactics for use.

However, it would be a mistake to rate the tank corps' counterblows as lacking in result. Paulus's army lost time and suffered perceptible personnel losses. The losses suffered by the Sixth Army's divisions in the fighting in the great bend of the Don are shown in the table overleaf.

What is striking are the high losses for Paulus's army in sick, which is atypical, for example, for the summer of 1941. In some formations the losses due to sickness are comparable to combat losses. However, it is also clear that those divisions that suffered heaviest were committed from the very beginning of the battle in the bend of the Don and essentially became victims of mistakes in evaluating the enemy. As early as 31 July, it was noted in the Sixth Army's war diary: 'The available forces seem very weak for subsequent operations against Stalingrad. The 297th, 44th and 113th Infantry Divisions and the 100th Jäger Division have been greatly weakened by losses.'[5]

All of this created a short-term situation in which the Sixth Army had insufficient forces to take the final, decisive step. In extremely unfavourable conditions, with a shortage of artillery and organic tank formations, the reserve armies methodically lowered the combat capability of the Wehrmacht's most powerful army on the Eastern Front.

Table 8: Losses by Sixth Army's (Army Group B) Formations Taking Part in Combat Operations in the Great Bend of the Don. 21 July–10 August 1942.[6]

Unit	Killed	Wounded	Missing in Action	Sick	Total
6th Army Headquarters*	15	28	0	3,011	3,054
XIV Panzer Corps Headquarters	35	100	6	13	154
16th Panzer Division	189	818	7	62	1,076
3rd Motorized Division	337	1,174	29	241	1,781
60th Motorized Division	219	912	38	101	1,270
VIII Army Corps Headquarters	43	199	7	44	293
100th Light Infantry Division	449	1,131	201	43	1,824
113th Infantry Division	313	1,058	40	89	1,500
305th Infantry Division	158	171	17	38	384
376th Infantry Division	101	357	47	290	795
384th Infantry Division	123	357	36	225	741
LI Corps Headquarters	12	25	0	15	52
297th Infantry Division	283	1,245	12	66	1,606
71st Infantry Division	264	1,115	18	46	1,443
44th Infantry Division	212	909	23	95	1,239
XXIV Panzer Corps Headquarters	4	31	0	57	92
24th Panzer Division	197	1,119	3	224	1,543
389th Infantry Division (1–10.8)	151	610	18	9	788
76th Infantry Division (1–10.8)	53	144	1	88	286
295th Infantry Division (1–10.8)	116	290	4	4	414
Total	3,274	11,793	507	4,761	20,335

* By 'headquarters,' we may understand in this context the headquarters and units, both combat and combat support, subordinated to it.

Chapter 4

The Elimination of the Sirotinskaya Bridgehead

As early as the height of the fighting in the Don bend the OKH[1] and the Sixth Army command were mulling over a plan for subsequent operations. In a telephone telegram on 7 August 1942, Paulus's headquarters quite unambiguously outlined its intentions and motives for launching an attack, namely in the Sirotinskaya area: 'A preliminary condition of any offensive against Stalingrad is the rout of the enemy in the Don bend facing the VIII Army Corps, insofar as in the opposite case any offensive will be flanked from the north and our major forces will be tied down. While still clearing out the cauldron, the army plans to gradually pull its mobile formations out of the fighting and to concentrate them behind the VIII Army Corps' front.'

As opposed to the thoughtless plan of 20 July for attacking toward Stalingrad, the new German offensive called for an attack along converging axes. These were 'asymmetrical Cannaes'[2] typical of the German school: 'The mobile formations must attack from the Dal'nii Perekopskii area along the spine of the heights to the Don, west and south-west of Kachalinskaya, while at the same time the infantry must cover their flanks. Along the southern flank, the infantry divisions must attack along the Don to the north, in order to cut off and destroy, insofar as possible, major Russian forces.'[3] This meant that the XIV Panzer Corps was to be directed at cutting the Soviet forces' front like a scythe, from the centre to the eastern flank. An infantry attack would be launched along the Don toward the tanks.

A mortal danger hung over those forces from which Stalin was demanding help for the 62nd Army's encircled forces. The stubborn resistance of the surrounded troops prevented the Germans from removing, as they had planned, the XIV Panzer Corps from the fighting even before the elimination of the 'cauldron'. However, this only delayed the attack against the Soviet 4th Tank Army. Possessing the strategic initiative, the German forces were able to secure their superiority along the axis of the main attack through the consecutive concentration of forces and to rout an enemy who did not possess an overall superiority of force. More often than not, the defending Soviet forces were unable to guess the axis of the next attack, insofar as it was extremely difficult to discover the mobile formations' regrouping.

It should be said that they were aware of the danger in the various Soviet headquarters. The 4th Tank Army had gone over to the defensive and was strengthening its line for the purpose of holding a bridgehead on the western bank of the Don River. What could the Soviet forces on the Sirotinskaya bridgehead put up against the enemy? The 4th Tank Army's formations, having suffered losses during the course of the unsuccessful counterblows, numbered at this time: 18th Rifle Division – 8,724 men; 184th Rifle Division – 3,950 men; 192nd Rifle Division – 4,965 men; 205th Rifle Division – 8,374 men; and the 321st Rifle Division – 7,544 men.[4] Army commander Kryuchyonkin no longer had any tank corps at his disposal. The 4th Tank Army's sole mobile reserve was the 182nd Tank Brigade, which had ten T-34s, six T-70s and twenty T-60s. Besides this, a number of new rifle and artillery units and formations were to be transferred to reinforce the army. These were the 22nd

Anti-Tank Brigade, the 39th and 40th Guards Rifle Divisions and the 343rd Rifle Division (8,677 men).[5] However, by the start of the German offensive they were still in the process of concentrating. The reasons for their late concentration were both the low mobility of the rifle units and the shortage of crossings over the Don.

As a result, four corps from Paulus's army (the XIV and XXIV Panzer Corps and VIII and XI Corps) were aimed at the 4th Tank Army's six rifle divisions. It was predominantly infantry that had been put into motion (the 24th Panzer Division had been transferred to Hoth's Fourth Panzer Army for an attack on Stalingrad from the south-east).

Exacerbating the defender's traditional problem of unearthing the enemy's plans, on 13 August a local offensive planned by Paulus by the XI Army Corps began along the right flank of the 4th Tank Army. Upon achieving a local penetration, the Germans confused the Soviet command regarding the axis of the main attack.

War contains all kinds of 'trifles' that determine who is to live and who is to die. There is the following entry in the 18th Rifle Division's war diary: 'An anti-tank regiment, consisting of 16 guns, arrived at 19.00 on 14.08. It arrived without fuel and was unable to take an active part in the defence.'[6] Had the anti-tank gun regiment had fuel, it would have materially strengthened the defence, but there remained only a few hours before the German attack.

The new German offensive began in the early morning of 15 August with a two-hour artillery and aerial preparation. The Soviet infantrymen along the axis of the enemy's main attack put up fierce resistance; hiding in the *balki* during the tank attack, they let the German tanks pass through and attacked the units following behind them. The tanks had to turn back in order to suppress the remaining centres of resistance. However, there was no miracle and as a result the 4th Tank Army's weak defensive centre was pierced. The 182nd Tank Brigade's few tanks, which had been brought up to face the German offensive, were soon wiped out. As early as the middle of the first day of the German offensive the lines of Kryuchyonkin's army had been split in two by the tank attack. The situation was exacerbated by an attack along the army's left flank by the German XXIV Panzer Corps (76th and 295th Infantry Divisions) along the Don. As early as the first half of the day on 15 August the 18th Rifle Division's 424th Rifle Regiment was encircled and routed. At 17.00 on 15 August began the 184th and 18th Rifle Division's disorderly withdrawal under pressure from the German infantry toward Trekhostrovskaya. By midnight the 60th Motorized Division had reached the crossing at Sirotinskaya. On 16 August the 16th Panzer Division broke through to the Don at Nizhnii Akatov, and during the second half of the day to the crossing at Trekhostrovskaya, thus depriving the retreating Soviet units of the opportunity of crossing the river in an organized manner. They were able to partially destroy the crossing over the Don at Trekhostrovskaya as German armoured personnel carriers were already racing across it.

In essence, the 4th Tank Army clearly demonstrated in August 1942 what would have happened had the tank armies not been in the Don bend in July. From the operational point of view, the condition of the divisions in Kryuchyonkin's army on 15 August was a repetition of the 62nd Army's formation by 23 July. Facing us are several rifle divisions, extended along a line with their flanks resting on the Don. Correspondingly, the Germans launch an attack and immediately break through to the main crossings. The rifle units, upon being cut off from the crossings, are either encircled or flattened against the bank of the Don. There was no standard scenario in which 'the Germans drive in a wedge, the tank corps rain down attacks on it and the clock ticks away' during the elimination of the Sirotinskaya bridgehead. Events developed with terrifying speed.

At the same time, as early as 17 August *Stavka* representative A.M. Vasilevskii issued an ultimatum to retain territory in the small bend of the Don, ordering the *front* command as follows: 'The *Stavka* considers it necessary not only to hold a bridgehead to the north-west of Sirotinskaya, but to now take back at all cost and maintain a bridgehead to the south-east of Sirotinskaya.'[7]

The idea of threatening the rear areas of the German troops moving on Stalingrad was a logical one, but one requiring resources. At the same time, the rapid collapse of the 4th Tank Army's defence spoiled the 1st Guards Army's concentration. The plan for employing it had to be changed on the fly. The army commander, K.S. Moskalenko, recalled:

> The decision by the *front* commander called for committing the 39th and 40th Guards Rifle Divisions into the fighting on the morning of 16 August, followed later by the 37th Guards Rifle Division, which had unloaded, under the command of Major General V.G. Zholudev, for the purpose of halting the enemy's offensive and keeping in our hands the bridgehead in this bend, to the Shokhin – Dubovyi area, and the 37th and 39th Guards Rifle Divisions to the southern part, to the Khlebnyi – Trekhostrovskaya sector. At the same time, the latter two divisions were to be subordinated to the 4th Tank Army. The remnants of the right-flank 321st, 205th and 343rd Rifle Divisions, which had lost contact with the army, were to be transferred to the 1st Guards Army.[8]

The 1st Guards Army's units were, of course, a powerful reserve. One cannot not but note that in the VIII Army Corps' reports to the Sixth Army, the rank and file of the 37th and 39th Guards Rifle Divisions are described according to the results of the first battles with them as 'made up primarily of young and fanatical communists'. The commitment of the Guards divisions of Moskalenko's army enabled us to avoid the complete loss of the bridgehead in the small bend of the Don. The main efforts of the German offensive were concentrated along the right flank, while the left-flank XI Army Corps was unable to achieve any great success in finishing off the retreating Soviet divisions.

After three weeks of fighting, only pitiful remnants were left of the full-strength divisions that had been committed into the battle as part of the 4th Tank Army at the beginning of August. The bloodiest period was 15–20 August. On 20 August 1,281 men remained in the 18th Rifle Division, 676 in the 184th Rifle Division, 1,238 in the 192nd Rifle Division and 4,356 in the 321st Rifle Division. The fresh formations that had been transferred from the Moscow area also suffered heavy losses. For example, as of 18 August the 39th Guards Rifle Division numbered 10,721 men but 4,158 on 20 August.[9]

At the same time, one should not assume that the Germans achieved success easily and without effort and that they only scattered the Soviet units by breaking through to the crossings. The 4th Tank Army was routed by superior forces. The expenditure of ammunition testifies eloquently to this. According to data from the VIII Army Corps' chief quartermaster, during the period from 15 through 22 August 8,724 light field artillery rounds and 4,566 heavy field artillery rounds were fired.[10] Correspondingly, during the fighting in the bend of the Don in the opening phase of the battle, from 18 July through 4 August 1942, 10,172 light field artillery and 2,230 heavy field artillery rounds were expended.[11] That is, during the course of routing the Soviet 4th Tank Army, the VIII Army Corps fired off, at a minimum, no less than during the tank battle in the great bend of the Don.

While defeating the 4th Tank Army, the Sixth Army's formations also suffered quite perceptible losses (see table).

Table 9: Losses by Sixth Army's Formations Taking Part in Combat Operations in the Elimination of the Sirotinskaya Bridgehead, 10–20 August 1942.[12]

Unit	Killed	Wounded	Missing in Action	Sick	Total
6th Army Headquarters*	4	49	0	1,005	1,058
XIV Panzer Corps Headquarters	7	27	0	6	40
16th Panzer Division	91	243	0	24	358
3rd Motorized Division	18	76	0	72	166
60th Motorized Division	38	140	2	74	254
VIII Army Corps Headquarters	0	8	0	3	11
100th Light Infantry Division	159	722	22	69	972
305th Infantry Division	164	540	27	39	770
XI Army Corps Headquarters	2	28	0	10	40
376th Infantry Division	99	314	28	132	573
384th Infantry Division	143	589	42	31	772
XXIV Panzer Corps Headquarters**	–	–	–	–	–
389th Infantry Division	170	631	42	28	788
76th Infantry Division	90	481	11	23	605
295th Infantry Division	51	239	3	10	303
Total	1,036	4,087	144	1,526	6,793

* By 'headquarters,' we may understand in this context the headquarters and units, both combat and combat support, subordinated to it.
** According to the report, there are no losses for this period of time.

As one can see from the data presented here and earlier, losses by German formations were significantly lower than Soviet ones. However, for the Sixth Army's infantry, the battle for the Sirotinskaya bridgehead was nevertheless quite bloody. While losses by the mobile formations were not large, the infantry divisions suffered tangible losses in the fighting against the encircled and cut off units of the 4th Tank Army.

Whatever the case, the large Soviet bridgehead on the right bank of the Don had ceased to exist. As early as 16 August the main goal became Stalingrad, only 60km away. In the Sixth Army's war diary the essence of the new mission was formulated as follows: 'The army must force the Don between Peskovatka and Trekhostrovskaya, with the main axis at Vertyachii. Under the infantry's cover of the northern flank, the mobile forces will break through along the line of the heights between Rossoshka and the headwaters of the Korennaya *Balka* to the Volga north of Stalingrad and simultaneously enter the city with part of its forces from the north-west.'

Somewhat later, on 21 August 1942, Wolfram von Richtofen,[13] the commander of the Fourth Air Fleet, noted in his diary while flying in the Kalach area: 'There are an unusually large number of knocked-out tanks and dead Russians.' This sounds particularly horrifying coming from the man who led the VIII Air Corps in the fighting in Belorussia in 1941 and also in the Vyaz'ma 'cauldron' in October 1941. However, one should admit that the open terrain in the great bend of the Don enabled one to see the battlefield better than the forests of Belorussia and the Moscow area.

Chapter 5

Reinforced Defence I. Abganerovo

The German command gradually augmented the scale of the attacks along converging axes. At first this was the offensive by the German Sixth Army's northern group of forces (XIV Panzer Corps and VIII Corps) along the 62nd Army's right flank. Then the scale of the 'Cannaes' was increased and attacks were launched by the northern and southern shock groups of Paulus's army in the direction of Kalach. The final step in increasing the scale of a possible encirclement of the Soviet forces along the distant approaches to Stalingrad became the drawing of Hoth's Fourth Panzer Army into the offensive. This would have enabled them to outflank the Stalingrad Front's southern flank, which was hanging in the air, and to outflank not only the 62nd, but also the 64th Army with an attack on Stalingrad.

'… is not occupied by any units'

On 30 July, on the day when the XL Panzer Corps of Hoth's army occupied a bridgehead on the Manych River, the Fourth Panzer Army was transferred from Army Group A to Army Group B. On this day Halder wrote in his diary:

> During the report to the Führer, the floor was given to General Jodl,[1] who bombastically declared that the fate of the Caucasus will be decided at Stalingrad. Thus it was necessary to transfer forces from Army Group A to Army Group B and that this must take place as far south of the Don as possible. Thus, the very same idea is served up in new crockery, which I expressed to the Führer six days ago, when the Fourth Panzer Army was forcing the Don. But the worthy company from the OKW didn't understand anything.

Insofar as Hoth's army was located between two operational axes, the Stalingrad and Caucasian, its formations were actively scattered between them. On 23 July the XXIV Panzer Corps was transferred to the Sixth Army and then the XL Panzer Corps was resubordinated to Army Group A. The *Grossdeutschland* Division was entirely removed from the German forces along the southern sector of the front. Before long it entered the fighting in the Rzhev area. Following these measures, the following formations remained in the Fourth Panzer Army:

The XLVIII Panzer Corps (14th Panzer and 29th Motorized Divisions);
The IV Army Corps (94th and 371st Infantry Divisions);
The Romanian VI Army Corps (Romanian 1st and 2nd Infantry Divisions) was en route.

In all, at the initial stage of its participation in the battle of Stalingrad, Hoth's army included one panzer, one motorized, and two German and two Romanian infantry divisions. Its combat strength was significantly less than Paulus's army. However, the Fourth Panzer Army was to operate along the Stalingrad Front's open flank and even small forces could cause major problems.

The Fourth Panzer Army's breakthrough to the southern bank of the Don essentially cut the 51st Army off from the North Caucasus Front's main forces. In the exact same way that the corps of Army Groups A and B were divided between two operational axes, a division of the Soviet forces opposing them also came about. According to *Stavka* VGK Directive No. 170539, the 51st Army was to be transferred to the Stalingrad Front at 12.00 on 31 July 1942. The forces of each side were finally divided between the Caucasus and Stalingrad. In the space between the Soviet and German armies along these two directions there remained only a thin screening membrane in the Kalmyk steppes. The 16th Motorized Division was allotted to the screen by the German command.

One should not say that the crisis along the boundary with the North Caucasus Front was an unexpected one for the Soviet command. The outflanking of the southern flank of the reserve armies' newly-formed line and an attack against the soft underbelly of the troops defending Stalingrad was an easily predictable move. As early as 16 July, Ya.N. Fedorenko informed A.M. Vasilevskii in a coded message: 'I consider the 62nd Army's left flank and the right flank of the N[orth] C[aucasus] F[ront] to be an especially dangerous area which is not yet secured by anything.'[2] Fedorenko proposed reinforcing this axis with a rifle division and a tank brigade and requested that Vasilevskii issue the corresponding instructions to the *front* command.

However, there lies a gulf between the realization of a danger and the technical possibility of taking countermeasures. In talks between the *front* headquarters and the *Stavka* VGK on 28 July 1942, in reply to the question 'Tell me, who is currently occupying the south-western front of the Stalingrad external line from Krasnyi Don station to Raigorod?' the laconic reply on the telegraph tape read 'The south-western front of the Stalingrad line is not occupied by any units'. Cadet regiments had been put into action at that time in the great bend of the Don and the divisions from the Far East were still en route. As a result, the decision was made to move up the 38th and 244th Rifle Divisions (2,000 men apiece) to the external line. They had been undergoing reformation as part of the 57th Army.

As the divisions arrived from the Far East and the tank brigades were reformed, Fedorenko's proposal to create a combat group from a rifle division and Tank Brigade was realized in practice. In the *front's* Combat Order No. 00166/op of 20.10 on 1 August 1942, the 208th Rifle Division, the 6th Guards Tank Brigade, an artillery regiment and an engineer battalion were to be detached to restore the situation along the 51st Army's front. All of these units and formations were to be transported to the Kurmoyarskii area by rail. In wire communications the next day (2 August) with Vasilevskii, Gordov reported that he was planning to move the 126th and 422nd Rifle Divisions to the 51st Army, in the second echelon behind the 208th Rifle Division. Thus, of the ten divisions arriving to the Stalingrad Front, Hoth's breakthrough along the Kotel'nikovo axis had drawn three onto itself. It was precisely here that events unfolded, which I would call one of the most terrible episodes of the battle of Stalingrad.

The failures around Voronezh caused a chain reaction throughout the entire country. Again, as around Moscow in 1941, divisions were needed from the Far East. One of these formations was the above-mentioned 208th Rifle Division. It had been formed as early as 1941, in the Maritime Province, but remained as part of the Far Eastern Front in the difficult winter of 1941–2. By the summer of 1942 the division numbered 13,360 men and was fully supplied with all necessary equipment and motor transport. There had been more than sufficient time to train the troops and commanders. The formation had received from *front* commander Apanasenko[3] the rating of 'good' during exercises in June 1942. The division was commanded by Colonel Konstantin Mikhailovich Voskoboinikov, who had been appointed in May 1942. He had no combat experience and had previously commanded a regiment in another Far Eastern division.

The 208th Rifle Division had been filled out by young cohorts, varying from 25 to 32 years of age and consisting of 80 per cent Russians and 20 per cent from other nationalities. The sudden changes in the fate of these young people, so full of life, began with the start of Operation Blau. On 12 July, on the *Stavka*'s orders, the 208th Rifle Division was removed from the Far East and sent to the Stalingrad area. It is hard to say with what sort of feelings the Far Eastern soldiers travelled to the west. However, I will probably not be too wrong if I suppose that they wanted to get into action as quickly as possible and to make their contribution to the war that had been going on for more than a year at the other end of the country. Following a lengthy trip throughout the entire USSR, Colonel Voskoboinikov's division was in Stalingrad on 31 July. Here the division commander received his orders in the *front's* headquarters: to move by rail through Kotel'nikovo to Tsimlyanskaya.

Actually, at the same time Colonel Voskoboinikov was at *front* headquarters getting his combat orders, trainloads of Far Eastern troops were moving along their assigned routes. Early on the morning of 1 August 1942 the two leading trains were pulling into Kotel'nikovo station. At that time the station had already been captured by Hoth's tanks. The battalions were forced to unload from the rail cars and accept battle under fire from tank guns and machine guns. At 08.00 on 1 August the third train came under attack from German aircraft at the Kurmoyarskii rail siding and was destroyed, without having the opportunity to get into the fighting. The soldiers and commanders traveling in the trains clearly imagined their first fight in a completely different manner than what actually happened. They thought of meeting the enemy in the trenches in defence, or of attacking him, deafened by artillery. But there were neither trenches nor artillery around Kotel'nikovo. There were railway cars, the sun-baked steppe and German tanks.

Only the 208th Rifle Division's fourth train unloaded in a relatively organized fashion. It arrived at Gremyachii station, the next one after Kurmoyarskii rail siding and 22km closer to Stalingrad, at 08.00. The division headquarters, an engineer battalion and a signals battalion were in this train. This makeup was well suited for organizing the formation's command post, but was ill-suited for the role of forward detachment. Nevertheless, it set out for Kotel'nikovo on foot and was several times subjected to air attacks along the road in the open steppe. The fifth train also successfully unloaded in Gremyachii. At this the Far Easterners' luck ran out. The 208th Rifle Division's sixth train, which arrived during the night of 1/2 August at Chilekovo station, was detained by the commandant 'for lack of a troop platform'. The delay proved fatal. At 05.00 on 2 August an attack by twenty German bombers blew the train to bits.

One may imagine Colonel Voskoboinikov's state when he caught up to the train with his staff in a car in Gremyachii at 11.00 on 1 August. He immediately left for Kotel'nikovo in order to gather together his subordinate units, which had been scattered across the steppe by German tanks and aircraft in a single hour. To top off all the disasters, the Far Easterners had to fight in conditions in which they were short of shells and bullets. Two trainloads of ammunition that had arrived at Gremyachii station had been smashed up by German aviation. By the morning of 2 August the scattered units of the 208th Rifle

Division had been thrown out of Kotel'nikovo, and by the morning of the following day – from the Kurmoyarskii rail siding, and the German advance were halted only 3–4km from Gremyachii.

The division's deployment along a particular line had essentially been foiled. The troops were being unloaded along the rail line to Kotel'nikov in one degree of chaos or another. Chuikov recalled:

> A battalion of soldiers from the 208th Rifle Division, which had deployed in a file with their front facing south, were digging trenches near the Nebykovskii rail siding. The battalion commander reported that having found out from those retreating from the south about the appearance of German tanks in Kotel'nikovo, he decided to take up defensive positions on his own initiative. He did not know where the regimental or division commander was, insofar as they had only just unloaded his battalion. I approved the actions of this battalion commander and ordered him to detain those retreating and promised to get him some communications from the nearest headquarters, which I hoped to find at Chilekovo station.

To be precise, Nebykovskii (Nebykovo) was next to Chilekovo. There's no such station on a railway map of that time. But this is not important. It's difficult to reproach the battalion commander for anything: it was necessary to occupy defensive positions in the face of a potential breakthrough by enemy tanks. However, ultimately less than half of the formation remained at Colonel Voskoboinikov's disposal. Four rifle battalions, one artillery battalion, an anti-tank battalion and a battery of field guns from the 208th Rifle Division gathered at Gremyachii. During the night of 3/4 August Colonel Voskoboinikov decided to pull the units he had gathered in the Gremyachii area back to the Chilekovo area. However, a withdrawal is a very dangerous manoeuvre in a battle with a motorized enemy. The final act of the drama followed early on the morning of 4 August. The Germans, who were advancing along the railway, first attacked the retreating units on the march and then threw those elements that had not had time to consolidate in the Chilekovo area out of their positions. Colonel Voskoboinikov and division commissar Malofeev died in the fighting around Chilekovo. The collection of the 208th Rifle Division's remaining units took place near Abganerovo and near the '74-kilometre' rail siding. The August fighting inflicted the final blow against it. The division was formally disbanded by order of the People's Commissariat of Defence of the USSR Order No. 00248 of 28.11.1942.

However, the scattered elements of the 208th Rifle Division, which accepted battle right in their trains, nevertheless played their role. Hoth abandoned an offensive strictly along the rail line and preferred to carry out a wide flanking manoeuvre across the steppe.

150km across the Steppe

But it was impossible to hold the enemy through a defence along axes in the open steppe, which was accessible to tanks, particularly in the summer. Having changed the axis of the attack, the attacking Germans broke through the 38th Rifle Division (with a strength of 1,685 men on 25 July), which was defending a 20–25km front and overcame the Stalingrad defensive line. This was accomplished by a broad flanking manoeuvre, which became a record of sorts not only for the 14th Panzer Division, but for the entire Eastern Front. It is described in the formation's history as follows:

On 3 August the division, with the rapid K64 [motorcycle battalion] once again in the lead, left the Remontnaya area for a long march that led it to the immediate vicinity of Stalingrad. The tropical sultriness in the steppe, without a hint of shade and the impenetrable and tangible dense screen of dust once again demanded from people and motors their maximum exertion of strength. A short rest at midday, and once again the rumbling of the march column in the steppe expanses. The vanguard reached its assigned goal by the rapidly falling night – through Zhutov 2 to the bridge near Aksai. The road was found with difficulty and the maps were a poor support for the travellers. One could rely only on a field compass. 150 kilometres were covered in 15 hours, 'a day's feat not yet observed in any panzer regiment in Russia', as it proudly sounded in the 36th Panzer Regiment's daily report. At the same time, however, fuel supplies had come to a halt. To have penetrated into the wide gap in the enemy front and to now stand without moving![4]

However, an unpleasant surprise awaited the German tank troops at the end of their 150km march: forty 'T-34 Stalingrad tanks'. The tanks had their weighty word in the battle with Hoth's attacking formations. In general, the Germans were very 'lucky' in that they had to attack a city in which a major tank factory was working at full throttle. The reformation of tank units took place at a rapid pace. Following the heavy July fighting along the Don, the 6th Guards Tank Brigade was pulled back to Stalingrad. It got its equipment directly from the factory and its personnel from the Stalingrad armoured centre. By 1 August the brigade had been brought up to authorized strength. It had a homogenous makeup, as opposed to many other brigades along the Soviet-German front – forty-four T-34 tanks without any kind of feeble light tanks. It received a doubtful acquisition in the form of T-70 tanks later, as part of reinforcements. On the night of 3 August the 6th Guards Tank Brigade was loaded onto trains and dispatched to the Kotel'nikovo – Dubovskoe area. However, the 6th Guards Tank Brigade did not make it to Kotel'nikovo. Without even making it as far as Abganerovo, the brigade was unloaded at Tinguta station and arrived in the area of Abganerovo station under its own power. The 'Siberian' 126th Rifle Division was located here. Actually, the 6th Guards Tank Brigade proved to be that 'lucky' weapon which was so lacking in repelling the Germans' first tank attacks along other axes. The enemy who attacked Abganerovo station on 5 August was met with fire from tanks in prepared positions. The tank troops reported ten knocked-out and burned German tanks. The 6th Guards Tank Brigade's own losses were only one tank, knocked out by artillery fire.

Having encountered fierce resistance along the approaches to Abganerovo station and experiencing a shortage of fuel, the XLVIII Panzer Corps went over to the defensive. The rapid breakthrough to Stalingrad did not take place. They were forced to wait for the Fourth Panzer Army to bring up its main forces and to break through the defence with infantry support. Lost in the burned steppe, the '74-kilometre' rail siding did not become just another locale that flashed by the dust-covered columns moving on Stalingrad. This rail siding, which was by no means noted on all maps, was fated for several days to become the arena of intensive tank battles.

Stavka VGK Directive No. 170554, regarding the creation of a new front, followed on the heels of the German Fourth Panzer Army's breakthrough of the Stalingrad line and its arrival at Abganerovo. The Stalingrad Front was to be divided in half 'for the purposes of ease of control' into two parts – the Stalingrad and South-eastern fronts. The distribution of the armies between the two *fronts* was as follows:

... the fronts are to have the following: Stalingrad – the 63rd, 21st, 62nd, and 4th Tank armies and the 28th Tank Corps; the South-eastern Front will contain the 64th Army (29th, 204th, 131st, 38th and 15th Guards Rifle Divisions, and the 6th Guards Tank Brigade), the 51st Army (138th, 157th, 91st, 302nd and 208th Rifle Divisions, the 115th Cavalry Division, and the 135th and 155th Tank Brigades), the 1st Guards Army (37th, 38th, 39th, 40th, and 41st Guards Rifle Divisions), and the 57th Army (35th and 36th Guards Rifle Division and the 126th, 244th and 422nd Rifle Divisions, and the 13th Tank Corps.

Simultaneously, the 64th and 51st Armies are to transfer to the South-eastern Front all of these armies' special services units, as well as all troops (schools, artillery units and units of the 118th Fortified Area) located along the southern front of the Stalingrad external line.

Half of the Stalingrad Front's aviation is to be transferred to the South-eastern Front.[5]

Colonel General A.I. Yeremenko was appointed commander of the new *front* and Major General G.F. Zakharov[6] his chief of staff. The *front* headquarters was formed from the disbanded Southern Front and that of the 1st Tank Army. One is particularly struck by the fact that the 1st Guards Army, which had been activated under duress in the great bend of the Don when the 'cauldron' happened, was subordinated to the South-eastern Front. The new army was hopelessly late in occupying positions along the southern front of the Stalingrad line. As a result, only the 64th, 51st and 57th Armies were subordinated to the South-eastern Front. In his memoirs, Yeremenko complains about the difficulties that arose as a result of drawing the boundary line between the *fronts* through Stalingrad, although in and of itself the division of the troops between the two *fronts* was entirely logical. The enemy's offensive on Stalingrad was developing along two axes and each *front* corresponded to an axis. One front was defending with its front facing to the north-west, and the second facing south-west and to the south. The Germans did not launch any attacks along the boundary between the *fronts*. In a word, Yeremenko's grievances against the supreme command appear unfounded.

From today's point of view the parrying of the XLVIII Panzer Corps' breakthrough at Abangerovo appears to be a great success and even lucky. Had the 6th Tank Brigade been late or even gotten farther, to Kotel'nikovo, the Germans' 150km march could have proven to be a catastrophe. And thus they ended up 30km from Stalingrad. But in August 1942 the overturning of the front line from positions that had been under construction for so long was considered a major breakthrough. On 6 August Stalin addressed to the Stalingrad Front command an irritated tirade dressed up in the form of *Stavka* Directive No. 170556:

The *Stavka* of the Supreme High Command is indignant over the fact that you allowed the enemy's tanks to break through the southern front of the Stalingrad line, without having put up the necessary resistance here and demands, on your personal responsibility, that you restore the situation today along the Stalingrad line at any cost, by destroying the enemy's tanks that have broken through or throwing them back to the south.[7]

It was perhaps already impossible to restore the front line along the Stalingrad line without the 1st Guards Army. One could speak only about stabilizing the situation and preventing a deep breakthrough by the German forces.

The absence of support from the Stalingrad line did not hinder the 64th Army in halting the enemy. The attacking Germans along the new axis of attack collided with a much more flexible form of combat than a fortified line – tanks. The 6th Guards Tank Brigade did not remain alone in the field. At the same time as the fighting raged on 5 August for Abganerovo station, the 13th Tank Brigade arrived at Tinguta station under its own power. Operating as part of the South-western Front since 1941, the tank brigade had been refitting in the Stalingrad area since the middle of July 1942. The tanks rolling off the assembly line were immediately put into units and formations that were waiting in line for equipment. The brigade received twelve tanks a day during 1–3 August. In all, the 13th Tank Brigade received forty-four T-34s (six companies of seven tanks each, plus two command tanks) and by 4 August was ready once again to go into battle. The brigade's motorized rifle battalion was also up to authorized strength. At 03.00 on 5 August it left for the area of Tinguta station. At midday on 5 August the brigade had concentrated to the south-east of the station. At midday on 6 August the attacking German units had occupied the '74-kilometre' railway siding and the 13th Tank Brigade immediately received orders to attack the siding and retake it. Met by fire and counter-attacks, the brigade halted. The number of tanks in the brigade declined by half during a day of fighting; by 7 August it already counted only twenty-two combat-ready tanks. During 7–8 August the brigade, in conjunction with the 38th Rifle Division (from the 57th Army) was holding by a mobile defence the enemy's advance toward Tinguta station, to the north of the '74-kilometre' railway siding. The 6th Guards Tank Brigade's tanks, which had been moved up in a timely manner to a new axis, repelled an attempt to attack from the '74-kilometre' siding to the south.

The 254th Tank Brigade became yet another participant in the fighting of 6 August. Of three brigades fighting near Abganerovo, it was the only newly-raised one. It had been formed in July 1942 and initially was to be part of the 1st Tank Army's 23rd Tank Corps, but it was ultimately subordinated to the 64th Army. In carrying out a 300km march, the 254th Tank Brigade lost tanks along the way due to technical difficulties. The brigade entered the fighting with fourteen tanks. The 254th Tank Brigade's first attack with eight tanks against the '74-kilometre' railway siding ended in failure, with one T-34 burned and six knocked out.

One of the Soviet command's first steps was the unification of the brigades operating in the Abganerovo area under a corps command. The headquarters of the 13th Tank Corps was ordered to concentrate in the area of Tundutovo station. It was now to be subordinated to the 64th Army. True to his habit of running the battle from the front, Colonel Tanaschishin arrived at the site and took over command of the brigade as early as 4 August. The corps headquarters arrived within two days, on 6 August. The corps headquarters was used by the command as a control instance familiar with the practice of employing tank troops. All of the brigades being transferred to the 13th Tank Corps were new to it. The 6th Guards and 13th and 254th Tank Brigades were subordinated to Tanaschishin. The completion of the tank corps' structure would have been achieved by the addition of a motorized rifle brigade to the three tank brigades. The 38th Motorized Rifle Brigade was promised by the *front* command, but it did not arrive. As a result, Tanaschishin's tank brigades operated with the rifle divisions' infantry.

The Battle for Abganerovo Continues

The Soviet command managed to gather a sufficiently powerful tank fist along the 64th Army's left flank. According to the 13th Tank Corps' documents, it had ninety-two tanks during the battle for the '74-kilometre' rail siding. Initially, two fresh brigades (6th Guards and 13th), with a strength of 44 tanks each, and were committed into the fighting. During 7–8 August both sides were accumulating their forces. The Soviet attack on the '74-kilometre' siding was initially scheduled for 8 August, but it did not take place because the 204th Rifle Division was detained on the march. M.S. Shumilov, the commander of the 64th Army, made the decision to postpone the offensive to 9 August. By that time (8 August) there were eleven T-34s in the 13th Tank Brigade and ten T-34s in the 6th Guards Tank Brigade, and six T-34s and four T-70s in the 254th Tank Brigade. The forced pause was employed for 'softening up' the enemy's defence. For example, the first armoured train from the 28th Armoured Train Battalion fired on the enemy's defensive positions on 8 August.

At 05.00 on 9 August the 13th Tank Corps, in conjunction with the 204th Rifle Division and the 133rd Tank Brigade, went over to the attack on the '74-kilometre' siding and captured it by 14.00. Several Soviet tanks stood for hours in one place and carried on an artillery duel with the enemy. As opposed to many other battles along the approaches to Stalingrad, during the course of the fighting for the '74-kilometre' siding we managed to organize cooperation between the artillery and tanks. The armoured train also fulfilled the role of a mobile battery. Massed artillery fire effectively suppressed the enemy's anti-tank defence. As a result, the 6th Guards Tank Brigade lost only one tank during the day's fighting. By 10 August twenty-four tanks remained in the German 14th Panzer Division, according to the formation's history. In conversations with Vasilevskii on the evening of 9 August, the *front* commander painted a colourful picture of the battle: 'The pilots I sent for observing the fighting reported that the Abganerovo area and the adjacent terrain was burning and that everything was enveloped in flames. I conclude that the rocket artillery did a bit of damage there …'

A peculiarity of the fighting for Abganerovo during this period was that the Germans did not shift the point of their attack, but rather launched attacks along a new axis as fresh forces came up. After the IV Corps' infantry came up, an offensive began to outflank Abganerovo from the west. On the morning of 11 August the 94th Infantry Division, having broken through the 126th Rifle Division's defence, cut the railway south of Abganerovo and seized the heights to the west of the station. In this manner a threat was created to the rear of the Soviet group of forces near the '74-kilometre' siding. The 6th Guards Tank Brigade was thrown in to meet the attacking Germans in order to parry the threat of their turning and outflanking our units. Attempts to counter-attack the enemy were not successful. The brigade tried for three days to take back the height, but without success. At the same time, the 13th and 254th Tank Brigades went over to the defensive. They were not involved in combat from 11 through 17 August and were improving their positions and receiving reinforcements.

The first round of the fighting for Abganerovo had been won by the Soviet troops on points. Formations had to be taken from the Sixth Army and sent to Hoth's army. Dërr writes:

> However, here, to the south of Stalingrad, it became clear that the Fourth Panzer Army would be unable to advance further without additional forces allotted to it.

Thus, on 12 August the Sixth Army, which was operating in the great bend of the Don, transferred two divisions (the 24th Panzer and 297th Infantry) to the Fourth Panzer Army, throwing them across the recently-constructed temporary bridge near Potemkinskaya. Upon receiving these reinforcements, the Fourth Panzer Army continued its offensive, following a regrouping; it shifted the axis of its main attack and on 17 August began to attack, having the task of reaching the high bank of the Volga in the area of Krasnoarmeisk.[8]

A breakthrough to the Volga at Krasnoarmeisk would split the Stalingrad Front's left wing in two.

Hoth Attacks

With the arrival of the divisions from the Sixth Army, the final stage of the struggle for Abganerovo began. At 05.00 on 17 August the Fourth Panzer Army went over to the offensive. The XLVIII Panzer Corps attacked south of the Tsatsa – Krasnoarmeisk line; the Romanian VI and IV Corps attacked along the line Abganerovo – Tundutovo, west and east of the railway, respectively. The IV Corps' attack struck against the boundary of the 126th and 204th Rifle Divisions and by 08.00 they had captured the Yurkin State Farm.

The task of halting the enemy's advance was given to the 13th Tank Corps. The rapid movement to the designated area did not take place without serious mistakes. The 6th Guards Tank Brigade's 2nd Battalion reached the Yurkin State Farm without security measures and exposed its flank to the enemy and was immediately punished for this: twelve tanks were immediately knocked out by the German anti-tank defence. The 13th Tank Brigade, which had arrived at 17.00 on 17 August, was also moved up to Abganerovo station. It had not had time to take part in the fighting on 17 August. The counteroffensive by the 29th Rifle Division and the 13th Tank Brigade began on 18 August. However, the Soviet forces were unable to retake the captured positions through a counter-attack.

Eight T-34s and a company of motorized riflemen, which comprised the heart of the resistance south-east of Abganerovo station, were surrounded. The 254th Tank Brigade's encircled tanks held out more than a day. The encirclement area was delineated by the Germans with the aid of rockets. Four tanks were knocked out and burned, while the remaining four were pulled out of the line by their crews as their fuel ran out. Six men of eight tank crews escaped from the encirclement, all from different vehicles.

The fighting on 18 August played out in quite a unique manner. The German tanks cruised along their forward line and fired. Neither side advanced: the Germans repulsed all counter-attacks, although they were themselves unable to advance.

On 20 August the Germans shifted the axis of their attack. This time the '74-kilometre' siding was once again designated the objective. This time they were unable to break the Soviet forces' resistance and capture the railway siding. Success was achieved only on 22 August, when the Germans were finally able to feel out a weak place in the defence (38th Rifle Division). The attackers managed to capture Tinguta station (closer to Stalingrad than the '74-kilometre' siding) and break through to Tundutovo by a broad outflanking of the positions around Abganerovo and the '74-kilometre' siding. The tanks once again played the role of 'fire brigade'. The 13th Tank Brigade, which bordered on Tinguta from the north and north-west, was immediately moved up to the station and prevented the enemy from advancing further. The 133th Tank Brigade carried out the role of strengthening the rifle units' defence around Tundutovo. It shored up the 422nd Rifle Division. The attempt to take back Tinguta station through a counterblow on the morning of 23 August did not bring any success. However, the enemy's further advance was halted. On 24 August the 13th Tank Corps numbered thirty-seven tanks. On 25 Halder wrote in his diary: 'Hoth's forces have run into the enemy's powerful defensive position around Stalingrad.'

The back-and-forth near Abganerovo continued for almost three weeks. The scenario was quite simple. The Fourth Panzer Army would launch attacks along a new axis as fresh forces came up and would grind up the rifle divisions' defence. However, the Germans were unable to develop the breakthrough and stream into the depth of the 64th Army's positions. Units from the tank brigades of Tanaschishin's corps would be brought up and they would seal off the breakthrough. The Soviet forces' subsequent attempts to restore the situation and return their lost positions (with the exception of the successful attack on the '74-kilometre' siding on 9 August) were unsuccessful. The infantry did not follow behind the tanks and the tanks, separated from the infantry, were unable to achieve a decisive result. Then the enemy would once again shift the axis of his attack. On the whole, the 64th Army's forces around Abganerovo managed to keep the situation under control. The tanks became a sort of support, maintaining the firmness of the rifle formations' defence. Within the confines of the manoeuvre battle between the Don and the Volga the enemy's advance, in three weeks of back-and-forth fighting around a railway siding in the middle of the steppe, was minimal.

Chapter 6

Serafimovich. The Foundation of Future Success

(Map 4)

O ne of the prerequisites for the later success of Operation Uranus – the Red Army's counteroffensive around Stalingrad – was the Soviet forces' hold on bridgeheads over the Don in the Kletskaya and Serafimovich areas. Moreover, the bridgeheads had sufficient depth to prevent the bombardment of the crossings by the enemy's artillery, as well as for the stationing of a sufficient amount of troops.

At the beginning of the fighting in the great bend of the Don, Serafimovich was on the periphery of the battle. The forces of the former South-western Front fell back to the Don and beyond the Don in July 1942 in quite a sorry state. The main force for defending and launching counterblows became the reserves moved up from the rear, although they were united by the headquarters of the 21st Army from the old South-western Front. From the very start, the Soviet command sought to employ the Serafimovich area for counterblows against the flank of the enemy group of forces aimed at Stalingrad.

In light of the appointment of V.N. Gordov as *front* commander, the 21st Army was commanded by Aleksei Il'ich Danilov,[1] a former ensign in the Tsarist Army and graduate of the Alekseev Military School. His service record was not bad and in 1931 he completed the M.V. Frunze Military Academy[2] and took part in the Soviet-Finnish War and had previously headed the 21st Army's staff.

The first episode in the fight for Serafimovich became the clash of the Soviet reserves with the Italians. The 63rd Rifle Division, which arrived at the 21st Army by rail, numbered 5,369 men, but only 1,751 rifles and seven heavy machine guns (the formation received reinforcements that lacked weapons and uniforms, but which were included in its ration strength). The low strength level forced it to operate in small detachments. For example, on 30 July the 63rd Rifle Division's 226th Rifle Regiment launched a tank landing consisting of 120 men and two companies of tanks from the 652nd Independent Tank Battalion. The detachment crossed the Don and entered the fighting south-west of Serafimovich.

In conditions of a porous front, it's possible that tank landings would have had a chance of success. But on 29 July 1942 the Italian 'Celere' Division arrived at the front around Serafimovich following a 400km march.[3]A brief but intense meeting engagement unfolded. A battalion from the Italian artillery regiment, which did not even have time to deploy, became the Soviet tanks' first victim. The fight against tanks was traditionally the 'Achilles heel' of the armies allied with Germany, but Italy was something of an exception in this regard. First of all, they already had German 75mm Pak97/38 anti-tank guns, and secondly, as an industrially-developed country Italy disposed of its own sufficiently capable artillery. The T-34s' most dangerous enemy was the model 75/32 (a 75mm gun with a 32-calibre long barrel), employing armour-piercing shells. They confidently hit T-34s. The Italians also had captured Soviet 76.2mm guns with regulation armour-piercing shells. Light T-60 tanks could also be hit by fragmentation-explosive rounds.

The 63rd Rifle Division's losses in the fighting from 30 July through 5 August were 517 men killed, wounded and missing in action. According to the memoirs of the commander of the Italian Expeditionary Corps (*Corpo di Spedizione Italiane*) in Russia, General Giovanni Messe,[4] the 'Celere' Division's losses were 1,000 men killed, wounded and missing in action. According to Soviet data, the 652nd Independent Tank Battalion had remaining in line only four T-34s and two T-60s. Eleven T-34s and seventeen T-60s were among the irreplaceable losses.

A regiment from the German 305th Infantry Division, reinforced by assault guns, was also operating with the Italians, but the Italians fought off the T-34s practically without its participation. The Germans' achievement in this fighting was throwing out of Serafimovich the remnants of the Soviet 304th Rifle Division, units of which fell back behind the Don. A relative quiet descended for a certain time along the front around Serafimovich. On 14 August the worn-out 'Celere' Division was pulled out of the front line and placed in the reserve.

The receipt and commitment of reinforcements into the fighting, as well as the arrival of a fresh formation, enabled the Red Army to launch a retaliatory attack against the Italian corps that had occupied positions along the Don. By 10 August the 304th Rifle Division had achieved a strength of 5,876 men, armed with 2,292 rifle, 33 heavy and 32 light machine guns and 217 Shpagin and Degtyaryov sub-machine guns. Of course, this was not the height of their dreams. The newly-arrived 'Far Eastern' 96th Rifle Division looked a lot better. It numbered 11,689 men, 8,190 rifles, 87 heavy and 195 light machine guns, and 391 Shpagin and Degtyaryov sub-machine guns. V.I. Kuznetsov's neighbouring 63rd Army was also brought in for a new offensive around Serafimovich. Its 197th Rifle Division (reinforced with a regiment from the 203rd Rifle Division) and 14th Guards Rifle Division were brought in for the operation. On 20 August the 14th Guards Rifle Division numbered 13,029 men, 107 heavy and 219 light machine guns, and 1,223 Degtyaryov and Shpagin sub-machine guns.

The offensive began at 03.00 on the night of 20 August with the forcing of the Don. An attack by the adjacent flanks of the 21st and 63rd Armies landed on the boundary of the Sixth Army's XVII Army Corps and the Italian XXXV Army Corps. I would like to immediately warn against regarding the Italian units as a mob incapable of combat and ready to run at the first sound of fighting. The 'Sforzesca' Division, which lay along the path of the 63rd Army's units, was in an unenviable position. The formation consisted of two regiments, disposing of only six infantry battalions and fairly weak artillery. The formation's overall strength on 1 July 1942 was 12,521 men.

In the 14th Guards Rifle Division's war diary the enemy was rated quite seriously and it was noted that the division advanced on the first day of the fighting, while 'overcoming stubborn resistance'. In the 197th Rifle Division's zone the Italians managed to hold the Soviet attacks for some time through a stubborn defence of the key Height 190.1, which loomed over the forcing area. The collapse of the defence by the six battalions of the 'Sforzesca' Division under the blows of eighteen well-outfitted battalions from two rifle divisions did not happen immediately.

General Messe employed 'Blackshirts'[5] – the Italian Fascist Party's militia formations – for counter-attacks. Despite their ideological stiffening, they were not a serious military force and suffered heavy losses. The counter-attacks rapidly bled the Italians dry and their resistance began to weaken. If on 21 August the 14th Guards Rifle Division reported taking 70 prisoners, then on 22 August they reported taking 226 prisoners, with its own losses for 22 August being 10 men killed and 35 wounded.

With the arrival of reserves ('Celere' and a battalion from the 'Pasubio' Division, the Croatian Legion, and the German 179th Infantry Regiment), General Messe decided upon a counterblow. One should say that the moment for launching a counterblow had been chosen quite fortunately by the Italians. On the morning of 23 August the division artillery and reinforcement artillery for the attacking Soviet divisions was still on the right bank of the Don. The counterblow forced the 197th Rifle Division to go over to the defensive and, as regards the 14th Guards Rifle Division, the commander of the 63rd Army, V.I. Kuznetsov, reported the following to *front* headquarters: 'Yesterday Gryaznov's (the commander of the 14th Guards Rifle Division) units abandoned their occupied line in confusion. A number of unit and battalion commanders have been put out of action and the situation was restored only in the evening.' Moreover, they managed to restore the position through artillery fire, and not a counter-attack.

If the hastily prepared and essentially improvised offensive by the 63rd Army began with the defeat of the 'Sforzesca' Division, then the 21st Army's offensive did not enjoy initial success, being met by a dense fire from the German infantry. An advance by the 21st Army's 304th Rifle Division followed only after the Italians retreated. As a result, the 304th Rifle Division's 812th Rifle Regiment was counter-attacked by the 'Savoy' Cavalry Regiment early on the morning of 24 August 1942 near Izbushenskii farm. The attack proved to be unexpectedly laden with results. In the 304th Rifle Division's operational report, it was admitted that 'The 812th Rifle Division's 1st and 2nd Battalions, having lost almost all their rank and file in the fighting with cavalry, destroyed up to 500 Italians'. According to the 21st Army's war diary, the 304th Rifle Division's losses from 20 August through 1 September were 94 men killed, 351 wounded and 603 missing in action. One must admit that the 304th Rifle Division lost at Izbushenskii at least several dozen men killed and no less than 300 captured. The Italians admit to losing 40 men killed and 79 wounded.

The counterblows only delayed the Soviet offensive for a time and bled the Italians white. On 25 August Messe ordered a withdrawal, without coordinating this with the Germans. This caused a scandal between the two allies, with the creation of 'Blumentritt's Group' as part of the XVII Army Corps and the Italians' refusal to subordinate themselves to Blumentritt as being inferior in rank. Nonetheless, the Germans were forced to react and try to close the 20km gap between the XVII Army Corps and the Italian Corps. For this, they had to abandon the Serafimovich area. The town, for which stubborn fighting had been waged for nearly a month, was at last liberated. The 22nd Panzer Division, the single mobile reserve in Paulus's army, was dispatched to the XVII Army Corps on Hitler's orders.

The paradoxical nature of the situation is that, first of all, there was no real Italian withdrawal on Messe's orders, and, second of all, as early as the evening of 25 August the Soviet 63rd Army command made the decision to halt the offensive and to consolidate. During 26–27 August this decision was confirmed by the development of events, when the 203rd Rifle Division, which had advanced with two regiments, fell back with heavy losses as a result of the 'Celere' Division's counterblow (this led to the relief of the formation's commander), while the 5th Guards Cavalry Division was thrown off the commanding Height 220.9 by the Germans' counterblow.

Simultaneously, the Germans' plans for restoring the situation by counterblows were foiled. A.I. Danilov, the energetic army commander, decided to galvanize the 21st Army's offensive by committing the 124th Rifle Division into the fighting, which had been removed from the neighbouring sector. The attack, combined with the forcing of the Don near Zatonskii, proved an unpleasant surprise for the Germans and forced them to employ reserves by no means for 'sewing up' the boundary with the Italians. Thus, for example, on 29 August the 79th Infantry Division lost 120 men and the 22nd Panzer Division lost two Panzer 38(t) tanks.

At the same time, one cannot but admit that the success with the formation of the Serafimovich bridgehead cost the Soviets quite dearly. The 63rd Army's shock group (197th and 203rd Rifle Divisions, 14th Guards Rifle Division, and the 3rd Guards Cavalry Corps) lost 1,913 men killed, 1,504 missing in action, 40 captured and 6,179 wounded – for a total loss of 10,124 men – from 20 August through 1 September 1942. The 203rd Rifle Division suffered the heaviest losses. According to the army's war diary, the formation lost 4,095 men. However, during the transfer of command, it was noted that 4,493 men were lost, including 698 killed and 1,410 (!) missing in action. The losses of the 21st Army's shock group (304th, 124th and 96th Rifle Divisions) from 20 August through 1 September 1942 proved to be significantly lower than that of its neighbour: 500 men killed, 670 missing in action and 1,683 wounded, for a total of 2,984 men for due to all causes.

On 1 September the Germans' and Italians' joint counterblow took place, with Messe putting into action his Alpine riflemen and a subunit of L6/40 tanks. The counterblow did not enjoy success and only slightly shook up the bridgehead's defence. As regards the fate of the L6/40 tanks, in the 14th Guards Rifle Division's war diary there is a note of them becoming separated from their infantry: 'Only the enemy's tanks managed to break through in the direction of State Farm No. 4, where they were met with fire from our anti-tank defence and routed.' In his memoirs Messe severely criticizes the Germans' 'uncomradely' behaviour, but from the Soviet documents' point of view the Alpine riflemen's penetration was eliminated on the first day of the fighting and the 14th Guards Rifle Division's regiment that had been pushed out of its position by the Germans, was unable to recover it in a counter-attack. In any event, the counterblow was not developed.

A particularly unpleasant thrust occurred on 6 September, when the 304th Rifle Division was caught off guard by a counter-attack by two groups of tanks from the Germans' 22nd Panzer Division while they themselves were attacking. On 4 September the 22nd Panzer Division numbered twenty-two Panzer 38(t)s, one Panzer III, one Panzer IV short-barrel tank, and three Panzer IV long-barrel tanks. The attack on the attacking Soviet infantry by the tanks on open terrain had very severe consequences. On 6 September the 809th Rifle Regiment lost 64 men killed, 14 wounded and 255 (!) missing in action, and the 807th Rifle Regiment 143 men killed, 40 wounded and 68 missing in action. This was perhaps the last effective attack by the Czechoslovak-produced Panzer 38(t) on the Soviet-German front.

However, the enemy's painful retaliatory attacks did not force A.I. Danilov to draw back from continuing the fight for the bridgeheads. The army commander decided to change the axis of the attack. The 304th Rifle Division was moved to the 21st Army's left flank and once again crossed the Don, but this time in the Kletskaya area. I should like to emphasize that the offensive plans were Danilov's own initiative and were not 'dropped' on him from on high.

At 05.00 on 16 September the 21st Army's offensive began in the space between Kletskaya and Raspopinskaya. The Soviet forces' enemy here was elements of the German 113th Infantry Division, which was being partially relieved by the Romanian 13th Infantry Division. The calculation of a surprise attack against the extended positions along the front proved justified. According to the 809th Rifle Regiment's war diary, as early as 08.00 the enemy, who had been occupying trenches and pillboxes 800m from the Don, 'ran away and abandoned his guns'. The attacked 113th Infantry Division managed to hold the key heights along the approaches to the Don, but before long the 79th and 113th Infantry Divisions were relieved by the Romanians (the 70th Infantry Division would before long be taking part in storming the factory areas of Stalingrad). Meanwhile, the Soviet offensive was renewed. The 63rd Rifle Division, having relieved the 304th Rifle Division, attacked on the evening of 22 September, threw the Romanians out of their positions and almost immediately reached the key Height 163.3. At the same time, by 20 September the 63rd Rifle Division was nearly as much of an 'invalid' as the 304th Rifle Division, disposing of 2,914 rifles for 6,583 men of the rank and file. The 647th Independent Tank Battalion, which had been attached to the division, was also nothing to write home about: it numbered six T-34s and eleven T-60s on 18 September.

According to data contained in supplements to the Sixth Army's war diary for 22–23 September, the Romanian 13th Infantry Division lost 50 men killed, 281 wounded and 84 missing in action, while the Romanian 6th Infantry Division lost 50 men killed, 152 wounded and 15 missing in action. The 63rd Rifle Division correspondingly lost 61 men killed and 251 wounded. The Romanians' attempts to counter-attack were unsuccessful. Yet one more bridgehead was now in the Soviet command's possession, this time near Kletskaya.

In tallying the results of the fighting for the bridgeheads at Serafimovich and Kletskaya, it is necessary to say the following. The result of the 63rd and 21st Armies' offensives was the formation of a propitious bridgehead, sufficiently deep for concentrating a large mass of troops, including mechanized formations. Simultaneously, the fighting for Serafimovich was quite illustrative in revealing the Italian army's qualities. The Italians put up resistance fully proportional to the forces put into action and were capable of a consequential counterblow. The Romanians, who had taken up positions around Kletskaya and Serafimovich, in place of the Germans and Italians, were not yet capable of this.

Chapter 7

The Formation of the 'Northern Covering Detachment'

For the Soviets, one of the most dangerous consequences of the rout along the Sirotinskaya bridgehead was the enemy's arrival at the Don River along sectors that were still poorly covered in the 4th Tank Army's rear. Although the line of the Don was being occupied by units of the fortified areas,[1] a continuous defence along the eastern bank of the river at the moment of the Germans' arrival simply did not exist. This considerably eased the task of Paulus's army of forming a bridgehead at Vertyachii for the final lunge toward Stalingrad. Simultaneously, the Don was being forced on the initiative of the tactical commanders. For example, on 16 August 1942 two companies from the German 384th Infantry Division occupied a small bridgehead near Nizhnii Akatov and by evening two battalions had already concentrated at it. On the night of 16/17 August the 389th Infantry Division seized yet another small bridgehead a little north of Trekhostrovskaya.

The Stalingrad Front was saved from complete disaster by the arrival of troops allotted for the 1st Guards Army (already mentioned above). For example, Major General V.G. Zholudev's fresh 37th Guards Rifle Division entered the fighting along the western bank of the Don almost 'from their vehicles', immediately following their unloading from their trains, and was defending along the approaches to the bridgehead at Trekhostrovskaya, allowing the remnants of the 4th Tank Army's defeated troops to pass through it. On 16 August the 37th Guards Rifle Division received orders to cross over to the eastern bank of the Don and to occupy it, while preventing the enemy from forcing the river. Major General S.S. Gur'ev's 39th Guards Rifle Division arrived in the same area. These two divisions were subsequently fated to play a significant role in the struggle for Stalingrad, including on the city's streets. The remnants of the 18th Rifle Division, which had lost part of their weapons while falling back and fording the Don, were also in the area of the German-occupied bridgehead. On 20 August they numbered only 1,281 men, with one (!) heavy machine gun. The 214th Rifle Division, which had been worn out in the July fighting in the great bend of the Don and pulled back into the rear of the 64th Army and reinforced, became the *front's* internal reserve. As of 20 August, already following the beginning of the fighting for the bridgeheads, it numbered 7,870 men, which was not bad for the time. As early as 16 August it received orders to move to the area of the disaster which had just arisen in the small bend of the Don. Following several corrections to the march route, the 214th Rifle Division was moved to Pan'shino and Verkhne-Gnilovskii, where it arrived on the night of 18/19 August. The 193rd Tank Brigade, which was armed with American tanks received through Lend-Lease,[2] was transferred to the 4th Tank Army for parrying the latest crisis. On 17 August it numbered twenty M3s General Lees and fifteen M3l Stuarts.[3]

The sector south of the bridgehead seized by the VIII Army Corps was in the sphere of responsibility of the 62nd Army, which had entirely fallen back behind the Don after the 'cauldron'. The fresh 98th Rifle Division (11,689 men as of 15 August) was in the immediate area of Vertyachii. They dispatched here the 40th Tank Brigade (three KVs, twenty-nine

T-34s and two T-60s), which had been restored following the fighting in the Don bend, and the fresh 134th Tank Brigade, which was yet another formation outfitted with Western-built tanks (nineteen Lees and thirty-two Stuarts as of the evening of 17 August). The first reaction by the *front* command to the 4th Tank Army's disaster was the hare-brained idea of forcing the Don in the Vertyachii from east to west for a counterblow in the Germans' flank, with its main strike force being the fresh 98th Rifle Division. The idea got as far as the working out of a detailed plan for a counteroffensive in the 62nd Army's headquarters (Combat Order No. 67 of 17 August 1942) and the inclusion of all the army's reserves in it. They had even begun moving four pontoon-bridge battalions up to the front for laying down a bridge over the Don. It was planned to force the Don on the night of 18/19 August. The attempt to carry out this plan would most likely have ended in disaster. However, the rout in the Don bend and the beginning of the river's forcing by the Germans cooled the Soviet command's ardour. The troops were switched to more realistic tasks. On 18 August the 98th Rifle Division received orders to defend with two regiments the bank of the Don in the Vertyachii area and to launch a counterblow with one regiment and the 134th Tank Brigade against the German-occupied bridgehead in the Verkhne-Gnilovskii area.

On the whole, the Stalingrad Front command managed to gather a sufficiently powerful group of forces, under the command of the 4th Tank and 62nd Armies, along the approaches to the bridgehead at Akatovo and Verkhne-Gnilovskii. Here we should note that the *front* command had been forced to allot reserves to the Stalingrad line's fortified positions along the approaches to the city. This defensive line was located approximately half-way between the Don and Stalingrad and its flanks rested on the Volga. According to its creators' idea, the line was supposed to prevent a rapid breakthrough to Stalingrad and the seizure of the city from the march. However, in order to carry out the task of reinforcement, it was necessary to occupy the line with troops. During the time of the events being described, the 87th and 35th Guards Rifle Divisions were to be allotted for this purpose. As of 15 August the 87th Rifle Division numbered 11,429 men and was well outfitted with heavy and light machine guns. In reality, well-equipped divisions were kept out of the fighting and held positions in the rear.

On the 19th the Soviet offensive began from various directions against the bridgehead occupied by units of the VIII Army Corps. The counteroffensive's limited result was predetermined by the limited forces – one complete division and one regiment apiece from three different divisions. The 214th Rifle Division operated in full strength in the counter-attacks against the bridgehead, although after an exhausting march. Only one regiment (the other two occupied defensive positions along the line of the Don) from the 37th Guards Rifle Division took part in the counter-attacks against the bridgehead on 19 August. The 120th Guards Rifle Regiment from the 39th Guards Rifle Division also took part in the counterblow. The remaining two regiments were still engaged in fighting along the western bank of the Don. All of the attacks by the 134th Tank Brigade's Western-built tanks against the bridgehead throughout 19 August were beaten off by the Germans, while the 384th Infantry Division claimed thirty Soviet tanks destroyed for the day. A Soviet report, delivered in the middle of the day, admits to two tanks lost, although these are clearly incomplete figures.

On 20 August the attack by the 98th Rifle Division's 166th Rifle Regiment, which had been allotted for the counterblows, was reinforced by a second tank brigade – the 40th Tank Brigade. However, the German forces in the bridgehead were reinforced at the same time by the crossing over of the 305th Infantry Division's 578th Infantry Regiment, which took up positions along the left flank. The fighting for the bridgehead lasted all day, but they could not manage to thrown the Germans off. One of the reasons for this was the VIII Corps' superiority in artillery. The corps disposed its divisions' artillery regiments as its own, with 150mm guns, as well as reinforcement artillery up to 210mm howitzers. The Soviet 4th Tank Army no longer disposed of 152mm guns, while reinforcement weapons were limited to anti-tank regiments with 76mm guns. In turn, tanks were quickly put out of action in the conditions of the summer of 1942, when the Germans disposed of effective anti-tank weapons. By the evening of 20 August the 193rd Tank Brigade had lost half of its tanks while six Lees and eleven Stuarts remained in line. In the 134th Tank Brigade the number of foreign vehicles in line had also fallen significantly, with only twelve Lees and twenty-one Stuarts still in service.[4] Moreover, according to one of the reports, five Lees were listed as having been lost to air attacks. At the same time, Soviet-made equipment was also knocked out at a fairly rapid pace. The 40th Tank Brigade lost two KVs and ten T-34s during the day's fighting, while one KV and ten T-34s were damaged.

While the fighting for the VIII Corps' bridgehead was going on, the Sixth Army was secretly preparing to force the Don along the previously designated axis of the main attack near Vertyachii with the forces of the LI Corps. The choice of Vertyachii was conditioned by the favourable terrain conditions for launching tanks toward the northern part of Stalingrad. Also, the Germans immediately made the decision to seize the bridgehead with infantry and only at the last moment commit tanks to it in order to secure the tank attack's surprise.

During reconnaissance, the Germans uncovered appropriate sectors for forcing the river for two infantry divisions subordinated to the LI Corps. Sectors along both sides of Luchenskii and south-west of Kalachkin for the 295th Infantry Division, and on both side of Akimovskii and at Perepol'nyi for the 76th Infantry Division. Despite the energetic attempts to drive the Germans from the VIII Corps' bridgehead, one cannot say that the Red Army did not pay any attention to the Vertyachii area. By order of the commander of the 62nd Army, A.I. Lopatin, the sector from the VIII Corps' bridgehead as far as Peskovatka was to be occupied by two of the 98th Rifle Division's regiments (with one in reserve). The commander ordered: 'The river must be kept under automatic weapons fire.' However, a serious mistake by the 62nd Army command was leaving a small space between the positions of the 98th and 399th Rifle Divisions covered only by the elements of a fortified area. This was the sector of the Don in the Luchenskii area, exactly where it was planned to force the river with the 295th Infantry Division. Colonel Selle, the chief of the Sixth Army's engineer troops, later wrote that the terrain along this sector 'was particularly favourable for a crossing, because the entire promontory along the southern bend was thickly overgrown and thus offered good opportunities for occupying jumping-off positions'. It's interesting to note that it was precisely here that the Germans decided to force the river on assault boats, without an artillery preparation, while calculating on a surprise attack.

The 76th Infantry Division's regiments allotted to the first echelon (correspondingly, the 203rd and 178th Infantry Regiments) and the 295th Infantry Division's 516th and 517th Infantry Regiments, received twenty-seven assault boats and twenty-four inflatable boats apiece. The LI Corps was allotted 17½ pontoon-bridge brigades for constructing two bridges with a capacity of 20 tons each, that is, capable of withstanding the weight of tanks.[5] Given the Don's width of about 250m, this was considered sufficient even taking into account possible losses. Jumping-off positions were occupied by German infantry on the nights of 19/20 and 20/21 August. Although there were no dense woods along the 76th Infantry Division's forcing sector, the *balki* that led down to the Don favoured the secret accumulation of infantry and boats. The artillery took up positions during the night of 20/21 August. Besides the divisions' own artillery and the corps' reinforcement artillery, artillery from the 44th Infantry and 16th Panzer Divisions was to be brought in to support the forcing of the Don.

Colonel Selle, the Sixth Army's chief of engineers, later recalled: 'The night before the offensive was clear. The wind was blowing from the south-east, but was favourable. A light fog lay over the Don. From 0.200 sharpshooters and engineers from the first wave stood at the ready by their assault cutters and inflatable boats and in the shelters of the jumping-off assault positions (in the willows, the hollows and the ruins of buildings).'

The crossing began at 03.00. Predictably, the most successful thrust over the Don was by the 295th Infantry Division. The first wave of infantry in its assault boats reached the opposite bank almost unopposed. Organized resistance along this sector was put up only after the breakthrough by the German infantry into the depth, toward Peskovatka. This allowed them to begin building a bridge over the Don as early as 05.00. Events developed far more dramatically along the 76th Infantry Division's sector. The crossing of the 178th Infantry Regiment over the Don near Perepol'nyi was carried out relatively successfully, but encountered fierce resistance along the bank. The forcing of the Don by the 203rd Infantry Regiment near Akimovskii suffered a failure. As Selle wrote in his report, 'again and again, the attempts we made to resume the crossing in the growing dawn suffered a failure'. The commander of the regiment's first battalion, Major Jordan was killed and chaos and panic broke out. The assault boats that returned for the second wave of infantry had to wait for their passengers – the soldiers and officers would not leave their shelters under the intense fire. All of the assault boats in this sector, with the exception of one, were out of action. The inflatable boats had also been shot up immediately upon departing their shelters. As early as 04.25 a note appeared in the 76th Infantry Division's war diary that 'The 203rd Infantry Regiment's crossing has been temporarily halted'. The German artillery laid down a smokescreen, hiding the disorganized elements of the 203rd Infantry Regiment from the Russian machine guns.

However, such a complex operation as the forcing of a major river always carries considerable risk. The German command's response was to move up its reserve – the same 76th Infantry Division's 230th Infantry Regiment – to the river along the sector which had already been relatively successfully crossed by elements of the 230th Infantry Regiment. The crossing by elements of the 230th Infantry Regiment began as early as 09.00, and closer to midday it was already attacking toward Vertyachii into the flank and rear of the Soviet units facing the front of the unfortunate 203rd Infantry Regiment. The main problem for the Germans at that moment was the necessity of building a longer bridge at Akimovskii itself. The Don is a bit wider at Perepol'nyi and should a longer bridge be needed the pontoon-bridge battalions would not have any reserve in the case of losses. Thus the decision was made to await the capture of Akimovskii. Subsequent events (a squall of Soviet air attacks and artillery bombardments) confirmed the correctness of this decision.

The reserve 230th Infantry Regiment, which had been committed by the Germans into the fighting, successfully stormed Vertyachii from the flank, despite 'powerful resistance by heavy machine guns, heavy mortars and anti-tank guns'. Assistance was also rendered to the 295th Infantry Division's attack against the Soviet strongpoint – a battalion from the 518th Infantry Regiment attacked Vertyachii from the south (its commander, Major Henze, was later awarded the Knight's Cross for this attack). At midday Soviet tanks appeared at the bridgehead, however, their actions were somewhat chaotic. The 76th Infantry Division's war diary contains the following note on that score: 'The commander of the 230th Infantry Regiment reports that enemy tanks evidently do not have a definite target and are simply firing in our direction.' Assault guns which had been brought up to the bridgehead, crossed as early as 13.00, and took up positions in the Vertyachii area, and anti-tank guns soon made the tank attacks a doubtful undertaking. According to day's results, the 76th Infantry Division's 230th Infantry Regiment claimed fourteen Soviet tanks knocked out. Only one T-34 burned and two T-34s knocked out from the 40th Tank Brigade are noted in the Soviet documents, and the 134th Tank Brigade's American tanks did not take part in the fighting on this day.

The forcing of the Don by the Germans and the formation of a solid bridgehead was immediately evaluated by the Soviet command as the failure of those commanders responsible for this sector. As early as midday on 21 August Major General I.F. Barinov, the commander of the 98th Rifle Division, was relieved and replaced by Colonel I.F. Seryogin, the commander of the 18th Rifle Division, which was being pulled back to the rear to refit. However, in retrospect one must admit that the bridgehead was seized as the objectively conditioned concentration of sufficient forces by the Germans for the resolution of the assigned task, and not as a result of the incompetence of an individual commander. Barinov later had quite a successful career in the Red Army and worked in the headquarters of the 65th Army at the concluding phase of the battle of Stalingrad.

The paradox of the situation lies in the fact that simultaneously with the forcing of the Don at Vertyachii, attacks by Soviet units continued against the VIII Corps' bridgehead and similar attempts by the Germans to expand this bridgehead. On the morning of 21 August the main units of the 62nd and 4th Tank Armies had been committed to the offensive against the VIII Corps' bridgehead. Two of the 98th Rifle Division's regiments were also committed against this bridgehead, while the remaining 308th Rifle Regiment was defending the Vertyachii area. In their reports, both sides in the fighting for the bridgehead claimed local successes achieved in heavy fighting. On 21 August the 305th Infantry Division's 578th Infantry Regiment lost seventy men killed and eighty wounded (losses comparable to those suffered by the entire 76th Infantry Division while forcing the Don). In any case, Soviet units, including tank units, committed to the attacks against the bridgehead, had first of all to be pulled out of the fighting, which was the reason for their delayed reaction to what was taking place near Vertyachii.

However, at 18.00 on 21 August, even before the completing the elimination of the Soviet forces' last centres of resistance near Vertyachii, the German engineer units began to lay down a bridge at Akimovskii. A pontoon bridge at Luchenskii was ready as early as 16.50 on 21 August, and the one at Akimovskii at 07.30 the following day. Correspondingly, the 16th Panzer Division was appointed to cross the bridge at Luchenskii, and the 3rd Motorized Division at Akimovskii.

A problem that exacerbated an already critical situation for the Red Army was the underestimation of the enemy. In the 62nd Army's morning report for 22 August, it was noted that: 'The enemy, having begun on the morning of 21.8.42 the crossing on boats and pontoons, crossed two regiments of infantry by the close of the day of 21.8.42.'[6] This was being written at the time when two German divisions had already crossed over the Don at Vertyachii. It's not surprising that in view of this low evaluation, only a rifle regiment from the 87th Rifle Division and the 137th Tank Brigade (three KVs, one T-34 and fifteen T-60s) had been committed for plugging up the breaches that had arisen as a result of the forcing of the Don. We should not fail to emphasize that the 87th Rifle Division's regiment was to be removed from the Stalingrad line – a risky but understandable move.

At 04.00 on 22 August the 137th Tank Brigade's few tanks, carrying infantry, attacked Peskovatka following a short artillery preparation. The weak counter-attack was predictably beaten back by the 295th Infantry Division and the Germans claimed six tanks knocked out, which corresponds with the 137th Tank Brigade's account (six tanks were also listed as knocked out or damaged). The 134th Tank Brigade also attempted to attack Vertyachii on 22 August, but without result, while eleven tanks remained in line of the thirty-three vehicles available the previous day. A report lists five Lees and three Stuarts as 'missing in action,' that is, that went into the attack but did not return.

In reporting the results of the day for 22 August, General Lopatin informed the *front* commander that the available infantry strength was insufficient to destroy the enemy that had crossed over the Don and requested permission to bring in the 35th Guards Rifle Division to carry out this task, or to completely remove the 87th Rifle Division from its positions along the Stalingrad line. At midday on 22 August the 35th Guards Rifle Division had occupied defensive positions along the north-western sector of the line, to the right of the 87th Rifle Division. As a result, the decision was made to, first of all, give up on continuing the 62nd Army's counterblows and go over to the defensive, and, second of all, to remove the two remaining regiments of the 87th Rifle Division from the defensive line by morning and to move them up to the approaches to the German bridgehead, thus strengthening the defence by the 1382nd Rifle Regiment, which was already engaged. This decision was not only late, but played a truly fateful role in the subsequent development of events. On the night of 23 August the 87th Rifle Division's two regiments left their prepared positions and began marching to the west, toward the Don.

At the same time, by midday on 22 August the German 16th Panzer and 3rd Motorized Divisions were concentrating near the pontoon bridges and the crossing of the armoured equipment to the left bank of the Don began unexpectedly. It was planned to free up and cross the 60th Motorized Division the following day. The strength of the XIV Panzer Corps' tank park at that moment is shown by the following figures (see table).

Table 10: The Strength of the XIV Panzer Corps' Tank Park on 22 August 1942.

	Panzer II	*Panzer III (short)*	*Panzer III (long)*
16th Panzer Division	–	11	57
3rd Motorized Division	8	–	27
60th Motorized Division	13	–	26

	Panzer IV (short)	*Panzer IV (long)*	*7.62cm Sfl*
16th Panzer Division	4	12	–
3rd Motorized Division	–	7	5
60th Motorized Division	–	3	7

By 18.00 on 22 August a panzer regiment from the 16th Panzer Division had crossed over the Don, but the complete concentration of the two divisions along the Vertyachii bridgehead was completed only in the early morning of 23 August. One of the most terrible days in the history of the battle of Stalingrad, which determined the nature of the armed struggle of the sides during the course of the subsequent weeks and even months, began early in the morning with air attacks.

Aside from the infantry's and artillery's positions, the march columns of the 87th Rifle Division's 1378th and 1379th Rifle Regiments came under air attack at about 05.00 Moscow time. In the open steppe they, as was pointed out in the operational report, 'having suffered heavy losses in men and materiel', scattered and were unable to put up serious resistance. At the same time, the tanks attacked in the Vertyachii area. The beginning of the offensive is described in bold colours in the 16th Panzer Division's history: 'At 04.30 [05.30, Moscow time, Author], the tanks of Sikenus's combat group emerged in a broad wedge from the bridgehead, like on a training ground, with Krumpen's and von Arensdorf's combat groups following behind them.'

The 16th Panzer Division's attack overthrew the 87th Rifle Division's 1382nd Rifle Regiment and the 137th Tank Brigade, and they fell back to the south, to the Dmitrievka area. At 08.00 [09.00, Moscow time, Author] the attackers reached Height 137.2 north of Bol'shaya Rossoshka and broke into the Stalingrad Line's empty positions, which had been abandoned a few hours earlier by the 87th Rifle Division's infantry. This was an enormous break for the Germans. As was noted in the XIV Panzer Corps' daily report, 'resistance substantially weakened following this'. The positions occupied by the 35th Guards Rifle Division along the line remained unmolested from the north. The offensive along the bridgehead's left flank by the 3rd Motorized Division's tanks and motorized infantry, reinforced by infantry from the 76th Infantry Division, finally finished off the 98th Rifle Division. As regards the division, it was later written in a report on 25 August that 'up to 300 men were gathered up, but no equipment'.[7]

Two German divisions were racing flat out toward Stalingrad, with Henschel Hs 129 ground-attack aircraft clearing a path for them. At about midday they crossed the railway line to Stalingrad at the 'Kilometre 564' and Konnyi rail sidings. A Soviet train was set on fire by the attack aircraft at a railway crossing and the German tanks moved east past the burning cars. The 3rd Motorized Division captured a train in the process of unloading and twenty American motor vehicles were seized. At 16.00 the 16th Panzer Division's forward detachment reached the heights north of Rynok, and at 17.00 reached the Volga south of Vinnovka. Along the bank of the Volga, along the railway near Latashanka, among piles of various equipment, the Germans discovered twenty-three 406mm naval guns that had been produced in the 'Barricade' factory in Stalingrad and destined for *Soviet Union*-class battleships that had not been completed.

The first enemy the Germans encountered right at the city's wall was the anti-aircraft batteries of Stalingrad's air defence forces. In the 16th Panzer Division's history there is mention of a fight with 'Russian anti-aircraft guns, served by women'. The tank troops from Hube's division claimed to have silenced thirty-seven anti-aircraft positions with a panzer battalion and motorized riflemen. The noted German historian and publicist Paul Carell paid particular attention to this episode in his description of the fighting for Stalingrad. Just how much does this story correspond with reality?

The guns of Lieutenant Colonel V.Ye. German's 1077th Anti-Aircraft Regiment were indeed positioned in the northern part of Stalingrad and along the approaches to the city from the north. His missions were to cover the Stalingrad Tractor Factory and the steam ferry over the Volga near Latashanka. The main mass of the regiment's rank and file consisted of men, but in the spring of 1942 directing and rangefinding crews, as well as the headquarters of batteries, battalions and regiments, were staffed by women. A certain number of women became crew members on the anti-aircraft guns, and in the list of those killed on 23 August are women who were listed at gun crew members.

The 1077th Anti-Aircraft Regiment's first foe early on the morning of 23 August was German aircraft, including dive bombers. At 14.30 a message was received that tanks were approaching the anti-aircraft guns' positions. The 6th Battery, which could rake the Sukhaya Mechetka *balka*, was well placed. The battery claimed twenty-eight German tanks knocked out. During the latter half of the day the hardest fighting was that of the 3rd Battery, which straddled the road from Yerzovka to Stalingrad. In the 1077th Anti-Aircraft's report on the results of the fighting, it is noted: 'The battery's girl-warriors manifested exceptional steadfastness and heroism.'[8] The battery was surrounded and was fighting, including with small arms. It was precisely this battery, to judge from a comparison of German and Soviet data, that was mentioned in the XIV Panzer Corps' report for 23 August: 'Several nests were not suppressed before nightfall.' In accordance with the 1077th Anti-Aircraft Regiment's report for 23 and 24 August, they lost thirty-five anti-aircraft guns, eighteen people killed, forty-six wounded and seventy-four missing in action.[9] Among those awarded the medal 'For Valour' in the 1077th Anti-Aircraft Regiment were two girls: A.A. Kondratenko and L.Ye. Popova. Thus, as a whole, the legend about women serving in anti-aircraft gun crews around Stalingrad has a documentary basis.

The Germans' lunge to the Volga, of course, radically altered the situation in the Stalingrad area. Major communications linking the city with the rest of the country had been severed. In explaining its success on 23 August, the German Sixth Army's war diary contains the following notation: 'The enemy is creating the impression that he expected the German offensive, but incorrectly determined its axis. His fresh divisions are concentrated to the west and south-west of Ilovlinskaya, where the German offensive was evidently expected.' However, this assumption does not correspond to reality. In an intelligence report by the headquarters of the Stalingrad Front on 21 August, the evaluation of the Germans' plans was, on the whole, accurate. 'The enemy's main group of forces (5–6 infantry divisions, 1–2 panzer divisions and two motorized divisions) has been concentrated against the 4th Tank Army and the 62nd Army's right flank, with the mission of forcing the Don River and operating against Stalingrad.'[10] Correspondingly, the forces being thrown into the Stalingrad area were gathering in the Ilovlinskaya area and at the neighbouring railway stations. They simply did not have time to reach their designated concentration areas. They were only one or two days late. The Germans essentially took advantage of the 'window of opportunity' offered to them by the Soviet command's underestimation of the bridgehead at Vertyachii and the denuding of the positions along the Stalingrad defensive line by the forward movement of two of the 87th Rifle Division's regiments.

On 23 August it seemed that the city that carried Stalin's name would be at the feet of the victors in no time at all. However, during the course of events the 'swing of the pendulum' by the German Sixth and Fourth Panzer Armies unexpectedly interfered. The Germans who were breaking through to Stalingrad at full tilt were running into formations which by no means had been identified by them. The first such formation was the 315th Rifle Division. It was formed in the Siberian Military District in the spring of 1942 and with the beginning of summer was transferred to the 8th Reserve Army. On the evening of 22 August, the day before the German offensive, the 315th Rifle Division received orders to occupy defensive positions along the southern portion of the Stalingrad defensive line in the Beketovka area by dawn on 24 August. The columns stretched out along the steppe proved to be directly on the path of the German offensive. One of the division's rifle regiments ended up to the south of the German wedge at the Volga and took part in defending the northern outskirts of Stalingrad. The remaining two regiments and the 315th Rifle Division's main forces ended up to the north of the axis of the attack by the 16th Panzer and 3rd Motorized Divisions. Here they joined up with several other formations that had by no means been designated for defending against Paulus's Sixth Army.

In order to repel the offensive by Hoth's Fourth Panzer Army to the south of Stalingrad, the *Stavka* of the VGK planned to allot not just infantry to the South-eastern Front. Tank corps were also to be sent to Yeremenko. In accordance with the combat Order No. 00369/op by the *front's* headquarters on 22 August, the 2nd and 16th Tank Corps were to unload in the Voroponovo – Yel'shanka area (2nd Tank Corps) and the Gumrak – Voroponovo area (16th Tank Corps). That is, the Soviet command planned to 'strengthen' the defence along the south-western approaches to Stalingrad with the aid of the tank corps.

The offensive by Paulus's army on 23 August overturned all calculations. The tank corps did not, for the most part, make it to their assigned areas. The 2nd Tank Corps ended up to the south, and the 16th Tank Corps to the north of the XIV Panzer Corps' wedge. Unfortunately, not one of them was able to get into the fighting as a planned surprise, that is, directly along the path of the Germans' breakthrough to the Volga. Only the 2nd Tank Corps' reconnaissance battalion came under attack in its train at the Konnyi railway siding, losing fifty-five men killed and wounded, including the commander and battalion commissar. Besides the formations destined for operations in the Stalingrad area, the *front* received a completely unexpected present – four rifle brigades, which were moving to the North Caucasus. These brigades were later fated to become some of the main participants in the fighting for the city on the Volga.

However, if fate decreed that an entire bundle of diverse formations, hindering its rapid seizure, should appear along the approaches to Stalingrad, then the city was defended far more weakly from the air. An extremely powerful air attack was launched against the city simultaneously with the Germans' arrival at the northern outskirts of Stalingrad. Hitler's Directive No. 45 of 23 July 1942 spoke of a massive attack against the city: 'The timely destruction of the city of Stalingrad has particularly great importance.'[11]

Stalingrad's anti-aircraft defence was significantly weaker than that of Moscow or Leningrad. By the start of the battle on 17 July 1942, the 102nd Air Division numbered only fifty-three fighters, of which only seventeen were new models. By 23 August the situation had not changed radically: the air division numbered forty-four planes of various types (fifty-one, according to other data) in line – I-16s, I-153s, MiG-3s, Yak-1s and Hurricanes. The situation was further exacerbated by the fact that two anti-aircraft regiments were based on the Rynok airfield (this was the Stalingrad Tractor Factory's airfield) in the northern part of Stalingrad. Accordingly, the breakthrough by the German tanks to Stalingrad led them right on to the positions of two of the city's anti-aircraft regiments. This significantly lowered the capabilities of Stalingrad's already weak anti-aircraft defence.

The results of all this were not long in manifesting themselves. A.I. Yeremenko recalled: 'I had to live through a lot during the recent war, but what we saw on 23 August in Stalingrad hit us like a bad dream. Here and there fire and smoke plumes would shoot up from the bomb explosions. Enormous plumes of flame lifted to the sky from the area of the oil storage facilities and rain down a sea of fire and bitter, caustic smoke.'[12] One cannot really call this a massive raid according to the number of aircraft involved, but its effect on the sun-baked city proved to be completely devastating.

On the evening of 23 August columns of the 2nd Tank Corps were moving through the burning city. As early as 15.20 on 23 August the corps commander, A.G. Kravchenko, received orders from the deputy front commander, Lieutenant General F.I. Golikov, to move to the Gumrak area in readiness to operate against the enemy's tanks and motorized infantry that had broken through to the Volga. Within 25 minutes the order had been transmitted to the brigade commanders. Between 17.00 and 18.00 the brigades moved out. As early as 20.00 they reached the area indicated by Golikov and the corps became part of Lieutenant General A.D. Shtevnev's (the deputy commander for armoured troops of the Stalingrad Front) so-called tank group. The strength of the tank park of Kravchenko's corps is shown in the following table.

Table 11: Strength of the 2nd Tank Corps' Tank Park on 23 August 1942.[13]

Formation	KV	T-34	T-70	T-60
26th Tank Brigade	–	37	5	23
27th Tank Brigade	–	42	5	24
148th Tank Brigade	15	–	5	27

The corps' 2nd Motorized Rifle Brigade had been torn in two and had been cut off to the north of the German breakthrough, while the other one managed to link up with the corps' main forces. The 148th Tank Brigade, together with the part of the 2nd Motorized Rifle Brigade and the remnants of the 12th Reconnaissance Battalion that had been attacked while on the train, had also ended up to the north of the XIV Panzer Corps' wedge.

The high command's first reaction to the Germans' breakthrough to the Volga was Stalin's order, which was formulated as *Stavka* Directive No. 170582, issued at 16.35 on 23 August:

> The enemy has broken through our front in small strength. We have sufficient forces to destroy the enemy who has broken through. Mobilise the armoured trains and turn them loose along the Stalingrad circular railway. Make generous use of smoke in order to confuse the enemy. Fight the enemy's breakthrough, not only during the day, but at night. Employ fully not only the artillery, but the rocket artillery as well.[14]

Smoke, night fighting and aviation were actually a weak hope. If some reports up the chain of command can be called 'panicky', then there also exist 'panicky directives' and *Stavka* Directive No. 170582 was undoubtedly one of them.

The paradox of the situation was that despite the directives from Moscow about 'confusing the enemy with smoke' and a fire storm in Stalingrad itself, the struggle continued for the VIII Corps' bridgehead. Moreover, a new player entered the struggle on the Soviet side – the 27th Guards Rifle Division, which had been transferred by rail from the Kalinin Front. The newly-arrived division went onto the attack as early as the evening of 23 August and the fighting broke out in full on 24 August. As shown in the daily report by the VIII Corps, a gap of 1km opened between the 384th and 389th Infantry Divisions on 24 August. The Soviet counteroffensive was upsetting the plan for a systematic advance by the VIII Corps' infantry behind the tanks of Wietersheim's corps that had gone on to Stalingrad. Paulus's plan for covering the flanks of the XIV Panzer Corps with the VIII Corps' infantry on the left and that of the LI Corps on the right was being thwarted.

As a result, the Germans' breakthrough to the Volga took place along a very narrow front, only about 6–8km wide. The 16th Panzer Division occupied the sector adjoining the Volga, with its front facing north, and the 3rd Motorized Division, adjacent to the railway, facing south. The first, one might say reflexive, action by the Soviet command was the attempt to close the 'window' in the Stalingrad defensive line, which had been opened the preceding night by the removal from the line of units of the 87th Rifle Division, with the forces of the 35th Guards Rifle Division. However unlikely, this attempt from the march proved successful – at about 02.00 on 24 August the 35th Guards Rifle Division broke into Bol'shaya Rossoshka, cutting the 8km corridor in the rear of the XIV Panzer Corps. Meanwhile, the 60th Motorized Division had crossed the Don by morning and in the middle of the day the greater part of it was trying to break through to link up with the main forces of Wietersheim's corps. The 35th Guards Rifle Corps fought all day in the area of Height 137.2 against German tanks and motorized infantry and restored the situation. In the XIV Panzer Corps' report on the results of the day's fighting, it states directly: 'The corps is in operational encirclement.' Actually, it was not a secure 'stopper' that had been inserted between the XIV and LI Corps, but a piece of territory, disputed by the two sides, about 6km wide between Height 137.2 and the area of Borodkin farm, Konnaya and the '564-kilometre' rail siding. Neither Soviet nor German units were able to reliably occupy this space without weakening their positions along other sectors.

One of the reasons for the unstable situation was the hurried formation of the 35th Guards Rifle Division. The division did not have a full-blown rear organization and had as much in the way of ammunition as the soldiers could take with them from their previous positions along the defensive line. They carried with them anti-tank rifles and mortars and ammunition for them. As regards the 35th Guards Rifle Division, the *front's* war diary admitted: 'The division was weak in firepower and could not wage a protracted battle.' This forced the Soviet command to bring up other units to save the 35th Guards Rifle Division, particularly the two regiments of the 87th Rifle Division which had come under attack while on the march on 23 August. It was precisely the battalions of these two regiments that occupied centres of resistance along the contested territory between Height 137.2 and the Borodkin farm. Their positions faced both east and west. At the same time, the Soviet command did not have much choice. The available reserves had been spent, including for forming a defensive line along the perimeter of the wedge that the XIV Panzer Corps had made to the Volga.

At this moment in the battle the Red Army had a pretty good chance of inflicting a defeat on the XIV Panzer Corps. What exactly did the Stalingrad Front command have at its disposal? Aside from the fresh corps to the north of Stalingrad, A.M. Khasin's 23rd Tank Corps, consisting of one tank brigade, was undergoing reformation, while the remaining brigades had already been strewn about for parrying crises along the *front's* southern flank. On 21 August, the day the bridgehead was formed near Vertyachii, the 56th Tank Brigade was removed from the corps and the 99th Tank Brigade on 23 August. The corps remained with the single 189th Tank Brigade, which numbered twenty-two T-34s, sixteen T-70s and five T-60s in line, with four T-34s, two T-70s and one T-60 undergoing repairs.[15] On the morning of 24 August three of the 189th Tank Brigade's tanks broke through to the Konnyi rail siding, but were unable to hold it due to the lack of infantry.

Stavka of the VGK Directive No. 170584, which was dictated by telephone by Stalin at 04.50 on 24 August, was already much calmer than the preceding advice to confuse the enemy with smoke. Evidently, they had already reported to Stalin that a pair of tank corps had 'fortunately gotten lost' in the area of the Germans' breakthrough. The supreme commander-in-chief ordered the *front* command and A.M. Vasilevskii: 'to without fail firmly close with our forces the hole through which the enemy has broken through to Stalingrad, to encircle the enemy who has broken through and destroy him. You have the forces for this, and you can and must do this.'[16] The second task assigned by the leader was to throw the enemy back beyond the confines of the Stalingrad defensive line.

A new stage in the actions of the Stalingrad Front was beginning. The main efforts were now being concentrated along the left bank of the Don and in the area between the Don and Volga. Having criticized the *front's* leadership, Stalin did not limit himself to words, but dispatched one of the Red Army's best operational minds – A.M. Vasilevskii, the chief of the General Staff – to organize a counterblow. This happened on 25 August. Vasilevskii recalled: 'On the morning of 26 August I arrived in the area where the 24th Army's forces were located and to where the troops of the 66th Army had begun to arrive, as well as those divisions designated for outfitting the 1st Guards Army.'[17] Here Vasilevskii is getting ahead of things, because according to the Stalingrad Front's war diary the headquarters of the 24th and 66th Armies arrived somewhat later.

It was planned to eliminate the XIV Panzer Corps' breakthrough to the Volga by the traditional method – an attack against the flanks. Two shock groups were created to carry out this plan. The first was to gather to the north of the breakthrough under the command of the deputy commander of the Stalingrad Front, Major General K.A. Kovalenko. It consisted of the 4th and 16th Tank Corps and the 84th, 24th and 315th Rifle Divisions. Kovalenko's group was assigned the task of launching an attack on the morning of 25 August in the direction of Sukhaya Mechetka *balka*. The second group, consisting of the 2nd and 23rd Tank Corps, under the command of Lieutenant General A.D. Shtevnev, was aimed through Orlovka in the general direction of Yerzovka. These two groups were assigned the task of encircling and destroying through joint actions the enemy group of forces that had broken through to the Volga in the area to the north of Stalingrad.

Singed by the heat of the Stalingrad fires, the 2nd Tank Corps launched its attack as early as the morning of 24 August. At 07.00 the 26th and 27th Tank Brigades reached their jumping-off positions and began the attack to the north-east. The object of the offensive was to reach Yerzovka and cut off the 'head' of the German tank wedge that had broken through to Rynok. The first success of Kravchenko's corps was the capture of Orlovka and the heights around it. Within a month, heavy fighting would unfold around them during the second assault on Stalingrad. The seizure and retention of these positions by the 2nd Tank Corps would later materially complicate the life of those German units assaulting the city. The 26th and 27th Tank Brigades were unable to advance father than the heights near Orlovka. Upon colliding with the enemy's reinforced defence, the corps changed the axis of its attack. At 17.00 on 24 August the 26th Tank Brigade was redirected to the east and received orders to occupy Rynok. By 23.00 the order had been carried out. Thus the 2nd Tank Corps not only prevented with its first counterblow the enemy's advance toward Stalingrad from the north, but also recaptured tactically important points within the city limits. There could be no kind of breakthrough to Stalingrad from the north, which was contained in Paulus's order of 19 August. The losses suffered by Kravchenko's corps during the first fight were relatively light: eight T-34s, one T-70 and one T-60 burned and sixteen T-34s knocked out, twenty-eight men killed and ninety-seven wounded.

On 25 August the 2nd Tank Corps was reinforced with the 56th Tank Brigade and attempted to expand the success achieved the preceding day. However, having recovered from the shock, the Germans organized a powerful anti-tank defence and the advance by the attacking units amounted to no more than 800m. Kravchenko showed caution and as early as midday ordered his forces to consolidate along the lines reached. The tanks stood in place and fired on the enemy's firing points that revealed themselves. The corps' losses amounted to only six tanks. They took Kravchenko's 56th Tank Brigade and replaced it with the newly-formed 99th Tank Brigade, which had fifty T-34s. When foreign researchers, especially Paul Carell, speak about unpainted T-34s directly from the factory, he is most likely speaking of the 99th Tank Brigade. The 2nd Tank Corps' tanks were produced far into the rear. To judge from photographs, these were T-34s with a hexagonal 'nut' turret, produced by Factory No. 183 in the Urals.

The attack by the brigades of Kravchenko's corps on 26 August was also unsuccessful and the corps' units went over to the defensive. Losses on this day amounted to eighteen T-34s in the 99th Tank Brigade, three T-34s in the 26th Tank Brigade, and six T-34s and one T-70 in the 27th Tank Brigade. One cannot but note the quite low rate of losses in the 2nd Tank Corps. The newly-arrived 99th Tank Brigade suffered heavy losses. The brigades of Kravchenko's corps held up well and managed to avoid losing their equipment in the first days of their stay in the Stalingrad area. On 27 August the 2nd Tank Corps received a regiment from the 315th Rifle Division to consolidate its positions.

If from the south the profile of the 'finger' stretched out to the Volga by the XIV Panzer Corps was formed by Shtevnev's group from units cut off by the German attack, then the northern face of the salient was formed by newly-arrived formations from without. At midday on 23 August the attacking German units passed through Yerzovka and, without slowing down, moved on further toward the Volga. No efforts had been made to consolidate Yerzovka. The Germans were immediately punished for their thoughtlessness. The 9th Motorized Rifle Brigade, which had been cut off from the 23rd Tank Corps' main forces, turned out to be in the right place at the right time. On the night of 24/25 August Yerzovka was captured by the brigade's motorized rifle battalion. The 148th Tank Brigade, which had arrived by the evening of 25 August, began to prepare for an attack to the south from the positions captured near Yerzovka. However, a few hours before the offensive, the brigade received orders to become part of Kovalenko's group, which was operating in the Spartak – Kotluban' direction. A brigade of KVs deployed and left for the north in the direction of Spartak. The fortunate motorized rifle battalion continued to hold Yerzovka until the arrival of the 64th Rifle Division. Who can tell? If the 148th Rifle Brigade had not been dispatched to Kovalenko's group, the communications of the Stalingrad Front's main forces with the 62nd Army would have been restored along the bank of the Volga, from Yerzovka to Rynok (recaptured by units of Kravchenko's corps).

As opposed to the 2nd Tank Corps, V.A. Mishulin's 4th and M.I. Pavelkin's 16th Tank Corps were still en route at the moment the Germans broke through to the Volga. The 4th Tank Corps was initially designated for the Stalingrad Front and unloaded from its trains during 22–24 August. The corps was outfitted with tanks during its movement along the railway, receiving equipment at intermediate stations.

According to an order by the Stalingrad Front of 22 August, the 16th Tank Corps was to unload south-west of Stalingrad. However, at 13.30 on 23 August an order was received to unload the corps before reaching the designated areas. As a result, the corps unloaded from trains and scattered over a distance of 70km along the railway line leading to Stalingrad. Part of the trains had not yet arrived and the unloading continued on 24 August. Finally, on 25 August Pavelkin's corps was moved up to the intermediate area Fastov – Zotov (to the north-east of the bridgehead 'uncovered' by the Germans). Here the order to counter-attack was received. The 16th Tank Corps was pulled out of the fighting in the middle of August and before being dispatched to the south managed to be reinforced with combat equipment. On 20 August it numbered 6,217 rank and file, 178 tanks (24 KVs, 82 T-34s and 72 T-60s), 12 76mm guns, three 45mm guns, and six 37mm guns.

According to the command's plan, the 4th Tank Corps' mission was to attack from north to south on Orlovka. Major General P.I. Fomenko's 84th Rifle Division, which had been transferred from the North-western Front, was supposed to cooperate with the 4th Tank Corps. The division had previously operated in wooded terrain and the steppe around Stalingrad, which was deprived of cover, was unfamiliar to the soldiers and commanders. At the same time, as opposed to many other reserves committed into the fighting, the 84th Rifle Division disposed of an experienced and battle-tested rank and file. The divisions transferred from other sectors of the front and from the reserve did not even have terrain maps of the appropriate scale, which made orientation extremely difficult. Major General P.I. Fomenko invited two collective farmers from Yerzovka to his headquarters for orienting himself in the terrain.

In its turn, the 16th Tank Corps was supposed to attack due south in the direction of Gorodishche. The latter was still being held by the 23rd Tank Corps from the direction of Stalingrad. Pavelkin's corps was reinforced by two regiments from the 315th Rifle Division, which had been cut in half. I should like to emphasize here that the two tank corps, reinforced by infantry, were being directed not at the boundary between the XIV Panzer Corps and the LI Corps, but at a frontal attack against the 16th Panzer and 3rd Motorized Divisions. The start of the offensive was set for 05.00 on 26 August. The troops were to move up to their jumping-off areas during the night before the offensive if only to secure the relative surprise of the attack. Both corps were in two echelons, with two brigades in the first and one in the second. the 84th Rifle Division was also in two echelons, which completely corresponded to the Soviet military theory of the time.

The Soviet offensive on the morning of 26 August began exactly at the designated time, but collided with a hurricane of fire and repeated air attacks. One of the 84th Rifle Division's regiments managed to advance 2km, but this success proved to be isolated and to advance further with open flanks was unrealistic. The 4th Tank Corps' two brigades taking part in the fighting in the first echelon suffered heavy losses: the 102nd Tank Brigade lost seven tanks knocked out and five burned, while another four tanks failed to return from the attack with their crews, and the 47th Tank Brigade lost ten tanks burned, twelve tanks knocked out and four tanks missing in action.[18] The 4th Tank Corps lost another eleven tanks on a

Soviet minefield, that is, the units of Kovalenko's group did not have maps or plans of the fortifications and obstacles erected by Soviet engineers along the approaches to Stalingrad.

The 16th Tank Corps, along with two regiments from the 315th Rifle Division, was also met with powerful fire, suffered losses and made no advance. The 16th Tank Corps' losses for 26 August were as follows:

107th Tank Brigade – 12 KVs, of which five were burned;
109th Tank Brigade – 13 T-34s, of which seven were burned;
164th Tank Brigade – two tanks went missing.

Despite the fact that the Soviet offensive was halted by heavy fire, the situation was seen by the Germans as critical. In supplements to the Sixth Army's war diary and notes on the activities of the XIV Tank Corps on 26 August, it was noted: 'In connection with the absence of supply the ammunition situation and fuel is becoming critical and panicked reports are issued one after the other. Wietersheim is demanding the immediate pullback of the corps from the Volga to the east behind the line of the railway.' They managed to stabilize the situation somewhat by having a supply convoy break through to the XIV Panzer Corps' position.

The supply of the XIV Panzer Corps was carried out by the Germans along the contested territory by convoys of motor vehicles escorted by tanks. The tanks usually launched an attack, forced the Soviet units to fall back, and then the trucks were passed through. Group Kaegler, consisting of a panzer battalion and a motorized infantry battalion from the 60th Motorized Division, was created for escorting convoys in the area of Height 137.2. The group was temporarily subordinated to the LI Corps' 76th Infantry Division. It should be noted that according to data from the Sixth Army's chief quartermaster, the isolated XIV Panzer Corps expended 95 tons of ammunition on 26 August.[19] By way of comparison, the LI Corps, which was outside the encirclement ring, expended 100 tons. Although this, of course, does not eliminate the deficit of individual types of ammunition in the XIV Panzer Corps, particularly of 50mm and 75mm shells for tank guns which were vitally necessary for tank battles.

Echoes of the crisis along the approaches to Stalingrad reached the highest levels. On 26 August Halder wrote in his diary: 'There is a very tense situation around Stalingrad because of attacks by superior enemy forces. Our divisions are no longer very strong. The command is too nervous. Wietersheim wanted to pull back his extended finger from the Volga. Paulus interfered with this.' The Sixth Army commander understood that no matter how difficult it was to hold the 'finger', it would be even harder to regain lost positions. Beside this, the retention of the positions by the XIV Panzer Corps would enable them to gradually grind up the Soviet tank reserves. However, the situation was truly close to critical.

The offensive by Kovalenko's group continued on 27 August. According to the proposal by the commander of the 84th Rifle Division's 201st Rifle Regiment, the direction of the 4th Tank Corps' attack was changed. Having reconnoitred the offensive zone for the tank troops, the regimental commander pointed out a deep *balka* which was interfering with the tanks' offensive in the zone of the forthcoming counterblow. It was proposed that they attack further to the east. The regimental commander's proposal was adopted. At 05.00 on 27 August the 4th Tank Corps' brigades went over to the offensive, but were met with the enemy's powerful artillery and mortar fire. The fighting lasted all day and at 17.00 the tanks fell back to their jumping-off positions. It was not possible to cut off the 16th Panzer Division that had reached the Volga. The tanks that broke into the depth of the enemy's defence fought in isolation until they were destroyed. The 45th Tank Brigade, which began the offensive with fourteen KVs and fifteen T-60s, emerged from the battle with five KVs and two T-60s (!).

On 27 August the 16th Tank Corps continued the fight for Kuz'michi together with two regiments from the 315th Rifle Division. The corps' brigades encountered a hail of fire and the Germans constantly launched counter-attacks, striving not to lose an inch along the 'land bridge' leading to the Volga.

The results of two days of fighting for Kovalenko's group proved to be disappointing. Of 160 available tanks, the 4th Tank Corps lost 140 (!), and 84 of the 16th Tank Corps' 180 tanks.[20] The 4th Tank Corps' offensive capabilities had fallen to practically zero. This was not unknown to the enemy. In a report to the OKH, the Sixth Army's headquarters stressed on 28 August: 'On the whole, the enemy's combat opportunities are worsening. There are a lot of defectors, particularly among the tank troops.' The tank troops, which in the USSR were recruited from among industrial workers, were, as a rule, the more reliable part of the army.

Essentially, the situation that had already been observed in the fighting in the great bend of the Don in July 1942, when the tank corps suffered heavy losses in attacks on the Germans positions, was being repeated. The tanks' success could be secured only by winning the artillery and tank duel with the enemy, and there were major problems with this. At the same time, one must admit that the Soviet command set itself the too ambitious task of routing the XIV Panzer Corps without applying sufficient efforts for holding the area dividing Wietersheim's divisions and the LI Corps.

The offensive by the 76th Infantry Division and Group Kaegler for the purpose of relieving the XIV Panzer Corps began at 09.00 (Berlin time). On the Soviet side, the attack hit the 87th Rifle Division's 1382nd Rifle Regiment, which was moving up to link up with its division. In this fighting the 87th Rifle Division proved to be uncommonly unfortunate and was always being attacked while on the march. The 1382nd Rifle Regiment was attacked by tanks and fell back to the south to Bol'shaya Rossoshka. The regiment's commander, Major M.F. Zaitsev, was killed. By 13.00 the German offensive had been crowned with success – a firm linkup had been established between the two corps in the Borodkin area.

The relief of the XIV Panzer Corps reduced the chances of its defeat to practically zero, but the attempt was nevertheless made by the Soviet command. On 28 August the 26th and 27th Tank Brigades received twenty-one T-70 tanks as reinforcements. On 29 August, on Shtevnev's orders, the 27th Tank Brigade (twelve T-34s, twenty T-70s and fifteen T-60s) and the 2nd Motorized Rifle Brigade attacked to the north-west at 16.00. The goal of the attack was the Opytnoe Polye State Farm. Units of the 16th Tank Corps had reached the area to the north-east of the state farm on the previous day (28 August). However, Kravchenko's corps was unable to break through to Kovalenko's group on 29 August. Met by powerful anti-tank fire, the tanks halted and fired in place. Having lost five tanks, the brigades fell back to their jumping-off position by evening. The success in defence and the offensive on 29 August was achieved by Paulus's army to no small degree thanks to the artillery: on this day the XIV Panzer Corps expended 167 tons of ammunition and the LI Corps 180 tons.[21]

In the evening of that same 29 August, when the Germans had managed to restore reliable communications with the XIV Panzer Corps, Paulus made the decision to evacuate the VIII Corps from the bridgehead. In his order to pull the units back, it was stated in particular that: 'The seizure and retention of this bridgehead cost us heavy losses, although it enabled us to carry out the task assigned by the Führer. The VIII Corps held down major enemy forces and inflicted heavy losses on him, enabling the army to accomplish the forcing of the Don along both sides of Vertyachii and to rapidly break through to the Volga.' There was no small bit of slyness in these words of consolation. The VIII Corps' divisions did not only hold the bridgehead, but also tried to attack from it (without any particular success). A major group of German forces had been tied down in fighting and suffered heavy losses. Yes, the bridgehead tied down several Soviet divisions, but the question is who needed reserves more at that moment in order to throw them onto the scales of battle.

At the same time that convoys were being escorted to the XIV Panzer Corps there were tank battles around Kotluban' and the 124th Rifle Brigade crossed the Volga on the night of 27/28 August. On 28 August its commander, Colonel S.F. Gorokhov, carried out a reconnaissance, and on the following day three of the brigade's battalions, with six tanks from the 99th Tank Brigade, attacked Rynok. The attack was supported by fire from artillery, tanks and anti-aircraft guns from the eastern bank of the Volga, as well as the gunboats *Usyskin* and *Chapayev*,[22] and armoured launches from the Volga Military Flotilla from the river. Within a few hours elements of the 16th Panzer Division's engineer battalion, which were defending Rynok, were falling back to Latashanka. Rynok would later become one of the 62nd Army's firmest defensive centres in Stalingrad, and S.F. Gorokhov may easily be called 'Colonel Steadfast'.

During 30–31 August the 2nd Tank Corps was defended its lines while gradually turning them over to K.M. Andrusenko's the newly-arrived 115th Rifle Brigade (4,329 men). During 1–2 September 1942 Shtevnev's tank group was disbanded.

The offensive capabilities of Kovalenko's group had also declined significantly. By the evening of 29 August the following remained in line in the 16th Tank Corps' brigades:

107th Tank Brigade – four KVs, seven T-60s;
109th Tank Brigade – six T-34s, nine T-60s;
164th Tank Brigade – 13 T-34s, eight T-60s.[23]

The 4th Tank Corps was reduced to the single 47th Tank Brigade, which on 29 August numbered three KVs, seventeen T-34s and sixteen T-60s. In contrast, the strength of the XIV Panzer Corps' tank park fell only by a small amount (see table).

Table 12: XIV Panzer Corps' Combat-Ready Tanks on 31 August 1942.

	Panzer II	*Panzer III (short)*	*Panzer III (long)*
16th Panzer Division	–	8	41
3rd Motorized Division	8	–	22
60th Motorized Division	9	–	14

	Panzer IV (short)	*Panzer IV (long)*	*7.62cm Sfl1*
16th Panzer Division	6	8	4
3rd Motorized Division	2	4	5
60th Motorized Division	1	2	6

Approximately twenty combat vehicles had been put out of action in each of the divisions of Wietersheim's corps.

The final chord in the counterblows by Kovalenko's group sounded on 31 August. The 39th Guards Rifle Division (transferred from the 4th Tank Army) and the 315th Rifle Division, supported by the 56th and 94th Guards Mortar Regiments, also took part in the offensive. Met by intense enemy fire, the rifle formations hit the ground and advanced only 300–500m. The 164th Tank Brigade's tanks that broke into Kuz'michi lacked infantry support and were forced to fall back to their jumping-off positions.

Although a decisive result was not achieved during the counterblows by Shtevnev's and Kovalenko's tank groups, they played no small role in the battle for the city. Hoth's Fourth Panzer Army, which was successfully attacking on 29 August, reached positions favourable for closing the 'pincers' of the two armies along the near approaches to the city. The Army Group B command immediately realized the new possibilities. At midday on 30 August Paulus received an order by radio which stated:

> In view of the circumstance that the Fourth Panzer Army seized at 10.00 today a bridgehead in Gavrilovka, now everything depends on whether the Sixth Army, despite the heavy defensive fighting which it is being forced to wage, can concentrate the maximum forces possible for an attack in the general direction of the south for the purpose of destroying the enemy forces to the west of Stalingrad in cooperation with the Fourth Panzer Army.

However, despite the orders from Army Group B, which followed one after the other, an attack by the Sixth Army's mobile formations toward the Fourth Panzer Army did not take place. Having broken into the wasp's nest of tank corps, Paulus showed firmness and did not authorize Wietersheim to pull the XIV Panzer Corps back, but the Sixth Army commander was not an adventurer. He did not consider it possible to remove so much as a single division from the 'land bridge', which was being pelted by attacks, for the sake of carrying out the encirclement along the eastern bank of the Don. Following the rapid breakthrough to the Volga, the Sixth Army's offensive on Stalingrad was essentially halted.

Simultaneously, August ended with the formation of positions which the Germans called the 'northern screen' (*Nordriegelstellung*), or the 'land bridge'. The wedge that had been driven into the Soviet troops' position by the XIV Panzer Corps divided the defenders of Stalingrad from the *front's* main forces. The desire to hold Stalingrad forced the Soviet command, time after time, to undertake offensives along this sector, of which more below.

Chapter 8

Reinforced Defence II. Beketovka

(Map 5)

T he South-eastern Front's defence, which remained without promised reserves in the form of the 2nd and 16th Tank Corps, before long had its durability tested. An attack by the Fourth Panzer Army to the south of Stalingrad was followed by the Sixth Army's breakthrough to the Volga. The 13th Tank Corps' 'reinforced defence' near Tundutovo station forced the Germans to once again change the direction of their main attack. Dërr writes:

> The army commander issued orders to pull the XLVIII Panzer Corps from the front at night, unit by unit, and to secretly concentrate it behind the army's refused left flank in the area to the north-west of Abganerovo station for launching a surprise attack to the north in the area to the west of Stalingrad. This meant giving up the capture of a group of heights in the Krasnoarmeisk area and giving up the converging attacks against the enemy planned by Army Group B.[1]

In describing these events, Dërr mourns the renunciation of continuing the offensive along the axis of the railway in the direction of Krasnoarmeisk. He justifies this exclusively by the terrain conditions:

> Near Krasnoarmeisk there is a high bank rising 150 meters over the level of the Volga and which falls back from the river and later turns to the south, passing into Yergeni. Here, if one looks downstream, is the final height near the bank. It commands the entire bend of the Volga, along with Sarpinskii Island. If it had been possible to break the defence of Stalingrad, then the attack should have been made precisely from here.[2]

Whatever the case, the decision had been made. During the course of two nights – 26/27 and 27/28 August – the IV Corps relieved the XLVIII Panzer Corps' divisions along the heights south-east of Tundutovo station. Meanwhile, the 13th Tank Corps was strengthening its defence along the railway. On 28 August Tanaschishin's corps received forty T-70 tanks as reinforcements, which were immediately distributed among the brigades and stationed along the centres of resistance. The 64th Army's defence, which relied on the 13th Tank Corps' tank brigades, was quite firm. However, the integration of the tanks into the defensive system of the rifle units secured the cover of only part of the 64th Army's defensive zone.

The subsequent attack by the XLVIII Panzer Corps on the morning of 29 August along the new axis was unexpected and crushing. The defence by the 29th and 126th Rifle Divisions, which was not supported by tanks, was shaken to its foundations. The XLVIII Panzer Corps' tanks attacked through Zety to outflank the 64th Army's positions in the direction of Stalingrad. As early as 06.00 on the first day of the new German offensive, M.S. Shumilov ordered the 6th Guards and 254th Tank Brigades to move to Zety. Thirty brand-new T-70s quickly moved forward to the Zety crossroads, which lay astride the path of the German offensive. True to his rule of managing the battle in the very thick of things, Tanaschishin himself left for Zety. The tank battle for Zety began at 10.00. The result of the confrontation of the T-70s and the German Panzer IIIs and Panzer IVs was predictable. By 14.00 units of the XLVIII Panzer Corps, having bypassed Zety, were continuing to advance toward Stalingrad. On the evening of 29 August Zety was captured by the 24th Panzer Division. In light of the deep turning of the 64th Army's left flank, the *front* command made the decision to pull back its troops. The tanks of Tanaschishin's corps cemented and put in order the withdrawal. Three tanks from the 254th Tank Brigade remained until the last moment, covering a passage through a minefield near the crossing over the Chervlenaya River. The withdrawal took place in an orderly manner and did not turn into a disorganized rout, despite constant air attacks.

However, they were nevertheless unable to maintain the integrity of the defence. The Germans managed to break through the internal line of the Stalingrad fortifications on the heels of the retreating troops. On 31 August tanks were once again thrown in to meet the German offensive. This was the 56th Tank Brigade. Here it makes sense to halt on its origins. One can always find in a major defensive battle units and formations which cut intricate circles in the rear elements of the fighting troops. They are transferred from one sector to another and lose tanks not from enemy fire, but from the endless forced marches. Crises arise here and there and these units, having not yet arrived at one concentration area, are force to leave for another. The 8th Mechanized Corps cut such circles in the border battles of June 1941.This role fell to the 56th Tank Brigade in the battle along the near approaches to Stalingrad.

The brigade, having been initially part of the 28th Tank Corps, and then the 23rd Tank Corps, had been reforming following the July fighting in Orlovka, to the north of Stalingrad since 19 August 1942. It received tanks directly from the Stalingrad Tractor Factory, as did many other tank brigades. To be sure, as opposed to the 6th Guards, 6th and 13th Tank Brigades, in the 56th Tank Brigade the T-34s were watered down with light T-70 tanks. On 21 August the brigade was dispatched to the southern approaches to Stalingrad and transferred to the 57th Army. It had no contact with the enemy during this period.

Following the German breakthrough from the Vertyachii bridgehead on 23 August the brigade was moved to the north. As a result of marches from north to south and back, the tanks began 'to fray'. At 20.00 on 25 August the brigade had the following:

Thirty-two T-34s, of which fourteen could move;
Nine T-70s, of which seven could move;
One M3 medium tank capable of moving.[3]

The only combat losses were from air attacks. On 24 August two T-34s were burned and one knocked out by German planes on the march.

The brigade was subordinated to the 2nd Tank Corps. By order of the corps commander, unit commanders began to reconnoitre routes for a counterblow against the flank of the enemy's XIV Panzer Corps, from Stalingrad to the north. The brigade took part in the fighting for one day as part of Shtevnev's tank group. However, on 26 August, by brigade was turned around 180° on Yeremenko's order and once again dispatched to the 57th Army along the southern approaches to Stalingrad. Once again the commanders prepared positions, this time for defence and counter-attacks. But on 30 August there arrived an order subordinating the 56th Tank Brigade to the 64th Army's headquarters. Late in the evening of the same day the brigade was concentrating along the line of the Chervlenaya River and once again was preparing a defence. It was only at 10.00 on 31 August that the brigade entered the fighting for the first time and was met by fire from ambushes by the XLVIII Panzer Corps' units rushing toward Stalingrad.

The enemy appreciated the defending units' stubbornness along the southern approaches to Stalingrad. Grams, the 14th Panzer Division's historiographer, writes:

> The division was sent at night through Aksai to a new concentration area. Early in the morning of 29 August the attack began once again, with powerful artillery support. Tanks and mounted panzer grenadiers overcame the entrenched enemy's positions and in one leap reached the enemy's artillery positions. Paying no attention to the revived enemy in its rear, the division used this local breakthrough and broke through to the Chervlenaya sector on 30 August. There it once more collided with a ready defence by the enemy who had occupied the commanding heights. The torturous struggle began once more, during the course of which the division, further and further enveloping toward the west through Nariman Plantator and Tsybenko, was supposed to gnaw through the enemy, all the way to Peschanka and Tri Kurgana. The enemy is becoming more stubborn and his anti-tank defence more effective.[4]

On 2 September the 56th Tank Brigade was transferred to the 13th Tank Corps. On 3 September, by order of Tanaschishin the brigade occupied defensive positions near the Gornaya Polyana State Farm. At this moment the brigade numbered nineteen T-34s, two T-70s and one M3 medium tank. The 64th Army's front was relatively quiet up to 7 September. The 13th Tank Corps was again distributed among various defensive sectors along the approaches to Beketovka. The 6th Guards Tank Brigade, 39th Tank Brigade, the 13th Tank Brigade and the 56th Tank Brigade occupied defensive positions (from north to south) along the line from Voroponovo to Yelkha.

Luck turned its back on the 13th Tank Corps at this stage of the battle. If in the beginning of August the 6th Guards Tank Brigade was fortunate enough to be in the right place at the right time, then a month later it was not removed from its positions in time. On 23.00 on 7 September the brigade was transferred from the 13th Tank Corps to the 62nd Army (to the 23rd Tank Corps). Tanaschishin decided to occupy the 6th Guards Tank Brigade's positions with part of the forces of the 39th Tank Brigade. However, at 23.00 on 7 September information reached the corps' headquarters that the 133rd Tank Brigade (62nd Army) would be moved up to the positions of the brigade being transferred to the 62nd Army. Accordingly, they did not hurry to occupy the positions of a brigade that had left for another army. Thus, to be sure, there remained a quite narrow corridor between the 13th Tank Corps and the 133rd Tank Brigade, which was not enfiladed by tanks, from Voroponovo station to Zelenaya Polyana. A breakthrough along this corridor would take the Germans directly to the bank of the Volga.

On the morning of 8 September there followed an attack by Hoth's Fourth Panzer Army from Voroponovo to Kuporosnoe. The intensity of the air and artillery preparation was even noted in German sources. Grams writes: 'Following a fire preparation of unheard-of strength, the division began its attack at dawn on 8 September, broke through the enemy positions and achieved a significant initial success.'[5]

At dawn on 8 September the 39th Tank Brigade's tank battalion was met with fire from enemy tanks upon approaching the designated area. Fresh from the march and not entrenched, the brigade's tanks were unable to hold the German offensive. In order to restore the collapsing defence, at 12.00 on 8 September, the 56th Tank Brigade's tanks were dispatched to positions in the area of Gornaya Polyana in accordance with Tanaschishin's oral command. Here the brigade prepared defensive positions and the tanks occupied their old trenches.

At German offensive in the direction of Kuporosnoe continued at dawn on 9 September. A General Staff officer with the 13th Tank Corps later wrote: 'Solid dust covered the ground on this day. Bombs were once again dropped on the 56th Tank Brigade's knocked out and burned tanks, but individual tanks which had been buried in the ground continued to fire and held the Gornaya Polyana State Farm, although they didn't believe this, even at the army's headquarters.' The 56th Tank Brigade lost seven T-34s and one M3 medium tank burned, with six T-34s knocked out.[6] The 56th Tank Brigade also lost its commander, Colonel V.V. Lebedev, in the fighting on 9 September. There are several legends regarding his death. According to one of the, German infantrymen broke into the brigade's command post and shot up the staff officers, and according to another Colonel Lebedev took a petrol bomb and set out for the area of the brigade's knocked-out tanks, where he was killed by a shell fragment. Lieutenant Colonel I.M. Babenko, who was fated to oversee its transformation into a Guards unit, became the new commander.

The 13th Tank Corps absorbed the enemy attack and deprived him of the opportunity of breaking through to Beketovka. In this way, the heights commanding the terrain near Beketovka remained in the hands of the Soviet forces. By the evening of 10 September only eight combat-ready tanks remained in Tanaschishin's corps. However, the fighting along the southern approaches to Stalingrad gradually died down. The units put themselves in order and restored their damaged equipment. On 20 September there remained twenty-three tanks (fourteen T-34s, eight T-70s and one T-60) capable of movement in the 13th Tank Corps.[7]

Given the relative stability of the front line, the 13th Tank Corps' repair services had the opportunity of restoring the damaged tanks. Forty-nine T-34s and forty T-70s had arrived at the corps as reinforcements in two months of uninterrupted fighting. One hundred and seventy-four tanks were repaired during this period. On average, three to five tanks were restored per day. This enabled them to maintain tank brigades with a strength of twenty to twenty-five combat vehicles the entire time.

Chapter 9

Conclusions to Part I

If we attempt to define the essence of the first period of the battle of Stalingrad in a single phrase, then this will be 'it's important when things come on time'. Both sides drew their conclusions from the experience of the summer-autumn campaign of 1941 and entered the 1942 campaign with the results of the creative rethinking of this experience. The Red Army employed the experience of 1941 in the formation and accumulation of reserves: reserve armies and tank brigades were formed from the spring of 1942. Accordingly, when the front around Millerovo collapsed it was restored by using the reserve armies, while the freshly-formed brigades were employed for counter-attacks. The German army, in its turn, eliminated its backwardness in the employment of anti-tank weapons, supplying its troops with new and effective weapons.

However, on the other hand, the Red Army and the Wehrmacht marched over old rakes with enviable stubbornness. The German command did not expect the appearance of the enemy's reserves 'out of nowhere' in the Don bend, while the Soviet command continued to dispatch inferior tank formations into battle with a steady hand.

Subjective factors also played no small role. Both sides entered the fight in the great bend of the Don with quite hazy notions of the enemy and his plans. Accordingly, both the operational plans for the Stalingrad Front and the Sixth Army revealed their groundlessness as early as the very beginning of the battle, or, at least how they failed to correspond to the situation. The Soviet plan proceeded from the idea that there was still time and that a supporting attack would be launched against Stalingrad. The *front's* long-term mission was to help the troops in the Caucasus by a counteroffensive against the enemy flank with the tank armies under formation. Paulus's headquarters proceeded from the assumption that it faced the remnants of South-western Front's forces routed around Millerovo, interspersed with reserves, and that Stalingrad was ready to fall into their hands like a ripe fruit.

Due to his underestimation of the enemy, Paulus at first threw in comparatively small forces and mobile formations with weak infantry support from the army corps into the offensive on Kalach. When it became clear that they had stirred up a hornet's nest and that the supply columns for the tank and motorized divisions were being destroyed by the enemy, he had no choice but to hold on and wait for the arrival of the infantry divisions in the great bend of the Don.

For the Stalingrad Front command, the German attack was also an unpleasant surprise that interfered with the normal restoration of the recently-collapsed front by means of the reserve armies. As a result, there was the attempt to crush the enemy's units that had broken through with counter-attacks by tank and rifle formations committed into the fighting as they arrived at *front* commander Gordov's disposal. However, there was no miracle: the troops that arrived to relieve the routed armies lacked sufficient combat experience and, besides, were extremely weak in artillery. There was only one full-fledged mechanized formation within the Stalingrad Front – the 28th Tank Corps – while the remainder suffered from a shortage of motorized rifle subunits.

All of this together did not make for favourable prerequisites for defeating the breakthrough by the haughty enemy's mobile formations. The XIV Panzer Corps' divisions, disposing of powerful artillery and air support (including air supply), proved to be the 'tough nut' which was too hard for the teeth of the Stalingrad Front's formations. Moreover, it was in the great bend of the Don that the realities of the summer of 1942 manifested themselves, when the German army received effective anti-tank guns. Now the T-34s and KVs were confidently hit by anti-tank artillery at the ranges at which fighting generally occurred, when an inexperienced crew might not recognize an enemy anti-tank gun. One may condemn the Soviet command as much as one wants for its hurried commitment of the 1st and 4th Tank Armies' tank corps into battle. However, the alternative to this was the encirclement of the 62nd Army at a minimum of a week earlier than actually occurred. The haste of committing them into the fighting and the tank corps' organic shortcomings are more likely the answer to the question 'Why did the fighting on the right bank of the Don not end in the Germans' defeat?' The elimination of the Soviet bridgehead in the Don bend during 15–20 August 1942 showed with horrible clarity the script for the development of events without tank armies.

The words of Winston Churchill in the House of Commons during the Battle of Britain are well known: 'Never in the field of human conflict was so much owed by so many to so few.' To a certain extent, these words may be addressed to the Soviet tank corps, which rained counterblows on the German formations attacking Stalingrad. There were about a thousand men in an average tank brigade, far less than in a rifle division. The brigades' tanks went into battle without infantry and artillery support and suffered heavy losses. But the tank brigades were the mobile weapon in the hands of the Stalingrad Front command for the operational reaction to the crises that sprang up. One could throw a tank brigade into a march of 200–300km toward the enemy's breakthrough. Moreover, one should not get the impression that the tank attacks were completely painless for the Germans. In breaking through the defence, they inevitably 'tore a strip' off the Germans' infantry units.

The loss of relative 'invulnerability' and the imperfect organizational structure led to heavy losses in armoured equipment during the counterblows. One could have parried the growing vulnerability of Soviet tanks by adopting the appropriate tactical forms, for which experience was required. This is exactly what the newcomers from the tank brigades formed in the spring of 1942 lacked. There is a note on this score in the history of the German 3rd Motorized Division: 'Even if our tanks are not superior to the Russians' in numbers and power, they will again and again emerge victorious thanks to their radio equipment, great mobility and better combat techniques.' Nonetheless, the tank attacks inflicted heavy losses on the enemy and slowed down his advance.

At the same time it is necessary to admit that the Stalingrad Front's defeat was to a significant degree conditioned by the concentration of large enemy forces against it. The German Fourth Panzer Army's turn toward Stalingrad swallowed up significant forces, both in rifle divisions and tank brigades. If they had remained in place, it is likely that we could have avoided the disaster of the 4th Tank Army along the Sirotinskaya bridgehead. Two armies, including the Sixth Army, the strongest one on the Eastern Front, were too much for the Soviet forces around Stalingrad.

Part II

The Verdun of the Steppes

The account of the battle for the city of Stalingrad itself usually begins on 13 September 1942. However, at the beginning of September there took place events which had a direct influence on the assault on the city. The defence of Stalingrad is one of the typical examples of defending a fortress not only with the forces of the defenders, but also through intensive pressure from the outside. Thus, as early as the beginning of September the fighting unfolded both along the near approaches to the city and along the front to the north-west of it. Moreover, the nature of the battle was in many ways determined by the presence of the Stalingrad Front's 'northern group'. Its presence and pressure dictated not only the distribution of the Sixth Army's forces, but also the axis of the attacks during the assault on Stalingrad.

Chapter 10

The Battle for the Semaphore. The Beginning

(Map 5)

The phrase 'the fight for the forester's hut' became the symbol for the First World War's positional battles. There wasn't much in the way of foresters and their huts, nor indeed forests, in the steppe country around Stalingrad. In the operational documents of the troops fighting to the north of the city another local reference point is mentioned – the semaphore along the railway from Kotluban' toward Stalingrad. It's amazing that this piece of railway property survived several cruel battles and was not knocked down by attacking tanks or blown to bits by shells or bombs. The semaphore near the '564-kilometre' railway siding may lay claim to being the symbol of the battle of Stalingrad to a much greater degree than Sergeant Pavlov's building. This is if only because it appeared at the centre of events far more often and was mentioned in operational reports up to the *front* level. Yes, and there are far more soldiers from both sides buried in the area of the semaphore than around any individual building in Stalingrad.

The expectations of the German command regarding the counterblows against the flank of the Sixth Army that had reached the city were justified as early as August 1942. However, if in the final days of August the formations that had turned up by chance took part in the counterblows, then in September the strategic reserves entered the fighting. Stalingrad once again demanded the commitment of the reserve armies into the battle.

However, until the concentration of the reserve armies' formations, the counter-attacks were launched by divisions arriving in detail and united by the headquarters of the 1st Guards Army. K.S. Moskalenko's headquarters could have simply been regrouped closer to Stalingrad together with part of the army's initial (August) strength. I believe that at that moment the *front* command, as well as the Soviet supreme command, cursed that hour when the 1st Guards Army was activated along the left bank of the Don. If Moskalenko's army had been left in reserve in the Ilovlya area, its divisions could have played an important role in the defensive battle in the final week of August 1942. Because of the premature employment of major reserves, the immediate employment of the 1st Guards Army against the XIV Panzer Corps in its breakthrough to the Volga was ruled out. They had to waste time regrouping and strengthening Moskalenko's army with formations from the reserve armies.

The decision to move the reserves to the Stalingrad area was made as early as 25 August. The forces of the 24th Army (five rifle divisions) and the 66th Army (six rifle divisions) began to arrive at the Stalingrad Front on 31 August. D.T. Kozlov's[1] 24th Army and R.Ya. Malinovskii's 66th Army were, respectively, the former 9th Reserve Army and the 8th Reserve Army. As we can see, both armies were commanded by generals who had previously commanded *fronts*. Kozlov was relieved of command of the Crimean Front in May 1942, and in July 1942 Malinovskii was removed as commander of the Southern Front for the loss of Rostov. This appeared to be a chance to restore trust in the command. By the beginning of September rifle divisions, artillery regiments, 'katyushas' and tank brigades began to arrive to the area to the north-west of the city. The number of tanks in the tank corps by the time of the Stalingrad Front's latest offensive is shown in the table.

Table 13: Numbers of Tanks in the Stalingrad Front's 4th, 7th and 16th Tank Corps on 31 August 1942.[2]

	4th Tank Corps				16th Tank Corps		7th Tank Corps[3]	
	45th Tank Bde	47th Tank Bde	102nd Tank Bde	107th Tank Bde	109th Tank Bde	164th Tank Bde	3rd Gds Tank Bde	62nd Tank Bde
KV	4	3	–	10	–	–	33	–
T-34	–	8	5	–	11	28	–	44
T-60	1	9	3	23	19	13	27	20
T-70	–	3	–	–	–	–	–	–
Total	5	23	8	33	30	41	60	64

It is clear that P.A. Rotmistrov's [4] corps comprised the real combat force. It was a newcomer to the 1st Tank Army. The remaining formations had lost a significant amount of equipment in the August fighting. A composite brigade, consisting of one KV, ten T-34s and fifteen T-60s, was formed from the 16th Tank Corps. In July 1942 Rotmistrov's corps took part in the unsuccessful counterblow by A.I. Lizyukov's[5] 5th Tank Army around Voronezh. The counterblow ended in failure and the corps suffered heavy losses. By August the corps had gradually restored the strength of its tank park.

The outfitting of the corps' motorized infantry was a typical problem for the Soviet tank troops during this period. Rotmistrov's 7th Motorized Rifle Brigade was at only 30 per cent strength. However, the command had no choice and reserves were committed into the fighting in the form in which they were found. The lull on the Bryansk Front enabled them to transfer troops from it on 28–30 August to the Stalingrad Front, which was being pelted by attacks. The 7th Tank Corps detrained in the area of Serebryakovo station and on the morning of 2 September, following a 200km march, concentrated in the area of the Rodnikovaya *balka*, to the north of Gorodishche and to the east of Samofalovka.

The 1st Guards Army's task was to capture the heights to the north of Gorodishche, cut the railway and link up with the units defending Stalingrad. The counter-attack was to be carried out by the 24th and 116th Rifle Divisions, with the support of the 16th Tank Corps' composite brigade, and the 7th Tank Corps, respectively. In the event the assigned task was carried out, the 7th Tank Corps was supposed to attack to the east, pushing the enemy to the Volga. The 671st Howitzer Artillery Regiment from the High Command Artillery Reserve (eighteen 152mm gun-howitzers), the 1184th Anti-Tank Regiment, the 23rd and 57th Guards Mortar Regiments and the 1140th Independent Guards Mortar Battalion were to cooperate with the corps and the 116th Rifle Division. Rotmistrov's tank corps was to be committed into the fighting from the march, with almost no time for preparation. The layout of the forward edge of the enemy, who had gone over to the defensive, had not been established. The problem was that not all commanders even had maps of the combat area. Only the brigade commanders had time to carry out reconnaissance.

According to the command's plan, the 7th Tank Corps was supposed to attack in a direction almost due south along the shortest distance and to link up with the Soviet forces operating in the Gorodishche area. By the start of the offensive by Rotmistrov's brigades, the 23rd Tank Corps' (62nd Army) 2nd Motorized Rifle Brigade was defending to the north of Gorodishche. The 23rd Tank Corps' 189th Tank Brigade and the 399th Rifle Division were defending along a front facing west in the Gorodishche area. Thus the 23rd

Tank Corps was holding positions which were, as they say, right around the corner. It was necessary to just cover a few kilometres. However, the 23rd Tank Corps was under constant enemy pressure and the prospects of holding the Gorodishche area were unclear. It was precisely this that forced them to hurry up the launching of the counter-attacks.

According to a report of 00.15 on 3 September the strength of the XIV Panzer Corps' tank park is illustrated by the following figures.

Table 14: Sixth Army's Tank Park as of 21 July 1942.[6]

	Panzer II	Panzer III (short)	Panzer III (long)	Panzer IV (short)
16th Panzer Division	–	8	45	6
60th Motorized Division	8	–	20	2
3rd Motorized Division	9	–	17	2

	Panzer IV (long)	Command Tanks	Marder Self-Propelled Guns	Total
16th Panzer Division	8	–	5	72
60th Motorized Division	4	1	6	41
3rd Motorized Division	2	–	7	37

However, as subsequent events showed, the most powerful element of the German forces defending the isthmus between the Volga and the Don was artillery. At that moment the XIV Panzer Corps included two battalions of 210mm howitzers, a battalion of heavy howitzers, a regiment of rocket launchers and several reinforcement batteries taken from other battalions in the high command artillery reserve.

At 05.30 on 3 September, following a 30-minute artillery preparation, the 1st Guards Army attacked with the forces of the 24th, 84th and 116th Rifle Divisions. The 3rd Guards and 62nd Tank Brigades were in the 7th Tank Corps' first echelon, with the 87th Tank Brigade and a motorized rifle brigade in the second. The attack began without supporting infantry. The first echelon's two brigades were not successful and at 12.00 Rotmistrov committed the 87th Tank Brigade into the fight. The corps' advance was halted by the enemy's powerful anti-tank fire. The Soviet tank troops' attempts to suppress and destroy the enemy's firing points brought no success. On 3 September the corps lost five KVs burned and seven knocked out, fifteen T-34s burned, seventeen T-34s knocked out, six T-60s burned and three T-60s knocked out.[7] Fifty-three tanks were put out of action on the first day of combat, almost a third of the corps' strength.

The following was noted in the Sixth Army's war diary: 'The XIV Panzer Corps' northern front in the area north of Bezrodnenskii was subjected to repeated powerful Russian attacks, who operated supported by more than 150 tanks. They were repulsed in heavy fighting with the assistance of tanks from the 16th Panzer Division and all of the 60th Motorized Division's artillery which was facing south. Our losses were significant.'[8]

Simultaneously, the Sixth Army's war diary describes the results of a visit to the front, in which the method of holding it was studied. Paulus was particularly displeased with the fact that the XIV Panzer Corps did not help the offensive on Stalingrad with its tanks, that is, 'The tank battalions of the 60th Motorized Division and other of the 14th Panzer Corps' divisions only took part in the fighting on this day along the northern front with a small part of their forces.'[9] That is, on the whole, a comparison of the number of the sides' tanks is in the present case insufficiently informative. The artillery propped up the defence. The author does not possess data on the XIV Panzer Corps' expenditure of ammunition on 3 September, although the expenditure of ammunition by the Sixth Army as a whole on that day was 575 tons.[10] A comparison with the data on the expenditure of ammunition for the following days enables us to evaluate the expenditure of ammunition by the XIV Panzer Corps at approximately 150 tons. This was more than sufficient to halt the Soviet infantry, while anti-tank guns, self-propelled guns and tanks were employed against tanks.

On the morning of 4 September the 1st Guards Army was already ready for a new offensive. However, an enemy counterpreparation fell upon it at 06.00. It would become one of the chief methods of the German formations defending to the north of Stalingrad. At 06.30 the German counterpreparation was supplemented by an air strike. The raid continued for an hour and a half. The 116th Rifle Division's infantry was pinned down under heavy enemy fire. Thus the 7th Tank Corps was deprived of infantry support. The preceding failed Soviet counter-attacks of themselves created the basis for the creation of a firm defence by the enemy. The knocked-out tanks remaining on the battlefield (including the tanks of the 4th Tank Corps, which was operating in this area during 26–27 August), had been transformed by the Germans into firing points. The knocked-out tanks' armour enabled the German infantrymen to survive during an artillery bombardment. The knocked-out tanks then became improvised pillboxes. The German soldiers holed up in the tanks rained a hail of lead on the attackers.

However, artillery became the main means of combat. The expenditure of ammunition by the XIV Panzer Corps on 4 September was 180 tons,[11] including 55 210mm shells, 308 150mm sFH18 rounds, and 325 10cm K18 shells.[12] There was essentially nothing with which to oppose this storm of heavy shells. On 2 September K.S. Moskalenko's army only contained the 671st Artillery Regiment and a battalion from the 1158th Artillery Regiment from the High Command Artillery Reserve – or a total of twenty-four 152mm gun-howitzers,[13] while the entire Stalingrad Front had only fifty-nine 152mm guns.[14] The air force also exerted a good deal of pressure on the attacking Soviet units, and the Sixth Army's war diary noted: 'Enemy attacks 15 kilometres north-west of Gorodishche along the XIV Panzer Corps' sector from 03.30, while the Luftwaffe operates against them with good effect.'[15]

As a result of two days of fighting, the 7th Tank Corps lost seven KVs, thirty T-34s and ten T-60s burned, and fourteen KVs, ten T-34s and six T-60s knocked out. The corps' offensive capabilities were practically exhausted. On 6 September twelve of the corps' tanks were attached to the 41st Guards Rifle Division for an attack along the previous axis. However, these attacks were unsuccessful and the Soviet forces along the front to the north-east of Stalingrad went over to the defensive. The hour of the corps' repair services had arrived: intensive work went on to restore the knocked-out tanks before the next offensive.

Chapter 11

A City Under Siege

(Map 5)

The rifle brigades' arrival in the northern areas of Stalingrad enabled the 2nd Tank Corps' units to catch their breath. The quiet life of the units of A.G. Kravchenko's corps did not last long. On the morning of 3 September the enemy broke through the 62nd Army's defensive front 18km from Stalingrad, near Pitomnik. By 12.00 the Germans were already in Talovaya, within a few kilometres of the city. At that same time Lopatin assigned Kravchenko the task, together with units of the 87th Rifle Division, of counter-attacking in the direction of the experimental agricultural station. What is interesting is that the commander of the 62nd Army assigned the mission somewhat 'ahead of time'. The Germans had not yet reached the experimental agricultural station, but most likely would have already been along this line at the time of the tank corps' regrouping. At 14.30 the 27th Tank Brigade set off on a march and by 15.40 was in the area of Stalingrad, to the north of the experimental agricultural station. At this moment the brigade included nine T-34s, seven T-70s and fifteen T-60s. At 17.00 the 99th Tank Brigade (twenty-three T-34s, seven T-70s and one T-60) set out behind the 27th Tank Brigade. The counter-attack was set for 05.00 on the following day. According to the final plan, Kravchenko's corps was supposed to operate along with the remnants of the 87th, 98th and 112th Rifle Divisions.

The counteroffensive began at 08.00 on 4 September and the day's events developed in a 'back and forth' manner – the tanks of Kravchenko's corps broke through to Gumrak, but in the second half of the day were forced to fall back to their jumping-off positions. One T-34, one T-70 and thirteen T-60s remained in the 27th Tank Brigade. On 5 September Gumrak was being held by the remnants of the 112th Rifle Division (285 active bayonets), the 27th Tank Brigade (eleven T-60s) and a reconnaissance battalion (two armoured cars and four armoured personnel carriers) from the 2nd Tank Corps. The 99th Tank Brigade (sixteen T-34s and four T-70s) was holding south of Gumrak, 'stiffening' the remnants of the 87th and 98th Rifle Divisions. For the time being, the Soviet command was managing to keep the enemy from breaking through to the streets of Stalingrad.

On 6 September there followed a breakthrough north of the positions occupied by the 2nd Tank Corps. A.I. Yeremenko described these events in the following manner:

> … on 6 September there took place an incident, the likelihood of which was even difficult to imagine. In carrying out a decision by the *Stavka* of the Supreme Commander-in-Chief, an order was issued by me 'Not a step back!' which was violated by General Lopatin – he personally pulled the 28th Tank Corps (the corps was actually without tanks and had been reinforced by an anti-tank battalion) three kilometres back to new positions without pressure on the part of the enemy, which the latter immediately took advantage of and advanced forward on our heels.[1]

Here some clarification is required. It was not the 28th Tank Corps, but the 23rd Tank Corps, which had been pulled back from its positions along the 62nd Army's northern flank. At that time it could only formally be called a corps: it included only the 189th Tank Brigade, with eight T-34s, five T-70s and two T-60s. The withdrawal was carried out during the night of 5/6 September, according to Order No. 122 from the headquarters of the 62nd Army. The withdrawal only somewhat shortened the front occupied along the approaches to the Konnyi railway siding. The positions that had been pushed forward were begging to be cut off by attacks along converging axes. To judge from events, A.I. Lopatin received news of the failure of the offensive by the *front's* northern group and made the decision to pull back his forces from the positions to which the 1st Guards Army had been breaking through to from the north. Their retention, in the absence of the prospect of a decisive breakout attack, threatened the 23rd Tank Corps and the remnants of the 399th Rifle Division with destruction.

However, the unfavourable development of events in any event brought about a negative reaction and a change of commanders. Thus the command of the 62nd Army was changed for the third time. Chuikov was appointed to command the army. As we recall, in July 1942 he occasioned doubts among the higher leadership. The relatively successful conduct of the 64th Army's defensive battle (in which Chuikov was the deputy commander) forced them to cast aside their doubts about the general who had away from the front for so long. However, before Chuikov's arrival the duties of the commander of the 62nd Army were temporarily carried out by its chief of staff, Major General N.I. Krylov.

By 7 September all of the tanks of the 2nd Tank Corps' two brigades were out of action. The commander of the 27th Tank Brigade had been wounded and the commander of the 99th Tank Brigade killed. On 8 September the 2nd Tank Corps was pulled back to the left bank of the Volga. On 11 September the 135th, 137th, 155th, 169th, and 99th Tank Brigades were subordinated to it and the task assigned of defending the eastern bank of the Volga along an 84km front. The 27th and 99th Tank Brigades' non-mobile tanks were transferred to the 23rd Tank Corps. As had happened repeatedly, following the loss of the tanks for 'stiffening' the defence, its defeat was only a matter of time.

Chapter 12

The First Assault on the City.
14–26 September 1942. The Beginning

Despite the collision with the Soviet reserves following the XIV Panzer Corps' breakthrough to the Volga, the German command at first viewed the prospects of the capture of Stalingrad quite optimistically. Late in the evening of 11 September 1942 Weichs, the commander of Army Group B, reported the situation at the front for his armies to the Führer. According to the results of this meeting, Halder wrote of the planned calculation for seizing the city: 'The storm of the urban part of Stalingrad is slated for 14 or 15.9, given good preparation. The time calculation: ten days for the capture of Stalingrad. Then 14 days for regrouping. The earliest end to the operation is by 1.10.'

Early in the morning of 12 September Friedrich Paulus, the commander of the Sixth Army, flew from Golubinka to Starobel'sk, where he boarded the plane of von Weichs, the commander of Army Group B. He arrived at the airfield in Vinnitsa at about noon. At approximately 12.30 von Weichs arrived by car at Hitler's headquarters. Immediately upon their arrival, the generals were ushered into the conference room, where the daily report on the situation at the front was heard. Hitler, Keitel,[1] Jodl, the army chief of staff, Colonel General Halder, the chief of the OKH operational section, Major General Hoisinger, and the OKH quartermaster general, Lieutenant General Wagner, were present at the conference. This was one of the most important conferences that determined not only the immediate tasks for Paulus's army, but the Wehrmacht's plans in the Stalingrad area as a whole.

Weichs and Paulus correspondingly reported on the situation in the Army Group B area, and that of the Sixth Army. The commander of the Sixth Army described the situation of the troops under his command in detail, up to the situation of each division. Hitler heard out both reports without any kind of substantial remarks and then asked Paulus: 'When will you have the city and the Volga's bank within the city in your hands? It's very important for me that this take place quickly.' The commander of the Sixth Army avoided giving a definite answer, referring to the troops' exhaustion. His answer was as follows: 'In light of the reported condition of our troops, who have been worn out in the fighting, as well as Russian resistance, I cannot name a final date. Quite the opposite, I must request reinforcements of three combat-capable divisions.'

In this matter Paulus failed to support Halder's optimistic calculation for the seizure of Stalingrad within ten days. Hitler agreed that the matter must be studied. Halder suggested a decision involving available forces. He stated that the high command neither had fresh forces nor the prospect of transferring them to Stalingrad in time. Halder's opinion was that there was only one way out: to transfer the formations of the Fourth Tank Army, which was south of Stalingrad, to the Sixth Army. The army chief of staff suggested delegating the resolution of this question to the Army Group B command.

The conference in Vinnitsa is usually linked to the planning for the capture of Stalingrad. However, in addition to this, plans were discussed for the crushing of the Soviet group of forces in the area between the Don and the Volga, to the north of Stalingrad (1st Guards, 24th and 66th Armies). Two operational variants were proposed to Hitler, defined as the 'big decision' and the 'middle decision'. Accordingly, the 'big decision' was directed at 'defeating and destroying the main mass of Russian forces between the Volga and the Don'.[2] The essence of the 'middle decision' consisted of 'a breakthrough by mobile formations from the area west of Yerzovka to the heights east of Prudka, from where it will be possible to turn to the west south of Tishanka and advance to the Don'.[3] This decision meant the turning of the Soviet shock group of forces in the 'battle for the semaphore' on the left, followed by its encirclement. Taking into account the fact that the tanks gathered in the reserve armies were gradually being put out of action, such an attack might have the most serious consequences – at a certain moment the Stalingrad Front command would not have readily available a sufficient number of combat-ready tank brigades for resisting an encirclement.

Hitler chose variant No. 2 – the 'middle decision' – at the Vinnitsa conference. According to Paulus's plan, this would require three panzer, two motorized and 9–10 infantry divisions in the area between the Don and the Volga north of the Tsaritsa River. It was planned to carry out the encirclement in 2–4 days, with 10–12 days to clear out the resulting 'cauldron'. It was precisely the difficulties in eliminating the encircled Soviet units that had arisen during the fighting in the Don bend that forced the Germans to forego the 'big decision'. However, at the same time it was admitted that the freeing-up of sufficient forces for a counteroffensive would be possible only after the capture of Stalingrad. Due to this, an unseen connection arose between the city's defenders and the Soviet group of forces around the semaphore. Stalingrad was to be stormed by the Sixth Army's worst divisions. The 'middle decision' was to be postponed as long as Stalingrad held out.

Simultaneously with the approval of the 'middle decision', Hitler made another decision which had far-reaching consequences: to forego the elimination of the bridgehead around Serafimovich. Thus was laid a delayed-action mine that would go off with a bang in November 1942, when the Soviet counteroffensive began from this bridgehead. There is the following notation in this regard in the Sixth Army's war diary for 13 September 1942: 'The commander has returned from making his report to the Führer. The Führer chose decision No. 2. The army will have to forego the complete clearing of the southern bank of the Don along the left flank in the XVII Army Corps' sector and concentrate forces there as quickly as possible for an offensive to the north between the Volga and the Don.'[4] One cannot but note the phrase 'as quickly as possible'.

According to the decision by the Army Group B command, an initial condition for the offensive operation was the clearing of Soviet forces from Stalingrad. In an order to the army group on 15 September, it was noted: 'Following the capture of Stalingrad, the army must as quickly as possible. and with the largest forces possible, attack in the area between the Volga and Don, to the north, for the purpose of defeating the enemy's forces along the XIV Panzer and VIII Army corps' northern front and, if possible, destroy them and occupy winter positions along the line Yerzovka – Varlomov – Pan'shino station – Pan'shino.'

In the event of the rapid collapse of the city's defence, the 1st Guards, 24th and 66th Armies might repeat the fate of the Crimean Front. It was an irony of fate that this could have taken place following the breakthrough of the defence along the left flank of D.T.

Kozlov's 24th Army, who was the former commander of the Crimean Front. The battle around Stalingrad could have turned out to be a terrible disaster for the Red Army.

The first practical result of the Vinnitsa conference was the transfer of three of the Fourth Panzer Army's divisions to the Sixth Army, with the simultaneous lengthening of the Sixth Army's front so far to the south that now all of Stalingrad, all the way to the southern approaches to the city, was in the zone of Paulus's army. During the course of its offensive to the east, the Sixth Army gradually lined up its corps facing the north-east approximately along the line of the course of the Don River. The XVII and XI Corps had been placed accordingly along this front. The latter corps occupied positions in the Don bend against several of the Soviet 4th Army's bridgeheads. Following the breakthrough to the Volga, the XIV Panzer and VIII Corps took up positions facing north-east. Accordingly, Paulus had only the LI Corps for storming the city. The transfer to him of part of the forces from Hoth's army was an absolute necessity. In evaluating the situation as a whole, one must say that Stalingrad would not be stormed by that army which had crushed the 62nd Army's defence in the Don bend. And the matter was not only and not so much in losses. The German command could bring in only part of the forces from Paulus's army for the storming of the city and, we should say directly, neither the best or largest part.

To a certain degree, the weakness of the LI Corps' formations could be compensated by a qualitative reinforcement. First of all, two battalions of assault guns were to be attached to Seydlitz's corps (see table).

Table 15: LI Corps' Armoured Equipment as of 05.00, 13 September 1942.[5]

Assault Gun Battalions	Combat-Ready	Undergoing Repairs	
	StuG III (short)	StuG III (long)	StuG III (short)
244th	3	3	9
245th	9	8	2

Earlier, a corps along the most important axis would immediately receive two battalions; for example, the VIII Army Corps during the defence of the shock group's flank in the Don bend. However, the LI Corps' subsequent artillery reinforcement was truly serious. Two 210mm howitzer battalions, a battalion of 10cm K18 guns and three battalions of 150mm sFH18 field howitzers were attached to it.[6]

The attackers' relative weakness was compensated to a certain degree by the defenders' weakness. The city was also defended by formations from the *Stavka* reserve which were by no means fresh. By the start of the assault the city's defenders were the 62nd Army's formations, which had been cut off from the Stalingrad Front's main forces by the 23 August attack and which had been pulled back from the front along the Don in the beginning of September.

Lieutenant General V.I. Chuikov, who took up command of the 62nd Army on 12 September 1942,[7] described in his memoirs the conditioned of the units entrusted to him in the following manner:

On the evening of 14 September a composite detachment from various brigades and divisions numbered about 200 bayonets, that is, less than one full-strength battalion: the strength of the neighbouring 244th Rifle Division did not exceed 1,500 men, while the number of bayonets in the division was not more than that of a full-strength battalion; the 42nd Rifle Division had 666 men, with no more than 250 bayonets. The other formations and units were of similar strength. The tank corps under the command of General A.F. Popov had 40–50 tanks in its brigades, of which about 30 per cent had been knocked out and were being used as firing points. Only Colonel A.A. Saraev's division and three rifle brigades had been fitted out more or less normally.[8]

This estimate was later repeated in the official Soviet historiography. A.M. Samsonov, citing Chuikov, writes: 'the divisions and brigades numbered 200–300 men'. If only 200–300 men had really been in the divisions, then Stalingrad would have fallen before 12 September. Both Chuikov and Samsonov exaggerate or, to put it mildly, are hurrying events. The 42nd Rifle Division, which Chuikov had hurriedly described as being ready to give up the ghost, numbered 5,032 men on 10 September. The 244th Rifle Division numbered 3,685 men on 10 September and 3,497 men on 15 September. It's not clear what 'composite detachment from various brigades and divisions' Chuikov is writing about, because the strength of the individual brigades and divisions in the 62nd Army was more than 200 bayonets. Complete data on the strength of the 62nd Army's formations before the assault can be found in the following table.

Table 16: The Strength of the 62nd Army's Rifle Formations on 11 September 1942.

Unit	Men	Horses	Rifles	Shpagin Sub-machine guns
33rd Gds Rifle Div	864	60	189	92
35th Gds Rifle Div	454	–	271	115
87th Rifle Div	1,819	315	509	40
98th Rifle Div	465	20	219	20
112th Rifle Div	2,297	638	1,181	117
131st Rifle Div	2,540	443	1,918	215
196th Rifle Div	1,004	107	605	162
229th Rifle Div	192	48	73	14
244th Rifle Div	3,685	860	989	141
315th Rifle Div	2,873	333	1,797	260
399th Rifle Div	565	18	–	–
10th Rifle Div (NKVD)[9]	8,615	406	7,069	1,080
10th Rifle Bde	1,912	280	1,148	18
115th Rifle Bde	4,868	308	2,625	113
149th Rifle Bde*	4,125	630	3,472	590
124th Rifle Bde	3,607	620	2,438	341
42nd Rifle Bde	5,032	336	–	–
9th Motorized Rifle Bde**	1,073	–	630	82
38th Motorized Rifle Bde	2,370	71	1,671	–

Unit	Light Machine Guns	Heavy Machine Guns	Mortars	Guns	Anti-Tank Rifles
33rd Gds Rifle Div	4	–	21	–	11
35th Gds Rifle Div	2	1	–	6	28
87th Rifle Div	1	–	13	–	–
98th Rifle Div	2	–	–	–	1
112th Rifle Div	5	6	11	–	–
131st Rifle Div	4	3	11	–	14
196th Rifle Div	3	–	3	1	6
229th Rifle Div	–	–	–	–	–
244th Rifle Div	14	5[10]	115	29	130
315th Rifle Div	15	10	6	23	126
399th Rifle Div	–	–	–	–	–
10th Rifle Div (NKVD)	129	38	102	12	63
10th Rifle Bde	11	34	26	–	24
115th Rifle Bde	100	40	93	30	69
149th Rifle Bde	115	29	51	23	78
124th Rifle Bde	84	22	56	25	68
42nd Rifle Bde	–	–	–	–	–
9th Motorized Rifle Bde	39	6	13	2	13
38th Motorized Rifle Bde	119	6	45	21	48

* According to data from 5 September 1942.
** According to a report by the brigade on 1 September 1942.

One can easily see that the 62nd Army contained a number of formations only formally worthy of their names. I draw your attention to the columns 'heavy machine guns' and 'light machine guns'. According to authorized strength table No. 04/300 of July 1942, which was in effect at that time, a rifle division was supposed to have 112 heavy and 337 light machine guns. The actual number of machine guns in the 62nd Army's formations was far below these requirements. The shortage of automatic weaponry doubtlessly reduced their chances of opposing the German offensive.

The rifle brigades that had not managed to make it to the Caucasus, and the division of NKVD [11] troops, had the greatest numbers at the start of the assault on the city. One should note that despite their similar strength, a rifle brigade and a worn-out rifle division have different combat worth. A significantly larger number of personnel of rear-area elements that do not take part in combat are in a worn-out rifle division. On the other hand, a division is certainly stronger in artillery. Before long, the remnants of several divisions were pulled back to the left bank of the Volga to reform.

The forces of the NKVD division's five regiments (approximately 1,500 in each) were spread relatively equally throughout the entire city, while occupying the so-called 'G' Line along the immediate approaches to the city. The line was built by the civilian population and engineers, but as was noted in a report on the engineer support for the defence of

Stalingrad, 'work in the city was begun late and thus on 10.9.42 820 structures had been built along the "G" Line, instead of the planned 1,310'. In all, thirteen battalion defensive areas were built along the city defence line. It was precisely these areas that were occupied by elements of Colonel A.A. Saraev's division. At the same time, one should not be deceived regarding the actual combat capabilities of the NKVD division – its artillery amounted to only twelve (!) 45mm guns and 50mm and 82mm mortars.

The most combat-capable rifle brigades, the 115th, 124th and 149th, were concentrated in the northern part of Stalingrad, forming a broad salient to the north-west from the Stalingrad Tractor, 'Red October' and 'Barricade' factories. Here the defence did not run along the city blocks, but in the open fields. The remnants of the 315th and 196th Rifle Divisions were here. The desire to hold positions in the northern part of the city was brought about by the expectation of a counterblow by the Stalingrad Front from the Kotluban' area. The situation demanded not only a stout defence. An attack toward the relief group of forces was not excluded. The defence of the southern part of Stalingrad, the elevator area, was the weakest. The weakened 35th Guards and 131st Rifle Divisions and the 10th Rifle Brigade had fallen back to this area. The fairly strong 42nd Rifle Brigade was defending to the west of the central part of the city, but its neighbours on the right and left were the 23rd Tank Corps' 6th Tank Brigade and the worn-out 244th Rifle Division. Data on the number of tanks in the units defending Stalingrad not long before the assault can be seen in the table.

Table 17: The Combat and Numerical Strength of the South-eastern Front's Armoured Units in Stalingrad as of 10 September 1942.[12]

Unit / Formation	Personnel		Motor Vehicles			Tanks	
	Authorized	*Actual*	*Autos*	*Trucks*	*Specialized*	*Heavy*	*Medium*
133rd Tank Bde	1,107	1,117	4	92	42	22	
23rd Tank Corps	7,592	5,494	12	331	53	–	38
27th Tank Bde*	1,181	768	2	71	19	–	13

*Attached to the 23rd Tank Corps on 12 September 1942.

Because the fighting was continuous (one may speak of the assault as a sharp increase in enemy activity), then by 13–14 September the number of the defenders' combat-ready tanks had decreased. For example, during the transfer of the 27th Tank Brigade to the 23rd Tank Corps on 12 September, the former included four T-34s, two T-70s and one T-60 mobile and six T-34s, seven T-70s and six T-60s immobilized. On the whole, Chuikov's description must be admitted as being close to the truth. The 133rd Tank Brigade, which consisted of twenty KVs which had earlier been defending the south-eastern approaches to the city, was added to the 62nd Army's tanks on the first day of the storming. The 26th Tank Brigade (twenty-two tanks) was also located south of the Tsaritsa River. Chuikov rightly raises the question of immobilized tanks, which were employed as fixed firing points. Because they were employed in the defensive system, the evacuation and repair of these vehicles was made more difficult. When the front line shifted they were simply lost or destroyed by their crews. For example, eighteen of the 26th Tank Brigade's immobilized tanks were abandoned in the Sadovaya area. The 27th Tank Brigade's immobilized tanks were dug in to the south of Gorodishche in the 23rd Tank Corps' and 112th Rifle Division's defensive system.

The German offensive against the centre of Stalingrad began according to plan at 04.45 Berlin time on 13 September. The Sixth Army's LI Corps, consisting of the 71st, 295th and 389th Infantry Divisions, went over to the attack. The corps' mission was formulated as follows: 'At 04.45 the LI Corps is to go over to the offensive from the area south of Gorodishche on Stalingrad, making its main attack along the Tatar Wall to the south-east.' That is, Seydlitz's corps was to move along the ancient wall directly on the centre of Stalingrad.

Units of the 23rd Tank Corps came under attack from German infantry on 13 September, particularly the 6th Tank and 38th Motorized Infantry Brigades. The major role of aviation in crushing the defence was mentioned in the 38th Motorized Infantry Brigade's war diary, 'when the enemy only bombed with his aviation the rank and file of the companies, he managed to break through to Avio-Gorodok'.[13] Here one cannot help but note that a Soviet motorized rifle brigade, even at authorized strength, was weaker than an ordinary infantry brigade in artillery and its defence overall was less secure. The 6th Tank Brigade's losses for the day were thirteen T-34s, with only three T-34s remaining in line in the brigade. As regards the 38th Motorized Rifle Brigade, in the 23rd Tank Corps' report it was written that 'having lost almost all of its equipment and personnel, it fell back to Height 107.5 with 30–50 men'.[14] By the evening of 12 September the brigade numbered 1,500 men 'ready for duty'. However, the corps headquarters nevertheless was a bit too quick to write off the 38th Motorized Rifle Brigade, and according to the war diary the brigade's losses for 13 September were 62 killed, 188 wounded and 132 missing in action.[15] That is, the losses were heavy, but did not signify the loss of the entire combat element. The LI Corps declared on this day the destruction of twenty-nine Soviet tanks. According to a report by the 23rd Tank Corps, the 6th Guards Tank Corps lost on 13 September eight T-34s and one T-70, the 189th Tank Brigade lost five T-34s and two T-70s, while the 27th Tank Brigade was fighting with immobilized tanks, having lost five T-34s and seven T-60s and T-70s.[16] In all, forty-one tanks were lost, and the German report even understated the losses, most likely at the expense of the immobilized tanks.

As was mentioned in the Sixth Army's war diary, the offensive developed according to plan on the first day: 'To the west of Stalingrad the LI Corps broke through into the depth of the Russian defensive line and, upon overcoming the stubborn resistance of the enemy, who disposed of particularly powerful artillery, occupied the dominating heights a little bit to the north-west of the city centre and the barracks there. In this manner the corps achieved its assigned objective for the day.'[17] The favourable development of events for the Germans can be explained in no small degree by their powerful artillery support: in total, the Sixth Army expended 760 tons of ammunition on 13 September, which something of a record for almost the entire preceding period.

A direct consequence of the Germans' breakthrough to the city centre was the loss of one of the crossings over the Volga. In all, there were four major crossings in the city: Central Crossing No. 1 (organized on 22 August 1942), Central Crossing No. 2 (organized 27 August), the crossing for wounded (along the Stalin quay, organized on 25 August), and the 'Red October' crossing (this was the 62nd Army's crossing, organized on 23 August). Central Crossing No. 1 ceased operating on 13 September.

The German offensive resumed on 14 September. Least successful were the attacks by units of the 389th Infantry Division, which encountered resistance by units of the 23rd Tank Corps, which rested upon the railway embankment. Quite the opposite, the 295th Infantry Division, which was attacking in the centre of the LI Corps' shock group, advanced successfully to the Volga and Mamaev hill. Its 518th and 516th Infantry Regiments, encountering no serious resistance, reached the railway north of the train station by 12.15.

Why did this happen? On 13 September elements of the 6th Tank and 38th Motorized Rifle Brigades were thrown back to the north, to the approaches to the workers' settlements. This opened the way for the German attack on defensive line 'G', where the 269th NKVD Regiment was occupying the fourth and fifth battalion areas. The account in the 269th Regiment's war diary was written in a quite unclear manner, with the accent on the soldiers' and commanders' feats. It's difficult to understand the unfolding of events from the war diary. However, in the NKVD 10th Rifle Division's report of 24.00 on 14 September, it is admitted that 'The enemy managed to drive a wedge into the depth of the defence along a number of sectors and penetrate into the city's confines'.[18] In the section on the 269th Regiment's activities, the report states that it 'accomplished a breakthrough along the road running from Gumrak station'.[19]

The 112th Rifle Division was in the second echelon along the approaches to Mamaev hill. At this time it was one of the weakest divisions in the 62nd Army. On 9 September its 385th Rifle Regiment numbered 136 men, its 416th Rifle Regiment 135 men, and its 524th Rifle Regiment 46 men, with its 436th Artillery Regiment numbering one 122mm howitzer and one 76mm Model 1939 gun. The 524th Rifle Regiment was occupying defensive positions along the forward edge, near Gorodishche, while the other two regiments formed the second echelon behind the 23rd Tank Corps' combat formation. On this first day of the assault, 13 September, matters were limited to the bombing of the 112th Rifle Division's positions.

The Germans' breakthrough as far as the railway during the first half of the day on 14 September signified a deep turning of the 112th Rifle Division's flank. It states in the 112th Rifle Division's war diary that as a result of the turning of its left flank, the 416th Rifle Regiment fell back to the north-eastern slopes of Height 102.0 (that is, it essentially abandoned Mamaev hill). For this the regimental commander was relieved of his position and replaced by the chief of the division's chemical services (!), Captain Aseev. As a result, the 295th Infantry Division's 518th Infantry Regiment, while advancing further to the east, reached the Volga by 15.00, while the 516th Infantry Regiment reached the south-western slope of Mamaev hill.

In describing the events of these days, Chuikov wrote:

> We decided to first of all defend the crossings against the enemy's artillery fire. For this, it was necessary to go over to a fixed defence, while in the centre occupy through frequent attacks the Razgulyaevka rail siding and the railway which runs from it to the south-west as far as the sharp turn toward Gumrak ... A tank corps, reinforced with infantry units, was assigned to carry out this assignment, supported by the main mass of the army's artillery. 13 September was for regrouping and the 14th for the attack, but the enemy pre-empted us.[20]

However, neither in the 62nd Army's war diary nor in the file of orders from the army's headquarters has there been found any kind of document resembling Chuikov's description. The new commander's first orders concerned strengthening the defence of the city and general questions of troop control. Chuikov's first order for a counterblow was Combat Order No. 145 of 22.30 on 13 September 1942.

The troops designated for the counterblow according to Order No. 145 were able to regroup and begin their offensive. This concerns most of all the units of the 23rd Tank Corps, which were supposed to counter-attack against Razgulyaevka. Yet another participant in the counterblow was the 272nd NKVD Regiment (minus one battalion), which had been transferred from the southern part of Stalingrad. It numbered 1,505 men on 13 September. However, the 272nd Regiment's counter-attack was not successful and the regiment went over to the defensive in the area of the cemetery near Height 112.5, south of the wall. There is a notation in the NKVD 10th Rifle Division's operational report: 'The regiment suffered heavy losses – up to 50–60 per cent. There are 170 men in the regiment.'[21]

Having repelled the counter-attack, at the 71st Infantry Division went over to the attack at 08.30 on 14 September and as early as 12.00, having crushed the Soviet forces' resistance along the edge of the city, broke through to the Stalingrad rail station (the so-called 'Stalingrad I'). Having resumed the offensive, at 15.15 the division reached the Volga east of the station with the forces of the 194th Infantry Regiment near the so-called 'water station' (*Wasserwerk* on German maps, the city water tower). However, one cannot say that the offensive was completely successful. As was pointed out in a report, the 71st Infantry Division's right flank was unable to overcome the Soviet defence, 'which was well fortified with armoured turrets and tank turrets'. Here the positions of the 42nd Rifle Brigade, under Hero of the Soviet Union Colonel M.S. Batrakov,[22] which had successfully repulsed the German attacks, were a small island of relative stability. By 'armoured turrets' we should probably understand immobilized tanks buried in the ground.

In summing up the events of 14 September, one can say that the LI Corps developed the first day's success, when elements of the 23rd Tank Corps were thrown back to the area of the workers' settlements. On 14 September the 269th NKVD Regiment and the remnants of the 112th Rifle Division were pushed back to the settlements. The strong artillery support was also traditional – on 14 September the Sixth Army expended 570 tons of ammunition.[23] In the Sixth Army's daily report, it was noted that: 'The enemy was obviously taken by surprise, that is, beside the numerous trucks captured, hundreds of tractors were seized at their stops.' To judge from this, this was the ready production of the Stalingrad Tractor Factory, STZ-3 tractors, which they simply did not have time to dispatch due to the break of rail communications with the centre of the country.

One must say that the new commander of the 62nd Army immediately began to institute iron discipline through the harshest methods. Later, in January 1943, Chuikov told a commission for studying the history of the Great Patriotic War, that 'We immediately undertook the most repressive measures concerning cowards. On 14 September I shot the commander and commissar of one regiment.'[24] This refers to the commander of the 399th Rifle Division's 1345th Rifle Regiment, Major Zhukov, and the regimental commissar, Senior Political Leader Raspopov. As is noted in the 62nd Army's order of 15 September 1942: 'Upon being attacked by the enemy, they showed cowardice in battle, abandoned their regiment and shamefully ran from the battlefield.'[25] Both were executed before soldiers and the order to this effect was read out in all of the army's units and subunits.

On the second day of the assault, 15 September, the defenders lost yet several more key positions. Around 12.00 two of the German 295th Infantry Division's regiments occupied Height 102.0 (Mamaev hill). Also, as a result of the offensive by the XLVIII Panzer Corps of Hoth's Fourth Panzer Army, Kuporosnoe was occupied. The 62nd Army had been separated from the 64th Army.

On 13 September the XLVIII Panzer Corps' 94th Infantry and 24th Panzer Divisions advanced toward Stalingrad from the south-east. In order to determine the attackers' strength, it is sufficient to note that on 11 September the 24th Panzer Division had a ration strength of 12,560 men, and with attached elements (anti-aircraft guns, the 670th Anti-Tank Battalion and *Reichsarbeitdienst*[26] personnel) 15,401 men. It was opposed by the 244th Rifle Division (3,288 men, 917 rifles, 124 Degtyaryov and Shpagin sub-machine guns, five heavy machine guns, 14 light machine guns, seven 122mm howitzers, and 15 76mm guns[27]), the 10th (160th) Rifle Brigade (1,912 men), and the 175th Independent Machine Gun-Artillery Battalion from the 115th Fortified Area (sixty-nine men, one light and eight heavy machine guns, three anti-tank rifles, and two 76mm guns on 3 September[28]).

On the first day of the assault the 10th Rifle Brigade and the 244th Rifle Division held their positions. On the following day, 14 September, the 24th Panzer Division was also unable to break the Soviet defence. As the division commander (by then already a Soviet captive), Major General von Lenski[29] later wrote in his report about the division's activities: 'Particularly heavy losses were suffered in the tanks that came upon a skilfully prepared minefield.' The powerful anti-tank artillery along this sector of the city's defence also became a serious problem for the Germans. A solution was found on the following day, 15 September, when von Lenski ordered an attack along the railway running from Sadovaya station. The narrow railway embankment was surrounded by *balki*, but nevertheless the tank attack along it enabled the Germans to overturn the 19th Rifle Brigade's defence on 15 September and break into the depth, as far as the 'Stalingrad II' station. The 10th Rifle Brigade, which had been pushed out of its position, fell back to the area of the elevator. The commander of the 244th Rifle Division, Colonel G.A. Afanas'ev bent back his left flank, moving up the 914th Rifle Regiment's second battalion and a reconnaissance company, but was unable to do more. The 24th Panzer Division's breakthrough resulted in the Germans getting into the rear of the 244th Rifle Division's units and cutting them off from the formation's rear establishment and headquarters. This led to a loss of troop control, while only scouts could get into the regimental lines at night. At the same time, the supply situation of the blockaded units left a lot to be desired even before they were isolated. As was noted in the evening report for 16 September by the 244th Rifle Division's headquarters, 'Thanks to the fact that the division's rear establishments are beyond the Volga and there are no crossings, the units have not received ammunition and food for several days already.'[30]

The main subject of the fighting on 15–16 September for the 24th Panzer Division was the battle for the so-called 'red barracks' on a high hill, around which were located the 244th Rifle Division's blockaded elements. Both combat groups of von Lenski's division and a motorcycle battalion were put into action against this position. As was noted in the XLVIII Panzer Corps' war diary, it was only during the second part of the day on 16 September that the Germans managed to capture the area of the 'red barracks,' taking it from 'a powerful enemy with anti-tank guns, artillery and 20 tanks'. The 244th Rifle Division and the 270th NKVD Regiment partially fell back from the area to the west of the Stalingrad II station behind the Tsaritsa River to the centre of the city. There was no solid front in the southern part of Stalingrad, in the area of the elevator.

Thus during the course of 13–15 September the Germans managed to crush the 62nd Army's defence through an attack by two corps, the LI Corps and the XLVIII

Panzer Corps, along the approaches to Stalingrad and to break through directly to the city streets. Logically, the next fighting for Stalingrad may be divided into the fighting in the centre of the city (the area of Mamaev hill and the Stalingrad I rail station) and the fighting in its southern part (the area of the elevator and the Stalingrad II station). These sectors are geographically divided approximately by the course of the Tsaritsa River and were organizationally in the offensive zone of the German LI and XLVIII Panzer corps, accordingly. It is expedient to observe the course of combat activities along each of these sectors separately, as an integral chain of events.

Chapter 13

The First Assault on the City.
14–26 September 1942. The Centre

(Map 6)

The 62nd Army's seriously undermined position could only be restored at the expense of the reserves. The commitment into the fighting by the Soviet command of fresh formations, brought up from the rear after refitting or from other sectors of the front, became routine in the struggle for Stalingrad. The 13th Guards Rifle Division became the first such reserve. It was among those formations which had been withdrawn into the reserve and which were being restored following the fighting near Khar'kov and Millerovo. As early as 25 July 1942 the division numbered only 1,235 men. However, the formation was gradually rebuilt. By the beginning of September the division numbered almost 10,000 men. The division's headquarters received the order to move to Stalingrad even before the assault, on 9 September 1942. On the night of 10/11 September the division drove across the steppe from the Kamyshin area to the Srednyaya Akhtuba area, along the left bank of the Volga to the east of Stalingrad. The commander of the 62nd Army, in his Combat Order No. 72 of 14 September 1942, ordered the following: 'The 13th Guards Rifle Division is to be crossed over to Stalingrad by 0300 on 15.9.42.'

The Guards troops arrived at the crossings at the height of the fighting. The divisional commander, A.I. Rodimtsev, recalled:

> The dark and foamy Volga water lapped at our feet. Standing on the shore, I viewed the badly wounded, destroyed and burning city. The weak wind slowly raised the crimson tongues of flame and back clouds of smoke to the sky, which were carried off on high and stretched out far above the Volga. It was difficult to make out what was going on along the far bank. One could only dimly make out the smashed boxes of buildings, the streets buried under piles of bricks, beams and iron, and the shortened and blackened tops of the trees.[1]

Chuikov describes the condition of the newly-arrived division as follows:

> Major General Rodimtsev informed me that the division was well outfitted and contained about 10,000 men. However, the situation with weapons and ammunition was bad. More than a thousand soldiers lacked rifles. The *front's* military council ordered the deputy *front* commander, Lieutenant General Golikov, to supply the division with the missing weapons no later than the evening of 14 September, by delivering them to the Krasnaya Sloboda area.[2]

Comparing Chuikov's words with the documents forces one to think deeply. On the one hand, the 13th Guards Rifle Division's war diary notes that on the night of 10/11 September the division was crossing over to the eastern bank of the Volga, 'numbering 9,500 men, not having finished fitting out and without weapons'.[3] On the other hand, the same war diary states: 'During 13–14.9.42 the division's units received weapons and ammunition.'[4] According to the report on the 13th Guards Rifle Division's combat strength on 13 September 1942, the formation numbered 9,603 men. There were 7,745 rifles, 170 Degtyaryov and Shpagin sub-machine guns, 30 light and 16 heavy machine guns.[5] The difference between the number of men and the number of personal weapons was more than 1,000. But the auxiliary elements were the worst supplied. For example, the 11th Guards Auto Supply Company had 59 rifles for 132 men. There were about 2,000 men in the rifle regiments of Rodimtsev's division, with about 1,800 rifles, that is, 90 per cent of the soldiers and commanders had rifles or automatic rifles. Of course, subunit commanders (armed with pistols or revolvers) don't need rifles. Artillery gun crews and rear-area workers, for example, and motor vehicle drivers and horse drivers, can do without rifles. Moreover, there's no problem at all in the absence of rifles in the artillery and mortar units or supply services. There were even 728 rifles for 926 men in the 13th Guards Rifle Division's artillery regiment. In a word, Rodimtsev's division was not badly outfitted by the standards of the middle and even the end of the war.

The 62nd Army's formations fighting in Stalingrad were outfitted with rifles no better than, and some somewhat worse than, the 13th Guards Rifle Division. Against this background, Chuikov's concern about the lack of weapons for the bakers in Rodimtsev's division appears quite strange. Thus on the basis of frivolous tales about the shortage of weaponry there appear movies similar to *The Enemy at the Gates*, in which soldiers are thrown into the Stalingrad fighting entirely unarmed.

However, Chuikov's tale nevertheless has some foundation. The 13th Guards Rifle Division differed for the worst from the other formations by its low supply of automatic weaponry. A Soviet division of this period had an authorized strength of 114 heavy machine guns, nine anti-aircraft guns, and 349 light machine guns, and 655 sub-machine guns. The 13th Guards Rifle Division had 14 per cent of its authorized heavy machine guns, 9 per cent of its light machine guns, and 26 per cent of its authorized sub-machine guns. There were no anti-aircraft machine guns in Rodimtsev's division at all. The reserve armies' formations that encountered Paulus's forces in the bend of the Don in July were far better outfitted. They had 200 light machine guns and 80 heavy machine guns apiece.

It is precisely here that we find indirect confirmation of the 62nd Army commander's words. In a report on its combat and numerical strength of 15 September, the 13th Guards Rifle Division numbered 8,009 men, 5,616 rifles, 36 heavy machine guns, 325 light machine guns, and 720 Degtyaryov and Shpagin sub-machine guns.[6] There also exists Combat Order No. 00110/op from the headquarters of the South-eastern Front of 13 September, in which it is proposed to supply the arriving 13th Guards Rifle Division, with instructions 'to the chief of artillery: to allot 450 Shpagin and 150 Degtyaryov sub-machine guns, 20 heavy machine guns, 100 light machine guns, and 1.5 combat loads'.[7] Yeremenko was the initiator of this order. The density of fire plays an important role in street fighting, and the sub-machine guns, along with light machine guns, become more necessary than ever. Rodimtsev's division was even outfitted with anti-tank rifles: there were 89 of them on 13 September, a number which grew to 229 on 15 September. As we see, the command regarded the formation entrusted to it seriously and tried adapt it as much as possible to the street fighting in Stalingrad. The documents confirm Rodimtsev's statement in January 1943 to the academic secretary of the commission for studying the Great Patriotic War, A.A. Belkin, about his conversation with Yeremenko. The commander of the 13th Guards Rifle Division also confidently stated that 'on 13 September I was fully armed, but rifle rounds and ammunition had not yet been distributed'.[8]

According to the initial plan, the 13th Guards Rifle Division's task was to defend the western outskirts of Stalingrad from the Stalingrad Tractor Factory settlement to Height 112.0 (along the approaches to the 'Red October' settlement from the south). However, in reality the formation began to operate in the fighting for the city centre. Z.P. Chervyakov's first battalion of the 42nd Guards Rifle Regiment, which crossed over first with a company of automatic riflemen, broke through to the train station and captured it. The regiment's second battalion crossed after it by the morning, while the third battalion and regiment artillery remained on the eastern bank of the Volga on that day. The battalion's breakthrough to the train station may appear to be a presumptuous move on the part of the commander of the 42nd Guards Rifle Regiment, I.P. Yelin. However, first of all, from the point of view of the overall situation, the battalion, which had moved from the bank of the Volga, was in direct proximity to the positions of the 10th NKVD Rifle Division's subunits, and secondly, control over the train station and the opportunity to fire on the railway line in the rear of the enemy who had already reached the quay was a serious advantage. Moreover, Chuikov's command post (the 'Tsaritsa underground'), with one exit to the course of the Tsaritsa River and a second onto Pushkin Street, was in close proximity to the train station. By the way, Chuikov put into action yet another battalion from Rodimtsev's division – the 3rd/34th Guards Rifle Regiment – for the direct defence of his command post which had unexpectedly come to be close to the front line.

After the commander of the 42nd Guards Rifle Regiment, Z.P. Chervyakov, was wounded in the area of the train station, the command was taken up by Senior Lieutenant Fedor Grigor'evich Fedoseev. He was, one might say, a veteran in Rodimtsev's division and had fought as early as Kiev in the 212th Airborne Brigade. He received the Order of the Red Star for those battles near Zhulyany. Fedoseev's battalion was reinforced with three anti-tank guns, a company of anti-tank rifles and a mortar company.

The traditional 'fire brigade' for the Soviet defence, including in the centre of Stalingrad, were the tanks. On Chuikov's order a battalion of KV tanks (eleven vehicles) from the 133rd Tank Brigade was removed from the southern approaches to the city and moved to the train station and entered the fighting on the morning of 15 September. Upon the tanks' approach to the train station, enemy tanks (according to brigade reports: they were probably StuG III self-propelled guns) appeared from under the bridge of the railway embankment. The KVs knocked out three vehicles on the fly and attempted to develop the success and attacked the enemy to the west of the embankment. However, here the tank troops encountered dense fire and armoured vehicles, which were identified as 'heavy tanks'. Again, these were most likely *Sturmgeschützen* from the 244th Self-Propelled Gun Battalion, which was supported the 71st Infantry Division's offensive. Having lost one tank knocked out and one burnt, the KVs turned back. Upon reaching the burnt-out buildings, the KVs camouflaged themselves and prepared to beat off the enemy attack.

One of the features of the 13th Guards Rifle Division's crossing into Stalingrad was that its elements landed along a broad front. Part of the second battalion's forces landed in the area of Mamaev hill and part in the centre of the city, and immediately set about clearing out the buildings nearest the crossing. In the second half of the day on 15 September, under cover of smoke from a burning barge near the western bank of the Volga, the 42nd Guards Rifle Regiment's third battalion and the division's headquarters, led by Rodimtsev, crossed. On the night of 15/16 September the artillery, a mortar battery and the remaining elements of the 42nd Guards Rifle Regiment crossed into the city centre. It was the third battalion that on the morning of 16 September began to advance toward the railway, while the under-strength second battalion remained in reserve. During the day on 16 September it was joined by elements landed near Mamaev hill. Also, on the night of 15/16 September two battalions of the 34th Guards Rifle Regiment crossed, one of which was initially put into action along the boundary between the 42nd Guards Rifle Regiment's first and second battalions, which were widely separated. Later, two battalions of the 34th Guards Rifle Regiment were moved from the area of 9 January Square to the Long *Balka*, where they also operated along a broad front. The 13th Guards Rifle Division's artillery remained on the eastern bank of the Volga and took up positions for supporting the subunits fighting in the city.

On the whole, one may note in the employment of the 13th Guards Rifle Division a definite inertia in the old plans imposed even before the beginning of the storming of the city by the Germans. The 39th Guards Rifle Regiment was crossed over the Volga as a whole to the area of the 'Red October' Factory, much further to the north of the centre, to a completely quiet sector which had not been subjected to enemy attacks. As a result, the formation turned out to be divided up along several axes. Being spread widely along the central part of Stalingrad, the battalions of Rodimtsev's division attempted to throw back to the line of the railway the enemy who had broken into the centre of the city. The only thing that saved these scattered battalions from immediate defeat was the fact that the enemy also lacked a continuous front in the centre of the city.

As early as 15 September it was decided to employ Major S.S. Dolgov's 39th Guards Rifle Regiment for a counter-attack in the area of Mamaev hill (Height 102.0). The question of the time this key height for the central part of Stalingrad was taken is controversial and here the sides' documents do not always coincide. In the LI Corps' combat report for 15 September, it is noted: 'At 11.40 the 295th Infantry Division's 516th Infantry Regiment, despite the enemy's stubborn resistance and the well-fortified positions, took Height 102 and its western slope.'[9] In its turn, the 112th Rifle Division's war diary notes that at 14.00 on 15 September it undertook a joint attack with the 39th Guards Rifle Regiment, as a result of which by 15.00 Height 102.0 was occupied by the 39th Guards Rifle Regiment.

In a later entry in a supplement to the Sixth Army's war diary, it is noted: 'In the intelligence section's intermediate report (19.10 hours), it was noted that the LI Corps lost Height 102 and its north-western slopes.' That is, Mamaev hill was lost by the Germans due to an attack by a fresh regiment (operating apart from the division) from the 13th Guards Rifle Division. However, the LI Corps' morning reports for 16 September already note that the 295th Infantry Division was occupying Height 102.0. Actually, there is no contradiction in this. In the Soviet 112th Rifle Division's war diary 'an attack to seize Height 102.0' is noted as the task for the day of 16 September.[10] This forces us to come to the conclusion that during the second half the day on 15 September or during the night of 15/16 September the key height was nevertheless lost. Unfortunately, the struggle was waged in different 'weight categories'. The Germans had the opportunity to support their attacks with far more powerful artillery fire. No changes in the situation of the 295th Infantry Regiment on Height 102.0 are noted in German reports. On the whole, the appearance of fresh forces in the city was an unpleasant surprise for the Germans. Despite all the unevenness of the 13th Guards Rifle Division's commitment into the fighting, it was already unrealistic to quickly crush it. In the Sixth Army's daily report it is noted: 'The LI Corps' combat capability, particularly during the last five days, has declined significantly. Losses from 13 through 15.9 are 61 officers and 1,492 other ranks.'

On the night of 15/16 September the headquarters of the 62nd Army moved 800m from the 'Tsaritsa underground', which was 800m from the front line, to a command post in the factory area, across from Zaitsevskii Island. The fighting in the centre of the city was clearly not developing in the Soviet forces' favour and Chuikov's headquarters risked being cut off from the army's main forces. It was actually already cut off and it was necessary to cross the headquarters to the eastern bank of the Volga, to Krasnaya Sloboda, and to then return to the western bank of the river on an armoured launch. One must also note that in his memoirs Chuikov dates the removal of his command post in the 'Red October' area as the night of 17/18 September. In the 62nd Army's war diary it is clearly written that 'At 24.00 on 16.9 the headquarters is to move to "Red October".[11] This was due to the movement of the headquarters by two trains.

The army headquarters spent two nights and the daylight hours of 16 September getting established in its new site. The dugouts for the 62nd Army's headquarters still had to be outfitted. Chuikov recalled the circumstances of the movement to a new command post: 'Oil tanks and a concrete pond for black oil were over us, along the steep bank. Machine tools, motors and other factory equipment, which had been prepared for evacuation beyond the Volga, but which remained here, lay piled up on a sand bar, Several half-destroyed barges and a lot of floatable wood stood near the bank's edge.'[12] N.I. Krylov, the army chief of staff, saw the surrounding chaos as an advantage: 'The enemy was not likely to suspect that the army's command post was deployed here.' And in fact this made it difficult for the Germans to interpret aerial photographs.

At the same time, one can see yet another important factor in the situation around Mamaev hill: the movement of the command post might have interfered with tracking the actual situation in the area of Height 102.0 and the capture of this key position. It was precisely on 16 September that this report was made: 'The 39th Guards Rifle Regiment is attacking Height 102.0 from the east and by 18.00 captured Height 102.0 and is continuing to attack to the north-west.'[13] This report had far-reaching consequences.

Actually, on 16 September, documents indicate attacks on Height 102.0 by the 112th Rifle Division's full-strength 416th Rifle Regiment (564 men), the 39th Guards Rifle Regiment and tanks from the 27th Tank Brigade (five T-34s, delivered from the factory and taking part in the fighting from midday). The attacks began at 08.00. In the 112th Rifle Division's war diary the result of the attacks is stated to be reaching the crest of the height and the capture of some 'small buildings' 200m north of the height. Of the five T-34s which took part in the attack on the height, one burned, one 'got stuck in a *balka* in enemy territory' and two were shot up, but returned from the fighting under their own power.[14] In the Germans' reports, the morning attacks are noted by the phrase: 'The enemy, who broke through along the boundary between the 516th and 517th Infantry Regiments, was thrown back by a counter-attack.'[15] The subsequent attacks were also reflected: 'The enemy's subsequent attacks on Height 102 at 13.00, 13.50 and 16.30 were beaten off, and two enemy tanks were destroyed.'[16] The number of T-34s left on the battlefield corresponds with Soviet data (two vehicles).

In the 112th Rifle Division's war diary the combat activities of 17 September are noted as fighting 'for Height 102.0'. The 27th Tank Brigade's tanks that were out of order supported the attack from immobile positions. At the same time, it was noted that the Germans undertook a counteroffensive, which threw the 416th Rifle Regiment from its previously-occupied positions (the 'small buildings' near Height 102.0). The German reports on this day do not indicate a counteroffensive, and it is possible that the 112th Rifle Division's war diary was drawn up later and the events were moved by a day. Whatever the reason, on 17 September Mamaev hill was already firmly in German hands.

In the meantime, events to the south of the Tsaritsa River, where units of the German XLVIII Panzer Corps had reached the area of the station (Stalingrad II) and the grain elevator, had begun to exert an influence on the situation in the centre of the city. Following the capture of the station, the 24th Panzer Division's tanks advanced on the morning of 16 September along the tracks further to the north, captured the railway bridge over the Tsaritsa River and formed a small bridgehead. Parts of the forces of the 270th and 272nd Regiments of the 10th NKVD Division were immediately deployed for attacking this bridgehead. The first regiment fell back from the southern bank of the Tsaritsa. In the XLVIII Panzer Corps' war diary it is noted that 'The enemy is continuously attacking the Tsaritsa bridgehead in great force'. The fighting for the bridgehead continued throughout the entire course of 16 September and ended in a success by the NKVD troops, while the XLVIII Panzer Corps' war diary wraps up the history of the bridgehead with the phrase: 'The Tsaritsa bridgehead had to be given up in the evening due to strong enemy pressure.'

The seizure of a bridgehead over the Tsaritsa, although it created a threat to the Soviet forces in the centre of Stalingrad, would not in and of itself have meant disaster. What did was when the main motorized infantry forces of the 24th Panzer Division reached the Tsaritsa and joined up with the LI Corps' neighbouring 71st Infantry Division, although at this stage at the level of fire contact. By the way, the tanks of the 24th Panzer Division, three of which were knocked out by 'friendly fire' from anti-aircraft guns supporting the 71st Infantry Division, were the first to suffer from 'fire contact'. Nonetheless, their arrival at the Tsaritsa signified the encirclement of the 42nd Rifle Brigade. Thus the 42nd Rifle Brigade's war diary notes that the encirclement arose from the sudden withdrawal, without warning, of its neighbours to its right and left. During the day on 16 September the brigade fought off attacks by the 71st Infantry Division, which was striving to eliminate the 'cauldron' and thus to free up forces for the storming of the centre of Stalingrad. However, the Soviets managed to beat off all the attacks and the 42nd Rifle Brigade sought to break through on the night of 16/17 September. The fact of the breakthrough is confirmed by German sources. One should note that the path of the breakthrough lay through the area of the railway bridge and the bridgehead just abandoned by the Germans. Had the bridgehead and bridge remained in the hands of the 24th Panzer Division's subunits, the breakthrough would have turned into a massacre of the 42nd Rifle Brigade's infantry from tank fire from the bridge and bridgehead. But this did not happen and as early as 05.00 on 17 September the 42nd Rifle Brigade had occupied defensive positions along the streets of Stalingrad. It is noted in the brigade's war diary that all of the wounded were evacuated to the crossing over the Volga.

Losses in the encirclement may be rated as moderate. According to the 42nd Rifle Brigade's war diary, losses for 17–18 September were 153 men killed, 308 wounded and 72 men missing in action.[17] In the LI Corps' daily report it was noted that in eliminating the 'cauldron' in the Dubovaya *Balka*, 'many prizes were taken, particularly in automatic weaponry, and more than 100 machine guns'. However, only twelve Shpagin sub-machine guns were declared among the 42nd Rifle Brigade's losses. The brigade remained fully combat-capable.

Map 1. Course of actions on the Soviet-German front on the eve of Stalingrad battle.

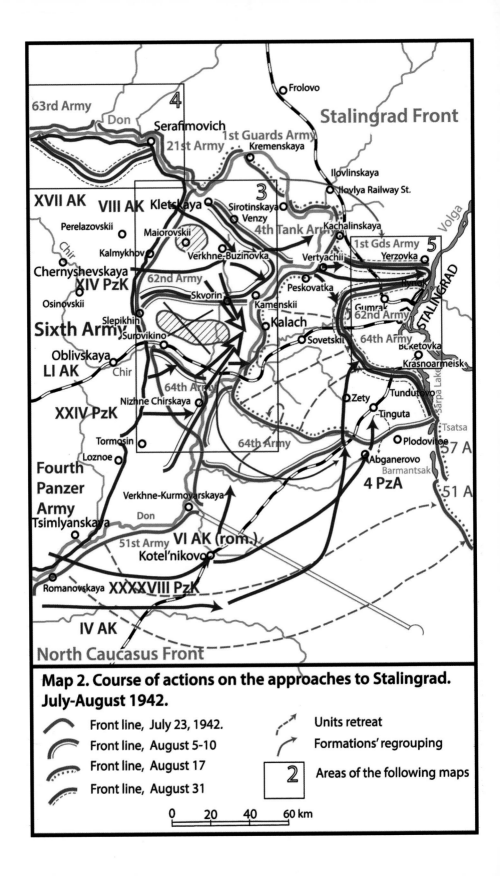

Map 2. Course of actions on the approaches to Stalingrad. July-August 1942.

Front line, July 23, 1942.

Front line, August 5-10

Front line, August 17

Front line, August 31

Units retreat

Formations' regrouping

Areas of the following maps

0   20   40   60 km

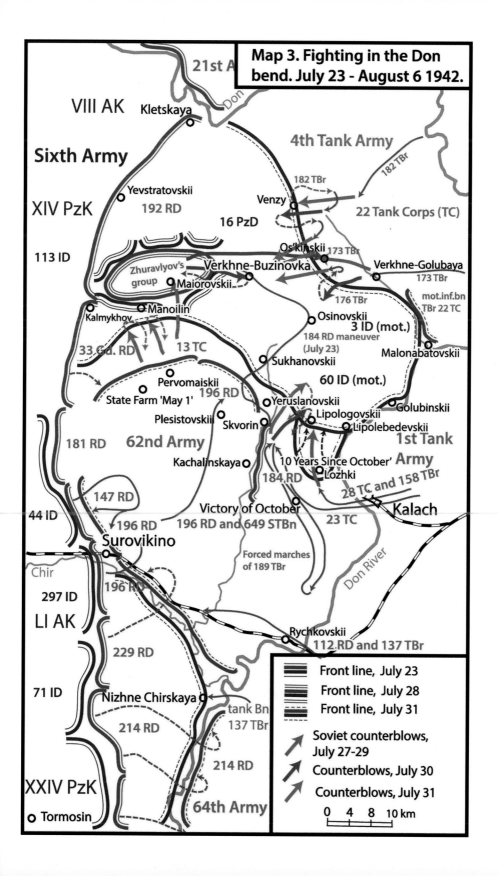

Map 3. Fighting in the Don bend. July 23 - August 6 1942.

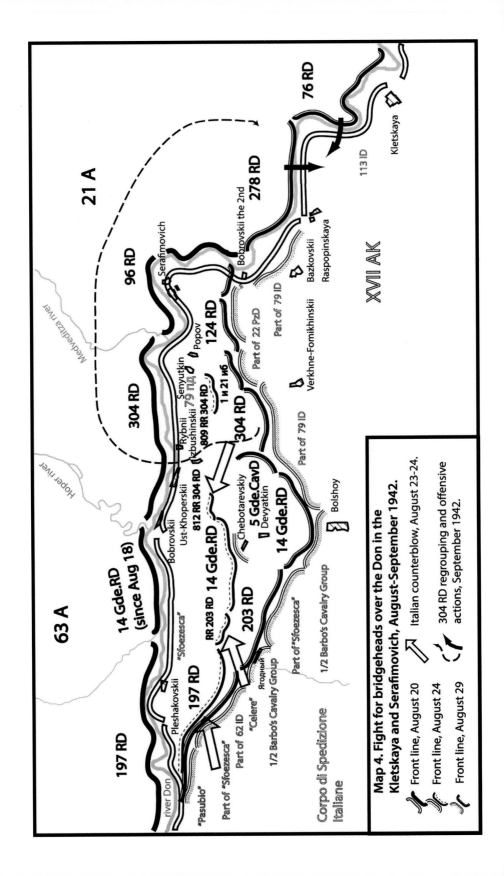

Map 4. Fight for bridgeheads over the Don in the Kletskaya and Serafimovich, August-September 1942.

Front line, August 20

Front line, August 24

Front line, August 29

Italian counterblow, August 23-24.

304 RD regrouping and offensive actions, September 1942.

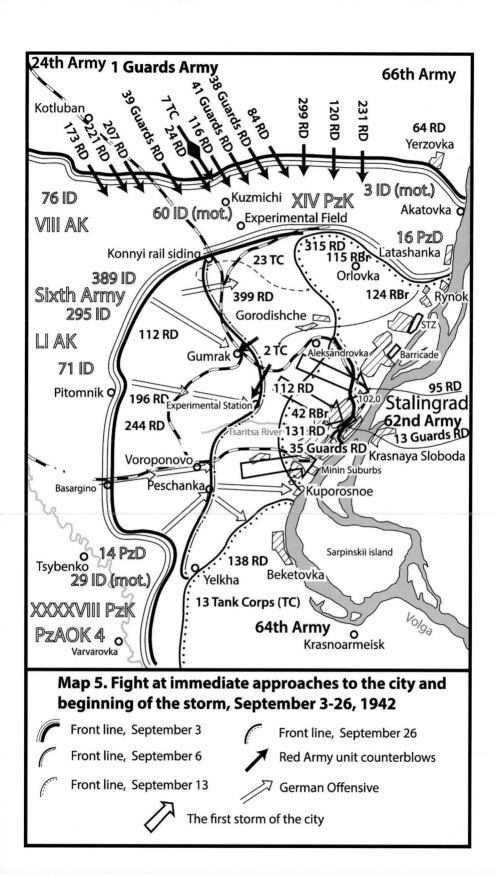

Map 5. Fight at immediate approaches to the city and beginning of the storm, September 3-26, 1942

- Front line, September 3
- Front line, September 6
- Front line, September 13
- Front line, September 26
- Red Army unit counterblows
- German Offensive
- The first storm of the city

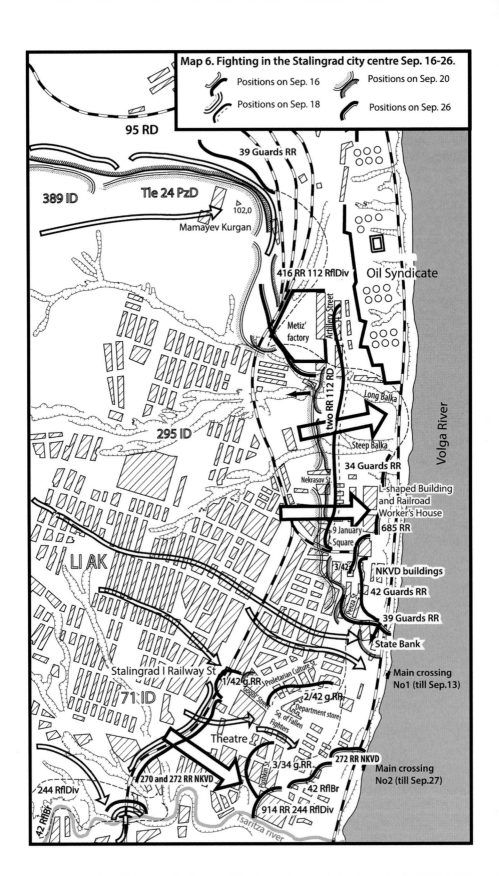

Map 6. Fighting in the Stalingrad city centre Sep. 16-26.

Positions on Sep. 16
Positions on Sep. 18
Positions on Sep. 20
Positions on Sep. 26

95 RD

39 Guards RR

389 ID

Tle 24 PzD

102,0
Mamayev Kurgan

416 RR 112 RflDiv

Oil Syndicate

Metiz' factory

Artillery Street

two RR 112 RD

Long Balka

Steep Balka

295 ID

34 Guards RR

Nekrasov St.

L-shaped Building and Railroad Worker's House

9 January Square

685 RR

Volga River

LI AK

3/42

NKVD buildings

42 Guards RR

Penza St.

39 Guards RR

State Bank

Main crossing No1 (till Sep.13)

Stalingrad I Railway St

1/42 g.RR

Proletarian Culture St.

Gogol Street

71 ID

2/42 g.RR

Sq. of Fallen Fighters

Department store

Theatre

Pushkin St.

3/34 g.RR

272 RR NKVD

Main crossing No2 (till Sep.27)

270 and 272 RR NKVD

42 RflBr

244 RflDiv

42 RflBr

914 RR 244 RflDiv

Tsaritza river

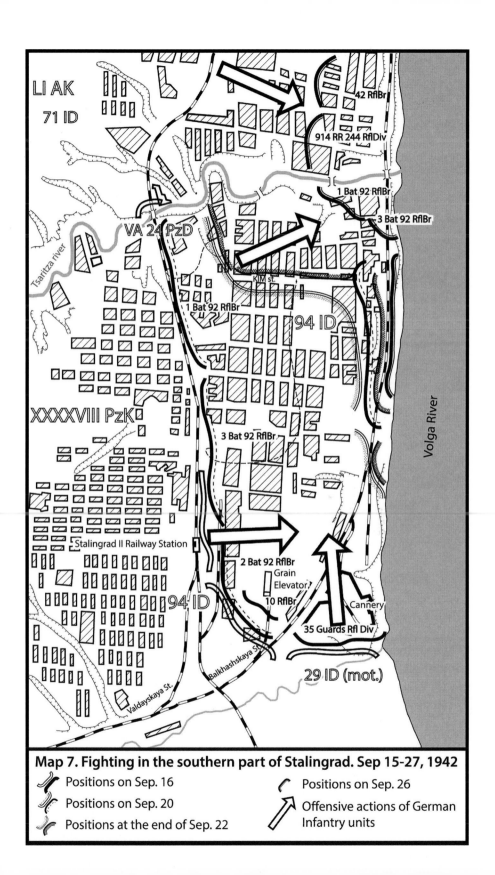

Map 7. Fighting in the southern part of Stalingrad. Sep 15-27, 1942

Positions on Sep. 16

Positions on Sep. 20

Positions at the end of Sep. 22

Positions on Sep. 26

Offensive actions of German Infantry units

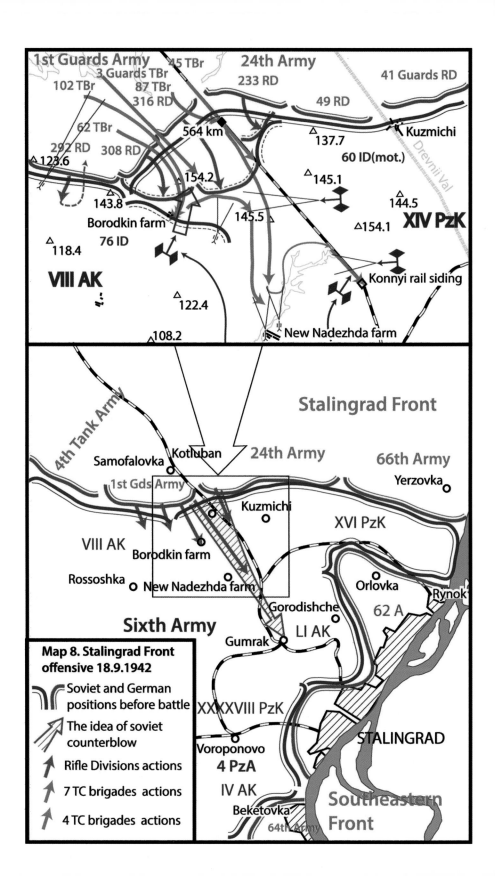

Map 8. Stalingrad Front offensive 18.9.1942

Soviet and German positions before battle

The idea of soviet counterblow

Rifle Divisions actions

7 TC brigades actions

4 TC brigades actions

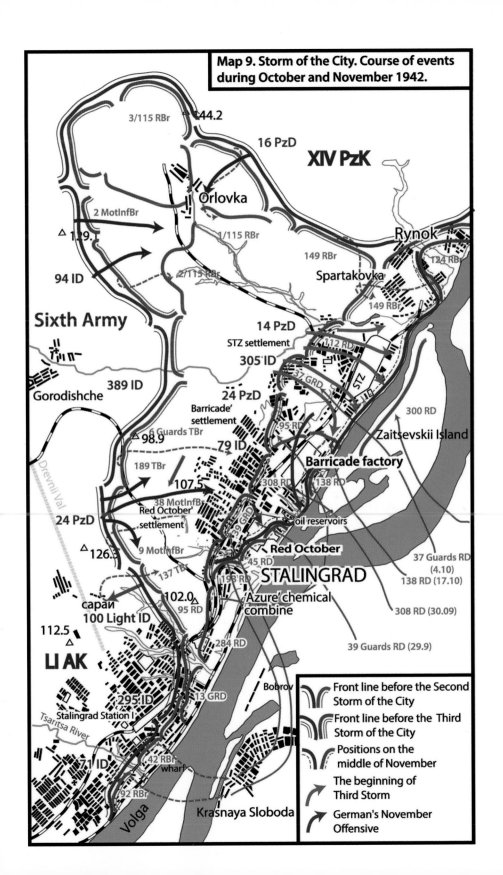

Map 9. Storm of the City. Course of events during October and November 1942.

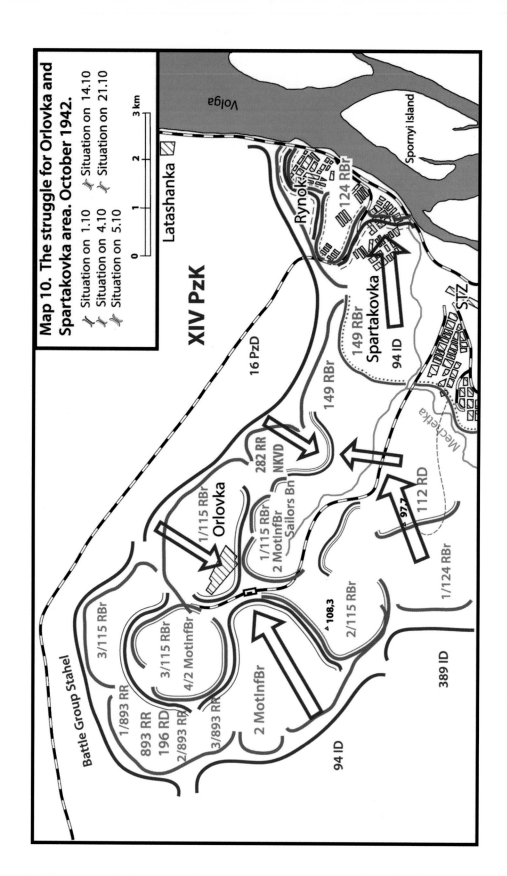

Map 10. The struggle for Orlovka and Spartakovka area. October 1942.

Situation on 1.10
Situation on 4.10
Situation on 5.10
Situation on 14.10
Situation on 21.10

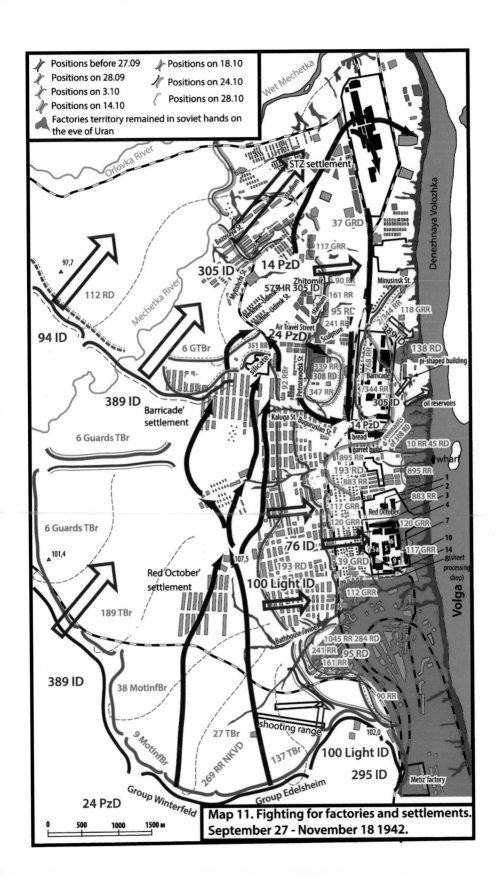

Map 11. Fighting for factories and settlements.
September 27 - November 18 1942.

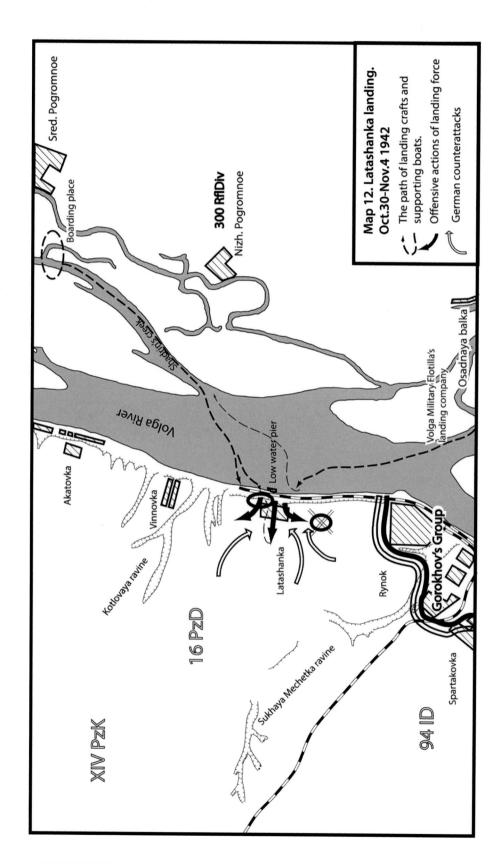

Map 12. Latashanka landing.
Oct.30-Nov.4 1942

The path of landing crafts and supporting boats.

Offensive actions of landing force

German counterattacks

Sred. Pogromnoe

Boarding place

300 RflDiv

Nizh. Pogromnoe

Shadin's creek

Volga River

Akatovka

Vinnovka

Kotlovaya ravine

Low water pier

Volga Military Flotilla's landing company

Osadnaya balka

Latashanka

Rynok

Sukhaya Mechetka ravine

Gorokhov's Group

Spartakovka

16 PzD

XIV PzK

94 ID

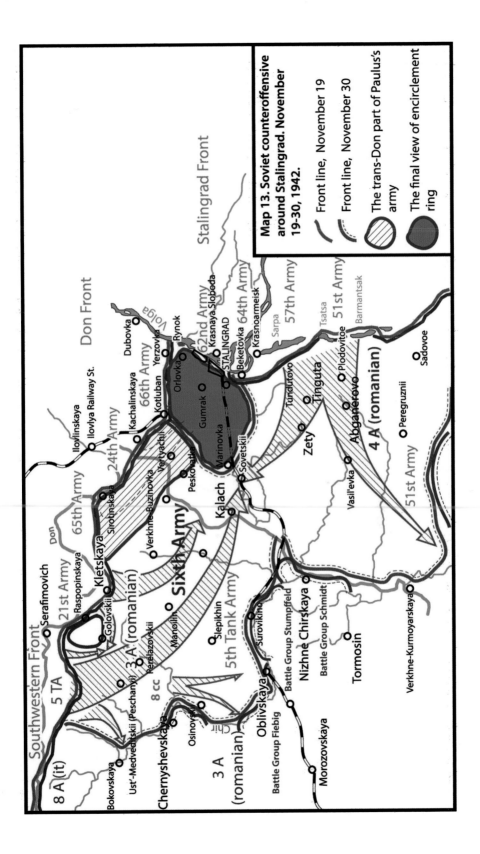

Map 13. Soviet counteroffensive around Stalingrad. November 19-30, 1942.

Front line, November 19

Front line, November 30

The trans-Don part of Paulus's army

The final view of encirclement ring

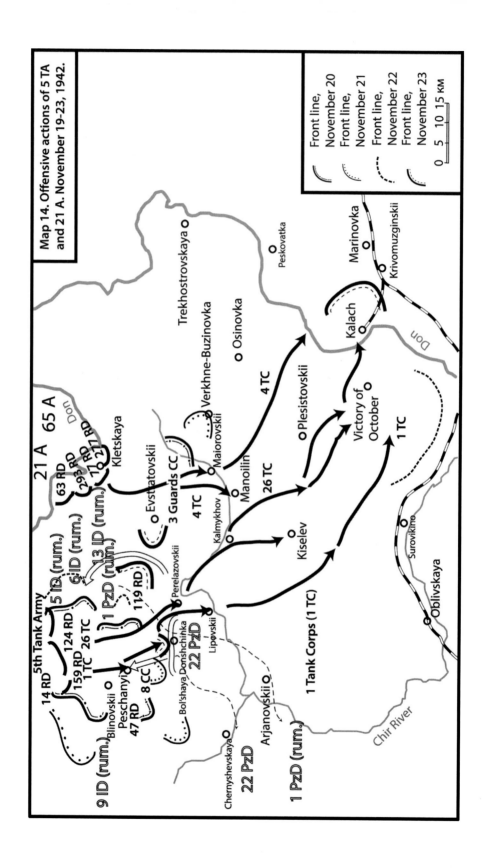

Map 14. Offensive actions of 5 TA and 21 A. November 19-23, 1942.

Front line, November 20
Front line, November 21
Front line, November 22
Front line, November 23

0 5 10 15 KM

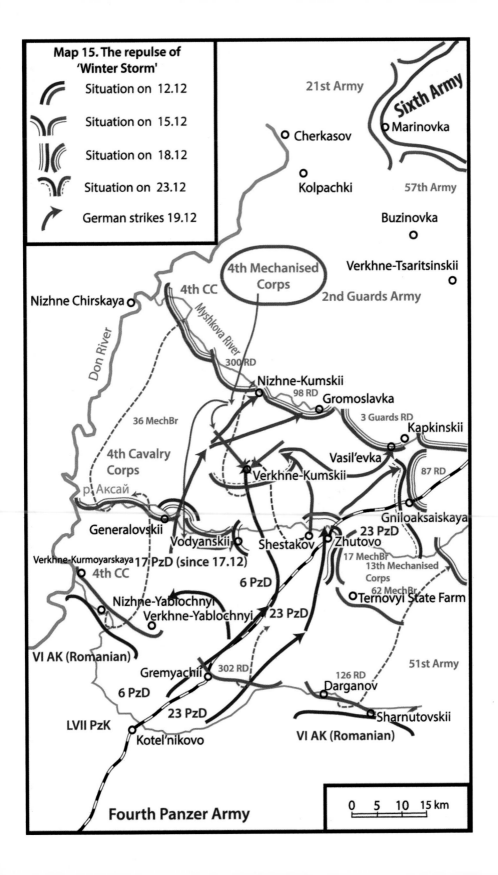

Map 15. The repulse of 'Winter Storm'

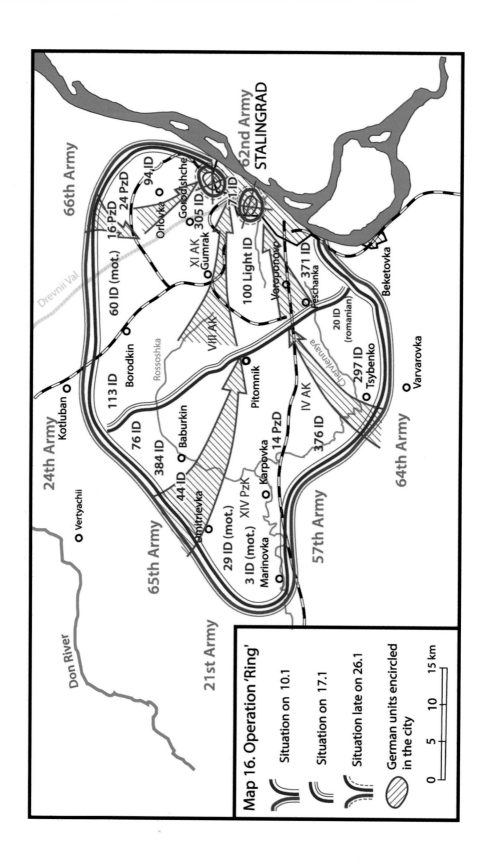

Map 16. Operation 'Ring'.

Situation on 10.1

Situation on 17.1

Situation late on 26.1

German units encircled in the city

0 5 10 15 km

However, the 42nd Rifle Brigade's withdrawal caused, in its turn, the exposure of the 244th Rifle Division's flank and the German infantry's breakthrough from the north, along the northern bank of the Tsaritsa into the division's rear, directly at its headquarters. As of 18 September, 765 men remained in the 244th Rifle Division, of which 195 were 'active bayonets' (for which there were 177 rifles, 24 Shpagin and Degtyaryov sub-machine guns and two light machine guns).[18] There still remained three 76mm guns and two 122mm howitzers in the division's artillery regiment. Nonetheless, the formation was put into order and occupied a defensive position with its front facing west. The headquarters of the 244th Rifle Division was located in the 'Tsaritsa underground', which had recently been abandoned by the headquarters of the 62nd Army.

Overall, it would be a great mistake to believe that the 13th Guards Rifle Division was the sole participant in the fighting that unfolded in the centre of Stalingrad. As was noted in the LI Corps' daily report for 18 September, 'Part of the city south of the train station as far as the Tsaritsa and Volga has been occupied by a strong enemy'. Here the Germans had in mind units of the 42nd Rifle Brigade, the remnants of the 244th Rifle Division and two NKVD regiments (270th and 272nd), which were defending south of the 13th Guards Rifle Division. Unfortunately, the documents of these units and formations were poorly preserved. The 42nd Rifle Brigade's war diary is not very informative and there is an enormous gap in the reports. However, in the absence of this mishmash of units immediately to the north of the Tsaritsa, an unenviable fate would have awaited the elements of the 13th Guards Rifle Division which had landed in the city.

It was precisely this group of forces to the north of the Tsaritsa that was attacked at 04.00 (Berlin time) on 19 September by the forces of two regiments from the 71st Infantry Division. As was noted in the corps' daily report, 'In heavy fighting against firing points located on the rail embankment, only the 191st Infantry Regiment, which reached the edge of a large square with party buildings, could advance forward a little.' The square with 'Communist Party buildings' was none other than the Square of Fallen Fighters, in which stood the city's executive committee and the department store. The offensive continued the next day with energetic support from the air, but the Germans, as they themselves admit, achieved only 'local successes'. At the same time, the LI Corps' expenditure of ammunition for 19 September was 240 tons, and 184 tons on 20 September.[19] In light of the limited success of the two days of fighting, the Germans paused, and a new offensive was slated for 24 September.

A reorganization of units and formations was carried out on the Soviet side along this sector. The remnants of the 244th Rifle Division was to be formed into a single 914th Rifle Regiment (411 men as of 20 September 1942), which was to be operationally subordinated to the commander of the 42nd Rifle Brigade. This was a regiment was pretty much in name only – a rifle company, a mortar company, a platoon of anti-tank rifles, and a machine gun platoon armed with 125 rifles, 39 Shpagin sub-machine guns, two heavy and two light machine guns, 12 anti-tank rifles and 12 50mm and 16 82mm mortars. The headquarters of the formations that were being pulled out of the fighting crossed over to the left bank of the Volga. One cannot say that this unconditionally told positively on the situation. The commander of the 244th Rifle Division's composite regiment, Major V.M. Shtrigol',[20] reported that the regiment had not been put on the 42nd Rifle Brigade's ration strength: 'The 914th Rifle Regiment has not received food for two days, while ammunition and medicine are absent.' In his turn, the commander of the 42nd Rifle Brigade complained that the command of the 914th Rifle Regiment refused to carry out his instructions, while suggesting that he approach him through the headquarters of the 244th Rifle Division. Here two regiments from Saraev's NKVD division were operating in the area directly to the north of the Tsaritsa. By the evening of 19 September 101 men remained in the 270th NKVD Regiment, so the remnants of the 270th Regiment were put into the 272nd NKVD Regiment.[21] On the morning of 22 September the regiment numbered 220 men.[22] On the whole, serious resistance to the Germans in the area immediately to the north of the Tsaritsa was put up by small units.

The next reserve committed into the fighting for Stalingrad was the 137th Tank Brigade. Before this it had been occupying defensive positions along the left bank of the Volga, among the other tank units which had been pulled out of the fighting and consolidated under the headquarters of the 2nd Tank Corps. At 02.00 on 17 September an order was received to cross the brigade over the Volga into Stalingrad. Actually, several brigades which had been acquired along the left bank of the Volga were formed into the 137th Tank Brigade. The brigade received 120 'dismounted' tank troops and motorized infantry as reinforcements from the 39th, 169th and 254th Tank Brigades. As early as 20.00 on the same day the brigade's units had gathered at the crossing. By 05.00 on 18 September the crossing on barges had been completed. In all, 764 men were crossed. The brigade concentrated in the area of the 'Red October' factory and by 07.00 on 18 September had occupied defensive positions. Actually, from the very first hours of its stay in Stalingrad the brigade was operating as infantry.

Up to the commitment of fresh formations into the fighting, the 39th Guards Rifle Regiment from A.I. Rodimtsev's division and the remnants of the 112th Rifle Division continued their attacks on Mamaev hill. The 13th Guards Rifle Division's remaining regiments were engaged in offensive and defensive fighting in the centre of Stalingrad. It is sometimes very curious to compare the sides' data about one and the same event. For example, in the 133rd Tank Brigade's report there is the following notation: '17.IX.42 the enemy's tanks, numbering up to twelve vehicles, broke through from the west and streamed along the Long *Balka* to reach the Volga. Because of this, three KV tanks were pulled out of the area of the train station and thrown onto Nekrasov Street [alongside the Long *Balka*, running from the west to the Volga – Author].'[23] It is further pointed out that the enemy tanks, which caused the KVs to be summoned, turned back. In the supplements to the Sixth Army's war diary this looks like a night raid by tanks along the city streets: 'With the onset of darkness, three enemy tanks broke through from the blocks south of the train station to the north-east, as far as the Volga, crushing two 3.7cm anti-tank guns.' This raid was a pretty risky venture, because a significant part of the city centre was controlled by the Germans.

On the whole, the remaining elements of the 13th Guards Rifle Division managed to achieve far less success than the 42nd Guards Rifle Regiment's first battalion, which broke through to the train station. By 18 September the 42nd Guards Rifle Regiment had been able to advance only as far as Penza Street, immediately adjacent to the Volga. The 34th Guards Rifle Regiment was also unable to advance very far – as far as Artillery Street, the Long and Steep *Balki*, and 9 January Square. However, these positions had been occupied in sufficient strength. In the LI Corps' daily report for 18 September the following was written: 'The 295th Infantry Division fended off numerous enemy attacks near the Volga.

It was necessary to halt clearing the part of the city near the Volga due to the enemy's strong resistance and two assault guns being put out of action.'

The three KV tanks that had been moved from the train station proved to be of great assistance to the battalions of Rodimtsev's division operating in the centre of the city. This enabled them to eliminate several points of resistance and advance and, according to the operational report of 01.00, on 20 September the 42nd Guards Rifle Regiment practically managed to link up its position with the battalion fighting in the area of the train station. The 42nd Guards Rifle Regiment's second battalion reached Proletarian Culture Street (not far from the department store and the Square of Fallen Fighters).

Yet one more measure for strengthening the situation of the 13th Guards Rifle Division's units in the centre of Stalingrad was the storming of one of the Germans' strongholds along the bank of the Volga – the State Bank building. Having been occupied by the enemy, at that moment this sturdy five-storey building was quite a headache – the crossing over the Volga came under fire from it. It's curious to note that in the literature the storming of the State Bank is usually attributed to the 42nd Guards Rifle Regiment.[24] However, there are no mentions of such an event in the regiment's war diary. According to a report by the 13th Guards Rifle Division, the division's blocking detachment stormed the State Bank on the night of 18/19 September, with the support of engineers. The blocking battalion numbered 383 men, armed with 301 rifles, nine Degtyaryov/Shpagin sub-machine guns and two light machine guns on 13 September. This is somewhat at variance with the movie version of ferocious blocking troops armed to the teeth with automatic weapons.

With the onset of darkness the engineers crept up to the State Bank along previously reconnoitred paths, pushing forward cases of TNT. Noticing this movement, the Germans opened fire which was suppressed by automatic rifles that had been distributed to the soldiers for this reason. The report also mentions blocking the building with fire from heavy machine guns (attached ones, as the battalion did not have its own 'Maxims'). The engineers made their dangerous trip several times until they had collected three 120–150kg charges of TNT each. The garrison was deafened by the resulting explosion and for several minutes did not fire a single shot. The assault groups broke into the building, knocking the enemy out with small-arms fire and grenades. In the 13th Guards Rifle Division's report the result of the attack was that 'half of the building has been blown up and several dozen automatic riflemen have been destroyed'.[25] Losses were twenty-three men killed and twenty-nine wounded. Aside from all of this, this shows the collapse of the very idea of blocking detachments in urban warfare. In the units pressed against the Volga they became the reserve employed for carrying out ongoing tasks. At the same time, one may assume that in 1944 it was considered incorrect to describe such an obviously inappropriate use of a blocking detachment.

However, it proved impossible to change the situation in the Soviets favour through the gradual pouring in of scanty reserves. This was the same as trying to put out a fire with buckets and bringing up the water by hand. By this time the idea had ripened with the command to launch a powerful counterblow into the flank of the enemy group of forces that had driven a wedge to the train station and Mamaev hill. At 18.00 on 18 September the *front* headquarters issued Order No. 122, in which Chuikov was given the following mission:

The commander of the 62nd Army, upon forming a shock group in the area of Mamaev hill of no less than three rifle divisions and one tank brigade, is to launch an attack in the direction of the north-western outskirts of Stalingrad with the task of: destroying the enemy in this area. The mission for the day: to destroy the enemy in the city of Stalingrad, while securely holding the line Rynok – Orlovka – Height 138.0 – Height 98.9 – the north-western and western outskirts of the city of Stalingrad.[26]

In order to carry out the planned operation, the fresh 95th Rifle Division was to be transferred to the 62nd Army at 18.00 on 18 September. The division was to be crossed over the Volga during the night of 18/19 September in order to concentrate in the 'Red October' area by 05.00. The division was initially designated for the group of forces to the north of the city, but was rerouted to the 62nd Army. The northern group of forces and the 62nd Army had been closely connected since the first days of the fighting for the city. The northern group of forces became the chief source of reserves for parrying crises in the city's defence. What is of interest is that in the introductory part of the order Yeremenko laid out an exceedingly curious motivation as to the necessity of a counterblow:

> Under attacks by the Stalingrad Front's formations, which had gone over to a general offensive to the south, the enemy is suffering heavy losses along the line Kuz'michi – Sukhaya Mechetka *Balka* – Akatovka. For the purpose of opposing our northern group of forces, the enemy is removing a number of units and formations from the Stalingrad – Voroponovo area and transferring them through Gumrak to the north.[27]

Thus Yeremenko's order addressed to Chuikov was not an isolated step within the framework of a narrow task of overcoming the crisis in the city's defence. It was a move in the command's game along with the 1st Guards, 24th and 66th Armies. On the one hand, the 62nd Army was supposed to attack the enemy group of forces that had been weakened (in the opinion of the *front's* intelligence units) by the removal of reserves. On the other hand, the army was supposed to prevent by a powerful counterblow the transfer of reserves from Stalingrad against the northern group of forces' attack. Unfortunately, by the time Chuikov received Yeremenko's order it was all over for the attack by the northern group of forces. There will be more about this later. There was also no redistribution of the Sixth Army's forces between the 'land bridge' and the troops in Stalingrad. Quite the opposite, Paulus was moving up the 24th Panzer Division, received from Hoth, into the centre of the city in order to strengthen the LI Corps' formations which were quite worn down. But, fortunately, both Chuikov and Yeremenko had more sense than to throw in their reserves for an attack toward the northern group of forces. Moreover, the 95th Rifle Division's 241st Rifle Regiment was intelligently left behind in the 62nd Army's reserve. On the whole, one may say that Order No. 122 took into account to a significant degree the interests of the defence of Stalingrad. The realization of its tenets would undoubtedly have made the life of the city's defender's easier.

Within a few hours after receiving Yeremenko's order, the commander of the 62nd Army relayed it down the chain of command, detailing the forces for carrying out the assigned task. Order No. 151, which was issued by the *front* headquarters at 23.50 on 18 September, defined the actions of the army's forces for the next few days. Chuikov's overall plan was 'to attack from the area of Height 102 in the general direction of the train station and to cut off and destroy the enemy who had penetrated into the central part of the city'. The 62nd Army's commander planned 'Cannaes' – attacks along converging axes against the flanks of the enemy who had broken into the central part of the city. The 95th Rifle Division, a regiment from the 13th Guards Rifle Division and the 137th Tank Brigade were to be included in the northern shock group. The southern shock group, consisting of the 42nd Rifle Brigade and the remnants of the 244th Rifle Division, were to attack towards it. Chuikov, who had recently been appointed commander of the 62nd Army, was full of optimism and the desire to achieve a decisive result during the first days of his occupancy of the post of commander. However, in reality his Order No. 151 had become outdated at the moment of its appearance: by 18 September the 42nd Rifle Brigade had been surrounded and had fallen back to the mouth of the Tsaritsa River. One can only rate the brigade's ability to attack after this as quite doubtful. A second problem was the Germans' capture of Height 102.0, which it was practically impossible to bypass in an attack on the train station.

However, Order No. 151 called for 'the 95th Rifle Division to attack from Height 102.0 toward the machine-tractor station with the following mission: to destroy the enemy in the attack zone and by the close of the day to capture the north-western part of the city of Stalingrad'.[28] I should point out the formulation 'from Height 102.0', that is, the order directly assumed the capture of Mamaev hill by Soviet forces. Actually, it was maintained in the 13th Guards Rifle Division's evening operational report of 18 September that the 39th Guards Rifle Regiment was occupying defensive positions 'along the line of Height 102.0'.[29] In the combat order by the commander of the 112th Rifle Division for 18 September the task of the 416th Rifle Regiment is indicated as 'to defend the north-eastern slopes of Height 102.0'. That is, the 112th Rifle Division was not aspiring to capture Mamaev hill with its own units. This was only a claim by the 39th Guards Rifle Regiment. Having failed to take into account the actual situation on Height 102.0, Chuikov's headquarters was now issuing essentially unrealizable orders.

The 'single tank brigade' mentioned in the *front* commander's order became the 137th Tank Brigade. It received orders to counter-attack along the western slopes of Mamaev hill. However, it may be called a tank 'brigade' only at a stretch – it contained only ten T-60 tanks. In all, it numbered 764 men. The beginning of the offensive was set for 12.00 on 19 September. Simultaneously with the preparations for a counter-attack and the arrival of fresh forces, the 62nd Army was getting rid of units that were no longer combat-capable, but which were being in danger of being destroyed: the remnants of the 87th and 315th Rifle Divisions were being moved to the left bank of the Volga.

The attack against the densely drawn-up enemy's shock wedge might have been successful given the presence of tanks. Had Chuikov's planned counter-attack been supported by only a single full-strength tank brigade, then it might have had a chance of success. Without tanks, a counter-attack by the forces of even a full-strength division could not meet expectations. By the way, the 133rd Tank Brigade's KV tanks in the city centre had been formally subordinated to the 137th Tank Brigade, but it proved impossible to take them away from Rodimtsev. Although formally attached to the 137th Tank Brigade, they remained in the centre of Stalingrad.

The Soviet counterblow began at noon on 19 September. The 137th Tank Brigade's motorized rifle battalion attacked as infantry and, as was noted in the brigade's report, 'As a result of insufficient preparation and the absence of smooth operations as riflemen, and not employing infantry tactics, the battalion suffered heavy losses and did not carry out its assigned task.'[30] The second battalion operated in the same spirit. The attack by the 137th Tank Brigade made no impression on the Germans, and the following was said of it in the daily report: 'The right flank of the 389th Infantry Division was attacked at 11.30 by infantry and four tanks. Following the destruction of three tanks by artillery, the enemy infantry fell back.'[31]

The 95th Rifle Division was to be committed into the fighting following a 40km forced march from Zaplavnoe station (to the east of Stalingrad). The division's 90th and 161st Rifle Regiments had concentrated on the western shore of the Volga by 05.00 on 19 September in the area of the 'Red October' factory. As early as 08.15 the division received orders to move up to the jumping-off point for an attack on Height 102.0. There had practically been no time to prepare for the attack and the divisional artillery, rear services and signals troops had fallen behind. Nonetheless, at 12.00 the 90th Rifle Regiment went onto the attack on Mamaev hill in the first echelon.

These are facts which raise no doubts. However, further on questions arise. In a report on the division's activities and the morning report for 20 September, which was signed by the division commander, Colonel V.A. Gorishnyi himself, it is maintained that Height 102.0 had been taken and the position of the 161st Rifle Regiment's third battalion is noted as 'the crest of Height 102.0'. It was written about two of the 90th Rifle Regiment's battalions that they were located along the 'slopes' of the height. However, the problem is that the enemy's documents do not indicate such a radical change of situation. The only thing noted was that the 295th Infantry Division's units beat off several attacks.

Another riddle is the type of losses: the 90th Rifle Regiment reported 48 killed and 1,135 wounded for 19 September, which is quite a strange correlation between those killed and wounded. Yet another piece of evidence can be found in the 13th Guards Rifle Division's morning report for 20 September: '... the 95th Rifle Division, which according to the order, was to attack to the south-west, has not yet passed through the 39th Guards Rifle Regiment's combat order and is still located behind the regiment.'[32] At the same time, there is an entry in the LI Corps' report on the results of the day for 19 September: 'According to the testimony of defectors and radio intercepts by the Red 62nd Army, we became aware of preparations for an attack at 11.00 between Height 102 and the air strip, and at 10.30 this offensive was foiled by an artillery attack.'[33] The chronology of events coincides – 11.00 Berlin time is 12.00 Moscow time. There is also the mention in the 137th Tank Brigade's report of the actions of its neighbour: 'The 95th Rifle Division's 161st Rifle Regiment, which came under heavy mortar and automatic rifle fire, suffered heavy losses, without advancing forward at all.'[34] All of this enables us to put forward the supposition that on 19 September the 95th Rifle Division's 90th Rifle Regiment (and most likely both regiments) came under enemy artillery fire while still in its jumping-off positions, which were behind the 39th Guards Rifle Regiment's lines, and suffered significant losses in wounded and concussed. This disorganized the attack. It required several hours for the unit to put itself back in order, after which it nevertheless attempted to renew the attack, and the Germans noted activity along this sector during the evening hours: 'At 17.20 along the 516th and 517th Infantry Regiments' sectors a new attack was beaten back, which was preceded by a powerful fire preparation.' As a result, Gorishnyi's staff preferred to report at least a partial success, assuming it could be made up for later. At the same time, they undoubtedly overrated their forces and underrated the sturdiness of the positions occupied by the enemy.

The very possibility of taking Mamaev hill by a 'cavalry attack' arouses great doubts in light of the structures on its top. They usually speak of 'cisterns,' but this doesn't convey their true nature. Later, Captain N. Aksyonov, from the 284th Rifle Regiment, had a chance to see these structures in January 1943. He described them in an interview with Mints's[35] commission:

> The walls were made of concrete and up to a metre thick, while on the outside they were sprinkled with earth in such a way that you got the impression that it was not a cistern, but a hill. There were two such hills, divided by partitions and there was water there earlier. A lot of embrasures had been built in these cisterns, which it was difficult to get into. This was an entire pillbox, modified by the Germans for firing with artillery. There were no less than 20 machine guns there.[36]

It is also clear that these pillboxes made out of water cisterns were excellent observation posts. The storming of the height, atop which such 'cisterns' stood, would be a difficult task even with artillery support, and in its absence appears to be impossible.

On the night of 19/20 September the 95th Rifle Division received ammunition and a battalion of anti-tank troops and a reconnaissance company crossed the Volga. This enabled the attacks to be resumed. On 20 September the commander of the 161st Rifle Regiment, I.V. Rudnev, was killed on the southern slopes of Mamaev hill. This might be a tragic accident, or due to a desire to personally lead one's troops into battle. Furthermore, the 95th Rifle Division's next operational report notes an advance south of Height 102.0 to the approaches to the city quarters south of Mamaev hill. That is, having announced a success on the first day of fighting, the 95th Rifle Division's headquarters was forced to 'develop' it. However, only 'a few forays' in the area of Height 102.0 were noted in the German reports.

It makes sense, however, to put forward a contending assumption: untruthful reports on the situation from the German side. If only the 295th Infantry Division had been statically at its positions, then this would appear sufficiently convincing. However, in the course of two nights, from 20–21 and 21–22 September, the 295th Infantry Division's elements were being relieved by the 24th Panzer Division, which had arrived from the XLVIII Panzer Corps and which was preparing for an attack against the workers' settlements. This decision was motivated by the desire to concentrate the efforts of the 295th Infantry Division on the offensive to the east, in the direction of the Volga. The commanders of the 24th Panzer Division's regiments had no interest whatsoever in covering the neighbouring corps' infantry. Thus the fact of taking up positions namely on Height 102.0 (it was occupied by the 24th Panzer Division's motorcycle battalion) is a weighty argument in favour of the fact that during these days Mamaev hill remained in German hands.

The following question might be asked: why did the commanders of the 13th Guards and 95th Rifle Divisions lie regarding the capture of the height? As to that, one may cite the following example. There is the following entry in the 13th Guards Rifle Division's war diary: 'In the fighting on 20.9 in the area of Height 102.0 a German soldier was captured from the 2nd Company/1st Battalion/267th Infantry Regiment/94th Infantry Division, who testified …'[37] Let us note – in the area of Mamaev hill. The war diary was drawn up after the fact (later events are mentioned in the description of the course of combat operations), but this same prisoner appears in the report by the 13th Guards Rifle Division for 18 September, which was signed by Bel'skii, the division chief of staff: 'A prisoner was taken, who testified: a private from the 2nd Company/2nd Battalion/267th Infantry

Regiment/94th Infantry Division.'[38] In reality, the soldiers of the 92nd Rifle Brigade took a prisoner from the 94th Infantry Division and sent him to the 13th Guards Rifle Division for the purpose of sending him to army headquarters. This is clearly stated in the 92nd Rifle Regiment's report for 18 September: 'An enemy prisoner from the 94th Infantry Division was taken, who was sent to army headquarters and by mistake turned over to the 13th Guards Rifle Division.'[39] The XLVIII Panzer Corps' 94th Infantry Division was at that moment unambiguously located to the south of the Tsaritsa River and was fighting against the 92nd Rifle Brigade outside the zone of Rodimtsev's division. In the 13th Guards Rifle Division they registered the prisoner as theirs and affirmed this in documents. Why was this done? After all, this would disorient the command as to the real state of affairs regarding an actual enemy division. Even Rodimtsev mentions in his memoirs that 'a soldier from the German 94th Infantry Division's 267th Infantry Regiment' was captured, although without openly maintaining that he had been captured by someone from his division.[40] The problem is that commanders at the tactical level could be confused in good conscience or consciously misinform the higher levels without fully realizing the consequences of their reports. We are dealing with just such an incident concerning the capture of Height 102.0.

Despite the 95th Rifle Division's doubtful achievements in the area of Mamaev hill, the commitment of a fresh formation enabled Chuikov to attend to restoring the integrity of his divisions in the centre of the city. In that same Order No. 151, Chuikov issued orders for an attack in the direction of the 'Stalingrad I' railway station to the 39th Guards Rifle Regiment to rescue Fedoseev's battalion, which had been defending it in isolation. Simultaneously, the 112th Rifle Division received a new assignment. The formation's task became the capture of the railway bridge over the Long Ravine. The idea was quite simple: to seize the bridge by an attack from the east along the ravine by the forces of the 112th Rifle Division and thus open a road to the railway station along the tracks for the 39th Guards Rifle Regiment. The 112th Rifle Division turned over its positions in the area of Height 102.0 and as early as 18 September was being moved to the area of the Long and Steep *Balki* along the approaches to the central part of Stalingrad. Here, as early as the second half of the day, it attempted to break through to the bridge and was fighting in the area of Artillery Street. Colonel Yermolkin's division had no success in achieving its assigned task on either 18 or 19 September. However, the division's losses may also be rated as moderate: 73 men killed and 125 wounded.[41] However, the division's strength was not great: on the morning of 19 September, despite having received reinforcements, all three of the 112th Rifle Division's regiments numbered only 644 men.[42] That is, losses accounted for up to a third of the units' strength.

By around 20 September the German divisions which were taking part in the assault on Stalingrad were far from being in the best condition, as a result of losses suffered. In the attachments to the Sixth Army's war diary there is a review of the condition of the army's formations on 20 September 1942, with the following data regarding the LI Corps' divisions.[43]

71st Infantry Division – seven infantry battalions (four weak and three exhausted), with the engineer battalion spent. The division is fit for defence;

389th Infantry Division – six infantry battalions (two spent and four weak), with the engineer battalion weak. The division is fit for defence;

295th Infantry Division – seven infantry battalions (two spent, four weak, one exhausted), with the engineer battalion spent. The division is fit for defence.

Despite the synonymous evaluation that 'The division is fit for defence', the 71st and 295th Infantry Divisions were given offensive tasks. The OKH signals officer with the Sixth Army, who on 23 September 1942 visited the troops in Stalingrad (295th Infantry Division, 71st Infantry Division, 194th Infantry Regiment, and the combined first and second battalions of the 194th Infantry Regiment and forward companies), was even more eloquent in his evaluation. He wrote:

> Both divisions, the 71st and 295th infantry, are very good, although they have been weakened to an extreme degree by losses, particularly among the infantry. The losses are high even during periods of quiet, while combat capability is falling from day to day. At present the strength of the rifle companies averages 10–15 soldiers. Losses are particularly high in officers, with a major shortfall in NCOs and experienced soldiers. Reinforcements are not top notch regarding experience, training and endurance in many cases. If the group commander dies,[44] in many cases the soldiers run back and only the personal intervention of officers brings them back to the front line. Without assault guns, these anaemic units, despite the self-sacrifice of individual soldiers, will be able to advance forward only with difficulty. The soldiers blame the command for the absence of assault guns in sufficient quantities. The soul of the battle are the regimental commanders, who personally lead their regiments into battle, although in practice these are already reinforced companies with a strength of 150–180 men. The battalion commanders in many cases are not up to the demands of the position. Because of the constant street fighting, which exceeds their capabilities; the soldiers are very tired and have become stupefied.[45]

If one moves from qualitative evaluations to quantitative ones, then the losses by the formations' which in one way or another were mobilized for the storming of Stalingrad, may be characterized by the following figures (see table).

Table 18: Losses by the Sixth Army's Formations Taking Part in the First Assault on Stalingrad, 11–20 September 1942.[46]

	Killed	Wounded	Missing in Action	Sick	Total
LI Corps	2	6	–	–	8
Headquarters					
295th Infantry Division	233	864	30	3	1,130
71st Infantry Division	188	763	20	10	981
389th Infantry Division	155	566	12	5	738

The breakthrough to the centre of the city and the capture of Mamaev hill cost the LI Corps' formations dearly, but they continued to assign them offensive tasks.

At the same time, they planned to 'develop' the 95th Rifle Division's 'success' on Mamaev hill at the *front* level. At 18.00 on 20 September Lieutenant Colonel N.F. Batyuk's 284th Rifle Division was to be subordinated to Chuikov. The formation was assigned an extremely ambitious mission: 'The division is to be employed for launching the main attack from Height 102.0 in the direction of the machine-tractor station, two kilometres east of Lesoposadochnaya.'[47] The machine-tractor station and Lesoposadochnaya were located on the outskirts of Stalingrad, halfway from Mamaev hill to the Tsaritsa River, in the rear of the German group of forces in the centre of the city.

Meanwhile, the task of 'developing' the success became more than illusory. Having taken up positions in the area of Mamaev hill, the 24th Panzer Division had a ration strength on 21 September of 11,756 men (15,143 men, counting attached units). In the review of the state of the Sixth Army's formations on 20 September, the following was written of the 24th Panzer Division: four panzer grenadier battalions (two average and two spent), one powerful motorcycle battalion, with the engineer battalion spent.[48] The division's combat capability was designated by the straightforward phrase: 'The division is fit for any offensive missions.' It's not surprising that the motorcycle battalion, which was designated as 'strong', occupied defensive position on the key Height 102.0. The division's tanks (twenty-two vehicles) had been gathered together for counter-attacks. Artillery observers had been placed in expectation of this in the cisterns on Height 102.0 Jason Mark, in his book on the 24th Panzer Division, gives the testimony of one of them, Lieutenant Nuschke, who wrote about his close proximity to the enemy – 'at the distance of a grenade toss'. Soviet snipers were also a constant danger. As an example, Nuschke cites the fact that the lenses of his stereo scope had been shot out by accurate fire. Nonetheless, the observation position allowed for an excellent view. As early as the night of 20/21 September the attacks on Height 102.0 were repulsed by the German artillery, partially in their jumping-off positions.

They did not know about this relief in the Soviet headquarters and the cogwheels of decisions adopted continued to turn. The 284th Rifle Division, which had been transferred to Chuikov, was a division hastily restored in the rear, typical of the struggle for Stalingrad. Following fighting along the Bryansk Front, it had been pulled into the reserve and was being brought up to strength in the town of Krasnoufimsk, in the Sverdlovsk Oblast'. The 284th Rifle Division had been transferred to the area of Lapshinskaya station by rail in the middle of September. From Lapshinskaya it was moved by motor transport to the Srednyaya Akhtuba area. The future famous sniper Vasilii Zaitsev[49] later recalled his first impression of Stalingrad: 'If you look from beyond the Volga, you see a tongue of flame here, and then in another place, which later coalesces into one, forming an enormous glow of fire.'[50] The 284th Rifle Division's 1043rd Rifle Regiment crossed the Volga on the night of 20/21 September and concentrated in the 'Red October' area. The simplest thing was to decide what to do with it – they pulled the regiment back into the army reserve.

Accordingly, the 241st Rifle Regiment, which had earlier been in the reserve, returned to the 95th Rifle Division on 21 September, although its artillery was running late (the artillery regiment arrived only on the night of 21/22 September). According to the division's operational reports, the 241st Rifle Regiment was not committed into the fighting on 21 September.

On the night of 21/22 September the 284th Rifle Division's 1045th and 1047th Regiments, a machine-gun battalion and small subunits crossed the river. As was mentioned earlier, it had been ordered to employ the division for a counter-attack against the Germans' flank from the as-yet untaken Height 102.0. The storming of Mamaev hill, which was occupied by strong elements of the 24th Panzer Division and supported by its tanks, would inevitably have become quite a costly affair for the 284th Rifle Division. The revelation of the fact that Height 102.0 remained in enemy hands and was being securely held by him could lead to extremely unpleasant consequences for Chuikov, who had commanded the 62nd Army for only a week. However, at that moment the German 295th Infantry Division, which had been regrouped from Height 102.0, began an attack under the plaintive howling of the 'Stukas' in the direction of the Volga quay. The dive bomber attacks and artillery preparation continued from 05.00 to 06.20 on 22 September. Although the German infantry advanced with difficulty, a threat arose to the central crossing. As early as 09.45 on 22 September Chuikov issued an order instructing the 284th Rifle Division to attack along the Volga.

At the same time, one cannot help but note that there was no instantaneous collapse of the front in the centre of Stalingrad during the 295th Infantry Division's attack. This is hardly surprising: at that moment the 295th Infantry Division was already weak and, as was already mentioned earlier, the conclusion on its capabilities was unambiguous: 'The division is fit for defence.'[51] This was partially compensated for by artillery: on 22 September the LI Corps expended 320 tons of ammunition,[52] which was quite a large amount, a total of 670 210mm shells being fired on Soviet positions in the city that day. However, the fact that it was planned to continue improving the 62nd Army's positions in the centre of Stalingrad played into the hands of the 13th Guards Rifle Division. Accordingly, during the second half of the day on 21 September, having turned over its positions to the 112th and 95th Rifle Divisions, the 39th Guards Rifle Regiment returned to the 13th Guards Rifle Division and took up a defence in the second echelon behind the 42nd Guards Rifle Regiment. Besides this, according to its war diary, on 21 September the 13th Guards Rifle Division received 898 reinforcements, which were distributed among the units and committed into the fighting.[53] This regrouping and the reinforcements strengthened the positions of Rodimtsev's division before the storm which was just about to break forth.

Despite a hurricane of fire and air support, it was only in the middle of the day that two of the 295th Infantry Division's regiments advanced toward the embankment road (that is, not even toward the Volga, while this took place not along the 34th Guards Rifle Regiment's sector, but that of the weak 112th Rifle Division). In the LI Corps' daily report, the following was noted: 'Because of the extremely stubborn resistance in the barricaded buildings and earthen bunkers, the bloody battle with flamethrowers and concentrated explosive devices, and with good support from assault guns and engineers, did not yield any result.'[54]

The 34th Guards Rifle Regiment of Rodimtsev's division, which had fortified itself in the city, came under attack. According to the division's operational report, the breakthrough finally occurred to the area of 9 January Square and the Long Ravine, along the 13th Guards Rifle Division's flank. According to the operational report, there remained 'up to 40 active bayonets' in the regiment.[55] The 13th Guards Rifle Division's overall losses for 22 September are listed in the war diary as 160 men killed and 370 wounded.[56] Fifteen heavy machine guns (of the thirty-six on hand as of 15 September) were lost immediately, along with twenty-six light machine guns. However, it's most likely that this data is incomplete.

In his interview with the Mints Commission, Rodimtsev described the course of the fighting as follows: 'At approximately 10.00 in the morning on the 22nd, the enemy attacked, crushed the forward edge, put six guns out of action, and captured 9 January Square. Here he suppressed a couple of anti-tank rifles and anti-tank guns and reached Artillery Street.' Artillery Street is in the area of the 'Metiz' factory, beyond the Long *Balka*, on the approaches to the oil syndicate's reservoirs. Rodimtsev threw in all his reserves to help the 34th Guards Rifle Regiment and, as one can judge from the cited German document, achieved an undoubted defensive success. As was mentioned in the operational report at 24.00 on 22 September, there remained the following in the 13th Guards Rifle Division's units:

34th Guards Rifle Regiment – 48 active bayonets;
39th Guards Rifle Regiment – 135 active bayonets;
42nd Guards Rifle Regiment – 298 active bayonets.

The units on the right bank of the Volga disposed of eight 76mm and eleven 45mm guns, and eight heavy and twenty-nine light machine guns. During the night Rodimtsev received about 500 reinforcements. According to a document that was compiled later (in January 1943), the 34th Guards Rifle Regiment alone received 1,388 reinforcements during 23–24 September. That is, it was completely reconstituted.

Despite its limited success, the German offensive of 22 September put the finish to the unification of the 13th Guards Rifle Division's elements in the centre of Stalingrad into a single whole. The 62nd Army's chief of staff, N.I. Krylov, evaluated the situation as follows: 'The hope remained all the way up to 21 September, that one of the street counter-attacks would enable the 42nd Regiment to link up with its first battalion.'[57] Under the threat of being turned and enveloped, Fedoseev's battalion fell back from the area of the train station toward the so-called 'nail factory' (the 'Red Picket' factory, called this because of its warehouse of nails), Gogol' Street and the department store. Fedoseev's strongpoint and headquarters were located in the department store. On 21 September his battalion had been semi-surrounded. On 22 September communications with the 42nd Guards Rifle Regiment's first battalion were lost. Attempts to learn of its fate by sending out scouts were unsuccessful. Rodimtsev later wrote about the battalion's fate in the area of the train station:

On one of the overcast October days a man, covered with wounds and overgrown with stubble, made his way to the left bank of the Volga. By a miracle he managed to make his way through the front line from the area of the train station. He reported that the first rifle battalion no longer existed. All of its soldiers and commanders died the death of the valiant in an unequal fight.[58]

The 13th Guards Rifle Division reported forty-three 'knocked out and burned' enemy tanks for 22 September.[59] In his memoirs, chief of staff N.I. Krylov also writes about the destruction of 'more than thirty' enemy tanks by the forces of the 13th Guards Rifle Division. How well founded is this claim? First of all, the participation of 'tanks' seems doubtful – the Sixth Army's tanks were propping up the defence of the 'land bridge' with the XIV Panzer Corps and that of Height 102.0 with the 24th Panzer Division. Thus we must be speaking of assault guns that had been attached to the LI Corps. Second, we now dispose of data from the enemy, so there is something to compare it with. One can put together data on the condition of the 244th and 245th Assault Gun Battalions' park (see table).

From the data shown here it is clear that no sharp reduction in the assault-gun park is observed. Moreover, in the report for 23 September the absence of irreplaceable losses in guns is clearly indicated.[60] In any case, tens of destroyed *Sturmgeschützen* seems a doubtful declaration. One may speak here of between five and ten vehicles.

Table 19: Combat Vehicle Strength of the 244th and 245th Assault Gun Battalions During the Fighting in the Centre of Stalingrad[61]

Date	Status	244th Battalion	245th Battalion
16 September	Combat-ready	7 long, 8 short	10 long, 9 short
	Under repair	2 long, 4 short	6 short
19 September	Combat-ready	6 long, 3 short	9 long, 5 short
	Under repair	3 long, 9 short	1 long, 16 short[62]
20–21 September[63]	Combat-ready	6 long, 3 short	9 long, 5 short
23 September (14.15 hrs)	Combat-ready	6 long, 8 short	8 long, 4 short
	Under repair	3 long, 4 short	2 long, 8 short

As was already stated above, the most dangerous penetration into the Soviet defence, as far as the road along the Volga is concerned, did not take place in the 13th Guards Rifle Division's sector, but in the sector of the neighbouring 112th Rifle Division. Overall, Lieutenant Colonel Yermolkin's division fell so often under German blows so fateful for the 62nd Army that it is hard not to note that the 112th Rifle Division attracted unpleasantness.

As of 24.00 on 21 September the division's units numbered:[64]

the 385th Rifle Regiment's combat strength was 141 men (in all 314 men, including 51 men from Gorokhov's 'composite battalion' and 50 men from a flamethrower company);

the 524th Rifle Regiment's combat strength was 67 men;

the 416th Rifle Regiment's combat strength was 278 men.

The most powerful unit, the 416th Rifle Regiment, was defending with its front facing west along the slopes of Mamaev hill and practically did not participate in the fighting of 22 September. In accordance with an order, on 21 September the 112th Rifle Division continued to attack in the direction of the bridge. The mission for 22 September was also an attack, but they did not have time to begin it, as the German attacks began at 05.30–07.30. Insofar as the jumping-off positions along this sector had been consolidated before the attack and not for holding powerful positions on the defence, these attacks were successful. Two of the 112th Rifle Division's regiments in the areas of the Long and Steep *Balki* were thrown out of their positions and pushed back to the 'asphalt highway' – a road along the Volga. Forty-four combat troops remained in the 385th Rifle Regiment and twenty-seven in the 524th Rifle Regiment.[65] In order to restore the situation here the 13th Guards Rifle Division was forced to activate the veterans of the storming of the State Bank – the blocking battalion and reconnaissance company. This is yet one more example of how in Stalingrad a blocking battalion was employed in a manner complete removed from its initial designation.

The attack and the 34th Rifle Regiment's retreat on 22 September led to the exposure of the 42nd Guards Rifle Regiment's right flank. This led to the encirclement of the 2nd Battalion's fifth company (it broke through to its lines on 23 September). At the same time, a defence facing south was established as early as the night of 22/23 September by the forces of the 39th Guards Rifle Regiment. On the night of 23/24 September there followed the German penetration, which they attempted to repel with their tested reserve from the blocking battalion (reinforced with a company), but unsuccessfully. The Germans had consolidated along the bank of the Volga.

Of course, the most serious argument against a German offensive in the centre of the city was a fresh formation. On 22 September the 284th Rifle Division was moving into the area of the 'Metiz' factory and went over to the attack with the forces of two regiments in the sector along the Volga. To judge from everything, it was precisely at this moment that the 'fiery attack' described in Zaitsev's memoirs took place. The path of the 1047th and 1045th Rifle Regiments' attack ran through a group of the oil syndicate's enormous cisterns along the bank of the Volga. In an interview with the Mints Commission, Zaitsev recalled the recent events: 'There were 12 fuel cisterns there. We captured these cisterns. Then 60 enemy planes took off and began to attack us. They blew up the fuel cisterns and we were covered with fuel. We fell back to the Volga and put out the fire in the water, tore all of the burning clothes off ourselves, remaining only in our striped undershirts, while some were even naked and covered themselves with their capes. With our rifles at the charge, we went into the attack.'[66] According to an operational report, the 284th Rifle Division's casualties for that day were 620 men, including 112 killed.

However, the commitment of the 284th Rifle Division in the area of the oil syndicate did not in and of itself mean an easing of the situation in the centre of the city. It was necessary to reinforce the positions of the 13th Guards Rifle Division, which had been attacked on 22 September. For this, it was decided to employ one regiment from another formation which was in the reserve – Major General F.N. Smekhotvorov's 193rd Rifle Division. The division had suffered heavy losses in the fighting on the Bryansk front in the Voronezh area in July 1942 and had been pulled back into the reserve for refitting in the Kurgan area (Urals Military District). On 8 August the division set about receiving reinforcements and equipment. During the course of a month the division received reinforcements and was earnestly engaged in training and knocking the units into shape. The division's strength was raised to nearly authorized levels – it left Kurgan with 10,655 men. The backbone of the privates and NCOs consisted of Russians and Ukrainians (5,861 and 1,338 men respectively). There were a lot of Kazakhs – 1,596 men. While still en route the designated station for the 193rd Rifle Division was changed and the trains turned on to the lateral railway to the east of the Volga with the destination of Leninsk. Having unloaded in the Kamyshin area, the 685th Rifle Regiment and an anti-tank battalion were moved to Stalingrad by motor transport. On 23 September the division received orders to cross the 685th Rifle Regiment into Stalingrad with the onset of darkness, to be attached to the commander of the 13th Guards Rifle Division. This had already become an 'evil tradition' of the battle of Stalingrad – the commitment of formations into the fighting in detail.

Two of the 685th Rifle Regiments were transported in motor vehicles as far as the area of Srednyaya Akhtuba and then reached the central crossing in the area of Krasnaya Sloboda on the march. The third battalion was moving separately and arrived on the following day, 24 September. The regiment's crossing over the Volga extended over three entire nights. On the night of 23/24 September the second battalion and two companies from the first battalion crossed. On the night of 24/25 September the remaining elements of the first and second battalions of the 685th Rifle Regiment crossed, and it was only on the night of 25/26 September that the third battalion joined them. The first losses were suffered during the crossing: seven men killed and 31 wounded. By this time the crossing was under

German artillery and mortar bombardment and the moorings on the right bank were under fire from 'automatic riflemen' (evidently machine-gun crews in the German-occupied buildings which towered over the bank). The regiment's 76mm battery remained on the left bank of the Volga, which did not favour the conduct of street fighting.

By this time the 13th Guards Rifle Division's right-flank elements had been pushed back to the bank of the Volga, and in places the forward edge was only 300–400m from the river bank. The 685th Rifle Regiment was accordingly given the mission of taking up defence on the right flank of Rodimtsev's division from the Steep *Balka* to the flour-milling factory along the second and third quays. Movement into these positions took place under fire and the 685th Rifle Regiment's first echelon was unable to capture the buildings along the quay. With the arrival of yet another battalion on the following night, the first series of buildings along the quay were recaptured and occupied. The arrival of the third battalion afforded a certain stability for the second echelon's defence, even if only hundreds of metres from the river. To be sure, the reserve immediately began to be tossed about in this critical situation: Rodimtsev removed a company and moved it to the left flank, which had become bared as a result of the collapse of a neighbouring units defence in the area of the mouth of the Tsaritsa River (see below).

Despite the 'stupefaction' of the German soldiers due to endless street fighting, mentioned by the OKH signals officer above, on 24 September the LI Corps nevertheless undertook its latest offensive for the purpose of routing the Soviet units defending south of the 'Stalingrad I' train station, located due north of the Tsaritsa River. As noted in the history of the 71st Infantry Division, a battery of anti-aircraft artillery was to be attached to support the planned offensive on 24 September. One of the reasons for employing anti-aircraft guns was the factor of the availability of shells: 'Anti-aircraft artillery, which disposed of an unlimited amount of ammunition, rendered particularly valuable assistance to the infantry.'[67] Despite the impressive absolute figures on the expenditure of ammunition by the Sixth Army's field artillery, the German command considered the troops' supply of ammunition insufficient. The offensive began at 07.00 on 24 September with vigourous air support. An infantry regiment from the 94th Infantry Division, which had been freed up south of the Tsaritsa River, was sent into the attack together with the 71st Infantry Division. The German attacks encountered the defence's fierce resistance. At that moment the 272nd NKVD Regiment was defending along the sector directly adjacent to the railway, to the south of the train station in the area of the city theatre (the building with the lions). The LI Corps' daily report notes: 'The enemy is putting up stubborn resistance in the stone, multi-storey buildings north of the mouth of the Tsaritsa. There is fierce fighting for every building.' Besides regular units, according to German data 'city militia numbering 80 men and comprised of workers and communists' took part in this fighting. A report on the employment of chemical weapons, introduced into the building following its bombardment by 'tanks', that is, assault guns ('according to military medical assistant Yefrosin'ina, who was at the command post and who was subjected to poisonous substances, chloropicrin was employed') in the storming of the 272nd NKVD Regiment's headquarters refers precisely to the fighting on 24 September. In spite of the serious resistance, the 71st Infantry Division and the regiment from the 94th Infantry Division managed to push back the defenders during the course of the day closer to the mouth of the Tsaritsa River.

On 25 September the fierce fighting at the mouth of the Tsaritsa River continued. As was noted in the LI Corps' daily report, 'We had to burn out several cellars with flamethrowers and blow them up with concentrated charges.'[68] However, resistance began to gradually weaken. On 25 September the 71st Infantry Division took 600 prisoners. The LI Corps' expenditure of ammunition was no longer at a record pace – 222 tons for 25 September (750 tons for the Sixth Army as a whole), although 335 210mm rounds were part of this total.[69] By this time it was already obvious that the days and hours of the bridgehead in the area of the mouth of the Tsaritsa were numbered. To the credit of the defenders, one should note here that on the night of 25/26 September the evacuation of almost 700 wounded (from the NKVD regiments and the 92nd Rifle Brigade) was organized on armoured launches.[70]

September 25th became to a certain degree a turning point in the fighting in the city centre – the German infantry had broken through to Central Crossing No. 2 (this is confirmed by the 62nd Army's war diary). 27 September is considered the formal date that the crossing ceased to function.[71] Also, the State Bank building was once again captured by the Germans. Rodimtsev's division held only a narrow strip of the Volga bank in its defensive zone, averaging about 500m in width. The division's strongest position at that moment was the complex of NKVD buildings on the corner of 9 January Square. It was bordered on the south by the State Bank, occupied by the Germans, and from the north by the 'Railway Workers' House' and the 'G'-shaped building, also occupied by the Germans.

The significance of the buildings commanding the Volga was noted straightforwardly in the 42nd Guards Rifle Regiment's war diary:

The enemy controlled the right and left banks of the Volga from the upper stories of these buildings, as well as the sector where our subunits were located. Movement during daylight within the defensive sector, as well as the carrying out of works, was linked to great losses among the rank and file, for the enemy, upon noticing any kind of movement or work, if he didn't get you with machine gun fire, would let loose with mortars and artillery, not with scattered fire, but short and frequent fire onslaughts.[72]

Supply was carried out across the Volga, but usually not along the 13th Guards Rifle Division's defensive sector – the 42nd Guards Rifle Regiment received ammunition and food from the 62nd Army's crossing near the 'Red October' factory, 7km (!) from its positions. It's not surprising that as early as 27 September the 42nd Guards Rifle Regiment attempted to take the 'Railway Workers' House' by storm with the forces of its second battalion, but unsuccessfully. The operation to capture this target would stretch out for many weeks.

Along its right flank, in the area of the Long *Balka*, Rodimtsev's division as yet maintained communications with the 62nd Army's main forces (which enabled them to move the 7km for supplies). The division's task was formulated in an order by Chuikov as follows: 'while holding the occupied area in the central part of the city – to successively destroy the enemy in the buildings captured by him'.[73] The capture and retention of 'Pavlov's building' on 9 January Square, which later became widely known, was a local success in this endeavour.

For the Germans the fighting in the city centre consisted for almost the entire period of a combination of offense and defence. At the same time as the Germans were attacking along the right flank of the LI Corps in the area of the mouth of the Tsaritsa, fighting continued along the left flank for Mamaev hill. The initial inaccurate reports about the true advance gave rise to an entire heap of problems. When the chief of the 62nd Army's artillery was ordered on 23 September 'to support the 95th Rifle Division's offensive with artillery fire from the central sector and the army group's guards mortar regiment', the artillery troops fired on the line 'attacked' by the 95th Rifle Division, that is, the central blocks along the line of the Long *Balka*, with almost zero results from the point of view of hitting the enemy's defence system on Mamaev hill.

The most productive attack in the area of Mamaev hill was undertaken on the night of 24/25 September. The following was written about this in the LI Corps' daily report: 'At 22.30 on 24.9 a powerful enemy attacked west of Marker No. 102 and penetrated into the defence. The penetration was blocked and at dawn the reinforced 26th Panzer Grenadier Regiment counter-attacked.' The counter-attack by the 24th Panzer Division's motorized infantry regiment enabled them to stabilize the situation by 10.00 (Berlin time) on 25 September.

The 24th Panzer Division's losses in the defence of Mamaev hill may be described as quite telling: on 23 September the division lost 32 men killed and 122 wounded, on 24 September 25 men killed, 76 wounded and one missing in action.[74] The 95th Rifle Division suffered heavy losses in numerous attacks in the area of Mamaev hill. According to a report by the formation's headquarters, from 19 through 25 September the division's units lost 5,186 men in killed and wounded.[75] The 241st Rifle Regiment, which was committed later, lost the most – 1,832 men.

A compilation of the reports and maps of the 284th Rifle Division's position reveals the doubtful nature of the 95th Rifle Division's reports about the capture of Mamaev hill. If the 95th Rifle Division's regiments had actually been fighting along the approaches to the Long Ravine, which separated Mamaev hill from the city centre, the 284th Rifle Division would not have been required to bend its right flank facing west during its attack along the Volga. However, on the 284th Rifle Division's maps the flank is bent, moreover, as far as an easily noticed reference point on a map or aerial photos – the pool with fuel oil in the area of the oil syndicate's cisterns.

During the night of 25/26 September the regiments of the 100th Jäger (light infantry) Division occupied positions on Mamaev hill in place of the 24th Panzer Division's elements. As regards its condition in the overall evaluation of the Sixth Army's formations on 20 September, the following was noted: the 100th Light Infantry Division – four strong jäger battalions, one strong Croatian battalion and an average engineer battalion. The conclusion on the division's condition corresponded to these evaluations: 'The division is fit for any offensive tasks.' To attempt to push it off its positions on Mamaev hill was almost a more difficult task than against the 24th Panzer Division's motorized infantry and motorcyclists.

The OKH signals officers attached to the Sixth Army wrote on 25 September what Stalingrad was like at that time:

The entire city has been heavily damaged and it is only in the suburbs that the buildings are partially fit for habitation. The tall buildings are all burnt out, although the cellars are still fit for use. The streets leading from west to east are partially enfiladed by artillery from the eastern bank, while the streets running north to south are under infantry fire from the parts of the city still occupied by the enemy. There are fires in many places, while the oil reservoirs have burnt out, but continue to burn here and there.[76]

On 25 September the strength of the 62nd Army's formations was as follows:[77]

13th Guards Rifle Division – 6,906 men;
95th Rifle Division – 5,455 men;
112th Rifle Division – 2,557 men;
193rd Rifle Division – 10,273 men;
284th Rifle Division – 7,648 men;
10th Rifle Brigade – 191 men;
42nd Rifle Brigade – 1,049 men;
92nd Rifle Brigade – 2,562 men;
115th Rifle Brigade – 4,023 men;
124th Rifle Brigade – 4,218 men;
149th Rifle Brigade – 3,119 men;
2nd Motorized Rifle Brigade – 883 men;
20th Motorized Rifle Brigade – 418 men;
9th Motorized Rifle Brigade – 705 men;
38th Motorized Rifle Brigade – 1,119 men.

By 25 September the fresh 13th Guards and 95th Rifle Divisions, which had been committed into the battle at the beginning of the assault, were now pretty worn out, although they had not lost their combat capability. However, the 284th Rifle Division, which was in good shape and capable of appreciably influencing the situation, still remained in Chuikov's hands. The 193rd Rifle Division also remained practically untouched.

The losses suffered in both the city itself and while attacking toward it, exerted an increasingly great influence on the condition of the German forces. The reserve divisions and the 'Far Easterners' time after time tore a strip off the German formations and by September 1942 quantity had turned into quality.

September 26th was the first day when the 62nd Army did not attack. In the evening Chuikov once again assigned offensive tasks to the 95th, 284th and 13th Guards Rifle Divisions, the 260th NKVD Regiment and the 137th Tank Brigade. This was most likely linked to the arrival of a new division. The enemy had its own plans in this regard: a new assault on the city was set for 27 September.

In summing up the results of the fighting for the central part of Stalingrad, one should first of all pay attention to the dilemma facing the Soviet command between the operational reaction to the changing situation in the city and the attempts to radically alter it. The first could be attempted by strengthening the city's defence and by transferring reserves to the 62nd Army. The realization of the second variant assumed the rout of the attacking enemy forces through a powerful counterblow. Despite the forced necessity of stabilizing the situation through the constant flow of reserves (and reinforcements), Yeremenko and Chuikov were drawn to the second variant and up to a certain moment sought to radically change the situation in the 62nd Army's zone and to inflict a major defeat on the enemy assaulting the city. The desire was logical and explicable, but it was first of all unsupported from the point of view of the correct choice of the operational variant. The mistaken evaluation of the situation of one's own forces in the area of Mamaev hill knowingly doomed any attempts to launch a counterblow against the Germans in the city centre to failure. At the same time, disposing of enemy documents, one cannot but admit that the LI Corps' 71st and 295th Infantry Divisions were a feasible target for a counterblow (despite the oppressive German superiority in artillery that hung over the defenders of Stalingrad). Quite the opposite, having occupied Mamaev hill, the 24th Panzer Division proved to be a 'tough nut'. The incorrect evaluation of the situation in the area of Mamaev hill led to failure and heavy losses for the fresh 95th Rifle Division, as well as the fouled up commitment of the 137th Tank Brigade and 284th Rifle Division into the fighting. The Soviet command's inclination for counterblows from the area of the 'Red October' factory can be explained to some degree by the proximity to the 62nd Army's main crossing.

It's difficult to call following the 'Mamaev hill' strategy a success. Positions were lost (particularly by the 42nd Rifle Brigade), which had been held since the Germans' first push on the city. Fedoseev's battalion from the 13th Guards Rifle Division, which had initially occupied a good position, was destroyed. The 13th Guards Rifle Division's scattered centres of resistance in the centre were eventually pushed back to the Volga with the partial blocking of supply through the capture of the commanding buildings (the 'L-shaped building' and the 'Railway Workers' House'). The fresh 95th Rifle Division had been ruined. The situation was made more acute by the 'roughness' in the conduct of the defensive operation, particularly in the crossing of the 13th Guards Rifle Division along a broad front, without concentrating efforts in the centre of Stalingrad, as well as the problems of supplying and supporting units in the city with artillery. For example, at the height of the fighting for the city centre, the 13th Guards Rifle Division's artillery regiment was firing on the area of the oil cisterns (to the south-east of Mamaev hill).

In retrospect, possessing information on the Germans' artillery 'fist', one must admit that a strategy of strengthening the city's defence through counterblows of tactical significance was more rational from the point of view of its practical realization. As practice showed, the resources available to the troops in sufficient quantity in the form of KVs and T-34s were quite applicable in urban warfare. At the same time, we should say outright that the picture of units bleeding themselves dry at the mouth of the Tsaritsa and in the city centre, alongside the unsuccessful attempts to attack Mamaev hill, calls forth contradictory feelings. The 'Stalingrad I' train station was just as important an objective as Mamaev hill from the point of view of controlling the central part of Stalingrad. All the more so as it was possible to take and hold the train station by a 'cavalry lunge'. The redirecting of the troops to the area of Central Crossing No. 2, closer to the mouth of the Tsaritsa, would have offered good prospects from the point of view of a strategy of exhausting the enemy in defence. This area again offers prospects from the point of view of command and control, for it was here that the sturdy 'Tsaritsa underground' was located, in which the headquarters of the 62nd Army was initially housed. Upon gathering a shock 'fist' along the approaches to the train station, Chuikov could have remained at his old command post. Of course, at the same time the question remains open as to whether Yeremenko would have agreed to allot reserves without the prospect of radically changing the situation.

There was still one more aspect to the 'Tsartisyn' strategy: cooperation with the forces in the southern part of the city, in the area of the grain elevator. We will speak in the next chapter as to how events developed in the areas south of the Tsaritsa River.

Chapter 14

The First Assault on the City. 13–26 September 1942. To the South of the Tsaritsa River

The symbol of the struggle for the areas of Stalingrad to the south of the Tsaritsa River became the massive concrete structure of the grain elevator, which towered over the surrounding buildings. Paulus even wanted to make it the symbol of the capture of the entire city, and one of the sketches of the proposed 'Stalingrad shield'[1] included an image of the elevator. However, in and of itself the elevator was just one of the episodes of the intense struggle to the south of Stalingrad.

The fighting for the elevator and its surroundings played out in connection with the breakthrough by the Fourth Panzer Army's XLVIII Panzer Corps to the city. One cannot stress enough that the very fact of the prolonged fighting for the elevator was the first consequence of the incorrect selection of priorities by the XLVIII Panzer Corps command. Following the capture of the 'Stalingrad II' train station on 16 September, according to an order from division headquarters, the 24th Panzer Division's tanks moved north toward the bridge across the Tsaritsa River and not to the grey mass of the elevator overlooking the railway toward the east. The bridge over the Tsaritsa was reached and captured intact as early as 16.15 on 15 September. The 24th Panzer Division's decision not to attack to the east enabled a small detachment of soldiers under the command of Senior Lieutenant M.P. Polyakov, from the 10th Rifle Brigade, to take back the elevator which had been occupied by a German forward detachment. The detachment was broken up into three groups. The first group, under the command of Lieutenant Satanovskii, drew the enemy onto it, while the second group under the command of Lieutenant Stepanov sought to turn the elevator from the rear. The third group, under the command of Polyakov himself, attacked from the flank. On the morning of 17 September the remaining Germans on the second floor were wiped out. Before long the defence of the elevator was reinforced, with elements of the 35th Guards Rifle Division and two brigades actually defending it. The defence of a sort of 'fortress', which lasted several days, had begun.

At the same time, one should note that the 24th Panzer Division's main task on 15 September was nevertheless the crushing of the 244th Rifle Division, which had been successfully withstanding the pressure from the German panzer division during the preceding days. The 24th Panzer Division would subsequently be removed from this sector in the area of the 'Stalingrad II' train station and moved to the LI Corps' sector. Thus stories about the division's participation in the fighting for the elevator during the subsequently days are untrue.

One of the props of the defence along the approaches to the elevator was the 133th Tank Brigade's second tank battalion, which included six KV tanks (two of which could not move).[2] The battalion was fighting in Yel'shanka, and then fell back to the area of the elevator. Here all six KVs were lost in the fighting with the XLVIII Panzer Corps by 17 September 1942 and the battalion's remaining rank and file crossed over the Volga. The 133rd Tank Brigade's first battalion, which included eleven KVs on 14 September, was shifted to the centre of the city and was fighting alongside with the 13th Guards Rifle Division's units (see above).

From midnight on 16 September the XLVIII Panzer Corps was subordinated to the Sixth Army and subsequently took part in the assault on Stalingrad. On 17 September the 94th Infantry Division and the 20th Motorized Division undertook the first attacks toward the area of the elevator and the canning factory, although as yet unsuccessfully. Simultaneously, elements of the 94th Infantry Division were advancing along the territory along the railway line as far as the Tsaritsa River. On the night of 17/18 September the elevator was attacked by assault groups from the 94th Infantry Division's 274th Infantry Regiment. As was noted in the XLVIII Panzer Corps' war diary, 'despite the employment of hand grenades and bundled grenades with a concentrated charge', the attack was not successful. One cannot help but note here the intelligent organization of the elevator's defence, when the garrison occupied not only the building itself, but also positions in the neighbouring buildings along the approaches to the elevator. This enabled us to uncover the approach of assault groups and to repel their attacks.

At 13.00–14.00 on 18 September the corps commander, General Kempf, ordered that the elevator be bombarded with fire from anti-aircraft guns, which had been attached to the 24th Panzer Division: 'I demand immediately that 50 rounds be fired from 88mm guns against the elevator.' Following a brief argument regarding the safety of the 94th Infantry Division's infantry, the anti-aircraft guns opened fire from a range of 800m. However, the hazily-formulated mission was carried out literally: the 'ack-ack' guns fired on the elevator without aiming or taking the defensive system into account. As the chief of the 24th Panzer Division's Ia reported, the anti-aircraft guns opened fire at 15.00 and fired fifty rounds, of which forty-four hit their target. Aside from forty-four half-metre deep holes in the building's façade, there was no visible effect. Despite the successful employment of 88mm guns even against the fully-fledged pillboxes along the Maginot Line and the Soviet fortifications along the old and new border in 1941, the guns' effect on the elevator's defence was close to zero. Later they fired on the elevator with 105mm guns from the 24th Panzer Division's artillery regiment with somewhat better results involving the destruction of its structures, but the elevator's defence maintained steadfast. During the day on 18 September the 94th Infantry Division's 274th Infantry Regiment was relieved near the elevator by the 29th Motorized Division's motorcycle battalion.

Despite the withdrawal of the 24th Panzer Division from the area south of the Tsaritsa and its transfer to another sector, a direct consequence of its attacks was the withdrawal to the north, partially behind the Tsaritsa, of the remnants of the 244th Rifle Division and the 270th NKVD Regiment and the formation of a pretty significant gap in the front along their positions, which enabled the Germans to reach the Volga.

The same tasks gave rise to similar decisions. Exactly the same as in the centre of Stalingrad, when we managed to stabilize the situation by committing the fresh 13th Guards Rifle Division, a fresh rifle brigade was committed into the southern part of the city. On orders from *front* headquarters, the 92nd Rifle Brigade was crossed over into Stalingrad during the night of 17/18 September, and Yeremenko immediately designated its defensive area – from the Tsaritsa to 'the railway triangle in the area of Valdai Street' (that is, as far as the railway's turn from Sadovaya Street to the Stalingrad II station, already occupied by the Germans). That is, to seal up the breach that had opened up on 16 September.

The 92nd Rifle Brigade was formed beginning on 18 August from sailors from the Northern and Baltic fleets in the town of Stupino near Moscow, and as early as 9 September, without having completed its formation, it left for the front. According to reminiscences of participants in the fighting, the soldier's naval dress was to be changed for army uniforms. However, the Soviet seamen requested they not change their uniform, as a result of which almost all retained their striped undershirts, their sailors' hats and belts, while many still had their pea-jackets. In the *front's* order the brigade is described as having '6,000 men',[3] that is, the brigade's actual strength at the moment of its arrival at the front was close to this figure. Lieutenant Colonel Pavel Il'ich Tarasov, who had earlier commanded a rifle regiment with the 137th Rifle Division, commanded the brigade.

By the morning of 18 September two of the 92nd Rifle Brigade's battalions had crossed over, with an anti-tank battalion, a signals company (two be sure, without equipment, which had been left at the unloading station), and two companies of 82mm mortars under the command of the chief of staff, Major N.F. Yemel'yanenko. According to his recollection, the crossing was made under fire, but without losses. Nonetheless, the haste of the movement and crossing told on the condition of the brigade. It was noted in the 92nd Rifle Brigade's morning report: 'The brigade has not had food for two days and there is no food.'[4] The battalions that crossed were involved in quite effective fighting on 18 September along the approaches to the Stalingrad railway station, destroying small enemy groups and capturing a prisoner from the 94th Infantry Division (he was mentioned previously). However, the intensive fighting led to the heavy expenditure of ammunition.

The relief of the elevator, which had just been won back from the Germans by the troops of the 10th Rifle Brigade, became the main achievement of the 92nd Rifle Brigade's subunits. A machine-gun platoon from the 2nd Battalion under Junior Lieutenant A.O. Khozyainov, and Lieutenant Z.G. Zozulya's rifle company were immediately dispatched to reinforce the defence of the elevator. As was noted in the history of the 92nd Rifle Brigade, *The Sailors Are True to Their Traditions*, Khozyainov's platoon disposed of two heavy machine guns, two anti-tank rifles, automatic rifles and grenades. The reinforcement of the garrison undoubtedly extended the defence of the elevator.

The crossing of the 92nd Rifle Brigade's rifle subunits and headquarters was completed on the night of 18/19 September. It was not possible to occupy the line indicated by Yeremenko and the brigade reached the approaches to the railway from the Tsaritsa River to the intersection of the railway lines on Balkhash Street. The 'triangle' of roads indicated in the *front* headquarters' order was already firmly in German hands. By this time the elevator was almost completely isolated. An attempt to reinforce its garrison on 19 September with a machine-gun battalion from the 92nd Rifle Brigade ended in failure – the company was surrounded and almost completely destroyed along the approaches to the elevator. By the morning of 20 September the brigade had occupied defensive positions with three battalions in the first line and one battalion in reserve. The appearance of the 92nd Rifle Brigade's battalions south of the Tsaritsa significantly changed the situation along this sector of the defence of Stalingrad. Now the XLVIII Panzer Corps would have to defeat not only the remnants of the 10th Rifle Brigade and the 35th Guards Rifle Division, but also four fresh battalions, although weakened by a shortage of supplies, in order to reach the Volga. As was noted in the evening report on 19 September by the Sixth Army's headquarters to the OKH's operational directorate: 'The occupation of territory near the mouth of the Tsaritsa and south of the southern railway station is being slowed down by the Russians' stubbornness and the weakness of our own infantry and it presumably will take another 1–2 days.' This evaluation proved to be extremely optimistic – the fighting continued for another week.

On the whole, the greatest problem for the 92nd Rifle Brigade was ammunition and supply over the Volga. The brigade's war diary contains an eloquent comment on this matter: 'Only a few brave souls managed to deliver ammunition to the right bank of the Volga River.'[5] They were not speaking about ammunition for the artillery, because the brigade's artillery[6] remained on the left bank of the Volga and rendered no support to the brigade. One of the reasons for this was the absence of radio communications. As was reported by the signals chief, 'There is neither radio communications nor food', and charging units were absent, although radio sets were available.

The arrival of the 92nd Rifle Brigade also enabled the command on 20 September to put in order a plan for the command and control of the troops south and north of the Tsaritsa. The remnants of the 10th Rifle Brigade, 35th Guards Rifle Division and the 131st Rifle Division were to be transferred to the 92nd Rifle Brigade. This could not be called a 'reinforcement'; the brigade was to receive weak subunits along with their defensive zones. For example, the remnants of the 10th Rifle Brigade, together with reinforcements, numbered only 200 men by 19 September. Perhaps the only valuable acquisition was a battalion from the 85th Guards Howitzer Artillery Regiment from the High Command Reserve, which was 'inherited' from the 35th Guards Rifle Division and supported the 92nd Rifle Brigade for a few days. On the whole, on 20 September the regiment numbered thirty-two 122mm howitzers on Stalingrad Tractor Factory tractors.[7] Several such guns were a fine acquisition for the 92nd Rifle Brigade.

The correlation of the sides' forces to the south of the Tsaritsa was obviously unfavourable for the Soviet troops. Strong Wehrmacht units operated against the 92nd Rifle Brigade's four battalions and the remnants of other units. As opposed to the 'invalids' of the LI Corps' formations that were storming the centre of Stalingrad, the XLVIII Panzer Corps' divisions were at that moment in good shape. In a review of the Sixth Army's formations on 20 September, the following was stated about the divisions in Kempf's corps:

- The 29th Motorized Division had six motorized infantry battalions (three average and three spent), one strong motorcycle battalion. The overall rating was that 'The division is fit for offensive tasks';
- The 94th Infantry Division had seven infantry battalions (seven average), while the engineer battalion was spent. The overall rating was that 'The division is fit for offensive tasks'.

Despite the problems with supply and artillery support, the sailors of the 92nd Rifle Brigade managed to hold the enemy's first effort against their positions, which followed on 20 September. It was admitted in the XLVIII Panzer Corps' daily report that: 'The 94th Infantry Division's attack to the south has bogged down in very heavy fighting.' However, this defensive success cost the 92nd Rifle Brigade quite dearly. In the second battalion along the left flank two companies were encircled by an attack along converging axes along the railway and from the elevator to the south, and an attempted counter-attack was met with 'powerful automatic rifle and machine-gun fire and intensive bombing by air', which led to heavy losses. As regards the first battalion, which was adjacent to the Tsaritsa, it was noted in the brigade's report that 'the battalion is suffering heavy losses from enemy aviation'. As early as the first day of the defensive fighting the reserve fourth battalion began to be thrown around in filling breaches in the defence.

A joint attack by the 94th Infantry and 29th Motorized Divisions was set by the XLVIII Panzer Corps against Soviet positions to the south of the Tsaritsa for 21 September. A combat group was being put together in the 29th Motorized Division from units of a motorcycle battalion, the 15th Motorized Rifle Regiment, as well as engineers and tanks (as of 20 September the division disposed of three Panzer IIs and five Panzer III long-barrelled tanks). The group was strengthened with the 29th Motorized Division's main mass of heavy guns (by weakening the subunits occupying defensive positions along the bank of the Volga). The canning factory was the object of the 29th Motorized Division's attack.

The German offensive on the canning factory began early on the morning of 21 September with an attack by dive bombers and a bombardment by the 94th Infantry Division's artillery on the Soviet positions facing the 29th Motorized Division's combat group. Such a massed attack against the canning factory ensured the advance of the 29th Motorized Division's units to the north. The 94th Infantry Division's offensive from west to east led to the link-up of the two division's elements. One encircled company remained of the 92nd Rifle Brigade's second battalion. The third battalion was pushed back to the east. On the evening of 21 September brigade commander Tarasov made the decision to shorten the front and pull back the third battalion to the line of Communist Youth International Street (running approximately parallel to the Tsaritsa from west to east).

The gradual collapse of the 92nd Rifle Brigade's defence led to a situation in which the elevator was completely isolated during the day of 21 September. On this day negotiators from the civilian population were sent by the Germans to the elevator with a proposal to lay down their arms and surrender. As the above-mentioned M.P. Polyakov wrote in his report, 'We shot these negotiators after they refused to take up arms and fight with us against the Germans'.[8] In view of the expenditure of ammunition and the small number of soldiers still able to fight, the decision was made to break out of the elevator, which was carried out on the night of 21/22 September. On 24 September a group of fifteen soldiers, headed by Polyakov,[9] reached their own lines. They probably managed to escape from the elevator along underground tunnels.

By all appearances, yet another important factor was the fact that as early as the evening of 21 September, between 21.00 and 22.00, German assault groups from the 29th Motorized Division's 15th Motorized Regiment broke into the elevator building. The first attempts to break out of the elevator were fixed at between 18.45 and 19.15 on 21 September, also according to German data. At 23.00 on 21 September the 94th Infantry Division was reporting on the raising the swastika flag on the elevator, although this could mean anything, all the way to raising the flag on the wall beneath the structure. In any event, at 04.00 on 22 September the elevator was considered by the Germans to be fully under their control.

The 92nd Rifle Brigade's strength was steadily melting away. On the morning of 22 September P.I. Tarasov was reporting that out of an initial strength of 865 men the brigade's third battalion had already lost 714 men and the second battalion had lost 745.[10] Elements of the second and fourth battalions occupied defensive positions along a narrow strip of the Volga bank, adjacent to a 'dike'. As regards this structure, the LI Corps[11] report on the results of the day noted that: 'Along the 276th Infantry Regiment's (94th Infantry Division) sector the enemy is still holding the bank along a 100-metre strip and he has fortified himself on the vertical mooring wall and cannot be destroyed by heavy weapons. Two assault sorties by an engineer battalion were unsuccessful.' In the XLVIII Panzer Corps' war diary this was noted as fighting 'against isolated nests of resistance, which have firmly ensconced themselves in the wall of the quay.' One should also not fail to note that along this sector the soldiers of the 92nd Rifle Brigade received artillery support from the left bank of the Volga, and in the XLVIII Panzer Corps' war diary it is stated directly that: 'Powerful mortar and artillery fire is coming from the left bank of the Volga on the 276th Infantry Regiment's sector.' However, it was namely on 22 September that the commander of the second battalion, Captain S.N. Zakharov, who was directing the fight for the 'dike'. was severely wounded.

The 92nd Rifle Brigade's situation could have improved if the situation in the centre of the city had stabilized. However, quite the opposite – it worsened and the establishment of communications between the 13th Guards Rifle Division and the troops in the area of the city theatre did not take place. On 22 September the 272nd NKVD Regiment numbered 220 men. At that moment the regiment was still located quite close to the train station, although it had already been pushed back from the bridge over the Tsaritsa (the bridgehead it had eliminated earlier). Moreover, on 24 September the Germans planned a general offensive to the area of the mouth of the Tsaritsa along both banks of the river. For this purpose one regiment from the 94th Infantry Division was to be transferred to the centre of the city and was supposed to attack along with the 71st Infantry Division. By the morning of 23 September it was being relieved near the 'dike' by elements of the 29th Motorized Division.

On 23 September brigade commander P.I. Tarasov was reporting that the commander of the brigade's first battalion, Captain A.L. Bereza,[12] 'having taken two clean pages of paper and a round official seal, left, together with his wife, for parts unknown'.[13] He is not listed as a prisoner of war, so most likely Bereza was banally killed while crossing over the Volga on his own. How could such a man have commanded a battalion? It was precisely the first battalion that was located along a relatively passive sector, adjacent to the Tsaritsa. The brigade's strength of 23 September was 2,391 men (including rear elements and the artillery on the left bank of the Volga).[14] At the same time, the weight of responsibility only grew: on 23 September, on orders from the 62nd Army, the headquarters of the 42nd Rifle Brigade was to be pulled back to the left bank of the Volga.[15] The rank and file were to be transferred to the 92nd Rifle Brigade (along with its sector and the very shaky situation there).

On 24 September the final stage of the struggle in the southern part of Stalingrad began. During this period reports from the 92nd Rifle Brigade are already absent from the appropriate files of the 62nd Army's headquarters, probably due to a loss of communications. As regards the two brigades, data from preceding reports is listed in the 62nd Army's war diary. The LI Corps' offensive began at 07.00 on 24 September with support from the VIII Air Corps. Its upheavals have already been described above. Stubborn resistance was also put up by the 92nd Rifle Brigade along the southern bank of the Tsaritsa, and the 94th Infantry Division's 267th Infantry Regiment 'advanced up to 300 metres toward the Tsaritsa in heavy street fighting'. The offensive continued the following day and, having broken through the 914th Rifle Regiment's defence, the Germans reached the 92nd Rifle Brigade's command post at the mouth of the Tsaritsa. South of the Tsaritsa, by evening the 94th Infantry Division had occupied the last two city blocks, having pushed the 92nd Rifle Brigade's soldiers out of them.

By the night of 26 September the remnants of the units defending in the area to the north and south of the Tsaritsa had grouped in the area of the mouth of the Tsaritsa (42nd Rifle Brigade,[16] 272nd NKVD Regiment, 914th Rifle Regiment and the 92nd Rifle Brigade's first and third battalions). The remnants of the 92nd Rifle Brigade's other two battalions occupied a narrow strip of the bank of the Volga south of the mouth of the Tsaritsa. This is confirmed by a report by the LI Corps for 25 September: 'The enemy continues to hold the mooring wall with a length of 600 metres, while being covered by fire from the eastern bank.' The finale of the 92nd Rifle Brigade's struggle proved to be quite unhappy. NKVD documents recount this as follows:

> On 26 September 1942, during the time of the offensive by the German-Fascist forces along the sector of the 92nd Independent Rifle Brigade, the brigade commander, Colonel Tarasov, and the brigade commissar, Senior Battalion Commissar Andreev failed to organize a defence and, manifesting cowardice, transferred the brigade's command post from the right bank of the Volga to … Island, without permission from the army command. Upon being arrested, Tarasov testified under interrogation: 'I confess my guilt in that I abandoned the brigade and moved to the island during an intense combat situation and without orders from the army's headquarters.'

P.I. Tarasov and G.M. Andreev were sentenced by a military tribunal to be shot as early as 6 October 1942. As was already noted above, the reason for the shift in the command post's location was the Germans' breakthrough to it on 25 September, when the German infantrymen had reached the mouth of the Tsaritsa River. Here one should note that Lieutenant Colonel Tarasov's mistake was the very stationing of his command post to the north of the Tsaritsa from the very moment of the crossing over into Stalingrad, instead of to the south of the river, where the battalions of his brigade were operating. This may be explained by the hope for an improvement in the situation in the centre, but led to a situation in which the 92nd Rifle Brigade's headquarters depended on the firmness of other units. The crossing over to Hungry Island on the night of 25/26 September worsened the situation and led to the collapse of command and control. It proved impossible to establish communications with the units during the course of the day, and those who crossed to the right bank of the Volga on the following night found the remnants of the brigade's elements along a narrow 50–70m strip of the bank near the mouth of the Tsaritsa. They crossed to Hungry Island on that same night. In the morning report by brigade commander P.I. Tarasov at 07.30 on 27 September, the number of those who crossed over the Volga from Stalingrad was estimated at sixty men.[17] At the same time, one should note that during the course of the 92nd Rifle Brigade's fighting in the city the system for evacuating the wounded was working and 468 wounded passed through the brigade's medical services.[18] On 30 September 1942 the 92nd Rifle Brigade numbered 1,100 men.[19] Artillery troops and rear area elements which remained along the eastern bank of the Volga were evidently included in this figure.

The remnants of the 272nd NKVD Regiment also crossed to the eastern bank of the Volga together with the 92nd Rifle Brigade. The last fighting along this sector took place early in the morning of 27 September. At 0700 elements of the 71st Infantry Division reached the bank of the Volga, capturing 400 prisoners (these were probably to a significant degree wounded). On the morning of 27 September the struggle for the 'dike' along the bank of the Volga was also concluded, comparable in its intensity to the fighting for the elevator. As was noted in the final report, at 06.00 the 94th Infantry Division's assault groups 'broke through to the mooring wall and destroyed the enemy behind it, completely clearing the bank of the Volga'. Elements of the 29th Motorized Division's 15th Motorized Regiment also took part in the storming of the 'dike'. It was noted in the XLVIII Panzer Corps' war diary that 'The enemy put up stubborn resistance'. During the course of the fighting 'numerous heavy and light infantry weapons' were captured. It's possible that they were speaking of the remnants of the 244th and 35th Guards Rifle Division's artillery. In the LI Corps' daily report the results of the concluding battles with the Soviet group of forces in the area of the 62nd Army's former command post were reflected as follows: 'The entire bank of the Volga from the army's boundary and to a point two kilometres north-east of the mouth of the Tsaritsa is securely in our hands.'

However, there was another side to this achievement. In the latest evaluation of the Sixth Army's formations on 28 September, the following was stated regarding the 94th Infantry Division: seven infantry battalions (seven weak), and the engineer battalion is spent. In contrast with 20 September, the evaluation of the division's condition had changed to 'The division is fit for defence'. At the same time, it was planned to employ the 94th Infantry Division for offensive missions in the area of the workers' settlements.

In toting up the results of combat activities in the southern part of Stalingrad, one is forced to admit that not all the possibilities for its defence had been fully employed. The tall elevator building offered excellent prospects for correcting artillery fire against the entire area along the approaches to the Tsaritsa. However, they did not take advantage of these. Moreover, the support for the activities of the 92nd Rifle Brigade's four fresh battalions with artillery left much to be desired. The brigade was essentially 'burned up' in several days of fighting. The extension of the struggle for the southern part of Stalingrad would have meant postponing the beginning of the storming of the factory settlements, which would have enabled us to strengthen their defence. Aside from this, the collapse of the defence at the mouth of the Tsaritsa signified the worsening of the 13th Guards Rifle Division's situation in the centre of Stalingrad.

On the other hand, for the Germans the area of the elevator also became an arena for mistakes and missed opportunities. The timely seizure and firm retention by elements of the 24th Panzer Division of this building that dominated the terrain could have significantly changed the course of combat activities in this area. The elevator definitely cost more than the bridge over the Tsaritsa, that is, the bridgehead that they nevertheless had to abandon. Also, available weapons, especially 88mm anti-aircraft guns, were employed quite irrationally.

It is also necessary to emphasize that the very fact of shooting the 92nd Rifle Brigade's commander and commissar in and of itself in no ways characterizes the firmness of its subunits. The sailors faithfully carried out their duty to the end, extending the fighting for the southern part of Stalingrad. The commander of the 92nd Rifle Brigade, Lieutenant Colonel Pavel Il'ich Tarasov and its military commissar Georgii Mikhailovich Andreev became, if one may express oneself thusly, the 'D.G. Pavlov'[20] and V.Ye. Klimovskikh of the fighting for Stalingrad. On the one hand, yes, there were undoubtedly mistakes in troop control, including the choice of the location for the command post. One the other hand, the crossing to Hungry Island took place under the threat of the rout of the brigade's headquarters and the exhaustion of its opportunities for resistance. The words in the sentence of Tarasov and Andreev that having left them without leadership, 'the troops and command-political element ... fled in panic from their defensive lines and began to cross to the left bank of the Volga',[21] may arouse only a bitter grin. How many men 'fled' this way? A few dozen left from four battalions from a full-strength brigade? They would have achieved nothing by remaining on the right bank and would most likely simply have perished, without inflicting any kind of tangible loss on the enemy.

Chapter 15

The Battle for the Semaphore II. The Counterblow of 18–19 September 1942

(Map 8)

itler's statement of 12 September 1942 as to the Red Army's incapability of launching 'retaliatory operations of a strategic nature' was accurate, but only partially so. The rifle divisions and tank corps undergoing reformation, in the best case, could have gone into action in October. However, the latest offensive by the ex-reserve armies around Stalingrad took place as early as the middle of September 1942.

Zhukov[1] writes in his memoirs about the meeting, at which Vasilevskii was present, that took place on 12 September in the Kremlin concerning the Stalingrad Front. However, a note about any kind of meeting with either Zhukov or Vasilevskii on 12 or even 13 September is missing from the entries in the journal of Stalin's visitors. The first time their surnames appear in September is only on 27 September. Therefore the conversations about 'another decision'[2] should be moved to the end of September. There was not even the outline of 'another decision' for the problem in the beginning of September. At that moment the Soviet command was searching for a decision of the problem in improving the quality of preparation for the latest offensive.

In Zhukov's report to Stalin of 12 September, cited above, the date for a new offensive was indicated: 'We have in mind beginning a new operation for 17.9.' Quite a lengthy pause was brought about by the expectation of the arrival of new formations. On 12 September 5–6 trains each, out of 14–15 overall, arrived with the four new rifle divisions. On 11 September the 95th Rifle Division didn't board at all and was still in Mozhaisk.

The amount of forces for the counterblow was not the only thing that had changed. Following the failure of the offensive at the beginning of September, the decision was made to shift the axis of the main attack. In order to get around the strengthened sector of the front, the 1st Guards Army was regrouped to the west of the railway running through Kotluban' to Gumrak. On the one hand, the mission of K.S. Moskalenko's army was to be made more complicated – it was necessary to cover a greater distance in order to link up with the forces of the 62nd Army in Stalingrad. On the other hand, there was the hope of turning the enemy's front that had not been pierced in the beginning of September.

The change in the axis of the main attack was accompanied by the redistribution of forces between the armies. The 1st Guards Army was to transfer part of its formations to its neighbours. The 39th Guards, 84th, 87th and 24th Rifle Divisions were to be transferred to the 24th Army and the 41st Guards Rifle Division to the 66th Army. The 173rd, 207th, 221st, 292nd and 308th Rifle Divisions, which were already located in the designated zone, were to be transferred to the new attack axis of Moskalenko's army. They had previously been part of the 24th Army. The 258th, 292nd, 260th, 273rd and 316th Rifle Divisions, which were arriving by rail, were supposed to increase the 1st Guards Army's offensive potential. These were fresh, major-strength divisions (see table). As we can see, Stalin and the *Stavka* were not only pushing Zhukov as regards the necessity of launching a counterblow. The supreme command was looking for and dispatching combat-capable reserves to the Stalingrad Front to resolve the assigned missions. Of the enumerated formations, the 260th, 258th and 273rd Rifle Divisions had been removed from the Voronezh Front. Stalin, in *Stavka* of the VGK Directive No. 170601 of 7 September, ordered 'Temporarily postpone the Voronezh Front's operation' and removed four full-strength divisions from N.F. Vatutin's[3] control. A fourth formation, the 233rd Rifle Division (13,028 men as of 15 September), was transferred to the Stalingrad Front's neighbouring 24th Army.

The new players would have enabled the Soviets to once again gather a ram for breaking the enemy's defence. The worn-out 221st and 207th Rifle Divisions (transferred from the 24th Army) were to be pulled out of the first line into the second. The 4th, 7th and 16th Tank Corps and the 3rd, 12th and 48th Tank Brigades were also supposed to operate along the new axis. As opposed to the offensive in the beginning of September, the 1st Guards Army received a powerful artillery fist, ten reinforcement artillery regiments. The most consequential addition was the howitzer and gun regiments. The army received twenty-four 122mm guns, forty 122mm howitzers and sixty-six 152mm gun-howitzers. This was a hefty reinforcement and a great step forward in comparison with all that had been done before. The army was also to receive eight Guards mortar regiments and three battalions, that is, about 100 M-8 and M-13 rocket artillery vehicles (predominantly M-13s). The 1st Guards Army was protected from air attack by six anti-aircraft artillery regiments (twelve 37mm guns each).

Table 20: The Strength of the 1st Guards Army's Rifle Formations on 15 September 1942.[4]

Unit	Men	Rifles	Heavy Machine Guns	Light Machine Guns	Shpagin Sub-machine Guns	Mortars	Guns	Anti-Tank Guns	Anti-Tank Rifles
173rd RD	7,194	6,179	53	166	679	188	44	30	198
207th RD	4,789	3,882	29	57	583	95	37	20	145
221st RD	5,724	6,341	56	142	653	230	41	28	215
258th RD	13,429	9,174	85	225	746	222	44	30	277
260th RD	13,303	8,913	80	207	649	207	44	30	269
273rd RD	12,770	9,001	81	200	739	222	44	30	279
308th RD	8,671	8,408	56	195	713	260	44	30	275
316th RD	10,495	6,820	46	188	858	180	44	30	239
292nd RD	9,970	6,212	81	210	911	188	44	30	228

Following the failure of the counterblows in August and the beginning of September, Stalin on 9 September wrote to Zhukov: 'I consider the restoration of the 4th and 16th Tank Corps to be inexpedient. Pavelkin and Mishulin, the tank corps commanders, are not suitable for their position.' Actually, the two corps were to be disbanded as punishment for their failure. It was planned to employ the corps' tank brigades 'in detail'. However, Zhukov managed to convince the supreme commander-in-chief to retain the corps, and as early as 11 September his proposal to keep them was approved by the *Stavka*. The corps commanders were replaced. A.G. Maslov was appointed commander of the 16th Tank Corps in place of Pavelkin. A.G. Kravchenko, who had displayed himself to good effect as commander of the 2nd Tank Corps, was appointed commander of the 4th Tank Corps in place of Mishulin. Having changed from anger to mercy, Stalin dispatched ninety-four T-34s to reinforce the tank corps of Moskalenko's army. It was not planned to disband Rotmistrov's 7th Tank Corps and it even kept its commander. The overall number of tanks in the 1st Guards Army's units and formations is shown in the following table.

Table 21: Tank Strength in the 1st Guards Army's Units and Formations by 18 September 1942.[5]

Unit/Formation	KV	T-34	T-70	T-60	Total
4th Tank Corps	11	38	–	31	80
7th Tank Corps	12	36	–	45	93
16th Tank Corps	11	22	–	37	70
148th Tank Bde	8	2	–	14	24
12th Tank Bde	–	22	13	–	35
3rd Tank Bde	–	23	15	–	38
Total	42	143	28	127	340

Soviet historiography has bored everyone to tears with complaints about the proportion of 'light and outdated' tanks. However, here we cannot but pay attention to the correlation of tank types in the Stalingrad Front's shock group of forces: 46 per cent of the tank park was made up of T-60 and T-70 light tanks, with T-60s predominating. The value of a T-60 in a standoff with a Panzer III and a September 1942 model Panzer IV was nil. Moreover, in the dusty air the T-60's already weak weaponry would break down. In a report about the 4th Tank Corps' 45th Tank Brigade's combat operations, it is noted that: 'The 20mm ShVAK on the T-60 tanks is not employed in battle in the majority of cases, because after a few shots it fails.'[6] That is, the T-60 would actually become a machine-gun platform, outfitted, moreover, with only a single magazine-fed machine gun. Given this configuration, the tank could only count on success on the fields of the First World War during 1916–18.

The 1st Guards Army arranged itself in three echelons for the offensive. There were five rifle divisions, three tank brigades and a tank corps (the 7th) in the first echelon. There were three rifle divisions and a tank corps (the 4th) in the second echelon. Finally, there was one rifle division and a tank corps (the 16th) in the third echelon (the army commander's reserve).

The shift of the attack axis did not signify the passivity of the remaining armies to the north and north-west of Stalingrad. The 24th Army was supposed to attack with its flank adjoining the 1st Guards Army. The army was to be reinforced with the 233rd and 49th Rifle Divisions and the 246th and 69th Tank Brigades. The latter were its Achilles heel, as they were quite weak. On 12 September the 246th Tank Brigade numbered six T-34s and seven T-70s, while the 69th Tank Brigade numbered four T-34s and one T-70 on the same date. The artillery fist of D.T. Kozlov's army was somewhat more modest than that of Moskalenko's. The 24th Army's offensive was to be supported by six reinforcement artillery regiments (thirty 152mm gun-howitzers) and four Guards mortar regiments (about fifty M-8s and M-13s). The 24th Army's anti-aircraft weapons were to be reinforced by two anti-aircraft artillery regiments (with twelve 37mm guns apiece). The Stalingrad Front's offensive was to be supported by 118 fighters, 84 ground-attack aircraft and 21 bombers from the 16th Air Army.

Unfortunately few, if any, documents showing the mechanism of adopting decisions have been preserved. Thus it is quite difficult to identify the authorship of these or other decisions. However, in September one can quite visibly track the gradually pumping up of the Stalingrad Front with artillery. This process began with Zhukov's arrival at the front, enabling us to link this pumping up of the shock groups with heavy guns as a decision by Zhukov, which was undoubtedly the correct one and corresponded to the situation.

On 15 September an instruction session was conducted for the formation commanders by the commander of the 1st Guards Army, K.S. Moskalenko. Zhukov was also present at the meeting. He was not a passive listener and at this meeting, along with Moskalenko and Malenkov,[7] Zhukov dispensed advice to the division commanders on how to conduct the forthcoming offensive. During the operation's preparatory phase a model of the terrain in the zone of the forthcoming offensive was built. On the morning of 16 September army commander Moskalenko issued assignments on this model to the commanders of the rifle divisions and tank corps. Zhukov was also present this meeting.

Not only were the Soviet troops preparing for a new battle, but the enemy was as well. According to a report at 22.45 on 17 September, the strength of the XIV Panzer Corps' tank park can be described by the following figures (see table).

Table 22: The XIV Panzer Corps' Armoured Strength on 17 September 1942.[8]

Unit	Panzer II	Panzer III (short)	Panzer III (long)	Panzer IV (short)
16th Panzer Division	–	8	50	2
60th Motorized Division	7	–	15[9]	1
3rd Motorized Division	5	–	27	4

Unit	Panzer IV (long)	Marder Self-Propelled Gun	Total Tanks and Self-Propelled Guns
16th Panzer Division	10	6	76
60th Motorized Division	4	9	36
3rd Motorized Division	7	5	48

The Germans transferred the 177th Assault Gun Battalion (ten long-barrelled and four short-barrelled StuG IIIs combat-ready on 16 September) to the VIII Corps not long before the start of the latest Soviet offensive for the purpose of raising its defensive capabilities.[10] Besides this, it was precisely here, in the defence of the 'land bridge', that the tank destroyers of the 521st Battalion, the most powerful on the Eastern Front, were put into action. They were also subordinated to the VIII Corps.

Aside from tanks, the XIV Panzer Corps and VIII Corps' units disposed of powerful infantry forces. In the 16th Panzer Division there were five middle-strength infantry battalions and six light and two heavy howitzer batteries. Other formations defending the 'land bridge' were the equal of the 16th Panzer Division.[11] The 3rd Motorized Division contained five battalions of medium strength, with the 60th Motorized Division having seven battalions of medium strength. The 76th and 305th Rifle Divisions contained nine medium-strength battalions apiece. Such an amount of infantry was a record among the Sixth Army's formations along the approaches to Stalingrad. For example, in the LI Corps' divisions there were from six to eight battalions, while in the eight-battalion 71st Infantry Division all of them were '*schwach*', that is, in a weak condition. Overall, by September 1942 a nine-battalion infantry division was already a relatively rare bird on the Eastern Front. As a result of losses, more and more divisions were going over to a six-battalion organization, that is, three regiments of two battalions each. In the autumn of 1943 this practice was codified as authorized strength. But in September 1942, Paulus put in nine-battalion 'dinosaur' divisions on the 'loud bridge', which were close relatives of those 'Tyrannosauruses' which swallowed up the Soviet mechanized corps in the summer of 1941.

Others of the Wehrmacht's formations in defence of the 'land bridge' were marked with the seal of exclusivity. Despite the fact that a Wehrmacht motorized division had a weaker authorized strength than the infantry ones, the 60th Motorized Division, with its seven average-strength battalions, exceed in strength many of the Sixth Army's infantry divisions. For example, the LI Corps' 389th Infantry Division had only six battalions, of which two were in a weakened condition. Just as was the case with the 16th Panzer Division's tanks, the 60th Motorized Division exceeded its authorized strength. Paulus's headquarters made an analogous choice in distributing its forces: the best formations were put in to defend the 'land bridge' and the worst were sent off to assault Stalingrad.

However, artillery was required to take the city and Paulus was forced to take two battalions of 210mm howitzers from the XIV Panzer Corps, which it had at the beginning of the 'Battle for the Semaphore'. The 100mm guns and 150mm howitzers remained subordinated to the corps. At this moment sufficiently strong artillery was at the disposal of the VIII Army Corps – a battalion of 210mm howitzers and two battalions of 100mm guns (minus one battery).

The Stalingrad Front's shock group, which was supposed to break the resistance of the north-facing front of the 'land bridge', was quite equal to its assigned task. The 1st Guards Army alone numbered 123,882 men. The 24th Army, which was to launch an attack along its flank with the 1st Guards Army, numbered 54,500 men on 10 September. In order to understand the true role of the battle in the steppe between the Don and the Volga, it is sufficient to compare these figures with the strength of the 62nd Army in Stalingrad itself. On 13 September 1942 the 62nd Army numbered 54,000 men, or less than half as many in the 1st Guards Army and more than three times fewer than the 1st Guards and 24th Armies together. The Stalingrad Front's offensive was generously supported by equipment. There were 611 guns and 1,956 mortars in the 1st Guards Army, making 71 guns and 194 mortars per kilometre of front along the axis of the main attack.

At 05.30 on 18 September the artillery preparation began, at 05.45 the 'katyushas' struck, and at 06.00 attack aircraft appeared over the battlefield. At 07.00 the artillery shifted its fire to the enemy's rear and the tanks and infantry moved into the attack. At 06.30 the 24th Army's right flank went over to the attack to the left of the 1st Guards Army.

To say that events developed dramatically along the axis of the *front's* main attack in the 1st Guards Army's zone is an understatement. Here the 308th and 316th Rifle Divisions attacked, supported by P.A. Rotmistrov's 7th Tank Corps. The 62nd Tank Brigade attacked together with the 308th Rifle Division, while the 87th Tank Brigade attacked with the 316th Rifle Division. The 3rd Guards Heavy Tank Brigade made up the corps' second echelon.

In the offensive's first hours Rotmistrov's corps managed to penetrate quite deeply into the enemy's defence. By committing the 3rd Guards Tank Brigade from the reserve into the fighting the 7th Tank Corps, together with the infantry, occupied Height 154.2, which dominated the terrain. However, having overcome the chain of heights in the area of Height 154.2, the brigades of Rotmistrov's corps got separated from their infantry and artillery. The infantry was pinned down by enemy fire and air attacks. What was far worse was that the success was at first limited to a wedge in the German defence by the tank corps and two rifle divisions.

The 292nd Rifle Division, which was attacking to the right, and the 12th Tank Brigade, made no progress. As was noted in the 12th Tank Brigade's report, 'upon the tanks reaching the Crow *Balki*, the brigade's combat formations were subjected to powerful artillery fire and air attacks by the enemy, as a result of which the 292nd Rifle Division's units were forced to go to ground, while the artillery, as the result of a break in communications and air activity against its firing positions, reduced to a minimum the pace of fire and the tanks were forced to carry on the fight isolated from the infantry and without artillery support, while suffering heavy losses'.

Lieutenant B.V. Nemov, the commander of a T-70 tank in the 12th Tank Brigade, recalled:

> … the roar of the artillery, the shell explosions or bombs from all sides. The rattle of rifle and machine gun fire. Many black columns of smoke rising to the sky. These were our tanks burning. This smoke was very far away and quite close. A T-34 was burning in a giant fire about 300 metres away. There were a large number of aircraft in the sky, both ours and German. There was aerial combat and several planes fell to the ground.

The 1st Guards Army's right-flank 173rd and 258th Rifle Divisions were also unable to overcome the chain of heights to the south of Kotluban'. The 24th Army's 233rd Rifle Division, which was attacking to the left, made only an insignificant advance. The narrow breakthrough front limited the space for manoeuvre and exposed the attacking units to fire from the flanks. In this regard, I would like to quote the Sixth Army's war diary, in which as early as 08.30 the situation was outlined as follows:

> … the expected enemy offensive for the purpose of easing the situation in Stalingrad from the area on both sides of Kotluban' station, began following a powerful artillery and aviation preparation. It led to quite a deep but narrow breakthrough by tanks and infantry along the boundary between the XIV Panzer and VIII Army Corps. Countermeasures by the XIV Panzer and VIII Army corps and the LI Army Corps' 389th Infantry Division are being taken and all of the VIII Air Corps' available forces are being thrown into the fighting.[12]

We should observe in parentheses that a division from the corps attacking Stalingrad was brought in to repel the Soviet offensive.

The attacker's main task was to develop the initial success and to shake up the enemy's defence to its entire depth. The success could also be developed toward the flanks, easing the forward advance of those neighbours who had stalled. At first all of these tasks were on the shoulders of the tank troops of the 7th Tank Corps. The 62nd Tank Brigade began to widen the breakthrough with an attack to the south-west in the direction of Borodkin farm. There were thirteen T-34s and eighteen T-60s by the start of the offensive. Of the T-34 tanks taking part in the attack, six vehicles were lost in the fighting for Height 154.2, while the remainder broke through to Borodkin farm. The lagging behind of the infantry prevented them from consolidating this initial success. The vehicles that broke through to the farm were counter-attacked by the enemy and burnt. Only a few crew members returned to their lines. As a result, the losses of the 62nd Tank Brigade for the day amounted to eleven T-34s and fourteen T-60s burnt, and two T-34s and one T-60 knocked out. The 87th Tank Brigade from Rotsmistrov's corps broke through deepest of all. By midday, when Height 154.2 had been taken, the brigade occupied rail siding '564'. Without halting, the brigade's tanks moved on further along the rail line. The next obstacle was a deep ravine, which limited the route of advance to the defile near the railway in the direction of the Konnyi rail siding. There was no time to stand around and think about it – anti-tank guns were firing from the New Hope farm on the right across the ravine. The only door to the depth of the enemy's defence seemed to the Konnyi rail siding (the same one which the 23rd Tank Corps was attempting to take back). They immediately 'knocked on the door'. The reply was not a friendly one – eight tanks from the 87th Tank Brigade's first battalion, which had gotten as far as the rail siding, were immediately counter-attacked by twenty enemy tanks which had arrived from Stalingrad and they were all burned out. Another battalion was attacked in the flank from behind the railway permanent way. The Germans' tank reserves, which had been reinforced by Paulus for defending the 'land bridge', joined the fighting. The 'heavy brigade' from Rotsmistrov's corps was the last to take part in the fighting. The 3rd Guards Tank Brigade began the fight with fifteen KVs and ten T-60s. It was committed at 07.30 along the boundary between the 62nd and 87th Tank Brigades and took part in the capture of Height 154.2.

Given the shallow depth of the defence, the penetration by Soviet tanks as far as the Konnyi railway siding created a crisis in the defence of the 'land bridge'. In the Sixth Army's daily report for 18 September we find a dramatic description of the situation in the XIV Panzer Corps:

> At 06.00 the enemy managed to penetrate along a sector of the 60th Motorized Division's northern front from both sides of Point 414 to the south, where he then penetrated to the area of Point 427 and to the west, where the division's command post, the main dressing station and the majority of the rear establishments were located. The enemy attack was halted through the cooperation of the division headquarters' rank and file and the signals battalion. A large number of German everyday articles and German weapons were found on the Bolsheviks captured in this fighting.[13]

Point 427 indicated by the Germans is the New Hope farm, to which the 87th Tank Brigade's tanks were breaking through to from the north.

The Germans also had to activate for the defence of the northern flank not only the 389th Infantry Division's units, but also other elements which were occupied with the assault on Stalingrad. According to an entry in the Sixth Army's war diary, the reserves were stationed in the rear of the XIV Panzer Corps and VIII Corps' attacked positions: 'Stiotta's and Meyer's groups: A defensive position along the line of the ravine north-east of Point 427 – the auto road south-west of it as far as the Nameless Ravine and Bol'shaya Rossoshka was occupied by both combat groups in concert with support elements from the 295th Infantry Division.' Colonel Max Stiotta was the commander of the LI Corps' engineers. An engineer battalion, a road construction battalion, a battalion of heavy howitzers, a mortar battery and a battalion of anti-aircraft guns and other small units were included in his combat group.

However, the final word in the battle on 18 September had not yet been spoken. There remained forces at the disposal of the Soviet command which it was planned to employ to exploit success. At 10.30 the 1st Guards Army chief of staff ordered the 4th Tank Corps to begin carrying out its mission. The corps was, together with the 207th and 221st Rifle Divisions (4,789 and 5,724 men in each on 15 September) to pass through the army's first-echelon combat formations and to attack in the direction of Gumrak. Formally, the 4th Tank Corps was to be committed into a 4km wide breach, which had been made by the 308th and 316th Rifle Divisions. As early as 12.00 the corps' 45th and 102nd Tank Brigades reached the positions that had been seized by the first echelon. The movement was carried out under air attack. The tanks did not suffer, but some of the soft-skin vehicles were knocked out by the bombs, including the headquarters vehicle of a motorized rifle battalion.

But the main trials were awaiting the tank troops ahead. As noted in the report by the Sixth Army's headquarters to the OKH, 'The enemy managed to break through along a 1–2km front along either side of the 564-kilometre halting point and he reached Nadezhda … The main mass of the XIV Panzer Corps' tanks are coming up from the east and south-east, and the VIII Army Corps' tank destroyers and assault guns from the west.'[14] As can be seen from later entries, the reserves arrived at the breakthrough area at about midday.

Before long the attacking Soviet infantry had been forced to hit the ground. The 45th Tank Brigade halted and did not move forward without infantry, strung out in a column along the railway. The 102nd Tank Brigade moved into the depth of the enemy defence. Despite the seizure of the commanding height the achievements of the morning offensive were limited to quite a narrow space to the west of the railway to Stalingrad. The narrowness of the breakthrough corridor enabled the enemy to enfilade it completely. Armour-piercing shells rained down from the right and left of the 102nd Tank Brigade's vehicles. The first blow was shells from the right flank, from the direction of Height 123.6, which remained in German hands. Four tanks were immediately set on fire. The four burning tanks and fire from anti-tank guns caused some confusion among the tank troops, but it was overcome and the tanks moved forward, leaving the firing sector of the enemy's guns. The next unpleasantness was the fire from the left, from the railway. Six German tanks were waiting in ambush behind a burnt-out train and were firing from behind the charred wagons. Another five of the 102nd Tank Brigade's tanks were put out of action. Borodkin farm and the ravine covered by anti-tank guns became obstacles for the breakthrough further on. That is, the brigade encountered the same obstacles as the 7th Tank Corps' tanks a few hours earlier. Another two tanks were lost in Borodkin, with three anti-tank guns destroyed and two headquarters vehicles captured. They were unable to get past the anti-tank guns near the ravine and all the tanks arriving there were destroyed. It should be noted here that of the twenty-eight T-34s, six T-70s and six T-60s in the 102nd Tank Brigade at the start of the offensive, only twenty T-34s, three T-70s and four T-60s took part in the fighting. The remainder were put out of action as the result of technical breakdowns. Thus every tank knocked out (especially the T-34s) was a significant loss.

However, from the Germans' point of view, the crisis had not yet been overcome. The retention of the commanding height in the Soviet forces' hands would mean the collapse of the defence in the coming days. If artillery could have been brought up, the defence visible from the height would have been subjected to a cruel bombardment from all weapons. It was necessary to restore the situation immediately. At 17.00 the counter-attack began from the area of the Borodkin farm. The 102nd Tank Brigade's tanks were already all knocked out and it was unable to put up any resistance to the enemy.

The defence of the captured height could only rely with great difficulty on the tank corps' second echelons. During the second half of the day the 3rd Guards Heavy Tank Brigade beat off attacks against Height 154.2. Its strength gradually melted away. The 3rd Guards Heavy Tank Brigade's losses for the day were seven KVs and three T-60s burned and seven KVs and three T-60s knocked out. By evening Height 154.2 had been retaken by the enemy. Attempts to throw the Soviet units back to their jumping-off positions failed – the 4th Tank Corps' 45th and 121st Tank Brigades repelled them. Both brigades did not cross the line of the heights and were not exposed to the murderous fire along the southern slopes. It's possible that it would have been better if they had supported their comrades in the fighting for Borodkin and Konnyi. But instead of this there was a duel at the foot of the lost height.

The consequences of a single day's fighting were truly destructive for the 1st Guards Army's tank formations. The 7th Tank Corps' tanks were practically mown down. Of twenty T-34s in the 4th Tank Corps' 102nd Tank Brigade which took part in the fighting, fourteen burned, two went missing in action and two were knocked out, of three T-70s, one burned, while all the T-60s were burned.

Major Matusevich, a General Staff officer with the 7th Tank Corps, wrote: 'One may state without mistake that the given offensive was foiled by enemy aviation.'[15] On 18 September the 16th Air Army carried out only 363 sorties. On this day the German air force, according to data by Soviet observation posts, carried out about 2,000 sorties. In the Sixth Army's war diary the high intensity of the employment of air power is noted: 'The VIII Air Corps directed all of its forces at effective and non-stop actions against the enemy who had penetrated into the area between the Volga and Don. 875 of our planes dropped 395 tons of bombs of all sizes.'[16] Besides aviation, the German artillery made no small contribution. Data on the expenditure of ammunition by the XIV Panzer Corps is unfortunately incomplete (there are no figures for the 60th Motorized Division, with the corps expending 40 tons without it), although it is known that the VIII Corps shot off 170 tons of ammunition on 18 September, including 254 210mm, 518 10cm K18 and 247 150mm sFH18 rounds.[17]

One could only escape the deadly air strikes and heavy artillery fire by closing with the enemy as much as possible. The infantry, which was pinned down at a safe distance from the German positions, became a 'sitting duck' for the enemy's planes and artillery. The tank brigades which broke through into the defensive depth, were counter-attacked by enemy tanks and burned.

The most unpleasant thing was that the losses were not recompensed even by the retention of the initial gains. One of the most important tactical practices in an offensive was the consolidation of the positions seized during the course of the offensive. In an account of the 1st Guards Army's combat activities, we find the following lines: 'On 18.9, following the breakthrough of the Germans' defence, the 316th Rifle Division and the 7th Tank Corps occupied the commanding Height 154.2, but did not consolidate there: they did not bring up reserves or weapons and did not organize consolidation detachments, which enabled the enemy to counter-attack and retake this height during the second part of 18.9.'[18]

It should be noted that the Red Army already had experience in consolidating captured positions. This circumstance was singled out in particular in instructions sent by Zhukov: 'Consolidation detachments, consisting of a company of engineers with obstacle equipment, and infantry ranging in size from a company to a battalion, and 2–3 repaired captured tanks apiece, should be allocated in each army for consolidating captured strongpoints.'[19] German assault groups during the First World War operated according to the same principle. They also took barbed wire with them into the attack and following the seizure of a trench they quickly built obstacles on the approaches to the newly-captured enemy trenches, in which the dead defenders' bodies were still warm.

The loss of Height 154.2 forced Zhukov to once again focus attention on the practice of consolidating captured lines. An order, signed by Zhukov and Malenkov, was sent to the commander of the Stalingrad Front, as well as the army, corps, division and brigade commanders:

> As a result of not adopting measures to consolidate, on the evening of 18.9, Height 154.2 was lost to the enemy. This is not the first case in which the Stalingrad Front has taken tactically favourable positions with heavy losses, but afterwards has failed to consolidate the captured site and failed to organize a good system of artillery fire and have not brought up tanks and failed to organize command and control, as a result of which they enable the enemy to once again throw our units from the captured positions. I consider that such an attitude by commanders to their responsibilities to consolidate sites and lines [captured] from the enemy to be equivalent to a crime.[20]

On the following day, 19 September, the 1st Guards Army attempted to renew the offensive. The tanks supported the attack with fire. The intensity of the struggle fell significantly. In the German daily report these attacks against units defending the 'land bridge' were evaluated as 'several disconnected but powerful reconnaissance attacks'. The chief reason for the sharp reduction in the northern shock group of the Stalingrad Front's offensive capabilities was the losses in tanks. The ammunition expenditure for the XIV Panzer Corps and VIII Corps fell significantly, but nevertheless remained at a high rate: the former fired off 200 tons on 19 September and the latter 161 tons.[21]

The merciless thinning out of the light tanks in the 1st Guards Army's offensive of 18–19 September was predictable. In the 148th Tank Brigade, following one day of fighting on 18 September, out of eight KVs, two T-34s and fourteen T-60s, there remained three KVs and five T-60s. In the 3rd Tank Brigade, out of twenty-three T-34s and fifteen T-70s, there remained eighteen T-34s and four T-70s. The number of tanks in the 1st Guards Army's tank brigades and corps following the latest attempt to break through and link up with the 62nd Army is shown in the table.

Table 23: The Condition of the Tank Park of the 1st Guards Army's Units and Formations by 18.00 on 20 September 1942.[22]

Unit / Formation	KV	T-34	T-70	T-60	Other	Total
16th Tank Corps	13	37	–	36	–	86
7th Tank Corps	3/3*	32**/10	0/2	8/28	–	43/40
4th Tank Corps	6/17	14/47	11/1	10/11	0/2+1***	41/79
148th Tank Brigade	1/7	0/2	–	4/13	–	5/22
3rd Tank Brigade	–	2/4	2/2	–	–	4/6
12th Tank Brigade****	–	2	2	–	–	4
Total	23/27	87/63	15/5	58/52	0/3	183/150

* Combat-ready tanks are in the numerator and tanks in repair in the denominator.
** The corps received twenty-one T-34s as reinforcements.
*** Two BT-5 tanks and one Mk III.
**** As of 21 September.

Thus of 340 tanks available at the start of the offensive, by 20–21 September there remained 183 combat-ready, taking into account reinforcements. Also, a certain amount could have been repaired. As opposed to manoeuvre battles, in positional fighting the repair park most often did not suffer and those tanks towed off the battlefield could be repaired.

The exhausting positional battles told not only on the tank park. Losses among the rank and file of the Stalingrad Front's three armies were also quite high (see table).

Table 24: Rank and File Losses of the Stalingrad Front's Armies Launching a Counter-attack during 1–20 September 1942.[23]

Army	Killed	Wounded	Missing in Action	Other Causes	Total
1st Guards	7,726	26,617	1,267	196	35,806
24th	5,747	20,061	6,629	67	32,504
66th	3,237	13,125	3,798	245	20,405
Total	16,710	59,803	11,694	508	88,715

At the same time, one cannot help but note that positional battles, despite their intensity and bloody nature, are not in any way comparable with the disasters associated with manoeuvre battles. In the manoeuvre phase of a battle a pitiful remnant of 700–1,500 men might remain of a fresh rifle division over a week from the sharp manoeuvrings of German panzer and army corps. Nevertheless, the pace of the lowering of the formations' strength is impressive. On 15 September 1942 the 308th Rifle Division numbered 8,671 men and the 316th Rifle Division 10,495 men. The counterblow launched during 18–19 September immediately knocked both formations out of the ranks of the up-to-strength. Correspondingly, on 20 September 1942 the 308th Rifle Division numbered 4,467 men, and the 316th Rifle Division 4,941 men. Nevertheless, they were not destroyed, as happened to the 62nd and 4th Tank Armies in the bend of the Don. Besides this, a significant share of the losses in the positional fighting were missing in action and wounded evacuated to the rear.

Following the unsuccessful offensive of 18–19 September, Stalin, in *Stavka* VGK Directive No. 170619, recommended to Zhukov that he shift the axis of the attack:

It seems to me that you should have shifted the main attack from the direction of Kuz'michi to the area between heights 130.7 and 128.9, eight kilometres north-east of Kuz'michi. This would have enabled you to link up with Stalingrad's defenders, to encircle the enemy group along the western bank of the Volga and to free the 66th Army for active operations toward Stalingrad. For this, you could have strengthened Malinovskii's left flank with three divisions and three tanks brigades from the 1st Guards and 24th Armies and to go over to an active defence in the 24th and 1st Guards armies' areas. So that these armies' defence was solid, you should have taken 2–3 reserve divisions from the 63rd and 21st Armies. This was all the more possible in that the enemy had already moved part of his forces from the 63rd and 21st Armies' area and shifted them to Stalingrad, leaving there a thin screen of Romanian and Italian units not capable of active operations. The rapid link-up of the northern group with the forces in Stalingrad is a condition without which your entire operation may become unsuccessful.

In the middle of September the tip of the attack shifted to the west. Now it was proposed by Stalin to shift it to the east. So it was said, so it was done. The 7th Tank Corps was concentrated in the zone of R.Ya. Malinovskii's army. Now it was supposed to operate in conjunction with the 64th and 99th Rifle Divisions (7,148 and 8,531 men respectively, as of 20 September), each with two brigades. The corps' composite 87th Tank Brigade numbered twenty-four T-34s and fifteen T-60s, and the attached 58th Tank Brigade another forty-three vehicles.

Questions of cooperation with the infantry and artillery were worked out in the most scrupulous manner. The commander of the 99th Rifle Division allocated two rifle companies to each tank battalion as tank riders. Besides the shift in the axis of the attack, it was decided to begin the offensive an hour and a half before the onset of darkness. At 18.00 on 24 September, following a 30-minute artillery preparation, the offensive began. Two brigades of the 7th Tank Corps moved into the attack and before long had broken through the forward edge of the enemy's defence. The infantry, under pressure from the Germans' artillery and mortar fire, slowed down the pace of its advance and fell far behind the tanks. The tank riders jumped off the tanks upon approaching the enemy's forward edge and contact with them was lost. Despite the onset of darkness, which hindered the activities of the Germans' death-dealing aviation, the infantry did not follow the tanks. Individual tanks that broke into the depth of the defence were set on fire. Several tanks lost their way in the darkness and arrived at Akatovka, where they captured a headquarters vehicle and returned to their jumping-off positions.

The offensive was renewed on the morning of 25 September, but without success. At the same time, German counter-attacks to restore the situation were also repulsed. In two days, of the eighty-nine tanks of Rotmistrov's corps that took part in the fighting, seventy-five were put out of action, including twenty-nine tanks lost irretrievably. The tanks, as the counter-attacks' main shock force, were put out of action and the offensive impulse faded away.

Despite the supreme commander-in-chief's instructions and the resulting launching of an attack in the 66th Army's zone, a major offensive was undertaken involving a shift of the main attack's axis to the west. Zhukov and Yeremenko did not follow the supreme commander-in-chief's instructions to the letter, insofar as they had their own opinion regarding the prospective axes. The famous aphorism 'And Vas'ka the cat listens, but eats all the same' is very *apropos* of the situation. The forces of the 1st Guards and 24th Armies were to be drawn into the operation. To be exact, the offensive in these armies' zones did not halt during 18–19 September. In particular, the night of 20/21 September was used for attacking under the cover of darkness. Insofar as the armies' tank units suffered heavy losses in tanks, the 91st Tank Brigade, which was being reformed following the July fighting, was brought up to the front.

The 1st Guards Army's 173rd, 273rd and 258th Rifle Divisions, independent tank brigades and the 16th Tank Corps were to be brought in for the new offensive. It was planned to commit the latter into the breakthrough following the smashing of the defence by the infantry. On 22 September the corps numbered 4,519 men and 87 tanks (14 KVs, 42 T-34s and 31 T-60s).[24] Aside from the exploitation echelon, each of the divisions taking part in the offensive was to be supported by a single tank brigade, operating in packets, from those available. These were, respectively, the 148th, 3rd and 12th Tank Brigades. The 1st Guards and 24th Armies' rifle formations were already pretty used up. The conviction that the German units had also suffered heavy losses under the blows by tanks and artillery in the preceding counterblows gave hope for the success of the undertaking. However, the enemy forces had also undergone changes. The 100th Jäger Division was removed from those troops attacking Stalingrad and made a part of the VIII Corps. It included four full-strength German battalions and one full-strength Croatian battalion.

The further development of events was quite typical for the Stalingrad Front's counterblows. The 16th Tank Corps was committed during the second half of the day on 23 September, but not into the breach, but into the fighting. The infantry advanced slowly and the front was not penetrated. The enemy lost the first ridge of heights (108.4 and 107.2), but the second ridge, consisting of Heights 130.1 and 130.4, became the line of stubborn resistance. The tanks surged ahead, destroying the enemy's centres of resistance with fire and tracks. However, the infantry was pinned down by fire and advanced extremely slowly. As was later stated in a report by the command of the 16th Tank Corps, 'the cooperating units of the 273rd Rifle Division, expecting to be completely destroyed by the enemy's tanks in the area of the heights, did not advance and failed to consolidate the tanks' success'.[25] At the same time, the corps' tank park was gradually melting away. On 24 September the 16th Tank Corps lost eleven KVs and twenty-eight T-34s, and by the close of 25 September there remained only three T-34s and eleven T-60s in line.

The Germans were holding on to the ridge of heights by their teeth, chiefly because the terrain was replete with favourable defensive positions. Colonel Dingler, who has already been quoted in von Mellenthin's telling, described German tactics as follows:

> We also came to the conclusion that it was not expedient to outfit positions along the forward slopes, insofar as it was impossible to defend them against tank attacks. One should not forget that tanks formed the basis of our anti-tank defence and that we concentrated all the tanks in the hollows immediately by the forward edge. They could easily hit the Russian tanks from these positions as soon as they reached the crest of the height. At the same time, our tanks were able to render support to the infantry, which was defending along the back slopes, while repelling the Russian tank attacks. The effectiveness of our tactics was proved by the fact that in two months of fighting our division put more than 200 Russian tanks out of action.[26]

Accordingly, the tanks of the Soviet brigades and corps located on the southern slopes of the heights were hit by German tanks occupying positions near the base of the heights.

During 25–27 September units of the 1st Guards Army carried out offensive operations daily and repeatedly carried out night attacks, but were unable to crush the enemy's resistance. During these days of fighting the divisions of Moskalenko's army were able to advance only 300–800m. Losses in the counterblows of 20–26 September were lower than during first twenty days of September (see table).

Table 25: Losses Among the Rank and File of the Stalingrad Front's Armies Launching Counterblows During 20–26 September 1942.[27]

Army	Killed	Wounded	Missing in Action	Other Causes	Total
1st Guards	2,009	7,097	1,320	186	10,612
24th	1,181	4,700	405	19	6,305
66th	432	1,273	99	17	1,821
Total	3,622	13,070	1,824	222	18,738

It is clear that Moskalenko's 1st Guards Army took the brunt of the continuing counterblow. The 66th Army, which was operating along an auxiliary axis, suffered insignificant losses.

One should not think that the enemy achieved his defensive success easily. There were nine battalions in the 76th Infantry Division as of 28 September, of which two were of medium strength, while seven were weak. They had begun the battle two weeks earlier with nine medium-strength battalions. On 28 September the 60th Motorized Division numbered seven motorized infantry battalions, of which four were of medium strength, two were weak, and one was 'worn out' (*abgekaempft*). The formation's engineer battalion was also listed as 'worn out'. The 60th Motorized Division had begun the battle with all of its motorized infantry battalions at medium strength. That is, the divisions' condition changed radically for the worse.

The positional battle to the north of Stalingrad gradually died down, but one of the last outbreaks of activity nevertheless is worthy of being highlighted. On the evening of 27 September a paper was sent to the commander of the 24th Army, D.T. Kozlov, marked 'extremely important' and signed by Yeremenko. The *front* commander was ordering him to regroup, to take in troops from the 66th Army and to go over to the offensive toward Orlovka on 30 September.[28] This order was evidently linked to the beginning of the latest assault on Stalingrad by the Germans. Two fresh tank brigades were to be transferred to the 24th Army for the new offensive: the 241st Tank Brigade (twenty-three M3s Lees and twenty-five M3l Stuarts) and the 167th Tank Brigade (twenty-nine Mk III Valentines and twenty-one T-70s.[29])

According to the *front* command's instructions, the 24th Army's staff worked out an offensive operation of limited scope. It was planned to launch the attack along the army's left flank for the purpose of 'chewing through the enemy's front during the course of two days and on the third day link up with the South-eastern Front's forces defending Stalingrad'.[30] Three rifle divisions and two tank brigades would constitute the breakthrough echelon. It was planned to employ the tanks of the two attached brigades for direct infantry support of the 343rd and 116th Rifle Divisions (6,540 and 4,950 men on 29 September, respectively).[31] The start of the offensive was set for 04.00 on 30 September.

The development of events with the start of the offensive was, on the whole, typical for this axis. The infantry fell behind the tanks under a hail of fire and did not advance. The tank-riders dismounted. This is hardly surprising: the ammunition expenditure for the XIV Panzer Corps for 30 September was comparable to that of the most intense days of the 'Battle for the Semaphore' and amounted to 198 tons.[32] Darting rapidly ahead, the tanks hid behind the crest of the heights and disappeared from view. Radio communications were maintained with the brigade until 11.30 on 30 September. Subsequent attempts to restore communications with the tanks that had broken into the depth of the defence continued until the end of the following day, but yielded no results. Two vehicles apiece returned from the battlefield and one vehicle from each was evacuated. The fate of the remaining vehicles remained unknown. German documents enable us to throw some light on the fate of the Lees, Stuarts and Valentines, which were received through Lend-Lease and which disappeared in just one hour. In the Sixth Army's war diary it was noted that the offensive was beaten off by the forces of the 3rd Motorized Division and sixty Soviet tanks were knocked out as far as behind the formation's defensive line. According to a report by the XIV Panzer Corps for 30 September, 24 Soviet and 100 non-Soviet tanks overall were destroyed and distributed as follows: two T-34s, three T-60s, nineteen T-70s, eight M3s Lees, forty-seven M3l Stuarts, and twenty-four Valentines.[33] The Germans noted the English-language lettering and accompanying documents in the tanks. On 29 September the 3rd Motorized Division numbered six Panzer IIs, ten Panzer IIIs (long), four Panzer IVs (short) and four Panzer IVs (long).[34] By the evening of 30 September the division numbered only one Panzer II, one Panzer III (long) and one Panzer IV (long).[35]

In the Sixth Army's daily report for 27 September the fighting along the 'land bridge' was rated as heavy: 'In the VIII Army Corps south of Kotluban' the 76th Infantry Division beat off in heavy fighting four enemy infantry-tank attacks, which were conducted in the space of 1–2 hours. During one of these attacks the Russians managed to penetrate the positions in the Big Thin *Balka*.' Fierce fighting, in which all of the Soviet attacks were repelled by the enemy, went on all day on 28 September. The losses testify eloquently to the intensity of the combat activities. During 26–30 September all of the Stalingrad Front's armies lost 3,767 men killed, 10,217 wounded, 878 missing in action, and 1,311 due to other reasons, for a total of 16,174 men.[36]

In absolute figures, the enemy's losses are as follows (see table).

Table 26: Losses of the Sixth Army's Formations Taking Part in the Defence of the 'Land Bridge,' 1–30 September 1942.[37]

Unit	Killed	Wounded	Missing in Action	Sick	Total
XIV Panzer Corps Headquarters	54	100	1	0	155
16th Panzer Division	481	1,513	88	69	2,151
3rd Motorized Division	395	1,217	35	300	1,947
60th Motorized Division	600	1,879	42	295	2,816
VIII Army Corps Headquarters	34	128	1	53	216
76th Infantry Division	419	2,435	44	72	2,970
Total	1,983	7,272	211	789	10,255

This data does not include the losses by detachments, which were employed in the struggle for the 'land bridge' (for example, units of the 389th Infantry Division). The compilation of losses by such episodes is extremely difficult. However, it is doubtful that these data would change the overall picture.

A comparison of the data presented with Soviet losses along this sector of the front (see above) produces, of course, a depressing impression. The correlation of the sides' irreplaceable losses in the 'Battle for the Semaphore' is 1:15. It should be stressed that a comparison of human losses in and of itself is not an index of the qualities of the sides' soldiers. The most terrible enemy of the soldiers and officers of the reserve armies were the German artillerists, who poured a hail of fire on the ranks of the attacking formations. The situation was much worse to the north of Stalingrad than around Rzhev, on the western front, where the attacking units were at least supported by artillery, up to 305mm inclusively.

In his memoirs, Zhukov quite accurately defined the reasons for the failures of the Soviet offensives (aside from the overall problems of the Red Army of 1942): 'Having occupied a series of commanding heights, he [the enemy, Author] had long-range artillery observation and could manoeuvre with fire in all directions. Aside from this, the enemy had the opportunity of waging long-range artillery fire from the area Kuz'michi – Akatovka – the 'Opytnoe Polye' State Farm. Under these conditions, the Stalingrad Front's 24th, 1st Guards and 66th Armies were unable to break through the enemy's front.'[38]

Indeed, the defensive front of the 'land bridge' was comparatively narrow, and the Sixth Army disposed of a large number of powerful and long-range guns (10cm K18s and 21cm Mörser 18s), capable of hitting practically any threatened sector. The artillery remained the 'god of war' and decided the fate of battles.

The series of counterblows to the north of Stalingrad, conducted since the end of August 1942, despite the major forces committed to them, remain insufficiently illuminated in our historiography. The *front* commander, Yeremenko, preferred altogether to distance himself from conducting the counterblows, citing that he was busy with the defence of the city. He wrote in his memoirs: 'I was unable to pay sufficient attention to this front, insofar as I was directly involved with the defence of Stalingrad.'[39] At the same time, he sharply criticized his deputies who were responsible for the front to the north of the city. The main object of his criticism was V.N. Gordov, who by then was dead and could not say anything in his own defence. The fault for the failure of the offensives was also broadly laid on Zhukov:

In September General of the Army Comrade Zhukov arrived at the Stalingrad Front as a *Stavka* representative. He took part in the organization of the above-named counterblows and undoubtedly was involved in the mistakes linked to them. He was neither in Stalingrad nor at the headquarters of the South-eastern Front and went directly to the headquarters of the Stalingrad Front, which was located 40 kilometres to the north of the city. Zhukov's arrival gave us some hope. We calculated that with his help the Stalingrad Front would be able to take advantage of the favourable position of its forces in relation to the enemy and render more effective assistance to the South-eastern Front, which was facing the enemy's main pressure in the city itself and along its southern flank. However, in many ways our hopes were not justified. As was the case before, the Stalingrad Front's attempts to eliminate the enemy breakthrough following Zhukov's arrival, remained unsuccessful.[40]

However, the plans preserved in the archives for the offensive operations bear Yeremenko's signature. Thus, for example, the above-mentioned plan for the 24th Army's offensive of 27 September was signed by Yeremenko and the deputy chief of staff of the Stalingrad Front, Major General I.N. Rukhle. Accordingly, for example, the 24th Army's military council drew up a plan for a counteroffensive with the remark in the 'Decision' section – 'basically instructed by the *front*'. Thus Yeremenko shares responsibility for the counterblows by the 1st Guards, 24th and 66th Armies with Zhukov, Gordov, Moskalenko, Kozlov and Malinovskii. The counterblows are just as much an inalienable part of the battle of Stalingrad as the fighting in the city. To forget them is at the very least unjust to those who took part in them. In essence, the Stalingrad Front's counteroffensives are indivisible from the fighting in Stalingrad itself. Chuikov threw newly-arrived reserves into the fighting in the same way, while trying to win back Mamaev hill and the central part of the city. With minimal tank support the successes of the 95th and 284th Rifle Division's counterblows were hardly less than that of the 1st Guards Army. The difference was only in the scale of the counterblows, that is, in the number of formations drawn in.

However, Yeremenko's and Gordov's activity as leaders of the Stalingrad Front did not satisfy the supreme command. Shifts in command and control along the Stalingrad direction went on practically the whole time from the moment a titan such as Timoshenko was removed from command. On 28 September *Stavka* VGK Order No. 994209 was issued, in which not only were the names of the two active fronts changed, but their commanders as well:

> In connection with the more complex situation around Stalingrad, the great extent of the fronts and the growing number of armies in them, as well as for the purpose of easing command and control, the *Stavka* of the Supreme High Command orders the following:
>
> 1. To form two independent *fronts* in the Stalingrad area with each of them directly subordinated to the *Stavka* of the Supreme High Command – the Don Front from the Stalingrad Front, including the 63rd, 21st, 4th Tank, 1st Guards, 24th, and 66th Armies, and the Stalingrad Front from the South-eastern Front, including the 62nd, 64th, 57th, 51st, and 28 armies.
> 2. To appoint Colonel General Comrade Yeremenko A.I. commander of the Stalingrad Front.
> 3. To appoint Lieutenant General Rokossovskii K.K. commander of the Don Front, relieving him of the post of commander of the Bryansk Front.[41]

In effect, *Stavka* precisely divided the forces which had earlier been under the command of A.I. Yeremenko between the two die-hard commanders. The new *fronts* inherited their armies from their predecessors – the Stalingrad and South-eastern Fronts. Gordov, the deputy front commander, and I.N. Rukhle, the chief of the operational section, were removed from their posts and put at the disposal of the people's commissar of defence. The *front* chief of staff, K.A. Kovalenko, was promoted to the post of deputy commander. K.K. Rokossovskii arrived at the post of commander of the Don Front with his chief of staff M.S. Malinin.

Chapter 16

The Second Assault on the City.
27 September–7 October 1942

(Maps 9 and 10)

On the German side, the most powerful players in the street fighting in Stalingrad were the formations transferred to Paulus from Hoth's army. The Sixth Army's LI Corps, which was the single formation which remained free following the occupation of defensive positions on the front along the Don and the 'land bridge' and thus put into the assault on Stalingrad, was in a woeful condition. According to a report of 26 September 1942 there were seven battalions in the 71st Infantry Division, of which four were weak and three 'worn out' (*abgekaempft*), and seven battalions in the 295th Infantry Division, of which two were of average strength, four were weak and one worn out, while the 389th Infantry Division contained six infantry battalions, two of which were at medium strength and four were weak. It was insanity to storm the city with these divisions given the constant strengthening of the defenders. They were only good for defence. The condition of the 24th Panzer Division and 100th Light Infantry Division was much better. As regards both formations in the ongoing evaluation of the condition of the Sixth Army's formations, it was stated that 'The division is good for any offensive missions'.

In the numerical sense, the situation appeared as follows. The strength of the 24th Panzer Division's subunits (*Gefechtsstaerke*) participating in the fighting on 21 September was 6,557 men, while the formation's ration strength was 11,756 men.[1] Taking into account attached units, the formation's ration strength amounted to 15,143 men.

By 27 September the LI Corps disposed of two battalions of 210mm howitzers, two battalions of 105mm guns, three battalions of 150mm howitzers, and the 244th and 245th Assault Gun Battalions as reinforcements.[2] The condition of the latter is shown in the table.

Table 27: The Condition of Armoured Equipment in the LI Corps on 26 September 1942.[3]

Assault Gun Battalion	Combat Ready		In Repair
	StuG III (short)	StuG III (long)	StuG III (short)
244th	11	9	1
245th	6	8	7

The plan for a new assault on the city was prepared by the German command as early as 19 September. The 24th Panzer Division, the 295th, 389th and 94th Infantry Divisions and units of the XIV Panzer Corps were supposed to take part in crushing the salient near Orlovka. As a result, the 24th Panzer Division and the 100th Jäger Division (five powerful battalions, including one Croatian) from the XI Corps were brought in for the new offensive. The latter division arrived at the streets of Stalingrad while transiting through the defensive battle for the 'land bridge'. The commitment of this division into the fighting was a signal event. This marked the beginning of the practice of removing divisions from the front along the Don for the assault on the city.

The 24th Panzer Division was divided into two groups for the offensive – Edelsheim's 'infantry' combat group and Winterfeld's 'panzer' combat group. Accordingly, all of the tanks and mechanized infantry, with a company of motorcyclists, were gathered into the 'tank' group, which was reinforced with a battalion from an artillery regiment. This was essentially an analogue of the Germans' 'armoured groups' of the war's second half, with only the Hummel and Wespe self-propelled guns, which appeared in 1943, absent for now. The remaining motorized infantry battalions, engineers and tank destroyers from the 24th Panzer Division formed Edelsheim's 'infantry' group. The division's first task was to break through to the railway line, and the second to break through to Height 107.5, while the 'infantry' combat group was to take advantage of the results of the 'tank' group's attack. In the event of a favourable development of events, it was planned to advance further to the north of Height 107.5. Von Lenski's division was reinforced with seventeen batteries from the High Command Reserve, including guns ranging from 100mm to 210mm, which to a significant degree compensated for the thinned-out ranks of tanks, while 88mm anti-aircraft gunners, whose armour-piercing and fragmentation and demolition shells had shown themselves to be quite effective against brick structures, were also to fire on the buildings on Height 107.5.

We completed the narrative about the defence of Stalingrad at that moment when Chuikov issued his latest order for an offensive on the evening of 26 September. According to the 269th NKVD Regiment's war diary, the order to attack was received only at 01.00 and transmitted to the subunits at 04.00. According to a report by the 137th Tank Brigade, the NKVD regiment at that moment numbered 602 men, of which 444 were 'active bayonets'. The 137th Tank Brigade itself numbered 534 men (390 'active bayonets') and disposed of approximately nine T-60s.

On the morning of 27 September the enemies faced each other in readiness for an attack. The passing of the initiative from hand to hand was rapid and accompanied by difficult consequences for the 62nd Army. According to the orders issued the previous evening by the command, the artillery preparation began at 05.00, to which the artillery of the 23rd Tank Corps' formations joined in. Units of the 137th Tank Brigade and the 269th NKVD Regiment attacked at 06.00.

The Soviet units' meeting engagement made a strange impression on the Germans. Correspondent K. Podewils wrote that 'It's most likely that the enemy intends to pre-empt the Germans' attack and that he knows its day and hour'.[4] However, the German artillery preparation of the forward edge began at that same hour. The German aviation simultaneously hurled itself against the enemy's artillery positions. Unfortunately, not only German artillery systems took part in repelling the Soviet attack. Three 122mm howitzers, captured by the Germans in the southern part of Stalingrad, also fired, showing the necessity of putting abandoned guns out of action. M30s captured by the Germans fired off about 300 rounds that had been captured along with them.

Immediately following the repulse of the Soviet attack, the tanks of the 24th Panzer Division attacked at 08.00. Later, in the LI Corps' daily report, the actions of the Soviet forces were described as follows: 'The Russians defended stubbornly from well-constructed positions, while being supported by powerful artillery of all calibres.'

The main attack hit the positions of the 9th and 38th Motorized Rifle Brigades. Before long the German tanks broke through the 38th Motorized Rifle Brigade's defence. Having cleared a path through these positions, part of the tanks turned south and reached the mortar and anti-tank positions of the 9th Motorized Rifle Brigade from the flank and rear. The vigorously-attacked mortar positions were quickly crushed. Left without mortars and anti-tank weapons, the brigade's defence was finished off by a frontal attack. The 9th Motorized Rifle Brigade's forward companies were cut off and no one from them returned. The brigade's remnants fell back to the silicate factory. Having broken the defence, the German tanks and motorized infantry also reached the rear of the 189th Tank Brigade, which was defending to the north. Under threat of complete destruction, the brigade fell back to the 'Red October' and 'Barricade' settlements.

The situation was saved by the commitment of tanks into the fighting. The 189th Tank Brigade, having received five T-34s from Chuikov's reserve, and the 6th Guards Tank Brigade seven T-34s, counter-attacked the enemy who was breaking through to the 'Red October' settlement. But this was only a temporary solution. At best, one could only hold one a day or two with tank counter-attacks.

The first day of the second assault was described quite jauntily in the Sixth Army's war diary:

> On 27.9 the army's southern flank began an offensive against the northern part of Stalingrad. While overcoming stubborn resistance, it achieved the goals assigned for the day. The western edge of the large railway loop, the commanding Height 107.5, and the quarters to the north-east of it, and the ravine north-west of Red October, were occupied and our units reached the railway south-east of Gorodishche along a broad front.

This success can be explained quite simply: the Germans would clear a path with a hurricane of artillery fire. The expenditure of ammunition by the LI Corps on 27 September was the impressive amount of 444 tons, including 346 rounds from 210mm howitzers and 2,044 rounds from 150mm field howitzers.[5]

One might raise the logical question: what could the defenders of Stalingrad put up against this hurricane of fire? It is well known that artillery batteries from the left bank of the Volga supported the 62nd and 64th Armies' units fighting on the streets of the city. In his memoirs, Chief Artillery Marshal N.N. Voronov,[6] while describing his visit to the Stalingrad area in September, writes: 'The characteristic whistle of heavy shells could be heard from time to time. This was the famous trans-Volga artillery group firing on the enemy. The heavy and super heavy artillery had been moved beyond the Volga in a timely manner.'[7] Further on, so as not to leave any doubts regarding 'heavy and super heavy' artillery, he writes of the presence of 203mm–280mm guns in this group.

However, Voronov's words, unfortunately, are not confirmed by documents. For example, on 1 October 1942 seven gun artillery regiments, armed with six 107mm guns, eighteen 122mm howitzers, ten 122mm guns (122mm model 1931 A-19 guns), and thirty-nine 152mm guns (the exact type is not indicated, but they are most likely ML-20 152mm gun-howitzers) were in the *front* artillery group.[8] A super-heavy artillery regiment with ten 203mm howitzers appears only in the reports from 20–25 October 1942.[9] As of 1–5 December 1942 this same single regiment is listed as being subordinated to the *front*, to be sure, with thirteen 203mm guns already.[10] According to data from the Red Army's Main Artillery Administration, the expenditure of 203mm shells was 1,800 rounds for the entire second half of 1942.[11] The other *fronts* along the Stalingrad direction did not expend ammunition of this type. In its turn, the German Sixth Army expended 4,318 210mm shells just during the period 1–20 September (the beginning of the assault on Stalingrad and the fighting in the Kotluban' area).[12] As they say, there's no need for commentary. During the period being described, the LI Corps fired an average of 200–300 210mm rounds per day. The Germans' weekly expenditure was 1,800 rounds.

Accordingly, one may state with a high degree of certainty that Voronov's words are an idealized presentation of the *front's* artillery group. 'As it should have been' and not 'as it was'. The reasons for this are most likely to be found in shell production. In the Red Army 203mm guns were fed with ammunition 'on the move', that is, production barely kept pace with expenditure. That is, there were heavy and super-heavy guns, but there were serious problems with supplying them with shells. The employment of 203mm howitzers was limited to the Western and Volkhov Fronts.

Only the stability of the front along those sectors where the 62nd Army's shock group of forces was located offered any consolation. The attack by the 100th Jäger Division in the area of Mamaev hill did not yield the Germans tangible results. At the same time, at that moment the 62nd Army commander already had quite a serious argument against the enemy's offensive. Chuikov's trump card was the 193rd Rifle Division, one regiment of which was already fighting in the centre of the city. With the start of the new German offensive, the decision was immediately made to cross the division's main forces to the city. General Smekhotvorov received an order stating: 'Despite all possible obstacles, the division is to cross during the night of 27/28.9 to the right bank of the Volga River and be subordinated to the 62nd Army, with the task of destroying the enemy in the area of the "Red October" settlement.'

The crossing of fresh forces into Stalingrad went astonishingly smoothly. Before the break of dawn on 28 September they had managed to cross both rifle regiments, an anti-tank battalion and the artillery regiment's gun batteries. The rear establishments were left along the left bank of the Volga, while the division's elements took with them only 1.5 combat loads of ammunition. To be exact, the soldiers gathered all their equipment before the crossing, while the rear-area elements and their vehicles were dispatched to their previous position. Thanks to the concealment measures adopted, the crossing was accomplished without losses.

The division was ordered to occupy defensive positions with the forward edge running along the western outskirts of the city. The occupation of positions by the division's 883rd Rifle Regiment, which was relieving the remnants of a tank and two motorized rifle brigades and the 269th NKVD Regiment in the Library Street – Bathhouse Ravine area was achieved relatively smoothly. The 895th Rifle Regiment's arrival at its assigned line passed far more dramatically. At 04.00 on 28 September, even before the completion of the crossing by all of the subunits, Major Vorozheikin's 895th Rifle Regiment began to move up to its assigned positions. However, instead of arriving at the assigned positions and entrenching there, a meeting engagement began with the Germans (the 24th Panzer Division's security detachment) already in the 'Red October' factory's settlement. This was essentially a meeting engagement. In reality, only the 895th Rifle Regiment's first battalion managed to reach its assigned defensive area, but it fell back before long as well. The employment of heavy infantry weapons became a problem. As was noted later in the regiment's report, 'the heavy and light machine guns and the 50mm and 82mm mortars, were clearly employed insufficiently during this period, that is, in their moving up to the defensive area the main part of these weapons did not arrive at their designated area and was partially destroyed by the enemy's artillery and mortar fire and by air strikes, and partially due to delays in its advance'.[13] Even worse was that the 193rd Rifle Division's battalions arrived at their supposed defensive line when it had already grown light, which prevented them from entrenching, while the engineer preparation of the positions was carried out badly.

At the same time, with the commitment of the 193rd Rifle Division's regiments, Chuikov managed to avoid the collapse of the defence, although the 24th Panzer Division was advancing slowly but surely. It was noted in the Sixth Army's war diary that 'The army's offensive against the northern part of Stalingrad achieved success today as well, despite the enemy's stubborn resistance. Half of the "Barricade" area has been captured, and to the north-west we have reached the Gorodishche creek from the south.'[14] The LI Corps' expenditure of ammunition for 28 September was less than for the previous day, but nonetheless was an impressive 331 tons, including 270 210mm and 1,328 150mm heavy field howitzer shells.[15] As before, the Germans cleared a path for themselves through the ruins of Stalingrad with a hurricane of fire.

One cannot but note that on 28 September a break in the strategy of conducting the defence occurred on Chuikov's part. This was all in all an important day in the battle of Stalingrad. It was precisely on 28 September that the division into the Don and Stalingrad fronts took place. Offensive tasks were to be entrusted to Rokossovskii. Naturally, defensive tasks remained in Yeremenko's hands. Chuikov went from the energetic flinging of reserves into the fighting with the task of achieving a decisive result to a strategy of stubborn resistance. Now the army commander would assign predominantly defensive missions. The regrouping of forces within the 62nd Army now also pursued the goal of strengthening the defence.

Yet another decision by Chuikov was the movement back into the city of rifle brigades which had fallen back from the southern part of Stalingrad. At 03.00 on 28 September his order appeared: 'Units of the 92nd and 42nd Brigades are to be concentrated by 19.00 on 28.9 along the left bank of the Volga River, near crossing No. 62 (Red October).'[16] Following their crossing, the 92nd and 42nd Rifle Brigades concentrated in the area of Mamaev hill on the night of 28/29 September to support the boundary between the 284th and 95th Rifle Divisions. Only Rodimtsev's division received very limited, even cautious, offensive tasks.

However, if a shift had occurred in Chuikov's mood, then the same cannot be said of the commanders of the 62nd Army's formations. Major General F.N. Smekhotvorov, the commander of the 193rd Rifle Division, had to be reproached for broadly interpreting Order No. 172 from the headquarters of the 62nd Army. 'To defend the zone' was interpreted by him to mean 'reach the assigned line and defend it'. Therefore he assigned his units offensive tasks for 29 September.

On one hand, the offensive by two regiments of the 193rd Rifle Division was planned taking urban conditions into account. Shock groups were created in the companies, consisting of a rifle platoon and a squad of automatic riflemen and an anti-tank squad. The groups were generously armed with 4–5 grenades (anti-tank RGD and F-1) per soldier. This compensated for the relative weakness of artillery support for the counter-attack and enabled them to advance and crush the 24th Panzer Division's flank security. A powerful attack hit the 26th Motorized Infantry Regiment's second battalion. As a retaliatory measure, the 24th Panzer Division command summoned tanks from Winterfeld's 'tank' combat group and a counter-attack was organized. Artillery and aviation also hit the 193rd

Rifle Division's attacking units. Smekhotvorov's attempts to reach the defensive line assigned to him essentially became a counterblow against the flank of the German shock group aimed at the factory settlements.

As a result of the 193rd Rifle Division's attack, part of the positions occupied by the Germans the previous day was won back. In the LI Corps' daily report for 29 September, it was noted that 'As a result of the enemy's powerful counter-attack in the first part of the day, a part of the city was lost in quadrant 51CD. At 13.00 a meeting attack began in the west part of the "Red October" settlement and the northern part of the "Barricade" settlement'. Also, during the second half of the day the 100th Light Infantry Division was drawn into the fight against the 193rd Rifle Division's regiments for the 'Red October' settlement. Smekhotvorov had no chance to reach his assigned defensive line in these conditions. The 100th Light Infantry Division suffered 346 casualties overall for 29 September, while remaining from 27 September onward at a consistently high rate of losses for the rank and file, the division inevitably began to lose its combat capability. The 24th Panzer Division, in its turn lost thirty-nine men killed, ninety-four wounded and eight missing in action on 29 September. These were the formation's highest losses for the entire period of the offensive in the northern part of Stalingrad. On the following day the Germans' combat formations in the 193rd Rifle Division's zone were significantly strengthened: a regiment from the 94th Infantry Division and units of the 100th Light Infantry Division occupied part of the 24th Panzer Division's flank security zone.

On 30 September the participation of the 27th, 137th and 189th Tank Brigades and the 9th and 38th Rifle Brigades in the fighting for Stalingrad ended. The 42nd and 92nd Rifle Brigades moved up to their positions. Correspondingly, the 'active bayonets', the artillery troops who had preserved their equipment and the mortar crewmen from the units being pulled out of the fighting, were transferred to the 6th Guards Tank Brigade. The brigades' headquarters, the 'horseless' artillery troops and rear establishments were crossed to the left bank of the Volga, as did the headquarters of the 23rd Tank Corps. The remnants of the corps' equipment and 'active bayonets' remaining in the line, which had been accumulated by the 6th Guards Tank Brigade, were subordinated directly to the commander of the 62nd Army.

As a result of the gathering of the remnants of the 23rd Tank Corps' brigades, by the close of 30 September the 6th Guards Tank Brigade had in line fourteen serviceable T-34s, five non-serviceable T-34s, one T-70, six T-60s, 268 'active bayonets', one anti-tank gun, four 76mm guns, six 120mm mortars and ten 82mm mortars.

At the same time, the *front* command made the decision to seize the initiative from the enemy. On the evening of 29 September the 39th Guards Rifle Division was subordinated to Chuikov and on the morning of 30 September the 308th Rifle and 37th Guards Rifle divisions were ordered to concentrate on the left bank of the Volga in readiness to cross over to Stalingrad.

The positional front along the 'land bridge' became a source for reserves. Major General S.S. Gur'ev's 39th Guards Rifle Division and Colonel L.N. Gurt'ev's 308th Rifle Division were removed from here. The first was taken from the 24th Army and the second from the 1st Guards Army. The 39th Guards Rifle Division was from those formations that had been reformed from airborne corps. It was one of the first of the 1st Guards Army's formations to arrive at Stalingrad and had taken part in combat operations since August 1941. The condition of the two divisions at the time of their movement from the positional 'meat grinder' was far from brilliant. However, as opposed to the manoeuvre battles from which the divisions emerged as a disorganized mob without heavy weapons, the retention of weapons was good in the positional fighting. On 25 September 1942 the 39th Guards Rifle Division numbered 4,082 men, 2,978 rifles, 695 Shpagin sub-machine guns, 24 light and 12 heavy and two anti-aircraft machine guns, 114 anti-tank rifles, 13 field and seven anti-tank guns, while the 308th Rifle Division numbered 4,248 men, 5,513 rifles, 476 Shpagin sub-machine guns, 106 light and 33 heavy machine guns, 119 anti-tank rifles and 45 field and 20 anti-tank guns. As we can see, Gurt'ev's division even had a slight excess of weaponry. The divisions did not receive reinforcements (at least a change in strength is not noticeable in their reports). On 1 October the 39th Guards Rifle Division numbered 3,745 men and the 308th Rifle Division 4,055 men. Major General Zheludev's 37th Guards Rifle Division, which was subordinated to the 4th Tank Army in September, was removed from the shock group to the north of the city. The formation was a bit more powerful than Gur'ev's and Gurt'ev's divisions which had been crossed earlier. On 25 September Zheludev's division numbered 6,695 men, 5,842 rifles, 1,157 Shpagin sub-machine guns, 154 light, 82 heavy and 10 anti-aircraft machine guns, 254 anti-tank rifles and 41 field and 29 anti-tank guns. The 37th Guards Rifle Division was also among those guards divisions which had been reformed from airborne corps. In August 1942 it had been committed into the fighting in the Don bend as part of the 1st Guards Army. Now the guards-airborne troops had to save Stalingrad.

Of course, under-strength reinforcing formations were no great present. Some rifle brigades in Chuikov's army had more men (see below). But it was at least stupid to look the *front* command's gift horse in the mouth. More and less powerful formations were in the Don Front's shock group to the north of Stalingrad. On the whole, two divisions were not a bad addition to the 62nd Army's combat strength.

The transfer of new formations to Chuikov simultaneously meant new tasks. In its Order No. 00142/OP at 20.45 on 30 September, it was demanded of the 62nd Army that it not only 'securely hold the city of Stalingrad and the Orlovka area'.[17] The army was assigned the task of winning back the settlements already captured by the enemy: 'The enemy is to be subsequently thrown out of the "Barricade" settlement and the "Red October" settlement, and from the Mamaev hill area, along with the adjacent blocks south of Mamaev hill by means of local operations.'[18] In spite of what was a sufficiently cautious formulation, these were nonetheless offensive tasks. Offensive tasks were also assigned to the 64th Army ('for the purpose of weakening the enemy pressure along the 62nd Army's front ... and it is to attack during the night of 1–2.10, launching its main attack with its right flank in the direction of Peschanka and Voroponovo'), as well as the 51st and 57th Armies.

The strength of the 62nd Army's formations on 1 October 1942 can be summed up by the following numbers:[19]

13th Guards Rifle Division – 6,076 men;
39th Guards Rifle Division – 3,745 men;
95th Rifle Division – 2,616 men;
112th Rifle Division – 2,551 men;
193rd Rifle Division – 4,154 men;
284th Rifle Division – 2,089 men;
308th Rifle Division – 4,055 men;
42nd Rifle Brigade – 1,151 men;

92nd Rifle Brigade – 92 men;
124th Rifle Brigade – 4,154 men;
149th Rifle Brigade – 3,138 men;
2nd Motorized Rifle Brigade – 1,312 men;
115th Rifle Brigade – 3,464 men;
6th Tank Brigade – 913 men;
282nd Rifle Regiment (NKVD) – 1,088 men.

During the night of 30 September/1 October the entire 39th Guards Rifle Division was crossed over to the western bank of the Volga and took up defensive positions in the second echelon. Simultaneously, part of the 308th Rifle Division's forces (351st Rifle Regiment) crossed over to the western bank of the Volga. The formation's two other rifle regiments and its artillery regiment were approaching the Volga.

On the evening of 1 October Chuikov, in his Order No. 179, assigned offensive tasks to the newly-arrived 42nd and 92nd Rifle Brigades and a reinforced regiment from the 308th Rifle Division.[20] The start of the infantry attack was set for 06.00 on 2 October, following a ten-minute onslaught by artillery and 'katyushas'. The main force of the attack was supposed to be the 351st Rifle Regiment, with an anti-tank battalion and a machine-gun battalion, which had been removed from the 308th Rifle Division on the personal order of Chuikov. The two brigades and the regiment were assigned the limited task of taking back the 'Barricade' settlement. One should note that the brigade had been hurriedly reinforced, and that if on 30 September the 92nd Rifle Brigade had numbered 1,100 men, then on 1 October it numbered 1,884 men.[21] Correspondingly, the 42nd Rifle Brigade grew from 600 men to 1,151 rank and file.[22] It was ordered to organize the offensive 'with crack groups and detachments with automatic rifles, hand grenades, petrol bombs, and anti-tank rifles'.[23] Attached to the text is a note in pencil by Chuikov on the necessity of consolidating the territory gained with the second echelon. However, this was essentially a frontal counter-attack against the 24th Panzer Division's two combat groups with extremely low prospects of success. For the time being, Chuikov left the 112th Rifle and the 39th Guards Rifle Divisions in his reserve. The 39th Guards Rifle Division was ordered to put together a defence in the immediate rear, along the approaches to the 'Barricade' factory. Chuikov directly ordered that 'All stone buildings are to be configured as pillboxes for street fighting'.[24] However, while disposing of the still combat-capable 6th Guards Tank Brigade, the 62nd Army commander did not insert it in the combat formations of the attacking subunits, limiting himself to ordering it to support the attack with fire from fixed positions. That is, in this case, it is difficult to reproach Chuikov for unrestrained 'offensiveness': he was seeking to hold the enemy with a counterblow, while simultaneously preparing to give battle in the defence on the city's streets.

Gurt'ev, the commander of the 308th Rifle Division, later spoke in an interview to the Mints Commission: 'I personally conducted the 351st Rifle Regiment to the jumping-off line at night, when we still were poorly orienting ourselves in the terrain. To be sure, in the army's headquarters they gave us guides from the division which was there.'[25] However, the counterblow of 2 October did not have the predicted success and did not make an impression on the enemy, and in the LI Corps' report the only mention was 'The 24th Panzer Division beat back one sortie'. Further advance was held up at that moment by the necessity of suppressing the resistance by scattered pockets of Soviet troops in the territory already occupied. The attacking 308th Rifle Division's losses were estimated at thirty men killed and eighty wounded.[26]

On the evening of 2 October Chuikov made his next move and moved troops up from the second echelon, strengthening the defence. The 308th Rifle Division's regiment received orders to occupy a strongpoint which had previously been prepared by the 39th Guards Rifle Division – the 'Sculpture' Garden. Another of the 308th Rifle Division's regiments was directed to occupy positions in the area of Nizhne-Udinsk and Verkhne-Udinsk streets (to the north of the silicate factory). The 39th Guards Rifle Division, in turn, was given part of the 193rd Rifle Division's sector, while moving up to the first line and leaving a single regiment in reserve. The 112th Rifle Division, which was fitting out the defence in the area of the two Udinsk streets, was to move to the north. The 112th Rifle Division received orders to occupy defensive positions by 05.00 on 3 October in the area of Height 97.7, in the space between the Orlovka and Little Mechetka rivers.[27] At about 20.30–22.30 on 2 October the 112th Rifle Division's regiments left for the designated area. A battalion each from the 124th and 149th Rifle Brigades, which were operating in this area, was operationally subordinated to the division. All of these measures were to be carried out according to Order No. 180 from the headquarters of the 62nd Army, at 19.35 on 2 October 1942.

Yet one more measure by the command for the purpose of strengthening the second line of defence on the streets of the city was the arrival in Stalingrad of the 37th Guards Rifle Division. However, upon arriving at the Volga on the night of 2/3 October, the division could not cross over into Stalingrad due to a shortage of crossing equipment. Only 175 men from the 118th Guards Rifle Regiment were able to cross over to the right bank during the night. It was insanity to remain at the crossing during the day, so they had to disperse, covering no small distance. For example, the 114th Guards Rifle Regiment was forced to hide in the woods 5km north of the crossing. To be sure, the bombardment of the columns on the march by the Germans was ineffective and there were no losses.

On the whole, Chuikov had undertaken a quite complex regrouping of his forces. Any lack of coordination here would create weak areas and breaches in the defence. The 308th Rifle Division's second regiment to arrive in Stalingrad (339th Rifle Regiment) crossed the Volga only at 07.00 on 2 October. The remaining units of Gurt'ev's division at that moment were still on the left bank of the river. The 339th Rifle Regiment began to carry out the first part of Chuikov's order addressed to the 308th Rifle Division – to occupy the 'Sculpture' Garden. Yet another regiment (the 347th) from Gurt'ev's division crossed over the Volga only by 04.30 on 3 October.[28] Correspondingly, their relief of the units of the 112th Rifle Division, which had already left the previous evening in the area of Verkhne-Udinsk and Nizhne-Udinsk streets, did not take place. This created a weakened sector in the structure of the 62nd Army's defence along this axis.

The German command, in turn, planned an attack by the 24th Panzer and 389th Infantry Divisions with the limited aim of seizing the approaches to the Stalingrad Tractor Factory. The 389th Infantry Division was to attack first, seizing the positions in order to secure the 24th Panzer Division's flank. Moreover, the start of the 24th Panzer Division's offensive depended upon the pace of the infantry's advance. In what had already become a tradition, the 24th Panzer Division was divided into Edelsheim's 'infantry' group (the division's main forces reinforced with additional units) and Winterfeld's 'tank' group (tank units with a battalion in armoured personnel carriers, a company of motorcyclists and a battalion from an artillery regiment). As of 2 October, the 24th Panzer Division numbered two command tanks, eight Panzer IIs, four Panzer IIIs (short), eleven Panzer IIIs (long), two Panzer IVs (short), and three Panzer IVs (long). The offensive was initially set for 1 October, but the beginning of the offensive was later shifted to 3 October. The shift of deadlines usually gives the defence time to consolidate its positions, but here it nevertheless came out just the opposite.

The relief of the units' positions and the delay with moving up and the regrouping of the reserves on 2–3 October had quite serious consequences. The structure of the city's defence being undertaken by Chuikov began to quickly fall apart. At 08.00 on 3 October the positions just occupied by the 112th Rifle Division were attacked by the 389th Infantry Division following an air and artillery preparation. There is mention of German tanks participating in the attack in the 112th Rifle Division's operational documents, but these were actually assault guns from the 244th Battalion (seven combat-ready self-propelled guns on 2 October).

In the 112th Rifle Division's war diary the condition of its units by the morning of 3 October is stated without beating around the bush: 'The division had only just arrived at its defensive line. The soldiers had not had time to entrench.'[29] The situation was partly ameliorated by the presence of the positions of a battalion from the 124th Rifle Brigade in the area of Height 97.7. As an example of the dominance of German aviation over Stalingrad during the daytime, Me 109 fighters actively participated in the attack on the Soviet units, firing on them with machine guns at treetop level. For those elements which had not had time to entrench, this was an extremely unpleasant factor, and the 112th Rifle Division's war diary mentions attacks by 'Messerschmitts' from a height of 100–150m. However, the biggest problem was the absence of a continuous front. A comparison of operational documents of the formations operating in this area leads one to the uncomfortable conclusion about the presence of a breach in the Soviet defence between the bridge over the Mechetka River and the northern part of the 'Barricade' settlement. The bridge itself was still controlled by machine-gun fire from the left-flank 385th Rifle Regiment, but an empty space yawned south of it. The 42nd Rifle Brigade's composite battalion was fighting for the silicate factory even further to the south. The presence of an unoccupied space led before long to a breakthrough by the Germans into the rear of the 385th Rifle Regiment and together with frontal attacks to the collapse of the defence in the area of Height 97.7. The 112th Rifle Division fell back to the east, behind the Mechetka River, to the Stalingrad Tractor Factory settlement.

During the first half of the day on 3 October the area of the silicate factory remained apart from the German offensive. Nothing, it seemed, portended the approach of the catastrophe. In the morning the shock group of the 308th Rifle Division's regiment and two brigades once again attempted to attack the 'Barricade' settlement, as noted by the Germans, 'with powerful support from artillery, mortars and salvos from rocket artillery'. However, at 15.00 (14.00 Berlin time) the 24th Panzer Division itself went over to the offensive with Winterfeld's and Edelsheim's two combat groups, respectively east and west of the silicate factory, enveloping the factory from the flanks.

The 24th Panzer Division's combat groups crushed the defence of the under-strength 42nd and 92nd Rifle Brigades. The first was thrown back by an attack by 'Group Winterfeld's' tanks to the woods north of the 'Barricade' settlement. The 6th Guards Tank Brigade was 'behind the back' of the 42nd Rifle Brigade. In the 6th Guards Tank Brigade's operational report, there are mentions of tanks fighting against tanks, although losses of combat vehicles in this fighting have not been determined on either the Soviet or German side. The 42nd Rifle Brigade's losses for 3 October were 292 men and 104 men remained in line, armed with 23 automatic rifles, 17 Shpagin sub-machine guns, two anti-tank rifles, and three 82mm mortars (that is, mostly headquarters and rear-area troops).[30] The 92nd Rifle Brigade, which reported '92 men together with medical workers' in line the previous evening was also not a serious force capable of putting up resistance to tank attacks. The attack by Edelsheim's combat group from the 24th Panzer Division simply finished it off. In the 92nd Rifle Brigade's operational report of 4 October, it was noted that 'The brigade essentially does not exist as a combat entity'.[31]

The formation of the group of forces for a counter-attack against the 'Barricade' settlement, with the 351st Rifle Regiment in the centre and two brigades along the flanks, played a negative role in the fate of the regiment from Gurt'ev's division, which was operating separately from the others. Having crushed the 42nd and 92nd Rifle Brigades' defence along its flanks, the Germans surrounded the 351st Rifle Regiment, and there is the following note in the 308th Rifle Division's war diary that 'being completely surrounded, the soldiers and commanders stoutly defended their positions and heroically perished south of the sili[cate factory] together with the staff and Commissar Frolov'.[32] Commissar Frolov was singled out in particular, as he had replaced the regimental commander, Major I.S. Markelov, who had been put out of action during the day. Only about thirty men from the regiment avoided encirclement, mostly artillery troops in their positions in the ravine behind the silicate factory. Also, part of the troops nevertheless emerged from the encirclement on the night of 3/4 October.

It should be noted that the expenditure of ammunition by the Germans on 3 October was comparatively small – the LI Corps fired off 'only' 294 tons on this eventful day, although among this total were 217 210mm shells.[33]

Insofar as one can judge from the surviving operational documents, the mainstay of the defence along the approaches to the Stalingrad Tractor Factory settlement, following the crushing of the 42nd and 92nd Rifle Brigades and the encirclement of the 351st Rifle Regiment, became the 6th Guards Tank Brigade. On the morning of 3 October the brigade numbered in line twenty-two tanks (fifteen T-34s, one T-70 and six T-60s). Due to the withdrawal of the 23rd Tank Corps to the left bank of the Volga, they transferred all the combat-capable tanks from several units to the brigade. In light of the overall collapse of the defence on 3 October, the 6th Guards Tank Brigade's lines ended up under bombardment, including from the flank (from the 112th Rifle Division's zone). It is significant that during the day of 3 October three T-34 tanks were listed as destroyed by air strikes (such a high result for air strikes was unusual), with another two T-34s knocked out.

According to an evening report (at 22.00 on 3 October), there still remained ten T-34s, one T-70, three T-60s and 125 'active bayonets' in the 6th Guards Tank Brigade.[34] In the evening the brigade received an oral order from Chuikov to defend the western outskirts of the Stalingrad Tractor Factory settlement from Bazovaya Street to Mytishchi Street and then further along the railway to Nizhne-Udinsk Street. The defence of this line stabilized the situation for a certain period of time and prevented the Germans from immediately breaking through to the Stalingrad Tractor Factory itself. They finished off the brigade as early as the morning of 4 October. As noted in the LI Corps' daily report, early on the morning of 4 October an assault group from the 389th Infantry Division destroyed two

Soviet tanks and in this way created favourable conditions for the division's offensive. They are evidently speaking here about the 6th Guards Tank Corps' tanks, as no other tank units were in this area.

A powerful artillery and air preparation presaged the Germans' attack on 4 October and the start of the attack by the 24th Panzer Division's combat groups was set for 09.00, at the time of the 'fall of the last Stuka's bomb'. Tank battles broke out among the skeletons of the burned-out buildings, often at a minimal distance. By midday eight T-34s, one T-70 and two T-60s from the 6th Guards Tank Brigade had already been destroyed by artillery fire and air strikes.[35] It is quite difficult to estimate the 24th Panzer Division's tank losses in the fighting with the 6th Guards Tank Brigade. The number of combat-ready tanks in the 24th Panzer Division by 4 October had even grown somewhat (by the return of tanks from the repair depots), by two command tanks, nine Panzer IIIs (short), seventeen Panzer IIIs (long), five Panzer IVs (short), and five Panzer IVs (long).[36] From 1 through 10 October one Panzer III (long) and one Panzer IV (short) were put out of action in the 24th Panzer Division (that is, they disappeared from the number of those combat-ready and undergoing repair).[37] The 6th Guards Tank Brigade's tank troops claimed to have knocked out eight enemy vehicles over two days.

On the night of 3/4 October the 37th Guards Rifle Division almost completely (minus its artillery) crossed over the Volga. The original plan foresaw its movement to the area of the Stalingrad Tractor Factory. However, the planned occupation of the defence by all units did not come about. The 114th Guards Rifle Regiment was assigned positions in an oral order for defence along the line of the railway to the west of the Sculpture Park. The 62nd Army's headquarters informed the commander of the 37th Guards Rifle Division that there was no enemy in the designated area and that a motorized rifle brigade was covering it. It was accordingly planned to reach the positions with two of the 114th Rifle Regiment's two battalions, leaving one in reserve. The Guards troops' mistake was in taking the information on the situation on faith and their own reconnaissance was not carried in the expectation of meeting and being oriented by the motorized rifle troops. While moving up to the railway, the regiment's second and third battalions were met by fire and an air strike and immediately suffered heavy losses. The battalions were forced to go over to the defence in the buildings, without reaching the designated defensive line.

In the 37th Guards Rifle Division's war diary there is a note reproaching the commander of the 114th Guards Rifle Regiment, Major F.Ye. Pustavgar,[38] to the effect that he failed to inform division headquarters about what had happened. However, the regimental commander himself did not receive information about the subunits that had left to occupy their positions. Lacking communications and news from the forward battalions, Pustavgar sent a company of automatic riflemen ahead, which also ran into the enemy, and this happened at 15.00 far in the depth from the designated line, upon leaving the Zhitomir Ravine. A picture emerges of the collapse and disintegration of the defence in the space between the 'Barricade' and 'Red October' factories. Major Pustavgar had to throw his last reserves – the first battalion and the training battalion – into the fighting. Having come into contact with the enemy, they were also subjected to an intensive bombardment and sustained losses estimated at 'up to 50 per cent of the rank and file'. However, the commitment of the reserves nevertheless cleared up the situation and stabilized the situation with the formation of two centres of resistance: one in the area of Verkhne-Udinsk and Nizhne-Udinsk streets and the second in the area of Air Travel Street. However, this in no way corresponded to the plan for commitment into the fighting. The situation was exacerbated by the absence of the as-yet uncrossed regimental artillery. It was noted in the 114th Guards Rifle Regiment's war diary that 'Our anti-tank rifles do not harm heavy tanks and the 45mm guns have not yet been crossed'.[39] This was linked to, among other things the lagging behind of transport and horses, about which the regimental commander reported as early as the evening of 2 October. This was tolerable in conditions of gradually closing up to the position, but seriously worsened the 114th Guards Rifle Regiment's situation upon entering the fighting from the march. The night of 4/5 October offered a brief respite.

The commander of the 37th Guards Rifle Division removed two battalions from the 118th Guards Rifle Regiment for restoring the integrity of the defence and attached them to the commanders of the 114th and 109th Guards Rifle Regiments, leaving only one battalion in reserve near the southern extremity of the Stalingrad Tractor Factory. However, the battalions arrived there only during the second part of the day. The infantry's movement during the day was discovered by the enemy and told on the circumstances of its commitment into the fighting in a bad way. As noted in the 114th Guards Rifle Regiment's war diary, 'Following an enemy air raid consisting of 23 planes and a bombardment by a six-barrelled mortar,[40] part of the battalion scattered and is being put back in order'.[41]

Aside from the rifle formations, Chuikov's army was also reinforced by Colonel D.N. Belyi's 84th Tank Brigade, which was to be transferred to the 62nd Army at 19.00 on 4 October. At that moment the brigade numbered five KVs, twenty-four T-34s and twenty T-70s. This was, of course, much better than committing tank troops into the city as infantry as was the case with the 137th Tank Brigade in September 1942. It was planned to employ the tanks as firing points for stationary fire. The brigade was to move into the 114th Guards Rifle Regiment's sector toward the buildings upon leaving the ravine along Zhitomir Street. By 7 October six T-34s and twenty T-70s had been crossed.[42]

However, at this critical moment the German command made the decision to halt for a bit the offensive in Stalingrad pending the arrival of fresh forces. In a report on the situation to the OKH operational section, the headquarters of the Sixth Army emphasized as early as the evening of 4 October that 'The infantry strength of the divisions involved in assaulting the city is very worn out. One must not expect rapid success without the infusion of new forces.'[43] The matter was given a practical coloration the following day when Paulus's headquarters reported to the OKH its decision to include the 305th Infantry Division into the storming of the city, freeing it up on the army's right flank.

As a result, it was planned to resume the assault on the city on 14 October. This, by the way, did not mean that a week of quiet set in. There is a notation in the Sixth Army's war diary on this score: 'During the course of the remaining time before the start of the offensive, it is necessary to make sure that the enemy cannot quietly reinforce his defence in the city.' It was proposed to 'carry out assault sorties' for the purpose of 'shaking up the enemy's defence, while simultaneously improving our jumping-off positions for an offensive'.

Of course, the 'assault sorties' did not cease during the course of the 24th Panzer and 389th Infantry divisions' offensive against the 'Barricade' settlement and the Stalingrad Tractor Factory either. Although the 100th Light Infantry Division remained to cover the flank, its units attempted to push the Soviet units to the east, into the depths of Stalingrad. In his report on the formation's actions on the results of the fighting, the commander of the 193rd Rifle Division, F.N. Smekhotvorov, noted an approach typical of the Germans: 'By the morning of 3.10 they had pulled their soldiers out of the bathhouse and adjacent buildings, and on the morning of 3.10 a whole avalanche of bombs, mortars and shells fell upon this strongpoint.' Such tactics were practically standard for the Wehrmacht. In this regard, Chuikov's approach, which is often mentioned in the literature, upon the approach of his own combat formations to the German positions, was by no means always efficacious.

According to a report at 16.20 on 3 October, the following remained in the 193rd Rifle Division's regiments:

685th Rifle Regiment – 150 men;
883rd Rifle Regiment – 60 men;
895th Rifle Regiment – 46 men.

Twenty-one heavy machine guns and only twelve light machine guns remained in the division. There remained four 76mm regimental and seven 45mm anti-tank guns (out of twenty-four at the beginning of the fighting) in the division's combat formations in Stalingrad. The division's artillery, which was operating from the eastern bank of the Volga, was pretty well preserved. On the whole, one must say that a full-bodied rifle division that entered the fighting for the city had turned into a ruin after less than a week. The reasons were laid out in the following manner: 'The division suffered such heavy losses as a result of the unrelenting and unpunished bombing by the enemy's strafing aviation with 250–500 kilogram bombs, and the unrelenting action of mortar fire.'[44]

Orlovka

The exhaustion of the strength of the Soviet forces attacking the 'northern covering detachment' from the north enabled the German command to deploy part of the XIV Panzer Corps' forces against the salient in the Orlovka area. This sector of the front had remained passive during the course of approximately two weeks. The core of the troops defending in the Orlovka area was the 115th Rifle Brigade, commanded by 42-year-old Colonel Kornei Mikhailovich Andrusenko. Following the fighting on the Western Front, the brigade was pulled out of the 16th Army on 14 August 1942 and was sent to Astrakhan'. However, it did not reach Astrakhan' and detrained at Leninsk station (to the east of Stalingrad) on 25 August, and then marched to Stalingrad. Andrusenko's brigade arrived at the front under strength (it was short 1,671 men) and subsequent skirmishes did not improve its condition. By the beginning of the events described, Andrusenko was heading an operational group consisting of the 115th Rifle Brigade, the 2nd Motorized Rifle Brigade and the 196th Rifle Division's composite regiment. As Andrusenko later wrote in his report on the results of the fighting near Orlovka, he proposed to the military council falling back along a few sectors and thickening his defensive front, but this proposal was not adopted. The group's single advantage was its long sojourn at the same positions and the opportunity of comprehensively preparing them. During the period of quiet Andrusenko also arranged his most reliable battalions in the first line.

On 27 September Andrusenko's operational group numbered 5,518 men, including 3,294 'active bayonets'.[45] The group disposed of 2,882 rifles, 32 heavy, four anti-aircraft and 89 light machine guns, 880 Shpagin sub-machine guns, 146 anti-tank rifles, and eight ampoule launchers. The group's artillery was represented by twenty-four 76mm guns, twelve 45mm anti-tank guns, two anti-aircraft guns, fourteen 120mm mortars, fifty-one 82mm mortars, and thirty-two 50mm mortars.[46] The group did not initially dispose of tanks and heavy artillery. Thus it is worth noting that on 25 September the Sixth Army's intelligence section characterized Andrusenko's brigade with the phrase 'The 115th Brigade (a lot of defectors)'.

The enemy was not particularly active along the front of Andrusenko's group before the evening of 28 September. However, the Germans worked actively against Soviet intelligence gathering. At 20.00 on 28 September the aviation preparation began, which was unheard of in its length. Bombs fell on the Orlovka area until 06.00. In all, according to the approximate figures of the defenders, about 1,700 bombs were dropped on them during the night. Following an hour's breathing space, the air bombardment resumed at 07.00. In his report Andrusenko noted that 'The entire area was shot up by machine guns and cannons from strafing aviation'.[47] He is most likely speaking of attacks by the latest Hs 129s from the 1st Assault Air Squadron's second group. The attack on Orlovka itself was carried out by the forces of the XIV Panzer Corps, which attacked in two shock groups, one from the north-east and the other from the south-west.

Units of the 16th Panzer Division, which had earlier been defending with their front facing north and had not taken part in the storming of Stalingrad, were drawn into the offensive. 'Stachel's Regiment' (named after the commander, Colonel R. Stachel), which had been transferred from the Luftwaffe, was also drawn into the offensive. The regiment had been reinforced with an engineer battalion and a tank platoon from the 3rd Motorized Division. The history of the 16th Panzer Division shows that by no means did the offensive develop smoothly and according to plan:

> The howl of the Nebelwerfers broke out on 29 September; the Ju 87s strafed Orlovka unremittingly, and artillery shells rained down on the enemy fortress. Then two companies from the 651st Engineer Battalion, which had been committed into the fighting for the first time, and the 79th Regiment's 8th Company moved forward. However, the Russians were still in place and holding on and had beaten off the attack by midday.[48]

These events were also described without enthusiasm in the XIV Panzer Corps' own daily report: 'The attack on Orlovka began in the morning. At first it proceeded at good speed, but was then halted by the stubborn enemy along well-fortified positions. Losses have been suffered.' Regarding the 16th Panzer Division's offensive, it was openly admitted that 'The offensive here was halted due to losses in men and tanks from defensive fire'. The XIV Panzer Corps' two groups were unable to link up and encircle the Soviet forces on 29 September. The 16th Panzer and 3rd Motorized Divisions' losses in armoured equipment on that day were one Panzer III (long), one Panzer IV (short), and one Panzer IV (long) from the 16th Panzer Division.

This defensive success cost Andrusenko's group very dearly. In his report on the results of the fighting, the commander of the 115th Rifle Brigade estimated the first battalion's losses in holding the 16th Panzer Division's attack on Orlovka from the east at 75 per cent of the officers and men. In order to hold the attack from the west (where the 2nd Motorized Rifle Brigade came under attack), it was necessary to expend Andrusenko's only available reserve – his fourth battalion. It was confirmed on the heels of these events that fifty-seven active bayonets remained in the 2nd Motorized Rifle Brigade on the first day of the fighting for Orlovka, with the remainder either killed or wounded. Yet another 100 men from the 2nd Motorized Rifle Brigade were listed as missing in action. Half of the available 120mm mortars (seven) were lost, as were almost half of the 82mm mortars (twenty-one). The link-up of the two attacking German groups on the first day of fighting was prevented by a timely counter-attack by the 115th Rifle Brigade's third battalion on Orlovka as early as the evening of 29 September. There really was not an encirclement at that moment – any kind of vehicle could move along the Orlovka *Balka* to the brigade's position. However, the distance between the tips of the enemy's shock wedges was only about 1,600m.

During the day on 30 September the men and officers fighting in the Orlovka area got a relative breathing spell due to the Don Front's attacks against the XIV Panzer Corps from the north (the attack by two brigades on Lend-Lease vehicles is described in another section). Chuikov viewed the deterioration of the situation in the Orlovka area very seriously. Although Andrusenko had not yet been forbidden to fall back, 350 reinforcements (four companies) were dispatched to him, which enabled him to restore the brigade's first battalion and reinforce the 2nd Motorized Rifle Brigade with a single company. The remnants of the 115th Rifle Brigade's recently-formed fourth battalion were transferred to the 2nd Motorized Rifle Brigade. The movement of soldiers within the group and the arrival of reinforcements enabled Andrusenko to carry out a counter-attack at midnight on 30 September for the purpose of improving his situation. However, as a result of the night fighting, he only managed to penetrate into the south-eastern outskirts of Orlovka. Communications with the subunits to the north-west of Orlovka continued to hang by a thread.

As the result of two days of fighting, Andrusenko's group claimed four enemy tanks that had hit mines, six knocked out by artillery and two burned by petrol bombs (a total of twelve). According to German figures, the 16th Panzer Division's loss of combat-ready vehicles for 29–30 September was one Panzer III (short), four Panzer IIIs (long) and two Panzer IVs (short). Taking into account the 3rd Motorized Division (whose losses are more difficult to calculate in light of the unknown distribution between the northern and southern sectors) and tanks returning from repair, the report by Andrusenko's group appears quite realistic.

The battle for Orlovka resumed on 1 October. There are various readings in the summary reports regarding the time of the final isolation of the 115th Rifle Brigade's third battalion and the 2nd Motorized Rifle Division's battalion, but the 115th Rifle Brigade's war diary precisely establishes that moment as 'by the close of 1.10'. This does not contradict enemy data, and in the XIV Panzer Corps' daily report it is maintained that Orlovka had been firmly taken by the evening of 1 October. An attempt to attack Orlovka with the forces of the 1/115th Rifle Brigade and to restore communications with those surrounded was once again made on the night of 1/2 October, but failed.

The surrounded troops had approximately 200 rounds per rifle and food for one to two days. The encircled group numbered 225 riflemen, six heavy and nine light machine guns, five 76mm guns (with a supply of 380 shells), sixteen 82mm mortars (350 rounds), four anti-tank guns (200 shells), and twenty anti-tank rifles.[49] That is, the surrounded troops were still fully capable of giving battle and holding out, which the subsequent days showed. One cannot help but note that measures were taken almost immediately to supply the surrounded troops by air, although the 8th Air Army's ability to organize an air bridge was slight. Five U-2s flew to the Sandy *Balka* (the location of the 3/115th Rifle Brigade) on the night of 2/3 October and seven U-2s flew to the Orlovka area on the night of 3/4 October and fourteen sacks of supplies were dropped. As usual, the pilots complained that the agreed-upon signal had not been laid out by the troops.

In the meantime, events in the Stalingrad's factory settlements began to exert an influence on the fate of Andrusenko's group. As was noted earlier, the lateness of the 37th Guards Rifle Division's regiments in crossing and reaching their positions led to a crisis and the collapse of the defence along the approaches to the Stalingrad Tractor Factory's settlement as early as 3 October 1942. A direct consequence of these events for Andrusenko's group became the turning of their left flank, which exacerbated the already poor situation of the 115th Rifle Brigade.

The first alarm signal rang out when on 2 October the 124th Rifle Brigade's first battalion was removed from its position along the 115th Rifle Brigade's left flank in the area of Height 97.7. Colonel Andrusenko appealed to army headquarters, but they assured the commander of the 115th Rifle Brigade that the 112th Rifle Division was moving up to its positions in the area of Height 97.7. As Andrusenko wrote later, 'I had complete confidence in the security of this axis'.[50] It's true that the 1/124th Rifle Brigade that had been occupying this defensive sector apart from its brigade was to be resubordinated to the 112th Rifle Division. However, on the morning of 3 October, first the artillery battalion's observer and then a cook (!) located in the 115th Rifle Division's administrative-supply unit reported that the enemy was infiltrating into the northern edge of the woods and even the approach of small groups of infantry toward the railway (running to the Stalingrad Tractor Factory). As was noted above, the fighting on 3 October led to the 112th Rifle Division and the 1/124th Rifle Brigade being pushed back from their positions in the area of Height 97.7 beyond the Mechetka River into the Stalingrad Tractor Factory settlement, which opened a path for the Germans into the flank and rear of Andrusenko's group. At that moment the commander of the 115th Rifle Brigade had almost no possibility of parrying the crisis. As early as 14.00 on 3 October the 115th Rifle Brigade's second battalion was encircled in the area of Height 108.3. This group of officers and men included about sixty riflemen, four heavy and six light machine guns, two 76mm guns, four 82mm mortars and two anti-tank guns.[51] The encircled battalion was also supported by artillery from outside the 'cauldron'.

On the night of 3/4 October Andrusenko organized a raid by the forces of a battalion of automatic riflemen, reinforced by elements of the brigade's headquarters, on Height 97.7. The raid proved to be quite successful and they managed to capture two machine guns, an automatic rifle, four rifles and food supplies for a company. During the raid they also met up with eight 'Hiwis',[52] who were engaged in defensive work for the Germans on Height 97.7. Six 'Hiwis' were shot on the spot 'while putting up resistance', while they took two of them prisoner and sent them back to the rear.

Even such an effective raid could not halt the overall worsening of the situation. The first attack on 4 October came from the north. As was noted in the XIV Panzer Corps' daily report, 'In the morning the 16th Panzer Division occupied the collective farm north-east of marker 85.1, following heavy fighting, and the greater part of the triangular grove east of marker 85.1'. The 16th Panzer Division's enemy in this fighting was the 282nd NKVD Regiment (operationally subordinated to the 149th Rifle Brigade). It numbered 1,060 men on 2 October 1942 and disposed of seven heavy and twenty-two light machine guns. Thus it really was a difficult task to push it from its positions. During the day on 4 October the Germans renewed their attacks from the south-west and a regiment from the 94th Infantry Division reached the railway one kilometre from Height 85.1, as a forward assault group. In this fashion 'visual communications' were established with the 16th Panzer Division advancing toward it. A 'naval battalion'[53] prevented the linking up of the two German shock groups along the edge of the Orlovka *Balka*. The 115th Rifle Brigade's first battalion (1/115th), the 2nd Motorized Rifle Brigade's main forces, as well as a small part of the naval detachment and an NKVD regiment ended up being encircled.

However, the isolation of the battalions of Andrusenko's group along various sectors did not automatically mean their defeat. In a report to the OKH operational section, the Sixth Army's headquarters described the developing situation in the following manner: 'A new cauldron has been created south-east of Orlovka. There are not as yet forces for clearing it.'[54] The 'cauldron' was actually ringed with covering forces from auxiliary units: 'The security of the cauldron has been entrusted to construction and transport units.'[55]

In the 115th Rifle Brigade's report on the results of the fighting there is a mention of the fact that on 5 October the Germans presented an ultimatum over the radio to the two surrounded battalions in the Orlovka area with a proposal to surrender, which was rejected. The situation, however, did not inspire confidence. There were only ten cases of ammunition and three sacks of food (which is not surprising given the small size of the 'cauldron') among the materiel dropped by the U-2s. They had to kill and eat their horses.

Having insufficient forces to defeat the surrounded Soviets, the Germans resorted to psychological warfare. As was noted in the 115th Rifle Brigade's war diary, the Germans broadcast 'waltzes, foxtrots and other music' to the encircled elements in the area of Orlovka, after which there followed directed propaganda, mentioning the names of the command and political contingent (probably received from deserters earlier). If they surrendered, the Germans promised to 'greet them as dear guests', and in the event of stubborn resistance, they threatened that 'Death awaits you!'. The messages from the loudspeakers intermingled with artillery fire. This psychological pressure had some effect on the tormented people in the encirclement. For example, in the XIV Panzer Corps' report for 4 October it was noted that 'The 3rd Motorized Division received 42 deserters from the cauldron south-west of Orlovka'. However, on the whole those surrounded held firm and the struggle continued.

There followed on the morning of 6 October the defeat of the weakest of the encircled groups – the 115th Rifle Brigade's second battalion. It was attacked by the forces of a regiment from the 94th Infantry Division, reinforced with armour. They saw the fighting in the positions of the 2/115th Rifle Brigade from other sectors, the explosions of grenades and the tanks crushing the positions (most likely they were speaking of assault guns). Scouts sent out that evening failed to find anyone in the battalion's positions. The Germans' attacks during the second part of the day against the south-eastern group (1/115th Rifle Brigade and the 2nd Motorized Rifle Brigade) had limited success. It was noted in the XIV Panzer Corps' daily report that 'The attempt to seize the heavily fortified *balka* north of marker 728 was repulsed by the fierce defence put up by the enemy, who employed mortars and anti-tank guns'.

However, the continuation of the attacks with the employment of armoured equipment meant the rapid defeat of the isolated group to the south-east of Orlovka. Thus it was decided to conduct a fighting breakout. It began at 02.00 on 7 October. Later on the choice of route along the Orlovka *Balka* was subjected to criticism. On the one hand, the *balka* hid one from observation, but on the other hand it was well illuminated by the Germans with rocket flares. In order to oppose the 'rocket men', Major Osipov, the commander of the 2nd Motorized Rifle Brigade, who was in charge of the breakthrough, instructed his men to kill those who were firing off rockets with fire from rifles and automatic rifles. This yielded some results when a squall of fire opened upon on the launching site of a rocket flare. The Germans had not yet had time to entrench along the perimeter of the encirclement, so this had a definite effect. The launching of the flares ceased for a while. In the morning eighteen men from the 1/115th Rifle Brigade and forty-three men from the 2nd Motorized Rifle Brigade reached their lines.[56] Nine men from the Volga Military Flotilla's 141st Naval Infantry Company emerged from the encirclement.[57] According to German data, during the first half of the day on 7 October, while eliminating the 'cauldron' south-east of Orlovka, units of the XIV Panzer Corps took 1,080 prisoners and captured 'a large amount of infantry weapons and ammunition'. A large part of the prisoners taken evidently consisted of those men from Andrusenko's group wounded in previous fighting.

During the day on 7 October there followed fierce attacks against the 3/115th Rifle Brigade and the 2/2nd Motorized Rifle Brigade, which had been isolated for a week to the north-west of Orlovka. At 18.00 the command element gathered together and made the decision to break out. At that moment in the encirclement of the two battalions there was still the hope that the integrity of the front of Andrusenko's group could be restored. With the defeat and pushing back of the group's main forces to the east, the continuation of the defence no longer made any sense. The idea of breaking out along the Orlovka *Balka* was rejected, as it would hamper manoeuvre and almost inevitably guaranteed a fighting breakout, for which there were no longer any forces. In accordance with the decision adopted before midnight on 7 October, a reconnaissance was conducted along the axis of the escape route. At 02.00 on 8 October, taking advantage of the darkness and the rainy weather, the column penetrated the Germans' encirclement ring without consequences.

Further on the group moved along the heights in the German rear. The next problem was to break through the front to their own people. Here the decision was made to turn into the Orlovka *Balka* after Height 97.7 and to then reach Stalingrad along it. This decision was motivated by the clearly visible concentration of the Germans' efforts in the Stalingrad Tractor Factory settlement. This decision to turn into the ravine, which they had earlier avoided, also justified itself. At 06.00 on 8 October a group of brave men reached their own lines from the encirclement without loss. According to German data, while eliminating the 'cauldron' north-west of Orlovka on 8 October, 619 prisoners were taken and three 76.2mm guns, one 76.2mm anti-tank gun, one 47mm gun, ten mortars, twenty-five machine guns, including two heavy calibre and two German ones, twenty anti-tank rifles, and other equipment was captured.

The 62nd Army's sole defensive sector which ran along open terrain had been lost. The front line now ran completely along the city's streets. In eleven days of fighting Andrusenko's group lost more than 3,000 men: 670 men killed, 521 missing in action, 1,810 wounded, 39 'captured,' and 18 'surrendered'.[58] The 115th Rifle Brigade had a ration strength of 1,210 on 10 October, including only 138 riflemen, three heavy and four light machine guns (four 76mm guns, one 45mm anti-tank gun, four 120mm and eight 82mm mortars were saved).[59] The 2nd Motorized Rifle Brigade had a ration strength of 607 men, including 185 riflemen.

Chapter 17

The Third Assault on the City. 14–19 October

(Map 11)

Beginning in the second half of October 1942 a battle unfolded for the Stalingrad factories. In Russian historiography they sometimes date the fighting for the Stalingrad Tractor Factory as running from 4–14 October. However, in the 62nd Army's war diary the start of the struggle for the factories is indicated precisely, beginning on 13 October. Further on there was fighting for the 'Barricade' factory from 15–23 October, and for the 'Red October' factory from 24 October almost to the beginning of the Soviet counteroffensive. The final goal of the German attacks was to have been the 'Azure' chemical industrial complex.

An important German advantage in the street fighting for Stalingrad was the ability to pick the place and axis of an attack. For the latest assault, it was decided to attack along a previously-unattacked sector of the front – the 62nd Army's northern flank and the area of the Stalingrad Tractor Factory. As was the case previously, the new offensive was to be conducted by pouring fresh forces into the shock group. Paulus removed the 305th Infantry Division from VIII Corps and subordinated it to LI Corps, which was assaulting Stalingrad. The division had earlier been placed at the 'land bridge', but its positions were not affected by the former reserve armies' powerful attacks. Thus the 305th was in good condition – in the middle of October it contained nine medium-strength battalions. The 14th and 24th Panzer Divisions were also to be brought into the offensive (see table).

Table 28: The Condition of the 14th and 24th Panzer Divisions' Tank Park on 13 October 1942.

	Panzer II	Panzer III (short)	Panzer III (long)
24th Panzer Division	6	7	13
14th Panzer Division	3	9	24

	Panzer IV (short)	Panzer IV (long)	Command Tanks
24th Panzer Division	3	2	2
14th Panzer Division	6	4	4

The 24th Panzer Division had been in the Sixth Army's reserve since 29 September and was located in the Plodovitoe area. The division's commitment into what was known to be a bloody struggle for the city was a risky move. Actually, this was one of the steps toward the coming disaster, when Paulus lacked any mobile formations at hand for counterblows against the Soviet tank and mechanized corps attacking toward Kalach. The number of formations that could effectively respond to a Soviet counteroffensive was inexorably diminishing. The 24th Panzer Division was employed during the second assault and suffered losses, and the 14th Panzer Division's turn came during the third assault.

The state of the tank park of the Sixth Army's shock group is not impressive, but a fresh nine-battalion infantry division was an important advantage. Paulus gathered the so-called 'Group Jaenecke' (named after the commander of the 389th Infantry Division), which included the 389th Infantry Division, the 305th Infantry Division, the 14th and 24th Panzer Divisions (eighty-three tanks in both), and thirty-one *Sturmgeschützen* from the 244th and 245th Assault Gun Battalions for the attack on the Stalingrad Tractor Factory. According to the plan, part of the tanks was to be employed for direct infantry support; that is, transferred from the panzer divisions to the infantry regiments.

Following a powerful German attack during 27 September–7 October, the commander of the 62nd Army made several attacks for the purpose of restoring his positions. Chuikov certainly did not underestimate the danger that threatened the factories. As early as 8 October he transferred the 95th Rifle Division to the Stalingrad Tractor Factory area, thus strengthening the 37th Guards Rifle Division's battle order. The 112th Rifle Division was also moved to the area of the Stalingrad Tractor Factory. The latter formation had been very worn out in its time, but Chuikov, evidently recalling his debut at the Stalingrad Front, which was connected with the 112th Rifle Division, left it in the 62nd Army. Unlike a number of other units of the 62nd Army's original formation, the 112th Rifle Division had not been pulled out of Stalingrad to refit.

On 10 October 1942 the 62nd Army's formations numbered:

13th Guards Rifle Division – 6,053 men;
37th Guards Rifle Division – 4,670 men;
39th Guards Rifle Division – 5,052 men;
95th Rifle Division – 3,075 men;
112th Rifle Division – 2,277 men;
193rd Rifle Division – 4,168 men;
284th Rifle Division – 5,907 men;
308th Rifle Division – 3,225 men;
42nd Rifle Brigade – 760 men;
92nd Rifle Brigade – 1,050 men;
115th Rifle Brigade – 1,135 men;
124th Rifle Brigade – 3,520 men on 5 October 1942;
149th Rifle Brigade – 2,556 men;
2nd Motorized Rifle Brigade – 569 men.[1]

As we can see, the 39th Guards Rifle Division had been visibly strengthened by reinforcements. Chuikov also managed to maintain the strength of the 13th Guards Rifle Division at a comparatively high level. In the days preceding the German offensive, however, the 95th and 37th Guards Rifle Divisions carried out a series of local counter-attacks and their strength had declined somewhat.

But the determining factor in the subsequent events became the offensive tasks assigned by the commander of the 62nd Army. The goals which Chuikov pursued were formulated by him in Order No. 196, issued at 01.43 on 14 October, literally a few hours before the start of the German offensive: 'To securely hold the occupied lines, to prevent the enemy from reaching the Volga and, by means of local operations, to clear the factory settlements of the Stalingrad Tractor Factory, and the "Barricade" and "Red October" factories of the enemy by 20.10 and, upon capturing Mamaev hill, to create secure and deep defence.'[2]

In his memoirs, Chuikov defined the goal of the counterblow as 'foiling the enemy's planned preparation of a new offensive'.[3] This statement contradicts not only the order's formulation, but its content as well. Almost all of the 62nd Army's formations received offensive tasks. There were only the provisos in the order that 'In the event of the enemy going over to the attack, hold …', with the defensive line indicated. By all appearances, Chuikov believed that assigning offensive tasks had been a mistake and puts forward yet another explanation in his memoirs: 'We aimed our counterblow at the enemy's main group of forces, believing that we could only foil his planned preparation for a new offensive by a counterblow.'[4] This thesis tallies poorly with the assignment of offensive tasks to all the formations in the area of the factories.

In justifying his offensive plans, Chuikov also cites orders from *front* headquarters. There really was an order from *front* headquarters with offensive tasks. It has already been cited before and stated: 'Subsequently, the enemy is to be thrown out successively through local operations from the "Barricade" settlement, the "Red October" settlement and from the Mamaev hill area, along with the adjacent blocks south of Mamaev hill.'[5] However, this order (No. 00142/OP) is dated 30 September and was issued in a somewhat different situation. Simultaneously, the 39th Guards Rifle Division and the 308th Rifle Division were to be transferred to the 62nd Army. Thus, active operations were first of all Chuikov's idea. Before long he had to reap all the consequences of this decision.

At the same time, we should emphasize that the offensive tasks did not arise at the last moment. Order No. 196, which was issued a few hours before the start of the German artillery and air preparation, was only a continuation of Order No. 190 of 11 October, which was addressed to specific formations. In Order No. 190 the 95th and 37th Guards Rifle Divisions were given offensive tasks. To be fair, one should not say that Chuikov was attempting to immediately achieve any kind of far-reaching goals through a local operation in the area of the Stalingrad Tractor Factory. In Order No. 190 the enemy's plans were estimated quite precisely as 'seeking to develop the attack toward the approaches to the Stalingrad Tractor Factory'.[6] The 37th Guards and 95th Rifle Divisions' offensive pursued the local goal of eliminating the enemy's wedge and capturing favourable positions for defence along the line of the two ravines and the defile between them. In the event of success, the Soviet forces' positions in the area of the Stalingrad Tractor Factory would doubtlessly have been strengthened. The neighbouring 112th Rifle Division was occupying defensive positions along the line of the Wet Mechetka River. The opportunities for a German tank attack on the Stalingrad Tractor Factor would have greatly narrowed.

The ambivalence in Chuikov's assignment of defensive and offensive tasks clearly manifested itself in the plan for employing the tank troops. Aside from rifle formations, there still remained in the 62nd Army the 6th Guards and 84th Tank Brigades. Colonel D.N. Belyi's 84th Tank Brigade was a new formation, the units of which had been crossed into the city to the area of the Stalingrad Tractor Factory during the first days of October. At the beginning of the brigade's active operations directly in the city the brigade contained twenty T-34s and twenty T-70s (the KV tanks were still on the left bank of the Volga).[7] But by the time the brigade met the Germans' new offensive it was already quite worn out: on 11 October it had only two T-34s in line and another knocked-out T-34 was being employed as a stationary firing point.[8] The brigade was still present in the order for an offensive, but as early as the night of 12/13 October it was pulled into the reserve, having turned over its battle-ready and unready vehicles to the 84th Tank Brigade. According to Order No. 190, the brigades were ordered to support the counter-attack by the 37th Guards Rifle Division and 95th Rifle Division with fire from their sectors. Getting ahead of ourselves, one may add – with part of its forces. A massed tank attack was not planned. In Order No. 196 the 84th Tank Brigade was listed in the army reserve. By the way, here is still one more operative factor: in *front* Order No. 00150/OP of 4 October, according to which the 84th Tank Brigade was to be transferred to Chuikov, it is clearly ordered that 'the tanks are to be used as stationary firing points'.[9] Chuikov was not inclined to violate these instructions from above.

It was planned to begin the offensive on the morning of 12 October. However, at the last minute it was determined that they had incorrectly evaluated the 37th Guards Rifle Division's situation in the 62nd Army's headquarters. Later, in his order of 12 October, Chuikov accused the division's headquarters of inaccurately indicating the situation of its units. As a result, it was necessary to advance farther than initially planned in order to arrive at the designated line (the so-called 'hexagonal building'[10] had not been occupied). Here one cannot but admit the justice of Chuikov's reproaches. In the 37th Guards Rifle Division's operational reports and the formation's war diary, the situation of the 114th Rifle Regiment was indicated as 'from the railway on Ustyug Street to the south as far as the Zhitomir Ravine',[11] that is, actually west of the 'hexagonal building'.

Having been really worn out in the September fighting, the 95th Rifle Division had been removed from its familiar and well-outfitted sector north-east of Height 102.0 (Mamaev hill) for carrying out the offensive. On the night of 8/9 October, having turned over its positions to the 284th Rifle Division, Gorishnyi's division was being moved to the area of the 'Barricade' settlement, where it took over the 37th Guards Rifle Division's sector. The change of subunits stretched out over two nights. There was no longer any opportunity for a thorough reconnaissance of the enemy.

The counteroffensive by the 95th and 37th Guards Rifle Divisions, which began on 12 October, did not develop very successfully. The attacking infantrymen were pinned down by enemy fire. The 84th Tank Brigade's tanks supported the attack with fire from stationary positions and in small groups of two or three moving tanks. The attack by the 95th Rifle Division's 90th Rifle Regiment along the Zhitomir Ravine was halted by 'powerful flanking fire from the enemy's wood and earth pillboxes, which were located along the right-wing neighbour's sector'. The regiment lost ten men killed, twenty-four missing in action and twenty wounded.

On the following day the 37th Guards Rifle Division was reinforced by the 39th Guards Rifle Division's 117th Guards Rifle Regiment with the task of resuming the offensive on 13 October. Chuikov continued to count on having time to reach favourable positions before the start of the German offensive. The offensive resumed during the second part of the day on 13 October. The 37th Guards Rifle Division's 114th Guards Rifle Regiment waged offensive operations until 03.00 on 14 October and occupied a few buildings along Botkin Street. The guards troops clearly had not had time to transform them into fortresses. By the evening of 13 October 24 there were twenty-four 'active bayonets' left in the 90th Rifle Regiment and another forty-three men in the mortar units.

Unfortunately, as we can see, they were unable to fully carry out their initially-assigned tasks. Quite the opposite, this failure and the accompanying losses weakened the defence along the approaches to the Stalingrad Tractor Factory. The attacking Soviet units were consolidating along the lines they occupied on the night of 13/14 October and the solidity of their defence was lower, due simply to the effect of the lesser amount of time spent preparing the positions. This is openly stated in the 37th Guards Rifle Division's war diary:

'Following the night attack, the division had only set about consolidating along the line reached and the defensive structures had not been completely by the start of the Germans' offensive.'[12] The Germans were also holding the line of the ravines and could freely move tanks through them, which happened before too long. One cannot but note that the penultimate order by the 62nd Army's headquarters immediately preceding the German attack was the order to the commander of the 37th Guards Rifle Division at 20.30 on 13 October 'To transform the unnamed height 200–300 metres south-west of the Stalingrad Tractor Factory into a strongpoint insurmountable for the enemy ...' Of course, they did not have time to carry out this order.

Jaenecke's group began its offensive with a lengthy 2½-hour artillery preparation at 07.30 on 14 October. The LI Corps fired off 859 tons of ammunition on 14 October, including 609 rounds from 210mm howitzers, 1,210 rounds from 100mm guns and 3,460 rounds from 150mm sFH18 guns.[13] In this way was set one of the records for ammunition expenditure for the entire period of the assault on Stalingrad. Major forces of the VIII Air Corps were also activated for supporting the offensive, and during the day the Luftwaffe's planes dropped about 600 tons of bombs on the Soviet positions. Later, in an account to a representative of the Commission on the History of the Great Patriotic War, Chuikov admitted: 'I've lived through a lot of bombings, artillery preparations and others in my life, but the 14th will remain in my memory.'[14] At that time his command post was located on the bank of the Volga in the area of the 'Barricade' factory, not far from the area of the German breakthrough. As Chuikov recalled, in coming out of the dugout visibility was not more than 5m due to the smoke and ashes.

Units of the 37th Guards, 95th and 112th Rifle Divisions came under the Germans' attack. It is interesting to note that along the left flank the Germans attacked not over open terrain, but along the city streets (Amber, Bauman and Botkin), crushing the 37th Guards Rifle Division's 109th Guards Rifle Regiment. The remnants of the 109th Guards Rifle Regiment, numbering twenty-six men, fell back over the river to Zaitsevskii Island during the night of 14/15 October. Having broken through to the stadium area, the Germans had the opportunity to attack into the rear of the 112th Rifle Division. The latter's position from the defender-friendly line of the Mechetka River had turned into a trap. On 13 October the 112th Rifle Division had already been quite weakened and was partially good for defensive actions. There were 109 men in the division's headquarters, 201 in the 385th Rifle Regiment, 263 in the 524th Rifle Regiment, 330 men in the 416th Rifle Regiment, 197 men in the 436th Artillery Regiment, and 131 in the engineer battalion.[15] To put up active resistance to the enemy with these forces was already problematic. A counter-attack by the stadium by a detachment of eighty men predictably had no success.

The second German attack followed along the boundary between the 37th Guards Rifle Division and the 95th Rifle Division. This attack also landed against subunits which had just been attacking and which had not yet consolidated along their new lines. The 95th Rifle Division's weak 90th Rifle Regiment in the area of the Zhitomir Ravine was easily crushed by the Germans, losing in a single day twenty-six men killed, wounded and missing in action, leaving only fifteen men in the regiment. It required somewhat more effort to collapse the 37th Guard Rifle Division's defence. In the formation's war diary it was noted that 'The attached anti-tank artillery, which was located in the defensive depth, did not manifest steadfastness in the struggle against the tanks and was crushed'. One of the 37th Guards Rifle Division's summary documents describes how the Germans managed to neutralize the 399th Anti-Tank Artillery Regiment, which had been attached to the formation: 'One enemy plane forced its [a battery of the 399th Anti-Tank Artillery Regiment] rank and file to take cover in a small ditch, which the German tanks took advantage of and shot up the guns at point blank range and took out the crews.'[16] Having smashed through the front, the attacking German units' forward detachments began to get into the rear of the 308th Rifle Division and to Chuikov's command post. The security detachment of the 62nd Army's headquarters got into a fight within 300m of the command post. The forcible rout of the units that came under attack was taking place. According to German data, on 14 October the entire Sixth Army took 387 prisoners, of which 49 were deserters, which is a comparatively small number.

In his account to a representative of the Commission on the History of the Great Patriotic War (the so-called Mints Commission), Chuikov noted in particular the role of the newly-arrived 84th Tank Brigade at the beginning stage of the struggle for the factories: 'As early as the previous evening I managed to bring up one tank brigade, bury all the tanks in the ground and put out an infantry security detachment, and the enemy didn't bomb them during the night.'[17] The brigade really did come under attack, but along a secondary axis for the Germans. Thus it was unable to prevent a breakthrough around Stalingrad Tractor Factory, but it prevented the Germans from taking the 'Barricade' factory in the same lunge. In the fighting on 14 October the 84th Tank Brigade's 201st Tank Battalion claimed twenty-five knocked-out German tanks at the cost of losing twelve of their own T-34s. Six T-70s were burned and four knocked out in the brigade's 200th Tank Battalion. Regarding human losses, there is an eloquent notation in the brigade's report of 'very great'. The victims of the 84th Tank Brigade's tank troops were most likely the 245th Assault Gun Battalion's assault guns, whose strength in combat vehicles fell for the day from thirteen (four short-barrelled and nine long-barrelled) to six (one short-barrelled and five long-barrelled).

Divisional commander Gorishnyi moved up a reconnaissance company of twenty men and a training battalion of forty men to the line of the railway, but in this way only prevented a German advance by 'cavalry lunge' to the Volga along Minusinsk Street. The Germans' objective at that moment was nevertheless the Stalingrad Tractor Factory and their main forces were being concentrated for seizing the factory.

The crushing of the 95th and 37th Guards Rifle Divisions' defences and the outflanking of the 112th Rifle Division's positions enabled the Germans to reach the grounds of the Stalingrad Tractor Factory in a single leap along the railway line. At 15.00 a panzer regiment from the 14th Panzer Division broke through to the factory and occupied a large shop in its southern part. Even after the onset of darkness on the evening of 14 October, the 14th Panzer Division's panzergrenadier regiment advanced toward the Volga south of the oil cisterns (on the river bank to the east of the Stalingrad Tractor Factory), where it took up an all-round defence. From this moment the 62nd Army had actually been cut in two. The 680th Railway Battery (three 152mm guns) became the victim of the Germans' breakthrough to the area of the Stalingrad Tractor Factory. On 14 October one of the trains was destroyed by air strikes, while the other two sustained damage. By the evening of 14 October, when the enemy had occupied the factory, the artillery troops who were still alive broke through to the Volga and crossed over to Zaitsevskii Island. The trains were blown up.

The enemy's arrival at the Volga in the area of the Stalingrad Tractor Factory put Chuikov in an extremely difficult position. The breakthrough to the river enabled the Germans to develop the offensive along the river and into the rear of the 62nd Army's forces, both to the north into the rear of the northern sector of the defence, and to the south, into the rear of those formations defending between Mamaev hill and the factories. As early as 16.00 on 14 October Chuikov made the decision to move units from the northern defensive sector to the area of the Stalingrad Tractor Factory. First of all, he ordered S.F. Gorokhov, the commander of the 124th Rifle Brigade, to move a full-strength battalion with anti-tank equipment to the northern part of the Stalingrad Tractor Factory. In carrying out this order, Gorokhov dispatched the 124th Rifle Brigade's first battalion, reinforced with a company of automatic riflemen and six anti-tank rifles with their crews, to the Stalingrad Tractor Factory. Secondly, an order was issued simultaneously to the 115th Rifle Brigade and the 2nd Motorized Rifle Brigade to take up positions from the bridge over the Wet Mechetka along the first ring road as far as the Stalingrad Tractor Factory. A battalion from the 149th Rifle Brigade was also deployed with its front facing south. The brigade's reserve from an automatic rifle company and a blocking detachment was moved up to meet the enemy.

The remnants of the 112th Rifle Division also fell back to the approaches to the northern part of the Stalingrad Tractor Factory. All of this taken together enabled them to stabilize the situation for at least some time. Chuikov later wrote in his memoirs that the 112th Rifle Division had been split into three groups: 'One part fell back to the north and linked up with Gorokhov's brigade in the Rynok area. Another, led by Lieutenant Shutov and Aleksei Ochkin, remained in the factory's foundry and assembly shops. The third, which political worker Boris Filimonov had formed, had concentrated in the basements of the Lower settlement.'[18] It was precisely these scattered groups and elements pulled from the northern sector that prevented the Germans from capturing the factory completely. It was noted in the Sixth Army's war diary that 'The 305th Infantry Division's offensive west of the northern part of the tractor factory was halted on the evening of 14.10 by the enemy's fierce resistance'.

The success of the offensive's first day cost the Germans quite dearly. The first day of fighting in Stalingrad caused the 305th Infantry Division heavy losses. On 14 October the formation lost 89 men killed, 283 wounded and 15 missing in action. The 14th Panzer Division also suffered appreciable losses – 33 men killed, 105 wounded and two missing in action. In a report by the Sixth Army's headquarters to the OKH operational directorate, the evaluation of the first day was cautious enough: 'The offensive by the LI Corps in Stalingrad was unable to achieve the tasks assigned for the day.'

One of the Soviet command's retaliatory moves was the sharp increase in direct air attacks at night on German units in the city. On the night of 14/15 October sixty-five planes (fifty-five U-2s, six SBs, one DB-3 and three R-5s) carried out 313 sorties, mostly by U-2 biplanes. Six hundred and one FAB-100 bombs, and many fragmentation and incendiary bombs were dropped without loss.[19] This activity was irritably assessed in the Sixth Army's war diary: 'The Russian aviation's night air superiority has tangible consequences. The troops are never left in peace and their strength is always under strain. There are human and equipment losses.' Chuikov also precisely singled out the effectiveness of night aviation in a conversation with an associate of the commission for studying the experience of the war: 'Our aviation worked well at night. Our U-2s – whoever invented them, they're invaluable. We called it the KA – the king of the air.'[20]

Meanwhile, the Soviet command was feverishly gathering reserves for building a new defensive line. At 01.00 Chuikov ordered the 92nd Rifle Brigade to be moved from its positions by lengthening the rifle division's front and the brigade transferred to the 37th Guards Rifle Division's position. However, the planned commitment of the brigade into the fighting did not take place. The 92nd Rifle Brigade's composite battalion, consisting of 147 'active bayonets',[21] arrived in the area of the 37th Guards Rifle Division's command post at 05.40 on 15 October and did not have time to take up defensive positions before the start of the German offensive. The battalion came under a heavy bombardment and suffered serious losses and its remnants, headed by the chief of staff, got into an encirclement. What happened was described thusly in the brigade's war diary: 'Upon encountering the enemy's tanks and lacking anti-tank equipment, the brigade's soldiers sacrificed themselves and destroyed the enemy tanks with grenades and petrol bombs.'[22] Twelve men remained in the brigade after the fighting.

However, the chief task of Jaenecke's group at that moment was to develop the 14th Panzer Division's success and the day of 15 October was spent by the Germans in occupying the Stalingrad Tractor Factory and the brick factory adjacent to it from the south by suppressing the remaining centres of resistance in the occupied area. As was noted in a report by the commander of the 112th Rifle Division to the commander of the 62nd Army, by 10.00 on 16 October there remained only 118 men in the 112th Rifle Division, including 42 officers and 76 NCOs and enlisted men. Only twelve men returned to their lines out of the first battalion of Gorokhov's brigade from the fighting for the Stalingrad Tractor Factory.[23] It was subsequently noted in a LI Corps report that 100 tank hulls and 35 tank turrets were captured, plus locomotives and other equipment. According to German data, 1,028 prisoners (including 31 deserters) were taken on 15 October, which was significantly more than on the previous day.

The LI Corps' tank losses may be evaluated by the decline in the strength of the tank park of the two divisions that took part in the fighting (see table).

Table 29: The Condition of the 14th and 24th Panzer Divisions' Tank Park on 15 October 1942.

	Panzer II	*Panzer III (short)*	*Panzer III (long)*
24th Panzer Division	6	6	10
14th Panzer Division	3	3	9

	Panzer IV (short)	*Panzer IV (long)*	*Command Tanks*
24th Panzer Division	4	0	2
14th Panzer Division	2	4	4

However, having concentrated on seizing the Stalingrad Tractor Factory, the LI Corps' units left the 95th Rifle and 37th Guards Rifle Divisions, which had been thrown back to the 'Barricade' factory, in peace for a while. In the 62nd Army's war diary for 15 October their condition was defined by the words 'have completely lost their combat capability'. To the credit of the 62nd Army's scouts, as early as the second day of the offensive they calculated that the factories had been attacked by units of the fresh 305th Infantry Division. A retaliatory move with the movement of a fresh formation (138th Rifle Division) was running late, about which more will be said later.

Perhaps Chuikov's best asset at that moment was the 84th Tank Brigade. The day of 15 October passed comparatively quietly for D.N. Belyi's brigade. Its heavy KV tanks, which had remained on the left bank of the river, were crossed over to the city with the start of the German offensive. On the evening of 15 October the brigade numbered five KVs, twelve T-34s (with seven in line) and five T-70s (with three in line).[24] The immobilized T-34s and T-70s were employed as stationary firing points.

By the morning of 16 October the LI Corps had regrouped with its front facing south for an attack on the 'Barricade' factory. The attack, in which the 14th Panzer and 305th Infantry Divisions were involved, began at 08.00 with intensive support from the air. Among the numerous bombs of all sizes, a few 1,800kg and 2,500kg bombs were dropped. However, the attack immediately ran into the buried Soviet tanks. It was noted in the LI Corps' report for 16 October that 'The attack by the 14th Panzer Division (one panzer battalion, the 64th Motorcycle Battalion and the 577th Infantry Regiment) against the north-western corner of the gun factory in quadrant 84D1 ran into enemy tanks. Sixteen enemy tanks (one KV, seven T-34s and eight T-60s) were destroyed during the fighting, and we lost 17 of ours.'

Unfortunately, the 84th Tank Brigade's report for 16 October is missing and the details of the fighting are unknown, but its combat vehicles, which turned out to be in the right place at the right time, became the nemesis of the German 14th Panzer Division. On the evening of 17 October the 84th Tank Brigade numbered one KV and one T-34 capable of moving, and another one KV, three T-34s and one T-70, which, being immobilized, were used as stationary firing points.[25] This forces us to conclude that the greater part of the 84th Tank Brigade's combat vehicles were lost in the tank battle on 16 October, having inflicted serious losses on the enemy. The Germans managed to crush the tank troops' resistance only by the middle of the day.

Thanks to the resistance in the area of the Stalingrad Tractor Factory and the success by the 84th Tank Brigade's tanks on the defensive, we managed to win time for the commitment of a new division into the struggle for the city. If before this the formations from the front to the north of the city had been the donor for the 62nd Army fighting in Stalingrad, then during the third assault a formation was removed from the 64th Army. The decision to move the division was made as early as the first day of the German offensive. By the close of 14 October Colonel I.I. Lyudnikov's 138th Rifle Division, according to an order from *front* headquarters, was to be subordinated to the commander of the 62nd Army. The division's units were undergoing combat training when at 15.00 on 14 October the order was received 'to be ready to cross over to the city of Stalingrad'. It's difficult at that moment to call the 138th Rifle Division's condition brilliant. It numbered 4,367 men, 1,019 rifles, 222 automatic rifles, 21 light machine guns, and three (three!) heavy machine guns. At the same time, the division disposed of a powerful artillery fist consisting of eleven 122mm howitzers, thirty-one 76mm guns and twenty-one anti-tank guns. However, these guns and mortars had an insignificant amount of ammunition. The division had recently received about 1,500 men as reinforcements, but lacked weapons and entrenching tools. Lyudnikov reported on all of this to the *front* commander. They accordingly corrected the formation's task 'to raise the most full-strength regiment, take the missing weaponry and cross it over to the right bank of the Volga River by 05.00 on 15 October'. It was ordered that the remaining units should await weapons and ammunition.

Major F.I. Pechenyuk's[26] 650th Rifle Regiment, consisting of 1,067 men armed with 591 rifles, 111 automatic rifles, 12 light and two heavy machine guns, 13 anti-tank rifles, and 17 50mm and 26 82mm mortars, was chosen to cross into Stalingrad. The regiment departed at 02.30 on 15 October but only arrived at the Staren'kii inhabited locale, 4km from the crossing, by 04.00–05.00. It became clear that the regiment was late to the crossing (it operated only until dawn, at 04.00) and the order to commit it into the city as early as 15 October was not carried out. *Front* commander Yeremenko arrived at 05.10 and his conversation with Lyudnikov lasted an hour and was probably not pleasant (the content of the conversation was not mentioned in the formation's war diary, and in his memoirs Lyudnikov was tactfully silent about all the difficulties of moving his division into the city). Meanwhile, during the day about 700 reinforcements arrived at the 138th Rifle Division. It should be mentioned in particular that in the 138th Rifle Division's war diary it was noted that the reinforcements 'were poorly trained and too young. Many were born in 1926.'[27] But they could not afford to be picky. They distributed the reinforcements, including 16-year-olds, between the 344th and 768 Rifle Regiments. They had to move immediately from their school desks to the hell of street fighting in Stalingrad.

It is difficult to call the crossing of Lyudnikov's division well organized. Closer to the evening of 15 October the 138th Rifle Division's regiments received an oral order to move to the 'Red October' crossing. The 650th Rifle Regiment moved up to the crossing at 20.00. The crossing proved to be occupied by elements of the 84th Tank Brigade (the KV tanks, see above), but nevertheless the regiment arrived in Stalingrad by 05.00. Major Pechenyuk's regiment departed for the area to the north of the 'Barricade' factory, in detail, as they arrived from the crossing. It was operationally subordinated to the 37th Guards Rifle Division.

The 138th Rifle Division's two other regiments arrived at the crossing and halted, lacking precise orders. As a result, the 344th and 768th Rifle Divisions stood around the entire day of 16 October near Staren'kii, and were subjected to air attacks and artillery bombardment. The crossing over the Volga took place only during the night of 16/17 October using ten armoured cutters and two motorized ferries from the Volga Military Flotilla. In this place it was first necessary to cross over the Volga to Zaitsevskii Island and then through Denezhnaya Volozhka into Stalingrad. The small bridge through Denezhnaya Volozhka had already been destroyed and the crossing of Lyudnikov's two regiments was carried out on the boats used for evacuating wounded from the city. To be fair, it should be said that that the division's headquarters crossed over as early as midnight on 16 October.

All of this lack of coordination in the 138th Rifle Division's crossing into Stalingrad could have had truly disastrous consequences if there had been perfect order on the other side of the front. But this was not the case. The LI Corps' daily report describes what happened:

> The LI Corps' attack on 16.10 with the 14th Panzer Division and the 305th Infantry Division was conducted against a stubbornly defending enemy with tanks in the dismantled building structures for the purpose of penetrating into the northern part of the armaments factory. But the goal set for this day was not achieved. The attack was not conducted with all of the 14th Panzer Division's and 305th Infantry Division's available forces, as well as the nearly impoverished presence of 100mm and 210mm munitions for the mortars. Experience has confirmed that in order to achieve complete success in a designated undertaking, the planned preparation of joint activities of infantry and artillery is necessary, while at the same time paying attention to fully supplying the troops with ammunition, which in the case of 16 October was neglected.

Actually, the LI Corps fired off 496 tons of ammunition (less than on the first day of the offensive) on 16 October, including 246 210mm howitzer rounds, 165 rounds from 100mm guns and 3,053 shells from 150mm sFH18s.[28] The 100mm guns, although they did not have a very powerful shell, nevertheless were actively employed by the Germans for counter-battery fire at long range.

The 'neglected' process of supplying the attackers with ammunition enabled the Soviets to commit the 138th Rifle Division into the city, with its front facing north and north-west. By order of the 62nd Army's military council, Lyudnikov's division was assigned the following task: 'The 138th Red Banner Rifle Division is to occupy and securely defend by 04.00 on 17.10.42 the line of the southern outskirts of Derevenki and Skul'pturnyi. It is to prevent the enemy from reaching the area of Lenin Prospect and the "Barricade" factory.'

Aside from the commitment of fresh formations into the fighting in Stalingrad, there was the ongoing process of pulling out of the city divisions that had lost their combat capability. With the arrival of the 138th Rifle Division, the long-suffering 95th Rifle Division was to be pulled back to the eastern bank of the Volga, but the 161st Rifle Regiment, with a strength of fifty 'active bayonets', was to remain in the city. The occupied positions were to be transferred to the arriving units of Lyudnikov's division.

The 138th Rifle Division's commander decided to construct his defence in two echelons. The 650th Rifle Regiment, which was already fighting along the approaches to the 'Barricade' factory, was to be allotted to the first echelon, as was the newly-crossed 768th Rifle Regiment. The 344th was to be allocated to the second echelon. However, the arrival of the 138th Rifle Division at its positions in Stalingrad did not take place very smoothly, as they had wanted. As a result, Chuikov's acquaintance with Lyudnikov began with a dressing-down of the division commander. The 62nd Army commander wrote him on 17 October: 'You have not carried out my order to occupy the railway station and the settlement to the west of Tramvainaya and Skul'pturnyi, by which you have failed to secure the 308th Rifle Division's right flank, as a result of which a gap has opened between your division and the 308th Rifle Division, which has enabled the enemy to effortlessly attack along the railway to the "Barricade" factory and to threaten to capture the "Barricade" factory and to advance further to the south.'[29]

Later on, Chuikov demanded that the commander repair the mistakes made: 'I hold you personally responsible for eliminating the gap with the 308th Rifle Division, to secure its right flank by establishing direct communications, and under no circumstances to all the enemy to penetrate onto the territory of the "Barricade" factory and into the boundary with the 308th Rifle Division. You are responsible for the boundary.'

One should say that in his memoirs Lyudnikov preferred to avoid descriptions of the details of the fighting for the 'Barricade' factory, citing the fact that 'The 138th Rifle Division is represented by a very skinny folder for this period in the USSR Ministry of Defence archives'.[30] There's an element of slyness in this: there is a quite detailed war diary for this period in the 138th Rifle Division's file, as well as operational reports for the time of the formation's being in Stalingrad. Chuikov's order that was 'cited' by Lyudnikov resembles the original (an order issued at 23.50 on 16 October) in only the most general sense and in several phrases. Only one thing can explain all of this: Comrade Lyudnikov did not want to discuss the details of what was going on in Stalingrad.

The reason for the dressing-down by Chuikov was the banal loss of orientation in the city. The 'Barricade' factory, as a secret plant, had been noted on the map of Stalingrad only by a white rectangle, with railway lines to the west. Major G.M. Gunyaga, the commander of the 768th Rifle Regiment, passed over several railway lines in the grounds of the 'Barricade' factory and believed that he had carried out his assignment of reaching the assigned line. However, in reality, the regiment's subunits remained on the territory of the factory.

The consequences of what one can without exaggeration call a fatal mistake were not long in coming. The Germans' 14th Panzer Division attacked along the railway running to the west from the 'Barricade' factory into the rear of the 308th Rifle Division. As was noted in the formation's midday report on 17 October, 'the enemy is easily infiltrating with infantry and tanks into the gap with our neighbour.' Moreover, the Germans undertook purposeful actions to create a 'cauldron': on the night of 16/17 October the 14th Panzer Division's 108th Motorized Regiment was shifted along the destroyed city blocks into the boundary between the 100th Light Infantry Division and the 24th Panzer Division and reinforced with the 'Messerschmitt'[31] tank group from the 24th Panzer Division. At 08.00 on 17 October, following an artillery preparation, the 108th Motorized Regiment began its attack along a ravine in the direction of the south-western corner of the 'Barricade' factory, and the 14th Panzer Division's 103rd Motorized Regiment moved forward to meet it along the railway. As early as midday the 108th Motorized Regiment reached the railway, thus closing the encirclement ring around two of the 308th Rifle Division's regiments.

The situation was made worse by the 24th Panzer Division's previously-planned pinning attacks from the front, which prevented the 308th Rifle Division's regiments from removing subunits in order to cover the flank. On the same day the 308th Rifle Division's command post came under attack and the commander's company went into battle. The difficult consequences of the envelopment of both flanks were outlined in the 308th Rifle Division's operational report of 12.00 on 18 October: 'The 347th and 339th Rifle Regiments' subunits, which were in an encirclement for a day and a half by an enemy outnumbering him by several times until the last minute, perished in their defensive areas without having retreated an inch.'[32] The 138th Rifle Division's situation also sharply worsened, although not as disastrously as that of its neighbour. Instead of defending along a comparatively narrow sector, with its front facing north and north-west in the northern part of the 'Barricade' factory, the units of Lyudnikov's division now had to defend the 'Barricade' factory as a whole, with their front facing to the west and north, in greatly depleted battle orders. The situation was exacerbated by a very powerful attack against the 650th Rifle Regiment, the situation of which on the evening of 17 October was described in a report as 'continuing to wage heavy fighting while encircled'.

The composite 161st Rifle Regiment from Gorishnyi's division (95th Rifle), which bestrode the fork in the railway lines near the south-western extremity of the 'Barricade' factory, held the Germans' breakthrough along the railway and further as far as the 'Red October' factory. Instead of a textbook defence in two echelons, Lyudnikov had to bring up his subunits in 'bits and pieces' to the perimeter of the 'Barricade' factory on the night of 17/18 October, thus dividing up his regiments by battalion. One battalion from the 344th Rifle Regiment was placed in the north-western corner of the territory of the 'Barricade' factory, with another one in the south-western corner, and between them the 768th Rifle Regiment was stationed facing west.

The stubborn resistance of the 308th Rifle Division's two regiments encircled to the west of the 'Barricade' factory basically saved Lyudnikov's units from an immediate rout. During the day on 18 October units of the German 14th and 24th Panzer and 305th

Infantry Divisions fought to eliminate the resistance on the ground occupied the previous day. According to German data, on 18 October the LI Corps took 537 prisoners (including ten deserters). At the same time, the less-than-happy debut of the 138th Rifle Division on the streets of Stalingrad resulted in appreciable losses. According to an evening operational report from 18 October, the 650th Rifle Regiment on the front line numbered only 86 men, and the 768th Rifle Regiment, also on the front line, numbered 424 men, with 577 men in the 344th Rifle Regiment. This critical situation was somewhat allayed by the holding of positions in the area of the northern extremity of the 'Barricade' factory, with the anchor of the flank on the river held by the remnants of the 37th Rifle Division's 118th Rifle Regiment. Aside from riflemen, it included the so-called 'Kiselyov group', made up of the crews of the 45mm and 76mm guns, who had lost their guns and were fighting as infantry. At that time it numbered about 300 men.

On the critical day for the Soviet forces in the area of the 'Barricade' factory of 17 October, the 8th Air Army attempted to operate more actively during the day, while covering its forces. Twenty-two fighters take off and seven were shot down or did not return from their combat assignment, while another two Yak-1s made forced landings due to damage. Another four La-5s from the 287th Fighter Air Corps take off to cover their forces in the area of the 'Barricade' factory, and two of them failed to return.

Meanwhile, the wave from the collapse of the front rushed back to the positions of the 193rd Rifle Division, which was defending along the approaches to the 'Red October' factory. On 17 October the withdrawal by its neighbour on the right – the 347th Rifle Regiment (308th Rifle Division) – was noted from the line of Petrozavodsk Street. A large part of the mines in the ravine north of Kaluga Street (along the flank of the 193rd Rifle Division's 685th Rifle Regiment) had been blown up by artillery fire and bombing. It was precisely here that the breakthrough by the 14th Panzer Division's 108th Motorized Regiment, which had been reinforced by tanks, took place while encircling Gurt'ev's division. The 193rd Rifle Division's right flank was open. In order to cover it, the remnants of the formation's training battalion were moved up, but that could only yield a temporary stabilization of the situation.

Chuikov saw that the 62nd Army's defence was crumbling before his very eyes. This forced him to attempt to 'tighten the screws', citing, among others, Order No. 227. Late at night on 18 October an order appeared from army headquarters, containing such statements as: 'Colonel Gurt'ev issued an order to pull back the 339th and 347th Rifle Regiments to the rear without my permission',[33] or that 'Colonel Gurt'ev has committed a crime against the Motherland'.[34] Accordingly, the commander of the 308th Rifle Division was ordered in no uncertain terms to return the regiments to their previous positions by morning. On the order, which was written with a simple pencil, the phrase 'failure to fulfil will be tried', was added following the instructions in crimson-coloured pencil. Chuikov's signature was appended in the same colour.

On the one hand, the words about the regiments' withdrawal contradict the fact of the encirclement of the 308th Rifle Division's regiments, the centres of resistance of which the Germans eliminated during the day on 18 October, which is confirmed by German sources. At 17.50 on 17 October the commander of the 193rd Rifle Division reported that 'According to a report by the commander of the 685th Rifle Regiment, the 347th Rifle Regiment (308th Rifle Division) is fighting in encirclement'.[35] On the other hand, part of the forces of the surrounded subunits was nevertheless able to receive the withdrawal order at the last moment. There are the following words in the 193rd Rifle Division's operational report, dated 22.00 on 17 October: 'According to a report by the commander of the 685th Rifle Regiment, individual groups from the 347th Rifle Regiment (308th Rifle Division) are being put in order in the area of the railway junction.'[36] Whatever the case, the 308th Rifle Division's integrated defence system had ceased to exist.

According to a later report by Gurt'ev, the encirclement of the two regiments took place as early as 13.00 on 17 October.[37] That is, at the time of the breakthrough by the Germans' 108th Motorized Regiment to the railway. Any communications with the units was cut, which prevented them from supporting the encircled regiments with at least artillery fire. The observation post of the division's artillery, along with radios, had also been crushed by the enemy. The 347th and 339th Rifle Regiments' command posts in the 'Barricade' factory in the area of the fork in the railway were cut off from their subunits, while the headquarters of the 339th Rifle Regiment was surrounded. Thanks to the arrival of reinforcements, Gurt'ev formed a battalion of 160 'bayonets', and the 339th Rifle Regiment received 50 men. With these forces Gurt'ev attempted to break through to link up with the encircled units, but was unsuccessful. By 12.00 on 18 October individual soldiers and commanders had gotten out of the encirclement. The headquarters of the 347th Rifle Regiment used the underground communications of the 'Barricade' factory for the breakthrough. The remnants of the 347th Rifle Regiment, numbering twenty-four men, took up defensive positions in the 'Barricade' factory's main office, while the regimental commander later reported that sixty men had gathered.[38]

One should say that the 62nd Army's headquarters did not limit itself to dressing down the formation commanders. The report by the commander of the 193rd Rifle Division, Smekhotvorov, about his flank being turned did not escape attention. On the morning of 18 October Krylov ordered the commander of the 39th Guards Rifle Division 'to set aside two rifle companies at the disposal of the commander of the 193rd Rifle Division for restoring the situation along the southern outskirts of the "Barricade factory"'.[39] A battalion of tanks (one KV and two T-34s), a motorized rifle battalion and a battery of anti-tank guns from the 84th Tank Brigade was also moved to the same area. The forces were, of course, small, but they could at least slow the Germans' advance.

The main consequence of the turning of the flank for the 193rd Rifle Division was its 685th Rifle Regiment being kicked out of its familiar and well-fortified positions by the evening of 18 October. As was noted in the 685th Rifle Regiment's report on the result of the fighting, 'The regiment's forward edge ran along the line of Protochnaya and Tupikovaya streets along open terrain and with hastily outfitted trenches, without shelters and communications trenches, and with the absence of powerful anti-tank weapons and machine guns ...'[40]

At 02.00 on 19 October reinforcements numbering 390 men, armed only with rifles, arrived at the 193rd Rifle Division, and, as it was noted in the operational report, 'they have not been under fire and are insufficiently trained, while the overwhelming majority are Kazakhs and Uzbeks'. It's not surprising that in these conditions (weak positions and a lack of time for knocking together the units that had received reinforcements) the 685th Rifle Regiment's defence collapsed under the enemy's attacks and the regiment's subunits fell back behind the railway toward the stone 'garret buildings' next to the bread-baking plant. In these conditions, on 19 October Major General F.N. Smekhotvorov was forced to pull back the 895th Rifle Regiment from its positions that had been outfitted during a quiet spell and to deploy it with its front facing north, closing ranks with the 685th Rifle Regiment, which had been thrown back to the area of the bread-baking plant. The 895th Rifle Regiment was now occupying defensive positions from the factory-kitchen (the 1/895th Rifle Regiment's strongpoint) as far as the positions of the 685th Rifle Regiment beyond the railway. On 19 October Major Vorozheikin, the commander of the 895th Rifle Regiment, perished in battle. The resumption of the fighting for the 'Barricade' factory to some extent rescued the 193rd Rifle Division's defence from further collapse, and the LI Corps' daily report notes that 'The planned offensive on the bread-baking plant and the bank of the Volga was postponed because of the situation in the arms factory'.

As a result of all of these events, Chuikov organized a real dressing-down in his order to the commander of the 193rd Rifle Division, with a mass of harsh words: 'You have begun to fall back without any reason, except from the threat of the enemy's expected attack …', 'such a feverish condition, such sudden and instantaneous changes in the situation were only possible for you'.[41] Chuikov reminded Smekhotvorov of the 'Not a step back' order and promised to help only with Army artillery. The 193rd Rifle Division's chief of staff, Chumakov, was criticized in a separate order: 'You are silent during the day [as in the document, Author] and everything seems to be going well with you, but later at night, when nothing can be done, you report "We have a disaster on our hands, the enemy has broken through …"'

It's difficult to agree here with Chuikov. As early as 17 October Major Chumakov openly stated 'I request you commit units from the army reserve into the newly-formed gap [in the area of the "Barricade" factory]'.[42] At 12.30 on 18 October, that is, during the middle of the day, he reported: 'Six tanks have broken through to the area of the school, which is between Buguruslan and Tiraspol' streets.' This was Stalingrad school No. 26, which was already located deep in the rear of the 193rd Rifle Division's positions. Only after this, at midnight on 18 October, did Smekhotvorov himself write the army commander a lengthy report (it was evidently him that Chuikov had in mind as the one who described the disaster) using statements that did not allow for an ambiguous interpretation: 'The enemy has almost completely destroyed the 685th Rifle Regiment and the training battalion', and 'a gap has developed between the 685th and 895th Rifle Regiments'.[43] Here Smekhotvorov wrote that 'I request you take immediate measures to eliminate the further development of the enemy's breakthrough'.[44] That is, the 193rd Rifle Division command informed Army headquarters about the unfavourable development of events and, one may say, was sounding the alarm. However, the reaction of the 62nd Army command to the gradual collapse of the front of Smekhotvorov's division was clearly delayed.

In the meantime, the weather got worse on 19–22 October, and rain mixed with snow poured down, and Paulus ordered that a new attack be postponed – in light of the exhaustion of the infantry's strength the German offensives had become more dependent on air support. According to the results of the third assault on Stalingrad, the 62nd Army's anti-tank gunners and tank troops can't be accused of bad shooting. The number of combat-ready tanks in the 14th and 24th Panzer Divisions of Paulus's army was inexorably falling (see table).

Table 30: The Condition of the 14th and 24th Panzer Divisions' Tank Park on 19 October 1942.

	Panzer II	*Panzer III (short)*	*Panzer III (long)*
24th Panzer Division	6	3	16
14th Panzer Division	3	1	4

	Panzer IV (short)	*Panzer IV (long)*	*Command Tanks*
24th Panzer Division	1	1	2
14th Panzer Division	1	2	4

Despite the pause taken by the Germans in the offensive on Stalingrad, sorties of a local nature continued, moreover with a large expenditure of ammunition. For example, on 20 October the LI Corps fired off 230 tons. Artillery and air attacks were launched on that day, particularly against the 193rd Rifle Division's 883rd Rifle Regiment, which was still holding out along its prepared positions. On 21 October the LI Corps fired off 293 tons of ammunition.[45] On this day the situation along the front of the 193rd Rifle Division's 895th Rifle Regiment worsened, when its first battalion was isolated in its strongpoint in the factory-kitchen. However, the deep envelopment and rout of this strongpoint did not take place and the opportunity for developing the success along this sector of the 193rd Rifle Division's defence was missed by the Germans at that moment. The 100th Light Infantry Division was not operating very energetically. On the other hand, units of the 14th Panzer Division were more active in the area of the bread-baking plant. In order to storm the buildings here, the Germans employed tanks, which were committed into the fighting following the artillery's working-over of the Soviet positions. As was indicated in the 685th Rifle Regiment's report, 'Three tanks were approaching the building at a distance of 70–100m and were positioned for mutual cover and were firing on the building from close range with guns and machine guns'.[46] The infantry took advantage of the results of the shelling. As a result, the first 'garret building' was captured on 21 October. However, the advance went on slowly through this method and before 24–25 October the Germans took five 'garret buildings'.

A hail of bombs and shells, even during the lulls in fighting, shook the Soviet defence. If on 21 October the 193rd Rifle Division's 883rd Rifle Regiment numbered 647 'active bayonets' and the 895th Rifle Regiment 373, then two days later there remained only 201 and 150 men respectively. An unpleasant consequence of the constant pressure on the part of German aviation and artillery was also the loss of anti-tank weapons such as 45mm guns and anti-tank rifles, of which, according to Smekhotvorov's report, 'literally a handful remain'.

Gorokhov's Group

In the northern part of Stalingrad there was defending a group from units of several rifle brigades, which from the beginning of September had acquired the name 'Gorokhov's operational group' or 'Gorokhov's group'. It was headed by the commander of the 124th Rifle Brigade, Colonel S.F. Gorokhov. The group proved to be the most stable of the operational groups created by the then-commander of the 62nd Army, Major General N.I. Krylov. Gorokhov's group had suffered seriously during the course of the German offensive on Orlovka, but in the middle of October it was still in comparatively good shape (see table).

Table 31: Numerical Strength of the Subunits Defending in the Northern Part of Stalingrad on 14 October 1942.

Name of Subunit	Overall Strength	'Active Bayonets'
1/124th Rifle Brigade[47]	146	77
2/124th Rifle Brigade	672	599
3/124th Rifle Brigade	488	369
4/124th Rifle Brigade	474	399
124th Rifle Brigade (all)	3,362	1,745
149th Rifle Brigade on 11 Oct	3,107[48]	1,331
115th Rifle Brigade (Andrusenko's group) on 12 Oct	1,401	no data[49]

By October there were no tank brigades left along the brigade's defensive sectors, but there was an unusual unit in the form of the Stalingrad tank factory's independent tank battalion. It consisted of various types of tanks, which had been brought to the Stalingrad Tractor Factory for repairs, but in light of the closing of the factory's work were employed predominantly as stationary firing points. On 11 October the battalion included twenty-three tanks: six KVs, eight T-34s, three T-70s and six T-60s. Of this number six tanks were in line and another two undergoing repairs.[50] The Stalingrad Tractor Factory battalion was broken up into three companies, which were occupying positions in the 124th and 149th Rifle Brigade's defensive system.

With the splitting of the 62nd Army in two and the attack on the Stalingrad Tractor Factory on 14 October the brigades in the northern part of Stalingrad were isolated. Gorokhov's group was shielded from an immediate attack into its rear from the south by the Wet Mechetka River. However, troubles arrived in the form of the XIV Panzer Corps, which joined in the general offensive by Paulus's army on Stalingrad on the morning of 15 October. The situation along the 'northern screen' in the middle of October was already sufficiently stable and this enabled the Germans to deploy the 16th Panzer Division to Stalingrad, as well as to activate the worn-out 94th Infantry Division for the attack. The XIV Panzer Corps began its attack a day later than the attack on the Stalingrad Tractor Factory, because the capture by its neighbour of the heights suitable for observation was expected.

However, the 115th, 124th and 149th Rifle Brigades were not included Chuikov's plan for a counteroffensive and for a lengthy period received only orders to defend. During the several days at their disposal following the fighting for Orlovka, the brigades had consolidated their positions well. As was noted in the daily report, the 16th Panzer Division's offensive 'was halted in the depth of the enemy's defence after a good initial success'. The Soviet defence in the Rynok and Spartakovka area was rated highly by the enemy: 'The enemy is fiercely defending along well-prepared positions, employing a large number of heavy infantry weapons. Flanking fire from the north and south led to our heavy losses. Numerous anti-aircraft and anti-tank guns are hindering the effective employment of tanks and assault guns.' At the same time, one should not say that Gorokhov's group disposed of a large amount of artillery. On 12 October the 124th Rifle Brigade had eight Stalin Factory-3 76mm guns, two 76mm regimental guns and twelve 45mm guns. There were sufficient armour-piercing shells for these guns. The 115th Rifle Brigade only disposed of three 76mm guns and one 45mm gun.

However, the collapse of the front in the area of the Stalingrad Tractor Factory and the loss of one of the 124th Rifle Brigade's battalions in the fighting for it nonetheless seriously weakened the situation of Gorokhov's group. On the second day of the offensive, 16 October, the Germans managed to break through to the mouth of the Wet Mechetka River and thus encircle part of the forces of the 62nd Army's northern group. Encircled were the 149th Rifle Brigade's third battalion, the remnants of the 282nd NKVD Regiment,[51] and also the remnants of the 115th Rifle Brigade. At night the encircled units broke out of the 'cauldron'. The headquarters of the 115th Rifle Brigade was pulled out of Stalingrad on 21 October 1942.

The Stalingrad Tractor Factory's tank battalion was destroyed during the first three days of the offensive. A company of T-60s was lost on 14 October and they were all burned by enemy artillery fire. By the evening of 15 October there were two KVs left in line. The remaining tanks had been knocked out by artillery fire or hit by bombs. By the close of day on 16 October both KVs had been encircled by the enemy. The infantry from Gorokhov's group fell back from the tanks. The KV crews fought until their ammunition ran out and with the onset of darkness they blew up their tanks and made their way back to their own lines.

According to German reports, as a result of three days of fighting against Gorokhov's group, they took 322 prisoners and captured 30 anti-tank guns, 16 mortars, one 'salvo installation,' and one tank was knocked out (this was evidently one of the stationary tanks from the Stalingrad Tractor Factory's battalion). The claim of having captured thirty guns was clearly exaggerated, as there were simply not that many guns in Gorokhov's group. The 124th Rifle Brigade's documents mention the loss of one 76mm gun and three 45mm guns. As regards personnel losses, the 124th Rifle Brigade reported 87 killed, 219 wounded and 55 missing in action from 15 until 22 October.[52]

At the same time, Gorokhov was complaining to army headquarters that Lieutenant Colonel Yermoklin, who was commanding the remnants of the 112th Rifle Division, had left for the eastern bank of the Volga without coordinating the move with him. As early as November Yermoklin was removed from command and sent to a military tribunal.[53] In January 1943 Chuikov singled him out for particular criticism, saying that 'All the division commanders retained their divisions, except for Yermoklin's 112th Rifle Division'.

The enemy's arrival at the Volga was creating the danger that the river would be forced by employing the two islands in this area. *Stavka* Order No. 157562 of 16 October commanded: 'In connection with the enemy's capture of the area of the Stalingrad Tractor Factory and his arrival at the Volga River, part of the 300th Rifle Division's forces is to be dispatched to temporarily reinforce the garrisons of Zaitsevskii and Spornyi islands.' This was a full-strength division numbering more than 10,000 men. Overall, the formation was the last reserve that the Soviet command could have thrown onto the streets of Stalingrad in what was truly a critical situation.

The situation of Gorokhov's isolated group stabilized during the second half of October. The XIV Panzer Corps was busy with the defence of the 'land bridge' and the LI Corps was attacking the factories, having turned their backs toward the small island in the northern part of the city. According to a report by Gorokhov, on 19 October 1942 he commanded 3,953 men and disposed of 15 heavy machine guns, 95 light machine guns and 57 anti-tank rifles. The group's artillery consisted of two 45mm guns, twenty 76mm guns, twenty-one 120mm mortars, forty-eight 82mm mortars, and twenty-three 50mm mortars. The group's core was the 124th Rifle Brigade, which numbered 2,640 men. The group's second formation was Lieutenant Colonel V.A. Bolvinov's 140th Rifle Brigade. The remnants of the 115th Rifle Brigade and the 112th Rifle Division were put into building up the two brigade's strength, although the morale of the two formations' soldier who had lived through a disaster gave rise to criticism. Supply over the Volga worked, but not flawlessly, Gorokhov complaining about the shortage of 120mm and 76mm shells, as well as of sniper rifles. The group's crossing was supported by a ferry and six armoured cutters from the Volga Flotilla.

On 19 October the Germans attacked the positions of Gorokhov's group once again. Early in the morning, following a powerful artillery and air preparation, Brendel's and Reimann's combat groups from the 94th Infantry Division attacked Spartakovka and penetrated into its western outskirts, thus capturing the city prison. This attack was not a decisive success, and in the XIV Panzer Corps' daily report it was noted that the offensive 'was halted by heavy fire from the mouth of the Wet Mechetka and the eastern bank of the Volga'. The 4/149th and 4/124th Rifle Brigades came under attack and lost on that day 248 men killed and wounded. An attempt to restore the situation by a counter-attack was not successful. Calm set in for a few days, while on the evening of 23 October Gorokhov decided to take back the occupied part of Spartakovka with a night attack.

The offensive was carried out by the forces of the 149th Rifle Brigade (450 'active bayonets'). Having launched the attack at midnight, by 05.00 the brigade's subunits had 'completely carried out their assigned mission'. However, as was often the case in Stalingrad, the Soviet forces' offensive activity ran into an enemy attack. On the morning of 24 October the 94th Infantry Division attacked the subunits of Bolvinov's brigade, which had not had time to consolidate. This led not only to a withdrawal from the recently-occupied positions, but also the loss of a significant part of Spartakovka. The Germans took back the prison by storm. According to a report by the 149th Rifle Brigade, its losses for 24 October were 91 killed and 223 wounded.[54] According to a corps report, the 94th Infantry Division's losses for the day were 175 men.

Having suffered heavy losses, the 149th Rifle Brigade was pushed back to the Volga and the so-called 'Bolvinov group' (named after the commander of the 149th Rifle Brigade) was formed from its remnants. However, the core of the defence of Spartakovka was the first and fourth battalions of the 124th Rifle Brigade. At that moment Gorokhov himself rated the situation as critical and reported to army headquarters: 'The situation is hopeless. Immediately send men, or explain a variant of operations.'[55] It is of interest to note that it was literally with these same words ('explain a variant of operations') that Model[56] around Rzhev had demanded reinforcements from Kluge.[57] Gorokhov's demands had an effect and within a few days he was given a battalion from the 300th Rifle Division's 1051st Rifle Regiment. They did not employ the 'foreign' battalion as a single whole, preferring instead to break it up and send its personnel and equipment to beef up the two brigades' units.

The next onslaught on Gorokhov's group followed on 27 October. In the XIV Panzer Corps' report the effective support from the air was particularly singled out: 'In the morning we had very good support from strafing Stuka dive bombers.' However, the Germans were unable to overthrow the defence of the northern sector. The 94th Infantry Division achieved only local successes. It is of interest to note that an example of its 274th Infantry Regiment's success on that day was that 'it destroyed in a close-quarters battle the crews of the enemy's anti-aircraft guns'. These were probably the remnants of the 1077th Anti-

Aircraft Regiment, which was covering the crossings in the northern part of Stalingrad and which had beaten back the attacks by German tanks on 23 August. In the reports by Gorokhov's group these anti-aircraft gunners are not mentioned. In Gorokhov's report of 27 October a three-hour 'bayonet and grenade' battle is noted in the foxholes and trenches, as a result of which they managed to hold their positions.

On 2 November 1942 there was another attempt to eliminate the Soviet bridgehead in Spartakovka. The 124th Rifle Brigade's second and third battalions rendered effective support to their comrades in the Rynok area, operating against the enemy with fire from the flank, and the advanced positions of the 3/124th Rifle Brigade favoured this. The German offensive can actually be rated a failure, and it is clearly stated in the XIV Panzer Corps' report that 'With the onset of darkness the 94th Infantry Division was forced to pull back its forces to their jumping-off positions and take up the defence there'. However, successful defence was not easily achieved. On this day Lieutenant Colonel Bolvinov, the commander of the 149th Rifle Brigade, died from a serious wound, and officers from the brigade's headquarters were wounded. On the whole, the 149th Rifle Brigade's losses were 53 men killed, one missing in action and 104 wounded, while the 124th Rifle Brigade lost 48 men killed and 108 wounded.[58] In a later report, a larger loss figure was listed for the group for that day – 116 killed and 212 wounded.[59] This was the highest daily loss figure from the entire period from 15 October to the middle of November. At that moment the 124th Rifle Brigade numbered 1,337 'active bayonets' and the 149th Rifle Brigade 436.

On 11 November the XIV Panzer Corps' 16th Panzer Division joined in the attempts to eliminate Gorokhov's bridgehead. However, the division's two assault groups, which had been sent into the attack on Rynok following a powerful artillery preparation, were not successful. It was noted in the corps' daily report that 'They managed to advance 200 metres into the depth of the settlement, but powerful barrage artillery fire halted further movement'. Soviet artillery, both Army and Brigade, lay down barrage fire from the left bank of the Volga. The 124th Rifle Brigade's artillery battalion was located on Spornyi Island in the Volga and carried out successful fire according to data supplied by observers in the brigade's positions. It's hardly surprising that Gorokhov even proposed petitioning the Presidium of the USSR Supreme Soviet to rename Spornyi Island[60] Artillery Troops Island.[61]

The final push against Gorokhov's group came literally on the eve of Operation Uranus – on 17 November 1942. The plan for the German offensive foresaw 'miniature Cannaes', with an attack along concentric axes from the north and west for the purpose of encircling Rynok's defenders and cutting them off from the Volga. In the 16th Panzer Division's history Rynok is described as 'a fire-breathing fortress, a labyrinth of trenches, filled with buried tanks, minefields and anti-tank rifles'. Tanks are not mentioned in the reports by Gorokhov's group and are not indicated on the maps of the defence, but their presence is not excluded among those vehicles which remained after being put out of action following the fighting at the end of August and beginning of September.

A battalion of motorized infantry from the 16th Panzer Division in armoured personnel carriers attacked Rynok from the west and managed to break through to the Volga as early as 09.30. However, a link-up with the group attacking from the north did not take place. One of the reasons for the failure of the offensive was the weather conditions, and it was pointed out in the XIV Panzer Corps' daily report that 'Poor visibility and powerful defensive fire hindered the two groups from linking up'. However, in Gorokhov's report, the conditions were also rated as favourable for the enemy: 'Thick fog, which reduces visibility to 100 metres, also favoured the enemy's concentration.' The Germans' breakthrough into the depth of Rynok's defence is confirmed by Colonel Gorokhov's report on the results of the fighting, but it was pointed out that they destroyed this group and took part of it prisoner. Prisoners were certainly taken by the 124th Rifle Brigade's soldiers: the brigade reported on the results of the day reported on the actual number of the 16th Panzer Division's units (which was not done earlier, or contained ridiculous errors such as the '94th Panzer Regiment' instead of the 94th Infantry Division). It is noted in the 16th Panzer Division's history that the subunits that broke through and consolidated in the settlement as an isolated group: 'There was no communication with the rear and Russian snipers had the road under fire. Smoke and snow. The light of explosions light up the night for a minute.' The detachment was later pulled back to the division's main forces.

In the XIV Panzer Corps' daily report for 17 November the effectiveness of the anti-tank defence of Gorokhov's group was singled out: 'Powerful fire from anti-tank defence and tanks led to heavy losses among our tanks.' The Germans' losses in armoured equipment proved to be truly impressive. On 15 November the 16th Panzer Division reported on the presence in line of thirty-nine Panzer IIIs (long), two Panzer IVs (short) and ten Panzer IVs (long). According to the results of the day on 17 November the division disposed of twenty-one Panzer IIIs (long), one Panzer IVs (short) and nine Panzer IVs (long). This yields a reduction of twenty vehicles (eighteen Panzer IIIs (long), one Panzer IVs (short) and one Panzer IV (long)). The Soviet side also claimed, which was unusual, a lower number of tanks put out of action – seventeen vehicles, including nine burned.[62] According to Soviet data, anti-tank riflemen claimed credit for some of the tanks. The infantry also distinguished themselves – a Soviet sniper killed Captain Mues, the commander of a mechanized infantry battalion, as well as mortally wounding Captain von Cramon, the commander of a tank battalion in the 16th Panzer Division in the fighting on 17 November. The death of two previously successful commanders made a painful impression on the rank and file of the German subunits taking part in the fighting. According to Soviet data, there were two enemy offensives on 17 November, with one being carried out in the morning and the other beginning at 15.30. The fighting continued until dark and quieted down only by 23.00. Losses for Gorokhov's group on 17 November amounted to 96 men killed and 119 wounded.[63]

On 18–19 November the Germans made attempts to resume the attacks, but without success. On the evening of 19 November, an order was issued by Army Group B in connection with the beginning of Operation Uranus: 'Halt all offensive operations in Stalingrad immediately.' Gorokhov's group had withstood and inflicted perceptible losses on an elite enemy formation. On the whole, one should admit that the sector of Gorokhov's group was the most effectively defended of all the 62nd Army's positions. One of the reasons for this was the absence of offensive tasks, which enabled it to consolidate, while erecting the 'fire-breathing fortress'.

Chapter 18

The Fighting for the 'Red October' Factory

Paulus transferred two regiments from the 79th Infantry Division (which had been subordinated to LI Corps as of 00.00 on 18 October) for the new offensive. These units, which were reinforced by a regiment from the 100th Jäger Division, seven tanks and the 244th and 245th Assault Gun Battalions, were supposed to launch their main attack, in conjunction with the 14th Panzer Division, from the west on the 'Red October' factory. The 24th Panzer and 305th Infantry Divisions were to launch supporting attacks against the 'Barricade' factory.

The offensive capabilities of the formations of Paulus's army were declining inexorably. The 24th Panzer Division, having become a ram with the assistance of which the salient near Orlovka was cut off, consisted by 19 October 1942 of five battalions, of which two were weak and three 'exhausted'. LI Corps' other formations were in no better condition. For example, the 71st Infantry Division had seven battalions (two of average strength, three weak and two exhausted), the 295th Infantry Division seven battalions (four weak and three exhausted), the 305th Rifle Division had nine battalions (all nine were weak), and the 389th Infantry Division had four battalions (one of average strength, one weak and two exhausted). The four battalions in the 389th Infantry Division were a record of sorts. The lowering of the 305th Infantry Division's potential from nine battalions of middling strength before the storming to nine weak battalions five days later appears to be a record as well. At that moment the formations with a good level of combat capability were the

Table 32: The Strength of the Sixth Army's Formations on the Approaches to Stalingrad on 24 October 1942.

Formation	Ration Strength	Combat Component	'Hiwis'
71st Infantry Division	12,277	4,723	1,764
295th Infantry Division	10,865*	2,887	2,553
305th Infantry Division	10,518	3,345	1,891
389th Infantry Division	8,604	2,736	1,176
94th Infantry Division	11,438	3,473	2,640
113th Infantry Division	12,458	5,169	1,897
76th Infantry Division	12,125	4,809	2,776
100th Light Infantry Division	11,700	5,765	1,851
3rd Motorized Division	10,442	4,196	1,041
60th Motorized Division	10,672	4,552	873
14th Panzer Division	12,070	5,462	523
24th Panzer Division	11,785	5,387	1,431
16th Panzer Division	13,126	5,164	467

* Counting a 912-man strong reinforcement battalion, which was not included among the combat component.

14th Panzer Division (five battalions in good condition) and the 79th Infantry Division (six battalions in good condition) that had just arrived from the front along the Don. This also took place due to reinforcements. Thus while it was being replaced by the Romanians near Kletskaya on 20 September, an entire battalion with a strength of three officers, 58 NCOs and 868 enlisted men arrived at the 79th Infantry Division. The absolute strength of the Sixth Army's formations is shown in the table.

From this table we can easily see the pointlessness of comparing Soviet and German formations. Even seriously worn-out formations had an overall strength exceeding the average strength of Soviet rifle divisions in good condition. On 20 October five StuG IIIs (short) and three StuG IIIs (long) were in the 244th Assault Gun Battalion and one StuG III (short) and five StuG IIIs (long) in the 245th Assault Gun Battalion. They were supposed to be the offensive's armoured battering-ram. The 79th Infantry Division's 208th and 212th Infantry Regiments received a battalion of assault guns each as support.

Contrary to normal practice, the new German offensive began at 01.00 on 23 October. The night attacks were beaten back, but they were merely an overture to the artillery and aviation attack that followed in the morning. However, this time there was no gift of fate in the form of a division that was prepared to attack, and the German units pushed forward with difficulty. The choice of a frontal attack from west to east meant the storming of positions that had been long and scrupulously prepared. Nonetheless, the hurricane of fire inflicted heavy losses on the 39th Guards Rifle Division defending the 'Red October' factory. LI Corps fired off 583 tons of ammunition on 23 October, including more than 10,000 rounds from 150mm sFH18 howitzers and 366 rounds from 210mm howitzers.[1]

According to German data, the two battalions of the 79th Infantry Division, having begun their attack at 08.10 on 23 October, within an hour had already reached the line of the railway to the west of the 'Red October' factory. On the other hand, the 100th Light Infantry Division's 54th Jäger Regiment was halted. The German offensive cut the 39th Guards Rifle Division's 120th Guards Rifle Regiment in two and communications were lost with the first and second battalions. However, according to Soviet operational reports, for several days 'automatic riflemen' had 'infiltrated' onto the factory grounds, but they were actually speaking of a breakthrough to the 'Red October' factory by two full-strength regiments. As early as the middle of the day on 23 October the German infantry burst onto the grounds of the 'Red October' factory from the west along a narrow front and captured shops No. 5, No. 5a, No. 3, and No. 6 (according to German terminology: these were, respectively, the shaping, mechanical, rolling and blooming shops). Later, No. 8 and No. 9 (the sheet processing shop) were also captured, as well as a group of structures from the scrap heap, the forge and the calibration shop). Soviet units managed to hold on to the popular goods and middle-shaping shops (Nos. 10 and 7 in German terminology), as well as the building in the northern part of the 'Red October' factory, the main office and garage and others. In these conditions the retention of the open-hearth shop in the centre of the factory (No. 4 on the German maps) was a significant achievement.

In supplements to the Sixth Army's war diary it was even maintained that with the onset of darkness on 23 October the 79th Infantry Division 'broke through to the Volga and reached the bank along a 500-metre front'. This was certainly an exaggeration which was contradicted by the following entries: it was noted in a report on 24 October that the 79th Infantry Division had captured shop. No. 7, that is, the middle-shaping shop and that it had been blocking the way to the Volga, and reaching the Volga without it being captured seems very unlikely.

On 25 October the subunits of the 79th Infantry Division which were breaking through to the 'Red October' factory's shops went over to the defence in light of the counter-attacks by Soviet units. According to German data, the counter-attacks were launched from the oil cisterns on the bank of the Volga toward shop No. 8 (the sheet processing shop) at 12.00 and with the forces of two battalions from the north-eastern part of the factory against shop No. 5 (blooming) at 14.00. This may be proof either of a loss of command and control and independent actions by scattered units, or of the conscious desire by the 39th Guards Rifle Division's command to disguise the real scope of the disaster and to attempt to eliminate its consequences with its own forces under the cover of fighting the 'infiltrating' automatic riflemen.

Everything was revealed early on the morning of 28 October, when Krylov, the 62nd Army's chief of staff, came down hard on the 39th Guards Rifle Division command: 'You lacked the courage to honestly confess that the factory has been surrendered to the enemy.'[2] Krylov did not beat about the bush, and wrote: 'It has been established that a large part of the "Red October" factory has been occupied by the enemy and only individual and unguided groups of the division continued to remain on the factory grounds.'[3]

Of course, one might conclude that Chuikov was unaware of what had taken place in the 'Red October' factory. However, this is contradicted by the following fact. On the night of 23/24 October 1942, on the basis of an oral order by the army headquarters, a battalion (1/34th Guards Rifle Regiment), numbering 115 men, was to be taken from Rodimtsev's division, which was located along a quiet sector, and personally subordinated to Chuikov for operations in the area of the 'Red October' factory.[4] The 39th Guards Rifle Division's reports for 23–24 October are simply missing from the folder preserved in the 62nd Army's file. In light of this, it's possible to put forth the assumption that stories about 'automatic riflemen' who had 'infiltrated' into the factory were not only the initiative of Major General Gur'ev's headquarters. Most likely, Chuikov himself decided to avoid 'hastily' informing the *front* command as to what had taken place. The reason for such behaviour could be the logical conclusion that Yeremenko would not forgive the loss of a third factory in a single day. The 'Barricade' factory had nearly been lost because of a loss of orientation, and now the Germans had almost taken the 'Red October' factory. In such a situation, the removal of Chuikov from the command of the 62nd Army was quite a reasonable prospect, while at the same time it only remained to hold out for just a few days before the start of Operation Uranus.

The fighting along the approaches to the 'Red October' factory and for the factory structures resulted in quite heavy losses. The 120th Guards Rifle Regiment, which came under German attack, reported 116 killed and wounded and 193 missing in action from 23 through 25 October.[5] On 26 October the regiment numbered 397 men, including 141 'active bayonets'. The 112th Guards Rifle Regiment's losses for 23–25 October were 223 men.[6]

Following the chewing-out by Krylov, there followed an admission of what had happened in the 39th Guards Rifle Division's report to the headquarters of the 62nd Army and a marking of the units' positions inside the factory: the 'remnants' of the 120th Guards Rifle Regiment are in the open-hearth shop and the 117th Guards Rifle Regiment was in the popular goods shop. It was precisely on this day, when the admission of the fact of the enemy's breakthrough into the 'Red October' factory's shops took place, that the 1/34th Guards Rifle Regiment was ordered by the 62nd Army's headquarters to return to the 13th Guards Rifle Division.[7]

It should be noted that they reacted to the crisis that arose during 19–20 October along the 193rd Rifle Division's defensive sector by setting aside a reserve by removing a battalion from the 300th Rifle Division. By the evening of 24 October the second battalion of the 300th Rifle Division's 1053rd Rifle Regiment, under the command of Senior Lieutenant Kolomeitsev, was concentrating toward Staren'kii and by 02.00 was crossing over to Stalingrad in order to be transferred to a representative of the 193rd Rifle Division. Information about the breakthrough to the grounds of the 'Red October' factory did not reach *front* headquarters and they did not activate a reserve in the fighting for the factory. The newly-arrived battalion numbered 604 men, armed with 1891/30-era rifles, 14 sniper rifles, 35 Shpagin sub-machine guns, six heavy and 21 light machine guns, nine 82mm and nine 50mm mortars, and nine anti-tank rifles and was supplied with ammunition for these weapons.[8] With the assistance of this battalion, they were able to eliminate the breach in the front of the 895th Rifle Regiment from Smekhotvorov's division.[9] It's clear that in the event of an admission by the headquarters of the 39th Guards Rifle Division of a breakthrough in the area of the 'Red October' factory, then a full-strength battalion would have been dispatched to the factory to assist the 120th and 117th Guards Rifle Regiments.

The next reserve of the *front's* headquarters was dispatched to the area of the bread-baking plant on 27 October at the disposal of the commander of the 193rd Rifle Division. This time two battalions were to be removed from the 45th Rifle Division (the first and second battalions of the 10th Rifle Regiment). Colonel V.P. Sokolov's division was being transferred to the *front* by *Stavka* VGK Order No. 170642 of 7 October for the defence of the islands in the Volga. However, in light of the worsening situation in Stalingrad, they began to move it all over the place for the fighting in the city. The 45th Rifle Division's two battalions numbered 1,588 men, armed with 1,127 rifles, 11 heavy and 42 light machine guns, and 36 anti-tank rifles.[10] This was also a serious force, the commitment of which into the fighting for the 'Red October' factory's shops had been consciously avoided by Chuikov.

Major General Smekhotvorov, upon receiving two full-strength (even if untried) battalions, decided to unite his available forces in two combat sectors. The first, under the command of the commander of the 685th Rifle Regiment, Colonel Drogaitsev, consisted of the remnants of the 685th Rifle Regiment, the 161st Rifle Regiment and the 1/10 Rifle Regiment, while the second, under the temporary commander of the 883rd Rifle Regiment, Senior Lieutenant Osyko, consisted of the remnants of the 883rd Rifle Regiment, the 895th Rifle Regiment and the 2/10th Rifle Regiment. The group's task was to create a continuous front in the space between the south-eastern corners of the 'Barricade' and 'Red October' factories. However, the groups, reinforced by the two fresh battalions, did not manage to reach their designated line on 28 October, as they were met with fire from the 100th Light Infantry Division's 54th Infantry Regiment, which was defending there. On the other hand, the attempt by the German 14th Panzer Division to attack was also unsuccessful. Both of the 193rd Rifle Division's combat sectors were consolidated in the first line of buildings along the quay. As was noted in the 193rd Rifle Division's war diary, the 1/10th Rifle Regiment lost 'up to 70 per cent of its rank and file' in the day's fighting.

Only the assembly shop remained in the hands of Soviets along the 308th and 138th Rifle Divisions' sectors in the area of the 'Red October' factory by 24 October, and by 25 October it was lost. A serious problem was also the Germans' penetration into the space between the two major enterprises, through the so-called 'bread-baking plant', to the Volga. The knocking out of the defenders' anti-tank artillery significantly reduced their ability to fight the German tanks, which more and more often began to be referred to as 'heavy' in the documents, although these were the usual Panzer IVs.

Having broken through to the factories' grounds, the Germans busied themselves with taking the city blocks. A report from the 95th Rifle Division on 24 October describes the Germans' tactics: 'During the day the enemy, covered by aviation, came almost face to face with the 161st Rifle Regiment's battle order and methodically blocked one building after the other, where groups of our soldiers were located. According to the battalion commander, Senior Lieutenant Selifanov, after the buildings were destroyed by tanks, the infantry would throw charges with poisonous substances (following the charge's explosion a yellowish-green smoke appears and it becomes impossible to breathe) at the remaining defenders.'[11] The reports also mention certain 'thin glass bottles, filled with phosphorous', which were evidently similar to Soviet petrol bombs.

In the 62nd Army's war diary the condition of the formations fighting in the area of the factories on 24 October was described in the following manner: 'As a result of the extremely heavy fighting, the units of the 138th and 193rd Rifle Divisions and the remnants of the 308th and 37th Guards Rifle Divisions have suffered heavy losses and have lost their combat capability as divisions and lost their artillery on the right bank. The above-named divisions are in need of relief by two combat-capable rifle divisions.'[12]

On the following day, 25 October, Chuikov approached the *front* commander about relieving the 308th, 193rd, 138th, and 37th Guards Rifle Divisions, which had suffered heavy losses in the fighting, with two full-strength divisions with anti-tank artillery. Despite the preparation for the conduct of Operation Uranus, which had already begun, Chuikov's requests for a new formation did not go unheeded. It would have been a shame to have lost Stalingrad, having invested so many forces in its defence. However, it would still be several days before a fresh formation arrived.

During the day on 29 October the 45th Rifle Division (6,358 men on 5 November) was placed completely at the disposal of the commander of the 62nd Army. Chuikov assigned the new division the task of occupying defensive positions between the remnants of the 308th and 39th Guards Rifle Divisions by 04.00 on 30 October. It was initially ordered to leave the 45th Rifle Division's divisional artillery on the left bank of the river 'in readiness to support by fire the subunits on the right bank of the river'. The first task of the newly-crossed units was to prevent the enemy's breakthrough to the Volga. According to the *front* commander's decision, the 95th Rifle Division, a veteran of the fighting in Stalingrad, was to be pulled back to Sarpinskii and Hungry islands instead in place of the 45th Rifle Division.[13] This was a pretty risky move, but Yeremenko, not without justification, considered it was unlikely that the Germans would undertake any major raids across the Volga. Accordingly, the headquarters and support elements of the 308th and 37th Guards Rifle Divisions, 'due to their complete loss of combat capability', were to be moved to the left bank of the Volga on the night of 31 October/1 November.

The commitment of the new formation was carried out in detail in the 'best' traditions of the fighting for Stalingrad. As has already been noted earlier, the two battalions and individual elements from the 45th Rifle Division's 10th Rifle Regiment were the first to be crossed over into the city. This took place in the space between the 'Barricade' and 'Red October' factories, to where the 193rd Rifle Division's regiments had been thrown back. They sought to furnish the commitment of the 45th Rifle Division's main forces into the fighting with the corresponding reinforcement weapons. The final days of October were the occasion for the final reinforcement by tank units of the defenders during the fighting in the city. This time flamethrower tanks from the 235th Tank Brigade were subordinated in detail to the 62nd Army. One company of flamethrower KV-8 tanks was crossed into Stalingrad on the night of 27/28 October. On this day the KVs went into battle, and, according to Soviet data, three enemy tanks were burned by flamethrowers in the tank battle in the city. Five KV-8 flamethrower tanks, which arrived during the course of 28 October, were placed in positions near the north-eastern corner of the 'Red October' factory. What then happened was described in the 84th Tank Brigade's operational report for 29 October: 'The enemy, having open approaches and poor cover of our tanks by the infantry, rolled up three anti-tank guns and fired thermite shells at point blank range for ten minutes at three KV tanks. One anti-tank gun was destroyed along with its crew.'[14] The two remaining tanks were immediately pulled back to a shelter, although the Germans had already managed to put the armament and optics of one of them out of order.

Chuikov, having a fresh division at his disposal and crossed it over into the city, decided to use the arrival of the 45th Rifle Division to clean out the grounds of the 'Red October' factory. According to Combat Order No. 217, aside from the 45th Rifle Division, the 39th Guards Rifle Division was also to be brought in for the offensive. The mission of the two formations was to reach the line of the railway running to the west from the 'Red October' factory and the bread-baking plant. This mission was, to put it mildly, ambitious. The attackers were ordered to move, 'without delaying at individual firing points and small enemy groups'.[15] The infantry attack was set for 12.30 on 31 October.

Great hopes were placed on the counterblow. As Krylov wrote later in his memoirs, 'the army was able to launch an attack on the enemy of which it had long been incapable', and 'our operational documents spoke of the army's launching a counteroffensive with part of its forces' (here Krylov is actually quoting word-for-word Combat Order No. 217).

The plan for a counterblow by Chuikov's staff collided with the offensive plans of Paulus's army. The 226th Infantry Regiment, with the participation of which the offensive began on 31 October on the grounds of the 'Red October' factory, arrived at the 79th Infantry Division. It was, as the corps' report stated, 'halted by heavy fire from shop No. 5, the clearing out of which had been unsuccessful that morning'. Also, according to German data, the 39th Guards Rifle Division's offensive (viewed as 'counter-attacks') led to a penetration into the German positions as far as the railway inside the factory.

An indirect consequence of the artillery preparation for the 45th Rifle Division's offensive was a powerful attack against the German 14th Panzer Division, and it was noted in the LI Corps' daily report that 'The division is suffering heavy losses from enemy artillery fire, which we are unable to properly suppress due to a shortage of munitions.'

The 45th and 39th Guard Rifle Divisions attacked on 31 October and were only able to improve their positions slightly, capturing a number of shops in the 'Red October' factory. The division subsequently held its captured positions. On the evening of 1 November Krylov addressed the latest chewing-out to the 39th Guards Rifle Division command, which began with the words 'When will the lying stop?' The 62nd Army chief of staff accused Gur'ev's staff of falsifying information that the calibrating shop and scrap heap had suddenly been noted as having been occupied by the enemy, although earlier they had been noted as being occupied by the 39th Guards Rifle Division. Accordingly, they were not subjected to a bombardment by the artillery at the disposal of the army and *front*.

In the meantime, self-propelled guns, specially created for urban fighting in Stalingrad, arrived with the Sixth Army on 28 October. They were officially designated *Sturminfanteriegeschütz 33* (infantry assault gun 33) and were armed with a 150mm gun with the ballistic qualities of the sIG.33 heavy infantry gun. Its story began at a Hitler conference on 20 September 1942, at which it was said: 'The fighting in Stalingrad has shown very clearly the need to have a heavy gun in a heavily armoured vehicle for firing a shell capable of destroying entire buildings with a few rounds.'[16] Simultaneously, instructions were issued: 'If it proves impossible to place an s.I.G in the turret of a Panzer III or Panzer IV, then it is necessary to try placing it in an assault gun.'[17] There were already 150mm guns available at the Skoda factories for mounting in a self-propelled gun, and they designed a very simple box-shaped superstructure with 80mm frontal armour at the Alkett factory. As a result, twelve self-propelled guns were ready as early as 13 October 1942. There is a notation in the Sixth Army's war diary for 28 October: 'The LI Army and XIV Panzer Corps have received orders to dispatch as quickly as possible the assault guns with s.I.G., which have arrived at Chir, to the 244th and 177th Assault Gun Battalions to take part in the fighting in Stalingrad.' However, the first six self-propelled guns arrived at the 245th Assault Gun Battalion on 30 October, with four guns to the 177th Assault Gun Battalion on 4 November. In any event, the overall plan for distributing the new self-propelled guns remained unchanged: one battalion for the LI Corps for the storming of the factories and one for the XIV Panzer Corps for the storming of the positions of Gorokhov's group.

At the end of October the Soviet air force began to fight more actively for the sky over Stalingrad. The number of fighter sorties increase steadily to 80–100 per day. On 24 October the war diary of Paulus's army noted nineteen Soviet planes shot down. According to the documents of the 8th Air Army, the loss of six combat aircraft was noted: one Pe-2 and one Yak-1 shot down by fighters, one Il-2 shot down by anti-aircraft guns, and three Yak-1s did not return from their combat mission.[18] The 16th Air Army's losses for 24 October were three Yak-1s shot down in air battles and five Yak-1s that did not return, while another three Yak-1s and one Il-2 made forced landings.[19] That is, in principle the German claim of nineteen planes shot down corresponds to reality. October 29th was a more difficult day for the 8th Air Army, when fifty-eight planes flew (five bombers, six ground-attack aircraft and forty-seven fighters), having carried out 110 sorties, including 95 by fighters. This cost them eight fighters shot down or failed to return. On 29 October the Sixth Army's war diary noted 'Very active enemy aviation all day'.

'The Battle for the Semaphore'. Rokossovskii's Attempt

At the height of the October fighting for the factories in Stalingrad, on the Don Front an operation had been planned, the mission of which was to break through to the city from the north. According to the *front's* war diary, orders for the conduct of the operation followed on 15 October 1942, on the day following the Germans' breakthrough to the Stalingrad Tractor Factory. Actually, this was the first major offensive planned at Rokossovskii's headquarters in his capacity as commander of the Don Front. This time it was planned to break through to the defenders of Stalingrad along the shortest distance. The mission was formulated in the following manner: 'For the purpose of rendering immediate assistance to Stalingrad, the 66th Army is to attack on 19.10, launching its main attack from the front Height 130.7 – the dairy farm – Height 123.9 in the general direction of Orlovka and Height 75.9 and to link up with the forces of the Stalingrad Front.'[20] The fresh formations

(62nd, 252nd, 212th, and 226th Rifle Divisions) arriving at the *front* were to be transferred to the 66th Army. As a result, the strength of Malinovskii's 66th Army for the new offensive was raised to 107,297 men, with 14 rifle divisions, including four fresh, full-strength ones with a strength greater than 10,000 men (the previously-mentioned 62nd, 212th, 226th, and 252nd Rifle Divisions). The four fresh divisions disposed of more than 80 heavy and 200 light machine guns each. Malinovskii was also to receive the materially reinforced 91st Tank Brigade (six KVs, eighteen T-34s and eleven T-70s), 121st Tank Brigade (nine KVs, eighteen T-34s and eleven T-70s) and the 64th Tank Brigade (five KVs, twenty-one T-34s and eighteen T-70s).[21] Against this, the 66th Army's own tank brigade – the 58th Tank Brigade (three T-34s and three T-70s) – looked quite pathetic. Together, they comprised over a hundred vehicles, but one should not think that this yielded a decisive superiority. The 3rd Motorized Division opposite them numbered on 19 October five Panzer IIs, twenty-one Panzer IIIs (long), four Panzer IVs (short) and four Panzer IVs (long), while the neighbouring 60th Motorized Division had four Panzer IIs, one Panzer III (short), thirteen Panzer IIIs (long), three Panzer IVs (short) and two Panzer IVs (long). Both German motorized divisions were listed as capable of offensive action, that is, they were in good shape. The 66th Army's reinforcement artillery included seventy-five 152mm guns. At this time the headquarters of the 1st Guards Army (a participant in the preceding 'fighting for the semaphore') was removed, with a redistribution of zones and formations between the remaining 24th and 66th Armies.

Three of the four fresh divisions were placed in the first echelon, while it was planned to employ one (226th Rifle Division) for the development of the success. This was not the decision of the army commander, Malinovskii, but was ordered in a directive from *front* headquarters on 17 October. Besides the newcomers, the shock group included the 116th Rifle Division (it was in good shape and numbered 8,493 men on 20 October). Each of the four divisions along the axis of the main attack received a tank brigade apiece.

At the same time, one has to say that the 66th Army's offensive was not a surprise for the Germans. The appearance on the front line of the 252nd and 62nd Rifle Divisions had been registered by the intelligence section of Paulus's army since at least 19 October. The regroupings and noise of motors behind the front line had also been fixed. The reaction to the signs of these offensive preparations was the subordination of additional anti-tank weapons to the XIV Panzer Corps: an anti-tank battalion from the 71st Infantry Division's Panzer Jag.Abt.171 and a heavy company from the Panzer Jag.Abt.4 (from the 14th Panzer Division).

The offensive began according to plan, on the morning of 20 October, but was unsuccessful. As was openly admitted in the *front's* war diary, 'The attacking units made almost no advance'. As was noted in the 62nd Army's war diary, the offensive by the formation was met with 'extremely heavy and aimed fire from automatic rifles, machine guns and mortars'. In the XIV Panzer Corps' report for 20 October, these events were described in a manner quite typical for the positional battles along the 'northern screen': 'The enemy tanks penetrated into the defence and partially broke through to the rear, where they were destroyed or put to flight. The enemy's infantry, numbering several thousand men, was halted in front of the forward positions by concentrated fire from all types of weapons.'

According to Soviet data, four of the 66th Army's brigades lost twenty-six tanks burnt, fifty-nine knocked out and nine missing in action (evidently from among those that broke into the enemy positions). Half of the KVs that took part in the fighting and two-thirds of the T-34s and T-70s were lost.[22] The 66th Army's 58th Tank Brigade effectively lost all of its equipment. It's difficult to blame the 16th Air Army for inactivity on the first day of the operation. Sixty-two Il-2s, 72 Yak-1s and five Yak-7s flew, carrying out 236 sorties. The assault aircraft launched strikes against the enemy's defence without losses, expending 238 100kg bombs. This uptick in activity cost thirteen Yak-1s fighters that failed to return, plus another three Yaks that made forced landings on their own territory.

Attempts to resume the offensive in the days that followed were unsuccessful. On 24 October an attempt was made to commit the fresh 226th Rifle Division into the fighting from the second echelon, but the result remained the same – 'an insignificant advance'. One of the regiments managed to break into the enemy's trenches, but no further. It's worthy of notice that the 226th Rifle Division's offensive was conducted in single-echelon formation in accordance with the recently issued Order No. 306 by the people's commissar for defence. By 25 October the fresh 62nd, 252nd, 212th, and 226th Rifle Divisions had fallen in strength to 7,210, 6,222, 6,926, and 8,389 men respectively. In total, the 66th Army's losses for 20–25 October amounted to 3,542 men killed, 1,064 missing and 10,474 wounded. The losses were mainly at the expense of the new divisions, but the 66th Army's 116th Rifle Division also suffered heavily, losing 1,658 men killed and wounded. By the end of the month the 66th Army had lost another 1,301 men killed, 84 missing in action and 4,839 wounded.

However, despite all the problems, the Don Front kept up an unrelenting pressure on the northern flank of the German forces attacking Stalingrad. For example, on 6 November there was only the single 245th Assault Gun Battalion in the LI Corps attacking the city, including two StuG IIIs and one s.IG. On the same day the 177th and 244th Assault Gun Battalions were in the VIII Army Corps with its front facing north. The first numbered six StuG IIIs (plus six in short-term repair) and the second nine StuG IIIs and four s.IGs. The *Sturmgeschützen* were an effective anti-tank weapon and were in demand for repelling the Don Front's tank-supported counteroffensives.

Chapter 19

The Landing in the Latashanka Area

(Map 12)

The flank of the German XIV Panzer Corps, which was open from the river side, formed a sector on the bank of the Volga in the area of Akatovka and Latashanka. A turning manoeuvre along the river appeared quite enticing, at least on paper. The prerequisites for carrying out a landing on the German-occupied bank of the Volga had been created with the arrival at the Stalingrad Front of the 300th Rifle Division (9,564 men on 16 October), which had been restored following the summer fighting, under the command of Colonel I.M. Afonin. The division's mission was the defence of the eastern bank of the Volga, but Yeremenko took the risk of employing individual elements of the newly-arrived division.

For the landing, Afonin set aside the 1049th Rifle Regiment's first battalion (1/1049), which was mentioned in the 300th Rifle Division's war diary as 'the best in the division'. Captain V.F. Bylda commanded the battalion. The landing force also included a detachment from the Volga Military Flotilla, six 45mm guns, two platoons of anti-tank rifles, four 37mm guns from the 115th Fortified Area,[1] an engineer platoon and a platoon of automatic riflemen. One barge, two civilian cutters, seven armoured cutters from the Volga Military Flotilla and twenty 'private boats' were to be used for the crossing. In all, 910 men, 604 regular and 16 sniper rifles, four heavy and 20 light machine guns, 135 Shpagin and Degtyaryov sub-machine guns, and nine 50mm and nine 82mm mortars.[2]

In the available operational documents the landing's mission was stated as assisting Gorokhov's group, which was being subjected to ceaseless attacks. The *front* command's motives for the landing operation are quite obvious. The German group of forces in the Latashanka area, which was being subjected to attacks by the Don Front from the north, attacked Gorokhov's group for several days. The assumption that the capabilities of the 16th Panzer Division, both offensive and defensive, had declined seemed quite logical and corresponded to reality. The 'trench strength' over 7km of front of Strehlke's combat group (an engineer battalion from the 16th Panzer Division named after the battalion commander, Major Ernst-Gunther Strehlke), which occupied positions in the area of Latashanka, was three officers, 23 NCOs and 163 enlisted. The greater part of them was located in positions along a 4km southern front facing toward Stalingrad. In Latashanka itself there were three scattered strongpoints, the garrisons of which together numbered fifty men.

The Soviet plan called for the preliminary destruction by artillery from the eastern bank of the wooden and earthen pillboxes on the bank, which had been designated as 'buried tanks'.[3] The detachment was divided into two groups with different boarding sites for the boats, with the battalion from Afonin's division in the area of Shadrin Creek and a company from the Volga Military Flotilla in Akhtuba. In its turn, the landing of the detachment was to be split into two trips, with the reinforcement equipment (the 45mm and 37mm guns) being landed together with the horses (!) during the second trip. Reconnaissance identified the most convenient sector for the approach to the bank – 250m north of the railway dead end. There were neither minefields, nor barbed wire or and other obstacles.

During the second half of the day on 30 October the detachment was concentrating in the woods near Shadrin Creek. The boarding of the first echelon (the battalion, minus a mortar company, the detachment of automatic riflemen, a medical detachment and a battery of 37mm guns) began at 23.00 and was completed within an hour. The boarding on the ships and boats was carried out in such a manner that the subunit on each cutter could fight independently following the landing. The first echelon boarded the *Revolutionary* (with a capacity of 75 men), *Labour Discipline* (270 men) and *Rudka* (75 men). The 8th Air Army was also drawn into the operation: five U-2 aircraft circled the Latashanka area from midnight to 02.00, masking the movement across the river with the noise of their engines.

By 01.00 on 31 October the first echelon had passed the jumping-off point (the mouth of Shadrin Creek) and in 15 minutes had crossed the Volga. But the boats were spotted by the enemy after they had covered two-thirds of the river's main channel. It should be pointed out that it was precisely the most powerful enemy – the tanks from Strehlke's group – that spotted them. Despite the shelling, all of the vessels reached the bank and within five minutes had disgorged their cargo of men and weaponry. The *Revolutionary* was damaged and the *Rudka* was sunk on the return journey. The *Labour Discipline* suffered ten direct hits, but was not put out of action. The barge was secured by the engineers on the right bank of the Volga as an improvised dock.

The boarding of the second echelon (an anti-tank rifle platoon, an engineer platoon, a mortar company and a battery of 45mm guns) began at 02.30 and by 03.45 armoured cutters *No. 11* and *No. 13* and the *Labour Discipline*, towing barges, had passed the jumping-off point. However, this time the mortar and artillery fire was so heavy that only the armoured cutters with the engineer platoon and anti-tank rifles could reach the shore. The report by the engineers attached to the landing paints a horrible picture of what happened: 'Mortar shells exploded on the barge's deck. Dead horses and people fell overboard and cases of ammunition caught fire.'[4]

In the end, it was not possible to land the battery of 45mm guns and the mortar company (82mm mortars) under fire from German tanks from the bank. The Volga Military Flotilla's landing company attempted to land from armoured cutter *No. 23*, but lost up to a quarter of its strength and fell back to Shadrin Creek. In all, they managed to land about 600 men (150 men on the armoured cutters and 450 by other means). In the report by Strehlke's group the support for the landing by artillery on the eastern bank of the river was singled out. In the 16th Panzer Division's history it was noted that 'The Russians supported their landing from the opposite bank with all of their barrels'.

As was later determined by questioning the soldiers and commanders who returned, the landing party landed without losses. V.F. Bylda, the battalion commander, attacked the centre of Latashanka with a group of automatic riflemen. The battalion commander's decision to lead the attack was allowable at the tactical level, but led to the loss of command and control of the companies. In the end, the attack proceeded in an uncoordinated fashion and the battalion broke up into three groups: along the northern outskirts, in the centre, and on the south-western outskirts of Latashanka. All four 37mm guns from the fortified area and a radio were lost on the first day. The loss of the radio immediately complicated coordination with the artillery on the left bank of the Volga. Overall, the matter of communications had become a major problem for the landing. In this regard, there is this note in the report by Strehlke's group on the results of the fighting in Latashanka: 'There are obviously capable and intelligent officers among the prisoners. However, their influence on the troops who had lost coordination was weak. The absence of command and control was very closely linked to a shortage of communications equipment.'

However, the landing party was not rapidly eliminated. As was noted in the XIV Panzer Corps' report, the counter-attack against the landing began only at 16.00, 'following the arrival of corps reserves'. Several companies from motorcycle units from the 3rd Motorized and 16th Panzer Divisions, as well as a company of tanks and artillery, with artillery forward observers, were included among the reserves. The Germans' real achievement on the first day was holding their positions, which enabled them to rake the river with fire and prevent the arrival of the landing's second echelon. The situation appeared uncertain from the Soviet side. There were no communications with the landing party and the radio did not reply. During the day on 31 October a signals officer was dispatched to the shore on an armoured cutter, who found a detachment of 114 men fighting along the north-eastern outskirts of Latashanka. The location of the remainder remained unknown.

In light of the absence of communications with the landed units, they dispatched the first deputy chief of staff (PNSh-1) of the 1049th Rifle Regiment, Senior Lieutenant Sokov, to the landing party. At 12.30 on 31 October he reached armoured cutter *No. 13* together with a landing company (sixty-eight men, plus five men from a reconnaissance company). As Petty Officer P.N. Oleinik, the assistant to the commander of *No. 13*, recalled, the conditions for a landing were not favourable: 'It was the middle of the night, and the night was lit up by the moon, when we, while cursing it, left for the right bank.' Despite the hurricane of fire from the bank, including from tanks, the cutter docked at the bank and unloaded. As Oleinik recalled, they managed to wait for the proper moment on the squat armoured cutter in the dead zone 'beyond the sunken trolley car', which had been sunk earlier in August or October, and the *Rudka*, which the current had carried downstream. At the same time, the armoured cutter picked up wounded from the shore. At 05.00 Sokov reported by radio that he had found the first company and had organized an all-round defence together with the landing company that had arrived with it.

A German counterblow with tanks followed during the day of 1 November, which finally cut the landing party off from the shore. The only choice in this situation was to break through in order to link up with friendly forces. Thus the commander of the landing detachment attempted to break through to the Rynok area. As one of the wounded commanders, who were evacuated to the left bank, reported: 'Senior Lieutenant Bylda ..., who had landed on the bank, is operating with the second company to the south in the direction of Rynok in order to link up with Gorokhov's group.'

I.M. Afonin insisted on dispatching the armoured cutters to the bank. As Senior Lieutenant Yu.V. Lyubimov, a signals officer with the Volga Military Flotilla, told the Mints Commission, Colonel Afonin 'always strengthened his orders with a threat to shoot someone on the spot' and forced two armoured cutters to go. They were unable to reach the bank. Lyubimov explained that as a result of a night raid, 'Armoured cutter *No. 23*, which had been dispatched by Afonin to the area of the landing, was fired upon in the centre of the river'. According to a report by the Volga Military Flotilla, *No. 23* was hit in the stern and sank up to its conning tower, losing one man killed and six wounded, while they removed the rifles and ammunition from the cutter.[5] Here it's worth noting that the Soviet cutters' enemy were the latest German self-propelled guns with a 105mm howitzer – *Geschützwagen* IVb fuer 10.5cm le.F.H.18/1 (Sf.) (Sd.Krz. 165/1). Six guns had reached the 16th Panzer Division in September 1942 for combat testing. According to a report by Strehlke's group, one of the self-propelled guns 'sank a gunboat that had been previously damaged by Gerke's tank platoon [engineer tanks, Author] on the first shot'.

At 05.00 on 2 November radio communications with the landing were broken. During the day on 2 November, as noted in the 300th Rifle Division's operational report, 'the firing of rifles and machine guns could be heard along the south-eastern outskirts of Latashanka' in the division's positions along the left bank of the Volga. According to German data, on that day a 'small but very stubborn enemy group' was routed by tanks and an armoured personnel carrier company in the northern part of Latashanka. The operation began with the first rays of the sun and concluded after two hours. Following this, only small and uncoordinated groups, which were hiding in the vineyards and among the railway cars, remained in the area of the landing.

On the night of 2/3 October two armoured cutters and seven rowboats were dispatched to Latashanka. The circumstances surrounding the dispatch of the two armoured cutters were quite dramatic. As Senior Lieutenant S.I. Barbot'ko (the commander of armoured cutter *No. 4*, with a rocket launcher) related to the Mints Commission: 'Colonel Afonin declared that the remnants of the landing are transmitting a signal to be removed from the shore. Cutters *No. 34* and *No. 381* took off to rescue the remnants of the landing. Lysenko tried to show that there was no landing party there and that the cutters would be leaving for nothing. Afonin then accused Lysenko of cowardice. Not wishing to shame the naval officer's uniform, Lysenko left himself on cutter *No. 34*.[6] Senior Lieutenant L.I. Moroz, the detachment commander, also left on the cutter …'[7] Considering that during the day on 2 November shooting could be heard in Latashanka, one can understand Moroz's insistence.

The intensive bombardment forced the rowboats to return, having lost one platoon commander killed. The armoured cutters tried to reach the shore under fire but, were forced to turn back 15m from the bank. On the trip back, a shell struck the conning tower of *No. 34* and wounded the commanders there. S.P. Lysenko was also seriously wounded. The out-of-control armoured cutter grounded on a sandbar and was immediately subjected to furious fire from the shore. The latest 105mm self-propelled guns entered the fighting. According to a report by Strehlke's group, during the night of 2/3 November, 'A gunboat was destroyed by nine direct hits from a self-propelled artillery mount'.

According to an operational report by the Volga Military Flotilla, the cutter hit the sandbar at the entrance to Shadrin Creek, that is, close to the Volga's left bank. Armoured cutter *No. 387* attempted to pull *No. 34* from the sandbar, but unsuccessfully, as the steel cables broke time after time. *No. 387* returned and they dispatched a small speedboat to the damaged *No. 34*, which rescued fourteen men from the vessel, including the wounded Lysenko and Moroz. They were unable to save Lysenko and he died in the Shadrin Creek within an hour of his return. Moroz died in hospital two weeks later. The wreck of *No. 34* bobbed above the water for some time, reminding people of the terrifying events at the end of October and beginning of November 1942.

On the night of 3/4 November Afonin dispatched five boats to the Latashanka area, of which four returned. The boats were fired upon from the shore. No fighting of any kind was observed during the day in the Latashanka area. However, the story of the Latashanka landing did not end here. On the night of 4/5 November, Dobroskokov, the political leader of the second company, and Lieutenant Martynov and an enlisted man, crossed from the western bank of the Volga. Dobroskokov reported the presence of a small group of soldiers along the railway lines under the trains and about the attempt being prepared to cross the remnants of the landing party over the Volga on a raft. Seven men, commanded by the battalion sergeant major Nikolenko, along with Junior Lieutenant Zlobin, passed through the 16th Panzer Division's positions on the night of 4/5 November to the line of the Don Front's 99th Rifle Division. Five of the seven were wounded. But even this was not the end of the story of the landing. According to German sources, a group numbering twenty men held out for seven days among the railway cars until they surrendered due to hunger.

According to a report by Strehlke's group, as a result of the fighting for Latashanka, 551 prisoners were taken, plus five anti-tank guns, 35 machine guns, eight mortars, eight anti-tank guns, and several hundred infantry firearms. It was also reported that approximately 250 men were found dead on the battlefield. According to calculations made on 7 November in the headquarters of the 300th Rifle Division, of the 910 officers and men involved in the operation, 171 returned (who did not make the landing).[7] As regards the calculation of losses for the period of the operation, from 30 October through 3 November, eighteen men were listed as killed (that is, the fact of their deaths was reliably known), with another fifty-five men wounded (evacuated).[8] The remainder (666 men) did not return and were listed as missing in action.

V.F. Bylda, the commander of the landing detachment, was listed as having perished, according to Soviet documents, but he was actually captured. During his interrogation he put forward one of the chief reasons for the landing's failure: 'The infantry was poorly trained and undisciplined. The officers, on the other hand, were well trained and have experience at the front.' The Germans, in generalizing the experience of the fight against the landing, noted: 'The resistance was extremely stubborn here and there, while in other places groups of the enemy surrendered even after a simple shot from a firearm.' For inexperienced soldiers from the depths of Russia the landing operation became an extremely serious test and not all of them passed it.

According to a report by Strehlke's group, losses on the German side (including elements attached to Major Strehlke) were 24 men killed and 98 wounded, for a total of 122 casualties overall. The number of the 16th Panzer Division's tanks during these three days fell by seven Panzer IIIs (long), one Panzer IV (short) and one Panzer IV (long), which one may call an outstanding result for a landing party armed only with anti-tank rifles, although some of these tanks were victims of the artillery bombardment from the left bank of the Volga.

'The operation was doomed from the very beginning', is always an insulting conclusion for the historian. But here we must draw just such a conclusion. The Latashanka landing had no chance of success even to consolidate on the bank of the Volga. At the same time, it cannot be said that the landing party was abandoned. It was energetically supported by fire from artillery and mortars, not to mention Afonin's insistence on dispatching cutters to the landing.

At the same time, one cannot say that the operation was poorly organized. There was the well thought-through division into detachments and the detachments into integral groups, the engineer reconnaissance of the landing sector, and even the masking of the cutters' approach by the noise of aircraft. In the report by Strehlke's group on the fighting near Latashanka, the following was stated: 'The landing operation was well prepared and quite nimbly carried out.' The plan for the Latashanka landing had one key shortcoming: it was built solely on the idea of the Germans' weak defence of the shore area, without considering the defence's reinforcement during the fighting. It's possible that the landing not of a battalion, but of a regiment, could have radically altered the situation; but, first of all, Yeremenko could not risk an entire regiment in the conditions of the crisis in Stalingrad, and, second of all, there was not enough available crossing equipment (considering the necessity of using the armoured cutters to supply the forces of the 62nd Army). The question of the landing party's equipment for fighting tanks also remained undecided.

Chapter 20

The Last Inch. November 1942

The latest target of the German offensive was to be the 'Azure' chemical plant. However, at that moment the Sixth Army's opportunities for removing formations from quiet sectors had been exhausted. In the war diary of Paulus's army three options for resolving this problem were outlined: 'The commitment of the 60th Motorized Division into the fighting following its relief by the 305th Infantry Division and the commitment into the fighting of two panzer grenadier regiments from the 29th Motorized Division. The third option was the transfer by the army group of five engineer battalions to the Sixth Army. The army's chief of staff replied that the third option is more desirable than the second.'

In the end, they chose the third option – five engineer battalions. It is believed that they were transferred by air from Germany, although this is a simplification of the situation. They were taken from Army Group B's formations, which were occupying defensive positions along the Don (see table). An undoubted advantage of these battalions was their experience of combat operations on the Eastern Front.

Table 33: The Condition and Origin of the Engineer Battalions Attached to the Sixth Army for the Assault on Stalingrad. 3 November 1942[1]

Battalion	From Which Formation	Officers	NCOs	Enlisted Men
45th (Motorized)	Second Army, Army Group B	9	30	246
50th	22nd Panzer Division, Army Group B	10	44	405
162nd	62nd Infantry Division, Army Group B	7	31	281
294th	294th Infantry Division, Army Group B	4	29	275
336th	336th Infantry Division, Army Group B	8	38	336

The operation received the code name Hubertus, the start of which was initially set for 10 November 1942. The 100th Light Infantry Division, reinforced by the five newly-arrived engineer battalions as well as a powerful artillery group (including rocket launchers), was supposed to be the main shock force for the offensive. The participation of a regiment from the 295th Infantry Division was also planned. The engineers were supposed to not only clear the minefields, but to also open routes through the railway lines and the destroyed railway trucks littering the grounds of the 'Azure' factory. However, the plans were changed not long before the already-designated date for the attack. On the evening of 6 November the chief of staff of the army group, von Sonderstern, approached Schmidt, Sixth Army chief of staff, with instructions from Hitler that 'the terrain to the east of the metallurgical and armaments factories should be occupied before the start of the offensive on the chemical factory'.

Sonderstern himself was not at all pleased with this plan, so the chief of the General Staff, Zeitzler,[2] was included in the discussion of this matter. Zeitzler was ready to appeal to the Führer, but requested an answer to the following questions:

1) When can you begin the offensive on the chemical factory, and is everything ready for this?
2) Can you begin the offensive against the area near the factories right now?
3) What reasons do you have for attacking the chemical factory first?'

Paulus replied in a neutral manner to the first two questions:

1) The offensive against the chemical factory may be undertaken as planned, on 10 November.
2) The offensive to the areas to the east of the foundry plant and the armaments factory may be carried out on 10 November. The offensive against these sites earlier than planned is not possible, because the infantry forces and heavy weapons have already begun their regrouping for the attack against the chemical factory and must be halted.

The reply to the third question began with the words 'I have no reasons to object to the plan proposed by the Führer'. However, further on, the commander of the Sixth Army pointed out that the 'Azure' factory was the 'most difficult site for an attack in Stalingrad'. Accordingly, the conduct of any kind of operations causing losses and reducing the troops' offensive capabilities was doubtful, insofar as they were already insufficient for storming the chemical factory. However, these obvious arguments were not listened to and Hitler's reply was unambiguous (as was noted in the supplements to the Sixth Army's war diary): 'The Führer has ordered the resumption of the offensive in Stalingrad for the purpose of seizing the "Azure" chemical factory and both sectors still held by the enemy east of the metallurgical and armaments factories. The sectors on the bank of the Volga must be occupied first, after which the chemical factory is to be attacked.'

In the end, LI Corps was informed by army headquarters that Operation Hubertus was being postponed. Instead of it, the very hurried planning of a new operation began. According to the initial plan, it was planned to carry out two attacks – one against the shop with the open-hearth furnace in the 'Red October' factory with the forces of Schwerin's group, and the second to the bank of the Volga to the east of the 'Barricade' factory, with the forces of the 305th Infantry Division and the southern wing of the 389th Infantry Division. However, Seydlitz, the commander of LI Corps, sharply objected to this division of force. In the end, the decision was made to concentrate all forces for an offensive by the 305th and 389th Infantry Divisions for the purpose of reaching the bank of the Volga east of the 'Barricade' factory.

The shock groups were to be reinforced with seven assault companies, chosen from various divisions of the Sixth Army, the five newly-arrived engineer battalions, two battalions of assault guns (with the new self-propelled sIG.33), and a tank company from the 14th Panzer Division. It should be noted that in a review of the Sixth Army's divisions on 9 November the 305th and 389th Infantry Divisions were rated 'good for defence'. Both formations consisted of six battalions. The main attack in the offensive was to be delivered by the 305th Infantry Division, which had been reinforced with three of the newly-arrived engineer battalions. The 389th Infantry Division was to launch a supporting attack. In confirming the plan for the LI Corps' offensive, Paulus wrote 'The most rapid regrouping of troops for the offensive against the "Azure" chemical factory will be required.'

The newly-arrived engineer battalions went through additional training in Kalach. Several captured T-34s were put into operation for anti-tank training purposes in order to develop skills in conditions as close to combat ones as possible. No one could have suspected that before long the presence of these tanks would play a cruel joke on the Germans. Offensive operations in urban conditions were practised in the ruins of the neighbouring villages.

The object of the German offensive was the positions occupied by I.I. Lyudnikov's 138th Rifle Division. As of 7 November it numbered 2,622 men, including 1,296 men on the right bank of the Volga. As of 10 November the 138th Rifle Division numbered 'active bayonets' (it's interesting that in the 138th Rifle Division's war diary there is the term 'combat strength', a loan word from the German *kampfstärke*):

> 344th Rifle Regiment – 207 men, 185 rifles, two heavy machine guns, 22 Shpagin sub-machine gun, seven mortars, four anti-tank rifles, and two light machine guns;

> 659th Rifle Regiment – 167 men, 137 rifles, two heavy machine guns, 28 Shpagin sub-machine gun, seven mortars, two anti-tank guns, and three light machine guns;

> 768th Rifle Regiment – 117 men, 95 rifles, 22 Shpagin sub-machine guns, three light machine guns, three anti-tank rifles, one Degtyaryov sub-machine gun, seven mortars, and one 45mm gun;

> 118th Rifle Regiment – 145 men, 95 rifles, 26 Shpagin sub-machine guns, three anti-tank rifles, two light machine guns, and one mortar.[3]

It has to be said that the condition of the units in Lyudnikov's division was not very impressive. The regiments disposed of a wholly insignificant number of heavy machine guns.

Krylov, the 62nd Army chief of staff, recalled the Sixth Army's offensive: 'At 06.00 on 11 November artillery fire fell upon our positions such as we had not seen for about two weeks. Once again the deafening roar of explosions swallowed up all other sounds and got into the ground under your feet. It became quite clear from the first minutes that this was the artillery preparation for a new assault.'[4] For the purpose of confusing the Soviet command, the Germans undertook attacks along a broad front by assault detachments from several formations.

The ruins of the factory, the numerous steel parts, stockpiles of gun barrels and T-beams had turned it into an area impassable for tanks. Thus it was logical that the attacks on Lyudnikov's positions fell north and south of the 'Barricade' factory. The main attack hit the boundary between Gorishnyi's 95th Rifle Division and Lyudnikov's 138th Rifle Division. On 11 November the 95th Rifle Division's 241st Rifle Regiment suffered losses up to 400 men killed and wounded. However, the Germans' first attempt to break through to the Volga was unsuccessful, and a group of 20–25 men that reached the river was surrounded and destroyed. Also, as early as the start of the offensive, two of the new sIG.33s were destroyed as the result of direct hits. The cornerstone of the 138th Rifle Division's defence along this sector was the administration building of the 'Barricade' factory, which was known by the Germans as the 'commissars' building', and in the 138th Rifle Division's documents as the 'pi-shaped building'. It's a paradox, but some of the defenders of the administration building were part of the 77th Army Blocking Detachment – yet another example of the 'inaccurate' employment of machine-gun detachments in actual fighting. It was this (prisoners' stories about the building's defenders) that became the reason for the appearance of the German term the 'commissars' building'.

The Germans' supporting attack hit the 118th Guards Rifle Regiment. There is a very eloquent entry in the 138th Rifle Division's war diary regarding its fate: 'The regiment was destroyed and seven men came out with the badly wounded regimental commander, Colonel Kolobavnikov.'[5] Even without taking into account the 118th Guards Rifle Regiment, which was crushed by the steamroller of the German offensive, the 138th Rifle Division's losses can be rated as quite heavy: 46 killed, 281 wounded and two missing in action. Essentially, one-third of the troops located along the right bank of the Volga were put out of action. But the crushing of the 138th Rifle Division in a single blow did not happen. Seydlitz, the commander of LI Corps, reported that 'The attack by both divisions was halted as a result of the enemy's cruel and stubborn resistance'. The first day's relative success cost the enemy quite dearly. The 389th Infantry Division, along with reinforcements, lost 48 men killed and 152 wounded, with 180 men immediately missing in action. The 305th Infantry Division, along with reinforcements, lost 13 men killed and 119 wounded.

The 62nd Army command attempted to hold its positions by moving a battalion from the 92nd Rifle Brigade to the sector of the enemy breakthrough. Two hundred and eight men from the battalion arrived by 18.20 on 12 November. At that moment the 241st Rifle Regiment numbered 40–50 men, having lost up to 90 per cent of its strength over two days of fighting.

The Germans took a break on 12 November, and on 13 November the offensive continued. By 12.15 on 13 November the 294th Engineer Battalion reached the Volga in the area of the so-called fuel cisterns (the remains of the long-burnt-out fuel containers). However, the main achievement on 13 November for the Germans was the successful storming of the 'Barricade' factory administration building. During the second part of the day on 13 November the remnants of a tank company from the 14th Panzer Division that had been attached to the 305th Infantry Division, three new self-propelled sIG.33 guns, and several *Sturmgeschütze* from the 245th Assault Gun Battalion, were brought up to the factory administration building. They opened fire on its upper floors. As was noted in the 138th Rifle Division's war diary, the fire proved to be quite effective: 'The building was blown up by the enemy from the upper floors and set afire'. The garrison's calling down fire on themselves only extended the struggle for the massive building slightly. The Germans had drawn lessons from the unsuccessful storming of the 'commissars' building' on 11 November. They noted that the Soviet defence had been concentrated on the first floor. In conformity with this, the breakthrough followed through the entrance to the building, followed by a dash to the second floor. Also, as was noted in the history of the 305th Infantry Division, the engineers of the 50th Engineer Battalion employed the stairs in order to get into the windows on the second floor. Having taken the second floor, the German engineers began to blow up the floors and throw grenades at the building's defenders and to set fire to the spaces on the first floor with flamethrowers and canisters of gasoline. The remnants of the garrison, numbering ten men, the majority of whom were wounded and suffering from burns, abandoned their fortress. The 138th Rifle Division's losses amounted to twenty-one men killed, ninety-one wounded and thirty-three 'due to other reasons' (it's unclear what is meant by this phrase).

The situation of the remnants of Lyudnikov's subunits, which had been squeezed into a limited space, was extremely difficult. An entry in the 138th Rifle Division's war diary for 15 November reads: 'The food has been consumed. There is no medicine. There are incidents of death. 250 heavily wounded men have accumulated.'[6] A.D. Bayandin, one of the participants in the defence of 'Lyudnikov's island,' recalled that the wounded tried to save themselves: 'Last night several men disappeared. They saw them on the ice floe. The chance of being saved was highly unlikely. Every suspicious object spotted on the ice was fired on by the Germans.' The ice on the Volga also interfered with supply and five boats that had been dispatched on the night of 19/20 November had been trapped by ice flows and carried downstream. The attempts by Gorishnyi's division, along with the 193rd Rifle Division's composite regiment, to restore the situation and to link up with Lyudnikov's division was unsuccessful.

The 138th Rifle Division was isolated on a piece of land 700m long and 400m deep. It was an extremely difficult matter to supply the 'island', even by air. Lyudnikov wrote:

> The pilots, those masters of night flight on their slow Po-2s,[7] also attempted to help the defenders of the 'Barricade' factory. They dropped sacks with ammunition and rusks over the 'island.' But our piece of land was so small that the sacks would fall behind the front line into enemy lines or into the Volga. And of those sacks which reached us, we extracted defective ammunition: they got damaged when they hit the ground.

The 138th Rifle Division's war diary contains figures on the effectiveness of these drops as of 17 November: 'During their entire period work airplanes dropped 13 packages, [of which] eight were received by us and the rest fell onto territory occupied by the enemy'.[8] As of 17 November rounds for Shpagin machine guns, mortar rounds and medical dressings were absent on Lyudnikov's Island. Batteries for the radio had only 2–3 hours of use left. The latter circumstance meant the threat of losing artillery support from the left bank of the Volga. The attempts to supply 'Lyudnikov's Island' by the 8th Air Army's U-2s began during the night of 13/14 November, when twenty sacks were dropped.[9] On the night of 15/16 November the 'night fliers' did not fly due to bad weather. On the night of 15/16 November twenty-three sacks of ammunition, four with grenades, two with medical supplies, and twenty-two with food, were dropped to the 138th Rifle Division. During the night of 16/17 November they dropped no less than sixty-six sacks in the area to the east of the 'Barricade' factory. However, to judge from entries in the 138th Rifle Division's war diary, only a small part of what was dropped actually landed on the 'finger of land' occupied by its subunits.

Nevertheless, the stubborn resistance of Lyudnikov's division meant that the offensive planned by the Germans on the 'Azure' chemical plant was postponed indefinitely. Even if the defence of 'Lyudnikov's Island' had quickly collapsed, the Sixth Army would still have required time to restore the combat strength of the formations and units for an attack on the 'Azure' combine, designated, as I should remind you, as a difficult objective for an attack.

They managed to turn the corner in the supply situation for 'Lyudnikov's island' as early as the beginning of Operation Uranus. On the night of 19/20 November armoured cutters from the Volga Military Flotilla broke through to the 138th Rifle Division. On the night of 23/24 November armoured cutters *No. 12* and *No. 13* broke through to Lyudnikov under covering fire from armoured cutter *No. 61* and delivered nine tons of cargo and evacuated 155 wounded.[10]

By 20 November 1942 the strength of the 62nd Army's formations was as follows:

13th Guards Rifle Division – 5,201 men;
37th Guards Rifle Division – 2,194 men;
39th Guards Rifle Division – 2,770 men;
45th Rifle Division – 4,696 men;
95th Rifle Division – 2,078 men;
112th Rifle Division – 659 men;
138th Rifle Division – 1,673 men;
193rd Rifle Division – 1,734 men;
284th Rifle Division – 4,696 men;
308th Rifle Division – 1,727 men;
42nd Rifle Brigade – 294 men;
92nd Rifle Brigade – 3,637 men;
115th Rifle Brigade – 271 men;
124th Rifle Brigade – 2,898 men;
149th Rifle Brigade – 848 men.

Some formations in this list (the 37th Guards and 308th Rifle Divisions) had been withdrawn from the right bank of the Volga due to exhaustion. The figures for these divisions were for the most part represented the strength of the combat support elements that were permanently located on the left bank of the Volga. In conditions in which the divisions and brigades were squarely pressed to the bank of the Volga, a significant part of their subunits was outside of Stalingrad. For example, on the night of 17/18 November 1942 in the 13th Guards Rifle Division on the right bank of the Volga, that is, in the positions in Stalingrad there were 3,118 men, and 2,071 men on the left bank of the Volga. Accordingly, in the units subordinated to the headquarters of the 95th Rifle Division (the 161st, 241st, 90th and 685th Rifle Regiments and the 92nd Rifle Brigade's third battalion) by the morning of 18 November there were 705 men on the right bank of the Volga. The 62nd Army's overall strength, along with artillery and flamethrower units, amounted to 41,199 men on 20 November.

Despite the fact that the Soviet forces, after more than two months of fighting, continued to hold their positions in Stalingrad, the German command looked to the future with optimism. On 17 November there followed an order by Hitler which Paulus transmitted to his subordinates down to regimental commanders:

> The difficulties of the battle around Stalingrad and the decline in combat strength are known to me. But now the difficulties for the Russians are even greater for the Russians, with the ice on the river. If we take advantage of this sliver of time right now, then we will eventually save more of our own blood.
>
> Thus I am waiting for the command, with its inherent energy, and the troops with their inherent boldness, will do everything so that they at least can break through to the Volga near the artillery factory and the metallurgical factory and seize these areas of the city.
>
> The air force and artillery must do everything in their power to prepare and support this offensive.[11]

Actually, with the onset of the cold and the beginning of the icing-up of the Volga the opportunities of holding the remaining pockets of resistance in the city were shrinking inexorably. In the Stalingrad Front's war diary on 13 November 1942 there appeared a troubling entry:

> The 62nd Army's forces are engaged in fierce fighting in very difficult conditions of command and control and communicating with the left bank of the Volga River. With the appearance of 'lard' on the Volga, the supply of food, munitions and the transport of reinforcements is going extremely intensely, considering the pressure of enemy fire and aviation the situation with the crossings is becoming close to catastrophic. Crossing equipment is suffering losses from 30–40 per cent and 60 per cent among the armoured cutters.[12]

There is no doubt that if the counteroffensive had not begun, then the Germans would have had every chance to eliminate the remaining centres of resistance in Stalingrad before the middle of December 1942. But they were not allowed to do that. The regrouping of forces for the conduct of Operation Uranus was proceeding full tilt. Just a few days were left before the beginning of the Stalingrad counteroffensive.

Chapter 21

Conclusions to Part II

Throughout the entire period from July to October 1942 the south-western direction was a terrible headache for the *Stavka* of the VGK. It endlessly swallowed up reserves, and not for the achievement of any positive goals but only to preserve the situation. During this period the south-western direction swallowed up seventy-two rifle divisions, or 69 per cent of the overall strength dispatched by the *Stavka* to various sectors of the front.[1] Sixty-three per cent of the tank brigades were dispatched here, to the Stalingrad area and the Caucasus. Holding Operation Blau (Braunschweig) demanded colossal efforts from the *Stavka* at the expense of reserves accumulated with great difficulty.

At the same time, one should not think that the German command did not commit reserves and scatter the clouds of 'Mongols' exclusively with the forces available at the beginning of the operation. Paulus was able to constantly feed the battle for Stalingrad with fresh forces by freeing up formations from the front along the Don, but this could only be done by replacing them with German allies. Accordingly, the Hungarian Second Army numbered 206,000 men on 31 July and occupied a 190km front, while the Italian army numbered 226,000 men (based on ration strength) on 9 September and occupied a 270km front.[2] All of this enabled them to support the offensive capabilities of the German troops in Stalingrad itself and the defence of the 'land bridge' between the Don and the Volga. The Romanian Third Army later joined the Hungarians and Italians.

Despite its complexity and the sharp turns in events, the battle for Stalingrad itself fits the proverb 'I turned to look to see whether or not she had turned to see if I had turned to look'. The opponents had learned a lot about each other in more than a year of war. Each of the sides more or less knew what could be expected from the other. Thus in the fighting for the city they made moves based on calculating the likely actions of their opponents and these calculations were mostly accurate.

Doubtlessly, being an educated staff officer, from the very beginning Paulus made the correct prediction regarding the Soviet command's next steps. The attacks against the 'land bridge' between the Volga and the Don were predicted by Paulus even before the appearance of the latest Soviet reserve armies in the Stalingrad area. Moreover, a very definite allocation of forces was carried out by the commander of the Sixth Army even before the receipt of intelligence data on the appearance of three new tank corps in the Stalingrad area. The necessity of defending the northern flank of the shock group attacking the city was pointed out as early as the order by the Sixth Army's headquarters on 16 August 1942. Thus, as opposed to the other battles for a fortress under attack from without, Paulus immediately stationed his forces proportionately to their missions. The redistribution of forces was not according to the number of formations, but according to their qualitative composition – the number and condition of the infantry and motorized infantry battalions. The best divisions stood with their front facing north in order to repel the attacks by the reserve armies' tank corps and rifle divisions. The lesser-quality divisions went to assault Stalingrad. They manoeuvred only with the efforts of the air force, which shifted from the streets of Stalingrad to Kotluban' and back again. Perhaps it was precisely because of this that the 'land bridge' withstood a squall of attacks. But because of this reason the assault on Stalingrad did not end with its defenders being pushed into the Volga.

A deviation from the script could have had fatal consequences for either side. If the Soviet command had not had tank corps available in August and the reserve armies in the beginning of September, then the screen to the north would have been dismantled for the storming of Stalingrad. The nine-battalion 76th and 305th Infantry Divisions would have entered the streets of Stalingrad as early as September and marched all the way to the Volga. Countermoves, such as the commitment of formations to the 62nd Army and the crossing over the Volga, would simply have been too late. Besides, the carrying capacity of the Volga crossings limited the strength of the city's defenders that could be effectively supplied. Also, the strength of the attacks by the Stalingrad Front's 'northern group' had to be at a certain level. Otherwise, the Germans would have placed somewhat weaker divisions facing north or reduced the number of formations defending the 'land bridge'. Accordingly, as the next move the strong formations would have made it check and checkmate for the 62nd Army in the city blocks and on the factory grounds. Aside from infantry, the 'land bridge' drew off assault guns which were employed like self-propelled anti-tank guns in the VIII Army Corps. Also, the Stalingrad Front's 'northern group' drew the German aviation's attention.

In their turn, the defenders of Stalingrad, by their stubborn resistance on the city's streets, at first stretched out and then made Operation Autumn Vine (the 'middle decision') – the Sixth Army's offensive operation which could have led to the encirclement of the 1st Guards and 24th Armies main forces, which would have been comparable to the defeat of the Crimean Front in May 1942 – entirely pointless. The condition for the beginning of the operation was the clearing of Stalingrad of Soviet forces.

The next stage in the struggle for the city became the gradual commitment of formations from the battle's periphery onto the streets of Stalingrad. Paulus removed divisions from the reserve (the 14th Panzer Division in October), from Hoth's army (the 24th Panzer and 94th Infantry Divisions), from the 'land bridge' (305th Infantry Division) and the Don front (the 100th Light Infantry Division in September and the 79th Infantry Division in November). It was also necessary to constantly maintain the defensive capability of the 'land bridge' in the face of unceasing attacks by Rokossovskii's forces. In its turn, the Soviet command pulled in formations from other sources – from the front along the Don (37th and 39th Guards Rifle Divisions), from the forces attacking the 'land bridge' (308th Rifle Division) and the 64th Army along the quiet front with Hoth's army (138th Rifle Division) to the 62nd Army. The symmetrical shifting of forces denied the Germans the opportunity of achieving a decisive result in the storming of the city. Despite the fact that the fighting in Stalingrad had the appearance (if one employs the formula in Hitler's order) of 'offensive activities of a local character', they exerted an influence on the overall situation by swallowing up Army Group B's reserves. This concerned, first of all, the mobile formations. Three panzer divisions (14th, 16th and 24th) and two motorized divisions (3rd and 60th) got mired in positional fighting. In this manner Army Group B's defensive capabilities were significantly reduced, which laid the ground for the approaching catastrophe.

However, the positional battle to the north of Stalingrad was, we should admit, a high price to pay for holding the city. One cannot but agree with the authors of the *Collection of Materials for Studying the Experience of the War*, which came out in the spring of 1943, who described the result of the operation in the following manner: 'In the final analysis, this operational success was achieved at a high cost in blood.'[3] Events proceeded in a circular fashion. The tank corps attacked, the infantry hit the dirt and did not follow the tanks and the latter were ground up in the depth of the defence. The subsequent infantry attacks, now without tanks, led to heavy losses and the loss of the armies' offensive capabilities. If in 1941 it was sometimes still possible to flatten the Germans' defence with the forces of T-34s and KVs that had broken away from the infantry, then in 1942 the enemy had weapons that were more than effective for countering this. In a report on the results of the September fighting in the Stalingrad area, the commander of the 7th Tank Corps pointed out: 'The situation on the battlefield has changed.' As a reason for the change in the situation on the battlefield, Rotmistrov pointed to the appearance among the Germans of a 'new anti-tank weapon produced by the "Rheinmetale" factory'. It's understood that this new weapon was the 75mm PAK-40.

The summer and autumn of 1942 became a time for the gradual formation of the Red Army's new infantry tactics, which to a greater degree included elements of assault actions. The all-round inculcation of the tactics of assault groups, in conjunction with the improvement in the tactics of the tank troops, enabled them to resolve tasks that would have been beyond the abilities of the divisions of 1942, including urban warfare. At the same time, in 1944–5 very under-strength divisions which were significantly inferior in strength to the reserve armies successfully carried out difficult tasks of breaking through the enemy's defence.

One of the main reasons for the formation of the positional front, 'the Verdun of the steppes', was the fact that the Red Army was seriously behind the Wehrmacht in employing heavy artillery. For example, Paulus's Sixth Army expended the following for September 1942: 3,137 155mm rounds from the captured French 414 (f) howitzer, 1,032 rounds from the 150mm K-39 gun, 83,459 rounds from the 150mm s.FH-18 field howitzer and 10,131 from the 210mm Mörser 18 howitzer.[4] The Stalingrad Front's 4th Tank, 1st Guards, 24th and 66th Armies replied to this hurricane of fire with 21,373 rounds from 152mm gun-howitzers. The Stalingrad Front did not expend heavier-calibre shells in September at all. Even taking into account the significant expenditure of ammunition by the Germans in the storming of Stalingrad itself, the picture, to put it mildly, is horrifying. The Germans replied with two to three rounds for every Soviet round fire from heavy guns. The artillery duel was being lost and the offensive expired.

The street fighting in Stalingrad, having become one of the legends of the Great Patriotic War, has simultaneously become overgrown with numerous myths and stereotypes. The image of the struggle for Stalingrad has become fixed in the social conscience as some kind of equal pressure on the Soviet defence on the city's streets for the purpose of reaching the Volga, from building to building, from shop to shop, and even from one open-hearth furnace (rolling mill) to another under sniper fire. The propaganda machine aided the strengthening of this stereotype, putting forth as typical episodes such as the struggle for 'Pavlov's building' and the sniper V. Zaitsev.

If one asks the question 'are the defence of "Pavlov's building" and the sniper war the typical and most widespread form of the struggle for Stalingrad?', then the answer will most likely be no. As often as not, the Soviet units had to attack the buildings occupied by the Germans. This happened either for the purpose of restoring the situation, or for the purpose of taking back positions that commanded the terrain.

Unfortunately, what was typical of the struggle for Stalingrad was the crossing in detail of formations being committed into the fighting for the city. The simultaneous crossing of an entire regiment into the city was most likely the exception rather than the rule. A crossing was often carried out by battalions, but from time to time they were even broken up by companies and would enter the fighting not as part of their battalion.

The reinforcements that arrived at Stalingrad almost immediately entered the fighting, without having had time to learn the situation. This, of course, was known to the command. As was noted in the 62nd Army's war diary for 27 October 1942, 'The periodic infusion of reinforcements into these divisions enter the fighting from the march and are not being mastered by the commanders and proper results are not being achieved.'[5]

It's hard to describe Chuikov's conduct of the struggle for Stalingrad as beyond reproach. His desire to attack was by no means a blessing. Essentially, it was the decision made by him to attack that created the prerequisites for the collapse of the front along the approaches to the Stalingrad Tractor Factory on 14 October 1942, a day which the commander of the 62nd Army himself rated as the most problematical. In its turn, the basis for the disaster of 14 October was laid by the ill-considered regroupings in the beginning of October, which led to the collapse of the defence along the approaches to Orlovka and the rout of the heretofore stout defence by Andrusenko's group. It is also difficult to rate Chuikov positively for the situation of the Germans' breakthrough to the 'Red October' factory. He either missed the disaster that was taking place in the immediate vicinity of his command post, or he consciously led the higher command astray, depriving Stalingrad of *front*-level reserves.

Krylov, the 62nd Army chief of staff, wrote in his memoirs: 'More aviation operated in the Stalingrad area, and we had at least a few tanks. However, here it was only the artillery that proved to be that force which was able to immediately support the rifle units along any sector.'[6] The key word here is 'able', because the practical realization of the system of troop support by artillery in the city left much to be desired and was inferior to that in Sevastopol' in 1941–2, which was familiar to Krylov.

From the point of view of equipment, it is interesting to note a description which was rendered about the equipment employed by the 84th Tank Brigade's command. It was precisely this brigade that was employed most actively in city conditions. In the brigade's report on the results of the fighting in Stalingrad it was noted:

> The employment of tanks by model showed that the heavy KV tanks in conditions of street fighting on a restricted bridgehead [he probably meant 'space', Author] for manoeuvre is not very effective and their employment is not expedient, because the tank's ability to move is extremely limited and it presents a big target, and to employ it as anti-tank defence is too expensive. The T-34 medium tanks, which are the most manoeuvrable, are less vulnerable and highly mobile, justify themselves best of all in street fighting.[7]

In the 24th Panzer Division's report on the results of the fighting in Stalingrad using tanks for urban warfare was mostly rated negatively. The narrow streets, impassable terrain and bomb craters were pointed out as an example of negative factors. In the 'Conclusions' the following was plainly stated: 'According to the experience of the fighting in Stalingrad, the employment of tanks in urban conditions should be avoided and only viewed as a last resort.'[8] Regarding the types of tanks employed, it was pointed out that the light

Panzer IIs were suitable for convoying supplies through areas not yet fully under control. Tanks with 75mm long-barrelled guns were valued as a weapon against armoured targets. It recommended destroying Soviet tanks and anti-tank guns, which had been located beforehand by ground troops, with their assistance before the attack. The 75mm short-barrelled 'cigarette butts', which were called the 'best weapon', received an unexpectedly high rating. Shells with delayed-action fuzes proved highly effective against wood and earth pillboxes and buildings. Panzer III and Panzer IV tanks were employed in mixed groups on a single street, covering each other.

The 24th Panzer Division's report singled out anti-tank rifles and snipers as the most dangerous enemy. It was recommended to blind the latter with smoke shells. It was also noted that it was best to communicate with motorized infantry through the tanks' side hatches and not through the commander's hatch, which was clearly a consequence of Soviet sniping.

Part III

Hot Snow

Chapter 22

The Father of the Gods: Uranus

(Map 13)

'A Different Decision'

The conference in the Kremlin about the situation in the Stalingrad area, which Zhukov dates as 12 September 1942 in his memoirs and at which the decision to launch a counteroffensive which changed the course of the war, was supposedly made, most likely took place between 27 and 29 September. According to Stalin's visitors' book, it was precisely then that Zhukov was in the Kremlin each day for several hours. As we know, despite the fact that the 18 September offensive had been prepared far better than the preceding counterblows, it did not succeed.

To judge from everything, the situation around Stalingrad was discussed on 28 September 1942, when Rokossovskii and Malinin were in the Kremlin. After Rokossovskii's and Malinin's departure, Zhukov and Vasilevskii spent about an hour with Stalin. What could they have discussed? On the following day, late at night (00.25–02.10), Zhukov was at the Kremlin together with Vasilevskii, Purkaev[1] and Konev.[2] Most likely, the outlines of the future plan for the autumn-winter campaign appeared precisely during those days. The outlines of the future Operations Mars and Uranus – two plans that called for the encirclement of major enemy groups of forces through flank attacks – were roughly defined.

What 'different decision' could there be? In and of itself, the defeat of an attacking enemy group of forces by flank attacks is a classic way of conducting a defensive battle. One may even offer as an example the defeat of Denikin[3] in 1919, in the preparation of which Stalin was directly involved. An offensive to a great depth to one degree or another always ended up swallowing up the attacker's forces in space and the lengthening of his flanks. Usually the situation became favourable for going over to a counteroffensive upon the slowing-down of the enemy's advance. The attacking steamroller would stop swallowing up reserves and they could be concentrated for a counterblow without looking back at the everyday demands of the defence.

The gap between the forces of Army Groups A and B in the Sal'sk steppes lent a peculiar piquancy to the situation around Stalingrad. When in August 1942 the German Fourth Panzer Army was attacking Stalingrad, Hoth left the remnants of the 51st Army on his flank. There was neither time nor forces to destroy them. Here the 57th Army gathered under its wing the remnants of the defeated units and part of the reserves arriving from elsewhere. One doesn't have to be a genius in order to think about launching a counterblow from the positions occupied by the 51st and 57th Armies.

In and of itself, the idea of an attack by the Stalingrad and Don fronts was hovering in the air. The question was the directions of the attacks and the amount of forces for launching them. In the final analysis, the success of the operation depended upon the time and place where the flank attacks were to be launched. The period of drawing up the plan for the November counteroffensive is practically ignored in the Soviet memoir literature. One might get the impression that a plan was ready, as early as September 1942, that later received the code name Uranus. The question immediately arises: 'So why then did they wait until November?' In reality, by no means did the plan for the Soviet counteroffensive come about immediately. Even if you move the conference about a 'different decision' from 12 to 27–28 September, almost two months remain until the beginning of the counteroffensive.

There were difficulties, not obvious at first glance, with both the northern and southern groups of forces for this 'Cannae' – the classical operation to double-envelop an enemy by an offensive against his flanks. The chief problem that the planning for the operation encountered on the Stalingrad Front's left flank (that is, to the south of the city) was the weakness of the road network. The railways which approached Stalingrad across the trans-Volga steppes from the east were having difficulty supplying the 62nd Army defending the city. Attempts to move a shock group of forces along these lines of communication would have been reckless. The 51st and 57th Armies could only be insignificantly reinforced and carry out a supporting mission. The main shock group of forces in the counteroffensive could rely only on the developed road network to the north-west of Stalingrad. That is, it was not necessary to create a group of forces for a crushing attack to a great depth there, against the obviously weak enemy flank – it was only necessary to supply it normally.

The 'Different Decision' from Below.

The next stage in the planning of the counteroffensive was an exchange of draft plans with the *front* commanders. On 6 October the Stalingrad Front command dispatched a document to the *Stavka* laying out the basic idea for a counteroffensive. In particular, it read: 'The resolution of the mission of destroying the enemy in the Stalingrad area should be sought for in an attack by powerful groups from the north in the direction of Kalach, and an attack from the south by the 57th and 51st Armies in the direction of Abganerovo and then to the north-west, that is, also on Kalach.'[4] If the candidate for conducting the counteroffensive from the south was already known, then it still had to be decided how and with what forces they were to operate from the north. The counterblow could be launched from the north by the forces of the Don Front. The *front's* forces hung over the Sixth Army's rear in Stalingrad. Communications with the Don Front's rear areas from the north possessed sufficient carrying capacity for supplying a major shock group of forces. But the defence of the enemy's flanks here was much stronger. However, the Don Front's main efforts during September 1942 were concentrated along the left flank, where attempts to break through and link up with the 62nd Army had not ceased.

The *Stavka* requested from Rokossovskii his thoughts on the possibility of launching a counterblow. In reply, he laid out his ideas regarding a new offensive for the purpose of linking up with the 62nd Army in Stalingrad. One can understand the commander of the Don Front. Before this, the attacks in the Kotluban' area had smashed themselves against the defensive wall of the Germans' VIII Army and XIV Panzer Corps. The proposed plan for linking up with the 62nd Army was clearly not what the *Stavka* had been expecting. On 11 October Vasilevskii tactfully replied to Rokossovskii: 'The operational plan presented by you cannot be confirmed by the *Stavka*. It is necessary to combine the attack from the north with an attack by the Stalingrad Front from the south, about which instructions will be forthcoming.'

On 9 October Yeremenko, the commander of the Stalingrad Front, approached Stalin with a new variant of his plan for a counteroffensive. The essence of his plan was as follows:

I have considered this matter throughout the month have calculated that the best axis of attack from the Don Front is the axis Kletskaya – Sirotinskaya to Kalach.

...

The launching of an attack east of the Don River from the Kotluban' area will not lead to any kind of success, because the enemy has the ability to throw everything from the Stalingrad area there and the operation will die out, of which we have had repeated experience.

How does one imagine the plan for conducting the operation?

In this operation the 3rd Guards Cavalry Corps and 2–3 mechanized brigades, which, despite all the difficulties of the march, must reach the Kalach area within a day, where it is to blow up all the crossings from the inhabited locale of Vertyachii to the inhabited locale of Kalach and to take up the defence with its front facing east. By this we can bottle up the enemy on the eastern bank of the Don with a single cavalry division, while a mechanized brigade will cover along the Lisichka River with its front facing west, to blow up all crossings along this river and mine the important axes along individual sectors.[5]

One cannot but recognize Yeremenko as one of the movers in the planning for the counteroffensive around Stalingrad. But, on the whole, his proposal to carry out an operation with cavalry strikes us as completely hopeless. This variant involves not so much a counter-offensive as a raid for the purpose of destroying the enemy's communications. Its success appears to be more than doubtful. The Germans had sufficient forces along the right bank of the Don to scatter the cavalry to the winds even in the event of the breakthrough to the crossings at Kalach and Vertyachii being successful. The 22nd Panzer Division had been left in the rear of the XVII Army Corps as far back as August. It was not in the best condition, but sufficiently strong to oppose a Soviet cavalry corps. Moreover, even a Romanian tank division with R-2 tanks could have successfully withstood cavalry. Even if the plan for breaking through to Kalach had been carried out, the prognosis for the development of events was not favourable. It was also unrealistic to expect to hold an internal encirclement along a broad front and to hold out against a relief attack from the west with cavalry forces and mechanized brigades. Even less realistically, the plan calculated on making the leap to Kalach in just one day. Such a lightning 'cobra strike', even by mechanized units, seems doubtful, and even more unlikely by cavalry forces.

As well as the cavalry raid, even the most sensible part of Yeremenko's plan – the attack by the 51st and 57th Armies toward Tinguta – makes no sense. The plan by the commander of the Stalingrad Front would not secure the formation of a sturdy 'cauldron'. The railway running from Stalingrad to the west through Surovikino and Oblivskaya would remain in the enemy's hands.

Perhaps the main step forward in Yeremenko's proposed plan was the overcoming of the psychological barrier against the stationing of the counteroffensive's shock groups along different banks of the Don. But in the end, neither Yeremenko's proposal for a cavalry raid from Kletskaya and Sirotinskaya nor Rokossovskii's proposals for breaking through to the 62nd Army found any support. A new plan was prepared, which was far more daring in its scope than all the previous ones. The bridgehead at Serafimovich was chosen as a jumping-off point for the counterblow against the flank and rear of the German Sixth Army.

Uranus Gets a Start in Life

In order to resolve the new task, the supreme high command created yet another major field force which was slated to play a key role in the counteroffensive around Stalingrad – the

South-western Front. In light of what has been related above, the story about delaying the formation of the South-western Front to the end of October in order to mislead the enemy regarding the Soviets' immediate plans looks extremely unconvincing. For example, A.M. Vasilevskii writes: 'The official formulation of the decision to create the South-western Front was moved to the end of October for the purpose of maintaining secrecy. It was planned to transfer the 63rd and 21st Armies from the Don Front to the South-western Front, plus the 5th Tank Army.'[6] But if the plan took shape as early as September 1942, then why was the new *front* for launching the main attack formed only at the end of October?

In July 1942 the entire space from the great bend of the Don to Tsimlyanskaya was entrusted to a single *front*. To be sure, a diehard like Timoshenko headed this *front*. In August the *front* was divided in two, although before long the command of both *fronts* was entrusted to a single man – Yeremenko. Only in September, with the appearance of such a figure as Rokossovskii, did the division of the *fronts* become a reality. The splitting-up was continued before the counteroffensive: on 22 October 1942 the South-western Front was reborn by order of the *Stavka* of the VGK. The new *front* received two old and one new army and a very weighty figure as commander:

The *Stavka* of the Supreme High Command orders:

1. The formation of the South-western Front by 31 October.
2. The South-western Front is to include the 63rd Army, 21st Army and the 5th Tank Army ...
3. The headquarters of the South-western Front is to be deployed on the basis of the 1st Guards Army's headquarters and be stationed in the area of Novo-Annenskii.
4. Appoint Lieutenant General Comrade Vatutin commander of the South-western Front, freeing him from the command of the Voronezh Front. Appoint Major General Stel'makh chief of staff of the South-western Front.
5. Appoint Lieutenant General Comrade Golikov commander of the Voronezh Front.[7]

Perhaps the date of the appearance of the South-western Front is evidence of the formation of a plan for Operation Uranus in the form in which it was later carried out.

In deciding the personnel matter for the new *front*, Rokossovskii's story of the previous month was repeated. Active operations on the Bryansk Front had ceased and Rokossovskii, who was commanding the *front*, was sent to the Stalingrad area. Offensives by the Voronezh Front were forbidden by *Stavka* VGK Directive No. 170627 of 28 September 1942. It was ordered only to consolidate the lines held, while the 17th and 24th Tank Corps were to be pulled into the reserve. Correspondingly, Vatutin, who had been commanding the Voronezh Front, was dispatched to the Stalingrad area. Major General G.D. Stel'makh, who had previously been the chief of staff of the Volkhov Front around Leningrad, was appointed chief of staff of the South-western Front.

Within a few days, on 25 October 1942, refinements followed regarding the distribution of forces between the South-western and Don Fronts. Of the seven rifle divisions which had initially been promised to Rokossovskii, four formations (226th, 293rd, 333rd and 277th Rifle Divisions) were to be transferred to the recreated *front*. Also, the South-western Front was to receive the 4th Tank Corps and the 3rd Guards Cavalry Corps (the one that Yeremenko proposed making the main strike force of the counterblow) from the Don Front, as well as a number of artillery units. Nor does this refinement jibe well with the idea of the previously-planned creation of the South-western Front. If it had actually previously been planned, then the entire complex of measures, which was spread over two documents, would have fitted into one *Stavka* directive.

Thus the version of the gradual evolution of the Soviet command's plans seems more convincing. The variants for the attacks on the eastern bank of the Don, which had been proposed in the beginning of October, were discarded. The cavalry raid proposed by Yeremenko along the western bank of the Don from the bridgehead near Kletskaya was also abandoned as unviable. The main shock force was shifted upstream along the Don, above Kletskaya. But instead of a cavalry corps, upon which Yeremenko had placed his hopes, a tank army had become the counteroffensive's main strike force.

One cannot but agree with Zhukov, who directly indicates the key role played by the *Stavka* VGK in preparing the operation: 'The chief and decisive role in the thorough planning and support for the counteroffensive around Stalingrad irrefutably belongs to the *Stavka* of the Supreme High Command and the General Staff.' The plans for offensive operations that were born in the *fronts*' headquarters had very limited value. A truly balanced and workable plan was prepared by the Soviet supreme high command. When Khrushchev writes, 'Zhukov came to see us. He told us that the *Stavka* had a plan similar to the one that Yeremenko and I laid out in our memorandum', he is using the term 'similar' far too broadly. The plan for a diversionary raid of cyclopean scale, proposed by Yeremenko and Khrushchev, has only a distant relationship to the plan for Operation Uranus. All of Yeremenko's and Khrushchev's claims of authorship are, at best, laughable. As regards the actions of the northern group of forces, their plan was simply monstrous.

From the point of view of strategy, Operation Uranus initially pursued quite ambitious goals. Later on, at a meeting at the headquarters of the 5th Tank Army on 3 November 1942, Zhukov formulated the operation's overall missions for the commanders:

a) to force the Romanians to leave the war by completely defeating the Romanian army;
b) to achieve a decisive turning point in the war in our favour;
c) to encircle and destroy the Stalingrad group of forces.

Later, while describing the battle of Stalingrad, they left out the task of knocking Romania out of the war. However, it was nevertheless assigned before the start of the operation.

The Geography of Uranus

The South-western and Stalingrad fronts, which occupied positions opposite the flanks of the Germans' Stalingrad group of forces, were to play the main role in Uranus. The Don Front was to carry out the task of tying down the encircled enemy and attacking along its right wing with limited aims.

The South-western Front's shock group, consisting of Lieutenant General P.L. Romanenko's[8] 5th Tank Army and Lieutenant General I.M. Chistyakov's[9] 21st Army, deployed along bridgeheads on the left bank of the Don near Serafimovich and in the Kletskaya area. It was to break through the Romanian Third Army's defence and develop the offensive with mobile troops to the south-east for the purpose of reaching the Don along the Nizhne-Chirskaya – Bol'shenabatovskii sector. The overall depth of the offensive by the *front's* forces was planned at 120km, with an offensive pace of 40km per day. Given an overall length of front of 245km, the shock group was deployed along the *front's* left flank along an 87km sector. By the start of the counteroffensive, the South-western Front counted twenty-three rifle divisions, three tank, one mechanized and two cavalry corps, three tank regiments, one motorized and one tank brigade, as well as thirty-nine artillery regiments, seven mortar regiments and seven regiments of rocket artillery from the high Command Reserve. Three of the 63rd Army's (which before long became the 1st Guards Army) rifle divisions were to launch a supporting attack for the purpose of supporting the 5th Tank Army. See the table for the strength of the South-western Front's armies.

Before November 1942 the experience of employing tank armies had been, if not uniformly negative, then by no means positive. The first employment of a major field force with the title 'tank army' was near Voronezh (A.I. Lizyukov's 5th Tank Army) had been a failure. The actions of the 1st and 4th Tank Armies in the Stalingrad area and those of the 3rd Tank Army around Kozel'sk also passed without noisy success. However, there was no disappointment in the mechanized major field force, as such, on the part of the Soviet command.

The 5th Tank Army, which had ceased to exist following the unsuccessful counterblows around Voronezh, had essentially been reborn. P.L. Romanenko, who in 1941 had commanded the 1st Mechanized Corps and who had headed the 3rd Tank Army in August and September, became the army commander.

Table 34: The Strength of the South-western Front's Armies on 20 November 1942.

	1st Guards Army	*21st Army*	*5th Tank Army*	*Front*	*Total*
Combat troops	142,869	92,056	90,600	6,423	331,948
Field guns	973	803	929	–	2,705
Mortars	2,293	1,554	1,456	279	5,582
Rocket artillery	14	40	–	164	218
Tanks	163	199	359	–	721
With rear establishments	155,096	103,270	104,196	27,340	389,902

The 5th Tank Army, or more accurately its tank and infantry core, was to be transported to by rail from the Bryansk Front (from the Plavsk area). For the soldiers and junior commanders, everything began as a usual training journey on 20 October 1942. But instead of exercises, with the onset of darkness they began to load the units onto trains. Everything took place in conditions of utmost secrecy. Even the formation commanders only knew the time and loading stations. By 6 November, following a 120km march from the unloading station, the army's units concentrated along the northern bank of the Don.

Upon its arrival, the 5th Tank Army received part of the 21st Army's sector, along with the formations occupying it: the 124th,[10] 203rd and 14th Guards Rifle Divisions. Before long the 203rd Rifle Division was transferred to the neighbouring 63rd Army (later the 1st Guards Army). In the end, by the start of Operation Uranus the infantry core of Romanenko's army consisted of six formations: the 14th, 47th and 50th Guards Rifle Divisions and 119th, 159th and 346th Rifle Divisions. They were divided into two echelons, with the 346th (minus one regiment) and the 159th Rifle Divisions assigned to the second echelon, while the remainder received zones of various width in the first echelon. Given the width of the army's front of 32km, the divisions along the axis of the main attack (47th and 50th Guards and 119th Rifle Divisions) were given zones of 4–6km in width, and 8km along the pinning axis (14th Guards Rifle Division) and 7km for the 346th Rifle Division's regiment. The strength of the 5th Tank Army's rifle formations varied greatly from formation to formation (see table).

Table 35: The Strength of the 5th Tank Army's Formations Before the Start of Operation Uranus.

14th Guards Rifle Division – 7,779;	47th Guards Rifle Division – 7,540;
119th Rifle Division – 9,574;	124th Rifle Division – 5,173;
159th Rifle Division – 3,494;	346h Rifle Division – 8,234.

As we can see, the stronger formations were among both the 'aborigines' and the 'Varangians',[11] who had arrived with the 5th Tank Army's headquarters. The 159th Rifle Division had been transferred to the Stalingrad area from the Voronezh Front.

By the end of 1942 a system had already practically come about in the Red Army in which the rifle divisions received tanks for direct infantry support. In the 5th Tank Army the forces for direct infantry support included the 8th Guards Tank Brigade (eighteen KVs, four T-34s, one T-70 and twenty-seven T-60s) and the 510th (ten KV-8s and eleven TO-34s) and 511th (eight KV-8s and ten TO-34s) Flamethrower Tank Battalions. There were also ten T-34s with mine-clearing rollers.

Insofar as the 5th Tank Army combined formations of varying mobility, it logically fell into two unequal parts. The rifle formations were in the first and the second received the name of the ERU's (success development echelon) mobile group. In this case, I use the term which was employed in the report by the 5th Tank Army's headquarters, which was written about the results of the fighting. The ERU's mobile group included the 1st and 26th Tank Corps, the 8th Motorcycle Regiment and the 8th Cavalry Corps.

The 5th Tank Army's plan for the offensive was broken down into three stages:

- the breakthrough of the front and the commitment of the ERU's mobile group;
- the development of the success, the destruction of the Romanian 9th, 14th and 5th Infantry Divisions and operational reserves in conjunction with the 21st Army's units and the arrival of the main forces at the Chir and Don rivers;
- the encirclement, together with the units of the Stalingrad Front, of the enemy's Stalingrad group of forces and the firm consolidation along the Chir River.

The depth of these tasks was 150km. According to the plan, all three stages were supposed to fit into a very short timescale – only three days. Moreover, the tank corps were supposed to break through to the crossings over the Don as early as the second day of the offensive. Accordingly, the 26th Tank Corps was supposed to seize the crossing at Kalach and the 1st Tank Corps one in the Nizhne-Chirskaya area. It was planned to 'come into contact with the Stalingrad Front's units, to complete the encirclement of the enemy group of forces and be ready to destroy it' as early as the third day of the offensive.

By 19 November the 1st Tank Corps numbered eight KVs, fifty-seven T-34s and sixty-five T-70s ready for combat. At 14.30 on 18 November the 26th Tank Corps numbered twenty-four KVs, sixty-seven T-34s and sixty-eight T-70s. It is worth noting that all of both corps' KV tanks had been grouped in one of the tank brigades. In Butkov's corps, this was the 89th Tank Brigade, which numbered eight KVs, ten T-34s and twenty-seven T-70s ready for combat. In Rodin's corps the 216th Tank Brigade was the 'heavy' one. It was noticeably stronger, containing by the start of Uranus twenty-four KVs, four T-34s and twenty-six T-70s (plus one undergoing repair). Such a decision regarding the KVs was quite logical, taking into account the fact that by no means could all the bridges bear their weight. Accordingly, one could employ a 'heavy' brigade in an offensive, first of all, like a ram, and secondly, dispatch it along its own route, taking into account the weight limits of the bridges. The KV tanks' manoeuvre would not tie down the other tank brigades. The 216th Tank Brigade's special role was laid out from the very start of the operation: it had been taken from the 26th Tank Corps and placed in support of the 50th Guards Rifle Division's infantry. However, this was the limit of the corps' being moved around. The 47th Rifle Division got the 8th Independent Tank Brigade as a mean of direct infantry support.

G.S. Rodin, the commander of the 26th Tank Corps, was not a newcomer to the Stalingrad direction and he had commanded the 28th Tank Corps during the summer. V.V. Butkov, the commander of the 1st Tank Corps, on the other hand, was a 'Varangian' from the western direction.

On the whole, in rating the 5th Tank Army's tank park, including direct support units and formations, the large proportion of light tanks is immediately apparent. Out of 408 tanks, 68 were heavy KVs, 168 medium T-34s and 172 light T-60s and T-70s. That is, light tanks accounted for 42 per cent of the overall strength of Romanenko's army. They could be quite easily handled by the anti-tank guns available to the Romanians, as well as the R-2 tanks armed with 37mm guns.

It's worth noting that the 5th Tank Army was a 'Varangian' – the 4th Tank Army, which had remained in the Stalingrad area, had been transformed into the 65th Army as early as October and remained part of the Don Front. It had lost its tank formations as early as August 1942 and the very designation of 'tank' was laughable. The army commander had been replaced even before the army's status had been changed – P.I. Batov[12] was appointed instead of V.D. Kryuchyonkin. Evidently the performance of Kryuchyonkin's headquarters in July and August had not been rated very highly at the top.

Insofar as in the early stage of the formation of the armoured troops the Soviet tank armies copied to a great extent the German panzer (motorized) corps, P.L. Romanenko's army received its own attack sector. The 5th Tank Army was supposed to attack along a 32km front with six rifle divisions, two tank corps and a single cavalry corps. The tank army was organized into two echelons. Four reinforced rifle divisions were in the first echelon, and another two rifle divisions, two tank corps and the cavalry corps in the second echelon. The latter were supposed to enter the breach made by the first-echelon formations. Following their commitment into the breakthrough, the tank corps (26th and 1st) were to develop the success in the direction of Perelazovskii and Kalach, toward the Stalingrad Front's mobile group. The cavalry corps, with the task of seizing the line of the Chir River and holding it until the arrival of the army's rifle formation, was to follow in the tanks' wake to support the tank corps' activities from the south-west.

Being a major encirclement operation, Uranus contained within itself a number of smaller 'cauldrons'. In this regard, a special role was assigned to the South-western Front's 21st Army. First of all, it was planned to encircle the Romanian Third Army by the adjoining flanks of the 5th Tank and 21st Armies. Secondly, it was planned to encircle the trans-Don part of the Sixth Army (XI Corps), which was located along the right bank of the Don) by the adjoining flanks of the South-western and Don Fronts. The South-western Front's 21st Army was to attack along a 40km front in the general direction of Zakharov, Novaya Buzinovka and Golubinskii. It included six rifle divisions and one tank and one cavalry corps. Four rifle divisions were to attack in the 21st Army's first echelon, and two rifle divisions, one tank and one cavalry corps in the second. Three rifle divisions, with an artillery density of about forty guns per kilometre of front, were to break through the enemy's defence along the main attack front of 12km. One rifle division was to attack along an auxiliary axis, with a single regiment occupying defensive positions along a 22km front, with the other two regiments attacking along a 3km front.

The 21st Army's mobile group (a tank and a cavalry corps) had the task of getting into the rear of the Germans' trans-Don group of forces, cutting off its path of retreat toward Stalingrad. On its arrival at the Don, the 21st Army was to be removed from the South-western Front and operationally subordinated to the Don Front.

The Don Front's shock group was to attack toward the 21st Army in order to form the encirclement around the left wing of Paulus's army. Sharing with the Stalingrad Front the weak centre of this 'Cannae', the Don Front's forces were, nevertheless, supposed to play an important role in the encirclement operation.

The Don Front's forces had the task of encircling the enemy group of forces, consisting of four infantry divisions and one cavalry division, which were defending west of the Don River, cutting it off from Stalingrad. The *pièce de résistance* of the plan for the *front's* operation was an attack along both banks of the Don. Along the right bank of the river, the 65th Army was to launch an attack with five rifle divisions and two tank brigades along a 20km front in the direction of Kletskaya. Along the left bank of the Don, the 24th Army was to launch an attack in the direction of Vertyachii, with the task of cutting off the enemy's trans-Don group of forces from the crossings over the Don. The 24th Army was to launch its attack simultaneously with 65th Army's arrival at the Don. In this fashion Rokossovskii's forces were to reach the crossings over the Don along both banks of the river, which would increase the chances of success for the plan to defeat the Sixth Army's left flank. The Don Front's single mobile formation – the 16th Tank Corps – was also supposed to operate as part of the 24th Army.

Table 36: The Strength of the Don Front's Forces on 20 November 1942.

	24th Army	*65th Army*	*66th Army*	*Front*	*Total*
Combat Troops	56,409	63,187	39,457	33,140	192,193
Field Guns	722	638	515	263	2,138
Mortars	1,123	1,230	1,023	786	4,162
Rocket Artillery	–	–	–	194	194
Tanks	48	49	5	152	254
With Rear Units	68,489	74,709	51,738	89,437	284,373

The Stalingrad Front was to launch its main attack with the forces of the 57th and 51st Armies, with the task of defeating units of the Romanian VI Army Corps and, in conjunction with the South-western Front's forces, encircle the Germans' Stalingrad group of forces. It was planned to launch two attacks in the *front's* sector. The 57th Army's shock group was given the task of breaking through the enemy front and committing the 13th Mechanized Corps into the breach. The latter was to operate as the success development echelon and to prepare the ground for creating the internal encirclement front. The 57th Army, together with the 64th Army's left-flank forces, was to develop the attack in the wake of the 13th Mechanized Corps to the north-west for the purpose of forming the internal encirclement front around the German Sixth Army.

Major General N.I. Trufanov's[13] 51st Army was to launch the second attack. The army was supposed to break through the enemy front along the isthmuses between Lakes Sarpa,

Tsatsa and Barmantsak and to commit the 4th Mechanized Corps into the breach in order to establish communications with the South-western Front's forces in the general direction of Kalach. The 4th Mechanized Corps was supposed to advance to the Abganerovo area to form the external encirclement front. For this purpose, part of the 51st Army's forces was to attack to the south-west following the breakthrough.

Table 37: The Strength of the Stalingrad Front's Forces on 20 November 1942.

	28th Army	*51st Army*	*57th Army*	*62nd Army*
Combat Troops	47,891	44,720	56,026	41,667
Field Guns	369	318	539	453
Mortars	816	698	962	744
Rocket Artillery	8	45	–	–
Tanks	80	207	225	23
With Rear Units	64,265	55,184	66,778	54,199

	64th Army	*Front*	*Total*
Combat Troops	40,490	27,523	258,317
Field Guns	356	162	2,197
Mortars	673	330	4,223
Rocket Artillery	–	–	53
Tanks	40	–	575
With Rear Units	53,742	73,775	367,943

The date for the start of the operation was established as follows: 9 November for the South-western and Don fronts and 10 November for the Stalingrad Front. The difference days for launching the offensive was conditioned by the lack of coincidence in the depth of the South-western and Stalingrad Fronts' forthcoming operations, the shock groups of which were supposed to reach the Kalach – Sovetskii area simultaneously.

On the whole, the plan for Operation Uranus was simple and even elegant. From the breakthrough sectors along the Don River to the north of Stalingrad, and from the chain of lakes to the south of the city, the attacking armies would spread out like a fan, forming external and internal encirclement fronts around the enemy. The tank and mechanized corps, possessing the greatest penetrating power, were to form the centre of the 'fan'. They were to break through toward each other first and prevent the enemy, in one way or another, from holding open a 'corridor' connecting it with the army group's main forces. The less-mobile infantry was to be along the flanks of the shock groups and nearest to the city. Cavalry formations would form the external encirclement front. The latter lacked penetrating power, but were less dependent on the rear services and could steadily advance into the depths of the steppe, pushing back the jumping-off positions of a possible relief attack as far as possible from Paulus's surrounded army. At the same time, a number of refinements had been added in the plan for Operation Uranus which scattered the forces of the attacking troops. Among these were the plan for splitting the encircled group in two (the encirclement of the trans-Don part of the Sixth Army), which required two tank corps for its realization.

Aviation

Three air armies were to provide aviation support for the forces of the three Soviet *fronts*. These were the Don Front's 16th Air Army, the Stalingrad Front's 8th Air Army and the South-western Front's 17th Air Army. Their quantitative and qualitative strength by the start of the operation is show in the following table.

Table 38: The Quantitative and Qualitative Composition of the Air Armies Involved in Operation Uranus.

Number of Aircraft					
Air Army	*Fighters*	*Attack Aircraft*	*Day Bombers*	*Night Bombers*	*Reconnaissance Aircraft*
16th	114	105	–	93	3
8th	284	273	65	122	7
17th	82	40	–	79	–
Total	480	418	65	294	10

The level of combat readiness in the air armies was about 75 per cent. That is, less than a thousand aircraft would be able to take off and take part in combat activities. Also worthy of attention is the small number of reconnaissance aircraft. The number of such aircraft in the Soviet air force was traditionally extremely small.

One has to say that the number of aircraft activated for Operation Uranus is extremely unimpressive, particularly when compared with the later operations of the Second World War. Then you might have 1,200 aircraft in a single air army, and not in three altogether. On the other hand, the enemy air force was equally unimpressive. On 20 November 1942 the Fourth Air Fleet, which was responsible for both the Stalingrad direction and the Caucasus, numbered 732 combat aircraft, of which only 402 were ready for combat. Moreover, a significant reduction in the German air force's numbers around Stalingrad took place literally two weeks before the start of the Soviet offensive. The start of the Allied landing in North Africa (Operation Torch) required them to activate major aerial forces in Germany. Von Richtofen immediately promised three groups of bombers and coolly dispatched them to the Mediterranean. As a result, on 20 November 139 bombers remained in the entire Fourth Air Fleet, of which only 64 were combat-ready. There had been 341 bombers (186 combat-ready) a month earlier. This is all the more surprising in that von Richtofen was one of the alarmists who warned about an impending Soviet offensive. However, the 1:2.4 correlation of combat-ready aircraft did not promise an easy victory for the Soviet air force.

The Winter Campaign's 'Window of Opportunity'

In order for Operation Uranus to succeed, aside from scrupulous preparation, a number of circumstances favourable to its realization had to come together. The first prerequisite for success was the choice of the axis of the main attacks aimed at the Romanian armies.

The Romanians are considered, and not without reason, one of the chief culprits in the disaster on the Volga. However, the Romanians had become hostages to the overall situation along the front of Army Group B. When on 10 September 1942 the Romanian Third Army, with a strength of 171,256 men, began to occupy its assigned defensive line, it ended up almost entirely along the steppe and not along the bank of the Don. Here were the bridgeheads at Serafimovich and Kletskaya, which the Red Army had won back from the

Germans and Italians in August 1942. On 24 September the commander of the Romanian Third Army, General Dumitrescu,[14] approached the German command with a proposal to eliminate the bridgeheads. He desperately needed the Don as an anti-tank obstacle. The Germans refused. At that moment they were too busy with the assault on Stalingrad and in repelling attacks against the 'northern screen' to the north of the city. Later, in a report by the D.V.K.15[15] (group of military advisors) with the Romanian V Corps, it was noted that 'If there had been German units to the east of the Romanian 6th Division and west of the Romanian 5th Division, or if the Romanian IV and III Corps had occupied a defensive front along the Don, then it's most likely that the Russians would not have achieved such a major breakthrough in the great bend'.[16]

On 19 November 1942 the Romanian Third Army consisted of the I (7th and 11th Infantry Divisions), V (5th and 6th Infantry Divisions) and IV (13th and 15th Infantry Division and 1st Cavalry Division) Corps and the XLVIII Panzer Corps (Romanian 1st Tank, German 22nd Panzer and Romanian 7th Cavalry Divisions). The army occupied defensive positions along a 170km sector. The overall strength of the forces subordinated to General Dumitrescu was 155,492 Romanians and 11,211 Germans. A Romanian infantry division in the Third Army occupied an average front of 20km, which clearly exceeded the defensive sectors recommended in the manuals. At the same time, all of the infantry divisions were in the first line, with one or two infantry battalions, at best, placed in the reserve. However, anti-tank weapons were the Romanian divisions' 'Achilles heel'. The chief anti-tank weapons were captured Soviet 45mm guns and Austrian-made 47mm Buckler anti-tank guns. The Romanian divisions received five or six 75mm anti-tank PAK-97.38 anti-tank guns each only in October 1942. Hollow-charge shells were the chief ammunition for these guns.

The most effective means for 'plugging up' tank breakthroughs was nevertheless not anti-tank guns, but independent mechanized formations. Formally, there existed just such a formation in Dumitrescu's army – the Romanian 1st Tank Division. As opposed to Soviet tank theoreticians, who imbibed progressive experience in the organization of tank troops through prisoner interrogations and captured documents, the Romanians were able to gain valuable first-hand knowledge. Thus the structure of a Romanian tank division had been copied from that of a German panzer division. It consisted of a tank regiment (two battalions), two motorized infantry regiments, an artillery regiment and auxiliary elements. The overall strength of the formation's rank and file was 13,600 men. Where they differed from the Germans was in equipment. The Romanian tank division had 109 R-2 tanks (a version of the Czech LT vz.35 tank with a 37mm gun) when it arrived at the front. During the course of training in Army Group B, the Romanian tank troops tested the capabilities of their guns against T-34s captured by the Germans. The results, as one might suspect, were disheartening. On 17 October the Romanian 1st Tank Division received eleven Panzer IV Ausf Gs and eleven Panzer III Ausf Ns (with a short-barrelled 75mm gun). They rearmed a single company apiece in the tank battalions with these vehicles. The German tanks with their Romanian crews underwent their first battalion exercises on 16 November 1942, three days before the start of the fighting.

The XLVIII Panzer Corps' German 22nd Panzer Division was not much different from the first Romanian mobile formation as regards its combat capabilities. It was precisely about this formation that they tell the story about the electric wiring being eaten by mice. As a result of this, of the formation's approximately 100 combat vehicles, only about 30 were ready for battle. However, if we remember that Panzer 38(t) tanks accounted for a significant part of the 22nd Panzer Division's tank park, then its combat value was doubtful, even without the brave action by the rodent saboteurs. In either event, the formation had been drawn into the preparation of a defence of the bridgeheads' perimeter at Kletskaya and Serafimovich. This took place literally a few days before the start of Operation Uranus. The division received orders on 10 November to move up to the Romanian Third Army's sector. The formation's last units began their movement to the appointed area on 16 November. Theoretically, the German panzer division could have become the 'cement' holding the German ally's defence. Yet one other attempt to pour 'fast-drying cement' into the Romanian troops' position was the so-called Battlegroup Simons. It was composed of mobile units from the 62nd Infantry Division: an anti-tank battalion, a reconnaissance battalion, a battalion from an artillery regiment and a headquarters with a signals platoon. Battlegroup Simons also included the 611th Independent Tank Destroyer Battalion (armed, according to various sources, with Marders or Panzerjäger Is with a 47mm gun). Such a combat group, with a strength of about a thousand men, might have become a support for the Romanian forces, which were weaker in anti-tank defence. Battlegroup Simons had trained for fighting to the south-west of Kletskaya and was subordinated to the headquarters of the XLVIII Panzer Corps. The XLVIII Panzer Corps was being further reinforced by the 670th Tank Destroyer Battalion (Panzer Jag. Abt.670) and the 849th Heavy Artillery Battalion (s.Art.Abt.849), taken from the Sixth Army on 14 November.

The Romanian forces to the south of Stalingrad had not had time to get an army headquarters. They were supposed to have been transferred to Hoth's Fourth Panzer Army and General Constantine Constantinescu's[17] Romanian Fourth Army on 21 November. The Romanian Fourth Army was to include the VI (1st, 2nd, 18th, and 4th Infantry Divisions) and the VII Cavalry (5th and 8th Cavalry Divisions) Corps and the 5th 'Rosiori' Regiment.[18] In all, the Romanian forces numbered 75,380 men. The Romanian forces taking part in the offensive against Stalingrad had suffered heavy losses – these divisions began the campaign with an overall strength of 101,875 men.

The 16th Motorized Division, which had been subordinated to the Fourth Panzer Army, had little in the way of cooperation with these forces. The division was securing Army Group B's flank and controlled a sector approximately 300km long all the way to the Terek River, where Army Group A's First Panzer Army was operating.

The chief disadvantage of Army Group B's defensive position, which offered a 'window of opportunity' to the Red Army for carrying out Operation Uranus, was the shortage of mobile reserves. On 15 November the 22nd Panzer Division and the Romanian 1st Tank Division were put into the army group's reserve and subordinated to the XLVIII Panzer Corps: the 22nd Panzer Division in the Perelazovskii area, and the Romanian 1st Tank Division behind the Romanian Third Army near Chernyshevskaya. The 294th Infantry Division was formally listed as being in the army group reserve, but as opposed to the mobile formations, its arrival at the right place and the right time was not guaranteed.

Army Group B's tank forces, which were concentrated in the Fourth Panzer and Sixth Armies by the start of the Soviet counteroffensive, were no longer in the best of shape. See table.

Table 39: The Condition of the Fourth Panzer and Sixth Army's (Army Group B) Tank Park.

Division	Panzer II	Panzer III (short)	Panzer III (long)	Panzer III (75)	Panzer IV (short)	Panzer IV (long)	Command
Fourth Panzer Army (16 November 1942)							
16th Motorized	8	–	16	7	–	11	1
29th Motorized	7	–	23	9	–	18	2
Sixth Army (18 November 1942)							
14th Panzer*	5	9	17	5	5	12	2
16th Panzer*	–	–	38	–	2	10	–
24th Panzer* (on 19 Nov)	5	13	18	5	5	12	2
3rd Motorized	3	–	22	3	–	4	–
60th Motorized	4	–	12	2	–	3	–
Army Group B Reserve							
22nd Panzer	2	5 Panzer 38(t)	12	10	1	10	–

Panzer III (short) is a Panzer III tank with a 50mm gun, and the Panzer III (long) is a Panzer III(75) with a 75mm gun.
Panzer IV (short) is a Panzer IV tank with a 75mm gun, and the Panzer IV (long) has a 43-calibre gun.
* Refined data from the Sixth Army's war diary.

There is no mention of 150 tanks in a panzer division, about which Soviet intelligence had been reporting. Even the 16th Panzer Division, which had long been the most powerful formation in Paulus's army, had by November 1942 lost its combat capabilities to a significant degree.

The capabilities of the motorized infantry of the Sixth Army's mobile formations had also declined significantly. There were five battalions (including a motorcycle battalion) in the 16th Panzer Division – three medium strength and two weak. Before the assault on the city there were five medium-strength battalions. There were five medium-strength battalions in the 3rd Motorized Division and seven in the 60th Motorized Division – four medium-strength battalions, two weak and one 'worn out' (*Abgekaempft*). There were five battalions, all of medium strength, in the 24th Panzer Division. Only the 29th Motorized Division was sufficiently powerful at that moment. It had been prepared by the Germans for an offensive on Astrakhan' and had not taken part in the bloody fighting for Stalingrad.

The only new formations were in Germany. As a result of the great extension of Army Group B's front, it was problematic whether or not the necessary forces could be brought up should a crisis suddenly arise. The transfer of only a single panzer division required 80–90 railway cars. Given the overloading of the rail lines connecting Germany with the Eastern Front, it would require at least three weeks from the moment the order to embark a single division from the Western Front was received until its arrival at the scene of combat activities on the Eastern Front. Actually, one division was already en route by the start of the Soviet counteroffensive. Recognising the threat to the Romanian Third Army, the Germans had dispatched the 6th Panzer Division, which had been reformed in Germany, to the East. But it simply did not have time to reach its destination in time. The appearance of a fresh German panzer division might have had a disastrous effect on the Soviet 5th Tank Army's offensive. The 'window of opportunity' for Operation Uranus would have been limited from above by the arrival of the 6th Panzer Division.

There was yet another threat. Without waiting for the arrival of the 6th Panzer Division from the West, on 14 November the Army Group B command ordered Paulus 'to prepare to withdraw all units of the 14th Panzer Division from Stalingrad and to transfer them to the XLVIII Panzer Corps as soon as possible, despite the retention of the main task of attacking in the city'. However, they were not able to fully carry out this plan.

What is interesting is that in the autumn of 1942 both Soviet and German intelligence were mistaken in their estimation of the enemy's real condition and capabilities. Soviet intelligence operatives underestimated the Sixth Army's strength, while the Germans underestimated the scope of the attacks along the front along the Don. Of course, the Soviet forces' movements during the run-up to the counteroffensive around Stalingrad were noticed by the Germans. Beginning from the middle of October the Army Group B command received a large amount of information regarding the concentration of Soviet forces in the Saratov area, which could be evidence of preparations for an offensive along the Stalingrad direction. By 3 November intelligence had reported that Soviet forces were preparing for an offensive against the Romanian Third Army. The intensive construction of crossings was also reported, which could not be fully explained by the necessity of improving troop supply. However, these reports were not perceived as preparations for an offensive on a colossal scale. The struggle for the bridgeheads near Kletskaya and Serafimovich was a satellite of the battle for Stalingrad and the Germans had already become accustomed to attacks along these axes. For example, the 21st Army attempted to take part through counter-attacks in the battle in the bend of the Don in July–August 1942. The repetition of the July and August offensives was not viewed as a serious danger.

The first major snowfall hit on 12 November 1942. The white flakes falling from the sky hid the enemies from each other. Almost nothing could be seen across the strip of no-man's land. The vague contours of positions, forward outposts and barbed-wire obstacles could only be spotted occasionally through the snowflakes. Intelligence yielded only vague outlines of the true composition of those forces with which they would soon collide in deadly battle.

Order No. 306

Among the numerous factors which were narrowing the 'window of opportunity' for the Red Army in the autumn of 1942 were, however strange this may sound, the instructions from above, from Moscow. On 8 October 1942 there appeared Order No. 306 by the Minister of Defence, on improving the tactics of the offensive battle and about the subunits', units' and formations' battle orders, signed by Stalin. The order postulated the imperfect organization of the formations and units in the offensive:

> As a rule, a rifle division, upon receiving an attack zone of one or one and a half kilometres along the front, organizes its regiments in two echelons, of which two regiments are in the first echelon and on behind them; a rifle regiment, in attacking along a 750–1,000 metre sector, is also forced to have, in the best case, two battalions in the first echelon and one in the second.[19]

At that moment echeloning was the accepted practice, laid down in manuals and instructions. However, in Order No. 306, Stalin pointed out the negative consequences of this practice, which had manifested themselves during the course of the fighting around Stalingrad and Rzhev (according to the results of which the order was issued):

> As a result of this, we have, first of all, extremely heavy and completely unjustified losses among the rank and file and in weapons from enemy artillery and mortar fire and aviation, which are suffered, first of all, by the elements of the second and third echelons even before they enter the fighting, as a result of which our offensive often misfires at the very first stage.[20]

True, the German artillery's hurricane of fire would hit not only the first echelon of the attacking formations, but the second and third echelons, which were still only waiting to enter the fighting. The soldiers and commanders could die under the blows of heavy and long-range artillery without ever having seen the enemy on the battlefield, while still in their concentration areas. It was planned to fight against this phenomenon in an original fashion – by renouncing echeloning. On the one hand, this would augment the power of the first attack, but on the other it would deprive the commanders of the opportunity to influence the development of the offensive. It was planned to retain no more than a company in reserve, and up to a battalion in the divisions. Operation Uranus was to become a full-scale test of the viability of Order No. 306, which was quite risky from the military point of view.

Chapter 23

The Tank Army. The First Success

(Map 14)

'Send an inspector to get fur mittens' was the telephoned telegram which was sent out between 16.00 and 17.00 on 18 November to the 5th Tank Army's formations. According to a prearranged code, this meant 'The beginning of the infantry attack is at 08.50 on 19.11.42'.

Artillery Day

At 08.50 on 19 November 1942, following an artillery preparation lasting one hour and 20 minutes, the forces of the South-western and Don Fronts went over to the offensive. The artillery's activities were made more difficult by the heavy snowfall and morning fog. Due to the poor weather, direct air support for the attack in the offensive sector of the *fronts*' shock groups was not carried out. The poor weather also prevented the air armies from carrying out active operations during the daylight hours of 19 November. However, if poor weather conditions proved in many ways fatal for Operation Mars,[1] then they most likely favoured the conduct of Operation Uranus. Many of the Red Army's operations subsequently began in poor weather.

Following an 80-minute artillery preparation, at 08.50 units of the 5th Tank Army attacked along the entire front. The first-echelon divisions attacking along the main axis encountered weak resistance along the forward edge of the defence. As they moved into the depth, the enemy's resistance grew and the infantry's advance slowed. The attack by the right-flank 14th Guards Rifle Division against the Romanian 9th Infantry Division had no success at all.

Operation Uranus was one of the first in which mine-clearing tanks were employed. However, of five tanks with mine rollers, two were out of action and only three vehicles flattened the minefield. As a result, four tanks in the 8th Tank Brigade were blown up by mines: two KVs, one T-34 and one T-60. The brigade's losses from mines exceeded those from enemy fire. On the first day of the battle, the brigade lost, besides the four blown-up tanks, one T-60 burned and three T-60s knocked out. The 124th Rifle Division lost 106 men on the first day of the offensive, while the 119th Rifle Division lost 183 men killed and wounded and the 47th Guards Rifle Division 271 men.

However, the infantry attack was only the prelude to an attack by major armoured forces. At 13.00 the tank corps reached the line of the attacking infantry and the 1st Tank Corps received a zone for operations 8–9km in breadth and the 26th Tank Corps one of 12–14km. The overall width of the tank corps' operations zone was therefore about 20–22km. The corps advanced shoulder to shoulder. Each directly entered the breach along a 5–6km sector, having their internal flanks adjacent and free zones of 5–6km toward the external flanks. By the time of the commitment of the tank corps into the fighting the enemy's defence had not yet been completely penetrated and the tank corps, overcoming the final centres of resistance on the march, began to rapidly advance to the south.

Plate 1: 'To your tanks!' Tank crews before boarding their tanks in the grounds of the Stalingrad Tractor Factory, summer 1942.

Plate 2: German soldiers filling a water barrel from a well. Drinking water became one of the major problems along the approaches to Stalingrad. (*NARA*)

Plate 3: Colonel General A.I Yeremenko, the commander of the Stalingrad Front, and N.S. Khrushchev, member of the military council.

Plate 4: T.I. Tanaschishin, commander of the 13th Tank Corps.

Plate 5: The German 733rd Artillery Battalion's 210mm howitzer. Heavy artillery became one of the Wehrmacht's main arguments in the fighting for Stalingrad. (*Author's collection*)

Plate 6: A Soviet prisoner of war from the 'cauldron' near Kalach. (*NARA*)

Plate 7: Soviet engineers build a bridge over the Don.

Plate 8: Soviet soldiers examine captured Italian L6/40 light tanks.

Plate 9: Guards anti-tank rifleman P. Makarenko by an Italian L6/40 tank he knocked out.

Plate 10: Friedrich Paulus, the commander of the Sixth Army at the 76th Infantry Division's command post in the area of Height 137.2, 25 August 1942. Sitting in front of the commander are General Seydlitz (LI Corps), General Rodenburg (76th Infantry Division) and Colonel Kaegler (commander of Battle Group Kaegler). (*NARA*)

Plate 11: 'It's me – Chuikov.' On 12 September 1942 Lieutenant General V.I. Chuikov took over command of the 62nd Army.

Plate 12: Paulus observes the advance of the LI Corps' units on Stalingrad, 14 September 1942. (*NARA*)

Plate 13: A pump house on the bank of the Volga: the Sixth Army reached this point on 14 September 1942. (*NARA*)

Plate 14: A T-34 from the 6th Tank Brigade, knocked out on Gogol' Street in Stalingrad. (*NARA*)

Plate 15: The Nazi banner atop the Univermag department store, end of September 1942. No one knew then that the department store would become the symbol of the Sixth Army's capitulation. (*NARA*)

Plate 16: The centre of Stalingrad shrouded in smoke. The building with the chimney in the centre is Gerhardt's mill, which has since become a memorial. (*NARA*)

Plate 17: German soldiers by the Stalingrad grain elevator, 21 September 1942. (*NARA*)

Plate 18: The fighting raged day and night. A German 210mm howitzer fires at night. (*Author's collection*)

Plate 19: How to hold the 'land bridge'? Paulus at his command post. To the right is the commander of the 76th Infantry Division, General Rodenburg and to the left is Elchlepp, chief of the operational section. (*NARA*)

Plate 20: In search of 'another decision'. G.K. Zhukov in the Stalingrad area, September 1942.

Plate 21: Colonel General Weichs (to the left), commander of Army Group B, in Stalingrad at the LI Corps' command post. Beside him are Paulus and Seydlitz (in the side-cap with a folder under his arm). 29 September 1942. (*NARA*)

Plate 22: Refugees from the combat zone. A photograph from a report by the Sixth Army's headquarters. (*NARA*)

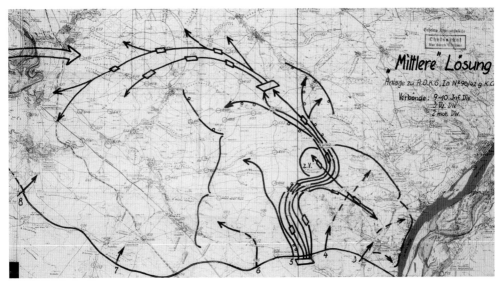

Plate 23: 'A middle decision'– a copy of a German map with the decision for an offensive to the north of Stalingrad.

Plate 24: Colonel Leontii Nikolaevich Gurt'ev, commander of the 308th Rifle Division.

Plate 25: War in the ruins of an industrial city. Soviet soldiers in position at the base of a gigantic destroyed smokestack in Stalingrad.

Plate 26: Yu.M. Maznyi, commander of the 120th Guards Rifle Regiment.

Plate 27: Colonel I.I. Lyudnikov, commander of the 138th Rifle Division.

Plate 28: At the 138th Rifle Division's command post. To the right is the commander, Colonel I.I. Lyudnikov. Opposite him from left to right are the division's military commissar, N.I. Titov, the chief of artillery, Lieutenant Colonel S.Ya. Tychinskii, and the chief of staff, Colonel V.I. Shuba.

Plate 29: I.M. Afonin commanded the 300th Rifle Division as a colonel. He later took part in the capture of Budapest.

Plate 30: 'The commissars' building': the administrative building of the 'Barricade' Factory, built at the beginning of the twentieth century for Vicker's Co. personnel.

Plate 31: An armoured launch – the workhorse of the Volga Military Flotilla. They were able to supply even the smallest bridgeheads in Stalingrad.

Plate 32: M.S. Shumilov, the commander of the 64th Army. This picture was taken after 1943, when epaulettes were introduced into the Red Army.

Plate 33: 'The hydraulic press'. A 152mm model 1909/30 howitzer from the 1st Artillery Division. (*TsAMO*)

Plate 34: A Churchill Mk III tank with the serial number T.31221R. This was one of the first tanks of this type to reach the USSR. It later served in the 47th Guards Heavy Tank Regiment around Stalingrad.

Plate 35: Saddles of the Sixth Army's killed and eaten horses. The Romanian cavalry that ended up in the 'cauldron' became a real gift for the soldiers of Paulus' army.

Plate 36: The most terrible enemy has fallen silent forever: a German 210mm howitzer abandoned in the 'cauldron'.

Plate 37: The monster's extracted teeth: German artillery abandoned in the Stalingrad 'cauldron'. In front is a sFH18 150mm heavy field howitzer. (*TsAMO*)

Plate 38: The victors. A group photo keepsake. These people will soon fan out along various fronts, carrying within themselves the knowledge that the Germans can be beaten.

The 26th Tank Corps' attack was the most powerful and vigorous. In a report by the German advisor with the Romanian 14th Infantry Division, it was noted that:

> Because of the fog, the artillery did not have the opportunity of firing on the tanks and suppressing their penetration. There were only six 7.5cm guns as effective anti-tank weapons in the division, but because of poor visibility and the attack's superior strength they were not in a condition to stop it. The 22nd Panzer Division's anti-tank battalion arrived too late and was unable to ease matters, as the collapse of the defence was fully under way.[2]

As a result, having defeated units of the enemy's 5th and 14th Infantry Divisions in its zone of movement, by dawn on 20 November the 26th Tank Corps had captured Novotsaritsynskii and Perelazovskii, where it routed the headquarters of the Romanian V Army Corps and captured a large amount of materiel. The tanks, upon reaching Perelazovskii, opened fire on the move, while the motorized infantry, by a rapid lunge, closed to small-arms range and enveloped Perelazovskii from the flanks and rear. The corps' attack was so overwhelming that the dazed enemy, having offered weak resistance, threw down their arms and began to surrender in groups. Only the 19th Tank Brigade, which was moving along the corps' left flank, was delayed by the enemy and was unable to link up with the corps in Perelazovskii until the morning of 21 November.

At the same time as the 26th Tank Corps was advancing rapidly, at 01.00 on 20 November the forward units of the 1st Tank Corps reached Ust'-Medveditskii (Peschanyi). However, an attempt to take it from the march suffered a defeat. The forward detachment fell back to a hollow north of the village. It was decided during the night to feel out the enemy with a reconnaissance. The enemy was the 22nd Panzer Division, which was moving up from the rear. One must say that Soviet intelligence was not able to determine in time the presence of the enemy's 22nd Panzer Division, and thus the collision with its units in the area of Peschanyi was to a certain extent a surprise.

If everything had gone according to plan then the division might not have ended up in the path of the Soviet tank corps. At first there weren't any kind of prerequisites for moving the army group's reserve toward the bridgehead at Serafimovich. At 09.00 on 19 November Heim, the commander of the XLVIII Panzer Corps, telephoned Army Group B and demanded that it immediately commit his panzer corps to the north-east toward Kletskaya. Heim justified his decision by the fact that a real danger to the Sixth Army's rear had arisen from Kletskaya. The army group chief of staff, von Sonderstern, agreed with the corps commander. At 09.30 the corps began to march toward Kletskaya, toward the axis of the South-western Front's supporting attack. However, at 10.45 Heim's corps received new orders, this time from the ground forces command: 'The offensive must be carried out not to the north-east, but to the north-west.' That is, the XLVIII Panzer Corps was redirected to the bridgehead at Serafimovich. The fact that all of these manoeuvres were carried out in a blizzard and along ice-covered roads only added to the acuteness of the soldiers' and officers' sensations. One has to say, however, that the supreme command made a correct decision and dispatched its most powerful reserve against the axis of the Soviet forces' main attack.

The activity of both sides' aviation on the first day of Operation Uranus was quite low, in view of the poor weather. The Soviet air force carried out only 44 sorties, chiefly in the

Kletskaya area. The VIII Air Corps carried out 120 sorties from airfields in the Karpovka area. Most of these were Stukas from the 2nd Assault Aircraft Squadron's first group.

It is traditional to describe the beginning of Uranus in bravura tones, although in fact what took place comes across in a somewhat different light. In a report, written in the 5th Tank Army on the heels of these events, it was noted: 'The rifle divisions, despite the well organized and conducted artillery offensive, were nevertheless unable independently to break through the forward edge of the defence and clear a path for the movement of the success development echelon.'[3]

The commitment of the tank corps into the fighting, and not in a 'clean' breach made by the infantry, led to quite significant losses. For example, on the first day of fighting the 1st Tank Corps lost forty-nine tanks and the 26th Tank Corps forty-six tanks. This accounted for about 30 per cent of their initial combat strength. Similar losses at the very beginning of the operation might have led to the loss of combat capability at the decisive moment the encirclement ring was being closed.

The second day of the 5th Tank Army's offensive was notable for the collision with the units of the XLVIII Panzer Corps, which were rushing about between the bridgeheads. At dawn on 20 November units of the 5th Tank Army resumed their offensive with the task of developing the first day's success and to destroy the Romanian Third Army together with units of the 21st Army.

The 1st Tank Corps, and the 8th Motorcycle Regiment and 8th Cavalry Corps which were following in its wake, was delayed before Ust'-Medveditskii (Peschanyi). A thick fog lay over everything. The weather was clearly not good for flying and the corps stationed its few motor vehicles, without dispersing them, in large masses in the open steppe. However, the same thick fog was also enveloping the enemy. Reconnaissance identified the enemy as 'the Romanian 1st Motorized Division's 6th Infantry Regiment, a blocking detachment up to a battalion in strength, consisting of Germans, up to three artillery battalions of various calibres in position, and up to 20 tanks'. It was decided to launch a frontal attack against such relatively weak forces. The reconnaissance did not report that the 22nd Panzer Division was located on the other side of the front.

The enemy's resistance was broken at midday; however, the offensive along the route indicated in the plan was now attended with great difficulties. Units of the 22nd Panzer Division fell back from Ust'-Medveditskii further to the south, consolidating on the heights south of the town. In order to advance further strictly according to plan the 1st Tank Corps, time after time, would have had to throw the enemy off each succeeding line, losing men and materiel. Romanenko had to order Butkov to turn and bypass the enemy's centre of resistance.

The 22nd Panzer Division subsequently fell back to the Medvezhii area. It should be noted that on 20 November it had not yet been surrounded. The division was fighting with open flanks, but there were no obstacles of any sort along its path of retreat to the west or south. With the onset of darkness, the corps' units were pulled out of the fighting and were supposed to move through Malaya Donshchinka and Bol'shaya Donshchinka to the area designated by the operational plan. Such a decision – bypassing the enemy's centre of resistance – was considered from the very beginning. They could have bypassed Peschanyi and hit the enemy holding it in the flank and rear. However, Butkov's corps rammed Peschanyi head-on, suffering personnel and equipment losses. The mission for the day was not fulfilled, and as early as the second day of the offensive the 1st Tank Corps was significantly behind schedule. According to the plan, it was to have broken through 25–30km south of the point where it was located on the evening of 20 November.

At least the 26th Tank Corps began 20 November well. Following the rapid seizure of Novo-Tsarintsynskii and Varlamovskii the corps' units encountered strong resistance in Perelazovskii. Here there followed a bold attack in the best traditions of the mobile formations. The tanks, having come up to Perelazovskii, opened fire from the march. The motorized infantry moved rapidly forward on trucks to within small-arms range, dismounted and began to envelop Perelazovskii from two sides, getting into the enemy's rear. Perelazovskii was taken by a vigorous attack. However, with this the day's success ended. The offensive on Zotovskii, which lay halfway to Kalach, did not take place. As was later written in a report by the headquarters of the 5th Tank Army: 'The 26th Tank Corps, intoxicated by success and the large amount of captured equipment, instead of moving forward and carrying out the day's task after turning over the area to the 119th Rifle Division, remained in Perelazovskii to await the 19th Tank Brigade and to count its spoils.'[4] The headquarters of the Romanian V Corps was in Perelazovskii, so it's likely that there was not much in the way of spoils. One may also call the refusal by commander of the 26th Tank Corps to attack in the flank and rear the group of forces delaying the advance of his neighbour, that is, the 1st Tank Corps, a serious mistake. However, to be fair, it should be said that there were good reasons for the delay in Perelazovskii. The neighbouring 1st Tank Corps had fallen well behind and a further advance, with open flanks, would have been risky. Rodin could have chosen not to do this and, speaking in general, had the right to do this. The commander of the 26th Tank Corps justified himself before the command for his stop in Perelazovskii with a nod toward his delayed neighbour.

Meanwhile, the 50th Guards and 119th Rifle Divisions, which were following in the wake of the tank corps, were subjected to attacks by the Romanian 1st Tank Division. It was seeking to break through and link up with the Germans' 22nd Panzer Division in Peschanyi. As a result, a regiment from the 50th Guards Rifle Division was thrown out of Zhirkov, while another, quite the opposite, took back Sredne-Tsaritsynskii, while a third held off an attack on Verkhne-Fominskii. The 119th Rifle Division's rear was also attacked in the Zhirkov area. It is possible that this explains the Romanian claims of having taken approximately 300 prisoners and destroying 60 motor vehicles. The losses in armoured equipment for the Romanian tank division amounted to twenty-five tanks, including four German and fourteen R-2s in the fighting. If the Romanian claim of prisoners and motor vehicles arouses doubts, then their claim to have destroyed sixty-two Soviet tanks seems completely unfounded. At that moment the tank corps had already moved far forward. However, the attempt by the Romanian tanks to break through gave birth to a certain amount of confusion and even panic at the tactical level. Colonel Kulagin, the commander of the 119th Rifle Division, reported to the headquarters of the 5th Tank Army that his division had been surrounded. For this Romanenko actually removed Kulagin from his post. In any case, the Romanians did not manage to break out to the west and the Romanian 1st Tank Division actually formed the western face of the planned 'cauldron' for the Romanian Third Army.

At that moment the Romanian units still had a chance to get out from under the attack by the 21st Army to the south. The counter-attacks by the Romanian 1st Tank Division prevented the 124th Rifle Division from linking up with units of the 21st Army and surrounding Dumitrescu's forces. Since the headquarters of the Romanian corps had been routed, General Lascar, the commander of the 6th Infantry Division and holder of the Knight's Cross for Sevastopol', took over command.

From the very beginning two divisions of Heim's corps had been operating without operational contact with each other. The Romanian 1st Tank Division's radio had been destroyed and the two formations ended up being divided as the result of the breakthrough by the 26th Tank Corps toward Perelazovskii. Instead of a flank attack, the 22nd Panzer Division was to enter the fighting in columns and in detail.

As early as the very beginning of the Soviet offensive, the Panzerwaffe[5] suffered failure. However, the Luftwaffe could still have transformed the Red Army's tactical success into an overall operational failure. Soviet aviation failed to operate at all on 20 November. That is, not a single sortie was noted. The Soviet pilots' opponents from the VIII Air Corps nevertheless made somewhat more than 100 sorties. Nevertheless, the activity of the German aviation had been sharply restricted by the poor weather. Aside from the absence of the possibility of influencing the course of combat operations, the weather hindered the evacuation of the airfields that ended up in the zone of the Soviet offensive. This led not only to the loss of planes, but also of valuable equipment, spare parts and engines. This later had a significant influence on the work of the Tatsinskaya and Morozovskaya air bases.

Weichs and Paulus take Countermeasures

At first the Sixth Army did not perceive the approaching danger. At 18.00 on 19 November the army command reported that it was planning to continue activities by reconnaissance elements in Stalingrad on 20 November.

However, an order by the commander of Army Group B, which was issued at 22.00, left no doubts as to the threat:

> The situation which is taking shape along the Romanian Third Army's front forces us to take radical measures for the purpose of very rapidly freeing up forces for covering the Sixth Army's flank and ensuring the security of its supply by railway along the sector Likhaya (south of Kamensk-Shakhtinskii) – Chir. In this regard, I order the following:
>
> 1. To immediately halt all offensive operations in Stalingrad, with the exception of actions by reconnaissance subunits, the information of which is necessary for the organization of defence.
> 2. The Sixth Army is to immediately detach two motorized formations (14th and 24th Panzer Divisions), one infantry division and, if possible, one headquarters (XIV Panzer Corps) and, also, as many anti-tank weapons as possible, and to concentrate this group of forces echeloned behind its left flank, for the purpose of launching an attack to the north-west or west.
>
> Signed: Baron von Weichs.[6]

Upon recovering from the first shock, the Sixth Army command displayed feverish activity to preserve the troops and to create jumping-off positions for a breakthrough out of the approaching 'cauldron'. At 14.45 on 20 November Paulus issued an order for forming a defensive line with its front facing west.

One has to acknowledge the coolness of the Sixth Army command. Decisions were rapidly made, but were completely logical. The Sixth Army's 'ace in the hole', the XIV

Panzer Corps, was to be removed from the front to the north of Stalingrad and shifted to the west. In one of Paulus's first orders following the start of Uranus, one can clearly perceive the desire to break out of the forming 'cauldron' – 'an offensive is called for from this line to the west'. But what is most interesting is that the designated positions were by no means located there where the front eventually stabilized along the western face of the 'cauldron'. The desire from the outset to rely on the old Soviet defensive line is absent in the order. It was planned to form a front to the west of the Don. The inhabited locales that were enumerated in the order – Sukhanov, Skvorin, Yeruslanovskii – were along the western bank of the Don to the north-east of Kalach. Kalach itself was to become an important staging post for the formations moving up to the new front. Paulus was evidently attempting to preserve for the trans-Don part of his army as much room as possible as the most favourable bridgehead for a breakout to the west.

However, the rapid development of events along the approaches to Kalach prevented the Sixth Army from forming a powerful bridgehead along the western bank of the Don. The XLVIII Panzer Corps, which had been drawn into a meeting engagement with the 5th Tank Army's corps, could not construct a stable defence. The attacking Soviet forces were, not without difficulty but quite rapidly, feeling out gaps in the enemy line.

The Soviet infantry's battle with the Romanian tank division continued on 21 November. The 50th Guards and 119th Rifle Divisions deployed with their front facing east and began to push the Romanians back from the road to Perelazovskii. In Perelazovskii itself a regiment from the 119th Rifle Division took up defensive positions to consolidate it. The 26th Tank Corps remained in Perelazovskii until 12.00. It's unclear whether the toting-up of the spoils continued for half a day or the corps was held up for some other more serious reasons. However, there were no major enemy forces along the corps' path. Thus when it set out from Perelazovskii at 13.00 Zotovkii, Kalmykov and Rozhki quickly fell under the treads of the Soviet tanks. Along the way, the Soviet tank troops routed the support elements of the units falling back before the 21st Army's front.

As opposed to its fortunate neighbour, the 1st Tank Corps on 21 November was unable to develop a vigorous offensive to the south toward Nizhne-Chirskaya, as was specified in the plan. By dawn on 21 November Butkov's corps had reached Bol'shaya Donshchinka. Here it ran into the same 22nd Panzer Division, which had taken up the defence. The right flank of the German formation's positions was hanging in the air in this area. All attempts by Butkov's tank troops to take Bol'shaya Donshchinka from the march were unsuccessful. Having established a cover, the corps deployed backwards and took a circuitous route through Perelazovskii, which had already been captured by its neighbour, and by the close of the day had reached Lipovskii. This was the same inhabited locale that, according to the plan, should have been captured as early as the evening of the offensive's first day. In the end, it was only on the third day of fighting that the 1st Tank Corps occupied this area and up to 24.00 was refuelling and bringing up its lagging vehicles. The 8th Cavalry Corps and the 8th Motorcycle Regiment got stuck together with the 1st Tank Corps. The latter was even temporarily pulled into the reserve in light of the hazy prospects of its commitment into the breakthrough and the fallen snow, which made the movement of motorcycles difficult.

On the night of 21/22 November Romanenko got a chewing-out from Vatutin. The *front* commander pointed out to the commander of the 5th Tank Army 'the lack of fulfilment of its tasks by the army and the unsatisfactory work by the 1st Tank Corps, the 8th Cavalry

Corps and the 119th Rifle Division'. At the same time, Vatutin established the missions for the following day:

1st Tank Corps – to capture Surovikino;
26th Tank Corps – to capture Kalach;
8th Motorcycle Regiment – to capture Oblivskaya;
8th Cavalry Corps – to reach the Osinovskaya – Novo-Stepanovskii area.

This order changed the tasks of the 5th Tank Army's mobile formations regarding what had been in the operational plan. The 8th Cavalry Corps was directed further to the south and the 1st Tank Corps was to be shifted from the Don to the Chir.

During the day on 22 November the 1st Tank Corps finally gained operational freedom. As one can see from the corps commander's order, in which the words 'Taking into consideration the enemy's disorganization and confusion, counting on panic', the Soviet command at that moment underestimated the enemy somewhat. Butkov spread his corps out in a fan along a front of more than 40km from Surovikino on the Chir to Pyatiizbyanskii on the Don. At the same time, only a single battalion of motorized riflemen was dispatched to Surovikino, which had been designated by Vatutin as the *schwerpunkt*.[7] The battalion attacked Surovikino at noon on 22 November, but was unsuccessful. Today we can say who was opposing the Soviet units at this moment. This was the Estonian 36th Police Battalion (the so-called *Schuma*), numbering about 450 men.[8] It had initially been dispatched to the Stalino (Donetsk) area to carry out its usual duties. However, due to the Soviet offensive, the collaborationists were sent to the front line. On 22 November they were fired upon at Surovikino station, where they detrained and took up defensive positions. If they had been attacked by tanks, the Estonian policemen would probably not have held out for an hour. Following the failure to seize the station in a 'cavalry lunge', the battalion of Soviet motorized riflemen first took up defensive positions and later gave up altogether the idea of storming the objective assigned by *front* headquarters. As noted in the corps headquarters' report, 'With the onset of darkness, it packed up and left'.

Meanwhile, the corps' units, which were scattered over a broad area, reached the Tuzov – Lysov area by the end of the day, although it was planned to reach this area as early as the second day of the operation. The main task of the day had not actually been carried out. This was the result of the back-and-forth between the new and old missions. The operational plan had directed the 1st Tank Corps to forcing the Don. The new objective of Surovikino, as ordered by Vatutin, lay along the Chir River. It is also possible that Butkov, due to inertia, was striving to break through over the Don, leaving Surovikino for later. It was precisely he who dispatched one of the brigades to Pyatiizbyanskii on the Don.

There is, however, one element that may serve as an explanation for the lack of attention paid by the commander of the 1st Tank Corps to Surovikino. The conversation between Butkov and Zhukov (as told by Butkov) not long before the beginning of Operation Uranus has been cited above. Zhukov, I should remind you, was orienting him regarding the German reserves in Nizhne-Chirskaya and the necessity of protecting the flank of Rodin's corps. The actions of the commander of the 1st Tank Corps on 22 November show that he was obviously gravitating toward Nizhne-Chirskaya, while also striving not to get separated from the 26th Tank Corps, the flank of which Zhukov himself had made him responsible.

The Romanian Third Army in the 'Cauldron'

On the offensive's third day, 21 November, the encirclement of the main forces of the Romanian Third Army was completed by the link-up of the 5th Tank and 21st Armies. The overall leadership of the encircled forces fell on the shoulders of General Lascar. The Third Army commander inquired of Antonescu[9] about subsequent activities (having in mind to get permission for a breakout for Lascar's group), but were told to obey orders from Army Group B.

The first surrender proposal to the Romanians came from the Soviet command at 02.30 on 22 November and was rejected. At first they sought to act like Germans. Five Romanian Ju 52s landed within the lines of the encircled troops and delivered ammunition and food and took away sixty wounded. However, the capabilities of the Romanian air force were less than modest. They were unable to support a real air bridge. The encircled Romanians had no more than forty rounds per gun and many soldiers had not eaten for three days.

The commanders of the encircled Romanian formations, Generals Lascar, Mazarini and Sion, made the decision during a meeting in Golovskii to break out at 22.00 on 22 November. But before long the attacking Soviet rifle formations interfered in the plans for a breakout. Soviet infantry attacked Golovskii from the west and General Lascar was taken prisoner. The loss of the 6th Infantry Division's headquarters resulted in the loss of the encircled units' radio communications with HQ. The last centres of resistance in the area of the encircled Romanian forces were destroyed by 25 November. Soviet forces took 27,000 prisoners.

The Crossing at Kalach is Seized

On the night of 21/22 November the 26th Tank Corps continued its dash toward Kalach. A forward detachment of two motorized rifle companies from the 14th Motorized Rifle Brigade, five tanks from the 157th Tank Brigade and one armoured car was dispatched to the bridge over the Don. The detachment commander was the commander of the 14th Motorized Rifle Brigade, Lieutenant Colonel Filippov. When at about 06.00 on 22 November the detachment reached the bridge over the Don at Kalach, the German guard of the bridge could not believe that enemy tanks could appear so far behind the front line. By the time they recovered it was already too late. The Germans did not have time to either blow up the bridge or to halt the T-34s approaching it. Dërr supplies an explanation for the ease with which the crossing was achieved: 'Another Russian tank unit reached the bridge and captured it from the march without a fight, because the bridge guards took it for a German training unit.'[10] On the whole, the episode was quite characteristic of manoeuvre operations. A breakthrough nearly always took troops guarding bridges by surprise and they would fall intact into the hands of the attacker. This was an enormous stroke of luck. The success of the South-western and Stalingrad fronts' offensive along converging axes depended to a great extent on the successful forcing of the Don, which divided the *fronts*.

Meanwhile, during the day on 22 November the 26th Tank Corps' main forces had been delayed along the approaches to the crossing along the line of the 'Victory of October' and 'Ten Years Since October' state farms. Here the soldiers and commanders of Rodin's corps encountered the ghosts of the summer's battles. About fifty knocked-out T-34s and T-60s, powdered with snow, stood on Height 162.9. Some of these were now being used by the Germans as firing points. Only in November 1942 the enemies had changed places: Soviet units were breaking through to Kalach, while the Germans were attempting to hold it. A serious advantage was that the forward detachment already held the crossing. However, it was surrounded and they could not break through to it for the time being. The 157th Tank Brigade's attempt to take the height by brute force was unsuccessful, so it was decided to bypass it from the right. By 14.00 the ghost-haunted height had been taken and the German units defending here fell back along the Don to the north, toward Rychkovskii. In the meantime, by 20.00 the 19th Tank Brigade had crossed the Don and concentrated in the woods north-east of Kalach.

The fight for the town of Kalach took place on 23 November. The defence was felt out by reconnaissance during the night. At 07.00 Kalach was attacked from the north by the 19th Tank Brigade. At 10.00 the tanks broke into the town, but the brigade's motorized riflemen were halted by fire from four earth and wooden pillboxes on its outskirts. The commitment of the corps' motorized rifle brigade also failed to bring success. The commander of the corps' 157th Tank Brigade pulled his tanks back to the height along the western bank of the Don and crossed the motorized riflemen over the ice. Accurate fire on Kalach and an attack from the rear forced the Germans to waver and begin to rush about. The garrison of Kalach did not withstand the latest attack and by 14.00 (by 16.00, according to other data) the town was entirely in the hands of Soviet forces. Numerous motor vehicles, tractors and other equipment in the town became the spoils of the Soviet troops. About 1,500 prisoners of war were also freed. However, their first stories somewhat darkened the joy of victory. According to the liberated prisoners, 'On the 20th and 21st [November], up to 100 tanks crossed over to the right bank of the Don. It is not known in what direction they went. They came from the Stalingrad area'.[11] A hundred German tanks in the rear, between the Don and the Chir, forced one to be careful. However, it should be noted that there was not this number of tanks in the combat groups dispatched by Paulus to Kalach. The fact that at that moment only thirty-five tanks were left in the 26th Tank Corps added a certain piquancy to these testimonies by the former prisoners of war. The corps made it to the offensive's final goal like a spent bullet. If the Germans had had sufficient forces in the Kalach area for establishing a secure defence, then Operation Uranus would have been on the brink of disaster.

From 04.00 on 24 November the 26th Tank Corps was to be transferred to the 21st Army. A division of missions had taken place between the 5th Tank Army along the external front and the 21st Army on the internal one.

The Marhabal of the Small 'Cauldron'

In the famous double-encirclement battle of Cannae in 216 BC, the commanders Marhabal[12] and Hasdrubal[13] commanded the right and left flanks of Hannibal's[14] forces, respectively. The 3rd Cavalry Corps, which Yeremenko had proposed employing for a lunge toward Kalach in his message to the *Stavka* on 6 October, nevertheless managed to take part in Operation Uranus. Of course, the task given to it was far more realistic than that proposed by the commander of the Stalingrad Front. It was planned to employ the cavalry in an offensive from the bridgehead at Kletskaya together with A.G. Kravchenko's 4th Tank Corps. They were supposed to carry out the same task as that of the troops of the Carthaginian commander Marhabal – to become the right flank of the 'Cannae' for the trans-Don group of forces of Paulus's army.

After nearly a month of fighting near the semaphore, the 4th Tank Corps had been pulled into the reserve and was replenishing its forces. By the start of the counteroffensive around Stalingrad General Kravchenko's corps was already in good shape. See table.

Table 38: Combat-Ready Tanks in the 4th Tank Corps Before the Start of Operation Uranus.[15]

Brigade	KVs	T-34s	T-70s	Total
45th Tank	22	–	26	48
102nd Tank	–	30	18	48
69th Tank	–	28	19	47
Total	22	58	63	143

The Soviet command logically concluded that there was no reason to expend mobile formations in the formation of the encirclement of the Romanian Third Army. Thus the 4th Tank and 3rd Guards Cavalry Corps were given the task of being the northern 'pincer' for the encirclement of the Sixth Army's trans-Don group of forces. The standard formation was adopted – 'the thread behind the needle' – with the tank corps in front and the cavalry corps behind it.

The 293rd and 176th Rifle Divisions were to punch through a breach in the Romanian forces' defence. At 07.00 on 19 November the roar of artillery announced the start of the 21st Army's offensive. Following a 50-minute artillery preparation, the infantry rose to the attack. However, the rifle units were unable to fully break through the enemy's defences. At 12.00 on the operation's first day the 4th Tank Corps was committed to complete the crushing of the Romanian forces. Having overcome the remnants of the enemy's defence without too much effort, the corps entered the breach in an 8km zone and rushed to the south-east, toward the Don, in two columns. Losses for the first day of the offensive were five KVs, nineteen T-34s and three T-70s. It's most likely that they fell victim to Simons's battle group, which was moving up to Kletskaya. By evening Kravchenko's tank troops reached the Manoilin–Maiorovskii area, having covered half of the way from Kletskaya to the Don. Having fully carried out the day's assignment, the tank corps spent 20 November putting itself in order and took on ammunition and refuelled. The 3rd Guards Cavalry Corps entered the breach behind the 4th Tank Corps. Pliev's[16] horsemen were somewhat delayed by the fact that the passages through the minefields made by the rifle units were not marked and it was necessary to feel their way through with their own engineers.

At 07.00 on 21 November the 4th Tank Corps continued its offensive. On this day there appeared on the western bank of the Don the first detachments of mobile formations from those dispatched by Paulus on 20 November (see above). However, they were unable to offer serious resistance and by 15.00 Kravchenko's corps had reached the Don from the west. Losses for the day were three KVs, three T-34s and ten T-70s. Their trophies for the day were 550 motor vehicles, an airfield with 25 planes and several depots, including one with captured weapons, in which 150 heavy Maxim machine guns were found.

Insofar as the 3rd Guards Cavalry Corps had also begun to collide with the enemy's detachments, consisting of tanks, during the course of their advance, Pliev's horsemen were allotted a company of T-70s and a platoon of T-34s, which accompanied them as far as the Don River. The cavalry reached the Don on 22 November, a day later than the tank troops.

However, the bringing up of a sufficiently numerous cavalry corps significantly reinforced the group of Soviet forces along the western bank of the Don.

The success of the crossing at Kalach is the most famous but not the sole incident of Soviet tank troops seizing crossings from the march during the November counteroffensive around Stalingrad. Kravchenko's tank troops distinguished themselves on the evening of 22 November, when the forward detachment for seizing a crossing successfully carried out its assignment and captured the crossing at Rubezhinskii, to the north of Kalach. The strategy chosen by Paulus of holding a bridgehead along the western bank of the Don by dispatching detachments from the mobile units was working against him. The crossings, despite the risk of their being captured, were not blown up, because units of the Sixth Army's panzer and motorized units, moving from east to west, were supposed to cross them. Following the seizure, the traffic moved in the opposite direction, and by 10.00 on 23 November the 4th Tank Corps had concentrated along the eastern bank of the Don.

Hasdrubal's 'Small Cauldron' Suffers a Reverse

Not all of the Soviet attacks were as successful as the attacks by the 21st and 5th Tank Armies. It was planned to employ the Don Front's single tank corps to split the enemy group of forces being encircled through a vigorous breakthrough along the bank of the Don. A 'Cannae' had been prepared for the trans-Don group of Paulus's army, and the role of Hasdrubal's cavalry was given to I.V. Galanin's[17] 24th Army.

Following the unsuccessful offensives of September 1942, by November 1942 the 16th Tank Corps had almost completely restored its combat capability. It numbered 5,654 men, 115 tanks, ten armoured personnel carriers, six armoured cars, 500 motor vehicles, and 30 motorcycles. The strength of the 16th Tank Corps' tank park by the start of the offensive is shown in the table.

Table 41: The Condition of the 16th Tank Corps' Tanks by 23 November 1942.[18]

Brigade	KVs	T-34s	T-70s	T-60s	Total
107th Tank	29/32*	–	–	11/17	40/49
109th Tank	6/8	17/19	–	14/14	37/41
164th Tank	–	20/28	5/10	3/12	28/50

* The figure in the numerator denotes combat-ready vehicles and the denominator the total number of tanks.

In November 1942 T-60 tanks looked, at best, ridiculous, but they were subsequently employed in the 16th Tank Corps as armoured ammunition carriers for KV and T-34 tanks. The allotment of radio tanks for artillery spotters was a great step forward. They were put through training and so the tanks in the offensive at least had the theoretical capability to get operational artillery support. It was planned to commit General Maslov's corps into the breach. According to the 24th Army's offensive plan, the 214th, 120th and 49th Rifle Divisions were to break through the enemy defences, while the 84th Rifle Division was to develop their success. The time for the 16th Tank Corps would come following the crushing of the enemy's defence throughout the entire depth. It was supposed to break through to the crossing and cut off the route to link up with the main forces of the Sixth Army's trans-

Don group of forces (XI Army Corps). The enemy of the 24th Army's formations was the 76th Infantry Division – a veteran of the battles for the 'land bridge'.

The 24th Army attacked on 22 November, but had no success and did not reach the line of the tank corps' commitment into the breach. The mission was altered. At 07.00 on 23 November two of the 16th Tank Corps' brigades attacked with the 24th Army's rifle formations. The corps was actually becoming a means for direct infantry support. The unpleasantness began as early as the first hours of the offensive. Passages through their own minefields were not designated properly. In conditions of flat terrain, without distinguishing features, the tanks missed the designated passages. As a result, the corps' brigades lost fourteen tanks in Soviet minefields and another twelve in German ones. The Germans' anti-tank artillery burned three KVs, two T-34s and two T-60s. Overall losses for the first day of the offensive were fifty-five vehicles (including those knocked out), which was nearly half of the tank park's initial strength.

The subsequent development of events calls forth a persistent felling of *déjà vu* regarding the Stalingrad Front's September offensives. At 08.00 on 24 November the 16th Tank Corps' remaining fifty-nine tanks attacked the enemy at top speed, firing from guns and machine guns. The motorized rifle units had been cut off by enemy fire. The radio tanks with their artillery spotters had been knocked out and there was no precise coordination with the artillery. Painfully familiar words were written regarding the 'queen of the battlefield' in the corps' report: 'The rifle formations' infantry did not rise up and remained lying down in front of the enemy's barbed wire obstacles.'[19] Losses during the second day of the offensive amounted to three KVs and four T-34s burned and seven KVs, three T-34s and two T-60s blown up on mines. Overall losses for the day amounted to thirty-three vehicles. As opposed to manoeuvre battles, the repair shops did not get flustered and thirteen tanks were returned to service on 24 November. This did not compensate for the heavy losses of the two preceding days, although it enabled them to keep the corps afloat. On 25 November thirty-one tanks took part in the offensive. On 26 November the corps' remaining tanks, numbering seventeen vehicles, were combined into a single brigade (the 164th). The composite brigade fought during the subsequent days, in direct support of the infantry. By the evening of 30 November only two T-34s and two T-60s remained. In a word, everything was very similar to the offensive two months before. Only the losses from minefields (their own and the enemy's) introduced an element of variety.

One of the chief reasons for the 24th Army's failures was the inaccurate definition of the outline of the enemy's forward line. Accordingly, the artillery preparation was carried out against positions occupied by combat security forces and not by the defending German units' main forces. What it interesting is that among the officers in the Don Front there was a man who was sounding the alarm and saying that the outline of the enemy's front line had been incorrectly delineated. This was Colonel Kosogorskii from a group of the Red Army General Staff's officers. As early as 10–12 days before the start of the operation, he was trying to prove with data from agent intelligence (which had gone through the area of the forthcoming offensive several times) that the enemy had either combat security forces or a dummy front line along the sector of the planned breakthrough. Kosogorskii took his point of view all the way up to the commander of the 24th Army, Major General Galanin, the 24th Army's chief of staff, Colonel Verfolovich, the member of the 24th Army's military council, Colonel Gavrilov, the commander of the 24th Army's artillery, Major General

Glebov, and the commander of the 16th Tank Corps, Major General Maslov. But they did not believe him. The headquarters of the 16th Tank Corps used aerial photo reconnaissance from the *front's* intelligence section of 4 November 1942, which did not reveal the enemy's true situation by the start of the Soviet offensive. A new period of the war was beginning, in which the Germans attempted to move their forces out from under the blow of the Soviet artillery preparation, while the Soviet command, on the other hand, sought to catch the enemy's soldiers and officers in their positions and destroy the greater part of them with the first blow.

The partial success in the struggle with the Sixth Army's trans-Don group of forces was achieved only due to the brilliant lunge to the Don by Kravchenko and Pliev's corps from the bridgehead at Kletskaya. Having seized a bridgehead on the left bank of the Don and having brought up cavalry to the river, the group from the two corps began to advance along both banks of the Don to the north-east, toward the forces of the Don Front. The threat of cutting off the crossings by this manoeuvre forced Paulus to make the decision to evacuate the XI Army Corps from the right bank of the Don. The cutting off of a large piece of the Sixth Army and its separate 'eating' did not take place. Quite the opposite: by means of pulling the XI Corps back, the Germans had at their disposal formations for building the stable western face of the 'cauldron'.

Chapter 24

Mechanized Pincers

A distinguishing feature of the Soviet 'Cannae's' southern 'pincer' was the large proportion of mobile formations. The weakness of the Stalingrad Front shock group's communications did not allow them to hope to break the enemy's defence with a mass of infantry with the subsequent commitment of tank formations into the breach. The accumulation of large masses of infantry and artillery in the 51st and 57th Armies' sectors and their subsequent supply with everything necessary was impossible. Thus along this axis the Soviet command relied on the mechanized corps.

The overall strength of all the 57th Army's units on 20 November 1942 was 39,400 men.[1] Of this number, 20,180 men were in the rifle units and 12,337 were part of the 13th Mechanized Corps.[2] The overall strength of the 51st Army on 20 November 1942 was 44,446 men.[3] Of this number, 15,651 men were in the 4th Mechanized Corps and 24,026 in the army's rifle formations. Thus the number of officers and men among the mobile troops of both armies was quite comparable to the strength of their rifle troops.

Aside from the 13th Mechanized Corps the 57th Army's tank troops also included the 90th and 235th Tank Brigades. The first included three KVs, fourteen T-34s and nine T-70s, while the second included twenty-six KVs and two T-34s. It was planned to employ these tanks exclusively for direct infantry support. Part of the 4th Mechanized Corps' forces was also included among them.

The story of the employment of tanks from freshly-formed mechanized corps as props for the rifle units deserves a separate description. On 17 November 1942, a few days before the offensive, Yeremenko approached Zhukov: 'I request permission to employ two of Comrade Vol'skii's regiments, and he will be compensated with the arrival [of the tanks].' Vasilevskii replied: 'The *Stavka* of the Supreme High Command orders you to take all measures for the most rapid transfer of independent tank regiments to the 51st Army and only in an extreme case authorizes you to employ Vol'skii's two tank regiments with infantry, but not at the expense of the mechanized brigade's regiments.'

To judge by this exchange, the 4th Mechanized Corps and the 13th Mechanized Corps were handled in a similar way. Tanks were taken from both formations. But as opposed to the 4th Mechanized Corps, there were no independent tank regiments in the 13th Mechanized Corps. Thus despite the ban on employing the mechanized brigades' tank regiments of the corps for breaking through the defence, they were activated as a means for direct support of the 57th Army's infantry.

The Stalingrad Front's offensive flowed like a wave from the right wing to the left. The first to attack was the 51st Army. The artillery preparation in the army's zone began at 07.30 and at 08.30 the army's units attacked and by 10.00 had broken in to the positions of the enemy's forward edge along all the attack sectors. The attack landed on the boundary of the Romanian 1st and 18th Infantry Divisions, which were occupying defensive positions along a broad front.

The tanks that had been removed from the 4th Mechanized Corps were employed for direct infantry support. The 158th Tank Regiment supported the attack by the 126th Rifle

Division and the 55th Independent Tank Regiment supported the 302nd Rifle Division. By 11.30 the mission had been carried out: the enemy's defence had been penetrated throughout its entire depth. One has to admit that the results of the tank regiments' work were impressive. On 20 November the 158th Tank Regiment destroyed eight guns and twenty-three wood and earth pillboxes along with their garrisons, while the 55th Tank Regiment destroyed twelve guns and forty-two pillboxes. Eighteen anti-tank guns were also captured. Losses for the 158th Tank Regiment were eight T-34s (five burned and three blown up on mines) and four T-70s, plus six T-34s that got stuck in a bog, while the 55th Tank Regiment lost two T-34s and three T-70s to enemy fire and three stuck in a bog.

At 11.20 on 20 November the 4th Mechanized Corps received orders to enter the breach. At 13.30 a mass of tanks and motor vehicles went into action. The corps moved into a clean breakthrough and the columns advanced without meeting resistance. By 19.30 units of Vol'skii's corps had reached the area of the Plodovitoe road junction. There were no local inhabitants in Plodovitoe and there was no one to guide them, while the bare steppe offered almost no orientation, forcing the mechanized brigades to feel their way forward. By dawn on 21 November units of Vol'skii's corps reached the Stalingrad – Sal'sk railway along the sector from Abangerovo station to Tinguta station.

The corps' main forces fell behind and thus Abganerovo station was taken by units of the corps' headquarters, the 44th Armoured Battalion (BA-64 armoured cars) and the 61st Motorcycle Battalion. A train with troops and artillery and depots, motor vehicles and other equipment was seized at the station. Among the captured prizes were also 150 Soviet-made guns, which had most likely been captured by the Germans during the defensive phase of the battle. Upon turning Abganerovo over to units of the 4th Cavalry Corps, the mechanized brigades of Vol'skii's corps continued the offensive. Tinguta and Abganerovo stations, the '74-kilometre' rail siding, and Zety were captured at midday. During 20–21 November the 4th Mechanized Corps captured ten tanks, 44 guns, 600 motor vehicles, and about 700 prisoners. The corps' own losses were sixteen killed and forty-five wounded.

The next to attack was the 57th Army. The artillery preparation here began at 09.30, or two hours later than its neighbour. At 10.30 the army attacked and as early as 12.00 the enemy's forward edge had been broken through. The attack hit the Romanian 2nd Infantry Division, which was defending along an 18km front. The first to attack were the 57th Army's rifle units, with support from tank brigades and tank regiments. The 169th Rifle Division attacked jointly with the 90th Tank Brigade. The offensive was no walk in the park. The Germans' operational reserve along this axis was the 29th Motorized Division. On the first day of the Soviet offensive they were preparing to dispatch it north to be subordinated to the XLVIII Panzer Corps. However, the beginning of the Soviet offensive to the south of Stalingrad forced them to throw the division into a counteroffensive. Upon seeing the tanks, the 169th Rifle Division's units began to fall back, but the 90th Tank Brigade's tanks saved the day, knocking out several enemy tanks. However, the Soviet forces' subsequent advance was halted. On 20 November the 169th Rifle Division lost 93 men killed and 257 wounded. The 90th Tank Brigade lost two T-34s burned and three KVs and one T-34 knocked out, while one T-34 and one T-70 were lost to mines. The 57th Army's other formations encountered less resistance. The 422nd Rifle Division lost seven men killed and 129 wounded, while the 143rd Rifle Brigade had seven men killed and 174 wounded.

If the 169th Rifle Division encountered resistance from enemy reserves in the form of the 29th Motorized Division, then a somewhat unexpected obstacle arose on the 422nd Rifle

Division's path. Upon receiving the signal 'Attack', the 176th Tank Regiment moved into the attack together with the 422nd Rifle Division's infantry. By 13.00 the enemy's defence had been broken through, but a blow followed from an unexpected direction. Following the breakthrough of the defence, the tank regiment ran into mines that had previously been laid (during the defensive phase of the battle) and remained in the rear of the Romanian forces. As a result, nineteen T-34s and three T-70s were lost. Losses to the enemy's anti-tank defence were one T-70 burned and one T-34 knocked out. Thus on the first day of the offensive the regiment was deprived of twenty-four tanks of the twenty-eight present at the start of the offensive. The regiment's participation in the Stalingrad Front's offensive was interrupted. Moreover, the 13th Mechanized Corps' 61st Mechanized Brigade, to which this regiment belonged, had lost its combat capabilities.

However, the chief figure in the 57th Army's offensive was the 13th Mechanized Corps. It was committed into the breakthrough on orders from the commander of the 57th Army at 13.30 on 20 November 1942. Units of the 29th Motorized Division, which had temporarily halted the Soviet infantry's offensive, were thrown out of their positions. Tanaschishin's attacking corps cut the railway to Stalingrad and was advancing further toward Nariman.

The 13th Tank Corps and the 169th Rifle Division, along with the 90th Tank Brigade, repulsed the last counter-attacks by the 29th Motorized Division on the approaches to Nariman. The Germans were thrown out of Nariman on 21 November. Dërr writes that 'The Fourth Panzer Army threw its reserve, the 29th Motorized Division, into the fighting. It initially restored the situation, but was subsequently unable to hold its positions.'[4] The 57th Army's forces were actually attacking along almost exactly the same route as Hoth had advanced on Stalingrad in August 1942.

At night on 22 November the 4th Mechanized Corps received an order from the deputy commander of the Stalingrad Front, M.M. Popov, to seize Sovetskii by the close of the day and push a forward detachment to Karpovka. At that moment the corps was moving forward blindly, in the literal sense of that word. There was no information arriving about the enemy along the axis of the offense either from the headquarters of the 51st Army or the staff of the Stalingrad Front. Requests for aerial reconnaissance were not met and because of the poor weather aviation was not operating. The corps had to rely on its own resources, dispatching reconnaissance detachments along all axes on motorcycles and in BA-64 armoured cars. Communications were also established with its neighbour on the right – the 13th Mechanized Corps. This cleared up the situation to an insignificant degree: sketchy information was received about the sector to the right of the offensive zone. There were simply no neighbours to the left, just the seemingly endless steppe. In such a situation a counterblow might follow from any direction. The 'fog of war' lay heavily over the battlefield. It remained to take all precautionary measures and wish on a lucky star. Vol'skii moved up a strong flank guard to the flanks and pulled the 60th Mechanized Brigade into the reserve.

Before long the already difficult situation was exacerbated by interference from above. Upon the approach of the corps' headquarters to Verkhne-Tsaritsinskii a plane delivered an order from the commander of the Stalingrad Front, Yeremenko, with the mission of seizing Staryi Rogachik, Novyi Rogachik, Karpovskaya and Karpovka. This would have materially changed the corps' initial task. Now it was supposed to turn away from its rendezvous point with the South-western Front at Kalach and attack into the rear of the Sixth Army's forces around Stalingrad. To be exact, the corps was to turn around to crush the Sixth Army's rapidly-building defence facing west.

Literally within half an hour following the plane's arrival, the deputy commander of the 51st Army, Colonel Yudin, arrived at the corps' headquarters by car from Yeremenko. The commander of the 4th Mechanized Corps was presented with an order by the commander of the 51st Army (to which it was operationally subordinated), confirming the mission assigned earlier. The mechanized corps was to seize Sovetskii and reach the line Karpovka – Marinovka, that is, approximately the line of the railway from Stalingrad to Kalach. Left with two orders in his hands, Vol'skii made the compromise decision and turned the 59th Mechanized Brigade on Karpovka. The attack against Karpovka had no result – the mobile units dispatched by Paulus had occupied the old Soviet fortifications. The remaining units of the 4th Mechanized Corps were moving on Sovetskii, carrying out the previous mission.

Sovetskii was finally captured by 12.20 on 22 November by the 36th Mechanized Brigade together with the 59th Mechanized Brigade's 20th Tank Regiment. Auto repair shops and the corps' spoils were located in the town. Depots with food, munitions and fuel were also captured. With the capture of Sovetskii the Sixth Army's communications were cut with the rear along the railway.

It is interesting to note that the 4th Mechanized Corps received its orders from communications officers. Moreover, the orders from different levels contradicted each other. In accordance with Russian historical tradition, it has been usual to angrily condemn the employment of communications officers in the summer of 1941 and to even paint them as one of the reasons for the catastrophe that occurred. However, this is an obvious case of putting the cart before the horse. Communications officers were employed successfully in the Red Army's successful operations. Corps were dispatched by the command to the necessary point without any particular problems and without the ideologically-approved radio communications.

The growth of the threat from the south was reducing the range of decisions enabling the Sixth Army to avoid a disaster. The first failures were already forcing them to think harder. The seizure of the bridge at Kalach and Rubezhnyi meant the failure of Paulus's plan to hold a major bridgehead on the western bank of the Don. The necessity of having to form yet another front to the south-west of Stalingrad would lead to the dispersal of the already scarce mobile reserves. If in his order of 20 November Paulus intended an offensive to the west, then on 22 November he was already proposing a breakout along the southern front. The western bank of the Don, which really dominated the eastern bank, represented a favourable position for defending with its front facing east. It was problematical whether this defence could be broken by mobile formations, while it would take a lot of time to bring up infantry divisions. On 22 November Paulus flew into the 'cauldron' from his headquarters which was located before this in Nizhne-Chirskaya. Schmidt, the Sixth Army's chief of staff, left with him.

As before, examples of both a successful defence and the successful preservation of the encircled troops' combat capability loomed before the supreme command of the German army and Hitler personally. The minuses of an immediate breakout ('heavy losses and, in particular, materiel losses'), which had been honestly pointed out by Weichs and Paulus, appeared to be a greater evil than the Sixth Army holding its positions in encirclement in the Stalingrad area.

Before long the threat of encirclement became a reality. At 16.00 on 23 November units of the 4th Mechanized Corps linked up with the 26th Tank Corps in the area of Kalach and Sovetskii. Before long the 4th Tank Corps' brigades arrived at Sovetskii. The

South-western and Stalingrad Fronts had securely linked up with each other, closing the encirclement ring. Now all communications linking the Sixth Army with Army Group B's main forces had been cut.

During the first days following the encirclement, Paulus insistently sought permission to break out of the 'cauldron' and abandon Stalingrad. At 01.15 on 24 November the commander of the Sixth Army sent Hitler a new radiogram with a proposal to break out. November 22nd was one of the decisive moments which determined the fate of Paulus's army. Hitler's order to Paulus to remain in Stalingrad and await a relief attack was one of the fateful mistakes of the German leadership which, in the final analysis, led to the collapse of the Third Reich. In this regard, it is worth pausing on the prelude to this decision. News about the breakthrough of Soviet tanks into the rear of the Sixth Army found Hitler in the Berghof, his mountain residence in southern Bavaria. Contrary to the widespread opinion that Göring[5] personally promised to supply the Sixth Army by air, the first Luftwaffe representative to arrive at the Berghof on 20 November was Hans Jeschonnek, the chief of the Luftwaffe general staff. Göring was 'too busy' to take part in the meeting – he was at an oil conference at Carinhall outside Berlin. Hitler explained to Jeschonnek that the Sixth Army would be cut off for some time while a new army group was being organized under Manstein for its relief. The Führer then demanded an answer regarding the possibility of supplying the Sixth Army by air. It was Hitler's habit to insist on an immediate answer and he very rarely gave anyone time to think the situation over and to calculate. Jeschonnek confidently replied that if bombers could be brought in and airfields prepared accordingly, then supply by air would be possible. He also cited the experience of the previous winter campaign, pointing out that the Luftwaffe had already supplied 100,000 men in the 'cauldron' around Demyansk. Hitler heard what he wanted to hear – abandoning Stalingrad was not part of his plans. Calmed by this reply, he ordered Paulus to remain in Stalingrad and wait and Manstein to prepare a relief attack. Actually, all of the decisions had been made before Hitler discussed for the first time the situation with Göring. Only on 22 November did Hitler and Göring meet. Actually, Hitler already had already made his decision and the Reichsmarshall could only agree with it. Also, while lacking any kind of figures regarding the necessary volume of cargo to be delivered to Stalingrad and the number of planes which could be brought in for an 'air bridge', Göring replied: 'Yes, the Luftwaffe can do this.' Hitler, having made one of the most important decisions determining the course of the war, left by train from the Berghof for the *Wolfschanze* ('Wolf's Lair'), his headquarters in East Prussia. Göring, in turn, left for Paris for a very important meeting with art dealers.

Thus from the very beginning one of the important factors for making a decision was the absence of any kind of calculations. When the first decisions were made for organizing an 'air bridge', its capabilities were not correlated with the volume of cargo necessary for the Sixth Army. Strict calculations show that in order to supply 250,000 men, 1,800 guns and 10,000 motor vehicles, not counting tanks, 946 tons per day were required. During the first days of the encirclement the Sixth Army command brought out the severely understated figure for the necessary volume of supply of 600 tons per day. Moreover, only 53.8 tons per day were delivered during 25–29 November. Wolfram von Richtofen, the commander of the Fourth Air Fleet, wrote in his diary as early as 21 November that 'I am putting forth all efforts in order to convince them that this cannot be achieved, because the necessary transportation resources are absent'. However, at the critical period of forming the decision, Hitler was en route from the Berghof to the *Wolfschanze*. He was deprived of the opportunity to hear out the Wehrmacht and Luftwaffe commanders directly responsible for carrying out operations on land and in the air in the Stalingrad area and only became firmer in his decision to organize a relief attack by Manstein and maintain the 'air bridge'.

Yet another one of Jeschonnek's unfounded assumptions was the very possibility of organizing an 'air bridge' in the conditions prevailing at Stalingrad. Aircraft only had to fly 60–80km in the Demyansk area. Around Stalingrad they had to fly several times that distance, 200–300km. Demyansk was a secondary sector of the front, along which the most powerful and numerous formations of the Red Army air force were not operating. Just the opposite, one of the most important battles was taking placing around Stalingrad and the Soviet command immediately began an active struggle with the 'air bridge'.

As yet unaware that the decision taken was based upon incorrect facts and figures, the Führer at the end of November viewed the future with optimism. Hitler, Göring and Jeschonnek were sure that Manstein would soon punch a corridor to Paulus's army.

Meanwhile, the Sixth Army's units and formations removed from Stalingrad were taking up defence with their front facing west. By 22–24 November Paulus's decision to rush the Sixth Army's units to the west began to bear fruit. The Germans, relying on the positions of the middle defensive line along the northern bank of the Chervlenaya River, halted the advance of the 57th Army's formations. The enemy of Tolbukhin's[6] army was the IV Army Corps (295th and 297th Infantry Divisions, the 29th Motorized Division and the Romanian 20th Infantry Division). Units of the 13th Mechanized Corps formed the internal encirclement front along the line of Chervlenaya River to the south of the Stalingrad – Morozovskaya railway. Here they consolidated and were defending before 27 November.

By 25 November the Sixth Army's front had shrunk to 200km. The following units were encircled:

The Sixth Army's headquarters;
the IV, VIII, XI, and LI Corps and the XIV Panzer Corps;
the 14th, 16th and 24th Panzer Divisions;
the 3rd, 29th and 60th Motorized Divisions;
the 44th, 71st, 76th, 79th, 100th, 113th, 295th, 297th 305th, 371st, 376th, 384th, and
    389th Infantry Divisions;
the Romanian 20th Infantry Division;
the Romanian 1st Cavalry Division;
the 243rd and 245th Assault Gun Battalions;
the 2nd and 51st Rocket Artillery Regiments;
the 91st Anti-Aircraft Regiment and more than 150 artillery subunits, engineer and
    construction battalions, military police battalions, and other auxiliary elements.

In all, on 25 November the Sixth Army's units in the 'cauldron' numbered 284,000 men. This figure includes the XLVIII Panzer and IV Army Corps, which had been subordinated to Paulus from the Fourth Panzer Army, as well as two Romanian divisions (1st Cavalry and 20th Infantry, numbering 12,607 men).

Chapter 25

The Failure of Winter Storm

(Map 15)

In and of itself the encirclement of the large group of German forces did not signify their immediate destruction. Moreover, the precedents for encircling the enemy by units of the Red Army available by the autumn of 1942 demonstrated the great resilience of the enemy who had gotten into a 'cauldron'. The Germans were in no hurry at all to surrender. Nor did they react in the same way as Soviet forces in 1941: the collapse of the 'cauldron' into individual centres of resistance and desperate attempts to break out of them as quickly as possible. For example, the XX Army Corps was isolated from the Ninth Army's main forces at Rzhev in January 1942. Before long communications were re-established with it with the aid of a counterblow. The garrisons of Kholm and Sukhinichi (von Gilsa's group) successfully held out and were later relieved by an attack from outside. The largest encirclement of German forces on the Eastern Front before Stalingrad was the encirclement of the II Army Corps at Demyansk. In all the cases described above the encircled forces were supplied by air. At the same time, a force numbering about 100,000 men was supplied in the Demyansk 'cauldron'. Transport aviation even brought in hay for the horses. At the same time, following the 'laying down of the bridge', that is, the punching of a corridor through to the encircled II Army Corps, supply by air did not completely cease and continued to the very end of the Demyansk saga. Speaking in general, transport aviation was employed by the Germans not only for supplying surrounded troops, but also for supporting formations having poor or extended lines of supply.

Thus by the winter of 1942/43 a firm plan of action had already been worked out:

1) the maintenance of the encircled troops' combat capability through the delivery of food, fuel and ammunition by air;
2) the restoration of communications with the main forces of the German troops operating in this area with the aid of a relief attack.

The Air Bridge Begins to Work

The beginning of operations according to the first point initially could only bring forth a smirk. On 25 November 1942, the commander of the Fourth Air Army, Wolfram von Richtofen, wrote in his diary: 'All of our "Junkers" are busy supporting the supply. But we only have a little more than 30 of them. Of yesterday's 47 aircraft, 22 were shot down and another nine today. So today we only managed 75 tons, instead of the required 300. We are short of transport aircraft.'[1]

Thirty planes instead of several hundred! But this was only the beginning. One of the original features of the German armed forces was the consistent fulfilment of even obviously stupid orders. The results achieved by this sometimes make us whistle in amazement. After Hitler made the fateful decision to supply the Sixth Army by air, the German air force command began to energetically gather up the forces of transport aviation. Not only were the transport subunits cleaned out, but the staffs, ministries and training units as well. The situation was made more complicated by the fact that about 250 transport aircraft were being used to supply the troops in North Africa.

By the beginning of December the following had been assembled for supplying Stalingrad:

1) ten groups of Junkers Ju 52s: the 9th, 50th, 102nd, 172nd, 500th, 700th, and 900th Special Designation Bomber Groups (*Kampfgruppe zur besonderen Verwendung*) and the I and II groups from a special designation bomber squadron;

2) four groups and two squadrons of Heinkel He 111s: the 5th and 20th Special Designation Bomber Groups, the I Group of the 100th Bomber Squadron, the III Group of the 4th Bomber Squadron, and the 27th and 55th Bomber Squadrons;

3) two groups of Junkers Ju 86s: the 21st and 22nd Special Designation Bomber Groups, with twenty-five and fourteen planes respectively;

4) one squadron of Heinkel He 177s: the 50th Bomber Squadron (it was actually a group of twenty He 177As);

5) one group of long-range transport aircraft, equipped with Focke-Wulf Fw 200s, Junkers Ju 90s and Junkers Ju 290s: the 200th Special Designation Bomber Squadron.

In all, these units numbered about 500 planes. Many of them were formed especially for the 'air bridge' to Paulus's army at the end of November 1942. As we can see, an entire 'menagerie' of different aircraft was brought in for supply work. Many of these were completely unsuited for transport missions, principally the outdated Ju 86 bombers and the He 177s, which were still suffering from 'teething troubles'. The latter carried a cargo that was even less than that of the more reliable He 111, and they were completely unsuited for evacuating wounded. The group of He 177s carried out only thirteen sorties, losing seven aircraft. The He 111s and the Ju 52s became the 'workhorses' for supplying Paulus's army. The former were primarily based at Morozovskaya and the latter at Tatsinskaya.

The statistics on supplying the Sixth Army appear as follows. On average, they were able to deliver the following per day:

25–29 November – 53.8 tons;
1–11 December – 97.3 tons;
13–21 December – 137.7 tons.

In total, this means that 269 tons were delivered during 25–29 November, 1,167 tons during 30 November–11 December, and 1,377 tons during 12–21 December. From the moment the 'air bridge' began to work, 18,410 sick and wounded from the Sixth Army were evacuated from the 'cauldron'.

It is of interest to note that they sent mail into the 'cauldron' and even took out mail in the other direction. Seventy-three tons of mail was sent into the 'cauldron' before 31 December. This meant that each day approximately two tons of mail was delivered to the Sixth Army. It is difficult to say how much this was extravagant – to maintain the morale of those in the 'cauldron' with letters from home. It is possible that this was simply the inertia of supporting those who were temporarily surrounded. Only 15 tons of mail went the other way, as the encircled troops did not have a lot to say.

Meanwhile, Back in the City …

The encirclement of Paulus's army was supposed to help improve the situation of Soviet units in Stalingrad itself. The 13th Guards Rifle Division got the opportunity to break out of the narrow stretch of the shore along the Volga. A powerful centre of resistance in the form of the L-shaped building, the 'Railway Workers' House' and School No. 38 lay across the path of Rodimstev's men.

A special detachment, numbering sixty men under the command of Senior Lieutenant V.I. Sidel'nikov, was formed in the 34th Guards Rifle Regiment for storming the L-shaped building. Sidel'nikov was only 21, but he had served in the Red Army since 1939 and had been fighting since June 1941. The detachment was divided into three assault groups. It was decided to break into the building while it was still dark and to fight in the labyrinth of its rooms as soon as it was daylight. The jumping-off line for the assault was 25m from the building being attacked from the southern half of the building. The building's narrow eastern wall had fewer firing points, while the short distance offered the opportunity of employing flamethrowers effectively against it. There were none of these in the regiment, but they sent two flamethrower operators from Division. The engineers and infantry dug a 130m trench in the frozen ground to reach the jumping-off line.

Training went on after dark under the cover of the Volga's high bank to plan the assault. A structure resembling the L-shaped building's eastern wall was chosen. A system of signals was worked out as a result of this training. The soldiers began to move up to their jumping-off positions at 04.00 on 3 December. The assault groups reached the designated line along the trench. Each participant in the assault had ten grenades and two anti-tank grenades. The groups also disposed of petrol bombs and thermite charges. At 06.40, according to a prearranged signal – three red rockets – the assault began with fire from flamethrowers against the machine-gun embrasures. Having thrown grenades into the building through the windows and breaches in the walls, the assault groups burst in. By 10.00 the eastern part of the building was in their hands. However, any subsequent advance was held by the enemy holed up in the basement. Upon consolidating in the captured part of the building, the soldiers of the assault group, as soon as it had grown dark, brought up 250kg of TNT and planted it over the cellar. As soon as the preparations had been completed, they pulled all the people in the building into a shelter. At 04.00 there was a resounding explosion and the remnants of the enemy garrison were buried under the rubble in the cellar. Sidel'nikov was awarded the Order of the Red Star for this assault.

If a night attack had been the *pièce de résistance* of the assault on the L-shaped building, then it was decided to assault the railway worker's building during daylight, following a powerful artillery preparation and under the cover of smoke. The building had already been partially occupied as early as November. A detachment numbering fifty men, broken up into eight groups of five or six men each, was formed for the assault. Heavy machine guns and anti-tank guns were supposed to provide fire support for the assault. Before dawn on 3 December the assault groups, taking advantage of the passages in the barbed wire obstacles and minefields which had been made earlier by the engineers, moved up to their jumping-off position. At 08.00, when the assault on the L-shaped building was at its height, the artillery preparation began. After a two-hour bombardment, the first-echelon groups threw themselves into the attack under the cover of smoke.

Having broken into the building, the assault groups got into a grenade fight. The second echelon, which had come up, set about methodically destroying the enemy in the cellars, corridors and rooms. The enemy's attempt to counter-attack from the neighbouring air force building was repelled by artillery fire. By 13.20 the 'Railway Workers' House' had been completely cleared of the enemy. Having taken the 'Railway Workers' House' and the

L-shaped building, the units of Rodiimtsev's division now had unmolested communications with the left bank of the Volga, not only at night but during the day as well.

However, the units of the encircled Sixth Army still retained their combat capability. An attempt to develop the success and seize yet another building in the same area – School No. 38 – was unsuccessful. On 26 December a detachment of thirty-two men broke into the school, but managed to seize only part of the first floor. The enemy's firing points outside the building were not silenced, as a result of which the second-echelon groups moving on the school were pinned down and then fell back. Several attempts during the course of the day to reinforce the detachment assaulting the school were unsuccessful for the same reason. According to the *front's* war diary, by 27 December 'The assault groups, which had broken into School No. 38, were thrown back to their jumping-off position by an enemy counter-attack'. Combat operations in Stalingrad had come to a standstill.

Much more successful were the actions of the 39th Guards Rifle Division in the area of the 'Red October' factory. The core of the enemy's defence was the sheet rolling shop – a stone L-shaped building 10m high, 200m long and 70m wide. The 'key' to taking this shop was the important reconnaissance in force, which was carried out on 13 December and which uncovered the enemy's fire plan. According to its results, on the night of 14/15 December the assault groups successfully penetrated into the shop, but the fighting for it continued for almost a week. Particularly vicious skirmishes took place in the cellar, where not only bayonets and grenades were used, but knives as well. They attacked the neighbouring medium shaping shop from the direction of the blind northern wall, in which they made several holes with a 76mm gun, which had been brought up and fired from a range of 30–40m, through which the assault groups penetrated into the shop. The calibrating shop was taken by storm, using one of the underground tunnels on the factory grounds, through which the assault group unexpectedly broke into the shop. By 24–25 December the grounds of the 'Red October' factory had been completely cleared of the Germans.

Manstein Prepares a Relief Attack

Army Group Don was created to plug the breach formed as a result of the offensive of the two Soviet fronts. It was supposed to punch a corridor to Paulus's surrounded army. In and of itself, the idea of creating yet another army group along the southern sector of the Soviet-German front arose even before the Soviet offensive. In the summer of 1942 Army Group South, according to the campaign plan, had been divided into Army Groups A and B. By November Army Group B contained seven armies, including four armies from Germany's allies. Such a large number of armies, which were moreover scattered over a broad front, made the work of Army Group B's headquarters quite difficult. This it was proposed to create Army Group Don under the command of Romanian Marshal Antonescu. However, the order, which had already been prepared by the OKH, was not issued and Army Group Don appeared as a fire brigade. Its core was the headquarters of Von Manstein's Eleventh Army, which had been hurriedly transferred from the central part of the front.

The first task of Army Group Don was the restoration of a continuous and relatively stable front. But it was impossible to build it out of various 'groups'. By 14 December three fresh divisions had arrived at Manstein's disposal: the 336th Infantry Division from Army Group B, the 7th Luftwaffe Field Division and the 11th Panzer Division from Army Group Centre. The 306th Infantry Division, 17th Panzer Division and the 3rd Mountain Division were also promised. The latter never arrived, as it was thrown around for parrying local crises in Army Groups A and B. The 17th Panzer Division arrived only on 17 December, already too late to play a significant role in the battle.

Army Group Don's second task was to punch a corridor to the Sixth Army. At first, Manstein planned to launch two relief attacks: one with the forces of the Fourth Panzer Army from the Kotel'nikovo area and another by Army Group Hollidt[2] from the line of the Chir River in the direction of Kalach. This variant was contained in an Army Group Don order of 1 December 1942 for an offensive for the purpose of relieving the encircled Sixth Army. The operation was given the code name Winter Storm (*Wintergewitter*).

It was planned to launch the main attack with the forces of the Fourth Panzer Army from the Kotel'nikovo area along the eastern bank of the Don River. The headquarters of the LVII Corps was to be transferred from the Northern Caucasus to control the divisions allotted for the offensive. The 6th and 23rd Panzer Divisions and the Romanian 5th and 8th Cavalry Divisions were subordinated to the corps.

The XLVIII Panzer Corps was to launch the second attack. The 11th Panzer, 336th Infantry and 7th Luftwaffe Field Divisions were to be subordinated to it. They were supposed to clear the heights to the west of the Don and seize the crossing at Kalach. Correspondingly, upon receiving the signal 'Thunderbolt' (*Donnerschlag*), the Sixth Army was to attack from inside the 'cauldron' to the south-east, toward the Donskaya Tsaritsa River, toward the Fourth Panzer Army, and to the west in the direction of Kalach. An exact date for the start of the offensive had not yet been determined on 1 December, but in any event it could begin no earlier than 8 December. A factor hindering an immediate offensive was the time needed to assemble the forces. In particular, a thaw in the Caucasus delayed the 23rd Panzer Division which was moving under its own power. A few days later the operational plan was given more detail. The LVII Panzer Corps' first mission was to force the Aksai River. Further on, the corps was to aim for Verkhne-Tsaritsynskii and was supposed to get into the rear of the Soviet forces along the internal front of the Stalingrad encirclement. It was planned to support the offensive's right flank with Romanian cavalry. The XLVIII Panzer Corps' forces were to be divided into two groups along different banks of the Don. The 11th Panzer and 7th Luftwaffe Field Divisions were to reach Kalach in the corridor between the Liski and Don rivers. The 336th Infantry Division was supposed to attack to the south of the Don from the bridgehead at Verkhne-Chirskaya. Thus, besides a breakthrough to Kalach, the XLVIII Panzer Corps was to support with an attack the LVII Panzer Corps' flank along the main axis of the attack. Following the punching-through of a corridor, transport columns which had been concentrated in the Verkhne-Chirskaya area were to move along it.

However, numerous crises along the Chir River soon interfered with Manstein's plan. In the end, the headquarters of the Romanian Third Army reported: 'At the present moment the XLVIII Panzer Corps' forces are insufficient for a simultaneous struggle against breakthroughs and the counteroffensive set for 12 December.'[3] Manstein reported to the OKH that 'the freeing-up of the 11th Panzer Division is not expected'. It was impossible to risk the stability of the Chir front. The Germans had to give up on two attacks and the main burden of the offensive fell on the LVII Panzer Corps.

A Mistake that was Almost Fatal

The Soviet command failed to correctly determine the axis of the relief attack. Thus the mistake of many of the Red Army's unsuccessful defensive operations was repeated. It was assumed that the attack would be launched along the shortest distance between the external and internal encirclement fronts. At that moment the distance between the Sixth Army's defensive line and the front along the Chir was about 40km. The commander of the South-western Front, N.F. Vatutin, should be recognized as the author of the version of the German attack along the shortest axis. As early as 25 November (that is, before Manstein's order) he was reporting to Stalin:

> On 24.11.42 the enemy began a forced transfer of troops by motor transport and to concentrate them in the areas of Solin, Bokovskaya and Popovka, and in the Tormosin – Nizhne-Chirskaya area. In all, by the close of 25.11.42 the enemy has concentrated in the Kruzhilin – Bokovskaya – Popovka area up to three new divisions and more than an infantry division, reinforced with tanks, in the Tormosin – Nizhne-Chirskaya area. The transfers are continuing. The concentration of reserves in the Bokovskaya and Tormosin area speaks to the enemy's possible intention to launch counterblows from Tormosin through Nizhne-Chirskaya to the north along the Don River for the purpose of breaking the ring being closed around his Stalingrad group of forces, and from Bokovskaya to the east for the purpose of getting in the rear of our forces.

Such an assumption appeared quite logical and well-founded. The external front had stabilized along the Don and Chir rivers. In the Nizhne-Chirskaya area, where the Chir flows into the Don, a salient had been formed facing Stalingrad that offered a good jumping-off position for punching a corridor through to the Sixth Army. However, the Army Group Don command preferred to launch a relief attack from Kotel'nikovo to Stalingrad. It was decided to use the bridgehead at Nizhne-Chirskaya for a supporting attack.

In the Stalingrad Front's war diary there is a cautious assumption in the entry for 4 December: 'The possibility of offensive operations by the enemy's Kotel'nikovo group of forces, in conjunction with the Tormosin group of forces, with the task of supporting the Stalingrad group of forces' exit from the encirclement is not excluded.'[4] Later this evaluation was altered only slightly. The entry for 9 December states that:

> Proceeding from the enemy's group of forces and the stubborn struggle to retain the area of the crossings in Nizhne-Chirskaya and the stubborn defence of the salient, facing the Don River at Marinovka and which significantly shortens the distance of the gap [between the external and internal encirclement fronts, Author], one may assume that the German command is planning to carry out an operation with the main attack axis from the Nizhne-Chirskaya area to Marinovka and a supporting attack along the Kotel'nikovo – Stalingrad railway.[5]

Thus Yeremenko's later assertion that 'From the very beginning of the formation of this group of forces, the Stalingrad Front command feared that the main attack would be launched precisely by this group from the Kotel'nikovo area'[6] is not supported by the documents. The *front* command agreed with the *Stavka*'s opinion that the main attack would be launched from the Nizhne-Chirskaya area. Here it's difficult to accuse the Soviet command of being unreasonable and hurried in its conclusions. It was 110km from Kotel'nikovo to the external front of the encirclement of the German Sixth Army. Nizhne-Chirskaya was 45km closer.

Nonetheless, one should not think that the Kotel'nikovo axis promised the Germans an easy ride. The pause that was granted by the German command was employed intelligently.

During 5–10 December 4,400 mines and 638 artillery shells used as mines were laid. Of this amount, 1,978 mines were laid in the 57th Army's zone along the internal encirclement front, while 1,208 mines and 638 artillery shells were laid in the 51st Army's zone. The 13th Mechanized Corps laid another 1,214 mines. At the same time, eleven bridges were mined.

The German offensive began on the morning of 12 December. The Soviet command's incorrect assumptions as to the enemy's plans secured the relative surprise and success of Operation Winter Storm's first blow. The 6th Panzer Division was broken up into three motorized infantry groups and one powerful panzer 'armoured group' for the offensive under Hunesdorf (the commander of a panzer regiment). The latter included a panzer regiment and a battalion of infantry in armoured personnel carriers, as well as supporting elements. The 'armoured group' was one of the variants of the combat groups. Subsequently, with the spread of armoured personnel carriers, the formation of 'armoured groups' became a common tactic for the German panzer troops. The Soviet defence was quickly crushed and the armoured group not only broke through, but also routed the defence's artillery and attacked the rear of the Soviet units in Verkhne-Yablochnyi, which were interfering with the neighbouring battle group's advance. The success of the offensive's first day even took the Germans somewhat aback. Horst Schaibert, then commander of a panzer company in the 6th Panzer Division, wrote:

> Taking into consideration our own strength, which was fully confirmed by the success of the breakthrough, we nevertheless expected more resistance, if not at the forward edge, then later in the depression near Nebykovo station. However, this depression, which was used for the railway to Stalingrad and bound by deep ravines, could hardly have been bypassed by motorized troops, as it offered definite advantages to the defenders.[7]

Incomprehension reigned in the 6th Panzer Division. 'Where were the Russians?' In the Wehrmacht supreme command's war diary the situation was assessed as follows: 'In Army Group B this morning Hoth's panzer group attacked and by 09.00 had achieved good results. The subsequent development of its offensive does not cause particular concern among the Army Group Don command, that is, the enemy units opposite Hoth suffered heavy losses in their strike force.'[8] As subsequent events showed, the Army Group Don command underestimated the capabilities of the Soviet mechanized formations along this axis.

The 302nd Rifle Division received the relief group's main attack on 12 December. It was still holding out at midday, but was later simply scattered. On the following day its condition was described as follows in the Stalingrad Front's war diary: 'It continues to gather in small groups in the Ternovyi State Farm Zhutovo station area.' That is, the formation ceased to exist as a part of the 51st Army's defence. A broad breach appeared in the army's formation. Time was required to restore the front's integrity. The mechanized corps and individual tank units could serve for a time as a means of holding the German offensive. They began to throw formations from the 5th Shock Army against the emerging axis of the main attack. As early as 12 December the decision was made to deploy the 4th Mechanized Corps to the Kotel'nikovo axis. Actually, Vol'skii's corps received the order on 13 December. The Soviet tank troops would have to fight the enemy in a manoeuvre battle. Up to now manoeuvre actions had not been the Soviet mechanized formations' strong suit. Moreover, the main enemy was to be the fresh 6th Panzer Division.

On 13 December the attacking Germans reached the line of the Aksai River and seized a bridge over the river with the forces of the 'armoured group'. To be sure, the joy was short-lived: following the crossing of one tank battalion, the bridge collapsed under the weight of the tank of the battle group's commander. They had to summon engineers and erect a pre-fabricated metal bridge over the Aksai for the tanks. Nevertheless, a tank detachment was thrown forward toward Verkhne-Kumskii. This inhabited locale was halfway to the final water barrier in front of the 'cauldron' – the Myshkova River.

On 13 December Yeremenko planned to launch a counterblow against the enemy's group of forces that had thrust ahead. It was intended to launch an attack along converging axes with two groups. The first consisted of the 4th Mechanized Corps, the 235th Tank Brigade, the 234th Tank Regiment, and the 87th Rifle Division. The mechanized corps and rifle division had been removed from the 5th Shock Army. The 13th Mechanized Corps was supposed to attack toward this group. Yeremenko's planned 'Cannae' contained a hint of a certain haste. All available units on hand were hurriedly thrown into repelling the relief attack. Nor did the 235th Independent Flamethrower Tank Brigade escape this. Regarding this brigade, very definite instructions were issued by the chief of staff of the Main Armoured-Tank Directorate, Colonel Kul'vinskii, in October 1942. It was ordered, in particular, that 'Flamethrower tanks are to be used only for their intended purpose and under no circumstances are they to be used as line tanks'. It was first planned to employ the flamethrower tank brigade against the encircled German forces. They were supposed to burn out the enemy infantry that was defending centres of resistance with the stubbornness of doomed men. But instead of this, they now had to face the German tanks head on.

The start of Winter Storm immediately brought about a reaction at the very top. As early as the evening of 13 December the initial plan for Operation Saturn was cancelled. Stalin explained the reason for the renunciation of the previously planned goals as follows: 'Operation "Saturn", with our forces' arrival at the line Kamensk – Rostov, was envisaged in a military situation more favourable for us, when the Germans did not have any reserves in the Bokovskii – Morozovskii – Nizhne-Chirskaya area.'[9] The main attack was now to be directed not to the south (toward Rostov), but to the south-east, on Morozovskii. Thus, as early as the second day of Winter Storm, the Soviet supreme command had abandoned the lunge at Rostov. That is, the destruction of the Sixth Army locked up in Stalingrad was preferred to cutting off Army Group A's path of retreat in the Caucasus. In connection with the change in missions, by Stalin's order, the 6th Mechanized Corps was to be removed from the forces designated for Operation Saturn. It was to be transferred to the Stalingrad Front for use against the forces advancing to save Paulus's army. Stalin's order to Vasilevskii followed on the evening of 14 December: 'In view of the altered situation in the south, the realization of the first stage of Operation Ring is to be postponed.'[10] It was ordered that the 2nd Guards Army, particularly its mechanized units, was to be shifted by forced march to the south. It was supposed to concentrate behind the 51st Army. In the event of the failure of the operations by the Stalingrad Front's mechanized corps along the path of Winter Storm, fresh forces would arise.

Everything would have been fine if the 2nd Guards Army had been ready to enter the fighting immediately in the event of the failure of the mechanized corps' counterblow, that is, by 15 December 1942. However, on that day it was by no means where they usually draw it on maps of the battle of Stalingrad. Rather, it should be depicted as being scattered like a cloud along the railways and dirt roads around the 'cauldron'. At that moment the Stalingrad Front, which had incorrectly predicted the axis of the enemy's main attack, had no guarantee of success.

The Guards Army

The new hero in the drama – 'a tall blonde man with aristocratic features' – is in need of a short introduction. The very name implies that the 2nd Guards Army belonged to the elite of the Red Army. However, this army began its life as the 1st Reserve Army, which had been formed on 1 September 1942 in Tambov. It was made up of the remnants of formations that had been withdrawn from the front for refitting. In particular, it initially included the 18th Rifle Division, which had been scattered along the steppe in the Don bend in August 1942. Later this division was removed and other formations, which had suffered heavy losses and lost their combat capability around Stalingrad – the 33rd Guards and 98th Rifle Divisions – took its place. One should say that Zhukov's protégé, Major General A.I. Utvenko, who became a division commander around Yelets as a major, demonstrated excellent qualities as a commander – his restored 33rd Guards Rifle Division demonstrated good results in exercises. On 23 October 1942, when by *Stavka* VGK Order No. 99427, the reserve army became the 2nd Guards Army, it included the following:

a) the 1st Guards Rifle Corps – 24th and 33rd Guards Rifle Divisions and the 98th Rifle Division;
b) the 13th Guards Rifle Corps – the 49th and 3rd Guards Rifle Divisions and the 387th Rifle Division;
c) the 2nd Guards Mechanized Corps (reformed from the 22nd Guards Rifle Division).

Ya.G. Kreizer[11] commanded the army while it was being formed and its chief of staff was Colonel M.D. Gretsov (the former chief of staff of Belov's 1st Guards Cavalry Corps). When it came time to enter the fighting, Lieutenant General R.Ya. Malinovskii (already known to us as the commander of the 66th Army in the fighting to the north of Stalingrad) was appointed commander, and Major General S.S. Biryuzov chief of staff. Kreizer became deputy commander and Gretsov chief of the army's operational section.

On 28 November 1942 preliminary instructions were received from the General Staff regarding the movement of the newly-minted army by rail. At that moment the 1st Guards Rifle Corps numbered 35,764 men, the 13th Guards Rifle Corps 37,664 men, and the 2nd Guards Mechanized Corps 17,136 men. The army's numerical strength almost exactly corresponded to the authorized strength tables. In all, the army numbered 90,564 men – quite a weighty force to be thrown into the scales of a major battle. Calculations for transporting the army were ready on 1 December and on 3 December orders were finally received for moving it. The moment was approaching for which the soldiers and commanders had been preparing over the long weeks of autumn, far from the cannonade along the front. As opposed to Rauss's 6th Panzer Division, the 2nd Guards Army had to cover not 4,000km to Stalingrad, but only approximately 700km. According to the plan, the army was supposed to fit into 142 trains.

However, in reality the transport of the 2nd Guards Army was far removed from the famous deployment of the German army in 1914, which went like clockwork. This is hardly surprising, as it was not conducted according to plans that had been worked out over decades. The trains did not always arrive on time and their loading was carried out on the ground along temporary gangways. The gangways collapsed, the motor vehicles fell off and the units wasted time lifting them back up. The low loading rates were often explained by the primitive conditions of the stations. Thus the army loaded not on the planned 142 trains, but on 156. The detraining area was a traditional one for reserves arriving in the

Stalingrad area – Archeda, Ilovlya, Lipki and Log stations to the north of the city. Here the Guards divisions had unloaded in August and the participants in the fighting for the semaphore in September. By the evening of 13 December, when the Germans had already reached the Aksai River, the 2nd Guards Army was still en route. Some units were in their trains and some were on the march to the unloading area. All of the army's units were still to the north of the Stalingrad – Kalach railway. Of the tank units, only the 22nd Tank Regiment had arrived.

It was only by 19.00 on 16 December that 120 of the 156 trains for Malinovskii's army had unloaded. But unloading to the north of Stalingrad was still only half the task. One still had to get to the area to the south-west of the city from the detraining places. The war diary paints an apocalyptic picture of the situation immediately following the units' arrival: 'Transport has fallen behind. Motor transport is not working due to the absence of fuel. There is no communication with the units that have detrained.'[12] In a word, the army was perfectly prepared to be routed in detail.

The Battle for Verkhne-Kumskii

By 14 December 1942 there was nothing astride the path of Hoth's attacking forces except for scattered rifle units and the 4th Mechanized Corps. This was one of those cases in which, in Churchill's memorable phrase, the fate of many depended upon the few. Corps commander V.T. Vol'skii had no right to make a mistake. He had to fight it out at Verkhne-Kumskii as long as possible, while delaying the German offensive until the 2nd Guards Army's main forces could be concentrated. The punching of a corridor to Paulus's encircled army would mean that all those who fallen on the sun-baked steppe in July and August 1942 and who went into the final battle in the destroyed city of Stalingrad had died in vain and would remain unavenged.

The 4th Mechanized Corps differed from the tank corps in the summer and beginning of autumn 1942, chiefly by a powerful motorized rifle element. With an authorized strength of 14,067 men, by 1 December it had 11,703 men on hand. The corps' tank park on that date numbered seventy-nine T-34s, seventy-seven T-70s and ninety-seven BA-64s. The corps' auxiliary equipment numbered 78 cars, 1,244 trucks and 119 specialized vehicles, three 'Voroshilovets' tractors, three Chelyabinsk Tractor Factory tractors, one 'Comintern' tractor, and 73 motorcycles with a sidecar and 23 without. The amount of motor transport inspires respect, as Vol'skii's mechanized corps was already a truly mobile formation. It could manoeuvre as a whole, and not 'in rolls'. If the corps had been forced to retreat in the style of 1941, then the Chelyabinsk Tractor Factory and the 'Comintern' tractors would probably not have been able to effectively evacuate knocked-out equipment. During 1–11 December the 4th Mechanized Corps was fighting along the line of the Don River and its strength fell somewhat.

One should say that from the very beginning that Vol'skii laid down the foundation for success – the 36th Guards Mechanized Brigade had been moved far forward, beyond the Aksai River, to the Vodyanskii area. By this means a threat was immediately created to LVII Panzer Corps' armoured 'finger', which had been moved forward. Rauss was forced to activate his Marders, anti-tank artillery and motorized infantry in order to secure the rear of his armoured group. On 14 December flamethrower tanks from the 235th Tank Brigade, together with the 234th Independent Tank Regiment, attacked Verkhne-Kumskii from the east. As opposed to their line brethren, the flamethrower KVs were armed with a 45mm gun and a flamethrower. Accordingly, they were completely helpless in a fight with the 6th Panzer Division's Panzer IVs. It was evidently about these tanks when Rauss spoke about the Soviet forces' unsuccessful attacks on Verkhne-Kumskii. The Germans claimed thirty-six Soviet tanks destroyed in this fighting.

However, on the morning of 15 December a counterblow was launched by the 4th Mechanized Corps' main forces against the 6th Panzer Division's elongated wedge toward Verkhne-Kumskii. At that moment the corps had 107 tanks in line. The corps' brigades attacked Verkhne-Kumskii from all sides. Even the flamethrower tank brigade and a battalion from the 87th Rifle Division took part in the offensive. The 6th Panzer Division's 'armoured group' had ended up in a rather sticky situation. It had little in the way of infantry, as the main mass of motorized infantry in Rauss's division was still on the southern bank of the Aksai and was covering the flanks. Hunesdorf, the commander of the armoured group, attempted to leave two companies of tanks in Verkhne-Kumskii and then move out and give battle with the forces of his tanks in the open field. However, this led to a situation in which while the main mass of Hunesdorf's tanks was fighting along the approaches to Verkhne-Kumskii, the town itself was attacked and taken by storm.

Nor did the fighting in the open field bring the Germans the desired result. The 55th Independent Tank Regiment constituted the reserve of Vol'skii's corps. During the counter-attack against the enemy with fire and short forays, the corps inflicted telling losses on the German panzer companies. Lieutenant Colonel Azi Aslanov commanded a regiment. The skilful manoeuvring of the regiment and fire in the open and from behind cover disrupted the Germans' combat formations and all of their counter-attacks were repulsed. Under attack from all directions and threatened from the rear to the crossing over the Aksai from the 36th Mechanized Brigade of Vol'skii's corps, the Germans were forced to abandon Verkhne-Kumskii by evening. One should mention that in his memoirs, the commander of the 6th Panzer Division, Erhard Rauss, described the 'wheeling battle' at Verkhne-Kumskii, in which many Soviet tanks were destroyed. Such claims have not yet been confirmed in Soviet documents: the 4th Mechanized Corps lost only twelve T-34s and nine T-70s knocked out and burned. Also, for some reason Rauss dates the 'wheeling battle' to 13 December, when Vol'skii's mechanized corps had not yet arrived at the battlefield. Schaibert, the author of the book *48 Kilometres to Stalingrad*, describes the events, while relying on documents. According to his data, during the fighting for Verkhne-Kumskii, the 6th Panzer Division lost irretrievably one Panzer II, thirteen Panzer IIIs and five Panzer IVs. Six Panzer IIs, twenty-eight Panzer IIIs (of all types), five Panzer IVs and two command tanks remained in line.

Whatever the case, in two days of fighting the Soviet mechanized corps managed not only to prevent the enemy's advance to the Myshkova, but to force the 6th Panzer Division to abandon Verkhne-Kumskii and fall back to the Aksai. Moreover, yet another day (16 December) had been spent by the Germans on eliminating the threat from the 36th Mechanized Brigade at Vodyanskii.

The next round of the battle at Verkhne-Kumskii took place on 17 December. The task of its defenders was to cover the deployment of the 2nd Guards Army along the Myshkova. By this time the 4th Mechanized Corps had been reinforced with the 85th Tank Brigade, consisting of seventeen tanks (on the morning of 16 December two KVs, six T-34s and six T-70s were in working order) and the 20th Anti-Tank Brigade, consisting of six or seven 76mm guns and several anti-tank rifles. Now the opponents had changed places: the Soviet mechanized corps was holding the heights south of Verkhne-Kumskii and the Germans were attacking them. At that moment the 17th Panzer Division joined the LVII Panzer Corps. It was quite weak and was far inferior to the 6th Panzer Division in striking power, but it was still a significant addition to Winter Storm's shock fist. At the time of its arrival at the front, it numbered 54 tanks and 2,300 men in the panzer grenadier regiments. The 17th Panzer Regiment occupied the offensive zone to the left of Rauss's division. Its enemy became the 4th Cavalry Corps.

Meanwhile, Winter Storm's main ram, the 6th Panzer Division, attempted to take back Verkhne-Kumskii. An armoured group from the neighbouring 23rd Panzer Division was attached to it for the offensive. The mission of the day was not even the seizure of Verkhne-Kumskii itself, but a breakthrough to the Myshkova and the seizure of a bridgehead at Gromoslavka. By the way, part of the 20th Anti-Tank Brigade's guns had remained at Gromoslavka. That is, for the Soviet command a possible attack on the brigade was not among the possible scenarios for the development of events. It is unlikely that the seizure of a bridgehead, even in the event of a success with the attack on Verkhne-Kumskii, would have been an easy matter for the Germans.

During the course of the offensive on 17 December the 6th Panzer Division's 'armoured group' carried out very complicated manoeuvres while attempting to attack positions along the approaches to Verkhne-Kumskii from the flank. In particular, the right flank of Vol'skii's corps was attacked near Height 146.9. Following this, the 'armoured group' deployed and headed west, to flatten the Soviet motorized infantry's positions. However, during this supporting attack, the Germans managed to push back the 20th Anti-Tank Brigade and force it to fall back on Gromoslavka, to the Myshkova. There appears in the Stalingrad Front's war diary an almost panicked entry that in the evening the enemy 'was advancing on Gromoslavka with a strength of about 100 tanks'. Fortunately, this assumption proved false.

Attacks along the actual axis of the main blow did not bring the Germans success. At 14.20 on 17 December the 'armoured group' radioed Rauss: 'The first attack on Verkhne-Kumskii was repulsed due to the unusually powerful anti-tank defence.' At that time the Fourth Air Fleet's capabilities were significantly lower than during the summer. The 'armoured group's' second attack did not even take place, due to the onset of darkness. The December days were short and did not enable one to quickly right a mistake or to make up lost time.

The motorized infantry of Vol'skii's corps played an important role in the success of the defence of the heights in front of Verkhne-Kumskii. In recounting the events of 17 December, Rauss wrote on the following day:

> The well masked Russian infantry hid in the deep slit trenches in groups of two to four men and simply allowed the two panzer regiments to roll right over their heads. Then, employing their numerous anti-tank rifles, each of which could be served by a single man, the Russians opened fire from a short range against the weakly armoured vehicles of Captain Kuper's battalion, inflicting heavy losses on it. Our panzers had to wait or even turn back to help the panzer grenadiers, who were forced to abandon their vehicles and wage combat as infantry with an unseen enemy. The enemy positions proved to be so well camouflaged in the yellow-brown steppe grass, which matched in colour the Red Army soldiers' uniforms, that one could only unearth their foxholes by falling into one. A number of unfortunate German soldiers were killed

before they could figure out from where they were being fired on. Even the Luftwaffe was unable to help in the struggle with these unseen ghosts. Never before had our panzer troops felt themselves so helpless, although they were able to beat off an attack by an enormous number of Russian tanks.[13]

The situation was fundamentally different from July and August 1942, when Soviet tank troops, short of infantry, were incapable of holding the enemy's mechanized formations independently. Now a mechanized corps, possessing tanks, infantry and a certain amount of artillery, had been rapidly moved against the axis of the German offensive.

On 18 December the 6th Panzer Division's attacks on Verkhne-Kumskii were local in scale. The German offensive had slowed down and the scales of the battle had begun to shift in favour of the Red Army. The 2nd Guards Army's newly-arrived divisions began to occupy defensive positions along the line of the Myshkova River. Now, even if the screen provided by Vol'skii's mechanized corps had been pierced, an unimpeded road to Paulus would not have opened up before the LVII Panzer Corps' formations. On 18 December the 4th Mechanized Corps became the 3rd Guards Mechanized Corps. It's amazing that the enemy immediately learned about this. As early as 14.00 a radiogram announced that 'Stalin has awarded the defenders of Verkhne-Kumskii the title of Guards'. It's possible that along the front, which was taking on the aspect of a positional struggle, the soldiers simply shouted the news across to each other from their trenches. Following the successful fight, the Red Army soldiers did not miss the opportunity to inform the enemy that their stubbornness had been recognized at the very top.

However, the augmentation of the strength of the LVII Panzer Corps' attack by the Germans ultimately led to the shattering the newly-christened Guards corps. As a result of a breakthrough along the right flank of Vol'skii's corps, where the 17th Panzer Division had entered the fighting, Verkhne-Kumskii ended up under immediate attack from two directions. As was later noted in a report by the headquarters of the 3rd Guards Mechanized Corps, 'The 1378th Rifle Regiment and the 59th Mechanized Brigade, having come under heavy attack, were half surrounded and partially destroyed', while the mechanized brigades, under the threat of encirclement, were forced to fall back to the line of the Myshkova River. However, the 6th Panzer Division had to undertake a turning manoeuvre, quite far to the east, toward Vasil'evka, in order to seize a bridgehead over the Myshkova.

The losses suffered by Vol'skii's corps around Verkhne-Kumskii were quite heavy: 994 men killed, 3,497 wounded and 1,075 missing in action or captured.[14] On 20 December there remained in the corps 6,833 men, 31 T-34s and 19 T-70s. Following the fighting around Verkhne-Kumskii, by 19 December the 85th Tank Brigade numbered only one T-34 and two T-70s, that is, it had lost almost all its equipment.

On the whole, the period from 11–20 December 1942 was noteworthy for the Stalingrad Front's comparatively low losses. During this ten-day period losses were 12,718 men (2,776 killed, 5,975 wounded, 2,304 missing in action, and 1,663 due to other causes).[15] The 4th Mechanized Corps' losses totalled, as we see, almost a third of the *front's* overall losses. During the preceding ten-day period, from 1–10 December, when the *front's* forces were attacking the enemy along the external and internal encirclement fronts, the losses were 14,513 men.

The Soviet forces achieved an undoubted success in the five days of fighting: time had been won for the concentration of the 2nd Guards Army. The mechanized corps' decisive actions at Verkhne-Kumskii enabled them to move rifle units to the axis of the German offensive. A quite powerful group of forces had been created even before the concentration of the 2nd Guards Army. As early as 18 December Vasilevskii was reporting to Stalin: 'The 300th, 98th, 3rd Guards, and part of the 87th and 38th Rifle Divisions have been deployed behind Vol'skii along the Myshkova River and further on toward Abganerovo (the external line of the former Stalingrad fortified area), with the task of securely covering along this line Yakovlev's [R.Ya. Malinovskii's pseudonym – Author] final concentration. On 17.12 two of the Stalingrad Front's tank brigades, having up to 80 tanks, have been brought up in the Gniloaksaiskaya – Vodinskii area.'[16] As we see, the 5th Shock Army was dispersed for constructing the screen: the 300th and 87th Rifle Divisions were part of it, according to a *Stavka* directive on the army's formation.

By the morning of 18 December 150 out of 156 2nd Guards Army trains had unloaded. At that moment the 98th and 3rd Guards Rifle Divisions from Malinovskii's army were already occupying defensive positions along the Myshkova, and the 2nd Guards Mechanized Corps was concentrating in the area of the famous '74-kilometre' railway siding, along the flank of Hoth's and Manstein's attacking group of forces. The plan for Winter Storm had been laid to rest.

Perhaps the only time when the relief attack might have been successful was from 14–16 December 1942. If Hoth had managed to quickly overcome the 4th Mechanized Corps' resistance, the 6th Panzer Division would have reached the rendezvous point accessible from inside the 'cauldron'. If Vol'skii's mechanized corps had suffered a defeat, then the LVII Panzer Corps would not have encountered any serious resistance on the road to Stalingrad. The Soviet command simply had no forces capable of halting the Germans' fresh panzer division. A powerful factor was the Don Front's attacks along the perimeter of the encirclement. In a conversation with Manstein on the evening of 19 December, Paulus said 'Today's fighting has temporarily tied down the main mass of our tanks and part of the army's shock force, and showed that the enemy is especially strong in tanks and artillery in the direction of Kalach'. As a result of all of these circumstances, Manstein no longer harboured any illusions regarding the prospects for Winter Storm. He reported to Hitler: 'It will be impossible for the LVII Corps alone to link up with the Sixth Army, not to mention maintaining this link. The final variant is the Sixth Army's breakout to the south-west. At least the greater part of the troops and mobile weaponry will be preserved.'[17]

There's no doubt that if this had occurred in 1944, then the Sixth Army would have made a dash for freedom, abandoning its heavy weaponry and equipment. This is precisely how Hube's[18] First Panzer Army broke out of encirclement in the spring of 1944. However, in December 1942 there were as yet no examples of the destruction of an encircled group of German forces by the Red Army. Stalingrad itself was fated to become that example. Meanwhile, there were no examples and Army Group Don's chief of staff, General Schultz, unsuccessfully attempted to convince the Sixth Army command to attempt a breakout, regardless of the relief group's successes.

In striving to convince the Sixth Army command of the necessity of immediately attempting to break out, Schultz promised Schmidt that he would deliver the necessary supplies from without following the punching through of a corridor.

As regards fuel, as well as food and ammunition, there's a transport column with 3,000 tons behind Hoth's army for these purposes, which may be put at your disposal as soon as communications are organized. In this case tractors for the operational movement of artillery pieces will be offered. Thirty buses stand ready for transporting the wounded. A large part of the wounded will be crossed over on trucks.[19]

Schmidt evasively replied: 'We'll report when we can begin the offensive.'

Thus the situation that had come about as of 19–20 December urgently demanded a change in the original plans. Paulus should have made an attempt to break out before the relief group reached the designated line (Buzinovka). Moreover, he should have made the breakout before accumulating the planned amount of fuel by air. This was staking everything in the hope of the breakthrough's success and the organization of the delivery of fuel for continuing the operation. Manstein writes in his memoirs about this option:

> An opportunity would have opened for creating a corridor between the Fourth Panzer Army and the Sixth Army in order to deliver fuel to the latter. For this purpose, the army group command was maintaining in readiness behind the Fourth Panzer Army a transport column with 3,000 tons of supplies, as well as tractors, which were supposed to secure the mobility of part of the Sixth Army's artillery.[20]

As we know, Paulus did not follow the admonitions of the army group command. Theoretically, Manstein had the right to send the Sixth Army the code word 'Thunderclap' in the hope that the Führer would confirm *post factum* the decision as being due to military necessity. However, the Army Group Don commander would have ended up, at least, looking stupid if Paulus had not obeyed this signal. Joint agreement between the Sixth Army command and that of Army Group Don was required for actions at odds with Hitler's instructions regarding the retention of Stalingrad and in violating the initial plans. In conditions when the Sixth Army command was not in agreement with an immediate breakout, justifying this by the presence of wounded and the shortage of fuel, there could be no talk of any kind of agreement. As to the big picture, the Sixth Army's breakout promised Manstein nothing. The Soviet armies standing along the perimeter of the encirclement would have hurled themselves upon Army Group Don with unpredictable results. On the other hand, the retention of Stalingrad meant the blocking of a major railway junction and the tying down of significant Soviet forces. Thus the resolution of the question about the breakout was left by Manstein on Paulus's conscience. In the final analysis, the salvation of the Sixth Army was its own commander's responsibility.

In the meantime, having become convinced that the mechanized corps was a tough nut to crack, the German command shifted its attack further upstream along the Myshkova, to the Vasil'evka area. A certain amount of success was achieved and a bridgehead along the northern bank of the Myshkova was seized. But the LVII Panzer Corps was simultaneously lengthening its left flank from the Don to Vasil'evka. In conditions of the 2nd Guards Army concentrating along the northern bank of the Myshkova, this was close to madness.

However, the Soviet forces did not have the opportunity to test the stability of the full-strength LVII Panzer Corps. On 16 December the forces of the South-western and Voronezh Fronts began Operation Little Saturn. The Soviet forces' offensive quickly created a threat to the German air bases at Tatsinskaya and Morozovskaya. On 23 December an order was issued by which the 6th Panzer Division was to be withdrawn from the Kotel'nikovo axis and dispatched toward Morozovskaya. At dawn on 24 December a column of tanks and motor vehicles, stretching 130km, set out for its newly-designated area. The hopes of relieving Paulus's army by an attack by the Fourth Panzer Army collapsed.

That same day, when the 6th Panzer Division's columns set out for Morozovskaya, the 2nd Guards Army went over to the offensive against the LVII Panzer Corps' extended front. At that moment the army included the 7th Tank and 6th Mechanized Corps. By 16.30 the 55th Tank Regiment of the newly-formed 3rd Mechanized Corps, together with units of the 24th Guards Rifle Division, once again took Verkhne-Kumskii. The Stalingrad Front began its offensive on Kotel'nikovo with the forces of the 2nd Guards Army and three mechanized corps. This was followed by an offensive on Rostov. But that is another story altogether.

The external encirclement front began to rapidly move away from the line of the Myshkova. An independent breakout by the Sixth Army along the Kotel'nikovo axis had become hopeless and even technically impossible.

Chapter 26

The Hydraulic Press. Operation Ring

(Map 16)

One of the chief reasons for carrying out measures to crush an enemy's surrounded forces is to free up one's own divisions and armies holding the perimeter of the encirclement. By surrounding them, a part of his forces are torn from his order of battle and for a certain time, until the arrival of newly-formed formations or transfers from other theatres, the attacker has numerical superiority.

As a result of these considerations, both sides sought to eliminate an encircled enemy as quickly as possible, even in a case when there was no threat of the 'cauldron' being relieved. The task of destroying Paulus's encircled army was entrusted to the forces of Rokossovskii's Don Front as early as 30 November 1942. However, at that moment the Don Front did not have the necessary men and materiel for carrying out the task in December. The 2nd Guards Army, which was designated to reinforce the Don Front, was instead dispatched to the Stalingrad Front and employed for repelling von Manstein's relief attack in the Kotel'nikovo area. Due to this, the beginning of the operation to eliminate the enemy encircled around Stalingrad was put off and the Don Front's forces were given the task of going over to the defensive along the entire encirclement front and preventing the enemy from creating a shock group to break out through offensive operations along individual axes.

Simultaneously, by the end of December 1942 the threat of a relief attack from without had been eliminated. By this time the Soviet forces' front ran along the line Novaya Kalitva – Markovka – Millerovo – Morozovskii – Zimovniki at a distance of 170–250km from the enemy's forces surrounded around Stalingrad.

By January 1943 the situation of Paulus's encircled army had deteriorated sharply. The territory occupied by the encircled forces had shrunk considerably and could be almost completely enfiladed by Soviet artillery. During the fighting in December the Germans were forced to expend all of their reserves to repel the attacks squeezing the 'cauldron' and almost all their divisions had been put into the front line. Supplies of ammunition, fuel and food were coming to an end. It should be noted that the Sixth Army's food supply relied to a significant degree on horsemeat. The numerous horses of the German infantry divisions and the Romanian cavalry gradually found their way into the soldiers' kettles. On 9 January 1943 the ration for a German soldier in the 'cauldron' was 75g of bread, supplemented by 200g of horsemeat.

The German command's plans for organizing the uninterrupted supply of the surrounded forces by air had collapsed. The transport and bomber aviation that had been brought in for this purpose in the middle of December 1942 and based at the Tatsinskaya, Morozovskii, Chernyshkovskii, Kotel'nikovo, Zimovniki and Sal'sk airfields, had by January 1943 suffered heavy losses from Soviet aviation and anti-aircraft artillery. With the loss of the majority of the above-named airfields at the end of December, as a result of the beginning of Little Saturn, the burden on air supply increased significantly.

Transport aviation was forced to shift its bases to Shakhty, Kamensk-Shakhtinskii, Novocherkassk, Mechetinskaya and Sal'sk, which increased the distance from the bases to the Sixth Army's landing fields by 100km. The main base of Fibig's He 111s became Novocherkassk. The Heinkels had to fly 330km to Pitomnik, which was 130km further than from Morozovskaya. For a time Sal'sk became the main Ju 52 base. However, the retreat of German forces from the Caucasus made it necessary before long to hurriedly evacuate the Sal'sk airfield. Colonel Fritz Morzik, an expert in transport operations who had been sent by Luftwaffe headquarters, chose a new airfield by flying his Storch around the countryside. As a result, snow-covered wheat fields around Zverevo, which was 65km to the north of Novocherkassk, were chosen. There a base for the Ju 52s was hurriedly created out of nothing. It began to operate on 16 January.

The supply of the surrounded enemy forces in Stalingrad by air worsened considerably and could in no way satisfy their requirements for food, ammunition and fuel. There could be no question of 600 tons per day. The Soviet air force and anti-aircraft artillery made a noticeable contribution to reducing the 'air bridge's' effectiveness. The 16th, 8th and part of the 17th Air Armies, troop anti-aircraft artillery and units of the corps area anti-aircraft defence (anti-aircraft artillery and the 102nd Anti-Aircraft Defence Fighter Division) imposed an air blockade on the encircled enemy. The means of carrying out this task changed in accordance with changes in the enemy's air tactics.

By the beginning of January 1943 a smooth system of carrying out the air blockade had been worked out. The struggle against enemy aviation was conducted in four zones: on airfields beyond the external encirclement front, in the air between the external and internal encirclement fronts, in the anti-aircraft artillery's fire zone, which was immediately adjacent to the encirclement area, and, finally, in the very area housing the encircled enemy. All of this turned the operation to supply Paulus's Sixth Army into a massacre of the Luftwaffe's transport aviation.

The situation that had arisen by January 1943 along the southern wing of the Soviet-German front had not only created favourable conditions for the final elimination of the enemy's forces surrounded in the Stalingrad area, but also required that this task be completed as quickly as possible. It was necessary to free up significant numbers of Soviet troops for operations along other directions in the Red Army's unfolding general offensive, as well as to liberate the Stalingrad railway junction and to restore rail communications with the forces which were attacking Rostov and the Donbas. Paulus's army had actually received its final mission: to hold on as long as possible and thus enable Army Group Don to restore the front and to avoid the encirclement of Army Group A retreating from the Caucasus.

The elimination of the enemy's encircled group of forces has entrusted to the forces of Colonel General Rokossovskii's Don Front. On 1 January 1943, in *Stavka* VGK Directive No. 170720, of 30 December 1942, the 57th, 64th and 62nd Armies, which had earlier been subordinated to the Stalingrad Front, were to be transferred to the Don Front. Accordingly, the Stalingrad Front was to be dissolved and replaced by the Southern Front. The latter was commanded by Colonel General Yeremenko, who was entrusted with the 2nd Guards, 28th and 51st Armies. The Stalingrad Front had existed for nearly half a year.

Stavka VGK representative, Artillery Marshal N.N. Voronov, took part in preparing and conducting the Don Front's final operation around Stalingrad. The marshal, in his memoirs, cites a document, according to which he received this appointment on 19 December 1942.

1. The *Stavka* of the Supreme Commander-in-Chief considers that Comrade Voronov has quite satisfactorily carried out his mission of coordinating the activities of the

South-western and Voronezh Fronts, and after the Voronezh Front's 6th Army was subordinated to the South-western Front one may consider Comrade Voronov's mission to have been fulfilled.

2. Comrade Voronov is being posted to the area of the Stalingrad and Don Fronts as Comrade Vasilevskii's deputy for eliminating the enemy's encircled forces around Stalingrad.

3. Comrade Voronov, as a *Stavka* representative and Comrade Vasilevskii's deputy, is obliged to present no later than 21.12.42 to the *Stavka* a plan for breaking through the defence of the enemy forces encircled around Stalingrad and eliminating them in the course of five to six days.[1]

Before long Vasilevskii was dispatched to coordinate the activities of the Southern and South-western Fronts and Voronov remained as the *Stavka*'s sole representative with the Don Front. The operation being drawn up was given the code name Ring. Voronov testifies that in the second half of December the Don Front command underestimated the strength of the encircled forces. He writes that Rokossovskii 'boldly and confidently named a strength figure of 86,000 men, which accounted for five infantry divisions, two motorized divisions, three panzer divisions, and three combat detachments of some sort'. The Soviet command only received completely reliable information on the Sixth Army's strength after the elimination of the 'cauldron'. The plan for the operation was presented by Voronov to the *Stavka* on 27 December 1942. The *Stavka* representative proposed launching the main attack against the western face of the 'cauldron' and driving the enemy from the west to the east. In his memoirs he formulates the operation's main idea as 'We decided to split in two the enemy's encircled group of forces by a powerful ramming blow from west to east with the accompanying destruction of its individual units'. The reason for choosing this axis in particular presents a great deal of interest:

a) In launching the main attack from west to east, we would be concentrating the main weight of our attack against the enemy's main forces located in the Marinovka – Zhirnokleevka – Malaya Rossoshka – State Farm No. 1 area and, splitting them in two, to subsequently and consecutively destroy the enemy's individual split-up groups.

b) Troops (76th, 44th, 376th, and 384th Infantry Divisions and the 14th Panzer Division) are defending along the main attack front, which have partially had a defeat inflicted on them during the South-western and Don Fronts' previous operation, among which the 44th and 376th Infantry Divisions have recently yielded the largest number of prisoners and defectors.

c) The defensive line occupied by the enemy in the western sector was prepared only following the withdrawal of his forces from beyond the Don, while the northern sector has been prepared for defence during the course of four months. Besides this, the best German divisions are occupying defensive positions along the northern sector and there are a lot of knocked-out German and our tanks, which are used by the enemy as armoured firing points.

d) The character of the terrain, which is cut by deep ravines running from west to east, guarantees our tank units freedom of manoeuvre into the rear, while an attack from north to south would limit their actions.

e) The favourable jumping-off position does not require a complex regrouping of forces.

The sole point which one may accept without reservation is point d. The length of the 'cauldron' from west to east was noticeably greater than from north to south. Besides this, in launching the main attack from the west to the east, a meeting attack was to be launched by the forces in Stalingrad, possessing miniscule offensive capabilities. The splitting of the 'cauldron' in two by converging attacks from north to south strikes us as more logical. However, the failures in the positional battles to the north of Stalingrad weighed heavily upon the Don Front command. Voronov presented several arguments in favour of leaving the former 'land bridge' in peace. Much water had passed under the bridge since the last attacks against the 'land bridge' and the powerful screen in the gap between the Don and Volga had been demolished. Of course, to attack through the numerous wrecks of burnt-out tanks would not have been pleasant. However, this equipment graveyard could have been overcome by advancing 3–5km into the depth of the German defence, that is, as early as the first days, if not hours, of the offensive. The idea of the attack from the western face of the 'cauldron' corresponds to a significant degree the situation of the first weeks following the encirclement of the Sixth Army, when it was necessary to place as much distance as possible between the external and internal encirclement fronts. In January, when the front had been, moved back 200–250km from the 'cauldron', the squeezing of the encircled group of forces from the west made no particular sense.

There's nothing surprising in the fact that the plan presented for Operation Ring was subjected to criticism on the part of the high command. On 28 December 1942, *Stavka* of the VGK Directive No. 170718, signed by Stalin and Zhukov, stated:

> The chief shortcoming of the plan presented by you for 'Ring' is that the main and supporting attacks move in different directions and do not meet anywhere, which makes the operation's success doubtful …
>
> The *Stavka* orders you to redo your plan on the basis of what has been laid out. The *Stavka* confirms the timetable for starting the operation proposed by you. The first stage of the operation is to be completed in the course of 5–6 days following its beginning.[2]

As we can see, the *Stavka* treated the decision by the front command to attack along the north-western face of the 'cauldron' with understanding. Voronov and Rokossovskii were considered sufficiently competent men for adopting decisions of this sort. Despite the basic idea of Operation Ring, which foresaw the splitting up of the group of forces into several parts and the subsequent destruction of each of them in isolation, this plan appeared to be difficult to realize. The shock groups would have to cover a comparatively long distance in order to link up with each other. Accordingly, the enemy might avoid the breakup of the 'cauldron' by falling back toward Stalingrad.

The 'Hydraulic Press'

The forces of the 21st, 65th and 24th Armies were to be brought in to launch the main attack. They were to be lined up like a trident. P.I. Batov's 65th Army was to have the leading role; it was supposed to attack in the centre of the shock group's formation along its own 12km front, with five rifle divisions in the first echelon and three in the second. The army was to receive massive reinforcements: twenty-seven High Command Reserve artillery regiments, four Guards heavy mortar brigades (M30s) and nine Guards mortar regiments. These would enable it to create an artillery density of 130 guns per kilometre of front along its sector. P.A. Batov's army was to also receive one tank brigade and six independent tank regiments. To the right of the 65th Army, I.M. Chistyakov's 21st Army was to launch an attack along its left flank along a 4km front with the forces of two rifle divisions, reinforced by a tank regiment, two artillery regiments and three High Command Reserve mortar regiments. To the left of P.I. Batov's army, I.V. Galanin's 24th Army was to attack along a 4km front. Its shock group included three rifle divisions, reinforced by one tank regiment, one High Command Reserve artillery regiment and two High Command Reserve heavy-calibre artillery battalions.

In all, 33 per cent of all the rifle divisions, 50 per cent of the artillery, 57 per cent of the guards mortar and 75 per cent of the tank regiments were concentrated along the axis of the main attack. This enabled significant densities of men and materiel along the axis of the main attack to be created. There was one division per 1.5km of front in the 65th Army's zone. There were 135 guns and mortars and ten tanks per kilometre of attack front. The density was raised to 167 guns and mortars per kilometre of front along the 9km breakthrough sector. The strength of the Don Front's armies is shown in the table.

Table 42: The Don Front's Combat and Numerical Strength on 10 January 1943.[3]

Army	Total Men	Mortars	Field Guns	Including 152mm Guns	Including 122mm Guns*
21st	34,878	541	243	–	–
24th	23,213	416	190	16	–
57th	23,571	424	123	21	20
62nd	26,486	610	234	6	18
64th	48,889	1,071	291	42	–
65th	75,503	1,814	272	170	126
66th	42,652	1,027	325	–	12
Front	5,966	344	24	–	–
Total	281,158	6,247	1,702	255	176

* 122mm guns, not howitzers.

Supporting attacks were to be launched from the north-eastern and southern sectors of the encirclement ring. The first – by units of the 64th and 57th Armies from the front Popov – Rokotino (12km), with the forces of four divisions, three naval infantry brigades and two tank brigades, reinforced by twelve High Command Reserve artillery regiments, four Guards mortar regiments (M-13s) and one Guards heavy mortar brigade (M-30s) in the general direction of Kravtsov and Voroponovo station. Given a favourable development of events, the 64th and 57th Armies were supposed to link up with the 65th Army and cut off part of the enemy's forces in the western part of the 'cauldron'. The second supporting attack was to be launched by units of the 66th Army (five rifle divisions, one tank, one artillery and two High Command Reserve regiments, and two Guards mortar regiments) in the centre along a 7km front in the direction of the Drevnii Val rail siding and Novaya Nadezhda. This attack was supposed to result in a link-up with the 62nd Army in Stalingrad and the cutting off of part of the enemy forces in the Orlovka area. It's clear that the 66th Army, attacking in the area of the epic battles for the Semaphore, would receive far more modest reinforcements than the 65th Army.

For the purpose of deceiving the German command as to the direction of the main attack, the Don Front command carried out the false concentration of a major group of forces behind the 24th Army's left flank in the Samofalovka area. Dummy tanks and guns were employed for this purpose.

The beginning of Operation Ring was set for 10 January. By the start of the operation the Don Front, consisting of seven armies, had thirty-nine rifle divisions, ten rifle and four tank brigades, twelve tank regiments, eighty-nine artillery, ten mortar and fourteen Guards mortar regiments, and five Guards heavy mortar brigades. The average strength of the divisions in the armies varied from 4,500 to 5,500 men. By the start of the operation the 65th Army was the strongest – it included on 5 January 1943 two formations with a strength greater than 6,000 men (23rd Rifle Division – 6,005, and 27th Guards Rifle Division – 6,029). Correspondingly, the 21st Army contained one division with more than 6,000 men (51st Guards Rifle Division – 6,483). At the same time, the strength of the 21st

Table 43: Tanks in Line in the Don Front's Tank Units at 22.00 on 9 January 1943.[4]

Army	Formation	KV	T-34	T-60	T-70	Valentine Mk III	Churchill Mk IV	Total
24th	8th Gds Tank Rgt	9	–	1	–	–	–	9
66th	7th Gds Tank Rgt	6	3	2	6	–	–	17
65th	91st Tank Bde	2	3	3	–	1	–	9
	47th Gds Independent Tank Rgt	–	–	–	–	–	21	21
	15th Gds Independent Tank Rgt	18	–	–	–	–	–	18
	14th Gds Independent Tank Rgt	21	–	–	–	–	–	21
	10th Gds Tank Rgt	16	–	–	–	–	–	16
	9th Gds Tank Rgt	4	–	–	–	–	–	4
	5th Gds Tank Rgt	22	–	–	–	–	–	22
21st	1st Gds Tank Rgt	10	6	–	2	–	–	18
62nd	Composite company	1	2	–	–	–	–	3
64th	90th Tank Bde	1	12	3	4	–	–	20
	166th Independent Tank Rgt	–	11	–	9	–	–	20
	35th Independent Tank Rgt	–	7	–	4	–	–	11
57th	235th Tank Bde	1	2	–	–	–	–	3
	234th Independent Tank Regiment	–	8	–	12	–	–	20
	254th Tank Bde	–	18	–	14	–	–	32
Total for the *front*		110	72	9	51	1	21	264

Army's remaining divisions varied from 3,612 to 4,907 men. The majority of the formations had taken part in the fighting, if not from the very beginning of the battle for Stalingrad in August–September 1942, then from the time of the counteroffensive in November 1942. The Don Front included 264 tanks, about 2,500 guns, more than 6,000 mortars (not including rocket launchers), and about 400 planes.

The basic organizational form of the Don Front's tank troops was the tank regiment. The tank corps had been activated for the offensive to the west, for the lunge to Rostov, and the Ostrogozhsk – Rossosh' and Voronezh – Kastronoe operations. Thus the most topical task for Rokossovskii's tank troops was direct infantry support. For the quantitative and qualitative strength of the Don Front's tank units, see the table opposite.

It's clear that the 65th Army was to receive not only the larger number of tank regiments, but also the most powerful regiments according to the number of combat vehicles in line. Also, one cannot but note that almost half of the Don Front's tank park was made up of heavy KV tanks. The second most numerous was, of course, the T-34. Besides this, a regiment of Churchill Mk IV tanks received through Lend-Lease took part in the destruction of the encircled Sixth Army. The single Valentine Mk III in the front's forces appears to be a real 'lone wolf'. Before 8 January the 254th Tank Brigade numbered two T-26s. They were later restored and put into action. Operation Ring was, perhaps, one of the last episodes in which tanks of this type were employed. The *front* also included the 2nd Guards, 4th Guards, 6th Guards, and 189th Independent Tank Regiments, the 121st Tank Brigade, and the 512th Independent Tank Battalion, which did not have any equipment.

Rokossovskii's forces, while not having a large superiority over the enemy in men, were significantly stronger than the Sixth Army in artillery and tanks. In the 65th Army's zone, along the axis of the main attack, the Soviet forces outnumbered the enemy by three times in infantry and fifteen times in artillery. The appointment of Artillery Marshal Voronov as *Stavka* VGK representative to the Don Front does not seem accidental. Given the weakness of the rifle divisions, it was planned to crush the enemy with a powerful artillery attack. Besides, a number of measures were carried out to increase the efficiency of the infantry's actions. It was planned to destroy the enemy's firing points with assault groups.

The German Sixth Army's panzer forces by the start of Operation Ring were, of course, not in the same condition in which they had ground up the Stalingrad Front's tank corps in July–September 1942. However, it was too soon to play Chopin's 'Funeral March' over them.

Table 44: The Strength of the Sixth Army's Tank Park on 9 January 1943.

	Panzer II	*Panzer III (short)*	*Panzer III (long)*
24th Panzer Division	–	1	1
16th Panzer Division	–	–	5
60th Motorized Division	–	–	2
60th Motorized Division*	–	–	5
3rd Motorized Division**	–	–	15
29th Motorized Division	–	–	8
Friedrich Company	–	–	3
II/Panzer Rgt.36***	–	–	1
160th Panzer Bn**** (60th Motorized Division)	–	–	3

	Panzer III 75mm	Panzer IV (short)	Panzer IV (long)	Command Tanks
24th Panzer Division	–	1	1	1
16th Panzer Division	–	–	3	4
60th Motorized Division	–	1	–	–
60th Motorized Division*	1	2	–	–
3rd Motorized Division**	–	2	5	–
29th Motorized Division	–	3	7	–
Friedrich Company	–	–	2	–
II/Panzer Rgt.36***	–	–	–	–
160th Panzer Bn**** (60th Motorized Division)	3	2	3	–

* Tanks transferred from the 24th Panzer Division.
** As of 8 Jan 1943.
*** Subordinated to the VIII Army Corps on 8 Jan 1943.
**** Subordinated to the VIII Army Corps on 7 Jan 1943; 11 tanks of unidentified type on 8 Jan 1943.

Besides tanks, the 29th Motorized Division disposed of four heavy and fourteen medium anti-tank guns and seven 88mm anti-aircraft guns. The 177th and 244th Assault Gun Battalions were also subordinated to the VIII Army Corps (113th, 76th and 44th Infantry Divisions). On 7 January the former disposed of seven *Sturmgeschütze* and two captured KVs, and the latter seven *Sturmgeschütze* and two self-propelled s.IG-33s.

As we can see, the most powerful tank fist was along the western face of the 'cauldron'. Voronov, in his justification for choosing the axis of the main attack, was quite wrong concerning the German troops' real combat capabilities along this sector of the encirclement perimeter. The axis of the Soviet forces' main attack lay along the boundary between the 29th Motorized and 44th Infantry Divisions. The first, as of 21 December 1942, was a real titan: an entire nine grenadier battalions (one strong, six of average strength, one weak, and one exhausted), with 90 per cent mobility. The 44th Infantry Division consisted of seven battalions (four weak and three exhausted). The 76th Infantry Division numbered six battalions (three of average strength and three weak). On the other hand, the 60th Motorized Division, which was defending along the 'favourite' axis near the Semaphore, that is, in the direction of Kotluban' and Konnyi rail siding, contained seven battalions (two weak and five exhausted). Thus an attack along the tested axis could have yielded a much better result. They could have immediately split the Sixth Army's group of forces in two and deprived it of the opportunity of employing the Gumrak and Pitomnik airfields. To be fair, one should note that the 3rd Motorized Division, which was the strongest in tanks, was on the most westerly sector of the 'cauldron' (which did not come under attack in Operation Ring), but it had only five grenadier battalions (one of average strength and four weak). In all, according to data for 18 December 1942, the Sixth Army had a ration strength of 249,600 men. This included 13,000 Romanians, 19,300 'Hiwis' and 6,000 wounded.

The forces of the Don Front attacked on the morning of 10 January. A direct aviation and powerful 55-minute artillery preparation preceded the infantry and tank attack. In the 44th Infantry Division's history, the beginning of the Soviet offensive is described as follows:

> The lower regions yawned wide on 10 January 1943. The Russians' offensive began. An hour-long artillery preparation – and for the first time of such length and power during the Second World War that, in the opinion of the participants in the battle of Verdun during the First World War, exceeded the artillery fire of that time – came down upon the German positions. The ground buzzed under the hail of iron and the firing of guns merged into an uninterrupted rolling dull roar. It was a miracle that in spite of this murderous fire and the weak shelters, the German troops did not suffer heavy losses. Then the waves of the attacking enemy went into action. A large number of tanks supported the infantry.[5]

Regarding the phrase 'did not suffer heavy losses', one must take the formation historian at his word – after 05.00 on 10 January there were no reports received of losses from the 44th Infantry Division.

By the close of the first day of the offensive the enemy's defence along a number of sectors had been pierced to a depth of 6–8km. The 65th Army made the greatest advance. On the evening of 10 January the Army Group Don commander was reporting to Hitler: 'The Sixth Army commander is reporting breakthroughs by major Russian forces in the north, west and south, aimed at Karpovka and Pitomnik. The 44th and 76th Infantry Divisions suffered heavy losses; the 29th Motorized Division has only individual units capable of fighting. There is no hope of restoring the situation. Dmitrievka, Tsybenko and Rakotino have been abandoned.' On 11 and 12 January the forces of the Don Front, while crushing the resistance of the enemy's individual combat-capable units, continued to advance, and by the close of 12 January the *front's* main shock group had reached the Rossoshka River. The enemy's defence had been penetrated along the Chervlennaya River, along the axis of the 64th and 57th Armies' attack, and the Soviet forces advanced 6–8km here. The attackers failed only in the 66th Army's sector. It was written about this army in the Red Army General Staff's operational report, that it 'attempted to attack with its centre units, but, upon encountering the enemy's powerful fire resistance, failed to achieve success'.

The first days of the offensive had already proved to be costly in losses for the Don Front's tank forces. In three days of fighting the strength of the Don Front's tank park fell by more than half. Many full-strength regiments lost a significant part of their equipment. For example, the 47th Guards Tank Regiment, which was outfitted with Churchills, to be honest, was burnt to a crisp. Of twenty-one tanks before the beginning of the operation, by the evening of the third day of the offensive there remained only three vehicles. Of course, in positional fighting, all the more so in conditions of the Soviet forces' offensive, a significant part of the knocked-out vehicles could have been restored. But the sharp drop in the number of tanks in the *front's* units reduced the pace of the offensive. Eleven combat-capable tanks still remained in the German 3rd Motorized Division on 12 January, and four Panzer IIIs (long), one Panzer IV (long) and one command tank in the 16th Panzer Division. Moreover, two KVs and one T-34 were being employed as static firing points in the 16th Panzer Division.

Table 45: Tanks in Line in the Don Front's Tank Units at 22.00 on 9 January 1943.[6]

Army	Formation	KV	T-34	T-60	T-70	Mk III	Mk IV	T-26	Total
24th	8th Gds Tank Rgt	1	–	1	–	–	–	–	2
66th	7th Gds Tank Rgt	3	1	–	3	–	–	–	7
65th	91st Tank Bde	14	2	2	–	1	–	–	19
	47th Gds Independent Tank Rgt	–	–	–	–	–	3	–	3
	15th Gds Independent Tank Rgt	4	–	–	–	–	–	–	4
	10th Gds Tank Rgt	6	–	–	–	–	–	–	6
	9th Gds Tank Rgt	8	–	–	–	–	–	–	8
	5th Gds Tank Rgt	6	–	–	–	–	–	–	6
	14th Gds Tank Rgt	8	–	–	–	–	–	–	8
21st	1st Gds Tank Rgt	3	2	–	–	–	–	–	5
62nd	Composite company	1	–	–	–	–	–	–	1
64th	90th Tank Bde	1	4	1	2	–	–	–	8
	166th Independent Tank Rgt	–	1	–	–	–	–	–	1
	35th Independent Tank Rgt	–	2	–	1	–	–	–	3
57th	235th Tank Bde	–	1	–	1	–	–	–	2
	234th Independent Tank Regiment	–	1	–	2	–	–	–	3
	254th Tank Bde	–	1	–	–	–	–	–	1
	189th Independent Tank Rgt	–	–	1	–	–	–	2	3
Total for the front		54	34	5	21	1	3	2	120

The German command's attempt to delay the further advance of the Soviet forces along the second defensive line, which mostly ran along the middle Stalingrad defensive line, was not successful. The 'hydraulic press' of 2,500 guns slowly but surely did its work.

The Don Front's troops, having carried out a regrouping of forces during 13–14 January, resumed the offensive on the morning of 15 January. The defence was pierced by the middle of the day. The remnants of the Sixth Army began to fall back to the ruins of Stalingrad.

As a last attempt to rescue the supply situation in 'Fortress Stalingrad', on 15 January 1943 Erhard Milch, who was known for his organizational abilities, left Rastenburg[7] for Army Group Don. He had not even managed to arrive when the 'air bridge' suffered a serious blow: during the night of 15/16 January the Pitomnik airfield was lost. This meant not only the loss of an airfield. Pitomnik was a well-equipped airfield for navigation. Not long before the capture of Pitomnik by Soviet units, Richtofen ordered a new air base to be outfitted in Gumrak. This had been a small Soviet airfield. The question of preparing it to receive transport aircraft had been raised a few weeks earlier. However, the Sixth Army command had not supported this idea. Paulus's headquarters was located there, as were the headquarters of two corps, a hospital and a depot. Thus the army did not want to attract the attention of the Soviet air force to Gumrak with any kind of construction work. Work here began only in light of the threat of Pitomnik being seized. At first Gumrak did not even have a radio beacon. Although it was formally ready to receive aircraft by 16 January, by the time of Milch's arrival Ju 52s could not even land there, only He 111s. On 16 January ten Heinkels landed at Gumrak. The Junkers switched over to dropping parachute containers for a while.

Milch was shocked by what he heard on 16 January at a meeting in the Fourth Air Fleet's headquarters train. The level of the transport planes' combat readiness had fallen to 20 per cent. The Fourth Air Fleet disposed of 140 Ju 52s at that moment, of which only 42 were combat ready. In turn, of those forty-two, twenty-seven were in the process of rebasing to Zverevo and were unable to immediately make flights to the 'cauldron'. As a result, the 'air bridge' was conducted with only fifteen Ju 52s. There were also 140 He 111 bombers, of which 41 were combat ready. Of twenty-nine Fw 200 Condors, only one was combat ready. This four-engine plane proved to be too sensitive to the harsh conditions of the Russian winter and the gruelling conditions of its employment.

Milch put forward an idea that had already been discussed by the Fourth Air Fleet command – to supply Paulus with the aid of gliders. But Richtofen and Fibig came to the conclusion that the conditions in Stalingrad were unsuitable for gliders. First of all, they were 'sitting ducks' for the Soviet fighters. The Fourth Air Fleet lacked fighters for escorting the Ju 52s, so to allot some for the gliders was simply unrealistic. Second of all, they had no capability for taking off from the 'cauldron'. That is, the gliders would be a 'one-time' thing. However, Milch busied himself for some time with this idea until it had to be abandoned due to the worsening of the situation.

By 16 January the territory of the Sixth Army's encirclement had shrunk to less than one-third of its original size. The Don Front's losses during the first five days of the offensive can be seen in the table.

Table 46: The Losses of the Don Front's Forces During 10–15 January 1943.[8]

Army	Killed	Wounded	Missing in Action	Other Causes	Total
21st	790	2,701	1	13	3,505
24th	466	1,242	7	103	1,818
57th	669	1,385	10	111	2,176
62nd	623	1,610	17	65	2,315
65th	1,899	6,379	21	121	8,426
66th	1,086	2,514	55	154	3,809
Total	5,533	15,832	111	567	22,043

In pursing the enemy's retreating units, by the end of 17 January the Don Front's forces had reached the line Bol'shaya Rossoshka – Gonchara – Voroponovo, where they encountered stubborn enemy resistance in the old Soviet fortifications along the approaches to the city. The 48th Independent Guards Tank Regiment, with Churchill Mk IV tanks, was dispatched on 16 January to strengthen the *front's* tank forces. It was subordinated to the 21st Army.

Bad news came one after the other in the German headquarters. On 17 January the recently-established Ju 52 base in Zverevo was attacked by Soviet aircraft. Nine Ju 52s were set on fire and another twelve were damaged. Only twelve planes remained operational. German air bases were usually well protected by anti-aircraft fire and the results of attacks against them were not very high. However, only a single battery of Romanian (!) 75mm guns and one battery of 37mm cannon were providing Zverevo's anti-aircraft defence. This rendered the Soviet fliers' success even more predictable.

On the morning of 19 January the commander of the XIV Panzer Corps, Hube, was summoned to continue work in Milch's special headquarters. He arrived on 20 January and immediately sent to the headquarters of the Sixth Army a list of effective officers, who were true to their oaths and who were to be recalled from the 'cauldron'. The German command essentially made the cruel but well-founded decision analogous to the attempt to extricate the Maritime Army's command echelon from Sevastopol' in June 1942. Hube himself would still cause no small amount of unpleasantness for the Soviet forces: he would receive one of the Third Reich's highest awards – the Diamonds to the Knight's Cross – for the fighting in the winter of 1944. Only an air crash on 21 April 1944 would cut short the career of the 'one-armed general', who had escaped from Stalingrad by a miracle.

Quite a lot of high-ranking officers and generals were taken out of the 'cauldron'. Thus, aside from the commander of the XIV Panzer Corps, General Hube, the commander of the 60th Motorized Division, Major General Kohlermann was taken out of Stalingrad. Among the commanders of the LI Corps' formations who abandoned the 'cauldron' were the commander of the 79th Infantry Division, Lieutenant General Count von Schwerin, the commander of the disbanded 94th Infantry Division, Lieutenant General Pfeiffer, and the commander of the 305th Infantry Division, Lieutenant General Steinmetz. Among the formation commanders of the XI Army Corps taken out of Stalingrad was the commander of the 384th Infantry Division, Lieutenant General von Gablenz. The list of officers from the IV Army Corps removed was headed by its commander, General of Engineers Jaenecke. The commander of the 9th Anti-Aircraft Division, Major General Pickert, who was one of Göring's favourites, also abandoned the 'cauldron'. To be exact, he flew out of the 'cauldron' and was supposed to return on the day when Pitomnik was lost. Thus Pickert never took off for Gumrak. The process of removing valuable cadres from the 'cauldron' affected not only the generals. Colonels Selle and Stiotta, who commanded the engineer troops, also left the encirclement. There were also less notable personages, for example, Major Willy Langk, who commanded a panzer regiment in the 14th Panzer Division and was later the commander of the 'Kurmark' Division in 1945. In a word, harsh military necessity forced them to preserve their command cadres and attempt to save then, tearing them away from the ranks of the army doomed to death.

However, one should not say that Milch's arrival was completely useless. For example, on 20 January he summoned an additional fifty qualified technicians from the Luftwaffe's testing centre in Rechlin. When they arrived and had familiarized themselves with the work of the airfield commands and crews, a remarkable thing was discovered. Only a few air crews who had been brought in for the 'air bridge' operation had been using the manufacturer's recommended procedure for starting engines in cold weather. This was understandable as regards the units transferred from North Africa, but these were in a minority and the practice of incorrectly starting engines was widespread. Draconian measures were adopted to make the pilots carry out the necessary procedure. As a result, the number of combat-ready planes grew from 20 per cent to 30 per cent. Nevertheless, Milch's innovation was already far too late. From the time of his arrival, the amount of freight delivered daily to the 'cauldron' had even fallen. Of course, this was not linked to his feverish activity, but to the overall worsening of the situation. If he had arrived earlier, it's possible that Paulus's troops would have been supplied somewhat better, if only by increasing the number of serviceable aircraft.

The preparation for an attack on the last line on the approaches to the city continued for four days. The operation's centre of gravity was shifted to the 21st Army's sector. The 65th Army's main artillery and rocket artillery forces were to be transferred to I.M. Chistyakov's army. A number of tanks were also received. On 22 January a train with twenty-three T-34 tanks arrived at Kachalino station to maintain the combat capabilities of the thinned-out ranks of the *front's* tank troops. The offensive by Rokossovskii's troops resumed along the entire front on the morning of 22 January. The enemy stubbornly held the fortifications of the inner line, but following crushing blows by Soviet artillery the enemy's defence was penetrated.

The Soviet forces' new successes reduced to nothing all the efforts to galvanize the 'air bridge'. Milch made great efforts to improve the working conditions at Gumrak. A radio beacon was installed there, as well as a radio homing device and a system for receiving freight was worked out. But it was lost on 23 January. Expecting the loss of Gumrak, on 21 January the Sixth Army began to outfit yet another airfield – Stalingrad. On 22 January it had been prepared to receive aircraft. However, the attempt to land He 111s there led immediately to the loss of six aircraft due to the thick snow and bomb craters on the landing strip. Moreover, the situation was worsening so rapidly that the Stalingrad airfield was lost literally within a few hours after Gumrak. Now the supply of the troops in the 'cauldron' was carried out only by parachute drops. There could no longer be any talk of evacuating the wounded. Moreover, the search for and gathering up of the containers was tied to many difficulties. Paulus reported that 'Many "bombs"[9] have not been found, because we do not have sufficient fuel to seek them out'. A significant proportion of the dropped containers were gathered up by the Soviets.

On 24 January, the day after the loss of the final airfield within the 'cauldron', Paulus reported: 'The 44th, 76th, 100th, 305th, and 384th Infantry Divisions have been destroyed. In light of the enemy's penetration the front has been torn apart along many sectors. There are strongholds and shelters only in the area of the city and further defence is senseless. Disaster is inevitable. I request you immediately authorize me to capitulate in order to save those people who remain.' No such permission was given by Hitler.

On 25 January the forces of the Don Front broke into Stalingrad from the west. By the close of 26 January the forces of the 21st and 62nd Armies linked up in the area of Mamaev hill and split the enemy forces into two parts: a southern part, pressed into the central part of the city, and a northern one, which ended up surrounded in the area of the tractor factory and the 'Barricade' factory.

The XI Army Corps had been surrounded in the area of the 'Barricade' factory and the IV, VIII and LI Corps and XIV Panzer Corps in Stalingrad itself, to the south and north of the valley of the Tsaritsa River. On 28 January the southern part of the encirclement area was, in its turn, torn in two. The Sixth Army, now split up into three parts, each isolated from the other, was living out its final days and even hours. The Sixth Army's evening report on 28 January stated:

The enemy's powerful breakthrough along the Gumrak – Stalingrad rail line has broken the army's front into sectors: a northern cauldron with the XI Army Corps, a central cauldron with the VII and LI Army Corps, and a southern cauldron with the command post and remnants of the army. The XIV Panzer and IV Army Corps have lost their units. The army is undertaking attempts to create a new defensive front along the northern edge of the cauldron and the western forward edge. The army assumes that its resistance will be finally crushed before 1 February.

One has to say that the forecast concerning the length of resistance was quite an accurate one. Paulus's headquarters was located in the basement of one of the buildings in the centre of Stalingrad. It is usually stated that the Sixth Army's headquarters was located in a department store, although in the Don Front's war diary the building of the executive committee is confidently named as the location of the headquarters and the place of its capture.

General Schmidt maintained contact with the other 'cauldrons' by radio. By this time the German forces' combat capability had declined sharply. Paulus's soldiers and officers began to surrender in droves. In just three days, 27–29 January, the 64th Army's units took 15,000 men and officers prisoner. The Don Front's own losses for 20–30 January 1943 can be seen from the following table.

Table 47: The Losses of the Don Front's Forces During 20–30 January 1943.

Army	Killed	Wounded	Missing in Action	Other Causes	Total
21st	1,759	5,478	48	56	7,341
24th*	355	845	–	82	1,282
57th	731	3,176	24	282	4,213
62nd	1,208	2,209	15	94	3,526
64th*	392	1,142	11	54	1,599
65th	900	3,376	26	217	4,519
66th	874	2,306	10	213	3,403
Total	6,219	18, 532	134	998	25,883

* Figures only for 20–25 January 1943.

It should be noted that the *front's* losses slowly but surely fell in the last ten-day period in January. For example, if during 20–25 January the overall losses were 16,444 men, then during 25–30 January overall losses were only 9,439 men. The 24th Army had left the *front* by that time.

On 30 January, on the tenth anniversary of the Nazi Party coming to power, Milch decided to make a gift to the remnants of the Sixth Army. Eighty-five aircraft left for a night flight to Stalingrad. They dropped 72 tons in parachute containers, predominantly on the northern 'cauldron', which was defended by the XI Army Corps.

On 30 January Paulus received a final radiogram from Hitler. It stated: 'I congratulate you upon being promoted to General Field Marshal.' This was essentially a veiled order to commit suicide. However, having carried out the order to hold on to the last man, Paulus did not consider it necessary to refuse to be captured. Moreover, Schmidt, the Sixth Army's chief of staff, on that day ordered a translator to go out onto the square with a white flag and find Soviet commanders to whom they could surrender. At first negotiations were held with the chief of the 38th Motorized Brigade's operational section, Senior Lieutenant F.M. Il'chenko. On the morning of 31 January a delegation from the headquarters of the 64th Army, headed by the army's chief of staff, Major General I.A. Laskin, the chief of the army's operational section, Colonel Lukin, and the commander of the 38th Motorized Rifle Brigade, Colonel Burakov, descended into the basement of the executive committee building. Upon arriving at Paulus's headquarters, they presented an ultimatum for the cessation of resistance and the complete capitulation of the encircled group of German forces. It should be emphasized that in the 64th Army's documents the place where they were captured was clearly stated to be the executive committee building. This was written in black and white in the 'Report on the Circumstances of the Capture of the Commander of the German Sixth Army, Field Marshal Paulus', which was sent to Rokossovskii by the 65th Army's military council. It stated:

> On the morning of 31.1.43 General Field Marshal Paulus was located in the executive committee building (the central part of the city of Stalingrad).
>
> During the fighting the building was surrounded by elements of the 38th Motorized Rifle Brigade under the direct command of the deputy brigade commander for political affairs, Lieutenant Colonel L.A. Vinokur.
>
> Following the encirclement of the building, von Paulus's personal adjutant arrived with a proposal to conduct negotiations.[10]

The report was signed by all the members of the army's military council, including Laskin, who personally went down to Paulus's headquarters. The word 'Department Store' was written in large letters on the façade of the department store and it would have been difficult for Comrade Laskin to confuse the two buildings on a clear winter morning. The executive committee building is even mentioned in the 64th Army's evening operational report.

At 10.00, Paulus was presented with an ultimatum to cease resistance and to completely surrender the encircled group of German forces. The ultimatum was accepted, but there was a hitch with the complete capitulation. The commander of the southern group of German forces in Stalingrad, Major General Fritz Roske, signed an order to cease combat activities and to surrender weapons. At that time Roske was carrying out the duties of the commander of the 71st Infantry Division in place of General of Infantry Alexander von Hartmann, who had perished on 26 January. It should be emphasized that it was Roske, not Paulus, who issued the order. Later, during an interrogation by Shumilov, Paulus emphasized that Roske made the decision on his own and that he (the commander of the Sixth Army) did not confirm it.

During the negotiations they demanded that Paulus issue an order to the troops of the northern group to cease resistance, but the commander of the Sixth Army refused. During the interrogation by Shumilov, Paulus justified his position as follows: 'I cannot issue orders to capitulate to troops not subordinated [directly, Author] to me. I hope you will understand the situation of a soldier and understand his duties.'[11] The commander of the 29th Motorized Division, Leyser, the chief of the LI Corps' artillery, Major General Vassoll, and the commander of the Romanian 1st Cavalry Division, General Bratescu, surrendered together with Paulus.

On 31 January, 12,800 men surrendered to the forces of the 21st Army during the capitulation of the southern group, including the commander of the 100th Jäger Division, Lieutenant General Sanne, the commander of the VIII Army Corps, Wilhelm Heitz, the commander of the 76th Infantry Division, Lieutenant General Rodenburg. Units of the 62nd Army captured the commander of the LI Corps, Lieutenant General Seydlitz, and the commander of the IV Army Corps, Lieutenant General of Artillery Pfeffer.

It's possible that they later reported Paulus's capture as being in the basement of the department store in order not to cast a shadow on the building where the organs of executive power were located. Unkind tongues would have immediately christened the dwelling of the people's servants as 'Paulus's house'. However, after the war the then executive committee building was torn down. The department store came up only on 5 February in a report by the headquarters of the 38th Motorized Rifle Brigade. However, in this very report, for some reason the German delegate is called 'the adjutant of the commander of the southern group, Major General Roske'. That is, in confirming the accepted version in one place, the report by the headquarters of the 38th Motorized Rifle Brigade places it upside down in another.

In a word, there is no unanimity in the documents, although the version of the executive committee building appears more often. So, where was Paulus captured? I personally prefer the version that on the morning of 31 January Comrade Laskin was in his right mind and memory when he was compiling the report to the *front* headquarters referring to the executive committee building. Post-war memoirs, written by both the participants in these events from the Soviet side, as well as by former Wehrmacht officers, who became citizens of East Germany, could have been subjected to editing for these and other reasons.

The northern group of forces held on a bit longer than the southern. On 1 February the Don Front's forces launched a powerful attack against its several isolated centres. The remnants of the 16th Panzer Division were located in the area of the silicate factory, the remnants of the 24th Panzer and 389th Infantry Divisions in the area of the Stalingrad Tractor Factory and its worker's settlement, and the 305th Infantry Division and remnants of other formations driven there from the worker's settlements in the area of the 'Barricade' factory.

On 2 February, following a powerful artillery bombardment, the XI Army Corps in the area of the 'Barricade' factory laid down its arms and ceased resistance. The corps commander, Lieutenant General Karl Strecker, surrendered. On 2 February the 21st Army's units took 17,964 men prisoner, among which were the commander of the 113th Infantry Division, Lieutenant General Sixt von Arnim, and the commander of the 305th Infantry Division, Lieutenant General Steinmetz. The 62nd Army's units added to this list the commander of the 389th Infantry Division, Major General Lattmann and the commander of the 24th Panzer Division, Lieutenant General von Lenski. In all, 15,000 men surrendered to the 62nd Army's forces. Only a few German senior officers committed suicide. Among them was Lieutenant General Gunther Angern, the commander of the 16th Panzer Division, who shot himself on 2 February 1943.

Following the elimination of the final centres of enemy resistance on 2 February, the forces of the Don Front began to load onto trains and gradually spread along the westward moving Soviet-German front. It was these very units that would have to form the southern face of the Kursk salient following the failure around Khar'kov.

Operation Ring ended up causing the Don Front's tank forces heavy losses. Following the intensive winnowing of the tank park during the first days of the offensive, its strength was never restored, despite the arriving reinforcements. The *front's* tank regiments and brigades were only a pale shadow of those which began the operation on 10 January 1943 (see table).

Table 48: Tanks in Line in the Don Front's Tank Units at 22.00 on 2 February 1943.[12]

Army	Formation	KV	T-34	T-60	T-70	Mk IV	Total
66th	7th Gds Tank Rgt	3	–	–	–	–	3
	8th Gds Tank Rgt	2	–	–	–	–	2
65th	254th Tank Bde	–	2	2	2	–	6
	91st Tank Bde	3	2	–	1	–	6
	121st Tank Bde	–	25	–	–	–	25
	47th Gds Independent Tank Rgt	–	–	–	–	4	4
	9th Gds Tank Rgt	10	–	–	–	–	10
62nd	90th Tank Bde	–	5	1	1	–	7
	5th Gds Tank Rgt	7	–	–	–	–	7
	Composite company	–	–	–	–	–	–
Front Reserve	1st Gds Tank Rgt	2	1	–	1	–	4
	48th Gds Tank Rgt	–	–	–	–	4	4
Total for the *front*		27	35	3	5	8	78

There remained less than a third of the initial strength of the Don Front's tank park. If you take into account the arriving reinforcements in military equipment, then by the end of Operation Ring there remained approximately a quarter of the combat vehicles that took part in the operation. Both regiments of Churchills (the 47th and 48th Guards Tank Regiments) suffered significant losses and only four vehicles remained from the full-strength regiments by the end of the battle.

However, despite the unevenness in planning and execution, Operation Ring consolidated the Red Army's success in the Stalingrad area. The entire world saw the crowds of forlornly wandering prisoners in the remnants of their clothing and the captured generals of the Wehrmacht who so recently had seemed invincible. In all, twenty-two enemy divisions were eliminated in the course of the Don Front's offensive operation from 10 January through 2 February 1943. A powerful blow had been inflicted on the German army's prestige.

Chapter 27

Conclusions to Part III

Regarding the success of Operation Uranus, it is first of all necessary to note that the Soviet command successfully took complete advantage of the 'window of opportunity', both in relation to the place and the time for launching the attack. Army Group B, as a whole, and the Sixth Army, were caught at a time when they did not dispose of sufficient mobile reserves, as well as men and materiel, for a stable defence of the front along the Don.

At the same time, one cannot but note that the 'window of opportunity' proved to be quite narrow and until the last moment the success of the operation remained uncertain. The defence commissar's Order No. 306, which was mentioned earlier, which basically reduced the Soviet infantry's shock capabilities, exacerbated the situation. Although no one formally rescinded the order, in practice they stopped being guided by it as early as December 1942. As the chief of the M.V. Frunze Military Academy, General A.I. Radzievskii, justly noted in a classified academic textbook in the post-war years: 'One should look to reduce losses not in a single-echelon formation, but in the more reliable suppression of the enemy's fire weapons, in changing the order of the displacement of the second (third) echelons before their commitment into the fighting, and in better cover against air attacks.'[1]

In evaluating Operations Uranus and Ring, it makes sense to go over those three points which were set out by Zhukov not long before the start of the Soviet offensive, on 3 November 1942. I should remind you that the mission of the three *fronts* was formulated in the following manner:

a) to force the Romanians to leave the war by completely defeating the Romanian army;
b) to achieve a decisive turning point in the war in the Soviets' favour;
c) to encircle and destroy the Stalingrad group of forces.

Despite the resounding defeat of the Romanian forces, Romania was not forced to leave the war. However, Stalingrad undoubtedly became the foundation for subsequent events. The turning point took place following the rout of the Romanian forces in the Crimea in the spring of 1944. In August 1944, on the fourth day of the Iasi – Kishinev operation, the Romanian king, Michael, summoned Marshal Antonescu to the palace and demanded an immediate armistice. Antonescu refused and was arrested. The king took negotiations with the Allies into his own hands. On the third day following Antonescu's arrest, the Romanian army turned on the Germans. Thus Romania left the war. But we should not forget that at that moment the Soviet 6th Tank Army was approaching Bucharest. At the end of 1942 and the beginning of 1943 the Germans and Antonescu himself possessed more than sufficient strength to maintain power in Romania. Thus we should admit that it was too much to expect Romania's exit from the war. Operation Uranus only led to the defeat and withdrawal from the territory of the USSR of two Romanian armies. On 7 January 1943 General Dumitrescu received orders to withdraw the remnants of the Third and Fourth Armies to Romania. On this date they numbered 73,062 men, consisting primarily of rear elements. But part of the Romanians at that moment were still scattered around various

German subunits. The Romanian army's losses from the start of Uranus were estimated at 140,000 men.

The turning point in a war is a difficult thing to determine. Nonetheless, one may confidently say that Stalingrad was one of the Second World War's turning points. It was not even a question of whether the Wehrmacht had achieved the goal of the campaign. The campaign in the Caucasus ended in a hurried withdrawal in the beginning of 1943. But the results of the battle of Stalingrad were not limited to this. The Wehrmacht suffered a major defeat. An entire army was eliminated at a single stroke. The Germans lost the strategic initiative for a long time.

November 1942 was a classic example of an incorrect definition of the enemy's plans. The Germans had prepared to wage a defensive battle, but not there and not with those forces where they were actually needed. Had the Germans been defending the defile between Lakes Tsatsa and Barmantsak, then there would have been every chance of it becoming the graveyard of Soviet armour. One might say the same thing about the perimeter of the bridgeheads at Kletskaya and Serafimovich. The shallow bridgehead at Kletskaya was particularly dangerous. The 21st Army's offensive from the Kletskaya bridgehead could have failed just like that of the 20th Army from the Vazuza bridgehead around Rzhev in November 1942. By an irony of fate, the group of forces attacking from the bridgeheads was the same: a tank corps and a cavalry corps. The difference was only in the troops who were occupying the perimeter of this and that bridgehead. The Germans also successfully repulsed the 24th Army's offensive. The Germans placed the Romanians where they considered the situation to be safe. They simply could not believe that there would be an immediate attack to a great depth and a meeting attack over quite deserted terrain.

The Soviet counteroffensive around Stalingrad was unprecedented on the Eastern Front. Never before had the Soviet forces tried to carry out an encirclement on such a scale. To be exact, major encirclement operations had been planned before this but had not been pushed to the closing of the 'pincers' in the enemy's rear. Correspondingly, the size of the 'fish' caught was such that its retention required great efforts. One cannot but agree with Manstein, who maintained: 'When on 22 or 23 December, he [Paulus] proposed breaking out with his army to the south-west, the appropriate moment, it is possible, had already been missed.'[2] The movement of such a mass of troops as the Sixth Army would have led to the breakthrough of the encirclement from within at the end of November 1942.

Soviet military specialists admitted the possibility of a breakthrough by the encircled forces. In the collection of materials on studying the experience of the war, which came out hot on the tail of these events in the spring of 1943, the following was noted:

> The situation might have developed otherwise, if the German high command had decided upon an independent removal of Paulus's group from the encirclement by an attack to the west and south-west. It's possible that in this instance part of the group's personnel could have been extracted from the encirclement ring, while losing its equipment and heavy weaponry. But the plan prevailed over reality, the expected help from the west did not arrive, and the encircled troops ended up completely isolated. The sole means for supply from the rear was transport aviation and radio communications. Given that situation which was arising along the Don Front at the end of November 1942, it was very important to have at *front* headquarters a correct idea of the strength of the enemy group of forces and its capabilities. Given different

behaviour by the encircled group of forces, that is, more decisive actions to break out of the encirclement at the very beginning, without the expectation of help from without, the miscalculation committed by the intelligence organs of the Don Front's headquarters in estimating the enemy would have led to serious complications of the situation in the area of the middle course of the Don.[3]

Actually, by no means did the formation of a sufficiently dense internal encirclement front happen immediately. The Kotel'nikovo axis was particularly weak, where the forces of the Stalingrad Front's 51st and 57th Armies were defending along the external and internal encirclement front. The 'Cannae's' southern wing was at first quite weak and the necessity of holding two fronts reduce its capabilities even further. The 4th Mechanized Corps occupied a zone of 60km along the internal encirclement front, which was quite a lot even for a formation with lots of infantry. In a word, during the first days following the closing of the 'cauldron' Paulus had a good chance of breaking out, with at least part of the Sixth Army's forces. Only the formations of the trans-Don part of Paulus's army were practically doomed to destruction.

According to Khrushchev's account, the possibility of a breakout was viewed as an inevitable evil:

> We were sure that the Germans would be surrounded in Stalingrad. I should repeat myself again, Zhukov and I had very good relations, and I told him: 'Comrade Zhukov, we'll do what we set out to do and surround the Germans. We should assume that the enemy's forces, when they find themselves surrounded, will want to break out. Where will they go? They won't try to break out of the encirclement to the north, but will move to the south. What will we hold them with? We don't have anything to hold them with. They will crush us, break out and get away.' Zhukov smiled and, looking at me, reacted with quite a strong and sharp flow of Russian words, adding: 'Let them go, we only need for them to leave and free up Stalingrad and the Volga.'[4]

However, this citation by Khrushchev doesn't dovetail well with Operation Uranus's tasks, as confirmed by documents, including removing Romania from the war.

From the operational point of view, the most striking thing in evaluating Operation Ring is the comparative lack of haste in carrying it out. Paulus's army had already been surrounded for a month and a half and was eliminated in only three weeks. One reason for this may be the exhaustion of the Don Front's forces, and another being the command's wish to avoid excessive losses. The first statement may be illustrated by a simple example. The 293rd Rifle Division entered the fighting at almost authorized strength. On 24 October 1942 the division had 10,420 men on hand. Following heavy fighting, its strength by 20 December had fallen to 3,797 men.

Nor was Paulus's army in better shape. On average they managed to supply the Sixth Army with the following amount of cargo per day. Up to 2,325 tons was delivered from 1 through 16 January, or an average of 145 tons per day. Only 790 tons were delivered or dropped into the 'cauldron' between 16 and 28 January, which yields an average per day of 60.75 tons. In all, during seventy days of aerial supply the Sixth Army received an average of 94.16 tons of cargo per day. This was far below even the minimal requirements in ammunition and food. With the start of Operation Ring, the Sixth Army's supply situation inexorably worsened.

The 'air bridge' for supplying Paulus's army became the last major operation by the Luftwaffe's transport aviation. Between 24 November and 31 January 1943 no less than 488 aircraft, which had been activated for supplying the Sixth Army, were lost: 166 aircraft were destroyed, 108 went missing in action, and 214 were written off as unrepairable. They were broken down in the following manner by type: 266 Ju 52s (a third of all such planes in the Luftwaffe), 165 He 111s, 42 Ju 86s, nine Fw 200s, five He 177s and one Ju 290.[5] Germany was no longer able to restore its transport aviation strength. The time when transport aviation could prevent all the efforts by Soviet forces to encircle large and small groups of German forces was irretrievably gone.

The weakness of both sides affected the languid development of the operation as a whole. The plan for the counteroffensive around Stalingrad called for splitting up the enemy group of forces into only two parts during the course of the encirclement. For this, an attack by the right-flank formations of the Don Front's 24th Army along the left bank of the Don in the direction of Vertyachii and Peskovatka was planned for the purpose of cutting off the enemy's forces operating in the small bend of the Don from the main forces in the Stalingrad area. We were not able to carry out such a splitting during the first stage of the counteroffensive.

All of this was the result of the fact that the armies of the Don Front's left wing and the right wing of the Stalingrad Front lacked sufficient men and material during the first days of the operation in order to split the enemy being surrounded; they had to limit themselves to just tying down a large number of enemy divisions which were opposite these armies. Attempts by the Soviet forces to eliminate the encircled enemy at the end of November by gradually squeezing his forces were unsuccessful. The enemy, who disposed of a large area of territory, was able to manoeuvre and reinforce.

In planning this operation, which began in January, the Don Front's headquarters miscalculated in estimating the encircled enemy's forces, which caused certain miscalculations in distributing men and materiel along axes. The idea of a splitting attack from north to south appears more appealing. A powerful attack might have disrupted the defence which the Stalingrad (and then the Don) Front had bumped up against in September and October 1942, while attempting to break into Stalingrad from the north. This is all the more so, since in January 1943 it was being occupied by far weaker forces. During Operation Ring the 66th Army's forces did not achieve a decisive success, that is, they disposed of minimal reinforcements. Twenty-seven artillery regiments might have had a far greater effect. The splitting of the Sixth Army in two would have undoubtedly shortened the time spent eliminating the resistance by the German forces in the 'cauldron'.

Conclusions

The most varied kinds of epithets are applied to the battle of Stalingrad, but one thing is obvious that this was a victory gained by the Red Army through much suffering. It was necessary to expend a great deal of strength in order to achieve an outstanding result in the form of the rout of a major enemy group of forces. The one who seized and held the strategic initiative was the one who called the shots in the summer campaign of 1942. It was impossible to transform the lengthy front from Leningrad to the Sea of Azov into an impregnable fortress.

The task of constructing a lengthy defensive front for the Red Army, which had only recently set about forming independent tank formations, was particularly difficult. As experience showed, holding the front required mobile reserves capable of rapidly moving to the axis of the enemy's attack and either 'sealing off' the breakthrough or launching an effective counterblow. As yet, the Soviet tank corps did not do this very well. If the breakthrough was not sealed, then the tank wedges would break into the depth of the troops' formation and close the lid of the 'cauldron' behind the numerous but low-mobility infantry formations. In these conditions a successful offensive and the seizure of the initiative was almost the only option. In the spring of 1942 the Soviet command was unable to tear the initiative from the enemy. Following the Crimea and Khar'kov and with the first attacks of Operation Blau, the fickle lady of the strategic initiative ended up in the embrace of the enemy for a long time. In practice, this turned into a hail of attacks, each following the other in those places where they were least expected.

In the summer of 1942 the reserve armies became USSR's 'security pillows'. The collapsing front around Voronezh and along the Stalingrad direction was re-established with their help. However, the Germans' seizure of the strategic initiative meant the continuation of the squall of attacks where they were not expected. Having attacked the 62nd Army's weak spot, the Germans rapidly crushed its front. Weak in infantry and artillery, the tank corps could only postpone the encirclement of the troops standing along the path to Stalingrad. Counterblows did not bring the desired results: the infantry did not follow the tanks and the tanks, left without infantry, were knocked out by the new 75mm guns which had arrived in the arsenals of the German anti-tank battalions. The 'thermite' shells sowed death in the ranks of the attacking T-34s and KVs. The Germans slowly but surely approached Stalingrad and in the middle of September broke into its streets.

Unfortunately, the city of Stalingrad was no exception in the achievement of success at the cost of great efforts and much blood. This was the case in the initial stages, as well as during the course of the fighting for the factory settlements and factories (the Stalingrad Tractor Factory, 'Barricade' and 'Red October'). In the beginning, the choice of a 'Mamaev' strategy with a powerful counterblow from Mamaev hill led to the defeat of the 62nd Army's units in the area immediately to the north and south of the Tsaritsa and to heavy losses among the fresh formations transferred to Chuikov. An indirect consequence of the 'Mamaev' strategy was the collapse of the front at the beginning of the Germans' attacks on the factory settlements. A number of mistakes were subsequently committed in the conduct of the defensive fighting, which subsequently led several times to a worsening of the situation in the city.

It was difficult for the Soviet troops around Stalingrad to win the artillery duel with the Sixth Army, if not impossible. The Red Army's capabilities in 1942 were objectively limited. Suffice it to say that in the USSR 67,698 tons of powder of all types were produced iin 1942[1], while 146,563 tons were produced in Germany.[2] This led to the USSR falling significantly behind in the number of shells produced and expended, particular large calibre ones.

But suddenly the moment arrived, which in hunters' stories begin with the words 'and then he came at me ...'. The Germans at first threw their most valuable mobile formations – the 14th and 24th Panzer Divisions – into the fighting in Stalingrad. Both were quickly reduced to ruins. They then moved to the south of Stalingrad the 29th Motorized Division, which it was planned to employ in the as-yet foggy plans to seize Astrakhan. After throwing in these trumps, the weak 22nd Panzer Division and the Romanian 1st Tank Division remained as Army Group B's reserve, subordinated to the XLVIII Panzer Corps. The powerful 6th Panzer Division simply failed to arrive at the front along the Don from France. The reformed Soviet tank and mechanized corps reached the front more rapidly.

The successful offensive around Stalingrad and the unsuccessful one around Rzhev, which was conducted at the same time, will be compared with each other. The successful Operation Uranus and the unsuccessful Operation Mars were not distinguished by the fact of who planned these operations and who carried them out. This is not the difference between a 'stupid Zhukov' and a 'smart Vasilevskii', but the difference between favourable and unfavourable conditions for conducting a major offensive. As opposed to Army Group B, Army Group Centre had combat-capable mobile reserves. It was precisely these that 'patched up' the Western and Kalinin fronts' penetration in November–December 1942. Also, around Rzhev and along the entire length of the front were German divisions which were far firmer against the Red Army's attacks of 1942. Tank and rifle formations for Operations Mars and Uranus arrived from the same source. The fate of the attacks against the Sixth Army's trans-Don group of forces shows the fate of Uranus in conditions when German troops occupied the entire front. It was not possible to cut off the XI Army Corps from the Sixth Army's main forces around Stalingrad. The 16th Tank Corps suffered heavy losses but did not achieve a decisive result. The exhaustion of this corps in Uranus is not any different that the 6th Tank Corps' attempts to break through the Germans' defence in Mars.

However, one should not think that the overall success of the Soviet forces' offensive in Operation Uranus was down solely to luck. The Soviet command single-mindedly created a situation for a future counteroffensive and, moreover, this process began long before the appearance of the plan for Uranus as such. Guided by the general principle of seizing and holding bridgeheads for the future, the Soviet command created bridgeheads at Kletskaya and Serafimovich. Through counter-attacks by the reserve armies and stubborn resistance on the streets of Stalingrad, the Soviet command placed the Sixth Army in the bottom of an operational 'hole' without major reserves. Further on, a certain amount of nerve was required for planning and carrying out an operation of unprecedented scale for the Red Army. The German command simply could not imagine such an operation.

Having surrounded Paulus's army, the Soviet command not only discovered that a far larger fish had fallen into its net than had been planned. Supply by air drew out the agony of those surrounded for another two and a half months. Stalingrad became one of the first *festungen* (fortresses) which slowed the pace of the Soviet forces' offensive by the fact of their location at a communications junction. According to a tradition which subsequently became widespread, a city became a *festung*. In the case with Stalingrad, the solid urban structures were augmented by defensive lines constructed along the approaches to the city.

The problem for the Red Army in 1942 was not manoeuvre actions, but breaking through the enemy's defence. In colliding with the German forces' prepared defences, Soviet units suffered heavy losses and failed to carry out their missions. This was typical not only of the well-fortified central sector of the Soviet-German front (Rzhev), but also for the thickening sectors of the front around Stalingrad. A more typical example was the Stalingrad Front's combat operations to the north of the city in September–October and those of the 24th Army in Operation Uranus in November 1942. The breakthrough of the Romanian forces' defence and the subsequent manoeuvre operations by the Red Army's forces were quite successful. Moreover, the manoeuvre duel with the German mobile formations at Verkhne-Kumskii during the repulse of Operation Winter Storm was conducted more than worthily. The Red Army would still have to demonstrate its skills in conducting manoeuvre operations. Stalingrad was just the first sign of this.

Notes

Chapter 1: Thermite Rain

1. Editor's note. Semyon Konstantinovich Timoshenko (1895–1970) was drafted into the Imperial Russian Army in 1914 and joined the Red Army in 1918. He later commanded Soviet forces in Finland and was appointed defence commissar in 1940. During the Second World War he commanded several *fronts* and high commands, but his lack of success led to his eventual eclipse and he never held an important command after 1942.

2. Editor's note. The *Stavka* of the Supreme Commander-in-Chief (*Stavka Verkhovnogo Glavnokomanduyushchego*), also known as the *Stavka* of the VGK, was the Soviet Union's highest military body during the Second World War. The *Stavka* was comprised of high-ranking civilian and military personnel and functioned as Stalin's military secretariat. Stalin, as supreme commander-in-chief, was the chairman of this body and the General Staff its executive organ.

3. Editor's note. Vasilii Nikolaevich Gordov (1896–1950) joined the Red Army in 1918 and fought in the Russian Civil War. During the Second World War he commanded a *front* and several armies. Gordov retired in 1946, but was arrested the following year on Stalin's orders and later executed.

4. Editor's note. This is a reference to Stalin, the chairman of the *Stavka* and the supreme commander-in-chief (*Verkhovnyi Glavnokomanduyushchii*).

5. Editor's note. Andrei Ivanovich Yeremenko (1892–1970) was drafted into the Imperial Russian Army in 1913 and joined the Red Army in 1918. During the Second World War he commanded armies and *fronts*. Following the war he commanded a number of military districts. He retired in 1958.

6. *Stalingradskaya Bitva. Khroniika, Fakty, Lyudi* (Moscow: Olma-Press, 2002), book I, p. 235.

7. Editor's note. Maximillian von Weichs (1881–1954) joined the Imperial German Army in 1914 and fought in the First World War. During the Second World War he commanded a corps, armies and army groups in Poland, the West, the Soviet Union, and the Balkans. Following the war, von Weichs was arrested for war crimes but was later released.

8. NARA T312, R1685, frame 19. Highlighted by the author.

9. Editor's note. Friedrich Wilhelm Ernst Paulus (1890–1957) joined the Imperial German Army in 1910 and fought in the First World War. During the Second World War he served in senior staff positions until his appointment as commander of the Sixth Army in early 1942. Paulus and his army were encircled at Stalingrad and forced to surrender in early 1943. While in captivity, Paulus became a critic of Hitler and joined the National Committee for a Free Germany. He was freed and returned to East Germany in 1953.

10. NARA, T312, R1685, frame 34.

11. Ibid.

12. On Soviet maps, Rychkovskii.

13. At first it was planned to transfer the 23rd and 24th Panzer Divisions to Paulus, but later the 23rd Panzer Division was retained as part of the group of forces attacking toward the Caucasus Mountains.

14. NARA T312 R1685, frame 187.

15. Editor's note. The OKW (*Oberkommando der Wehrmacht*) was established in 1938 to coordinate army, navy and air force operations. As the war progressed, the OKW came increasingly to operate as Hitler's military staff in opposition to the army high command (*Oberkommando des Heers* – OKH).

16. Editor's note. Vasilii Ivanovich Kuznetsov (1894–1964) was drafted into the Imperial Russian Army in 1915 and joined the Red Army in 1918. During the Second World War he commanded several armies and was a deputy *front* commander. Following the war, Kuznetsov commanded an army and a military district and served in the central military apparatus.

17. Editor's note. Vladimir Yakovlevich Kolpakchi (1899–1961) joined the Red Army in 1918 and fought in the Russian Civil War. During the Second World War he served in higher staff positions and commanded a number of armies. Following the war, Kolpakchi commanded a number of military districts and served in the central military apparatus. He died in an air crash.

18. Editor's note. Vasilii Ivanovich Chuikov (1900–82) joined the Red Army in 1918 and fought in the Russian Civil War. During the interwar period he commanded an army during the 1939–40 war with Finland and was a Soviet military advisor to Chinese leader Chiang Kai-shek. During the Second World War he commanded an army in the defence of Stalingrad and held this post until the end of the war. Following the war, Chuikov commanded Soviet occupation troops in Germany, served as commander-in-chief of the Ground Forces, and was chief of national civil defence.

19. Editor's note. Fedor Vasil'evich Tokarev (1871–1968) was a Russian-Soviet firearms designer whose career encompassed both the Tsarist and Soviet regimes. The single-shot rifle referred to here is his 7.62mm 1938/40 model.

20. Tsentral'nyi Arkhiv Ministerstva Oborony Rossiiskoi Federatsii, fond 206, opis' 280, delo 10, list 9. This archive is hereafter abbreviated as TsAMO RF.

21. TsAMO RF, f. 81, op. 12074, d. 8, l. 160.

22. TsAMO RF, f. 220, op. 220, d. 71, l. 48.

23. TsAMO, f. 206, op. 280, d. 0, 11. 13–14.

24. *Russkii Arkhiv. Velikaya Otechestvennaya Voina: Stavka VGK: Dokumenty i Materialy: 1942 God* (Moscow: Terra, 1996), vol. XVI (5-2), p. 294. This publication is hereafter referred to as *Russkii Arkhiv*.

25. Editor's note. The Sovinformburo (Soviet Information Bureau) was the leading Soviet news agency from 1941 to 1961.

26. NARA, T312, R1448, frame 839. The XIV and XXIV Panzer Corps, which were transferred later, were not counted here.

27. *Velikaya Otechestvennaya Voina, 1941-1945 gg. Kampanii i Strategicheskie Operatsii v Tsifrakh* (Moscow: Ob"edinennaya Redaktsiya MVD Rossii, 2010), vol. I, p. 441.

28. Ibid., vol. I, p. 430.

29. TsAMO RF, f. 220, op. 220, d. 71, l. 48.

30. NARA, T312, R1448, frames 120-2.

31. The 75th Infantry Division was armed with guns of both types.

32. NARA, T312, R1685, frame 105.

33. Ibid.

34. NARA, T312, R1448, frame 156.

35. NARA, T312, R1685, frames 95, 102.

36. NARA, T312, R1683, frame 899.

37. NARA, T312, R1685, frames, 258-9, 301.

38. Editor's note. Aleksandr Mikhailovich Vasilevskii (1895–1977) joined the Imperial Russian Army in 1915 and the Red Army in 1918. During the Second World War he served primarily in the General Staff apparatus and was chief of the General Staff during 1942–5. He was also a *Stavka* representative to several *fronts* and commanded troops in Europe and the Far East. Following the war he again served as chief of the General Staff and was later minister of the armed forces. Vasilevskii's career went into decline after Stalin's death and he was forced to retire in 1957.

39. TsAMO RF, f. 220, op. 220, d. 18, l. 259.

40. TsAMO RF, f. 3430, op. 1 d. 34, l. 29.

41. TsAMO RF, f. 220, op. 235, d. 6/2, l. 457.

42. *Sbornik Boevykh Dokumentov, Velikoi Otechestvennoi Voiny*, Vypusk No. 33. (Moscow: Voennoe Izdatel'stvo, 1957), p. 169.

43. Ibid.

44. TsAMO RF, f. 220, op. 235, d. 6/2, l. 423.

45. Editor's note. Yakov Nikolaevich Fedorenko (1896–1947) was drafted into the Imperial Russian Navy in 1915 and he joined the Red Army in 1918. During the Second World War he headed the Main Armoured Administration and was simultaneously the chief of the Red Army's mechanised and armoured forces.

46. TsAMO RF, f. 38, op. 11360, d. 120, l. 135.

47. Editor's note. A Guards mortar regiment consisted of rocket artillery, commonly known as 'Katyushas'.

48. Editor's note. Kirill Semyonovich Moskalenko (1902–85) joined the Red Army in 1920 and fought in the Russian Civil War. During the Great Patriotic War he commanded a brigade, corps and armies. Following the war, Moskalenko commanded an army and military district and was also commander-in-chief of the Strategic Rocket Forces.

49. Editor's note. Vasilii Dmitrievich Kryuchyonkin (1894–1976) was drafted into the Imperial Russian Army in 1915 and he joined the Red Army in 1918. During the Second World War he commanded a cavalry division, a cavalry corps and a number of armies. Following the war, he served as deputy commander of a military district, before retiring in 1946.

50. NARA, T312, R1683, frame 34.

51. TsAMO RF, f. 220, op. 220, d. 22, l. 31.

52. NARA, T312, R1683, frame 50.

53. NARA, T312, R1683, frame 48.

54. Editor's note. Hermann Hoth (1885–1971) joined the Imperial German Army in 1903 and served during the First World War. During the Second World War he commanded a mechanized corps, a panzer army and a field army. Hitler relieved him of command at the end of 1943. Following the war, Hoth was convicted of war crimes, but was released from prison in 1954.

55. *Russkii Arkhiv* (1996), vol. XVI (5-2), p. 322.

56. Editor's note. Anton Ivanovich Lopatin (1897–1965) joined the Red Army in 1918 and fought in the Russian Civil War. During the Second World War he commanded corps and armies. Following the war, he commanded a rifle corps and served in staff positions in several military districts. he retired in 1954.

57. Editor's note. Mikhail Stepanovich Shumilov (1895–1975) was drafted into the Imperial Russian Army in 1916 and joined the Red Army in 1918. During the Second World War he commanded a corps and an army. Following the war, Shumilov commanded armies and military districts.

58. TsAMO RF, f. 3430, op. 1, d. 34, l. 30.

59. NARA, T312, R1683, frame 258.

60. Editor's note. The Maginot Line was an extensive system of concrete fortifications built along the Franco-German border during the 1930s and named after the defence minister André Maginot. The Germans bypassed the Maginot Line in 1940 and it has since become a metaphor for expensive failure.

61. NARA, T312, R1685, frame 258.

62. NARA, T312, R1683, frame 899.

63. NARA, T312, R1683, frame 832.

64. Ibid.

65. Ibid.

66. Ibid.

67. V.I. Chuikov, *Srazhenie Veka* (Moscow: Sovetskaya Rossiya, 1975), p. 33.

68. Ibid., p. 35.

69. TsAMO RF, f. 220, op. 226, d. 19, l. 116.

70. TsAMO RF, f. 220, op. 220, d. 71, l. 100.

71. Editor's note. This is a reference to the 5th Guards Tank Army's counter-attack on 12 July 1943 at Prokhorovka station, in which the army lost more than 50 per cent of its armoured strength in ten hours. The name has since become a synonym for a counteroffensive launched at the wrong place and the wrong time, leading to heavy losses.

72. NARA T312 R1448, frame 856.

73. TsAMO RF, f. 3430, op. 1, d. 34, l. 23.

74. NARA, T312, R1683, frame 74.

75. TsAMO RF, f. 220, op. 226, d. 19, ll. 119–20.

76. According to the 158th Tank Brigade's report, the enemy's strength included tanks buried in the ground.

77. See D. Glantz, *To the Gates of Stalingrad: Soviet-German Combat Operations, April–August 1942* (Lawrence, KS: University Press of Kansas, 2009), p. 234.

78. NARA, T312, R1448, frame 878.

79. NARA, T312, R1683, frame 84.

80. TsAMO RF, f. 3430, op. 1, d. 34, l. 30.

81. TsAMO RF, f. 3430, op. 1, d. 34, l. 30a.

82. NARA, T312, R1683, frame 84.

83. TsAMO RF, f. 3430, op. 1, d. 34, l. 30a.

84. NARA, T312, R1683, frame 82.

85. NARA, T312, R1448, frame 883.

86. NARA, T312, R1448, frames 1148, 895.

87. TsAMO RF, f. 3418, op. 1, d. 6, l. 1.

88. Ibid.

89. TsAMO RF, f. 220, op. 226, d. 19, l. 123.

90. Editor's note. Nikita Sergeevich Khrushchev (1894–1971) joined the Communist Party in 1918 and served as a political commissar during the Russian Civil War. He later gained Stalin's favour and rose rapidly through the party's ranks. During the Great Patriotic War he served as a political commissar with various *fronts*. Following the war, he was party boss in Ukraine and Moscow. After Stalin's death he gradually pushed aside his rivals and occupied the top posts in the party and government. Khrushchev was removed from his offices in 1964 and sent into retirement, where he wrote his clandestine memoirs.

91. K.S. Moskalenko, *Na Yugo-Zapadnom Napravlenii. (Vospominaniya Komandarma)* (Moscow: Nauka, 1969), p. 279.

92. Compiled from data in TsAMO RF, f. 220, op. 220, d. 8, ll. 302-3, and d. 18, ll. 233-4.

93. TsAMO RF, f. 324, op. 4794, d. 3, l. 4.

94. TsAMO RF, f. 220, op. 220, d. 18, l. 238.

95. NARA, T312, R1683, frame 118.

96. Editor's note. The Wehrmacht ('defence force') was the German term for the unified armed forces (army, navy air force) and existed from 1935 to the end of the war.

97. Editor's note. Franz Halder (1884–1972) joined the Imperial German Army in 1902 and fought in the First World War. He was named chief of the army (OKH) staff in 1938 and served in this position until relieved by Hitler in 1942. Halder spent two years in prison following the war and worked for the US army historical branch.

98. This term was used in conversations by the *front* headquarters with the Red Army General Staff.
99. TsAMO RF, f. 38, op. 11360, d. 120, l. 153.
100. Editor's note. The Russian word for gully or ravine is *balka* (plural, *balki*) and will be used from this point on.
101. TsAMO RF, f. 220, op. 220, d. 8, l. 306.
102. NARA, T312, R1683, frame 1277.
103. NARA, T312, R1683, frame 1168.
104. TsAMO RF, f. 324, op. 4794, d. 3, l. 4.
105. NARA, T312, R1683, frame 1348.
106. TsAMO RF, f. 220, op. 220, d. 82, l. 130.
107. TsAMO RF, f. 38, op. 11360, d. 120, l. 154.
108. NARA, T312, R1683, frame 1283.
109. NARA, T312, R1683, frame 1393.
110. G. Dërr, *Pokhod na Stalingrad (Operativnyi Obzor)* (Moscow: Voennoe Izdatel'stvo, 1957), p. 44.
111. NARA, T312, R1449, frame 135, R1448, frame 1153.
112. This is evidently a reference to ammunition for the *Sturmgeschützen.*
113. Editor's note. Paul Ludwig Ewald von Kleist (1881–1954) joined the Imperial German Army in 1900 and fought in the First World War. During the Second World War he commanded armoured troops in Poland, the West, the Balkans, and the Soviet Union. Hitler relieved him of command in 1944. The Americans extradited von Kleist to the Soviet Union, where he was imprisoned until his death.
114. Editor's note. The State Defence Committee (*Gosudarstvennyi Komitet Oborony*, GKO) was organized shortly after the start of the German invasion in June 1941. Chaired by Stalin, the State Defence Committee was the country's highest wartime body and supreme decision-making organ.
115. Editor's note. Rodion Yakovlevich Malinovskii (1898–1967) joined the Imperial Russian Army in 1914 and fought in the First World War in Russia and France, before returning home to join the Red Army. During the Second World War he commanded a corps, armies and *fronts* in Europe and the Far East. Following the war, Malinovskii remained in the Far East before returning to Moscow to command the ground forces and serve as defence minister from 1957 until his death.

Chapter 2: Heat: The Cauldron

1. TsAMO RF, f. 3418, op. 1, d. 6, l. 8.
2. TsAMO RF, f. 220, op. 220, d. 71, l. 131.
3. TsAMO RF, f. 345, op. 5512, d. 10, l. 4.
4. TsAMO RF, f. 220, op. 220, d. 77, l. 69.
5. TsAMO RF, f. 220, op. 220, d. 71, l. 126.
6. Dërr, *Pokhod*, p. 44.
7. NARA, T312, R1683, frame 200.
8. TsAMO RF, f. 220, op. 220, d. 71, l. 139.
9. TsAMO RF, f. 220, op. 220, d. 71, l. 141.
10. Ibid.
11. TsAMO RF, f. 320, op. 4522, d. 8, l. 213.
12. Editor's note. Konstantin Mikhailovich Simonov (1915–79) was a noted Soviet author, playwright and war correspondent whose works chiefly chronicled the events of the Great Patriotic War and other conflicts. Following the war, Simonov held a number of high-ranking posts in the Soviet literary establishment.
13. NARA, T312, R1683, frame 240.
14. NARA, T312, R1683, frame 848.
15. TsAMO RF, f. 345, op. 5487, d. 16, l. 22.
16. *Russkii Arkhiv*, vol. XVI(5-2), p. 362.
17. TsAMO RF, f. 345, op. 5487, d. 48-49, l. 70.
18. NARA, T312, R1683, frame 242.
19. NARA, T312, R1683, frame 244.
20. TsAMO RF, f. 220, op. 220, d. 71, l. 171.
21. Dërr, *Pokhod*, p. 44.
22. NARA, T312, R1683, frame 246.
23. Editor's note. Here the document's compilers clearly made a mistake and are speaking of the XIV and XXIV Panzer Corps.
24. NARA, T312, R1683, frame 246.
25. Editor's note. Filipp Ivanovich Golikov (1900–80) joined the Red Army in 1918 and served in its political organs before taking up command assignments, including that of chief of the army's Main Intelligence Directorate (GRU). During the Great Patriotic War he headed the Soviet military mission in Great Britain and the United States. He also commanded a number of armies and *fronts*, before being assigned to various posts in the army's administrative apparatus, including that of head of the armed forces' Main Political Directorate.

26. Moskalenko, *Na Yugo-Zapadnom*, p. 295.
27. Editor's note. The Komsomol (*Kommunisticheskii Soyuz Molodezhi*) was the Communist Party youth auxiliary.
28. S.P. Ivanov, *Shtab Armeiskii, Shtab Frontovoi* (Moscow: Voennoe Izdatel'stvo, 1990), p. 313.

Chapter 3: The Results of the Tank Battle in the Great Bend of the Don
1. F. Hahn, *Waffen und Geheimwafffen des Heeres, 1933-1945* (Koblenz: Bernard & Graefe, 1986), vol. I, p. 80.
2. TsAMO RF, f. 345, op. 5512, d. 10, l. 6.
3. TsAMO RF, f. 5512, op. 1, d. 34, pp. 54–5.
4. Editor's note. Erich von Manstein (1887–1973) joined the Imperial German Army in 1906 and fought in the First World War. During the Second World War he served as chief of staff of an army group and commanded corps, an army and an army group. He was relieved by Hitler in early 1944 and never held a command afterward. Following the war, Manstein was convicted of war crimes, but served only a few years before being released.
5. NARA, T312, R1683, frame 132.
6. Compiled by the author according to data from NARA T312 R1448, frames 1106, 1241, 1304, and 1393.

Chapter 4: The Elimination of the Sirotinskaya Bridgehead
1. Editor's note. The OKH (*Oberkommando des Heeres*) was the German army high command.
2. Editor's note. The Battle of Cannae was fought on 2 August 216 BC in south-eastern Italy during the Second Punic War between Rome and Carthage. At Cannae the Carthaginian forces under Hannibal defeated the Romans with a double envelopment. The idea of 'Cannae' was later elevated by Schlieffen and others to the acme of the military art.
3. NARA, T312, R1683, frame 246.
4. TsAMO RF, f. 220, op. 220, d. 71, l. 150.
5. Ibid.
6. TsAMO RF, f. 1085, op. 1, d. 7, l. 5.
7. TsAMO RF, f. 220, op. 220, d. 87, l. 36.
8. Moskalenko, *Na Yugo-Zapadnom*, p. 298.
9. TsAMO RF, f. 220, op. 220, d. 71, l. 175.
10. NARA, T312, R1449, frame 135.
11. NARA, T312, R 1448, frame 1153.
12. NARA, T312, R1449, frames 63, 105.
13. Editor's note. Wolfram von Richthofen (1895–1945) joined the Imperial German Army in 1913 and fought in the First World War. During the Second World War he commanded an air corps and an air fleet before retiring in 1944 for health reasons. He died in Allied captivity.

Chapter 5: Reinforced Defence I. Abganerovo
1. Editor's note. Alfred Josef Ferdinand Jodl (1890–1946) joined the Imperial German Army in 1910 and fought in the First World War and served in the interwar Reichswehr. In 1939 he was appointed chief of the OKW operations staff. Jodl signed the German surrender at Reims on 7 May 1945. He was convicted of war crimes at Nuremberg and executed.
2. TsAMO RF, f. 38, op. 11360, d. 120, l. 131.
3. Editor's note. Iosif Rodinovich Apanasenko (1890–1943) was drafted into the Imperial Russian Army in 1911 and he joined the Red Army in 1918. During the Second World War he commanded the Far Eastern Front and was later appointed deputy commander of the Voronezh Front. Apanasenko was killed in action.
4. R. Grams, *Die 14.Panzer-Division 1940-1945. Herausgegeben im Auftrag der Traditionsgemeinschaft der 14. Panzer-Division* (Bad Neuheim: Verlag hans-Henning Podzun, 1957), p. 50.
5. *Stalingradskaya Bitva*, bk. I, p. 297.
6. Editor's note. Georgii Fedorovich Zakharov (1897–1957) joined the Imperial Russian Army in 1915 and the Red Army in 1919. During the Great Patriotic War he commanded armies and fronts. Following the war, he commanded a number of military districts.
7. *Stalingradskaya Bitva*, bk. I, p. 305.
8. Dërr, *Pokhod*, pp. 38–9.

Chapter 6: Serafimovich. The Foundation of Future Success
1. Editor's note. Aleksei Il'ich Danilov (1897–1981) joined the Imperial Russian Army in 1916 and the Red Army in 1918 and fought in the Russian Civil War. During the Second World War he commanded armies and served in high-ranking staff positions. Following the war he commanded an army and a corps was also a deputy military district commander.

2. Editor's note. The academy was founded in 1918 and renamed the Frunze Military Academy in 1925, in honour of the recently-deceased war commissar. The academy is roughly equivalent to the US Army's Command and General Staff College. The academy was renamed the Combined Arms Academy of the Armed Forces of the Russian Federation in 1998.

3. Strictly speaking, the name 'Celere', which is often encountered in the literature, is incorrect. 'Celere' means 'rapid'. The formation was officially known as the 3rd Rapid Division 'Principe Amadeo Duca d'Aosta.' As of March 1942, the division consisted of two three-battalion regiments of bersaglieri (motorized rifles), and a motorized artillery regiment. It is more correct to refer to it as the Italian Motorized Division.

4. Editor's note. Giovanni Messe (1883–1968) joined the army in 1901 and fought in Libya and the First World War. During the Second World War he commanded a corps in Greece and the Italian Expeditionary Corps on the Eastern Front. He was captured in Tunisia in 1943, but was later appointed chief of staff of the Italian Co-Belligerent Army on the side of the Allies. Messe retired in 1947 and later served as head of the veterans' association.

5. Editor's note. The Blackshirts were paramilitary units organized under the auspices of the Italian fascist movement after the First World War. In theory at least, they were seen to be more ideologically reliable than the average army recruit, much like the German SS units.

Chapter 7: The Formation of the Northern Covering Detachment

1. This was a Red Army formation designated for occupying fortified positions, including field defences. The 54th Fortified Area along the eastern bank of the Don numbered about 3,000 men, armed with 123 heavy machine guns.

2. Editor's note. Lend-Lease was an American aid programme that delivered food, military equipment and raw materials to the Allies during the Second World War. In all $50.1 billion of aid was delivered, including $11.3 billion to the USSR.

3. In the Red Army American tanks were given the designation 'M3 medium' (abbreviated M3s) and 'M3 light' (M3l).

4. TsAMO RF, f. 220, op. 220, d. 13, l. 229.

5. The VIII Army Corps received another three brigades and the 71st Infantry Division one.

6. TsAMO RF, f. 1246, op. 1, d. 7, l. 67.

7. TsAMO RF, f. 220, op. 220, d. 72, l. 7.

8. TsAMO RF, f. 1077 zen. polka, op. 708695, d. 1, l. 3 (back).

9. TsAMO RF, f. 1077 zen. polka, op. 708695, d. 1, l. 5.

10. TsAMO RF, f. 220, op. 220, d. 78, l. 109.

11. *Stalingradskaya Bitva*, bk. I, p. 236.

12. A.I. Yeremenko, *Stalingrad* (Moscow: AST, 2006), p. 148.

13. TsAMO RF, f. 3403, op. 1, d. 8, ll. 3-4.

14. *Stalingradskaya Bitva*, bk. I, p. 413.

15. TsAMO RF, f. 38, op. 11360, d. 77, l. 31.

16. *Stalingradskaya Bitva*, bk. I, pp. 418–19.

17. A.M. Vasilevskii, *Delo Vsei Zhizni* (Moscow; Politizdat, 1978), p. 219.

18. TsAMO RF, f. 3403, op. 1, d. 11, l. 36.

19. NARA, T312, R14491, frame 122.

20. TsAMO RF, f. 220, op. 220, d. 87, l. 30.

21. NARA, T312, R1449, frame 230.

22. Small river craft, each armed with two 100mm naval guns.

23. TsAMO RF, f. 3414, op. 1, d. 24, l. 5 (back).

Chapter 8: Reinforced Defence II: Beketova

1. Dërr, *Pokhod*, p. 40.

2. Ibid., p. 40.

3. TsAMO RF, f. 3430, op. 1, d. 8, l. 47.

4. R. Grams, *Die 14.Panzer-Division 1940-1945. Herausgegebenim Auftrag der Traditionsgemeinschaft der 14.Panzer Division* (Bad Nauheim, 1957), pp. 52–3.

5. Ibid., p. 53.

6. TsAMO RF, f. 3430, op. 1, d. 8, l. 68.

7. TsAMO RF, f. 48, op. 468, d. 25, ll. 71-2.

Chapter 10: The Battle for the Semaphore. The Beginning

1. Editor's note. Dmitrii Timofeevich Kozlov (1896–1967) joined the Imperial Russian Army in 1915 and the Red Army in 1918 and fought in the Russian Civil War. During the Second World War he commanded a number of *fronts*, but was blamed for the Soviet disaster on the Kerch' peninsula and reduced in rank

and appointed to command an army and other posts. Following the war he was a deputy commander of a military district until his retirement in 1954.

2. TsAMO RF, f. 220, op. 220, d. 71, l. 192.
3. The data for the 7th Tank Corps are taken from a corps report and can be found in TsAMO RF, f. 3401, op. 1, d. 8, l. 2.
4. Editor's note. Pavel Alekseevich Rotmistrov (1901–82) joined the Red Army in 1919. During the Great Patriotic War he commanded a tank brigade and then a tank corps. He later commanded tank armies, including the 5th Guards Tank Army during the fighting around Kursk. He was removed from command in 1944 and relegated to central administrative duties. Following the war, Rotmistrov served with the Soviet occupation forces in Germany and worked in the central military-educational apparatus.
5. Editor's note. Aleksandr Il'ich Lizyukov (1900–42) joined the Red Army in 1919 and fought in the Russian Civil War. During the Second World War he commanded a division and various corps, as well as a tank army. Lizyukov was demoted to the post of corps commander following the unsuccessful Soviet counteroffensive around Voronezh and he was shortly afterwards killed in action.
6. NARA, T312, R 1685, frame 509.
7. TsAMO RF, f. 3401, op. 1, d. 3, l. 2.
8. NARA, T312, R 1683, frame 486.
9. NARA, T312, R1683, frame 480.
10. NARA, T312, R 1449, frame 357.
11. In total, the Sixth Army expended 575 tons.
12. NARA, T312, R1449, frame 388.
13. TsAMO RF, f. 220, op. 220, d. 10, l. 3.
14. Ibid., l. 8.
15. NARA, T312, R1683, frame 490.

Chapter 11: A City Under Siege
1. Yeremenko, *Stalingrad*, p. 196.

Chapter 12: The First Assault on the City. 14–26 September 1942. The Beginning
1. Editor's note. Wilhelm Keitel (1882–1946) joined the Imperial German Army in 1901 and fought in the First World War and served in the interwar Reichswehr. Hitler appointed Keitel chief of the OKW in 1938 and he held this post to the end of the war. Keitel signed the German surrender in Berlin. He was tried for war crimes at Nuremberg and executed.
2. NARA, T312, R1685, frame 847.
3. NARA, T312, R1685, frame 849.
4. NARA, T312, R1683, frame 572.
5. NARA, T312, R1685, frame 1019.
6. NARA, T312, R1685, frame 1166.
7. According to the army's war diary.
8. Chuikov, *Srazhenie Veka*, p. 111.
9. According to the division's report, TsAMO RF, f. 345, op. 5487, d. 8, l. 3.
10. Including three out of action.
11. Editor's note. The NKVD (*Narodnyi Komissariat Vnutrennykh Del*, People's Commissariat for Internal Affairs) was the name of the Soviet secret police between 1934 and 1946. This agency had the task of carrying out repression against the regime's domestic and foreign enemies.
12. TsAMO RF, f. 48, op. 468, d. 25, ll. 33–35.
13. TsAMO RF, f. 3368, op. 1, d. 2, l. 22.
14. TsAMO RF, f. 3418, op. 1, d. 6, l. 26.
15. TsAMO RF, f. 3368, op. 1, d. 2, l. 24.
16. TsAMO RF, f. 3418, op. 1, d. 6, l. 26.
17. NARA, T312, R1683, frame 572.
18. TsAMO RF, f. 345, op. 5487, d. 8, l. 5.
19. Ibid.
20. Chuikov, *Srazhenie Veka*, pp. 112–13.
21. TsAMO RF, f. 345, op. 5487, d. 8, l. 7.
22. Awarded the title of Hero of the Soviet Union for the fighting near Yel'nya.
23. NARA, T312, R1449, frame 591.
24. *Stalingradskaya Bitva: Svidetel'stva Uchastnikov i Ochevidtsev* (Moscow: Novoe Literaturnoe Obozrenie, 2015), p. 390.
25. TsAMO RF, f. 345, op. 5487, d. 5, l. 351.

26. The national labour service.

27. TsAMO RF, f. 345, op. 5487, d. 24, l. 9.

28. TsAMO RF, f. 220, op. 220, d. 20, l. 10. By the start of the German offensive, the independent machine gun-artillery battalion numbered somewhat more men due to the transfer to it of the remnants of other battalions from fortified areas.

29. Major General Arno von Lenski was appointed commander of the 24th Panzer Division in place of the previous divisional commander, Major General von Hauenschild, who had been wounded. Von Lenski had earlier headed the panzer forces school in Krampnitz. He took up his command on 14 September 1942.

30. TsAMO RF, f. 345, op. 5487, d. 24, l. 31.

Chapter 13: The First Assault on the City. 14–26 September 1942. The Centre

1. A.I. Rodimtsev, *Gvardeitsy Stoyali Nasmert'* (Moscow: DOSAAF, 1969), p. 25.

2. Chuikov, *Srazhenie Veka*, pp. 120–1.

3. TsAMO RF, f. 1075, op. 1, d. 4, l. 4.

4. Ibid.

5. TsAMO RF, f. 48, op. 451, d. 41, l. 69.

6. TsAMO RF, f. 48, op. 451, d. 41, l. 67.

7. TsAMO RF, f. 48, op. 451, d. 3, l. 142.

8. *Stalingradskaya Bitva*, p. 424.

9. NARA, T312, R1685, frames 1123–4.

10. TsAMO RF, f. 1309, op. 1, d. 7, l. 27 (back).

11. TsAMO RF, f. 345, op. 5487, d. 48-49, l. 136.

12. Chuikov, *Srazhenie Veka*, p. 136.

13. Ibid, p. 136.

14. TsAMO RF, f. 3109, op. 1, dl. 13, l. 23.

15. NARA, T312, R1685, frame 1200.

16. Ibid.

17. TsAMO RF, f. 1840, op. 1, d. 8, l. 19.

18. TsAMO RF, f. 345, op. 5487, d. 24, l. 40.

19. NARA T312, R 1449, frames 707, 723.

20. He subsequently commanded the 92nd Rifle Brigade and became a hero of the Soviet Union (1944).

21. TsAMO RF, f. 345, op. 5487, d. 8, l. 20 (back).

22. Ibid., l. 29.

23. TsAMO RF, f. 38, op. 1136, d. 77, l. 112.

24. V.M. Kravtsov and M.V. Savin, *Boi v Stalingrade. Kratkii Operativno-Takticheskii Ocherk* (Moscow: Voennoe Izdatel'stvo, 1944), p. 12.

25. TsAMO RF, f. 345, op. 5487, d. 9, l. 10 (back).

26. TsAMO RF, f. 345, op. 5487, dd. 48-9, l. 136.

27. Ibid.

28. TsAMO RF, f. 345, op. 5487, d. 5, l. 361.

29. TsAMO RF, f. 345, op. 345, d. 9, l. 5 (back).

30. TsAMO RF, f. 38, op. 1136, d. 77, l. 149.

31. NARA, T312, R1686, frame 121.

32. TsAMO RF, f. 345, op. 5487, d. 9, l. 12 (back).

33. NARA, T312, R1686, frame 121.

34. TsAMO RF, f. 38, op. 1136, d. 77, l. 149.

35. Editor's note. Isaak Izrailevich Mints (1896–1991) served as a political commissar during the Russian Civil War. Following the war he embarked upon an academic career and later became one of the mainstays of the official Soviet school of historiography, despite a brief eclipse in the latter years of Stalin's reign during the campaign against 'rootless cosmopolitans' (Jews) in the Soviet Union.

36. *Stalingradskaya Bitva*, p. 476.

37. TsAMO RF, f. 1075, op. 1, d. 4, l. 25.

38. TsAMO RF, f. 345, op. 5487, d. 9, l. 7.

39. TsAMO RF, f. 345, op. 5487, d. 31, l. 3.

40. Rodimstev, *Gvardeitsy*, p. 65.

41. TsAMO RF, f. 345, op. 5487, d. 16, l. 56.

42. Ibid.

43. NARA, T312, R1686, frame 262.

44. Meaning an infantry section.

45. NARA, T312, R1686, frame 523.

46. Compiled by the author from data in NARA T312 R1449, frames, 759, 851.
47. TsAMO RF, f. 48, op. 451, d. 3, l. 165.
48. NARA, T312, R1686, frame 265.
49. Editor's note. Vasilii Grigor'evich Zaitsev (1915–91) joined the Soviet navy in 1937 and transferred to the army when the Second World War broke out. He made his mark as a sniper and is credited with more than 200 kills during the battle of Stalingrad alone. Following the war, Zaitsev worked as an engineer and factory director.
50. *Stalingradskaya Bitva*, p. 503.
51. NARA, T312, R1686, frame 262.
52. NARA, T312, R1449, frame 753. The overall expenditure by the Sixth Army was 865 tons.
53. TsAMO RF, f. 1075, op. 1, d. 4, l. 25.
54. NARA, T312, R1686, frame 302.
55. TsAMO RF, f. 345, op. 5487, d. 9, l. 25.
56. TsAMO RF, f. 1075, op. 1, d. 4, l. 23.
57. N.I. Krylov, *Stalingradskii Rubezh* (Moscow: Voennoe Izdatel'stvo, 1979), p. 167.
58. Rodimtsev, *Gvardeitsy*, p. 79.
59. TsAMO RF, f. 1075, op. 1, d. 4, l. 28 (back).
60. NARA, T312, R1686, frame 335.
61. NARA, T312, R 1685, frame 1205; R 1686, frames 139, 188, 335.
62. To judge from everything, the figure of sixteen vehicles includes seven cannibalized self-propelled guns at the vehicle salvage point near Kalach (without motors and guns), which are shown separately in the report of 23 September, but it's unclear where they ended up.
63. According to the report of 21 September, the condition of both battalions' self-propelled guns remained unchanged in comparison to the preceding day.
64. TsAMO RF, f. 345, op. 5487, d. 16, ll. 70-70 (back).
65. TsAMO RF, f. 345, op. 5487, d. 16, l. 72.
66. *Stalingradskaya Bitva*, pp. 503–4.
67. *Die 71. Infanterie-Division im Zweiten Weltkrieg 1939-1945. Gefechts-und Erlebnisberichte aus den Kaempfen der 'Glueckhaften Division' von Verdun bis Stalingrad, von Monte Cassino obis zum Plattensee* (Eggolsheim: Nebel Verlag GmbH, 1973).
68. NARA, T312, R1686, frame 499.
69. NARA, T312, R1449, frame 832.
70. TsAMO RF, f. 345, op. 5487, d. 8, l. 44.
71. TsAMO RF, f. 48, op. 451, d. 36, l. 8.
72. TsAMO RF, f. 6223, op. 671790, d. 1, l. 65 (back).
73. TsAMO RF, f. 345, op. 5487, dd. 48-9, l. 163.
74. J. Mark, *Death of the Leaping Horseman. The 24th Panzer Division at Stalingrad. 12th August-20th November 1942* (Mechanicsburg, PA: Stackpole Books, 2014), pp. 205, 208.
75. TsAMO RF, f. 345, op. 5487, d. 15, ll. 30-1.
76. NARA, T312, R 1686, frame 522.
77. TsAMO RF, f. 48, op. 451, d. 41, l. 129.

Chapter 14: The First Assault on the City. 13–26 September 1942. To the South of the Tsaritsa River

1. The Wehrmacht had the unofficial practice of allowing military personnel who participated in certain battles (successful or conditionally successful) to wear sleeve patches in the form of a small stylized shield. There were the 'Kholm shield', the 'Crimean shield' and the 'Kuban shield'. However, in view of the rout of the Sixth Army around Stalingrad the idea of a 'Stalingrad shield' was buried. Author's note.
2. TsAMO RF, f. 38, op. 1136, d. 77, l. 110.
3. TsAMO RF, f. 48, op. 451, d. 3, l. 157.
4. TsAMO RF, f. 345, op. 5487, d. 31, l. 4.
5. TsAMO RF, f. 1904, op. 1, d. 1, l. 2 (back).
6. According to a report of 20 September, the brigade disposed of twelve 45mm anti-tank guns, four 76mm regimental and sixteen 76mm divisional guns.
7. TsAMO RF, f. 48, op. 451, d. 41, l. 61.
8. TsAMO RF, f. 345, op. 5487, d. 56, l. 20.
9. M.P. Polyakov perished on 9 October 1943 as the commander of the 271st Guards Rifle Regiment's third battalion.
10. TsAMO RF, f. 345, op. 5487, d. 31, l. 15 (back).
11. At 18.00 on 22 September the 94th Infantry Division was to be transferred from Kempf's corps to LI Corps.

12. According to the 'Memorial' database, Aleksandr Luk'yanovich Bereza, born 1905, is listed as a deserter (missing in action).

13. TsAMO RF, f. 345, op. 5487, d. 31, l. 18.

14. TsAMO RF, f. 48, op. 451, d. 41, l. 58.

15. TsAMO RF, f. 345, op. 5487, d. 5, l. 374.

16. According to the reminiscences of N.I. Krylov, 62nd Army chief of staff, the commander of the 42nd Rifle Brigade, M.S. Batrakov, was wounded and evacuated across the Volga on 21 September.

17. TsAMO RF, f. 345, op. 5487, d. 31, l. 22.

18. TsAMO RF, f. 345, op. 5487, d. 31, l. 26.

19. TsAMO RF, f. 48, op. 451, d. 41, l. 103.

20. Editor's note. Dmitrii Grigor'evich Pavlov (1897–1941) fought in the First World War and joined the Red Army in 1919. During the interwar period he commanded armoured forces in Spain. During the Second World War he commanded the Western Front until he was blamed for the disaster of the opening days and relieved of command. Pavlov was executed a month later, along with his former chief of staff Klimovskikh.

21. TsAMO RF, f. 345, op. 5487, d. 5, l. 467.

Chapter 15: The Battle for the Semaphore II. The Counterblow of 18–19 September

1. Editor's note. Georgii Konstantinovich Zhukov (1896–1974) was drafted into the Imperial Russian Army in 1915 and joined the Red Army in 1918. In 1939 he defeated a major Japanese incursion in Mongolia. During the Great Patriotic War he served as Chief of the General Staff and commanded several fronts. In 1942 he was appointed deputy supreme commander-in-chief, directly under Stalin. Following the war, he was relegated to several minor posts. After Stalin's death he served as defence minister and was a member of the Communist Party Presidium. Nikita Khrushchev removed Zhukov from all his posts in 1957 and he lived as a 'non-person' until Khrushchev's own removal in 1964.

2. Editor's note. This is a reference to a radically new idea for the Soviet counteroffensive around Stalingrad.

3. Editor's note. Nikolai Fedorovich Vatutin (1901–44) joined the Red Army in 1920. During the Great Patriotic War he served as chief of the General Staff's operational directorate, deputy chief of staff and a *Stavka* representative. From 1942 he commanded a number of *fronts* along the South-Western Strategic Direction. Vatutin died from wounds received in a partisan attack.

4. TsAMO RF, f. 220, op. 220, d. 72, l. 36.

5. TsAMO RF, f. 38, op. 11360, d. 8, l20. 13.

6. TsAMO RF, f. 3403, op. 1, d. 8, l. 64.

7. Editor's note. Georgii Maksimilianovich Malenkov (1902–88) joined the Red Army in 1918. Thereafter he quickly rose through the party ranks and became a protégé of Stalin. He played an active role in the party purge of the late 1930s and was head of the party's cadre directorate and a secretary of the Central Committee. During the Great Patriotic War he was a member of the GKO in charge of aircraft production. Following Stalin's death, he briefly held the top government and party posts, but was later eclipsed by Khrushchev. Following an attempt to overthrow his rival, Malenkov and several others were stripped of their posts.

8. NARA T312, R1686, frame 37.

9. In the division's report of 15 September one Panzer III with a 75mm long-barrelled gun was reported.

10. NARA T312, R1685, frame 1205.

11. The index of a battalion's combat capability ranged from *stark* (strong) to *schwach* (weak).

12. NARA T312, R1683, frame 522.

13. Florian Freiherr von und zu Aufsess, *Die Anlagenbander der Kriegstagebucher der 6.Armee* (Moscow: Voennoe Izdatel'stvo, 2006), p. 30.

14. NARA T312, R1683, frame 622.

15. TsAMO RF, f. 3401, op. 1, d. 3, l. 4.

16. NARA, T312, R1683, frame 708.

17. NARA, T312, R1449, frame 708.

18. TsAMO RF, f. 292, op. 6911, d. 42, l. 23.

19. TsAMO RF, f. 220, op. 220, d. 17, l. 10.

20. TsAMO RF, f. 3401, op. 1, d. 7, l. 89.

21. NARA, T312, R1449, frame 707.

22. TsAMO RF, f. 38, op. 11360, d. 120, ll. 14, 16, 16 (back).

23. TsAMO RF, f. 220, op. 220, d. 72, l. 85.

24. TsAMO RF, f. 3414, op. 1, d. 25, l. 16.

25. Ibid.

26. F.V. Mellentin, *Tankovye Shrazheniya 1939-1945. Boevoe Primininie Tankov vo Vtoroi Mirovoi Voine* (Moscow: Inostrannaya Literatura, 1957), p. 148.

27. TsAMO RF, f. 220, op. 220, d. 72, l. 86.

28. TsAMO RF, f. 220, op. 220, d. 8, l. 400.
29. TsAMO RF, f. 206, op. 262, d. 25, l. 57.
30. TsAMO RF, f. 220, op. 220, d. 8, l. 405.
31. TsAMO RF, f. 220, op. 220, d. 72, l. 87.
32. NARA, T312, R1449, frame 1043.
33. NARA, T312, R1686, frame 805.
34. NARA, T312, R1686, frame 725.
35. NARA, T312, R1686, frame 763.
36. TsAMO RF, f. 220, op. 220, d. 72, l. 85.
37. NARA, T312, R1449, frames 63, 105.
38. G.K. Zhukov, *Vospominaniya i Razmyshleniya* (Moscow: Olma-Press, 2002), vol. 2, p. 79.
39. Yeremenko, *Stalingrad*, p. 231.
40. Ibid., p. 231.
41. *Russkii Arkhiv*, vol. XVI (5-2), p. 403. Konstantin Konstantinovich Rokossovskii (1896-1968) was drafted into the Imperial Russian Army in 1914 and fought in the First World War. He joined the Red Army in 1918 and fought in the Russian Civil War. He was arrested in 1937, but released before the war. During the Second World War he commanded a corps, an army and several fronts. Following the war, Rokossovskii commanded Soviet forces in Poland and served as Polish defence minister.

Chapter 16: The Second Assault on the City. 27 September–7 October 1942

1. NARA, T315, R804, frame 434.
2. NARA, T312, R1686, frame 590.
3. NARA, T312, R1686, frame 610.
4. K. Podevil's, *Boi na Donu i Volge. Ofitser Vermakhta na Vostochnom Fronte, 1942-1943* (Moscow: ZAO Izdatel'stvo Tsentrpoligraf, 2010), p. 169.
5. NARA, T312, R1449, frame 912.
6. Editor's note. Nikolai Nikolaevich Voronov (1899–1968) joined the Red Army in 1918 and fought in the Russian Civil War. During the Second World War he served as chief of the Red Army's artillery and head of National Air Defence and also was a *Stavka* representative to several *fronts*. Following the war, Voronov continued as armed forces artillery chief and also headed the main artillery academy.
7. N.N. Voronov, *Na Sluzhbe Voennoi* (Moscow: Voennoe Izdatel'stvo, 1963), p. 256.
8. TsAMO RF, f. 48, op. 451, d. 41, l. 95.
9. TsAMO RF, f. 48, op. 451, d. 41, ll. 122, 166.
10. TsAMO RF, f. 48, op. 451, d. 41, ll. 226-9.
11. TsAMO RF, f. 81, op.12075, d. 28, l. 10.
12. NARA, T312, R1449, frames 690, 884.
13. TsAMO RF, f. 345, op. 5512, d. 53, l. 107.
14. NARA, T312, R1683, frame 718.
15. NARA, T312, R1449, frame 930.
16. TsAMO RF, f. 345, op. 5487, d. 5, l. 390.
17. TsAMO RF, f. 48, op. 451, d. 3, l. 185.
18. Ibid.
19. TsAMO RF, f. 48, op. 451, d. 41, l. 104.
20. TsAMO RF, f. 345, op. 5487, d. 5, ll. 403-5.
21. TsAMO RF, f. 48, op. 451, d. 41, ll. 103-4.
22. Ibid.
23. TsAMO RF, f. 48, op. 451, d. 41, l. 405.
24. TsAMO RF, f. 48, op. 451, d. 41, l. 404.
25. *Stalingradskaya Bitva*, p. 255.
26. TsAMO RF, f. 1330, op. 1, d. 6, l. 62.
27. TsAMO RF, f. 345, op. 5487, d. 5, l. 406.
28. TsAMO RF, f. 1330, op. 1, d. 6, l. 63.
29. TsAMO RF, f. 1309, op. 1, d. 7, l. 34.
30. TsAMO RF, f. 345, op. 5487, d. 29, l. 44.
31. TsAMO RF, f. 345, op. 5487, d. 31, l. 34.
32. TsAMO RF, f. 1330, op. 1, d. 4, l. 15.
33. NARA, T312, R1449, frame 1110.
34. TsAMO RF, f. 345, op. 5487, d. 44, l. 12 (back).
35. TsAMO Rf, f. 345, op. 5487, do. 44, l. 13 (back).
36. NARA, T312, R1686, frame 948.
37. NARA, T315, R804, frames 498, 521.

38. He is not listed in the reference books, but the regiment's reports were signed by him. See also N.I. Volostnov, *Na Ognennykh Rubezhakh* (Moscow: Voennoe Izdatel'stvo, 1983), p. 55.
39. TsAMO RF, f. 6438, op. 279610, d. 1, l. 7.
40. A 150mm rocket launcher.
41. TsAMO RF, f. 6438, op. 279610, d. 1, l. 10.
42. TsAMO RF, f. 345, op. 5487, d. 30, l. 19 (back).
43. NARA, T312, R1686, frame 955.
44. TsAMO RF, f. 345, op. 5512, d. 34, l. 20.
45. TsAMO RF, f. 345, op. 5487, d. 37, l. 84.
46. Ibid.
47. Ibid., l. 89.
48. W. Werthen, *Geschichte der 16.Panzer-Division 1939-1945* (Bad Nauheim: Verlag Hans-Henning Podzun, 1958), p. 113.
49. TsAMO RF, f. 345, op. 5487, d. 37, l. 100, and f. 1936, op. 1, d. 5, l. 12.
50. TsAMO RF, f. 345, op. 5487, d. 37, l. 81.
51. TsAMO RF, f. 345, op. 5487, d. 37, l. 100.
52. Editor's note. The 'Hiwis' (from the German *Hilfswilliger*, or 'willing helpers') were personnel employed by the German army during the Second World War from the civilian population of Eastern Europe and the Soviet Union, or from Soviet POWs. The 'Hiwis' mainly carried out auxiliary tasks in the rear and grew to be quite numerous by the end of the war.
53. The Volga Flotilla's 141st Independent Naval Infantry Company, which numbered twenty-eight men by the evening of 28 October.
54. NARA, T312, R1686, frame 955.
55. Ibid.
56. TsAMO RF, f. 345, op. 5487, d. 37, l. 150.
57. TsAMO RF, f. 48, op. 451, d. 29, l. 148.
58. TsAMO RF, f. 345, op. 5487, op. 37, l. 151.
59. TsAMO RF, f. 345, op. 5487, op. 37, ll. 168-9.

Chapter 17: The Third Assault on the City. 14–19 October

1. TsAMO RF, f. 48, op. 451, d. 41, l. 136.
2. TsAMO RF, f. 345, op. 5487, d. 5, l. 434.
3. Chuikov, *Srazhenie Veka*, p. 215.
4. Ibid.
5. TsAMO RF, f. 48, op. 451, d. 3, l. 185.
6. TsAMO RF, f. 345, op. 5487, d. 5, l. 419.
7. TsAMO RF, f. 345, op. 5487, d. 30, l. 9.
8. TsAMO RF, f. 345, op. 5487, d. 44, l. 33.
9. TsAMO RF, f. 48, op. 451, d. 3, l. 207.
10. A filtration station.
11. TsAMO RF, f. 1128, op. 1, d. 9, l. 12.
12. TsAMO RF, f. 1128, op. 1, d. 20, l. 19.
13. NARA, T312, R1450, frame 239.
14. *Stalingradskaya Bitva*, p. 394.
15. TsAMO RF, f. 345, op. 5487, d. 16, l. 162.
16. TsAMO RF, f. 345, op. 5487, d. 54, l. 46.
17. *Stalingradskaya Bitva*, p. 394.
18. Chuikov, *Srazhenie Vekai*, p. 224.
19. TsAMO RF, f. 48, op. 451, d. 11, l. 187.
20. *Stalingradskaya Bitva*, p. 397.
21. TsAMO RF, f. 345, op. 5487, d. 31, l. 37.
22. TsAMO RF, f. 1904, op. 1, d. 1, l. 5.
23. TsAMO RF, f. 345, op. 5487, d. 32, l. 179.
24. TsAMO RF, f. 345, op. 5487, d. 30, l. 29 (back).
25. TsAMO RF, f. 345, op. 5487, d. 30, l. 32.
26. Pechenyuk was born in 1906 and was a veteran of the Soviet-Finnish War. He ended the war in the Far East in August 1945.
27. TsAMO RF, f. 1205, op. 1, d. 16, l. 2.
28. NARA, T312, R1450, frame 304.
29. TsAMO RF, f. 345, op. 5487, dd. 48-49, l. 206.
30. I.I. Lyudnikov, *Doroga Dlinoyu v Zhizn'* (Moscow: Voennoe Izdatel'stvo, 1969), p. 26.

31. It was named after its commander Sr. Lieutenant Hans Messerschmitt and in no way was it connected to the aircraft.
32. TsAMO RF, f. 345, op. 5487, d. 26, l. 56.
33. TsAMO RF, f. 345, op. 5487, d. 5, l. 442.
34. Ibid.
35. TsAMO RF, f. 345, op. 5512, d. 34, l. 89.
36. TsAMO RF, f. 345, op. 5512, d. 34, l. 67.
37. TsAMO RF, f. 345, op. 5487, d. 54, l. 8.
38. TsAMO RF, f. 345, op. 5487, d. 54, l. 9 (back), 13.
39. TsAMO RF, f. 345, op. 5487, d. 5, l. 448.
40. TsAMO RF, f. 345, op. 5512, d. 53, l. 61.
41. TsAMO RF, f. 345, op. 5487, d. 5, l. 451.
42. TsAMO RF, f. 345, op. 5512, d. 34, l. 85.
43. TsAMO RF, f. 345, op. 5512, d. 34, l. 70.
44. TsAMO RF, f. 345, op. 5512, d. 34, l. 73.
45. NARA, T312, R1450, frame 477.
46. TsAMO RF, f. 345, op. 5512, d. 53, l. 62.
47. The 124th Rifle Brigade's first battalion.
48. Of these, 346 were on the left bank of the Volga.
49. One hundred and forty-eight riflemen, 230 artillery troops, 211 mortar troops, seven chemical troops, 38 engineers, 155 signals troops and 61 headquarters personnel.
50. TsAMO RF, f. 345, op. 5512, d. 15, l. 6.
51. TsAMO RF, f. 345, op. 5487, d. 33, l. 63.
52. TsAMO RF, f. 345, op. 5487, d. 32, l. 180.
53. TsAMO RF, f. 48, op. 451, d. 6a, l. 33.
54. TsAMO RF, f. 345, op. 5487, d. 32, l. 206.
55. TsAMO RF, f. 345, op. 5487, d. 32, l. 200.
56. Editor's note. Walter Model (1891–1945) joined the Imperial German Army in 1910 and fought in the First World War. During the Second World War he commanded a division, corps, army and army group on various fronts. He was highly valued by Hitler for his prowess in defensive battles. Model committed suicide in the Ruhr pocket.
57. Editor's note. Gunther Hans von Kluge (1882–1944) joined the Imperial German Army in 1901 and served during the First World War. During the Second World War he commanded an army and an army group and was briefly commander-in-chief of German forces in the West. Kluge was implicated in the July 1944 plot to assassinate Hitler and committed suicide.
58. TsAMO RF, f. 345, op. 5487, d. 32, l. 220.
59. TsAMO RF, f. 345, op. 5487, d. 32, l. 249.
60. This is still its name.
61. TsAMO RF, f. 345, op. 5487, d. 32, l. 250.
62. TsAMO RF, f. 345, op. 5487, d. 32, ll. 247, 249.
63. TsAMO RF, f. 345, op. 5487, d. 32, ll. 247.

Chapter 18: The Fighting for the 'Red October' Factory

1. NARA, T312, R1450, frame 512.
2. TsAMO RF, f. 1133, op. 1, d. 6, l. 77.
3. Ibid.
4. TsAMO RF, f. 1075, op. 1, d. 4, l. 43.
5. TsAMO RF, f. 345, op. 5487, d. 12, l. 103.
6. Ibid.
7. TsAMO RF, f. 345, op. 5487, d. 5, l. 469.
8. TsAMO RF, f. 48, op. 451, d. 25, l. 209.
9. By the beginning of November there were eighteen men remaining in line from this battalion. Senior Lieutenant Kolomeitsev had been wounded.
10. TsAMO RF, f. 345, op. 5487, dd. 48-9, l. 225.
11. TsAMO RF, f. 345, op. 5487, d. 15, l. 97.
12. TsAMO RF, f. 345, op. 5487, dd. 48-9, l. 217.
13. TsAMO RF, f. 48, op. 451, d. 82, l. 108.
14. TsAMO RF, f. 345, op. 5487, d. 30, l. 65.
15. TsAMO RF, f. 345, op. 5487, d. 5, l. 442.
16. T. Jentz, *Sturmgeschütz-s.Pak to Sturmmörser. Panzer Tracts*, No. 8 (Boyds, MD, 2000), p. 46.
17. Ibid., p. 46.

18. TsAMO RF, f. 48, op. 451, d. 11, l. 219.
19. TsAMO RF, f. 206, op. 262, d. 62, l. 47.
20. TsAMO RF, f. 328, op. 4852, d. 273, l. 70.
21. TsAMO RF, f. 206, op. 262, d. 27, l. 32.
22. Ibid.

Chapter 19: The Landing in the Latashanka Area
1. These were probably 1930 model 37mm anti-tank guns, or captured German ones.
2. TsAMO RF, f. 1247, op. 1, d. 14a, l. 41.
3. Strehlke's group really did dispose of five 'engineer' tanks, that is, three Panzer IIIs and two Panzer IIs.
4. TsAMO RF, f. 1247, op. 1, d. 14a, l. 35.
5. TsAMO RF, f. 48, op. 451, d. 29, l. 219.
6. Ibid.
7. TsAMO RF, f. 1247, op. 1, d. 14a, l. 41.
8. TsAMO RF, f. 1247, op. 1, d. 14a, l. 38.

Chapter 20: The Last Inch. November 1942
1. M. Kehrig, *Stalingrad: Analyse und Dokumentation einer Schlacht (Beitrage zur Militar-und Kriegsgeschichte)* (Stuttgart: Deutsche Verlags-Anstalt, 1974), p. 41.
2. Editor's note. Kurt Zeitzler (1895–1963) joined the Imperial German Army in 1914 and fought in the First World War. During the Second World War he served in a variety of senior staff positions until his appointment as chief of the OKH General Staff in 1942, during the battle of Stalingrad. However, Zeitzler was dismissed by Hitler in 1944 and never held another command.
3. TsAMO RF, f. 1205, op. 1, d. 16. l. 39.
4. Krylov, *Stalingradskii Rubezh*, p. 286.
5. TsAMO RF, f. 1205, op. 1, d. 16, l. 39 (back).
6. TsAMO RF, f. 1205, op. 1, d. 16, l. 45.
7. Lyudnikov, *Doroga*, p. 48.
8. TsAMO RF, f. 1205, op. 1, d. 16, l. 46.
9. TsAMO RF, f. 48, op. 451, d. 11, l. 298 and further.
10. TsAMO RF, f. 48, op. 451, d. 29, l. 226.
11. *Stalingradskaya Bitva*, book one, p. 894.
12. TsAMO RF, f. 48, op. 451, d. 98, l. 44.

Chapter 21: Conclusions to Part II
1. *Velikaya Otechestvennaya Voina 1941-1945 gg. Kampanii i Strategicheskie Operatsii v Tsifrakh*, vol. I, p. 378.
2. *Germany and the Second World War* Vol. VI: *The Global War* (Oxford: Oxford University Press, 2001), pp. 1073, 1075.
3. *Sbornik Materialov po Izucheniyu Opyta Voiny* Vypush No. 6. April–May, 1943. (Moscow: Voennoe Izdatel'stvo, 1943), p. 33.
4. Compiled by the author according to NARA, T312, R2449, frames 688-90, R1450, frames 32-42.
5. TsAMO RF, f. 345, op. 5487, dd. 48-49, l. 224.
6. Krylov, *Stalingradskii Rubezh*, p. 98.
7. TsAMO RF, f. 345, op. 5487, d. 30, l. 95.
8. Mark, *Death of the Leaping Horseman*, p. 329.

Chapter 22: The Father Of The Gods: Operation Uranus
1. Editor's note. Maksim Alekseevich Purkaev (1894–1953) was drafted into the Imperial Russian Army in 1915 and joined the Red Army in 1918. During the Great Patriotic War he served as a *front* chief of staff and later commanded a *front*. After the war, Purkaev commanded military districts.
2. Editor's note. Ivan Stepanovich Konev (1897–1973) was drafted into the Imperial Russian Army in 1916 and joined the Red Army in 1918. During the Great Patriotic War he commanded an army and several fronts. Following the war he commanded Soviet troops in Germany and Austria, and also commanded the ground forces and a military district. He later served as first deputy minister of defence and commander-in-chief of the Warsaw Pact forces. Konev briefly commanded Soviet forces in Germany in 1961–2.
3. Editor's note. Anton Ivanovich Denikin (1872–1947) joined the Imperial Russian Army in 1892 and fought in the Russo-Japanese War and First World War, rising to high rank in the latter conflict. During the Russian Civil War Denikin led the anti-communist Volunteer Army until 1920. Following the White defeat, Denikin went into exile and eventually emigrated to the United States.
4. Yeremenko, *Stalingrad*, p. 352.
5. *Stalingradskaya Bitva*, book 1, p. 706.
6. Vasilevskii, *Delo*, p. 223.

7. *Russkii Arkhiv*, 16(5-2), p. 440.
8. Editor's note. Porfirii Longvinovich Romanenko (1897–1949) joined the Imperial Russian Army in 1914 and the Red Army in 1918 and fought in the Russian Civil War. During the Second World War he commanded tank and combined-arms armies. Following the war, Romanenko commanded a military district.
9. Editor's note. Ivan Mikhailovich Chistyakov (1900–79) joined the Red Army in 1918 and fought in the Russian Civil War. During the Second World War he commanded a brigade, division, corps, and armies. Following the war, Chistyakov commanded armies and was the deputy commander of a military district.
10. Before long it became the 50th Guards Rifle Division.
11. Editor's note. The Varangians (Russ. *Varyagi*) was the name of the Scandinavian adventurers who arrived in ancient Russia during the ninth century to rule over the indigenous Slavic tribes. The term, as used here, denotes someone who is invited in.
12. Editor's note. Pavel Ivanovich Batov (1897–1985) joined the Imperial Russian Army in 1915 and the Red Army in 1918, and fought in the Russian Civil War. During the Second World War he commanded a corps and several armies. Following the war, Batov commanded armies and a military district.
13. Editor's note. Nikolai Ivanovich Trufanov (1900–82) joined the Red Army in 1919 and fought in the Russian Civil War. During the Second World War he commanded an army and a corps. Following the war, Trufanov served in the Soviet military occupation administration in Germany and also served in the Far East. He retired in 1960.
14. Editor's note. Petre Dumitrescu (1882–1950) joined the Romanian army in 1901 and he served in the First World War. During the Second World War he commanded the Third Army for the duration of the war against the Soviet Union. He was later tried for war crimes, but acquitted.
15. Literally, the *Deutsches Verbindungs-Kommando*, or German communications command.
16. NARA, T311, R271, frame 283. This paragraph was singled out with a coloured pencil in the original.
17. Editor's note. Constantine Constantinescu-Claps (1884–1961) joined the Romanian army in 1903 and fought in the Second Balkan War and the First World War. During the Second World War he commanded an army on the Eastern Front, but was relieved in 1943 and retired the same year. Constantinescu-Claps was arrested by communist authorities in 1951 and sentenced to prison, but was freed in 1955.
18. A cavalry regiment that had been converted into a motorized one, numbering 1,047 men.
19. *Russkii Arkhiv. Velikaya Otechestvennaya*, vol. 13 (2-2), p. 324.
20. Ibid.

Chapter 23: The Tank Army. The First Success

1. Editor's note. Operation Mars was the code name of a major Soviet offensive conducted between 25 November and 20 December 1942. The operation, carried out by the Western and Kalinin fronts, was supposed to cut off the Rzhev salient, but was a costly failure.
2. NARA, T311, R271, frame 309.
3. TsAMO RF, f. 232, op. 590, d. 17, l. 31.
4. TsAMO RF, f. 232, op. 590, d. 17, l. 37.
5. Editor's note. A command within the German army responsible for armoured and motorized forces.
6. Dërr, *Pokhod*, p. 69. With a refinement from the Sixth Army's war diary.
7. The point of applying maximum effort.
8. Editor's note. *Schuma* is the shortened form of *Schutzmannschaft*, which were subunits of the Germans' auxiliary police in the occupied territories.
9. Editor's note. Ion Victor Antonescu (1882–1946) joined the Romanian army in 1904 and served in the Second Balkan War and the First World War. During the interwar period he rose rapidly through the ranks and became defence minister. He early on associated himself with the fascist Iron Guard and came to power in a coup in 1940. He aligned Romania with Nazi Germany and took his country into war against the Soviet Union. Antonescu was deposed in August 1944 and arrested. He was later tried and executed.
10. Dërr, *Pokhod*, pp. 70–1.
11. Yu. Mashenko, citing TsAMO RF, f. 331, op. 5041, d. 29, l. 5.
12. Editor's note. Marhabal (third century BC) was a Carthaginian general and cavalry commander. He was second in command to Hannibal Barca during the Second Punic War (218–201 BC).
13. Editor's note. Hasdrubal Barca (245–207 BC) was a Carthaginian general during the Second Punic War and brother of Hannibal Barca. He was killed in battle.
14. Editor's note. Hannibal Barca (247–181 BC) was an outstanding Carthaginian general who led his armies against Rome during the Second Punic War. Despite many victories, he was decisively defeated at the battle of Zama (202 BC) and forced to flee. He continued to resist the Romans from exile, but was betrayed and forced to commit suicide.
15. TsAMO RF, f. 3403, op. 1, d. 7, l. 39.
16. Editor's note. Issa Aleksandrovich Pliev (1903–79) joined the Red Army in 1922. During the Great Patriotic War he commanded a cavalry division and corps and later a cavalry-mechanized group in Europe and the

Far East. Following the Great Patriotic War he commanded armies and a military district and was the commander of Soviet forces in Cuba during the Missile Crisis.

17. Editor's note. Ivan Vasil'evich Galanin (1899–1958) joined the Red Army in 1919 and fought in the Russian Civil War. During the Second World War he commanded a corps and several armies. Following the war, Galanin served as a deputy corps commander until his retirement in 1946.
18. TsAMO RF, f. 3414, op. 1, d. 25, l. 22.
19. TsAMO RF, f. 3414, op. 1, d. 25, l. 31.

Chapter 24: Mechanized Pincers
1. TsAMO RF, f. 48, op. 451, d. 41, l. 212.
2. Ibid.
3. TsAMO RF, f. 48, op. 451, d. 41, l. 211.
4. Dërr, *Pokhod*, p. 72.
5. Editor's note. Hermann Wilhelm Göring (1893–1946) joined the Imperial German Army in 1912 and became a decorated fighter pilot during the First World War. Following the war, Göring joined the Nazi Party and became one of Hitler's trusted lieutenants and his designated successor. He commanded the Luftwaffe before and during the Second World War until relieved by Hitler during the war's closing days. Göring was sentenced to death at the Nuremberg war crimes trials, but committed suicide before the sentence could be carried out.
6. Editor's note. Fedor Ivanovich Tolbukhin (1894–1949) joined the Imperial Russian Army in 1914 and the Red Army in 1918. During the Great Patriotic War he served as a *front* chief of staff, and Army commander and a *front* commander. Following the war, Tolbukhin served as commander-in-chief of the Southern Group of Forces and commanded a military district.

Chapter 25: The Failure of Operation Winter Storm
1. V. Gerlits, *Paulyus: Tragediya Fel'dmarshala* (Smolensk: Rusich, 2006), p. 295.
2. Editor's note. Army Group (*Heeresgruppe*) Hollidt was an ad hoc formation thrown together after the encirclement of the Sixth Army. It was led by the commander of the XVII Army Corps, Karl-Adolf Hollidt.
3. D. Sadarananda, *Beyond Stalingrad: Manstein and the Operations of Army Group Don* (Westport, CT: Praeger, 1990), p. 27.
4. TsAMO RF, f. 48, op. 451, d. 125, l. 16.
5. TsAMO RF, f. 48, op. 451, d. 125, l. 34.
6. Yeremenko, *Stalingrad*, p. 417.
7. Kh. Shaibert, *Do Stalingrada 48 Kilometrov. Khronika Tankovykh Srazhenii. 1942-1943* (Moscow: ZAO Tsentropoligraf, 2010), p. 65.
8. *Kriegstagebuch des Oberkommandos der Wehrmacht (Wehrmachtführungsstab)*, Band II (Frankfurt am Main: Bernard & Graefe Verlag fur Wehrwesen, 1961), p. 1120.
9. *Stalingradskaya Bitva*, bk. 2, p. 204.
10. Ibid., p. 211.
11. Editor's note. Yakov Grigor'evich Kreizer (1905–69) joined the Red Army in 1921. During the Second World War he commanded a division and several armies. Kreizer's career stalled after the war under Stalin, but he advanced rapidly under Khrushchev and commanded several military districts.
12. TsAMO RF, f. 303, op. 4005, d. 75, l. 17.
13. E. Rauss, *Tankovye Srazheniya na Vostochnom Fronte* (Moscow: ACT, 2005), pp. 262–3.
14. TsAMO RF, f. 48, op. 468, d. 24, l. 221.
15. TsAMO RF, f. 48, op. 451, d. 125, l. 113.
16. *Stalingradskaya Bitva*, bk. 2, p. 232.
17. Sadarananda, *Beyond Stalingrad*, p. 42.
18. Editor's note. Hans-Valentine Hube (1890–1944) joined the Imperial German Army in 1909 and fought in the First World War. During the Second World War he commanded a regiment, division, corps, and an army. He died in a plane crash.
19. KTV AOK, Band 2, p. 298.
20. E. Manstein, *Uteryannye Pobedy* (Moscow: AST; St. Petersburg: Terra Fantastica, 1999), p. 375.

Chapter 26: The Hydraulic Press. Operation Ring
1. Voronov, *Na Sluzhbe Voennoi*, pp. 299–300.
2. *Stalingradskaya Bitva*, bk. 2, p. 299.
3. TsAMO, f. 206, op. 262, d. 189, l. 102.
4. TsAMO RF, f. 206, op. 262, d. 173, l. 11.
5. W. Haupt, *Army Group South. The Wehrmacht in Russia, 1941-1945* (Atglen, PA: Schiffer Military History, 1998), p. 245.

6. TsAMO RF, f. 206, op. 262, d. 173, l. 13.

7. Editor's note. Rastenburg (Polish, Ketrzyn), now in Poland, was the site of Hitler's military headquarters, the 'Wolf's Lair' (*Wolfsschanze*) during the Second World War.

8. TsAMO RF, f. 206, op. 262, d. 189, l. 131. There is no data for the 64th Army during this period.

9. This is what Paulus called the parachute containers.

10. TsAMO RF, f. 341, op. 5312, d. 185, l. 206.

11. TsAMO RF, f. 341, op. 5312, d. 185, l. 204.

12. TsAMO RF, f. 206, op. 262, d. 173, l. 35.

Chapter 27: Conclusions to Part III

1. A.I. Radzievskii, *Razvitie Teorii i Praktiki Proryva (po Opytu Velikoi Otechestvennoi Voiny). Uchebnoe Posobie* (Moscow: Voennaya Akademiya im. M.V. Frunze), vol. I, p. 177.

2. Manstein, *Uteryannye Pobedy*, p. 340.

3. *Sbornik Materialov po Izucheniyu Opyta Voiny*, Vypusk No. 6. Aprel'-Mai 1943 (Moscow; Voennoe Izdatel'stvo, 1943), p. 74.

4. N.S. Khrushchev, *Vremya. Lyudi. Vlast' (Vospominaniya)* (Moscow: IIK 'Moskovskie Novosti', 1999), bk. 1, p. 415.

5. F. Morzik, *German Air Force Airlift Operations* (USAAF Historical Division, 1961), p. 195.

Conclusions

1. I. Hahn, *Waffen*, p. 214.

2. I.I. Vernidub, *Na Peredovoi Linii Tyla* (Moscow: TsNIINTIKPK, 1993), p. 406.

Bibliography

I. Archival Holdings
NARA T311 Heersgruppe B.
NARA T312 Armee Oberkommando 6. KTB Ia. OQu, Ic.
NARA T314 R1159 XXXXVIII PzK.
NARA T315 R804 24 Panzer Div.
TSAMO RF, f. 38, GABTU.
TsAMO RF, f. 81, GAU KA.
TsAMO RF, f. 220, Stalingradskii Front.
TsAMO RF, f. 48, Yugo-Vostochnyi Front.
TsAMO RF, f. 206, Donskoi Front.
TsAMO RF, f. 232, Yugo-Zapadnyi Front.
TsAMO RF, f. 303, 2-ya Gv. Armiya.
TsAMO RF, f. 324, 4-ya Tankovaya Armiya.
TsAMO RF, f. 335, 21-ya (6-ya Gv.) Armiya.
TsAMO RF, f. 345, 62-ya (8-ya Gv.) Armiya.
TsAMO, RF, f. 312, 63-ya Armiya.
TsAMO RF, f. 341, 64-ya (7-ya Gv.) Armiya.
TsAMO RF, f. 3403, 4-i Tankovyi Korpus.
TsAMO RF, f. 3430, 13-i Tankovyi Korpus.
TsAMO RF, f. 3418, 23-i Tankovyi Korpus.
TsAMO RF, f. 3401, 7-i Tankovyi Korpus.

II. Literature
Adam, V., *Trudnoe Reshenie. Memuary Polkovnika 6-i Nemetskoi Armii* (Moscow: Progress, 1967).
Aufsess, Florian Freiherr von und zu, *Die Aulageubander der Kriegstagebucher der 6.Armee* (Moscow: Voennoe Izdatel'stvo, 2006).
Anan'ev, I.M., *Tankovye Armii v Nastuplenii. Po Opytu Velikoi Otechestvennoi Voiny 1941-1945 gg* (Moscow: Voennoe Izdatel'stvo, 1988).
Axworthy, M., *Third Axis. Fourth Ally. Romanian Armed Forces in the European War 1941-1945* (London: Arms and Armour, 1995).
Boevoi Sostav Sovetskoi Armii. Chast' 2 (Yanvar'-Dekabr' 1942 g.) (Moscow: Voennoe Izdatel'stvo, 1960).
Boevoi Ustav Konnitsy RKKA (BUK-38) (Moscow: Voennoe Izdatel'stvo, 1938).
Boevye Deistviya v Ispanii i Kitae (Opyt Issledovaniya) (Moscow: Izdatel'stvo NKO SSSR, 1940).
Chuikov, V.I., *Srazhenie Veka* (Moscow: Sovetskaya Rossiya, 1975).
Dashichev, V.I., *Bankrotstvo Strategii Germanskogo Fashizma* (Moscow: Nauka, 1973).
Dërr, G., *Pokhod na Stalingrad (Operativnyi Obzor)* (Moscow: Voennoe Izdatel'stvo, 1957).
Dettmer, F., *Die 44. Infanterie-Division. Reichs Grenadier Division Hoch-und-Deutschmeister. 1939-1945* (Friedberg: Podzun-Palas-Verlag, 1958).
Die 71. Infanterie-Division im Zweiten Weltkrieg 1939-1945. Gefechts-und Erlebnisberichte aus den Kaempfen der 'Glueckhaften Division' von Verdun bis Stalingrad, von Monte Cassino obis zum Plattensee (Eggolsheim: Nebel Verlag GmbH, 1973).
Dierich, W., *Kampfgeschwader 55 Greif* (Stuttgart: Motorbuch-Verlag, 1973).
Fronty, Floty, Armii, Flotilii Perioda Velikoi Otechestvennoi Voiny 1941-1945gg. Spravochnik (Moscow: Izdatel'stvo 'Kuchkovo Pole,' 2003).
Gal'der, F., *Voennyi Dnevnik. Yezhednevnye Zapisi Nachal'nika General'nogo Shtaba Sukhoputnykh Voisk* (Moscow: Voennoe Izdatel'stvo, 1971).
Gerlits, V., *Paulyus: Tragediya Fel'dmarshala* (Smolensk: Rusich, 2006).
German Report Series. The German Campaign in Russia – Planning and Operations 1940 – 1942 (Uckfield, UK: The Naval and Military Press, Ltd., 2003).
Germany and the Second World War: Volume I: The Global War (Oxford, UK: Oxford University Press, 2001).
Glantz, D., *To the Gates of Stalingrad: Soviet-German Combat Operations, April-August 1942* (Lawrence, KS: University Press of Kansas, 2009).
Gor'kov, Yu.A., *Gosudarstvennyi Komitet Oborony Postanovlyaet (1941-1945). Tsifry, Dokumenty* (Moscow: Olma-Press, 2002).

Grams, R., *Die 14.Panzer-Division 1940-1945. HerausgegebenimAuftrag der Traditionsgemeinschaft der 14.Panzer Divison* (Bad Nauheim: Verlag Hans-Henning Podzun, 1957).

Gudmundisson, D., *Stormtroop Tactics. Innovation in the German Army, 1914-1918* (New York: Praeger, 1989).

Hahn, F., *Waffen und Geheimwaffen des Heeres, 1933-1945* (Koblenz: Bernard & Graefe, 1986).

Haupt, W., *Army Group South. The Wehrmacht in Russia, 1941-1945* (Atglen, PA: Schiffer Military History, 1998).

Hayward, J., *Stopped at Stalingrad. The Luftwaffe and Hitler's Defeat in the East, 1942-1943* (Lawrence, KS: University Press of Kansas, 1998).

Jentz, T., *Panzertruppen. The Complete Guide to the Creation & Combat Employment of Germany's Tank Force, 1933-1942* (Atglen, PA: Schiffer Military History, 1996).

Jentz, T., *Panzertruppen. The Complete Guide to the Creation & Combat Employment of Germany's Tank Force, 1943-1945* (Atglen, PA: Schiffer Military History, 1996).

Jentz, T., *Sturmgeschuetz-s.Pak to Sturmmoerser. Panzer Tracts*, No. 8 (Boyds, MD, 2000).

Kardashev, V., *Rokossovskii* (Moscow: Molodaya Gvardiya, 1972).

Karel', P., *Vostochnyi Front. Kniga Pervaya. Gitler Idet na Vostok. 1941-1943* (Moscow: Izografus, EKSMO, 2003).

Kehrig, M., *Analyse und Dokumentation einer Schlacht (Beitrage zur Military-und Kriegsgeschichte)* (Stuttgart: Deutsche Verlags-Anstalt, 1974).

Keitel', V., *Razmyshleniya Pered Kazn'yu* (Smolensk: Rusich, 2000).

Khrushchev, N.S., *Vremya. Lyudi. Vlast'. (Vospominaniya)* (Moscow: IIK 'Moskovskie Novosti,' 1999).

Kokunov, V.L., and Stupov, A.D., *62-ya Armiya v Boyakh za Stalingrad* 2nd expanded and revised ed. (Moscow: Voennoe Izdatel'stvo, 1953).

Kravtsov, V.M., and Savin, M.V., *Boi v Stalingrade. Kratkii Operativno-Takticheskii Ocherk* (Moscow: Voennoe Izdatel'stvo, 1944).

Krylov, N.I., *Stalingradskii Rubezh* (Moscow: Voennoe Izdatel'stvo, 1979).

Kto Byl Kto v Velikoi Otechestvennoi Voine 1941-1945. Lyudi. Sobytiya. Fakty: Spravochnik (Moscow: Respublika, 2000).

Lannoy, F. de and Charita, J., *Panzertruppen. Les troupes Blindees allemandes, 1935-1945* (Damigny: Heimdal, 1945).

Lelyushenko, D.D., *Moskva-Stalingrad-Berlin-Praga. Zapiski Komandarma* (Moscow: Nauka, 1973).

Lemelsen/Schmidt, *29.Division.29 Infanteries-Division (mot.). 29. Panzergrenadier-Division* (Friedberg: Podzun-Pallas-Verlag, 1960).

Lyudnikov, I.I., *Doroga Dlinoyu v Zhizn'* (Moscow: Vysshaya Shkola, 1985).

Manstein, E. von., *Uteryannye Pobedy* (Moscow: Voennoe Izdatel'stvo, 1957).

Mark, J., *Death of the Leaping Horseman. The 24th Panzer Division at Stalingrad. 12th August-20th November 1942* (Mechanicsburg, PA: Stackpole Books, 2014).

Mellentin, F.V., *Tankovye Shrazheniya 1939-1945. Boevoe Primininie Tankov vo Vtoroi Mirovoi Voine* (Moscow: Inostrannaya Literatura, 1957).

Messe, D., *Voina na Russkom Fronte. Ita'yanskii Ekspeditsionnyi Korpus v Rossii* (Moscow: Kniizhnyi Mir, 2009).

Morzik, F., *German Air Force Airlift Operations* (Montgomery, AL: USAAF Historical Division, 1961).

Moshanskii, I. and Smolinov, S., *Oborona Stalingrada. Stalingradskaya Strategicheskaya Oboronitel'naya Operatsiya. 17 Iyulya-18 Noyabrya 1942 Goda* (Moscow: BTB-MN, 2002).

Moskalenko, K.S., *Na Yugo-Zapadnom Napravlenii. (Vospominaniya Komandarma)* (Moscow: Nauka, 1969).

Myuller-Gillebrand, B., *Sukhoputnaya Armiya Germanii 1933-45 gg* (Moscow: Izografus, 2002).

Newton, S., *German Battle Tactics on the Russian Front, 1941-1945* (Atglen, PA: 1994).

Oborona i Polevye Fortifikatsionnye Sooruzheniya Nemetskoi Armii (Moscow: Voennoe Izdatel'stvo NKO SSSR, 1942).

Operatsii Sovetskikh Vooruzhennykh Sil v Velikoi Otechestvennoi Voine 1941-1945. Voenno-Istoricheskii Ocherk (Moscow: Voennoe Izdatel'stvo, 1958).

Otkroveniya i Priznaniya. Natsistskaya Verkhushka o Voine 'Tret'ego Reikha' Protiv SSSR (Smolensk: Rusich, 2000).

Pliev, I.A., *Pod Gvardeiskim Znamenem* (Ordzhonikidze: Ir, 1976).

Po Prikazu Rodiny. Boevoi Put' 6-i Gvardeiskoi Armii v Velikoi Otechestvennoi Voine 1941-1945 gg (Moscow: Voennoe Izdatel'stvo, 1971).

Podevil's, K., *Boi na Donu i Volge. Ofitser Vermakhta na Vostochnom Fronte. 1942-1943* (Moscow: ZAO Izdatel'stvo Tsentrpoligraf, 2010).

Polevoi Ustav RKKA (PU-39) (Moscow: Voennoe Izdatel'stvo, 1939).

Portugal'skii, R.M., Domank, A.S., and Kovalenko, A.P., *Marshal Timoshenko* (Moscow: Izdatel'stvo MOF 'Pobeda-1945 God', 1994).

Razvedivatel'nyi Byulleten' No. 25. Germanskaya Taktika (Po Opytu Voiny SSSR s Germaniei) (Moscow: Voennoe Izdatel'stvo NKO SSSR, 1942).

Raus, E., *Tankovye Srazheniya na Vostochnom Fronte* (Moscow: AST, 2005).

Raus, E., *Panzer Operations. The Eastern Front Memoir of General Raus, 1941-1945.* Compiled and translated by S.H. Newton. (Boston: Da Capo Press, 2003).

Reese, R., *Stalin's Reluctant Soldiers. A Social History of the Red Army* (Lawrence, KS: University Press of Kansas, 1996).

Rodimtsev, A.I., *Gvardeitsy Stoyali Nasmert'* (Moscow: DOSAAF, 1969).

Rokossovskii, K.K., *Soldatskii Dolg* (Moscow: Voennoe Izdatel'stvo, 1988).

Rotmistrov, P.A., *Stal'naya Gvardiya* (Moscow: Voennoe Izdatel'stvo, 1984).

Russkii Arkhiv. Velikaya Otechestvennaya Voina. Stavka VGK: Dokumenty i Materialy 1942 God Vol. XVI (5-2) (Moscow: Terra, 1996).

Sadarananda, D., *Beyond Stalingrad: Manstein and the Operations of Army Group Don* (Wesport, CT, 1990).

Safronov, V.G., *Ital'yanskie Voiska na Vostochnom Fronte. 1941-1943 gg* (Moscow: Veche, 2012).

Samchuk, I.A., *Trinadtsataya Gvardeiskaya. Boevoi Put' Trinadtsatoi Gvardeiskoi Poltavskoi Ordena Lenina Dvazhdy Krasnoznamennoi Ordenov Suvorova i Kutuzova Strelkovoi Divizii (1941-1945)* 2nd expanded edition (Moscow: Voennoe Izdatel'stvo, 1971).

Samsonov, A.M., *Stalingradskaya Bitva* 4th revised and expanded edition (Moscow: Nauka, 1989).

Sarkis'yan, S.M., *51-ya Armiya (Boevoi Put')* (Moscow: Voennoe Izdatel'stvo, 1983).

Sbornik Materialov po Izucheniyu Opyta Voiny No. 6. Aprel'–Mai 1943 G (Moscow: Voennoe Izdatel'stvo, 1943).

Sbornik Materialov po Izucheniyu Opyta Voiny No. 9. Noyabr'– Dekabr' 1943 G (Moscow: Voennoe Izdatel'stvo, 1943).

Sbornik Voenno-Istoricheskikh Materialov Velikoi Otechestvennoi Voiny, Vypusk No. 18 (Moscow: Voennoe Izdatel'stvo, 1960).

Schmitz, G., *Bildband der 16.Panzer-Division, 1939-1945* (Bad Nauheim: Podzun, 1956).

Schrodek, G., *Ihr Glaube galt dem Vaterland. Geschichte des Panzer-Regiments 15 (11.Panzer-Division)* (Munchen: Schild Verlag, 1976).

Senger under Etterlin, F. von, *Die 24.Panzer-Division vormals 1. Kavallerie-Division, 1939-1945* (Heidelberg: Kurt Vowinckel Verlag, 1962).

Shaibert, Kh., *Do Stalingrada 48 Kilometrov. Khronika Tankovykh Srazhenii. 1942-1943* (Moscow: ZAO Tsentrpoligraf, 2010).

Shreter, Kh., *Stalingrad* (Moscow: Tsentrpoligraf, 2007).

Shtemenko, S.M., *General'nyi Shtab v Gody Voiny* (Moscow: Voennoe Izdatel'stvo, 1989).

Stalingradskaya Bitva: Svidetel'stva Uchastnikov i Ochevidtsev (Moscow: Novoe Literaturnoe Obozrenie, 2015).

Stalingradskaya Bitva. Khronika, Fakty, Lyudi (Moscow: Olma-Press, 2002).

Stalingradskaya Epopeya: Materialy NKVD SSSR i Voennoi Tsenzury iz Tsentral'nogo Arkhiva FSB RF (Moscow: 'Zvonitsa MG', 2000).

Stoves, R., *Die 22.Panzer-Division, 25 Panzer-Division, 27.Panzer-Division and die 233.Reserve-Panzer Division* (Friedberg: Podzun-Palas-Verlag, 1985).

Vasilevskii, A.M., *Delo Vsei Zhizni* (Moscow: Politizdat, 1983).

Velikaya Otechestvennaya 1941-1945 gg. Kampanii i Strategicheskie Operatsii v Tsifrakh, two vols (Ob"edinennaya Redaktsiya MVD Rossii, 2010).

Volostnov, N.I., *Na Ognennykh Rubezhakh* (Moscow: Voennoe Izdatel'stvo, 1983).

Voronov, N.N., *Na Sluzhbe Voennoi* (Moscow: Voennoe Izdatel'stvo, 1963).

Wagener, C., *Die Heersgruppe Sued. Der Kampf im Sueden der Ostfront, 1941-1942* (Friedberg: Podzun-Palas-Verlag, 1981).

Werthen, W., *Geschichte der 16.Panzer-Division, 1939-1945* (Bad Nauheim: Verlag Hans-Henning Podzun, 1958).

Yeremenko, A.I., *Stalingrad* (Moscow: AST, 2006).

Zhukov, G.K., *Vospominaniya i Razmyshleniya*, two vols (Moscow: Olma-Press, 2002).

III. Internet Resources

https://forum.axishistory.com
https://nordrigel.livejournal.com/
https://www.obd-memorial.ru/
https://pamyatnaroda.mil.ru
https://podvignaroda.ru/
https://waralbum.ru